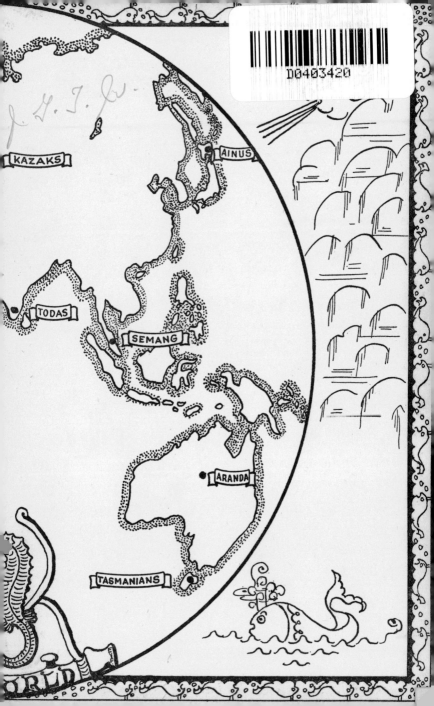

KAZAKS

AINUS

TODAS

SEMANG

ARANDA

TASMANIANS

D0403420

OUR PRIMITIVE CONTEMPORARIES

THE MACMILLAN COMPANY
NEW YORK · BOSTON · CHICAGO · DALLAS
ATLANTA · SAN FRANCISCO

MACMILLAN AND CO., Limited
LONDON · BOMBAY · CALCUTTA · MADRAS
MELBOURNE

THE MACMILLAN COMPANY
OF CANADA, Limited
TORONTO

A POLAR ESKIMO BELLE.
Photograph by Donald B. MacMillan.   Courtesy of the American
Museum of Natural History

OUR PRIMITIVE CONTEMPORARIES

BY GEORGE PETER MURDOCK, PH. D.

PROFESSOR OF ANTHROPOLOGY
YALE UNIVERSITY

THE MACMILLAN COMPANY · NEW YORK

COPYRIGHT, 1934,

BY THE MACMILLAN COMPANY

ALL RIGHTS RESERVED—NO PART OF THIS BOOK MAY BE
REPRODUCED IN ANY FORM WITHOUT PERMISSION IN WRITING
FROM THE PUBLISHER, EXCEPT BY A REVIEWER WHO WISHES
TO QUOTE BRIEF PASSAGES IN CONNECTION WITH A REVIEW
WRITTEN FOR INCLUSION IN MAGAZINE OR NEWSPAPER

Set up and electrotyped. Published February, 1934.
Reprinted June, 1935; April, 1936; May, 1938; May,
1940; June, 1943; August, 1945; April, December, 1946;
October, 1947; June, 1948; January, 1949.

Printed in the United States of America

TO

THE TRAVELERS, MISSIONARIES, GOVERNMENT OFFICIALS, AND
ANTHROPOLOGISTS, BUT FOR WHOSE PAINSTAKING
RESEARCHES AND PENETRATING OBSERVA-
TIONS THIS BOOK COULD NOT HAVE
BEEN WRITTEN

INTRODUCTION

How does the "savage" actually live? The general reader who is curious on this point can turn to scores of books about "primitive man" with selections on religion, marriage, and other institutions culled from hundreds of diverse peoples. Or he can read one of the systematic ethnographies which attempt to cover the whole world by devoting a few lines to each of some thousands of tribes. Or he may pick up a work on some particular region and acquire a general idea of the distribution of "culture traits" in that area. But in none of these books, however excellent, can he gain any adequate conception of the actual mode of life of a primitive people. For this he must turn to the original descriptive monographs themselves. Many of these, because they are rare, out of print, or buried away in obscure scientific journals, will be unavailable to him. The others, if they are really authoritative, he will find so freighted with masses of detail, of interest only to the professional anthropologist, that he will turn from them in discouragement, if not in boredom.

The present work springs from an appreciation of this gap in the literature, and seeks to remedy it. There are here gathered together, within the compass of a single volume, brief descriptions of eighteen different primitive peoples representative of all the great regions and races of the world and of all the major types and levels of culture. Each account, though short, aims to cover with reasonable adequacy every important aspect of economic, political, and social life, with some reference also to the racial, geographic, and historical background. An insight into the drama of life, as it actually unfolds among a number of diverse peoples, should yield, the author strongly feels, a truer picture of aboriginal civilizations than any generalized account of "primitive man."

The tribes selected are not always either "primitive" or "contemporary" in a literal sense. The Aztecs and Incas, for instance, are primitive only in the sense that they are usually studied by the anthropologist rather than by the historian and the sociologist. The descriptions, though usually couched in the present tense for greater vividness in presentation, depict the culture of each tribe, in so far as possible, as of the time of its first contact with western civilization. The cultures are contemporary, therefore, only in the broad historical or evolutionary perspective, which regards a century as but a moment in the immense span of human history.

The book is frankly addressed to the general reader and the college student. It therefore abjures footnotes and the other badges of scholarship. It includes, however, a bib· liography at the end of each chapter to guide the reader who may wish to learn more about a given culture. Aster- isks indicate the most reliable comprehensive works; highly technical or specialized contributions, however excellent, are not thus marked. Primitive culture is intrinsically in- teresting, as the author knows from years of teaching ex- perience with classes in anthropology and sociology. The facts of ethnography need no sugar-coating. Only facts, therefore, will appear in the text—not broad generalizations, or speculative reconstructions, or romantic idealizations, but the specific customs by which a number of primitive peoples actually order their lives.

The intelligent lay reader of this volume will, of himself, doubtless arrive at certain general conclusions which most specialists accept as axiomatic. He will, for example, fail to discover any direct correlation between race and cultural development. He will note that cultures are adjusted to their geographical environments, as is notably the case with the Polar Eskimos, but that vastly different cultures can flourish in similar environments, *e.g.*, the diverse adaptations of the Aranda, the Hopi, and the Nama Hottentots to an arid habitat, and he will conclude that geography exerts a selective or conditioning rather than a determining influence on civilization.   He will observe that simpler cultures differ amongst themselves at least as markedly as, for example, European civilization differs from Chinese, and he will conclude that there is no one distinctive "primitive culture" nor even any single series of cultural types. He will note, however, that there is no culture which does not possess some form of religion, marriage, economic organization, and the other major social institutions, and he will conclude that all cultures, including our own, are built according to a single fundamental plan, the so-called "universal culture pattern."   He will perceive that a culture is something more than an accidental congeries of traits; it is a unified whole, with its constituent parts consistent with and adjusted to each other.   It presents the aspect of a system in equilibrium—an equilibrium which is continually being disturbed and readjusted as new elements are borrowed or invented, and which may be completely destroyed by too sudden and fundamental a series of changes, as through white contact, with resulting cultural disorganization and decay.   The reader may even come to the realization that his own culture is but one of many, and not in any vital respect different from the others. We are perhaps fortunate in having chosen applied science for special elaboration, rather than religious ceremonial, or war, or the potlatch, but only an incurable optimist could assert that our religious beliefs, our attitude toward sex and reproduction, and our political institutions are uniformly more rational than those of our primitive contemporaries.

Though addressed to the general reader, this volume raises certain questions of theory and method, to which the professional anthropologist and sociologist may legitimately demand an answer. The layman and the student, therefore, are advised to turn directly to the text, while the author pens a

NOTE TO THE SPECIALIST

In the selection of the eighteen tribes, the aim has been to achieve a representative geographical distribution and at the same time to illustrate all the major variations in the primary social institutions as well as such notable specialties as the couvade, the potlatch, and cannibalism. These criteria have led to the inclusion of certain comparatively poorly documented tribes, *e.g.*, the Tasmanians, the Semang, and the Witotos, in preference to others about which a richer literature exists. Geographic distribution has been disregarded to some extent in the selection of a disproportionate number of tribes from native North America, partly because of the special interest of American readers in their own aboriginal predecessors, but mainly as a practical demonstration of the tremendous diversity of primitive culture even on a single continent and within a comparatively homogeneous race.

The nature of the material in the individual case, and not any hard-and-fast rule, has determined the arrangement of the facts in each chapter. The aim is always to present first those elements of the particular culture which can be understood without anticipation of what is to follow. So far as possible, all aspects of culture receive treatment. Some subjects, however, notably folklore and ceremonial and to a lesser extent language and kinship systems, require so much space for adequate presentation that, in a short chapter, they can be treated only with regrettable brevity.

The facts have been derived from extensive reading in the literature on each of the tribes. Experience has demonstrated the danger of relying upon any single author, no matter how excellent his work. Each writer has his blind spots and his limitations. A trained anthropologist, for example, may give complete data on the kinship system and religious ceremonies but fail to record the incidents of everyday life, which the sympathetic missionary, who has lived amongst the people for years, describes at length in his memoirs. The early explorer and the colonial administrator make their own unique contributions. Each writer, moreover, has his prejudices—the official's consciousness of the superiority of his own race, the missionary's abhorrence of savage "idolatry," the anthropologist's preoccupation with the theories of his own particular school of thought. With wider reading, personal biases tend to cancel out, the lacunæ are filled, and a complete picture of the culture emerges.

The author has not, of course, exhausted the literature. He has surveyed all the more important contributions and sampled the rest, including in the bibliographies only the works actually read and found useful in compiling the chapter. In general, he has placed little reliance upon writers who have not had personal contact with the peoples they describe. Secondary sources have been drawn upon only incidentally or where a preliminary review of the primary sources has demonstrated the accuracy and thoroughness of the writer, as in the cases of Roth on the Tasmanians and Schapera on the Hottentots. One important exception should be noted. In writing the chapters on the Aztecs and the Incas, the author, not being himself a specialist on these civilizations, has preferred to depend upon the scholarly compilations and reconstructions by qualified students of the original sources, rather than trust to his own more immature judgment.

The text, though designed for the layman, strives for accuracy. It makes no statement of fact without authority, or without weighing the relevant circumstances where the authorities conflict. Statements by authors of doubtful reliability, such as those of Vaughn Stevens on the "soul bird" and "name tree" of the Semang, have been accepted only in so far as they seem consistent with the context and have been partially substantiated. Nevertheless, some errors of fact and of interpretation must inevitably have crept in. All corrections thereof will be gratefully received.

Though largely the product of library research, the volume is not exclusively so. The chapter on the Haidas incorporates a considerable amount of original material gathered by the author in 1932 on a field trip sponsored by the Institute of Human Relations in Yale University. The chapters on the Samoans and the Dahomeans have benefited by the authoritative criticisms and suggestions of Professor Peter H. Buck (Te Rangi Hiroa) and Professor Melville J. Herskovits respectively, and those on the Iroquois and Hopi have similarly profited through the alterations suggested by two former students of the author's, Mr. W. N. Fenton and Mr. J. Spirer, on the basis of their respective field experience with the tribes in question. That these readers have suggested only minor changes in the four chapters augurs well, perhaps, for the essential accuracy of the others. The chapter on the Haidas has undergone an even severer test. Composed two years before the author's visit to the tribe, it was read in the original form at the close of his trip to an intelligent native of the old régime, whose manifest surprise gave additional weight to his confirmation. That the chapter required no fundamental revision or correction, but only expansion on the basis of new material, while primarily a tribute to the soundness of the pioneer work of Dr. John R. Swanton and others, was nevertheless highly gratifying.

The present work has no ax of anthropological or sociological theory to grind; it is concerned only with facts and description. Some interpretation, to be sure, is unavoidable. When it becomes necessary, the author gives preference to the views of his most reliable authorities, unless they seem naïve, inconsistent with the facts, or influenced by theoretical presuppositions.   Hoernlé's conception of *!nau* among the Nama Hottentots, for example, seems, on the basis of the cited facts, to be forcibly crammed into the mold of Van Gennep's "rites of passage" theory, and to be more readily reconciled with the widespread notion of ritual uncleanness.

Certain theorists will doubtless criticize the treatment of religion for virtually ignoring the concept of *mana* or impersonal supernatural power. To the scientist, the reason for this omission should be sufficiently cogent.   The author began with the intention of making full use of the concept. In tribe after tribe, however, he found it inapplicable, the more so the more deeply he dug into the facts, and he ended without being able to use it at all.   To choose but one example out of many, he could find little relation between Handy's reconstruction of Polynesian religion in terms of *mana* and the reported facts on Samoan religion.   In science, when a theory, however plausible, parts company with the facts, there is no choice; the theory must yield.   Thus, though the author still feels the inadequacy of animism as a universal explanation of religious phenomena, he is now convinced that it must be supplemented by something more substantial than *mana*.

In the field of social organization, British usage has been followed in preference to American.   The term "clan," since it lends itself readily to the formation of compounds such as "clansmen," is used for a unilateral kin-group in place of the more awkward "sib" and "gens."   The Americanist who is startled to read of a "patrilineal clan" or to find the present tense used for the now decadent culture of a tribe which he himself has studied, need only remember that the work is addressed, not to him, but to the general reader.   The specialist may be interested in the Haida chapter as a summary report of the author's own field work, and he will find the Inca chapter probably a more integrated survey of Peruvian social organization than appears elsewhere in English, but in other cases he will naturally prefer to consult the original sources. The lay reader and the student, however, may conceivably profit from a brief, non-technical description of a number of living, functioning, primitive cultures as of a date when they were actually in full flower.

The teacher who adopts this volume as a text in a course in anthropology will doubtless find it most suitable when used in conjunction either with one of the standard textbooks dealing with anthropological theory or with lectures covering the same subjects. Since it concerns itself entirely with fact, the book should not conflict with any reasonable theoretical position. Teachers of sociology will perhaps find it useful as a background against which to project their analysis of present-day social phenomena. There is, of course, no virtue in assigning the chapters in the exact order of their presentation. The arrangement adopted is purely geographical, beginning with Oceania simply because the Tasmanians happen to have had the lowest culture of modern times, and ending with Africa chiefly because, contrary to popular prejudice, the Negro peoples display, on the average, a more complex development of government, art, industry, and material culture than the non-literate inhabitants of any other great continental area.

GEORGE PETER MURDOCK.

YALE UNIVERSITY,
December, 1933.

ACKNOWLEDGMENTS

FOR permission to reproduce illustrations in this volume, the author wishes to thank the American Museum of Natural History, New York, for the frontispiece and Figs. 40, 48, 53, 54, 60, 67, 68, 69, 73, 74, 75, 77, 78, 80, 82, 86, 89, 91, 93, 94, and 95; the Bernice P. Bishop Museum, Honolulu, for Figs. 17, 18, and 19; Hon. Hiram Bingham, Washington, for Fig. 92; F. A. Brockhaus, Leipzig, for Figs. 22, 24, 26, and 27; Verlag von Gustav Fischer, Jena, for Figs. 101, 102, and 104; Friederichsen, De Gruyter & Co., Hamburg, for Figs. 96, 97, 98, and 100; the Göteborgs Museum, Gothenburg, for Fig. 88; William Heinemann, Ltd., London, for Figs. 49 and 108; Professor Melville J. Herskovits, Evanston, for Figs. 111, 113, 115, and 117; Hutchinson & Co., Ltd., London, for Figs. 22, 24, 26, and 27; Kegan Paul, Trench, Trubner & Co., London, for Figs. 1, 2, 3, and 4; The Macmillan Company, London, for Figs. 5, 8, 10, 12, 28, 30, 31, 32, 105, 109, and 110; E. Schweizerbartsche Verlagsbuchhandlung, Stuttgart, for Figs. 13, 15, 17, 19, 20, and 21; the Smithsonian Institution, Washington, for Figs. 41, 44, 58, 59, 76, and 79; the Staatliches Museum für Völkerkunde, Berlin, for Fig. 65; Strecker und Schröder Verlagsbuchhandlung, Stuttgart, for Fig. 35; and Mrs. Jessie A. Whiffen, Aldwick, Sussex, England, for Fig. 99.

For reading various of the individual chapters and offering invaluable criticisms and suggestions, the author is under the deepest obligations to Dr. Edward M. Weyer, Jr., of New York; to Professor Melville J. Herskovits, of Northwestern University; to his former students, Mr. William N. Fenton and Mr. Jess Spirer; and to his colleagues, Professors Peter H. Buck, Maurice R. Davie, Albert G. Keller, James G. Leyburn, and Edward Sapir, of Yale University. To Professor Carter A. Woods, of Wells College, he is most grateful for assistance rendered during the early stages of the work. To Mrs. Edna Yates Ford he wishes to express keen appreciation of her artistry and interest in making the line drawings, maps, and colored plate which illustrate the book. And to his wife, Carmen Rothwell, he is profoundly indebted for her sympathetic assistance throughout the preparation of the work.

G. P. M.

ACKNOWLEDGMENTS

My thanks are tendered for permission to use illustrations to this volume: to ... for the frontispiece and Figs. 40, 41, 57, 58, 80, 67; to the Mrs. ... Soc. to Figs. 65, 88, 90, and 97; the Rev. ... Walton for ... Hopkins for Figs. 35, 36, and 76; Dr. ... Rushton Armitage ... Figs. 89, P. A. Brooke and Son for Figs. 52, ... and 95; ... Cassell Publishing Co., for Figs. 101, 102, 103, and 104; Messrs. A. Constable & Co., Longmans ... Co., Figs. 42, 44, and 54; the Fitzwilliam Museum, Cambridge ... the Walton Studio and Ltd., Longman for Figs. 38 and 108; ... and the ... Heliotype Company, for Figs. 11, 12, 13, ... C. ... Maclehose and Co. Ltd., London, for Figs. 97, ...; ... Fig. ... the ... Joseph Hughes Teacher for ... ... Figs. 1, 2, 3, and 4, the Macmillan Company, London, for Figs. 6, 8, 10, 16, 29, 37, 59, 101, 104, and 110; E. Scott ... for ... Woodbury Company Stonegraft, for Figs. 15, 17, 51, 57, 80, and 30; the Smithsonian Institution, Washington, for Figs. 74, 75, 76, and 79; the Stanford ... Museum, for ... ... Berlin, for the ... Studio ... ... and Son, London, A. Witthers, Albert and Sons.

My thanks are also tendered to ... for their invaluable assistance in the work. And to ... Charman Blaikie ... been constantly indebted for his sympathising assistance ... the preparation of the work.

C. F. M.

CONTENTS

ILLUSTRATIONS

Our Primitive Contemporaries

OUR PRIMITIVE CONTEMPORARIES

CHAPTER I

THE TASMANIANS

TASMANIA is an island of some 26,000 square miles—about half as large as the State of New York—situated approximately 150 miles off the southeastern coast of Australia, from which it is separated by Bass Strait. The island is mountainous, but fertile and well watered, and is plentifully supplied with forests. Animal life abounds—chiefly marsupials like those of Australia. Tasmania possesses, moreover, one of the finest temperate climates in the world. The character of the environment, therefore, cannot explain the culture of the aboriginal inhabitants, which was unquestionably the lowest of any people known to modern man. Not climate or topography, but isolation is responsible for this condition. The continent of Australia forms a barrier on the north, and has kept Tasmania remote from all cultural influences emanating from Asia and Oceania. The culture of the aborigines, therefore, could consist only of elements originally brought by the first immigrants, those developed independently on the island, and perhaps a few which filtered through from Australia, where civilization had advanced but a trifle farther.

The native population of the island, before the coming of the whites, has been conservatively estimated at 2,000, or less than one inhabitant to every ten square miles. Almost certainly it never exceeded 5,000. Racially, the Tasmanians belonged to the Oceanic branch of the black race. Different authorities have sought in turn to relate them specifically to the Australians, the Melanesians, the Papuans of New Guinea, and the Negritos of the Andaman Islands. Probably, however, they should be classed as a distinct subrace. Though sometimes erroneously classed as pygmies, they actually attained a medium stature, the men averaging five feet five or six inches and the women four feet eleven inches. Their skin was a dull black in color. Their black hair hung in corkscrew curls but was not kinky. The eyes of the Tasmanians were dark, the nose broad with a depression at the root, the nostrils full, the jaws projecting, the teeth large, and the head moderately long and narrow (cephalic index approximately 75). The cranial capacity was low (averaging 1,200 c.c. for both sexes), but not the lowest on record.

The natives of the island were divided into numerous tribes and subtribes, which lived in a state of perpetual antagonism and hostility and carried on no trade or other mutual intercourse. Each tribe had its recognized hunting grounds, which were owned by the group as a whole; there was no individual ownership of land, although private property was acknowledged in such objects as weapons, amulets, and ornaments. To trespass on the territory of another tribe was equivalent to a declaration of war.

War, the most serious business of the men, characterized intergroup relations. The chief weapons were the spear and waddy. The bow and arrow—even the boomerang and spearthrower, with which the Australians were familiar—were entirely unknown in Tasmania. The spear, a slender piece of hard wood about ten feet long with its ends merely sharpened and then hardened by fire—the natives had no knowledge of the attachment of stone or bone points—could be thrown with accuracy over distances up to forty yards. The waddy or throwing-stick, made of a piece of similar wood about two feet in length, somewhat thicker at one end, was grasped by the slender end and could be used either as a club or as a missile. The Tasmanians also hurled stones in battle, and employed a flat wooden shield as a defensive weapon. Of metal as a material for tools and weapons they were entirely ignorant.

Every adult male was a warrior. Military organization did not exist except for an indefinite sort of subordination to a war chief. The principal causes of war were trespassing on the hunting grounds of another tribe, stealing women, and revenge. When the men of a tribe sallied forth to fight, the women and children were hidden in the bush, partly for safety and partly because the women were pacific and opposed to excessive violence. The natives never attacked except in superior force. A large party of strangers was safe from aggression; only single individuals or small groups were ordinarily attacked.

Military tactics almost invariably followed the principle of surprise. A favorite method was to divide into a number of small bands, one serving as a decoy to lure the enemy into an ambush where the others fell upon them. Employing another characteristic ruse, a Tasmanian would advance upon his unsuspecting enemy apparently unarmed, with his hands clasped over his head, but dragging his spear along the ground with his toes. By a quick movement the spear was transferred to the hand and hurled before the hapless victim was put on his guard. The first white man killed by the natives met his death in this way.

Battles consisted mainly of skirmishes with little loss of life. The whole attacking party usually withdrew if one of its members was killed, making every effort, however, to carry off its own wounded. Women were ordinarily spared. The killing of an enemy gave occasion for dancing and great rejoicing. The body was commonly mutilated, especially the head, and the finger joints were broken.

Within the tribe, peace and a primitive equality prevailed. In the absence of any social stratification, leadership was vague and undefined. Certain men were tacitly recognized as chiefs for their courage, strength, and prowess. The office was not hereditary, and scarcely existed except in war. The elders possessed a measure of authority, but there was no tribal council.

Law was as rudimentary as government. If a member by his actions gained the ill-will of the tribe, he had to stand while they hurled spears at him. These he dodged as best he could by contortions of the body—a defense at which the Tasmanians were adept through long practice. Ridicule was utilized for social control. A man who had violated a tribal custom was made to perch on the low branch of a tree, while his fellows gathered round and jeered him. Disputes between individuals were often settled by regulated duels; each of the adversaries in turn struck the other over the head with a waddy. The report does not state, however, who had the right to the first blow.

Under this simple form of social and political organization, the Tasmanians lived the life of nomadic hunters. They were ignorant of agriculture and possessed no domesticated animals—save the vermin which throve on their bodies and were from time to time picked off and eaten! Even the dog, the almost universal companion of savage man, was unknown until introduced by the whites. The quest for food, in brief, was confined to collecting, fishing, and hunting.

Wild plants, roots, seeds, berries, fruits, fungi, and birds' eggs were assiduously gathered, and formed a significant part of the Tasmanian diet. Oysters, crabs, and other shellfish, constituting another important item of subsistence, were obtained by the women. True fish, however, were tabooed as food, and the fishhook was unknown. Animal foods formed the real staff of life. Snakes, lizards, ants, and grubs were eagerly sought and eaten. A stranded whale provided a rare and welcome feast. The women, by means of a rope and a sharp stone for cutting notches, climbed trees after opossums. Larger or fleeter animals, like the kangaroo, wallaby, bandicoot, and wombat, were hunted by the men, often accompanied by the women to carry their spears and bring home the game. A favorite method of catching kangaroos consisted in surrounding a herd with a circle of fire and spearing them as they tried to escape. The larger animals were also hunted by stealth; a man would creep up from behind and dispatch them with a spear. Certain food taboos were observed; in addition to abstaining from fish, some tribes refused to eat the male wallaby, while others spared the female. That cannibalism was ever practiced is highly improbable.

The Tasmanians were nomads. Each tribe followed a regular annual migration, usually spending the winters near the seashore. On the march, the women carried the household

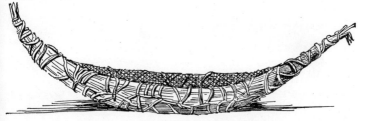

After Roth

FIG. 1. MODEL OF A TASMANIAN BOAT.

utensils, the food, and the children as yet too young to walk. There were, of course, no roads—only beaten paths or trails —but the aborigines possessed a remarkably accurate knowledge of the country in which they lived. Their boats were mere rafts, constructed of several rolls of buoyant bark bound together with rushes, and propelled by poles rather than paddles. While capable of holding several men, they were not water-tight and were navigable only in calm waters and for short distances. All the women and some of the men were expert swimmers.

Since the Tasmanians rarely stayed in one place for more than a day or two, their dwellings were frail and temporary structures. The usual shelter was a simple windbreak, constructed of interlaced boughs or strips of bark in the form of a crescent and open on the leeward side. A few tribes in the west of the island built superior huts, shaped like a beehive and consisting of a framework of boughs covered with grass or bark. A number of these rude shelters formed a village or camp, located as a rule on the bank of a river or lagoon. Each family occupied its own hut and had its own fire. At night its members slept about the latter in a sitting position with their heads between their knees.

It is probable, though by no means certain, that the Tasmanians knew how to generate fire. Their use of the friction of two sticks and of the simple fire-drill may have been borrowed from the Australian aborigines who were

After Roth

FIG. 2. TASMANIAN SHELTERS.

brought over to the island in the early days of its settlement. In any event, they employed these methods only in emergencies, for they made every effort to preserve their fire. They tended their campfires with the utmost care, carried a lighted brand from one camp to the next, and even kept a small blaze burning on their rafts. They used fire for warmth, in hunting, and for shaping wood, but above all for cooking. They prepared meat by roasting the animal whole over the fire. Of boiling as a method of food preparation they were totally ignorant.

The material equipment of the household was meager in the extreme. The art of pottery had never been acquired, but competent twined baskets and nets, used chiefly for carrying shellfish, were woven from grass, reeds, and bark. A utensil for holding water was manufactured by folding a large kelp leaf and fastening the ends with wooden skewers. Shells sometimes served the same purpose. The natives made thread and string, and twisted ropes from long strands of wire-grass. They used teeth for perforating shells, and a wooden spatula for detaching shellfish from the rocks. Animals were skinned with stone knives and scrapers. These lacked handles, for the art of hafting was unknown. They were given a sharp edge by striking off flakes—usually on one surface only—with another stone, or were made simply by

After Roth

FIG. 3. TASMANIAN BASKET AND KELP-LEAF VESSEL.

dashing one rock on another and selecting a sharp fragment. There was no chipping by pressure and no grinding or polishing of stone implements, for in their stone technic the Tasmanians were still in the early Paleolithic Age.

Clothing was exceedingly scanty. Ordinarily both sexes went about entirely naked. Only occasionally, as in sickness or exceptionally cold weather, was a minimum of clothing worn—an opossum or kangaroo skin thrown over the shoulder. Sometimes, too, the women wore a skin across the shoulder and around the waist to support their infants. The head was uncovered, but rude moccasins often protected the feet.

It was into such a primitive society that the Tasmanian child was born—if, that is, it was born at all, for abortion was not uncommon. Crude physical means, like thumping on the abdomen, were employed to terminate an unwelcome pregnancy. Infanticide was likewise practiced. Scarcity of food and the cares of maternity occasionally led mothers to kill their newborn infants. And if a mother died in childbirth her child was often buried alive with her. Early travelers, however, frequently commented on the large number of children, and it is probable that abortion and infanticide were unknown or exceedingly infrequent before the coming of the whites.

The birth of a child seems to have been attended by no special religious observances. A woman taken in labor dropped behind with another woman. When the child was born, the mother took it to the river and bathed it, after which she caught up with the rest of the party as best she could. The parents selected a name for the infant—usually one taken from some object in the environment that caught their fancy, such as an animal, a tree, a shell, or a tuft of grass.

The entire care of the children devolved upon the women. Mothers sometimes carried their babies astride the shoulder, holding them by the hands. More often they slung them in a kangaroo skin on the back, in which case they usually suckled them by tossing their pendulous breasts back over the shoulder. They normally nursed their children for two years or more before weaning them. Parents displayed great fondness for their offspring, and rarely punished them.

During the years of childhood the young Tasmanian absorbed the culture of his tribe through conscious inculcation and unconscious imitation. In this way, for example, he acquired the language—a simple agglutinative speech unrelated to any other, consisting chiefly of nouns, verbs, and adjectives, characterized by a paucity of abstract terms, and supplemented to a marked degree by tone and gesture. He also learned to count as high as five—the Tasmanians possessed no higher numerals. A major part of his education consisted in becoming familiar with the economic functions and duties of adult life. The girls learned that woman's work was to collect vegetable foods, dive for shellfish, climb trees for opossums, serve as pack animals, make the baskets and boats, build the huts, care for the children, and tend the sick. Boys learned that the chief duties of the men were to hunt, fight, and make weapons. They were taught by their elders the use and manufacture of weapons and the art of tracking men and animals, and they also acquired a knowledge of local geography.

When a boy reached the age of puberty, he underwent a ceremony of initiation into manhood, in which he was scarified on the shoulders, thighs, and breast, was given a secret name, and was presented with a fetish stone, which he kept carefully concealed from the women. There seems to have been no corresponding ceremony for girls. A system of age-grades apparently prevailed among the Tasmanians. Promotion from one grade to the next was determined by age and merits recognized by the tribe. Secret ceremonies accompanied initiation into each, but an unusual degree of mystery centered about admission to the third and highest grade, the members of which possessed certain regulatory powers.

When a man was of age to marry, he usually seized a woman by stealth or force from another tribe. In other words, marriage was exogamous and by capture. Sometimes, however, females were betrothed to a man from childhood, and marriages for love were not unknown. No definite wedding ceremonies have been reported of the Tasmanians. Polygyny was permitted, and was practiced mainly by the older men. Many, of course, were monogamous by necessity. A married man and his mother-in-law studiously avoided one another. Morality, by our standards, was relatively high. Delicacy marked the intercourse of the sexes. The women, though naked, were modest. As one writer quaintly observes: "It appears a point of decorum with the ladies as they sit with their knees asunder to cover with one foot what modesty bids them conceal." Fidelity in marriage was strictly insisted upon, especially in the wife. Adultery was extremely rare before the coming of the whites; it was punished in the man by piercing his legs with spears, while the woman was cut to pieces with stones. Women occupied a comparatively low status. Husbands often mistreated their spouses, they appropriated the choicest foods for themselves, and they could lend or otherwise dispose of their wives. Divorce was permitted, dependent mainly on the will of the husband, and some men had a succession of wives. Widows, if they did not remarry, are said to have become the common property of the men of the tribe into which they had married.

With advancing age, the lot of the Tasmanian was not an enviable one. To be sure, the old men enjoyed a certain prestige on account of their wisdom and experience, their plurality of wives, and their knowledge of the mysteries of the highest age-grade, and the old women possessed a similar measure of authority within their own sex. But the exigencies of a wandering life made it impossible to care for the sick and the infirm. So the aged, when they had grown feeble, were provided by their fellows with a little food and left behind to die. Similarly a sick comrade, if the ministrations of the medicine man and the women had not succeeded, was given food and a purgative and left to perish, unless he recovered in time to overtake his fellows.

When a Tasmanian died, his friends made haste to dispose of the body. Funerals were usually held at sunset, since it was commonly believed that a person was not completely dead until the sun went down. Some of the eastern tribes placed the corpse in an upright position in a hollow tree and built a fence around it. Cremation seems, however, to have been more common. The body was placed on a pile of logs and burned, after which the ashes and charred bones were collected, buried in a shallow grave, and covered with grass. Over the whole was then erected a conical monument of bark. During the first night the entire tribe sat around the remains, keeping up a continuous low wail or lamentation.

In token of mourning widows plastered their heads with pipe clay, smeared their faces with grease and charcoal, lacerated their bodies with shells, burned their thighs, and cut off their hair and threw it on the grave. The skull and bones of the deceased were often worn in mourning by the relatives.

Every individual was thought to possess a shadow or soul, which lived on after death as a ghost. The belief in an after-life found expression in the practice of placing a spear beside the body of a dead man, "to fight with when he is asleep," as one native expressed it. Life in the next world was thought to resemble life in this, save that it was divested of the evils of the latter. The realm of the departed was located in some distant region, where it was commonly believed a dead man would "jump up white fellow." For this reason Europeans were often regarded as dead Tasmanians returning from the spirit land.

A cardinal principle of Tasmanian religion was a belief in ghosts and in their influence on the living. Occasionally the spirits of the dead were regarded as benevolent, and their bones were worn by their relatives for protection. Usually, however, they were considered malevolent, and were greatly feared as the source of all manner of evils. Hence burial places were strictly avoided. The natives preferred to make detours of many miles rather than pass close to a grave. For a similar reason the survivors never pronounced the name of a dead person. To have done so, of course, would have been to attract the attention of his ghost—and the attentions of ghosts are rarely considered salutary. Instead, devious circumlocutions were resorted to, and it was considered a grave offense to mention to a man the name of one of his dead relatives.

The Tasmanians also believed in a hierarchy of spiritual beings of an order higher than the ghosts of the dead, some of them benevolent, but the majority evil in disposition and responsible for most human afflictions. These spirits were thought to inhabit rocky caves and crevices, hollow trees, and a variety of natural objects, and to hide in the woods during the daytime and wander about at night. Consequently the natives were vastly afraid of the dark. Whether they believed in actual gods or not is uncertain, though some of their spirits, like the thunder demon and the moon spirit, stood out above the rest in power and prestige.

Magic and witchcraft played a prominent part in Tasmanian religion. Sickness and death were not regarded as natural, but were always attributed to some supernatural cause—the malevolence of divine beings or the operation of witchcraft. To harm an enemy one needed only to obtain something belonging to him, like a few hairs, wrap them in fat, and place them near the fire. As the fat dissolved before the heat, so the body of the unfortunate man was thought to waste away and die. The bones of the dead and peculiar stones were regarded as charms capable of counteracting malevolent agencies, curing disease, and even causing injury to one's enemies.

Primitive as they were, the Tasmanians nevertheless had professional medicine men or shamans, to whom they attributed magical powers, especially in the cure of disease. The shaman had his regular paraphernalia, notably a rattle made of dead men's bones. Healing was in theory accomplished entirely by supernatural means. The medicine man induced in himself a state of spasmodic muscular contractions, considered an evidence of spirit possession, and in this condition was able to work cures. The therapeutic methods were various. A favorite one was bleeding, called "letting out the pain," in which the skin of the affected part of the body was deeply gashed with a stone knife. Sometimes the shaman would feign to suck a small stone or bone out of the affected part, producing it as the presumptive cause of the ailment. Other methods were baths, massage, the application of wet bandages, and cauterization. A number of vegetal remedies also found favor. A native skin disease was cured by wallowing in ashes. Snake bites were treated by thrusting a charred stick into the wound, stuffing the hole with fur, and then singeing off the surplus to the level of the skin.

The Tasmanians showed a measure of artistic development. They were fond of making rude charcoal drawings of animals, human beings, boats, geometrical figures, and the like, on the bark of trees and of their huts. Music was simple and monotonous. Their songs, though pitched largely in a minor key, were soft, plaintive, and melodious. Impromptu solos or duets reciting the mighty deeds of the singers or their ancestors constituted a favorite form. The only instrumental music was percussive—marking rhythm by beating two sticks together or thumping on a crude drum consisting simply of a rolled kangaroo skin.

Vanity found rich expression in personal adornment. The face was blackened with charcoal, and the body smeared with grease, clay, and red ocher. The hair of the men was matted with grease and red ocher, and hung down in ringlets over the shoulders, neck, and face. The women, on the other hand, usually cropped their hair short, at least in spots, with stone knives, and removed all body hair. Both sexes delighted in wearing bright-colored flowers, feathers, and berries on the head. Around the neck were hung strings of blue spiral shells and necklaces of kangaroo sinews dyed with red ocher. The men often wore strips of fur around the neck, body, arms, and legs. A favorite form of ornament in both sexes was scarification. The skin of the arms, legs, shoulders, and breast was gashed, and charcoal rubbed in; when the wounds healed they left rows of knobby scars. Other mutilations, like circumcision, knocking out teeth, and cutting off finger joints, were not practiced.

For recreation, the men were fond of setting up marks and throwing their spears and waddies at them. In this game they showed great proficiency, and it kept them in practice for war. The Tasmanians, low as they were, understood how

FIG. 4. PORTRAIT OF A TASMANIAN MAN.
From Roth, *The Aborigines of Tasmania.* Courtesy of Kegan Paul,
Trench, Trubner & Co., Ltd.

to make and enjoy a fermented liquor. They tapped a species of gum tree and allowed the sap to collect in a hole at the base, where it was left to undergo natural fermentation. The result was a crude but evidently palatable wine.

The principal amusement of the Tasmanians, however, was their corroborees or tribal dances, of which the most important was celebrated annually in November. They were usually held at night around a large fire under a full moon. The men danced—naked, of course, and well smeared with clay, grease, and red ocher—while the women beat time with sticks and drums. The performers sang as they danced, starting with soft tunes and slow paces, advancing to louder sounds and quicker steps, and finally rising to shrieks and whoops of excitement and a frenzy of motion, which lasted until they fell exhausted. The dances usually assumed a dramatic character, depicting hunting scenes, courtship, and heroic deeds of war. Some were religious, and at these the women were not allowed. The latter had, however, their own secret dances, which seem to have enacted in dramatic form the events of a woman's life—clambering for opossums, diving for shellfish, digging for roots, nursing her children, and quarreling with her husband.

The Tasmanians lived only for the passing moment. Their wants were few and in general easily satisfied. They indulged in their simple animal pleasures without thought of the future. Thus when food was plentiful, they gorged themselves and were happy, but they accumulated no stores. In bad winters, consequently, they suffered severely from hunger, and were even forced at times to gnaw on kangaroo skins. Mercurial in temperament and emotionally unstable, they were quick to laugh and as readily provoked to anger, but a burst of rage could melt immediately into a sunny smile. Their natural curiosity and imitativeness were manifested in their early contacts with European sailors. Their interest being aroused by the white skins of the latter, they sought to explore under their clothing to discover whether they were white all over and to verify their sex. They delighted in mimicking the actions of the sailors, and would laugh immoderately when one of them mispronounced a Tasmanian word. Their naïve sense of humor found expression in childish pranks, such as hiding their guests' belongings. On one occasion, when a sailor had been mystifying a group of natives by sticking a pin into his leg without drawing blood or giving evidence of pain, one of them, who had received a pin as a present, slyly and surreptitiously jabbed it into the leg of the unsuspecting magician, evoking a startled cry of pain to the great merriment of the onlookers.

The advent of the white man was an event fraught with sinister consequences for these gay and improvident children of nature. The island was discovered by Tasman, the Dutch navigator, in 1642, but was not again visited by Europeans until 1772, when Marion du Fresne, commanding a French expedition, explored the coast. The first Tasmanian to be killed by a white man was shot by the members of this party. In 1803 the English established the first European settlement on the island. In the following year a panic seized the colonists, and they brutally shot down a party of native men, women, and children, who were approaching them with every sign of friendship. This act precipitated hostilities between the whites and the natives, which lasted for twenty years.

The colonists regarded the aborigines as a degenerate race, not so much human beings as wild beasts to be ruthlessly exterminated. Even more barbarous in their treatment of the natives were the bushrangers, convicts who had escaped into the bush where they lived a life of brigandage. These outlaws hunted the blacks for sport. They stole their women, chaining them up, outraging them, and in the end killing them. In one case a bushranger discovered a native woman, far gone in pregnancy, hiding in a tree after her comrades had fled. He deliberately fired at the defenseless creature and brought her tumbling to the ground, dead.

Another ex-convict used regularly to hunt natives in order to provide his dogs with meat.

The aborigines, though naturally disposed toward peace and friendship with the whites, were roused to fury by these outrages, and retaliated in kind. But spears and waddies were no match for firearms. The blacks were driven steadily back as the settlements advanced, and their numbers were decimated. The slaughter of a group of natives, surprised by a band of whites as they sat peacefully around their campfire at night, is vividly described by one author: "The wounded were brained; the infants cast into the flames; the bayonet was driven into the quivering flesh; the social fire around which the natives gathered to slumber became before morning their funeral pile."

Finally Governor Arthur, realizing that the depredations of the natives were simply acts of vengeance for the injuries they had received, resolved to put an end to the prevailing anarchy. To discourage killing the natives, he offered a reward of £5 for every adult captured alive and uninjured, and £2 for every child. This plan had unanticipated consequences. It sanctioned and encouraged the formation of capture parties, and in the excitement of a man-hunt the participants were not always scrupulous about sparing the lives of their prey. Arthur then turned to another plan. Nearly five thousand soldiers, police, and civilians, armed with guns and handcuffs, were formed into a cordon stretching across the island. In October, 1830, this line started to move southward to drive all the natives into the Tasman Peninsula and pen them there. But when this human dragnet had closed in, at an expense of £30,000, it had caught only one native man and a boy. The others had all slipped through the line "like a sunbeam through a butterfly net."

What this great drive had failed to do was accomplished single-handed by a Methodist bricklayer, George Robinson by name, who had a warm sympathy for the natives and was one of the few white men they trusted. Unarmed and accompanied only by a few friendly natives, he went into the bush to reason with the aborigines and to explain that, however the settlers and bushrangers might treat them, the government desired to protect them. At the imminent risk of his life he tramped hundreds of miles from one secret retreat to another. Through his unaided efforts all the surviving blacks—now only 203 in number—were gathered together in 1835 on Flinders Island in Bass Strait. Thus the "Black War" came to an end

Though kindly treated from then on, the natives could not withstand the changed conditions of life. Unsuitable food, catarrhal disorders, and pneumonia, aggravated by close confinement and the wearing of clothing, and the restrictions of captivity, caused them to pine and sicken and die. Twelve years later, in 1847, when their numbers had been reduced to forty, they were transferred to a reservation near Hobart. But they were already doomed to extinction. The last aboriginal male died in 1869, and in 1876, with the death of the woman Truganina or Lalla Rookh, the Tasmanian race became finally extinct. This in brief is one chapter in the history of the triumph of "civilization" over "savagery."

BIBLIOGRAPHY

BARNARD, J. "Aborigines of Tasmania." *Australasian Association for the Advancement of Science*, Vol. II. Melbourne, 1890.

BONWICK, J. *Daily Life and Origin of the Tasmanians*. London, 1870.

——. *The Lost Tasmanian Race*. London, 1884.

CALDER, J. E. "Some Account of the Wars of Extirpation, and Habits of the Native Tribes of Tasmania." *Journal of the Anthropological Institute of Great Britain and Ireland*, Vol. III. London, 1874.

GIBLIN, R. W. *The Early History of Tasmania*. London, 1928.

HAMBLY, W. D. "Types of 'Tronattas' or Stone Implements Used by the Aborigines of Tasmania." *American Anthropologist*, New Series, Vol. XXXIII. Menasha, 1931.

LORD, C. "Critical Notes on the Observations Made by the Early Explorers concerning the Aborigines of Tasmania." *Australasian Association for the Advancement of Science*, Vol. XVII. Adelaide, 1924.

QUATREFAGES, A. DE. *Hommes fossiles et hommes sauvages*. Paris, 1884.

*ROTH, H. L. *The Aborigines of Tasmania*. London, 1890.

SCOTT, E. *A Short History of Australia*. London, New York, 1928.

SOLLAS, W. J. *Ancient Hunters and Their Modern Representatives*. Third edition. New York, 1924.

TYLOR, E. B. "On the Tasmanians as Representatives of Palæolithic Man." *Journal of the Anthropological Institute of Great Britain and Ireland*, Vol. XXIII. London, 1894.

CHAPTER II

THE ARANDA OF CENTRAL AUSTRALIA

In a region of approximately 40,000 square miles at almost the exact geographical center of the Australian continent reside the Aranda or Arunta, a large tribe or nation numbering originally at least two thousand members. In physique, the Aranda may be taken as fairly representative of the Australian branch of the black race. Their lithe, erect, well-proportioned bodies attain an average stature of over five feet six inches in adult males, about four inches less in females. Their full lips and chocolate brown—not black—complexions align them with the African Negroes, but they differ markedly from the latter in their hair, which, though black, is wavy rather than kinky, and in their beards, which in males are abundant and heavy. A receding forehead and prominent supraorbital (brow) ridges are seemingly primitive characteristics. The nose, broad and depressed at the root, often shows a pronounced curve which lends it a superficially Jewish appearance, though no enthusiast seems yet to have derived the nation from the Lost Tribes of Israel. The form of the head, though variable, is usually moderately narrow or dolichocephalic, with an average cephalic index of slightly less than 75, like that of many northern Europeans. Some authorities, indeed, rank the Australian aborigines closer to the white race than to the African Negroes.

The Aranda speech shows little kinship in either grammar or vocabulary with the languages of the tribes to the east, south, and west, which belong to the great South Australian linguistic stock. Its affinities are rather with the heterogeneous linguistic region of northern Australia. An extensive sign language, closely resembling our own deaf and dumb language except that the positions of the fingers and hands represent words rather than letters, is widely used by the Aranda both amongst themselves and for communication

FIG. 5. AN ARANDA MAN.
From Spencer and Gillen, *The Arunta*

with other Central Australian tribes of alien speech. Time is reckoned by "sleeps" and "moons," and an erudite native can count as high as five.

Geographically, the Aranda inhabit a semi-desert region

embracing a major portion of the watershed of the Finke River. This stream with its tributaries rises north of the Macdonnell Ranges, traverses the three main ridges of the latter at right angles through deep and narrow gorges, descends through the foothills, and meanders slowly across an undulating sandy or stony plain in a south-southeasterly direction until it reaches the Macumba River. The altitude of this region ranges from only seventy feet above sea level in the south to nearly five thousand feet in the highest peaks of the Macdonnell Ranges. A warm temperate climate prevails, the temperature occasionally falling as low as 20° F. on cold nights in July and August, and rising as high as 115° in the shade on hot days in December, January, and February. Winds are strong, and whirlwinds common. For weeks or months on end the sun shines hotly from a cloudless sky on a parched and withered landscape. The streams shrink to mere rills or isolated pools, the Finke itself drying up in sandy flats long before it reaches the Macumba. The soil supports only wiry shrubs, grass so sparse that each tuft stands out from its neighbors, and an occasional desert oak or acacia tree, except in the north where small patches of evergreen and deciduous forest occur. Rain falls infrequently and at irregular intervals, temporarily filling the streams. On extremely rare occasions it is sufficient to cause the latter to overflow their banks. The flood rapidly subsides under the scorching sun, but the thirst-quenched land, suddenly transformed, blossoms out with a rich and luxuriant vegetation, and birds, frogs, lizards, insects, and other fauna appear as if by magic where previously scarcely a sign of animal life had been visible.

To this environment the economic life of the Aranda represents a good adjustment. When water and food are reasonably plentiful, they range far and wide over their territory in tiny bands of two or three families each, a family consisting of a man, his wives, and children. Temporary camps are pitched beside a water-hole. Each family occupies an individual wurley or hut, a simple lean-to consisting of two forked sticks set upright in the ground six or eight feet apart supporting a horizontal pole against which leafy boughs are leaned on the side toward the prevailing wind (see Fig. 12). The household equipment is extremely meager—a grinding stone, a crude spindle for twisting thread, and a few wooden troughs or basins, one to three feet in length, hollowed out of wood. Except for an occasional bag woven from vegetable fibers or strips of fur, the Aranda have no knowledge of basketry; none whatsoever of pottery. In front of the wurley—inside in cold weather —burns a small fire, at which the cooking is done and around which the family sits, eats, talks, and sleeps. On chilly nights tiny fires are built between the sleepers and replenished by any one who wakes. Early on a summer morn-

FIG. 6. ARANDA WOVEN BAG.

ing—later in the winter—the camp is astir. Time has no value to the Aranda, and the men and women may linger for hours watching the children play. If food is urgently required, however, the camp breaks up to obtain it.

The Aranda practice no agriculture and possess no domestic animals save the half-wild dingo or native dog. They catch a few fish in the water-holes, either with spears or by means of brushwood weirs. But their existence depends mainly on collecting and hunting.

The women, accompanied and assisted by the children, scour the country for plant foods such as grass seeds, lily roots and stems, Cyperus bulbs, yams and other tubers, acacia pods, fungi, vegetables of all sorts, berries, and fruits like the quandong. Each carries a pointed wooden staff for digging roots, and a wooden trough, balanced on the head or slung at the hip, for bringing home the fruits of her labor (see Fig. 10). The women and children likewise gather small animals such as rats, small marsupials, lizards, snakes, frogs, snails, and even beetles, caterpillars, certain flies, and grubs, for practically everything edible in nature is eaten—including pounded ant-hill clay.

The men hunt birds and the larger animals. The weapons of the chase—and of war—are manufactured mainly of stone and wood. Stone technic ranges from crude chipping through careful flaking by the pressure method, to grinding and

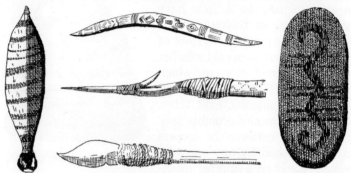

FIG. 7. WEAPONS OF THE ARANDA: SPEAR-THROWER, BOOMERANG, SPEARS, AND SHIELD.

polishing. Knives are of chipped stone, either held in the hand or attached with resin to a wooden handle. An ax or an adze consists of a carefully ground stone head hafted with resin to a piece of wood forked at the end. A point of stone or wood spliced and bound with tendons to a wooden shaft about ten feet in length, the whole often equipped with barbs, constitutes the Aranda spear. A unique and exceedingly useful implement is the spear-thrower, a leaf-shaped and often concave piece of hard wood about two feet long tapering at one end to a narrow handle and at the other to a blunt point, to which is attached by a tendon a short sharp wooden point. This fits into a hollow in the end of the spear and propels it with much greater force and leverage than the arm alone could impart. On the handle end is fixed with resin a sharp piece of quartz, which forms the principal cutting implement of the natives. The spear-thrower is at the same time the chief fire-making instrument. Two men grasp the ends of the weapon, saw back and forth on a piece of soft wood, add sand to increase the friction, blow on the smoldering sawdust, and ignite some shredded bark tinder—all in a minute and a half. This process is rarely resorted to, however, since the natives much prefer to preserve their fires and always carry a burning brand from one camp to the next. As projectile weapons the Aranda also use flat curved sticks or boomerangs, not, however, of the returning type. Shields are fashioned of light wood or bark with a concave inner surface and a longitudinal bar as a handle.

The men kill brush turkeys, pheasants, snipe, geese, ducks, pigeons, cockatoos, eagle-hawks, and other birds with their boomerangs. They usually stalk the kangaroo, creeping up cautiously and halting when the animal looks up, until they are close enough to hurl their spears. Sometimes several hunters combine to drive a kangaroo into an ambush, and occasionally fire is employed for a similar purpose. To catch the rock wallaby, which follows definite runs, a man will lie in wait patiently for hours. To trap the emu or Australian ostrich, a pit is constructed on its feeding grounds, a spear fixed upright at the bottom, and the top covered with brush and earth. Sooner or later a bird steps on the bushes, breaks through, and is transfixed by the spear. Sometimes a native poisons a water-hole frequented by emus with pituri, a narcotic drug, and hides in the vicinity until a bird drinks and becomes stupefied. Occasionally, too, relying upon the natural inquisitiveness of the emu, a man carries a pole resembling the long neck and small head of the bird and imitates its aimless movements, until it advances to investigate and he can throw his spear at close range.

Most foods are thoroughly cooked by roasting. The natives dislike underdone food, and eat nothing raw except a few vegetables. Insects are roasted. The seeds of a species of Claytonia are winnowed, pulverized on the grinding stone, mixed into a paste with water, and baked into a sort of bread in the embers. Nearly all animals are roasted whole in hot ashes. Their entrails are drawn, cooked in hot sand or ashes, and eaten. The natives may eat at any time of day, but they usually take their principal meal toward evening. The father cuts up the meat with the blade of his spear-thrower and tosses portions to the women and children. If the food is abundant, visitors flock in to enjoy the customary hospitality, and every one eats to repletion. Nothing is stored for the future, except for a few days before a festival, and in bad times the Aranda "tighten their belts" and starve philosophically.

As special sweetmeats, the natives relish the nectar of flowers, certain sweet gums, and the honey ant, but the supreme delicacy is honey. The men, who alone may gather it, in their greed not infrequently eat the bee itself. Though they make no intoxicating beverage, the Aranda chew pellets of pituri for their narcotic effect. The men are extremely fond of the warm blood of freshly killed animals.

The idea of using skins as clothing seems never to have dawned upon the Aranda. Under ordinary circumstances both sexes go about stark naked save for a few ornaments. The women sometimes wear a string of red beans around the neck, an ornament on the forehead, and in rare instances a small fur apron suspended from a cord about the waist. The men don a belt of human hair, arm bands of twisted fur strips, and a small pubic tassel, which serves rather to attract attention than to conceal. Both sexes commonly wear necklaces of fur string, greased and dyed, and head bands of similar material. Of other apparel there is none. The women cut their hair short; the men grease theirs, dye it with red ocher, dress it into a chignon, and adorn it with feathers. Partly for ornament and partly for religious reasons the Aranda submit to a number of mutilations. The men undergo circumcision and subincision at puberty, pierce the nasal septum for a bone ornament, and pluck out the hairs on the forehead. Both sexes occasionally knock out an upper incisor tooth, and invariably raise scars on the body and arms by gashing the skin with a flint and rubbing ashes or down into the wound.

But one gains only a partial and warped conception of Aranda culture if one views it merely as an adaptation to the natural environment. The life of the people is molded and directed and influenced even more fundamentally by an all-pervasive man-made environment of traditions, social arrangements, and religious and magical presuppositions, which, however artificial and exotic they may appear to us, possess to the native all the objective reality of physical nature itself.

The social organization of the Aranda consists first of all in a primary division of the tribe into two halves or "moieties." These are not local divisions, for any group of moderate size will contain members of both. Each moiety is subdivided in turn into two "sections," likewise not local in character. Exogamy prevails with regard both to the moiety and to the section, *i.e.*, a man cannot marry a woman of his own moiety, and consequently not of his own section either. He must obtain a wife from the other moiety— indeed from one particular section of that moiety. Descent in the moiety is patrilineal, *i.e.*, a child belongs to his father's moiety, not to his mother's. Curiously enough, however, a child does not belong to his father's section, but to the other section in the same moiety. In other words, descent is only indirectly patrilineal. This arrangement may be clarified by a diagram, showing by name the two constituent sections under each moiety, and representing by horizontal arrows the section from which a man may take his wife and by vertical arrows the section to which his children belong.

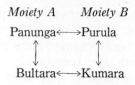

Thus a Panunga man necessarily marries a Purula woman and begets Bultara children, a Purula man weds a Panunga woman and has Kumara children, a Bultara man marrying a Kumara woman begets Panunga children, and so on.

The above, however, tells only half the story. Each section is further subdivided into two subsections or "classes." A man must marry a woman of one particular class in the proper section of the other moiety, and his children belong to one particular class in the other section of his own moiety. Another diagram will illustrate the situation among the northern Aranda, who have retained the section names for four of the classes and have invented new names for the other four. Horizontal arrows point to the class into which a man marries and vertical (angled) arrows to the class to which his children belong.

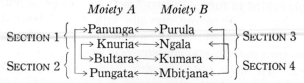

A Panunga man, for example, marries a Purula woman; their daughter, a Pungata, marries a Mbitjana man and bears Ngala children, who in turn find their spouses in the Knuria subsection, and so on. The whole arrangement is known to specialists as an "eight-class system with exogamy and indirect patrilineal descent."

This system of intermarrying classes is not an arbitrary invention but grows directly out of the native method of classifying relatives. With us, kinship terms are individual; we have, for instance, one particular wife, mother, father, or mother-in-law.   The Aranda, however, follow what is called a classificatory system of relationships; they lump whole groups of relatives together under the same term. When they use a term for a man, they always apply the same term to his brother and sometimes also to his sister, and they extend the term indefinitely to his cousins in the paternal line of descent.   Thus the term "father" (*oknia*) is used, not only for the speaker's own father, but also for the father's brother, the father's first cousin (*i.e.*, his father's brother's son), and so on *ad infinitum*.   All relatives in each generation are grouped into four categories.   For the second ascending (grandparental) generation every one is either (1) *arunga*, father's father or his sister; (2) *apulla*, father's mother or her brother; (3) *chimmia*, mother's father or his sister; or (4) *ipmunna*, mother's mother or her brother. The four categories in each succeeding lower generation include, respectively, the children of the men in the several categories of the next higher generation.   Since, moreover, grandparents call their grandchildren by the same terms (*arunga, apulla*, etc.) as the latter call them, alternate generations are grouped together and the total number of categories is reduced to eight.   The members of each of these eight great groups of kinsmen form a subsection or class in the eight-class system.

The Aranda, moreover, do not distinguish between blood relatives and relatives by marriage. The term "wife" (*anua*), for example, refers not only to an actual wife but indiscriminately to any woman belonging to the particular category of blood relatives, the particular subsection, from which a man may choose a wife.   To a Panunga man, for example, any eligible woman in the Purula class is his "wife."   Similarly his "mother-in-law" (*mura*) is any woman, and his "father-in-law" (*irundera*) any man, who is a parent of any of his actual or possible "wives."

These systems are not mere theories or empty forms; they are very practical matters going to the very core of the life of the people. They involve serious duties and rigid formalities, which carry with them severe penalties for infraction. A man is expected, for instance, to provide all his "fathers-in-law," whether or not he has actually married their daughters, with a share of all the game he procures, and he must mourn the death of any of them by gashing himself till the blood flows freely, even if the deceased is a personal enemy. And he must never approach, speak to, or even look at any of his "mothers-in-law." Even the details of camp life reflect these all-pervading systems. In a large camp, for example, the two moieties are separated, pitching their wurleys on different levels or on opposite sides of a stream. In such a camp there are usually two exceptionally large wurleys, used as primitive club houses, one by the men and one by the women. Each is rigidly tabooed to the opposite sex, and even the visiting of private wurleys is governed by strict regulations. Women, for example, though they may at all times visit the huts of the other moiety (their husband's) and may visit the wurleys of their own section when the owners are absent, may under no circumstances approach the huts of the other section of their own moiety, for they are *mura* (mothers-in-law) to the owners thereof. Severe penalties, like death and social ostracism, await the individual rash enough to violate these rules.

Each Aranda belongs from birth, not only to a particular class, section, and moiety in the eight-class system, but also to a particular totem group. The members of such a group regard themselves as intimately associated with, and in a way descended from, some natural object, usually an animal or plant. Totem groups are not units in or parts of the class organization; they form an independent system and frequently include individuals of different classes and sections. They have no connection with marriage; a man may marry a woman of any totem, provided she is of the proper class. And they are only partially hereditary; a child usually, but not always, belongs to his father's group.

Over each local totemic group presides a totem chief (*inkata*), whose duties are mainly religious in character. In

FIG. 8. ARANDA CEREMONIAL COSTUME REPRESENTING
THE EMU TOTEM.
From Spencer and Gillen, *The Arunta*

many Australian tribes a strict taboo forbids eating one's own totem animal or plant. An Aranda, however, may eat his totem, though sparingly and not the best parts. Each group is thought to control the numbers of its totem, and from time to time holds a special ceremony designed to promote the increase of the animal or plant in question. These Intichiuma ceremonies, as they are called, involve bloodletting rites, much imitative magic, and the ritual eating of a little of the totem by the chief and other members of the group. But for these ceremonies by the various totem groups, it is thought, the food supply of the Aranda would soon be exhausted. Each group also claims certain rights in its totem animal or plant. The members of other groups, though they may partake of it freely, must not cook and eat it outside the camp, but must bring it in, else the men of the totem will be angry and the supply will fail.

Each local group has its totem center where it stores, in a cave, crevice, or other hiding place, the various *churinga* of its ancestors and living members. A *churinga* is a fetish object, taboo to women and children. Most of them are flat

slabs of stone or wood, oval or elongated in shape, varying from a few inches to several feet in length, and incised with designs having a definite meaning to the initiate. Some have a hole at one end, to which a string is attached, and can be whirled so as to produce

FIG. 9. ARANDA CHURINGAS.

a roaring noise. The women and children attribute the sound of these "bull-roarers" to a great spirit; only the men are privy to the secret. Each man, woman, and child possesses one personal *churinga;* men but not women can inherit others. The attributes of a dead man are thought to reside in his *churinga* and to be imparted to its owner. To lose such a possession is the greatest evil that can befall a man. The totem chief has full charge of all the *churinga* in the storehouse; none may be touched without his permission. A strict taboo protects plants growing in the vicinity of the storehouse and animals living or fleeing there. Even a man pursued by enemies can find there a sanctuary which none dare violate.

Behind the totemic system lies a vast body of tradition, rehearsed in dramatic form from time to time by the various totem groups in special ceremonies. These myths deal in the main with olden times, the so-called Alchera age, and with the deeds of the semi-divine totemic ancestors who inhabited the earth at that time. Originally springing from different plants and animals, or at least intimately associated with them from the first and capable of assuming their forms and characteristics, these Alchera ancestors fashioned men out of inert and formless lumps, grouped them in moieties and classes, gave them their weapons, and instructed them in their various customs and ceremonies. They wandered over the earth, creating its natural features and halting frequently to perform ceremonies. At each stopping place certain of them died, their bodies descended into the ground, and a tree or rock arose to mark the spot. But they left their *churinga* behind, and with them their souls. Thus were established the various totem centers, each consecrated to the group honoring the totem animal or plant associated with the ancestors who died there, and each with its storehouse containing the *churinga* of those ancestors and their descendants.

The souls of the Alchera ancestors, lingering behind with their *churinga*, split into two parts. One part always clings to the *churinga* in the storehouse. The other seeks restlessly to enter the body of a passing woman and be reborn as a human child. Thus each human being is the reincarnation of a totemic ancestor and naturally belongs to the totem group of that particular ancestor regardless of his parentage or class affiliation. The spirit remaining in the *churinga*, the double of the soul that is temporarily residing in an individual, acts toward that individual as a familiar or guardian spirit. It is usually well disposed toward him, and if he is gifted with the power of seeing spirits he can even converse with it.

The Aranda have no conception of physical paternity. Pregnancy results, not from any act of the father, but from the entrance into the mother's body of the spirit of some totemic ancestor, whose identity is determined by the old men. A father regards his child, not as his offspring in our sense, but rather as his property, on a principle similar to that by which we recognize the owner of a cow as the owner of her calf. An Aranda, therefore, shows no surprise or concern when his wife gives birth to a half-caste child; he attributes it, perhaps, merely to her eating white flour obtained from the Europeans. Pregnant women observe a variety of food taboos and are segregated from the men in special huts near the women's club house.

Women occasionally produce an abortion by tying a belt very tightly about the abdomen. Infanticide, though rare, is practiced under certain circumstances, more commonly with girls than with boys. If the mother is still suckling an older child, and is thus unable to rear the infant, she chokes it to death with sand immediately after birth. Twins are always killed. Now and then a child a few years of age is slain and its body fed to an older but sickly child, not as food, but in order to impart its strength to the other. Actual cannibalism exists today only in this special instance, though its former prevalence is attested by tradition and by practices of bloodletting and blood drinking.

Childbirth is usually easy, and the mother goes about her duties in an hour or two. If difficulties arise, the father assists by acts of ritual magic. The mother severs the umbilical cord with a stone knife, burns the afterbirth, and places the baby in a wooden trough without bathing it. After a few days she makes a necklace for the infant from the remainder of the cord, and paints a black line over its eyebrow to ward off illness. In the meantime, the paternal grandfather takes a piece of wood from a sacred tree near the storehouse, retires into the bush with a few old men, makes a personal *churinga* for the child, and deposits this in the storehouse. A woman never sees her personal *churinga;* a man not until initiated. Each individual possesses two names, a totemic name known to everybody, and a secret *churinga* name bestowed shortly after birth by the totem chief in consultation with the older men and uttered only on the most solemn occasions. These sacred names are known only by the very old men; women do not even know their own.

Infants, before they can sit up, are carried in a wooden trough; afterwards they ride astride the mother's hip or shoulder. They are suckled until at least three years of age. Women nurse each other's children, and disputes often arise over who shall stay in camp for this purpose while the rest go out after food. Parents treat their children with uniform kindness. They sometimes scold them, but never punish them except in rare bursts of passion. Uninitiated boys camp with the women and girls, play with them, and accompany them on their rambles for plant foods and small animals. Through observation and imitation of their elders, the young acquire a knowledge of the tracks of animals, the location of the best sources of food, the respective duties of the sexes, and the economic aspects of life generally. The older men and women reserve the choicer foods for themselves by means of a variety of taboos imposed upon uninitiated boys and girls. Boys, for example, may not eat lizards and emu fat or they will grow up deformed, and girls must abstain from the echidna, brush turkey, and eagle-hawk else their breasts will not develop.

The transition from childhood to the status of an adult is effected in both sexes by ceremonies of initiation. In the girl these are relatively simple, consisting mainly in a ritual rubbing of her breasts with fat and ocher. The boy, however, must undergo a long series of complicated rites, often of a highly painful or even dangerous nature and always charged with a magical import. Their object is partly to test his fortitude and qualifications for manhood, and partly to inculcate habits of obedience to his elders, to impart the

FIG. 10. AN ARANDA WOMAN WITH HER CHILD,
DIGGING STICK, AND WOODEN TROUGH.
From Spencer and Gillen, *The Arunta*

traditional lore of the tribe and the secrets of the men, and to teach the necessity of absolute observance of all tribal customs.

The first of these ceremonies, held at the age of ten or

twelve, marks the lad's departure from the company of the women and his entrance into economic community with the men. The central rite consists in his being tossed several times into the air by the men, while the women dance and shout. Any "father-in-law" whom he has insulted or neglected can beat him with a club as he falls. When he has reached puberty, a corroboree is held, and he witnesses several days of ceremonies designed to acquaint him with the legends of the Alchera ancestors. He is then circumcised, and the exuviæ eaten by his younger brother to promote growth and vigor in the latter. He is taught the secret of the bull-roarer, and retires into the bush to recover. Here he is visited by a delegation of men, who bite his scalp till the blood flows freely. This helps his hair to grow. Five or six weeks later comes the ceremony of subincision, from which the women are rigidly excluded. While the women at their club house gash themselves severely on the shoulders and abdomen, the men seize the youth and, with a stone knife, slit his genital member to the urethra underneath. At an indefinite later time is held a great Engwura ceremony, which may last for several months and is attended by all neighboring groups. Beginning with a monotonous succession of corroborees and special ceremonies, this celebration terminates in a period of unrestrained license. At its high point the neophytes must undergo a series of fire ordeals—defending themselves with branches while the women throw burning grass and sticks on their heads, lying down for five minutes on green boughs laid over a huge fire, and kneeling unprotected for half a minute in the blazing coals of a smaller fire. Now at last they are men.

They are not full men, however, for a man must wait some time after his initiation before he sees his own *churinga*, and before he is shown the sacred storehouse he must prove himself worthy of receiving and capable of keeping the tribal secrets. Sometimes he must even undergo a further ordeal, such as having his forehead gashed or a thumb-nail torn out.

Girls are married when they reach puberty, nearly always to men considerably older than themselves. This disparity in age results from the peculiar manner in which marriage is normally contracted. Neither party has a voice in the transaction. Two men agree to establish a *tualcha mura* relation between their children, the son of one and the daughter of the other. But, curiously enough, this makes the girl, not the wife, but the mother-in-law of the boy. It gives him the right to marry her as yet unborn daughters. The relation is established by a definite ceremony in which the mothers of the children smear them with grease and red ocher and shear the girl's hair to make a belt for the boy. A man may possess several such mothers-in-law, all of them, of course, so related to him that their daughters will be of the class into which he is permitted to marry. (Normally they are daughters of the brothers of his maternal grandmother.) If a man thus acquires more wives than he wants, he may give away the extra ones or simply waive his right. There is, however, no objection to polygyny.

When a girl is of age to marry, certain male relatives of her allotted husband, including the men eligible to marry her, transport her into the bush, deflower her with a stone knife, have connection with her, paint and decorate her, and return her to the groom. After this wedding ceremony she is his private property, and no man may have access to her without his permission. The wife always joins her husband's local group.

While a *tualcha mura* arrangement is the normal mode of marriage, it is not the only recognized one. A man may take a wife—from another man—by capture, elopement, or magic. The capture of a woman from another group usually follows the murder of her husband in blood-revenge. Elopement involves the consent of the woman and requires considerable hardihood, for the wandering wife is severely lacerated, and the man is forced to stand on guard against the weapons of the offended husband without being allowed to retaliate.

If he proves strong and clever enough, he keeps the woman. Magic, a favorite and legitimate method, is employed in various ways. If, for example, a man croons magical love ditties all night over a *churinga*, the lady of his heart feels irresistibly drawn toward him, her internal organs quiver with emotion, and she steals away from her husband to join him.

Considerable laxity prevails in sexual relations. Though a husband will inflict horrible punishment upon his wife for any infidelity on her part, he will lend her readily to a friend or guest. Women may also be offered to enemies to avert hostilities. Messengers to distant groups are often accompanied by women; the strangers manifest their acceptance or rejection of the proposal by visiting or refusing them. Promiscuity reigns at certain corroborees. Occasionally even the class restrictions are temporarily suspended, and only actual fathers and daughters, mothers and sons, and brothers and sisters are taboo to one another. In general, however, marriage or intercourse with a person of a forbidden class is the greatest of all crimes or sins. It incurs the penalty of immediate death, for it corresponds precisely to incest amongst ourselves.

In view of their virtual exclusion from all ceremonial, religious, and governmental matters, women cannot be said to enjoy a high position in Aranda society. A man may easily dispose of his wife. A woman, however, cannot secure a divorce; she can only run away. Widows are inherited by the next younger brother of the deceased husband. Women, though they work hard, are not treated with harshness or cruelty; they are physically ill-used only for breaches of tribal custom.

The Aranda never abandon or kill their aged and infirm. On the contrary, they treat them with especial kindness and respect, reserving the choicest foods for them through taboos, and providing for those who are unable to care for themselves. The old men, in particular, enjoy great prestige and a considerable measure of authority. If an old man is sick, he may regain his strength by drinking the blood of a younger man or by scraping some chips from his *churinga*, mixing them with water, and drinking the potion. When a person is seriously ill, the women in their anxiety throw themselves on his body. "But for this habit," sighs a missionary, "some might recover."

When a man dies, his soul flies away temporarily in the form of a whistling bird. The relatives set up a loud lamentation, disarrange their hair, and strew sand and ashes over one another. The father throws himself on the body and is cruelly beaten by the women with their digging sticks. All "sons-in-law," actual and possible, gash themselves severely on the shoulder. If the deceased is a woman, her "mothers" lacerate their heads in similar fashion. Burial ensues with all possible haste. The hair of the dead man is cut at the grave and made into a belt for his eldest son. The body is interred in a sitting position, properly oriented, and covered loosely with brushwood and earth, leaving a hole by which the soul may enter and leave. Over the grave is reared a small mound, covered with fresh twigs, and the ground nearby is cleared of all stones, grass, bushes, and débris so that the ghost may have no landmarks to find its way about. Immediately after the funeral, the hut of the deceased is burned, his property destroyed, the camp abandoned, and a new one erected.

While mourning lasts, the survivors must not mention the name of the dead; certain relatives may never do so. The widow smears her hair, face, and breasts with white pipe clay, isolates herself, tends the grave, and observes a taboo of silence. Mourning terminates after twelve or eighteen months in a second funeral, at which the widow is crowned with a hideous chaplet of animal bones, hair, and feathers. The men visit the abandoned camp and seek to banish the haunting ghost by dancing, shouting, and brandishing their weapons. They then proceed to the grave and trample upon it, while the female relatives spill blood over the sacred spot. At the conclusion of the ceremony the soul of the deceased departs to join its double, the *churinga* spirit, at the totemic storehouse, where it waits to be reborn.

Such property as is not destroyed at the funeral is inherited by the eldest son, or in default of sons by a younger brother. Possessions thus inherited include a man's *churinga*, the belt made from his hair, in which his qualities inhere, and certain totemic ceremonies in which private property is recognized. A woman's *churinga* descends to her younger brother, never to another woman.

The Aranda cannot conceive of death from natural causes. To him it is always due to the magical operations of an enemy. He knows many ways of producing death by magic. One of the commonest is "bone-pointing." A man mutters incantations and curses over a sharp bone or stick tipped with resin, and points it at his unsuspecting enemy as the latter sits by the campfire. The victim shortly sickens and dies. A wound from a spear that has been "sung over" is especially dreaded. No matter how slight the wound, if the victim suspects magic, he refuses food, pines away, and dies. Nothing can save him, not even European medicine, for faith can kill as well as cure. The deadliest magic of all, however, is that worked by a sorcerer who has undergone a sinister ceremony involving the dislocation of the joints of his little toe. Such a man can spread secret death while wearing invisible "debbil-debbil" shoes made of emu feathers and human hair matted with blood. Other methods of sorcery are too numerous to mention, but the Aranda are exceptional in never practicing exuvial magic with hair and nail clippings.

But magic has other uses than causing death—for example, curing disease, acquiring a wife, punishing crime, and cowing the women. Indeed, as Sir Baldwin Spencer points out, the Aranda lives in an environment suffused with magic. "Everything that is of importance to him in life, whether it counts for pleasure or discomfort, for good or for evil, is a matter of magic. Drought and flood, the periodic increase of animals and the mysterious springing up of plants out of the ground, even his own birth and

FIG. 11. POSITION ASSUMED BY THE ARANDA
IN "BONE-POINTING."
From Spencer and Gillen, *The Arunta*

death and that of all the people around him, are not to him due to what we call natural causes, they are all, in his mind, simply the result of magic of some form or another." He believes so implicitly in magic that he never thinks of putting it to the test. Cases of failure he attributes solely to stronger adverse magic.

Though all persons, including women, may practice magic, the shaman or medicine man is a specialist in the art, and he alone can counteract the magic of an enemy. A man becomes a shaman through a bloody initiation at the hands either of the spirits themselves or of his fellow practitioners. In either case he has a hole pierced in his tongue, dresses distinctively, observes various taboos, employs special paraphernalia, and holds intercourse with the spirits, mostly evil or at least mischievous, which throng in every locality. Upon him devolves the duty of ascertaining the identity of the sorcerer who has caused a death. He also cures disease, which likewise comes only through magic. He proceeds by rubbing and sucking the affected part and producing with practiced legerdemain the pieces of stone, wood, or bone allegedly introduced by the sorcerer's magic. He receives no reward for success. Neither is he blamed for failure; the patient did not call him in time, or the enemy's magic is too potent. The shaman is also called upon to dispel an eclipse of the sun. With his magic chants and fetish stones he exorcises the evil spirit who is obscuring the light—invariably with success.

Death, being due to magical rather than natural causes, is in all respects like actual murder and is dealt with as such. It imposes upon the near relatives of the deceased the obligation of blood-revenge against the sorcerer or his kindred. Hence, in the natural course of things, every death is followed by the slaughter of a second person.

The political, judicial, and military institutions of the Aranda are very rudimentary. Tribal government does not exist. The natives are divided into innumerable independent local groups, which are identical with the totem groups. Each has its recognized hunting grounds as well as the totem center about which its ceremonial life revolves. Only within these atomistic groups does anything resembling political organization prevail. Each local group acknowledges the leadership of a totem chief, whose authority is vague, dependent upon his personal prestige, and mainly, as we have seen, of a religious character. The office is hereditary, descending from father to eldest son provided the latter belongs to the same totem. On all important matters, such as the conduct of ceremonies, the totem chief consults with a council of the oldest and most respected men of the group. This council of elders exercises the few strictly regulative functions—dealing with strangers and organizing parties to punish crime and execute blood-vengeance.

FIG. 12. ARANDA ELDERS MEETING BEFORE A WURLEY.
From Spencer and Gillen, *The Arunta*

Law is no less rudimentary. In general, peace prevails within the group. Occasionally, to be sure, quarrels arise between individuals. If women fight, etiquette demands that they belabor each other alternately with their clubs or digging sticks. The men usually look on indifferently. If two men come to blows, however, their respective mothers and sisters step in to shield them and often bear the brunt of the battle. Such quarrels, however, are rare and easily settled. Definite judicial machinery is called into being only in the case of serious crimes, such as marrying a woman of the wrong class, unauthorized acquisition of totemic secrets, actual murder, and especially causing death through sorcery. Death, the penalty in each case, is invariably executed in the same way, namely, by an avenging party organized by the council of elders.

Relations between groups, even of different tribes, are almost equally amicable. No such thing as a chronic state of hostility exists. Couriers with messages or invitations travel with impunity from group to group. Local trade is extensively carried on among the different branches of the Aranda, war clubs and magic knouts are bartered from the Warramunga and other northern tribes, and pituri is obtained by exchange from the interior of Queensland, hundreds of miles away. Local groups sometimes lend *churinga* to friendly neighboring groups. This brings luck to the borrower and prestige to the lender—besides presents, which always accompany their return. Visiting between groups, even aside from special ceremonial occasions, is quite common. Men may go alone, in parties, or with their families. The presence of women and children gives evidence of friendly intentions. The visitors wait outside the camp until an old man comes out, converses with them, and invites them in. The women and children stay at the women's club house, the men at the men's club. The latter are frequently provided with temporary wives. The guests take pot luck with their hosts, and after a day or two go out with them in search of food. Visits by large parties sometimes precipitate noisy and acrimonious disputes, but very rarely a resort to force. Under normal conditions, therefore, intergroup relations of trade and friendly intercourse prevail.

Actual warfare is all but unknown. A number of local groups have been known to unite temporarily under an elected war chief against an enemy, but such instances are rare indeed. Under ordinary circumstances the only approach to war is found in the expeditions organized for blood-revenge and the punishment of crime. When a death has occurred and the shaman has accused a member of another group, the avenging party selected by the council prepare themselves by various ceremonies. They may, for example, rub themselves with the dead man's hair-belt to strengthen them in their purpose, or open their veins and spurt blood on one another to unite themselves more closely and prevent treachery, or enact magical dances representing the slaying of the culprit. They may accomplish the actual deed by stealth, or they may advance openly against the enemy in battle array. In the latter case, nothing more than a battle of vituperation may result. Often, however, after a conference between the elders, the victim is treacherously slain with the connivance of his fellows. If the criminal is a member of the group, a party from a neighboring group may be called in to execute the murderer. The members of a successful avenging party disguise themselves against the ghost of the murdered man by painting themselves with charcoal and wearing green twigs on their heads and in their noses. Even blood-revenge, therefore, rarely leads to actual fighting.

The Aranda have shown themselves equally friendly to the whites. Aside from a certain amount of cattle raiding in retaliation for the inroads of the settlers on the hunting grounds and water-holes of the aborigines, there has been little violence. In other ways, however, the natives have suffered from contact with the alien race. Tuberculosis and venereal disease, contracted from the whites, have reduced the population of the tribe from more than two thousand at the end of the last century to barely three hundred in 1928, and they threaten it ere long with complete extinction.

BIBLIOGRAPHY

BASEDOW, H. *The Australian Aboriginal.* Adelaide, 1925.

EYLMANN, E. *Die Eingeborenen der Kolonie Südaustralien.* Berlin, 1908.

GILLEN, F. J. "Magic amongst the Natives of Central Australia." *Report of the Eighth Meeting of the Australasian Association for the Advancement of Science.* Melbourne, 1900.

GILLEN, F. J. "Notes on Some Manners and Customs of the Aborigines of the McDonnell Ranges Belonging to the Arunta Tribe." *Report on the Work of the Horn Scientific Expedition to Central Australia*, Vol. IV. London, 1896.

HOWITT, A. W. *The Native Tribes of South-East Australia*. London, 1914.

LEONHARDI, M. VON. "Über einige religiöse und totemistische Vorstellungen der Aranda und Loritja in Zentralaustralien." *Globus*, Vol. XCI. Braunschweig, 1907.

MATHEWS, R. H. "Notes on the Arranda Tribe." *Journal and Proceedings of the Royal Society of New South Wales*, Vol. XLI. Sydney, 1907.

———. "Marriage and Descent in the Arranda Tribe, Central Australia." *American Anthropologist*, New Series, Vol. X. Lancaster, 1908.

PORTEUS, S. D. *The Psychology of a Primitive People*. New York, 1931.

RADCLIFFE-BROWN, A. R. "The Social Organization of Australian Tribes." *Oceania*, Vol. I. Melbourne, 1930–31.

SCHMIDT, W. "Die Gliederung der australischen Sprachen." *Anthropos*, Vols. VII–XIII. Wien, 1912–18.

———. "Die Stellung der Aranda unter den australischen Stämmen." *Zeitschrift für Ethnologie*, Vol. XL. Berlin, 1908.

SCHULZE, L. "The Aborigines of the Upper and Middle Finke River." *Transactions and Proceedings of the Royal Society of South Australia*, Vol. XIV. Adelaide, 1891.

SPENCER, B. *Wanderings in Wild Australia*. 2 vols. London, 1928.

*SPENCER, B., and GILLEN, F. J. *The Arunta*. 2 vols. London, 1927.

———. *The Native Tribes of Central Australia*. London, 1899.

———. *The Northern Tribes of Central Australia*. London, 1904.

STIRLING, E. C. "Anthropology." *Report on the Work of the Horn Scientific Expedition to Central Australia*, Vol. IV. London, 1896.

STREHLOW, C. *Die Aranda- und Loritja-Stämme in Zentral-Australien*. Frankfurt a.M., 1907–11.

CHAPTER III

THE SAMOANS

IN the heart of the romance-laden South Seas, about 14° below the equator and 171° west of Greenwich, lies Samoa, a group of fourteen volcanic islands with a total land surface of nearly 1,200 square miles, mostly accounted for by the three large islands of Savaii, Upolu, and Tutuila. The native Samoans are typical representatives of the Polynesian race and exhibit scarcely a trace of admixture with the darker Melanesians. Physically well-proportioned, athletic, and often handsome, the men attain an average stature of nearly five feet eight inches, the women some four inches less. They are characterized by a light brown complexion, straight or wavy black hair, comparatively scanty beards and body hair, dark brown eyes, a medium (mesorrhine) nose, a rather flat face, and a moderately broad or brachycephalic head (average cephalic index 81). The vexed problem of the racial affiliations of the Polynesians does not concern us here.

The Samoan language, which from its soft and liquid character has been termed "the Italian of the Pacific," is a dialect of the Polynesian branch of the far-flung Malayo-Polynesian linguistic stock. Striking cultural similarities ally the Samoans with the Polynesians in general and the neighboring Tongans in particular—a proof that their culture owes its origin largely to migration and borrowing rather than to independent development.

From the coast, paralleled by barrier reefs, the land rises sharply toward the interior, culminating in extinct or quiescent volcanic peaks from two to four thousand feet in height. Samoa lacks rivers, but springs abound, fed by a rainfall which averages well over 100 inches annually. The prevailing trade winds, occasionally interrupted by typhoons, gratefully

FIG. 13. A SAMOAN CHIEF.
From Krämer, *Die Samoa-Inseln.* Courtesy of
E. Schweizerbartsche Verlagsbuchhandlung

moderate the otherwise oppressive tropical heat and humidity. Though the temperature varies remarkably little in any month from the annual mean of 78° F., two seasons are distinguishable: a fine season from April to October, and a rainy season from November to March. The extremely fertile soil supports a luxuriant tropical vegetation, which swarms with bird and insect life.

Nothing could be more erroneous, however, than the popular conception of Samoa as a tropical paradise where man has nothing to do but idle, while nature, unsolicited, drops her bountiful fruits into his lap. To be sure the waters teem with fish, but in other respects nature is niggardly indeed. Except for a few wild roots and fruits, the land provides no plant foods which man may collect, and no animals larger than snakes, lizards, and land crabs for him to hunt. If life is comparatively easy in Samoa, it is because man, not nature, has made it so. Man brought with him to the islands, not only poultry and the dog, but also the pig, which he keeps in pens and fattens on coconuts. He also introduced the various plants and trees whose cultivation furnishes him with his primary means of subsistence.

Breadfruit trees, coconut palms, and banana trees are planted in or near the villages, and yield abundantly with comparatively little attention. On the other hand, taro, a starchy root, and the yam, a coarse imitation of the potato, which are grown in swamps and harvested with digging sticks, require arduous clearing of the land and careful, laborious tillage. A sixth staple crop—the least esteemed—is the sweet potato. In addition, the Samoans cultivate the ti tree, the paper mulberry, pandanus, arrowroot, kava, and sugar cane. The men clear the land and plant the fields; the women weed and harvest the crops.

Hunting, in default of any large indigenous animals, consists chiefly in catching or snaring birds, and frequently assumes the aspect of a noble sport rather than a task. On certain occasions the chiefs foregather in the bush for a period of sport and festivity, bringing with them pigeons which they have caught, tamed, and trained as decoys. Concealing themselves under brush shelters around a cleared space, the hunters allow their decoys to circle about at the end of strings. The wild pigeons, attracted by their tame cousins, are readily caught in elongated nets fastened to bamboo poles. Great rivalry prevails among the hunters as to who can catch the most.

Next to the soil, the sea provides the natives with their principal means of subsistence. Fish are caught in an almost endless variety of ways: by hand, with snares and nooses, in baskets and traps, with spears, in nets of excellent quality and various sizes and shapes, with weirs and dams, by rod and line with ingenious hooks of wood and shell, by stupefac-

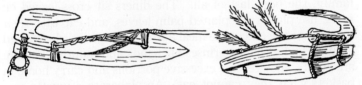

FIG. 14. TYPES OF SAMOAN FISHHOOKS.

tion with vegetable poisons, and with the bow and arrow, which, curiously enough, are not used in warfare. The women and older girls, armed with sticks, comb the shores of the lagoons for small fry—lobsters, crabs, shrimps, mollusks, sea urchins, and octopuses. One of the choicest aquatic delicacies is the palolo, a marine worm which rises to the surface of the sea in early November to breed. The natives turn out *en masse* to scoop them up in baskets, eating them cooked or raw with equal relish. The men alone fish with boats and tackle, which are strictly taboo to the women. They often spear fish at night by torchlight, and they even attack the shark with nooses and clubs. They go out to sea in special boats to troll the bonito, a game fish which provides exciting and dangerous sport. It is caught with an unbaited hook of tortoise shell, concealed with feathers and attached to a piece of mother-of-pearl made to resemble a small fish. Finding a turtle floating on the surface of the water, a man will dive beneath it and flip it over on its back, rendering it helpless. A head fisherman in each village controls all communal fishing activities.

On a normal day the Samoans rise at dawn, disperse to their various labors with no food save perhaps a lump of cold taro, assemble for a late breakfast or lunch at about eleven o'clock, take a siesta during the noonday heat, return to their tasks after a visit or two, gather at dusk for the principal meal of the day, and spend the evening in conversation, dancing, singing, and love-making. The evening meal is a ceremonious affair, beginning with a libation to the gods. The head of the household is served first, then the rest of the family, the boys last of all. The diners sit cross-legged on mats, use platters of plaited palm leaves, and eat with their fingers. At the end of the meal a wooden finger bowl is passed around, and every one rinses his hands and mouth. If there are guests, they receive excessive portions and carry home in baskets what they cannot eat. An elaborate etiquette surrounds the sharing and giving of food, and hospitality is both a virtue and an obligation.

Though the women prepare the food, the men cook it. Even old men and chiefs do not consider the culinary art beneath their dignity. A shallow pit in a special cookhouse serves as an oven. Fire is generated by the plowing method— pressing a pointed stick of hard wood back and forth on a softer piece until the sawdust is ignited by the friction. The cook then heats a number of round stones in the fire, rakes away the ashes, places the food over the hot stones, covers it with green leaves, and allows it to bake for an hour or two. In the absence of pottery, boiling is done in wooden vessels by dropping in heated stones. Coconuts are eaten raw, but breadfruit, yams, taro, and even bananas are always thoroughly cooked. Coconut cream, the oil expressed from the kernel of the nut, finds the same uses in Samoan cookery that butter does in ours, and taro takes the place of potatoes on their bill of fare. Surplus breadfruit is stored in shallow pits, where it ferments into a sour evil-smelling mess, to be baked into small cakes when other food is scarce. Many kinds of puddings and other special dishes are prepared from vegetable products. Fish, when not eaten raw, are either cooked in coconut cream or wrapped in leaves and baked like vegetables. The Samoans are said to eat dogs, but they despise eggs and do not even esteem chickens very highly. They regard pigeons, turtles, and pork as the choicest of meat foods. A pig is throttled, trussed up on a pole, singed, scrubbed clean, dressed, stuffed with hot stones, and baked whole in the oven till half done. The entrails are removed, cleaned, separately cooked, and eaten.

From the kava plant, a variety of pepper, the natives prepare a stimulating but non-alcoholic drink. The girls cram pieces of the dried root into their mouths, chew them thoroughly, and spit out the juice and pulp into a special wooden bowl. The mess is then stirred, mixed with water, strained through a bark strainer, and the first cup poured out as a libation to the gods. Kava is made and served according to an elaborate and intricate ritual as a necessary preliminary to every event or undertaking of social, economic, political, and religious importance.

The Samoans dwell in substantial elliptical houses about twenty-five feet in height and thirty in diameter. On a few stout central posts and an ellipse of short outside pillars, is erected a complicated superstructure of beams, plates, purlins, rafters, and struts, all bound firmly together, not by nails or pegs, but by decorative lashings of sennit. On this framework, sheets of sugar-cane thatch are carefully laid and lashed, one overlapping the next, from the eaves to the ridgepole. A raised stone platform, covered with mats, serves as a floor. There are neither walls nor doors—only screens plaited from coconut leaves, suspended from the roof between the outside pillars and lowered by cords in inclement weather. Privacy, therefore, does not exist; every word and act of the occupants is the property of any interested spectator.

Though women prepare the thatch, plait the screens, and fetch the gravel, the actual construction of the house falls to a specialized and highly honored craft of male artisans. The carpenters are organized into guilds, each with its

Fig. 15. Kava-Making in Samoa.
From Krämer, *Die Samoa-Inseln.* Courtesy of
E. Schweizerbartsche Verlagsbuchhandlung

chief, its masters and apprentices, its trade-mark, and its special ceremonial. The artistic tastes of the individual craftsman are given free rein in the matter of details, and slavish imitation is frowned upon, but any substantial deviation in style or plan from the accepted standards arouses antagonism and leads to expulsion from the guild. The builder of a house supplies his carpenters with food and all materials; he feasts them at various stages in the construction; and he pays them lavishly. A ceremony of consecration, with prayers to the tutelary divinities of the family and the carpenters' guild, marks the completion of the building.

Furniture is limited to mats, mosquito curtains, and bamboo pillows, but the implements and utensils of the household are varied and well adapted to their uses. Among the more important are: knives of bamboo and chipped stone, shell scrapers, hafted adzes of polished stone, a wooden horse for grating coconuts, files of shark skin for polishing wood, a pump drill, an adze-shaped wooden implement

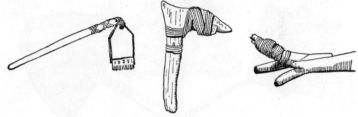

FIG. 16. SAMOAN TOOLS: TATTOOING IMPLEMENT, ADZE, AND COCONUT GRATER.

for splitting breadfruit, netting needles, carved wooden combs and fans, brooms, tongs for handling hot stones, ropes, plaited baskets, carved wooden bowls, and coconut-shell drinking cups and water bottles. An open hearth in the center of the house, a lamp consisting of a crude wick in a coconut shell filled with oil, and strings of candlenuts furnish light at night.

The Samoan women manufacture two outstanding textile products—mats, and tapa or bark cloth. Mats, used as carpets, bedding, and clothing, are plaited from various vegetable substances, especially pandanus leaves scraped clean and slit into thin strips. The finest mats, which resemble the best Panama hats in texture, are often fringed and decorated with feathers, and require several months to make. They are the natives' choicest possessions and serve as a sort of medium of exchange, a fine specimen with historical associations being as valuable as a house or a boat. To prepare tapa, the women strip and scrape the inner bark of the paper mulberry, lay it on a wooden anvil, beat it to the thickness of paper with a mallet, and stretch it to dry. Various designs are rubbed or painted on the finished product with vegetable or mineral dyes.

Neither sex, as a rule, wears any clothing above the waist, children nothing at all. The usual costume is a mere kilt

After Buck and Krämer

FIG. 17. SAMOAN FANS.

of ti leaves, extending to the knees with women, much more abbreviated with men. Sometimes, especially in the evening or during illness, the natives wear robes of tapa, which, since it cannot be washed, quickly becomes filthy. On special occasions the women don fine mats in place of their leaf girdles. Head and feet are ordinarily unclad, though chiefs wear dancing headdresses of feathers or human hair. The body is anointed with a mixture of coconut oil and turmeric, which gives it a stylish yellow sheen. The men pluck out all facial hair. The women cut their hair short, but often stiffen it with scented oil and gum. Men of rank wear theirs long, gather it into a knot on the crown, and sometimes bleach it light brown with lime. Both sexes delight in wearing garlands of flowers and necklaces of bright shells and beads, but strings of whale ivory are valued most highly.

Like all Polynesians, the Samoans are at home both in and on the sea. Expert at swimming and diving, they spend much time in the water, taking especial pleasure in riding the surf on a board. With only the simplest tools, such as the stone adze and pump drill, the native carpenters

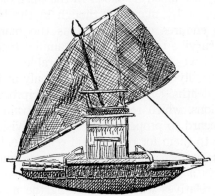

After Buck

FIG. 18. MODEL OF A SAMOAN DOUBLE CANOE.

build canoes varying in size from small dugouts hollowed from a single log, to vessels fifty or sixty feet in length, constructed of small planks neatly fitted and lashed together with the interstices caulked with gum. In view of their exceptional narrowness—a three foot beam is unusual—all canoes, to prevent capsizing, are equipped on the port side with an outrigger, a wooden float attached to the vessel with spars. They are propelled both by paddles and by triangular mat sails. The larger sea-going canoes possess keels, gunwales, and small decks fore and aft. Enormous double canoes with thatched cabins on platforms, though now fallen into disuse on account of their unwieldiness, are said to have been capable of transporting an entire village.

The strongest social tie in Samoa is the bond of kinship. Actual degrees of relationship in our sense are recognized, but such distinctions carry little weight. Kinship terms are not employed in social intercourse; a child, for instance, addresses his parents by their personal names rather than as "mother" and "father." In practice all relatives are lumped together under one term, *ainga*, irrespective of whether they are allied by blood in the male or female line, by adoption, or by marriage, though in the last case the relationship endures only so long as the marriage exists or children survive to bind the two families together. This body of relatives, though of considerable theoretical importance, actually functions as a group only at births, marriages, and deaths. Kinship involves reciprocal privileges and obligations, which reflect a marked strain of communism with regard to property. People may visit their kinsmen, or flee to them for refuge, and remain as long as they like without compensation. When any one builds a house or boat, pays a fine, or assembles a dowry, it is assumed that all his relatives will aid in raising the necessary sum. No one, for fear of being thought stingy, will refuse to give or lend an object for which a kinsman expresses a desire, even though it be a piece of tapa just completed after weeks of painstaking labor. The recipient is expected eventually to render some approximately equivalent favor, so the privilege is rarely abused. Though this system may dull individual initiative, it removes the fear of poverty. The aged and incapacitated can never lack food, shelter, and clothing. "How is it?" the natives incredulously exclaim when Europeans speak of a man as poor, "No food! Has he no friends? No house to live in! Are there no houses belonging to his friends?"

Rank in Samoa depends upon the possession of titles. Untitled individuals or commoners differ little in status except as distinguished by age or sex. The nobles, however, form an extensive hierarchy, each successive rank of which is associated with the possession of a title carrying with it specific privileges, duties, and responsibilities. Each title involves the headship of a household and a definite status in the community; likewise, depending on its degree, certain civil, political, military, and religious functions and prerogatives. Nobles or title-holders fall into two main classes—chiefs (*alii*), and orators or "talking chiefs" (*tula-fale*)—each with numerous grades. A chief is hedged in by thousands of minute rules of etiquette. For example, he may not climb his own coconut tree if any one of lesser rank is present. His person is taboo to commoners. He is addressed in a special ceremonial language. He remains silent in public, allowing his orator to speak for him. He alone may eat certain tabooed foods. At feasts he receives favored positions and choice portions, and is served first with kava and food. His authority may be real and tyrannical, or it may be merely nominal, depending upon his personal qualities and the dignity of his title. The talking chiefs are the custodians of tradition, the censors of etiquette, the masters of ceremonies. They act as spokesmen, advisers, ambassadors, and marriage brokers for the chiefs. For their services they receive fine mats on ceremonial occasions when property is distributed. They wield great power, sometimes greater even than the chiefs themselves.

A Samoan is never born to a title; he must acquire it. To be sure, birth into a family with a high title improves his chances. Nevertheless, the succession falls only occasionally to the eldest son. Nomination is vested in the kindred group, and its choice is affected by personal preferences, intrigues among the mothers and sisters of candidates, and the natural desire for a strong and capable leader. The community, moreover, exercises a veto power. Thus the successor may quite likely be a younger or an adopted son, a brother or nephew, or even a brother- or son-in-law.

The mode of selection, though it lends itself to intrigue, places a premium less on descent than on personal qualities of courage, charm, integrity, skill, and leadership.

The unit of social and economic life is the household. Unlike our own biological family of parents and children, the Samoan household may embrace as many as fifty persons occupying several adjoining houses. It is really a large joint family, patriarchal in character, acknowledging the authority of one headman (*matai*), to whom the members are usually related by blood, adoption, or marriage. This family head invariably holds a title of some kind, and is treated with the respect due his rank. He performs the ceremonial and religious duties of the household with dignity and decorum. Though in theory he holds the power of life and death over his subordinates, his authority really depends largely on his personal qualities, and if unpopular he may be deposed. Theoretically exempt from petty domestic tasks, he is seldom so in actuality. He directs, and takes a leading part in, the economic activities of the household. He owns the land tilled by the members and can alienate it by sale or gift, but the live stock and domestic implements and utensils belong to the household in common, and the fine mats and choicest pieces of tapa are the property of the *ainga* or larger kindred group.

Ten or more households are united by kinship or for mutual protection into a village, a self-governing political unit. Each village owns its own communal fishing grounds, and definite boundaries separate its territory from those of its neighbors. It recognizes the man with the highest title in the village as its head chief and accords him special honors. A large round house serves as a communal meeting place and a reception hall for visitors. Here all the village nobles or chiefs, *i.e.*, the heads of households, meet in a general assembly (*fono*), which combines the functions of a legislature and court of justice and organizes all community enterprises. The actual meeting usually follows a formal routine, since the members consult privately in advance to exchange views and thresh out differences. Decisions are made, not by a majority vote, but by certain chiefs whose titles give them this right in particular cases. The decrees of the assembly are strictly enforced; disobedience is punished by banishment and the confiscation or destruction of property.

A number of villages commonly unite, especially in periods of stress, to form a district or petty state. The chief with the highest title becomes the prince or overlord of the district, and his village is made the capital. His person is rigidly taboo and is thought to radiate deadly influences. The ranking chiefs of the several villages constitute a district *fono* or parliament, whose primary function is to adjust differences and prevent strife among the members of the league. The villages are entirely independent as regards the conduct of their internal affairs, and are at liberty at any time to sever their relations with one district and join another. There is no permanent kingship over all Samoa. Occasionally, however, one man may unite in his person the titles of the four ruling districts of Upolu and Savaii and thus become in effect the king of the whole island group. But the position is not hereditary; on his death the titles are scattered and the kingship dissolves.

In Samoa, the community intervenes to punish crimes or redress injuries only in the case of offenses considered particularly heinous. For minor wrongs, such as theft, the injured individual or family is forced to resort to self-help, or even to blood-revenge. Satisfaction may be exacted either of the culprit himself or of his kinsmen, for a household is jointly responsible for the acts of all its members. Theft of crops from a plantation is the commonest crime; stealing property from a house, a capital offense, is practically unknown, and taking property left outside the house is considered perfectly legitimate. To guard what he cannot and the community does not protect, the owner of a plantation has recourse to supernatural agencies. Taboos, in particular, furnish very effective protection. The owner places one of a wide variety of taboos on his plantation and indicates the fact by a special token. To place a "white shark taboo" on his breadfruit grove, for example, he plaits coconut leaflets into the form of a shark and fixes this symbol to a tree; a trespasser, when he next goes to sea, will be devoured by the god incarnate in the white shark. Supernatural means may also be used to detect the culprit. Suspected persons are called upon to take oath of their innocence before the village god; refusal to risk divine vengeance marks a man as guilty. Or the owner, on discovering a theft, may shout out a curse against the thief; fear often impels the latter to make restitution, especially if he begins to feel ill.

Offenses against the village or high chief, grand larceny, murder, and slander, *e.g.*, casting reflections on a family's ancestry or calling a man "a stinking swine," constitute major crimes in which the community may intervene to prevent blood-revenge. A village assembly convenes to fix the penalty, which, depending on the crime, may be death, mutilation, confiscation or destruction of property, hanging up by the heels, exposure while naked to the full glare of the tropical sun, or a variety of other special punishments. A scandalmonger, for instance, may be forced to bite into a poisonous root which causes the mucous membranes of the mouth to swell so that no solid food can be taken for weeks. A particularly humiliating punishment consists in trussing up the culprit like a pig and subjecting him to a mock cooking in a cold oven—a practice vividly reminiscent of cannibalism. Punishment extends to the criminal's family, which must pay heavy fines or even suffer banishment or the destruction of their houses and plantations. As a rule, the kinsmen of the culprit proceed before dawn to the house of the injured party, bearing gifts by way of restitution, and remain outside with their heads bowed in the dust until forgiven. To render their humiliation even more abject, they may be required to bring stones, leaves, and firewood—as much as to say: "Here we are, your pigs, to be cooked if you please; and here are the materials with which to do it."

The Samoans live in a chronic state of war. Rarely is there a time when neighboring villages somewhere in the islands are not in arms, and great wars involving two or more districts are not infrequent. The causes include trespassing on alien territory, retaliation for real or imagined wrongs and insults, the murder of a chief, ambition for power, disputes over titles, and marriage with the divorced

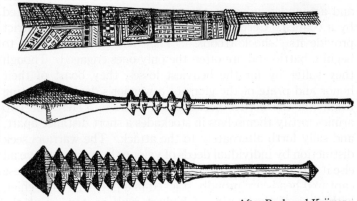

After Buck and Krämer
FIG. 19. REPRESENTATIVE SAMOAN WAR CLUBS.

wife of a chief. The natives fight with barbed wooden spears, sometimes tipped with the sting of a ray, with slings for throwing stones, and especially with artistically carved wooden war clubs equipped with sculptured knobs, blades and spikes in a bewildering diversity of patterns. For security they build refuges on commanding eminences, with high stone walls and platforms from which stones can be rolled or spears hurled at an approaching enemy.

Before precipitating a fight, a chief seeks allies among his relatives and friends, offering fine mats as bribes for assistance. Every man and boy strong enough to wield a club takes up arms. Non-combatants and movable property are removed to strongholds or neutral places, though women occasionally accompany their husbands to nurse them if wounded, or to carry their weapons in battle. The warriors don their finest apparel and trinkets, blacken their faces, and bind their heads with turbans as a protection against club blows. A feast is held, and the village gods are consulted by divination. If the auspices seem favorable, the war party starts out; it returns immediately, however, if any bad omen, like the squeaking of rats, is observed.

If several villages are allied, each has its own commander and acts independently, though operations may be directed by a council. Certain villages near the borders of a district provide its "shock troops." They have the sole right to begin a battle and are often the only ones engaged. Though they suffer by far the heaviest losses, they boast of their honor and prate of the glory of a warrior's death. Fighting begins on the border between the districts. Here the two armies fortify themselves in stockades a short distance apart, and sally forth alternately to the attack. The warriors seek distinction by individual deeds of valor or bravado. Above all else it is commendable to cut off the head of an enemy. These captured heads are proudly stacked in a pile before the chief, with that of the victim of highest rank on top. But the Samoans much prefer tactics of surprise and stratagem to open fighting. A foraying party, for example, will descend by sea or overland upon an outlying enemy village, slaughtering all the inhabitants, pillaging and destroying property, then retreating to safety.

Male prisoners are slain, unless held as hostages. Sometimes, as the acme of revenge, they are cooked and certain parts of their bodies eaten. Women, however, are usually spared and distributed among their captors. The victors treat the vanquished with extreme severity, laying waste their property, levying tribute in fine mats and tapa, and exacting the same humiliating penance as that required of the families of criminals. There are even tales of the imposition of human tribute for the table of cannibal chieftains.

But peace soon heals the ravages of war. Houses are rebuilt, fields replanted, friendly relations reëstablished. Normally, a lively trade flourishes between the islands; certain districts or villages specialize in the manufacture of fishing nets, paddles, canoes, turmeric, mats, and the like, and barter their products with their neighbors. Trade relations are even maintained by canoe with Tonga and Fiji. Visiting between friendly villages is an established custom. Each village maintains a special guest house for the lodging and entertainment of strangers. Here they are received with great ceremony and cordiality, and are provided with kava, food, and even women—usually the divorced wives of chiefs.

The arrival of a visiting party is the signal for a holiday. On all such festive occasions the Samoans find diversion in a variety of games, often of a competitive nature: boxing—by both sexes—and wrestling, fencing, throwing discs and spears for accuracy and distance, fishing and tree climbing matches, canoe racing, etc. Other amusements include hide-and-seek, forfeits, riming and guessing games, riddles, string figures, and practical jokes. But the favorite pastime is dancing. Not only visits, but weddings and all other special occasions provide excuses for dances, which may be large and formal or small and informal, depending on the circumstances. The dancers usually divide into two parties, the one singing, clapping, or beating time on wooden gongs while the other performs. Neither age, sex, nor rank debars one from the floor. Individuality and skill are encouraged, and to be a poor dancer is no small social handicap. Dances vary in type; some are stately and dignified, others athletic and noisy, still others burlesque or clownish. They are never symbolic, though they are frequently suggestive or even frankly obscene.

Such is the world into which a Samoan child is born. Children, even if illegitimate, are considered a blessing rather

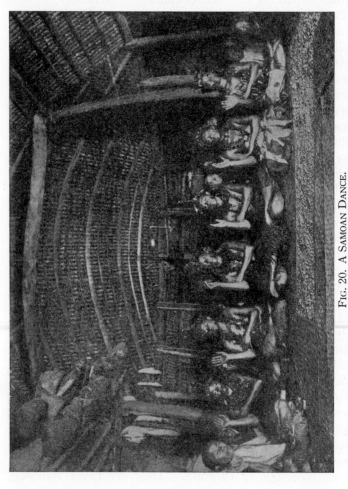

FIG. 20. A SAMOAN DANCE. From Krämer, *Die Samoa-Inseln*. Courtesy of E. Schweizerbartsche Verlagsbuchhandlung

than a burden, and the average mother has four or five. Abortion, though occasionally induced by violent massage from motives of fear, shame, or laziness, is rare, and infanticide unknown. A pregnant woman observes a number of taboos; she must shun haunted places, heavy burdens, and, above all, solitude. If not living with her parents, she must return to their home for the birth of her first child. Childbirth takes place in the presence of twenty or thirty interested spectators of both sexes and all ages. The mother makes it a point of honor not to writhe unduly or cry out in pain. Her mother, a special midwife, and other old women render the necessary assistance. Prayers and sacrifices are offered to the divinities of the father's and, if labor is difficult, also of the mother's family. The newborn infant is wiped off and wrapped in a special piece of tapa. The umbilical cord is cut with a bamboo knife and bound with a string amid rites of sympathetic magic designed to promote valor or industry. A few hours later the mother takes the child to the sea to bathe it, and after the third day she is up and about her usual tasks. The relatives remain until the baby's umbilical cord drops off—the signal for a grand feast. For months the mother's relatives have been collecting fine mats and tapa; the father's, pigs and other property. Now, with much ceremony, the two families exchange these gifts, the actual parents receiving nothing but the honor. After feasting, games, and dancing, the visitors depart—to reassemble for special ceremonies at various stages of the child's development.

For a short period after birth the mother bandages the infant's head and binds it with flat stones to broaden it—a narrow head being considered ugly—and for months she continues to mold it with her hands. She bathes the child frequently, anoints it from time to time with coconut oil, and carries it on her left hip or her back. She suckles it herself, unless unable to do so, and abstains from intercourse with her husband during lactation. Mother's milk is supplemented with other foods at an early age. Indeed, the newborn babe is fed the juice of chewed coconut kernels until the midwife adjudges the mother's milk fit. Children are sometimes weaned in six months. Usually, however, nursing continues for two years, supplemented by solid foods like starch puddings and chewed bananas. Improper feeding results in a high infant mortality rate.

As soon as possible, a mother turns her child over to its elder brothers and sisters, who become solely responsible for its care and discipline. By the time it learns to tyrannize over its young guardians, it finds itself saddled with responsibility for a still younger child. Strict obedience to parents is insisted upon, and is enforced by constant scoldings and occasional cuffings. In this way children soon learn to observe certain taboos—not to stay in the sun, not to touch the kava vessels, not to stand up in the house or when addressing elders, etc. They are given definite tasks to perform, graded according to their age and ability, and thus by the age of six they become a positive economic asset to their families. Boys of about the same age in contiguous households tend to form into gangs and wander about the village and plantations together. Girls form similar groups, and marked hostility develops between the gangs of the two sexes. Within a gang, individual friendships spring up. Thus if one boy finds a fallen coconut, he asks his special friend to join him in eating it and tells the rest to "go and catch butterflies."

At about the age of nine or ten, brothers and sisters—and cousins of opposite sex—learn to feel shy in each other's presence and to avoid one another, for Samoan custom interposes elaborate restrictions between them. They may not touch one another, converse familiarly, sit or eat together, use one another's possessions, walk together, dance on the same floor, or even be together except at home or in a crowd. In each other's presence they preserve an exaggerated decorum. This special relationship between a brother and his sister extends to her children and is reflected in certain peculiar beliefs and practices.   Thus a brother dreads his sister's ill-will with a superstitious fear; a man on succeeding to a title distributes valuable presents to his sister and her descendants; a sister's son (*tamasa*) makes free with his uncle's property.

Upon the young in Samoa devolves most of the petty, disagreeable, unskilled, and humdrum labor—fetching water, gathering leaves, cleaning house, building fires, lighting lamps, serving drinks, running errands, and—that most onerous burden of all—tending babies.   Every child is at the beck and call of all its older relatives, who have the right at any time to criticize its conduct, interfere in its affairs, or demand personal service.   Boys escape this monotonous drudgery by the age of eight or nine, when they begin to follow their fathers and learn to cook, fish, and handle weapons.   Girls, however, are not released or given an opportunity to learn the finer domestic arts until puberty.   Children find relief from this nagging repression in two ways. One is in dancing.   Here, and here alone, the young are encouraged to be independent and original.   The other escape is in running away.   Children are free to leave home at any time and go to live with relatives under the guise of a visit. Rarely, in fact, do they live continuously in one household; they are always testing out other, and possibly more congenial, residences.   The fear of losing an economic asset operates as a strong check on parental tyranny.   Parallel with this practice is that of formal adoption, the giving away of children to friends or relatives in exchange for valuable presents.

Boys, at about eight or ten years of age, submit informally to a kind of circumcision at the hands of a specialist.   This makes them men, but they cannot marry until they have been tattooed—an elaborate and painful operation performed, when a lad is about sixteen years of age, by the members of a specialized guild.   The artist works with a number of bone implements shaped like a small rake.   These he dips into a mixture of candlenut soot and water and taps into the taut skin of the patient with a small mallet, applying the pigment in a series of bands and other designs extending from the waist to the knee. The whole operation requires several months, during which time the father boards and lodges the artist, pays him in instalments with fine mats and tapa, and invites friends and relatives for a series of feasts and revels. The youth now joins the *aumaga*, a non-secret organization of all the young men of the village together with the older untitled men. This association performs coöperatively most of the heavy work of the community—fishing, taro cultivation, cooking, and the like. Also, under the leadership of the *manaia* or heir presumptive to the head chief, it entertains visitors and conducts most of the social life of the village.

When a girl reaches puberty, she is inducted with a feast and a distribution of property into the *aualuma*, a similar organization of the young unmarried women and the wives of untitled men. She, too, may be tattooed, though with scantier and more delicate designs. Freed from drudgery, she now enjoys the pleasantest period of her life. The *aualuma* is a looser organization than the *aumaga*. Though occasionally assembled for communal labor, such as preparing thatch or cultivating and harvesting a paper mulberry crop, it functions chiefly as a body of entertainers and as a court of honor to the *taupou* or "village princess." The high chief of the village has the right to name some girl in his household as *taupou*. She is elevated above the girls of her age to a position and prestige superior even to that of the wives of ranking chiefs. Though exempt from the grosser female tasks, she is surrounded by chaperons and elaborate restrictions on her freedom. She acts as ceremonial hostess and entertainer to visitors from other villages—waiting upon them, preparing their kava, dancing for them—and in this finds her chief pleasure.

With privacy an unknown luxury, no child reaches the

FIG. 21. A SAMOAN TAUPOU OR VILLAGE PRINCESS.
From Krämer, *Die Samoa-Inseln.* Courtesy of
Schweizerbartsche Verlagsbuchhandlung

age of puberty ignorant of "the facts of life." The nudity of infants, the practice of bathing unclad in the sea, and the use of the beach as a latrine leave no secrets about the human body and its functions. Children witness again and again the phenomena of birth and death. From salacious conversation, suggestive dances, and curious spying upon lovers, they acquaint themselves with the facts of sex. There is no ignorance, no repression. With a complete absence of shame they experiment casually with a variety of practices which we term "unnatural," and in a year or two after puberty, when shyness and the childhood antagonism of the sexes have worn off, they are ready to experiment with sex itself.

The daughters of chiefs, and especially the village princess, are carefully guarded and are severely punished for any lapse from the path of virtue, but otherwise chastity is a fiction rather than a reality. Clandestine amours between the unmarried "under the palm trees" even receive the tacit sanction of society. Both sexes exercise complete freedom in the choice of partners, though a girl's first lover is usually an older man and a boy's first sweetheart a more experienced girl. Love is considered an art, and clumsiness marks a youth as an object of ridicule. Convention demands romantic protestations of devotion, but affairs are rarely of long duration, and either party may be carrying on several at the same time. The Samoans laugh incredulously at tales of passionate jealousy and lifelong fidelity.

A youth needs a confidant or go-between (soa) to gain the ear of a girl, sing his praise, quiet her fears, and arrange a rendezvous. The choice of a soa requires care. A young or awkward lad may fail; a bold and handsome wooer may win the lady for himself. A brother makes a good agent, but a female confidante is the best of all, though difficult to obtain on account of avoidance restrictions. If the girl is favorably disposed but afraid to venture outdoors at night, the lover may remove his girdle, grease his body to make it slippery, and steal into her house under cover of darkness, exercising all caution not to disturb the dogs and other occupants. This practice renders possible an abuse known as "sleep-crawling." Disgraced or unpopular lads, and sometimes angered or jilted lovers, employ this means to steal the favors they cannot otherwise obtain, relying upon the girl's complaisance or her expectation of another visitor. If she suspects or resents the intruder, she raises a cry, and the whole household turns out to give chase. If caught, he is beaten and ridiculed, and no self-respecting girl will thereafter entertain or marry him. Needless to say, "sleep-crawling" provides the girl with an excellent alibi if her real lover is unlucky enough to be caught at her side.

These clandestine love affairs frequently lead to matrimony; in effect, therefore, they constitute a form of trial marriage. Like marriage, they are subject to definite incest taboos. Severe social censure, even banishment, is the penalty for any sexual union between relatives by blood, marriage, or adoption. If a youth seriously desires to wed a girl, he pays her formal court. With his *soa* or go-between, he calls at her home with a ceremonial present of food. Acceptance of this gift by her family indicates that they look with favor upon his suit. He is received with ceremony and invited to dine and spend the evening. While the go-between attends the girl, paying her ostentatious court and pleading the cause of his friend, the lover sits apart, watching the proceedings out of the corner of his eye. After repeated visits of this sort, a formal proposal is made. The decision rests with the family, though the girl's consent is asked. She usually employs every artifice of coquetry to delay matters, for she is naturally loathe to exchange her easy life for the cares of matrimony, and no stigma attaches to her if she remains single for years. Once accepted, the suitor often comes to live with the girl, though the actual wedding is deferred for a few months to enable the two families to assemble the requisite gifts. At the ceremony, the kinsmen of the groom present the bride's relatives with foodstuffs, pigs, and other property, and receive tapa and fine mats in return. The groom rewards his go-between with a particularly handsome gift. The residence of the newly married couple depends largely on circumstances. Except in the case of titled men, however, the groom very commonly lives with the bride's family for a year or until the birth of the first child, after which he removes with his wife to his own home.

Especially elaborate ceremonies attend the marriage of a village princess. She may wed only a chief of another village or his heir, and her personal preferences are little heeded. Between the formal betrothal and the wedding, the groom's talking chief remains with the bride's family, from whom he receives a succession of costly presents. The wedding takes place in the groom's village before a multitude of friends and relatives. The bride, draped with fine mats and decked with garlands and trinkets, walks majestically down a pathway of tapa to the groom, while the onlookers gash and bruise their heads with stones. She then submits to a public defloration or test of her virginity. If found unchaste, she is clubbed and stoned, often to death, by her outraged relatives. Otherwise, after an exchange and distribution of property, the ceremony terminates in an orgiastic riot of festivities, and the bride retires to a home specially prepared for her.

As an alternative to formal courtship and marriage, a couple may elope, either for sheer ostentation or because one family opposes the union. Elopement, however, involves the danger, not only of corporal punishment, but of social disgrace in case the objecting family refuses to relent and legalize the match by a formal exchange of property. To elope with the *taupou* or princess of another community brings a man and his village great distinction. The humiliated parents of the girl may make the best of the situation, or they may refuse to sanction the union and try to coerce the girl.

The Samoans regard marriage more as an economic than
as a sexual union. Though fidelity is expected, adultery is
not uncommon and, while punished severely, especially in
the man, it does not usually break up the home. Adultery
with the wife of a chief, however, is a serious offense. The
woman is cast out, and the man is either killed, mutilated,
or forced to pay heavy fines and render ritual humiliation.
Monogamy prevails, except in the case of chiefs, but it is
sometimes associated with a form of concubinage. Chiefs
marry frequently—sometimes as often as fifty times—owing
to the importunity of their orators, who profit hugely thereby.
Rarely, however, do they live with more than two or three
wives at a time, for the women commonly return to their
homes because of quarrels or merely to escape a marriage
of convenience.

Divorce is easy. Either party may terminate the union
at any time and, except in the case of the divorced wife of
a chief, seek a new partner. If the couple have been long
married, they arrange a fair division of property. If there
are children, the younger follow the wife, the older, the husband. Remarriage is also permissible for either party after
the death of the other. A widow, indeed, customarily marries the brother of her deceased husband, even if he already
has a wife, but she is not forced to do so.

Once married, a woman has a comparatively uneventful
life to look forward to. Her rank depends upon that of her
husband and fluctuates with his fortunes. Hence she lacks
the stimulus of ambition, though she may exercise considerable influence through wire-pulling. She keeps busy
with household duties, child-bearing, domestic arts, reef
fishing, and agricultural labors, but she is far from a drudge.
Indeed, the heavier tasks fall to the men. She labors under
few disabilities other than certain mild taboos observed during menstruation and the prohibition against touching the
men's fishing tackle and canoes. Though theoretically subservient to her husband, she is in practice consulted on all

household matters, and she may even exert indirectly a large measure of influence in the community. She enjoys, therefore, a satisfactory—in some respects an enviable—status. As she grows old, she acquires special skill in the arts, especially in the manufacture of baskets, tapa, and fine mats, and becomes the teacher of the younger women. An old woman, likewise, may qualify for one of the two specialized female professions, midwifery and medicine. The influence of the old women in the household is often very great. The sisters and paternal aunts of the *matai* or headman, for example, have a veto right in elections, the sale of land, and the distribution of dowries.

The lure of a title creates among the young men an atmosphere of competition lacking in the opposite sex. A man rarely secures his first title, usually a low one, before the age of thirty, often not before forty. He must, therefore, demonstrate his worthiness over a long period of years. He seeks to excel his companions in economic pursuits—not so markedly, however, as to arouse envy and hatred. He strives to cultivate propriety in deportment, facility in oratory, proficiency in ceremonial, and qualities of leadership. He may apprentice himself to a master in some specialized profession, such as carpentry, or he may cultivate special skill as a wood carver, barber, tool maker, or the like. Demonstrated merit finds its logical reward in a title and a place in the village assembly. This suffices for many men. The more ambitious, however, prefer to play politics for higher titles and greater wealth, power, and prestige. Old men normally resign their titles, reserving only a minor seat in the assembly. They remain at home, supervising the children, braiding sennit, and offering advice. With extreme age, taboos are relaxed, and an old man may even sit beside and converse with his sister.

The sick are invariably treated with the greatest consideration. The physicians who minister to them are often old women, each with her secret lore which she imparts only to her chosen successor, but there are also male shamans or medicine men. The therapeutic methods employed include emetics, ointments, massage, bleeding, and lancing. Cuts are bathed with salt water and bandaged with leaves. Fractured bones are set with considerable skill. These seemingly rational practices, however, by no means stand alone. Disease is in the main attributed to supernatural causes, actuated by human or divine malevolence, and is treated accordingly. Thus, when a man falls ill, his sister must take oath that she has wished him no harm. Or his relatives assemble to confess and expiate their sins, and thereby avert divine wrath. Or a shaman exorcises the evil spirit. Or a priest is called in to ascertain the cause and to advise as to the proper sacrifices for propitiating the angry divinity.

When a man lies on his deathbed, his relatives assemble with valuable presents, and at the moment of death they begin a frantic lamentation—the louder, the more they have hated and feared the deceased. They rend their clothes, beat their heads, and gash their bodies with stones and firebrands till the blood flows. The object of all this is to impress upon the deceased, who is now a ghost with incalculable powers for evil, how greatly he is loved and honored by his survivors. The widow and daughters shear their hair, and, if the deceased was a chief, all labor in the village ceases. A female relative anoints the body with oil and turmeric, wraps it in tapa, and lays it out in state.

The funeral is usually celebrated on the following day. Every one attends, bearing gifts of fine mats. Four or five men bear the body to the grave. Here it is sometimes dissected to discover the cause of death, and any suspicious substance is cut out and burned to prevent further contamination. The corpse is then buried in a shallow grave lined with stones or mats, and beside it are deposited the articles used by the deceased during his last illness and occasionally also other valuable property. Over the grave is erected a simple mound of earth or a cairn of stones, surmounted, in the case of a chief, by his club or spear. A funeral feast follows the interment. The gifts brought by the mourners are redistributed, each receiving something. The night is devoted to kava drinking, speeches, songs, games, and dancing. For days thereafter, fires illuminate the grave and the house of death. All who have come into contact with the deceased, his corpse, his house, or his fire are unclean and must touch no food until the fifth day, when they undergo ritual purification.

The women of one noble family practice the art of embalming. They remove the viscera, cut off the hair, anoint the body repeatedly with oil, and puncture it daily with a needle to drain off the accumulated fluids. When the odor subsides—in about two months—they affix the hair, stuff the abdominal cavity with tapa, clothe the body, and deposit it in a special building. If oiled from time to time, the mummy keeps almost indefinitely.

The Samoans believe that each man has a soul, which leaves the body in death and takes up its abode, in the case of a chief, on a pleasant island to the west, or, in the case of a commoner, in an underworld beneath the sea. From here the ghosts of the dead rise at night to visit their former haunts and spread mischief among the living. Consequently the natives hesitate to venture abroad at night without a light, and travelers scatter food in the dark forests. Especially feared is the restlessly wandering ghost of a drowned or otherwise unburied man. His survivors spread a sheet of white tapa near the spot where the body disappeared, and offer up urgent prayers. The first living thing to light on the sheet—whether a grasshopper, ant, butterfly, or lizard— is carefully wrapped up and buried with all the proper ceremonies, for in it the spirit of the deceased is thought to have become incarnate.

The Samoans likewise believe in a vast hierarchy of superior spirits and gods, many but not all of whom are apotheosized heroes and ancestors. These spiritual beings, though they vary widely in nature and function, are but vaguely defined; one and the same spirit may be a great war god to one village, a tutelary local deity to another, and a household divinity in a third. Of whatsoever origin or nature, however, they all possess one characteristic in common—each is regarded as visibly incarnate in some material object or class of objects, which may be called its fetish.* The object may be some natural phenomenon, or a human artifact, or a plant; most commonly, however, it is an animal.

In spite of vagueness and overlapping, one may roughly distinguish the base of the spiritual hierarchy in a class of *genii* or tutelary divinities of the household, which, almost without exception, have their residence in certain animal species—pigeons, turtles, fish, lizards, centipedes, crabs, octopuses, and the like. With them is associated a sort of quasi-totemism. The members of a family may not eat the animal fetish of their divinity. If they violate this taboo or even witness an outsider violating it, they must do penance to avert disaster. One member is selected as a scapegoat to be trussed up like a pig and subjected to mock cooking in a cold oven. Moreover, each individual has his private guardian spirit—the particular divinity that was being invoked at the moment of his birth—and toward its fetish he observes a similar taboo. The tutelary divinity protects the household from malevolent spirits. In return, it is propitiated before fishing, planting, and other industrial enterprises, and receives as sacrifices the first fruits of the taro crop, the first basket of food from the oven, the first cup of kava, etc. The

* The term "fetish" has, unfortunately, been so often loosely used to refer to any object treasured or held sacred by man, that it requires definition. As used here and throughout the book, it has the specific meaning given it long ago by Julius Lippert (*Kulturgeschichte der Menschheit*, II, 364. Stuttgart, 1887). Properly speaking, a fetish is any thing, inanimate or animate, in which an alien spirit resides; it is an object worshiped or treasured, not for itself or even for any vague or mystical power associated with it, but solely by virtue of its "possession" by a definite spiritual being. So useful a term does not deserve oblivion.

headman acts as household priest, performing the sacrifices, fixing and conducting special feasts, and ascertaining the will of the god by divination.

Each village and district similarly has its special protecting deity—likewise incarnated as a rule in some animal. If a member of a village protected by an owl-god finds a dead owl, all the inhabitants assemble to gash their foreheads with stones and burn their bodies with firebrands. Most villages erect to their deities a special house or temple, often surrounded by a sacred grove where fugitives may find sanctuary. In addition to its animal fetish, the village god is thought also to dwell in a man-made idol in the temple— a wooden bowl, a basket, a sacred stone, a crude human figure, or the like. The god is served by a priest, who is usually the high chief of the village. There exists also a special class of diviners or augurs, frequently hunchbacks, epileptics, or otherwise abnormal persons, who foretell the future by means of omens. The village gods enforce the above-mentioned property taboos. They are invoked, propitiated, and even coerced in order to control the weather, avert evil, obtain success in war, etc. Thus, to bring rain, the priest dips a fetish stone into water, and to banish a calamity threatening a village, its members assemble to confess and expiate their sins. Ceremonies are held at the appearance of the new moon and on special occasions. Once a year, in the spring, a great festival is celebrated with sacrifices, games, dancing, and enforced rest from all labor. Parties who cherish grudges against one another commonly take advantage of this occasion to fight them out under the auspices of the community.

Certain deities enjoy more than a local cult. Among them are gods presiding over special human activities— gods of agriculture, fishing, hunting, childbirth, etc., the tutelary divinities of the crafts and guilds, and especially the numerous and prominent gods of war. By observing the behavior of the animal incarnations of the war gods, the success or failure of a military expedition can be predicted. If, for example, an owl, heron, kingfisher, or other fetish bird of a war god flies ahead of an advancing party, it is an omen of victory; if, however, it flies across the path or toward the rear, it is a bad omen, and the party immediately retreats. Other deities are associated with natural phenomena and reside on an island to the west. Among them are gods of the earth, sea, heavenly bodies, rain, lightning, and whirlwinds. At the head of the Samoan pantheon stands Tangaloa, creator and benefactor of man, who approaches the stature of a supreme being. The worship of these higher gods differs little from that of the inferior divinities. About them, however, has been woven an elaborate and interesting mythology and cosmology, for a description of which space is here unfortunately lacking.

The Samoans have fared comparatively well in their contact with European civilization. Though discovered in 1722 by a Dutch expedition under Roggeveen, the islands received no white settlers until 1830, when the London Missionary Society established a mission there. Traders followed the missionaries, and governments the traders. Great Britain, Germany, and the United States asserted rival claims to the islands during the last quarter of the nineteenth century. These were settled in 1900 by giving the United States sovereignty over Tutuila and the smaller eastern islands, and Germany control over the remainder—now held by New Zealand under a mandate from the League of Nations. The missionaries and traders introduced influenza and other diseases, which once ravaged the islands. Recently, however, under intelligently administered public health measures, the population has been increasing, and it is now rapidly approaching 50,000, nearly what it was before the arrival of the whites.

The native culture of Samoa, as it has been described above, has naturally been modified by European influences. It has not disintegrated, however, as has been the case elsewhere in Polynesia. Competition between the English missionaries and German traders, and between the three rival nations, prevented any one group gaining the upper hand in exploiting the natives, and in recent years intelligent and sympathetic colonial administrators have conscientiously sought to preserve the best elements of aboriginal culture. The most outstanding cultural changes have been the extirpation of the more barbarous practices, such as warfare, cannibalism, defloration, and blood-revenge, and the complete conversion of the natives to Protestant Christianity. On the benefits of the latter change, we can do no better than to quote, in somewhat condensed form, the proud boast of a missionary writing in 1861: "Soon after the arrival of the missionaries, a marked change took place. Coats, waistcoats, trousers, neckerchiefs, and straw hats came into use. The women commenced wearing loose calico dresses, and were rarely seen without an upper garment of some kind. Much was thus done to further the commercial interests of civilized countries. The demand for cotton goods alone, apart from other articles of foreign manufacture, amounts to about £15,000 per annum, and is every year increasing."

BIBLIOGRAPHY

BASTIAN, A. *Inselgruppen in Oceanien.* Berlin, 1883.

BROWN, G. *Melanesians and Polynesians.* London, 1910.

*BUCK, P. H. (TE RANGI HIROA). "Samoan Material Culture." *Bernice P. Bishop Museum, Bulletin 75.* Honolulu, 1930.

BÜLOW, W. VON. "Beiträge zur Ethnographie der Samoa-Inseln." *Internationales Archiv für Ethnographie,* Vols. XII–XIII. Leiden, 1899–1900.

——. "Die Ehegesetze der Samoaner." *Globus,* Vol. LXXIII. Braunschweig, 1898.

——. "Notizen zur Ethnographie, Anthropologie und Urgeschichte der Malayo-Polynesier." *Internationales Archiv für Ethnographie,* Vol. XVIII. Leiden, 1908.

——. "Das ungeschriebene Gesetz der Samoaner." *Globus,* Vol. LXIX. Braunschweig, 1896.

CHURCHILL, L. P. *Samoa 'Uma*. New York, 1902.

ELLA, S. "The Ancient Samoan Government." *Australasian Association for the Advancement of Science*, Vol. VI. Brisbane, 1895.

———. "Samoa." *Australasian Association for the Advancement of Science*, Vol. IV. Hobart, 1892.

FRIEDLAENDER, B. "Notizen über Samoa." *Zeitschrift für Ethnologie*, Vol. XXXI. Berlin, 1899.

HANDY, E. S. C. "Polynesian Religion." *Bernice P. Bishop Museum, Bulletin 34*. Honolulu, 1927.

HANDY, E. S. C., and W. C. "Samoan House Building, Cooking, and Tattooing." *Bernice P. Bishop Museum, Bulletin 15*. Honolulu, 1924.

HESSE-WARTEGG, E. VON. *Samoa, Bismarckarchipel und Neuguinea*. Leipzig, 1902.

KRÁMER, A. *Die Samoa-Inseln*. 2 vols. Stuttgart, 1901–02.

KURZE, G. "Die Samoaner in der heidnischen Zeit." *Mitteilungen der Geographischen Gesellschaft (für Thüringen) zu Jena*, Vols. XVIII–XIX. Jena, 1900–01.

MARQUES, A. "Notes pour servir à une monographie des iles Samoa." *Boletim da Sociedade de Geographia de Lisboa*, Vol. VIII. Lisboa, 1889.

MEAD, M. *Coming of Age in Samoa*. New York, 1928.

———. "The Rôle of the Individual in Samoan Culture." *Journal of the Royal Anthropological Institute of Great Britain and Ireland*, Vol. LVIII. London, 1928.

———. "Social Organization of Manua." *Bernice P. Bishop Museum, Bulletin 76*. Honolulu, 1930.

PRITCHARD, W. T. "Notes on Certain Anthropological Matters Respecting the South Sea Islanders (the Samoans)." *Memoirs Read before the Anthropological Society of London*, Vol. I. London, 1863–64.

———. *Polynesian Reminiscences*. London, 1866.

REEVES, E. *Brown Men and Women*. London, 1898.

REINECKE, F. "Zur Kennzeichnung der Verhältnisse auf den Samoa-Inseln." *Globus*, Vol. LXXVI. Braunschweig, 1899.

RIVERS, W. H. R. *The History of Melanesian Society*. 2 vols. Cambridge, 1914.

SCHULTZ, E. "The Most Important Principles of Samoan Family Law." *Journal of the Polynesian Society*, Vol. XX. Wellington, 1911.

STAIR, J. B. *Old Samoa*. St. Paul's, 1897.

SULLIVAN, L. R. "A Contribution to Samoan Somatology." *Memoirs of the Bernice Pauahi Bishop Museum*, Vol. VIII. Honolulu, 1921.

THILENIUS, G. "Die Fahrzeuge der Samoaner." *Globus*, Vol. LXXX. Braunschweig, 1901.

TURNER, G. *Nineteen Years in Polynesia*. London, 1861.

*———. *Samoa*. London, 1884.

WATSON, R. M. *History of Samoa*. Wellington, 1918.

WILKES, C. *Narrative of the United States Exploring Expedition during the Years 1838, 1839, 1840, 1841, 1842*. 5 vols. Philadelphia, 1845.

WILLIAMSON, R. W. *The Social and Political Systems of Central Polynesia*. 3 vols. Cambridge, 1924.

CHAPTER IV

THE SEMANG OF THE MALAY PENINSULA

As a potpourri of heterogeneous racial elements, probably no region on earth can compare with the southern or British half of the Malay Peninsula. The aboriginal inhabitants were overrun, from the twelfth century on, by successive waves of a conquering race from central Sumatra, the Malays, who today constitute slightly less than half of the total population of 3,500,000. Arab traders made the port of Malacca a center for their lucrative spice trade during the Middle Ages, converted the Malays to Islam in the fourteenth and fifteenth centuries, and are still prominent figures in the seaport towns. The Portuguese, Dutch, and English, who, since 1511, have successively exercised an increasing measure of sovereignty over the peninsula, have contributed their share to the present population of 15,000 Europeans and 12,000 Eurasians. Dark-skinned Tamils and kindred peoples from southern India, to the number of nearly half a million, have been imported as laborers for the tin mines and rubber plantations. Chinese traders and coolies have immigrated in such numbers that they now constitute approximately one-third of the population. To these diverse groups we may add the Siamese, who hold political sway over the northern half of the peninsula, the merchants of all nations, and the flotsam and jetsam which great ports like Singapore and Penang invariably attract from all corners of the earth.

Submerged by this alien flood, and driven back into the interior, are the aborigines, who comprise today less than one per cent of the total population. Even they, however, do not constitute an ethnic unit. On the contrary, they fall into three entirely distinct racial groups. The pagan Jakun, Malayan in race and language but related only distantly to the dominant Malays, are the remnants of an old indigenous stock. The Sakai, sharply differentiated from the Jakun by their dwarf stature, narrow heads, and wavy or curly hair, find their closest racial relatives in the Veddahs of Ceylon. More primitive than either, and distinguished from both by the possession of definitely negroid characteristics, are the Semang, a race of true pygmies, descended probably from the earliest inhabitants of the land. It is with the 2,000 survivors of this ancient Negrito race that we are here concerned.

Adult males among the Semang do not exceed five feet in average stature; females are three or four inches shorter. The bodies of these pygmies, however, exhibit no trace of deformity, but are well proportioned and sturdy. The skin is a dark chocolate brown in color; the hair short, black, and woolly; the beard and body hair extremely scanty; the forehead low and rounded; the eyes a deep brown; the nose short, flat, and exceptionally broad (nasal index nearly 100); the face rounded and prognathous; the head mesocephalic in shape (cephalic index 79). Speculation has evolved many bizarre theories as to the racial affiliations of the Semang. One early authority even regarded them as descendants of "escaped negro slaves brought over by Alexander the Great." It is definitely established today, however, that they are racially akin to the Negritos of the Andaman and Philippine Islands, with whom they also reveal many points of cultural similarity.

In language, on the other hand, the Semang show no relationship to the other Negritos. Their speech, though often classed by itself as a distinct linguistic stock, exhibits marked resemblances to the Mon-Khmer languages of Burma and Indo-China, not only in the basic elements of its vocabulary, but also in the monosyllabic character of its roots and in its use of prefixes and infixes in grammatical composition. The Semang possess no form of writing, and, except where they have come into contact with the Malays, they are unable to count beyond three.

Fig. 22. A Semang Youth of Eighteen Years.
From Schebesta, *Bei den Urwaldzwergen von Malaya.* Courtesy of F. A.
Brockhaus, Leipzig, and Hutchinson & Co., Ltd., London

Before the alien invaders, the aborigines have retreated to the interior of the peninsula, to the foothills of the jagged ranges which rise in places to an altitude of over 7,000 feet. The Semang themselves, save for a few scattered groups, inhabit the states of Kedah, Kelantan, and Perak, and are mainly concentrated in the area between 101° and 102° east longitude and between 5° and 6° north latitude. The temperature is tropical, varying with season and altitude from 68° to 90° F. in the shade. A torrential rainfall of approximately 100 inches annually renders the climate excessively humid; the sun rarely penetrates the morning mists before ten o'clock. The heavy precipitation also gives rise to innumerable short rivers and streams, extensive mangrove swamps, and a rank tropical vegetation. Trees, thorny underbrush, poisonous plants, creeping, climbing, and trailing vines, bamboos, ferns, mosses, and parasitic growths create such a profusion of plant life that the jungle can often be penetrated only with a knife, and even the animals usually follow the stream beds or beaten trails. The forests swarm with an unparalleled abundance and diversity of insect fauna, of which the worst are the mosquitoes and leeches. Crocodiles infest the streams. Frogs, lizards, turtles, pythons, cobras, and other reptiles abound. Bird life is even more profuse and varied. The mammalian fauna, mostly characterized by protective coloration, includes the elephant, rhinoceros, saladang or wild bull, tiger, panther, leopard, sloth bear, deer, wild boar, tapir, otter, wild dog, gibbon, macaque and other monkeys, lemur, and flying squirrel. Among the numerous fishes, there is one species that walks overland and another that shoots flies by expelling a jet of water.

In this environment the Semang pursue the life of nomadic hunters and collectors. Rarely remaining in one place for more than three days, they wander restlessly about in search of game and the wild roots and jungle fruits which constitute the mainstay of their existence. They practice no agriculture except under Malay influence, and possess no domestic animals save a half-wild reddish dog. They make pets, however, of young captive monkeys and other animals, and it is a common sight to see a woman nursing her baby at one breast and a little monkey at the other. Animals thus suckled, though they may be sold or given away, cannot be killed or eaten by their owners and friends.

The Negritos catch fish in ingenious traps and with rod and line, but they never employ nets or poison. They scoop up small fry in pools and sluggish streams with baskets. For larger fish and turtles they use a spear or a long harpoon made from the leafstalk of a large palm.

Hunting is, in the main, subsidiary to the collection of yams, durian, and other wild roots and fruits. An occasional

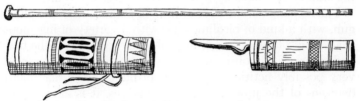

FIG. 23. SEMANG BLOWGUN AND QUIVERS.

hunter employs a bamboo spear, four or five feet in length, pointed with a bamboo sliver. A much more important weapon is the blowgun, which the Semang have borrowed from the Sakai. It consists of a delicate inner tube of bamboo, about seven feet long, protected by an outer casing, and frequently provided with a mouthpiece of gutta-percha. By means of this instrument, an explosive puff of breath can project a poisoned dart with accuracy a distance of twenty-five yards. The dart is a sharp needle-like sliver of bamboo, a foot or more in length, equipped at the base with a conical plug of pith fitted exactly to the tube, and nicked near the head so that the point will break off in the wound. The poison, which is capable of killing a man, is concocted over the fire from various ingredients, chief among which is the sap of the upas tree. The native weapon of the Semang—one unknown to the other aboriginal tribes—is, however, the bow and arrow. The bow is of plain wood, six or seven feet in length, strung with a waxed cord of vegetable fiber. The arrows are of bamboo, barbed, winged, poisoned with upas, provided with detachable heads, and carried, like darts, in decorated bamboo quivers. The Semang apparently do not understand the principle of feathering, or else use it for magical rather than utilitarian purposes, for they clip the feathers close to the quill and fasten them to the arrow in various positions and pointing in either direction. The natives seem to find compensation for the resulting inaccuracy, however, in other ways, for, as one of them explained: "If I shoot the arrow at a wild pig, the feathers whirr through the air, the pig stands transfixed by fear, looks around, and is hit."

The Semang obtain birds and small animals with the blowgun, with a kind of birdlime, and with a variety of ingenious snares and pitfalls. Larger animals they secure with the bow and arrow. Early observers report a number of curious—and very possibly fictitious—methods of hunting the mammoth denizens of the jungle. Thus the natives, it is alleged, approach an elephant from the rear and, as it lifts its foot, drive in a sharp poisoned splinter of bamboo. The animal, thus crippled, falls an easy victim to their spears. The rhinoceros, which loves to wallow in the mud of a marsh, is sometimes imprisoned when the sun hardens the surface into a thick crust. On finding such a helpless beast, the natives are said to build a fire over its body and roast it to death.

The Negritos generate fire by friction—either by the simple method of rubbing two sticks together, or by sawing back and forth on a dry branch with a strip of rattan. They use fire for warmth, in tool-making, and especially for cooking, though meat is occasionally eaten raw. Birds, fish, and small animals are inserted in a cleft stick tilted over the fire, and thus roasted. Poisonous yams and other roots are grated, treated with lime, kneaded into dough, wrapped in leaves, and baked or roasted. Though the women cook, they do not eat until the men and boys have finished. Bamboo vessels and coconut shells serve as drinking cups, and leaves as plates.

Adults wear a minimum of clothing, children nothing at all. The women, more as a prophylactic against disease than as an article of apparel, wear an elaborate and tasteful girdle made from the glossy black strands of a special fungus growth. These are woven into a long narrow braid, coiled several times about the body, in such a fashion that the ends of the strands hang loose and form a handsome bushy fringe. The men usually content themselves with a simple waist-

After Schebesta

FIG. 24. THE SEMANG SHELTER: FRAMEWORK FROM THE FRONT AND COMPLETED STRUCTURE FROM THE REAR.

string of palm fibers, into which they insert leaves as a fringe. Both sexes wear fillets of leaves, armlets and bracelets of fiber, and necklaces of palm or fungus strands, strung with shells, teeth, bones, leaves, roots, seeds, etc. The body is painted, but for magical purposes rather than adornment. Though both sexes commonly shave the head, the women leave a narrow fringe on the forehead and a circular patch of hair in back—the latter for the reception of elaborate bamboo combs richly and artistically decorated with incised designs. With respect to mutilation, circumcision and tattooing are unknown and scarification rare, but filing the teeth and piercing the ear lobe are general.

The dwellings of the Semang, as one might expect from their nomadic mode of life, are frail shelters scarcely deserving the name of huts. To three or four stout sticks, planted in the ground at an angle and supported by forked sticks and bamboo uprights, palm leaves are lashed to serve as a roof. The whole forms a structure intermediate between a mere windbreak and a lean-to. A camp consists of several of these shelters arranged roughly in a circle. The natives inhabit caves and rock crevices only in emergencies, and superior huts only under Malay influence. Before pitching a camp, they always build a fire; if the smoke rises straight in the air, the site is favorable, but if it drifts off into the jungle, another location is sought, for there is danger of tigers.

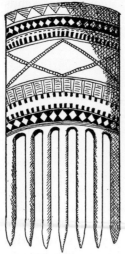

FIG. 25. DECORATED BAMBOO COMB OF THE SEMANG.

The Semang make no pottery and possess no objects of metal except through trade with the Malays. They manufacture no stone implements, though they use stones as they find them for hammers, knives, files, and whetstones. With regard to their industrial arts they still linger, as one authority expresses it, in "a primitive period, a bamboo age." The uses of bamboo are manifold; they have been illustrated rather than exhausted in the instances already cited—blowguns, arrows, darts, quivers, spears, spearheads, combs, drinking vessels. The native knife is a sharp sliver of bamboo. Strips of bamboo and rattan are woven into baskets. Raised platforms of split bamboos serve as beds. The Negritos use no boats except bamboo rafts. They make a variety of magical objects from the same material. Even their musical instruments consist of a bamboo drum, bamboo sticks for beating time, mouth and nose flutes of bamboo, and a bamboo jew's-harp. Many of these articles—especially the quivers, combs, and blowguns—are richly decorated with attractive incised designs, which frequently serve a magical as well as an ornamental purpose. Though occasionally realistic, the patterns are usually conventional or symbolic. A bat, for example, is represented by wavy lines suggestive of its wings.

The assertion that the Semang hold all property in common is true only in so far as it applies to food. Each family shares the foodstuffs which it has collected, prepared, and cooked with every other family in the camp, even though this leaves them with insufficient for themselves. In other respects, however, private property prevails. Clothing and implements are individual possessions and cannot be used by another without permission. Each adult male owns several wild upas and durian trees, which no one else dares molest, while women enjoy a property right in everything they manufacture, including the shelter. A man's property is inherited by his children or relatives, never by his wife; a woman's by her children or, in default thereof, her brothers and sisters, never by her husband.

Economic specialization, other than a division of labor between the sexes, does not exist. A certain amount of trade, however, is carried on with the Malays; wax, resin, gums, and other jungle products are exchanged for salt, beads, cloth, and metal articles. Formerly, this trade always assumed the form known as "dumb barter." The timid Negritos would deposit their goods at an appointed spot and retire, returning in a few days to remove the articles which the Malays had meanwhile left in exchange. Ignorant of the true value of their forest products, they were invariably cheated by their crafty civilized neighbors.

An extreme degree of atomism prevails with regard to political organization. Not only do the Semang as a whole possess no unified government, but even the individual tribes, of which there are eight, are territorial and linguistic rather than political units. Each tribe is subdivided into a number of independent bands. The band consists, on the average, of about six families united by kinship ties or for mutual aid. Within the family the father exercises a mildly patriarchal authority over his wife and children, but it is decidedly questionable whether any authority higher than this is actually recognized. To be sure, bands are frequently reported to possess "chiefs," but these seem to be, not political heads, but men respected for their age, personal qualities, or supernatural powers. Indeed, the so-called chiefs are almost invariably medicine men. They possess no actual power to control or command others. In short, a condition of practically complete equality prevails.

In default of anything resembling formal laws, crime consists in the violation of divinely sanctioned customs and is so rare as to be practically unknown. The community as a whole exacts punishment. If a thief does not make restitution in kind, he is severely berated or even flogged by his fellows. Murder and adultery are punished either by death or by a kind of wergild.

The economic and social life of the Semang centers in the band. Each band has its own territory, roughly defined as the area containing the wild fruit trees belonging to its adult male members, and it camps and moves as a unit. A minimum of formality prevails. Individuals never greet one another in any way, even after prolonged separation. They address one another by kinship terms, never by name. For recreation, dances are frequently held at night. The women alone perform, while the men beat time and provide the musical accompaniment. The dancers execute a curtseying step with undulatory movements of the arms and hands in time to the music. The songs, mainly descriptive of animals and plants, are chanted in an archaic dialect. In general, a measure of geniality and good humor, coupled with a certain matter-of-factness, pervades the everyday life of these people.

The various bands live at peace with one another. They roam with perfect freedom over the territories of other groups in the same tribe—always, of course, respecting their fruit trees. War, or any other form of hostility, is absolutely unknown, not only between the different bands and tribes of the Semang themselves, but also with the Sakai, and even with the Malays, by whom they are not infrequently harassed. They never react to ill-treatment with treachery, much less with open violence. They merely withdraw and avoid their oppressors. As a result, self-preservation has developed in them a marked timidity and suspicion of all strangers. Sympathetic visitors find great difficulty in breaking through this barrier of shyness, but when they succeed, they find the Negrito a friendly little being, cheerful and brimming over with curiosity.

The Semang apparently trace kinship in both the male and female lines, and they certainly recognize the rôle of the father in conception. Although they thus, correctly enough, attribute the body of the child to sexual reproduction, they are said to possess a curious belief as to the origin of its soul. The soul of an unborn child is thought to reside in a bird. When a woman becomes pregnant, she visits the nearest tree of the species after which she is named, and decorates it with leaves and flowers. The soul-bird, attracted by these tokens, alights on the tree and is killed. By eating the bird the mother provides her unborn child with its soul. The expectant mother continues to work until the child is born, but she observes various taboos, especially prohibitions against eating large fish, monitor lizards, squirrels, wild boars, mawa monkeys, argus pheasants, or any animal killed with the bow and arrow. Occasionally the father submits to similar taboos. The Negritos welcome children and seem never actually to practice either abortion or infanticide, although they claim to know means both of preventing conception and of producing miscarriage.

Childbirth, which is rarely difficult, takes place in the dwelling on a special bamboo seat provided with a back rest. All the men save the husband leave camp, and the mother is attended by her female relatives and by a special midwife, of which each band includes at least one. The midwife severs the umbilical cord with a bamboo knife, bathes the infant in warm water, pierces its ear lobes with

Fig. 26. A Semang Medicine Man Imitating a Woman in Childbirth.

From Schebesta, *Bei den Urwaldzwergen von Malaya.* Courtesy of F. A. Brockhaus, Leipzig, and Hutchinson & Co., Ltd., London

a thorn, and names it after some neighboring tree. The father cuts a series of notches on the name-tree to identify it, and it is never felled. All trees of the same species are taboo throughout life to the individuals named after them.

After delivery, the mother rests for several days, drinking certain supposedly restorative decoctions, and then returns to work. She nurses the infant for at least two years, and normally has another child after an interval of about three years. She carries the baby on her back, often slinging it from the bough of a tree while at work. The Negritos are a cleanly people; they bathe their children frequently, and even train their dogs to assist in keeping them clean. One instance will suffice. "A suckling child had just performed a very human action. The mother held her darling up and called the house dog, which dashed up eagerly and licked the child clean." Children up to the age of five sleep between their parents, thereafter on separate beds. The harsh conditions of life result in a heavy but not exceptional infant mortality. One observer found that the twenty-six women over thirty-five years of age whom he studied, had sixty-six living children as against forty-five who had died.

Parents display great fondness for their offspring. They never beat them, and, though they scold them, they never permit outsiders to do so. Mothers fondle their infants, dandle them on their knees, prattle to them, and decorate them with ornaments. The principal care of the children falls to the mother, but the father also plays with them and tends them in the mother's absence. No such thing as conscious education exists; children learn solely through imitation and play. A girl discovers how to weave baskets by observing her older sisters and cousins. A boy watches his father make a bow, then makes a toy one himself and plays with it. Even tiny tots follow their fathers into the jungle in search of game. Children undertake serious economic activities as soon as they are able, and become assets rather than liabilities at an early age. No secret or ritual ceremonies are held at puberty for either sex.

Sex relations are by no means unregulated. The unmarried, to be sure, enjoy a considerable measure of freedom in this respect, but fidelity is rigidly insisted upon in the married—on penalty of death or severe fines and corporal punishment. Modesty and secrecy surround sexual intercourse, which takes place only at night. Strict avoidance restrictions separate a man and his mother-in-law and also a woman and her father-in-law. Under no circumstances may such persons speak to or approach one another, nor may they occupy adjoining shelters. These restrictions persist even after divorce, and they result, not only from marriage, but from any sexual union. A certain degree of avoidance likewise prevails between father and daughter and between mother and son, after the children have reached about five years of age.

Girls usually marry at the age of fifteen or sixteen, men three or four years later. Although occasionally, because of laziness or the like, a man or a woman cannot find or keep a partner, voluntary celibacy is unknown and incomprehensible to the Semang. They asked a Catholic priest who was visiting them why he had deserted his wife; they laughed incredulously when he tried to explain that he had no wife and wanted none, and became frankly skeptical when they saw the picture of a woman in a book he was reading.

A man invariably seeks a wife in another band, rarely, however, in another tribe. Marriage takes place, moreover, by mutual consent without compulsion or hindrance from the parents of either party. When a couple have reached an understanding, the man gives his prospective father-in-law a number of gifts as a sort of bride-price, and presents his betrothed with a girdle. The bride and groom eat together at a wedding feast and then retire for several days into the forest, where they build a shelter, gather food, cook, eat, and make love. On their return from their honeymoon they take up their residence for a year or two in the band of the bride, where the groom works for his father-in-law. Then, as a rule, they join the husband's band, returning from time to time, however, to visit and work.

Marriage is a brittle monogamy. Polygyny, though not
forbidden, is extremely rare, and where a man has two or
more wives, as occasionally happens, they always live in

FIG. 27. THREE GENERATIONS OF SEMANG: GRANDMOTHER,
MOTHER, AND CHILD.
From Schebesta, *Bei den Urwaldzwergen von Malaya.* Courtesy of
F. A. Brockhaus, Leipzig, and Hutchinson & Co., Ltd., London

different bands. Though customarily monogamous, the
Semang can and do change partners with great frequency,
especially where there are no children. Either party can
divorce the other with equal facility. The husband simply
leaves or is told to leave the shelter, which is the woman's

property. If the wife terminates the union, her father must restore the bridal gifts or their equivalent to the husband, but if a man leaves his wife he forfeits the bride-price. The children normally remain with their mother. Either party may remarry, except that marriage between a man and the divorced wife of his younger brother is forbidden.

Women enjoy a comparatively high status. They are never beaten or otherwise oppressed by their husbands. Though they work rather harder than the men, the division of labor by sex is not manifestly inequitable. The men hunt, trap, fish, gather fruits and firewood, and make and decorate their tools and weapons. The women dig roots, cook, tend the children, make mats and baskets, and erect the shelters, but even here the men often assist them, especially in the heavier labor. Far from being a drudge, the wife is practically her husband's equal.

The aged are honored and respected, as is shown by the fact that they are never contradicted. When they are incapable of working, their children provide for them, and frequently carry them on their backs in moving camp. Never are the sick and infirm harshly treated, much less abandoned or killed.

The Semang attribute death, disease, and most of the ills of life to black magic or the malevolence of supernatural beings. One may injure an enemy by conjuring an evil spirit to plague him or enter his body, and this is most readily accomplished if one can secure some article belonging to the victim, for example, in the case of a woman, her girdle. An effective means of producing death is by "pointing" a bamboo. The sorcerer, after performing a ceremony with a taper of beeswax, places a short pointed sliver of bamboo on his palm and commands it to go and kill his enemy. It flies through the air—as far as a two days' journey—and pierces the victim to the heart. If notched, it is even more deadly, for it will "twist itself round his heart-strings." The Malays, in particular, live in great dread of this aboriginal magic. The Negritos seek to protect themselves by an extensive use of charms and amulets. Painting the body is thought to avert disease; wearing certain leaves and blossoms on the head, to protect against falling trees. Expectant mothers wear special incised bamboo tubes under their girdles as a charm against nausea. The men believe that the incised designs on their blowguns and quivers possess magical efficacy both in warding off disease and in bringing down game.

The shaman or medicine man is the most influential individual in the band. He wears a distinctive costume, observes special food taboos, carries an emblematic wand, and often receives a special burial. The office is transmitted from father to son. By means of a magical stone, a quartz crystal, the shaman can, amongst other things, see a tiger lurking near the camp and give his people warning. He is an expert at bamboo pointing and other magic, and knows how to make an unfailing love charm from a rare jungle flower. He can communicate with supernatural beings and assume the form of a tiger. Disease, to the Semang, is caused by an evil spirit who has gained entrance into the body. The shaman alone can determine the specific cause and prescribe means for exorcising the demon. To accomplish this he builds a special hut, makes use of his quartz crystal, massage, and a variety of medicines, and sometimes works himself into a trance. To cure a woman seized with pains in her limbs, a medicine man in one reported case uprooted two saplings, rubbed her abdomen and back with soil from the holes, expectorated on her, and caused the saplings to be hurled violently into the jungle. That he thus succeeded in expelling the demon was proved by the fact that the woman recovered.

According to a typically animistic belief of the Semang, not only men but all living beings—animals, birds, fishes, etc.—possess souls. The human soul is a miniature replica of its owner, except that it is red like blood. It can leave the body in dreams and wander abroad. What one sees in a dream, therefore, is the actual experience of one's soul, and its reality is not to be doubted. "If I have dreamed that I killed a wild pig," asserted one Negrito, "it is true. In the morning I tell all the camp and we set out to look for the pig, and we find it too." In death, the soul takes final leave of the body in the form of a bird.

Though a Malay tradition states that the Semang once ate the bodies of their dead and interred only the heads, they certainly do nothing of the sort today. They bury the dead on the day of their death, except in the case of prominent medicine men, whose bodies they deposit in trees or leave unburied. Deep silence is preserved at the funeral. The corpse is placed in the grave on a mat with its head oriented toward the setting sun. A crude roof of stakes and palm leaves serves to keep the earth from immediate contact with the body. Above the grave a shelter is erected for the reception of all the charms and other possessions of the deceased except such valuable objects as blowguns and metal articles obtained by trade. Fires are lighted beside the grave. Water is poured into the mouth of the corpse, placed in a vessel beside it, and sprinkled over the grave, that the departed spirit may not thirst on its journey. For a similar reason, food is also occasionally deposited in or on the grave. Immediately after the funeral, the survivors abandon the old camp and pitch a new one, preferably across a stream, for a ghost cannot cross water. For several days the relatives mourn with loud lamentations and abstain from singing, dancing, and the wearing of ornaments. On the last day of the moon during which the death occurred, the period of mourning terminates with a feast and a dance.

The ghosts of the departed inhabit a spirit world on an island in the western sea, where sickness and tigers are unknown and trees bear abundant fruit the year round but life is otherwise much the same as on earth. To reach this land, however, they must cross a flimsy rope bridge over a boiling sea. At the farther end stands a horrible monster, whose aspect so frightens the timid and wicked that they fall off and must swim about in agony until a god graciously lowers his great toe to enable them to climb out. The souls of deceased shamans frequently enter the bodies of tigers, elephants, or rhinoceroses, where they reside for a time before journeying to the hereafter. The ghosts of the dead return from the spirit world at night in the form of birds and haunt their graves, which are therefore carefully shunned. Especially do the ghosts of bachelors inspire fear, for, peevish at being deprived of wives in the spirit world, they roam the earth with malice toward men. When the Negritos hear their cries at night, they extinguish their campfires and huddle with fear in their shelters.

The Semang likewise believe in a variety of supernatural beings not—at least directly—of human origin. These include nature spirits in the sun, earth, water, and other natural phenomena, the malicious demons responsible for disease, and a class of tiny sprites or elves who inhabit flowers and are well disposed toward men. Of actual gods there are several, but with one exception they are purely mythological beings receiving no cult or worship of any sort. Towering vastly above all the rest in practical importance—as is not inexplicable under the environmental conditions—looms Karei, the god of thunder. Invisible, superhuman in size, omnipotent, omniscient, he created men, gave them their souls, and is aware of their every transgression. Though sometimes kindly and well disposed, he grows angry when they do wrong and warns or slays them with his thunderbolts.

Sin is the violation of a taboo imposed by Karei. The category of sins includes, curiously enough, not theft or murder, but such things as familiarity with one's mother-in-law, killing a sacred black wasp or certain tabooed birds, mocking a tame or helpless animal, sexual intercourse in the daytime, playing with birds' eggs, drawing water in a vessel blackened by fire, watching dogs mating, combing one's hair during a thunderstorm or the mourning period, and throwing a spear in the morning—quite permissible in the afternoon! The sound of thunder, the sign of Karei's anger, gives warning that some one has sinned. All who are conscious of guilt, or at least one person representing the band, must hasten to render atonement by a blood sacrifice. The performers gash their shins, mix the blood with water in a bamboo vessel, and toss it to the angry elements with prayers of "Stop! Stop!" This is by far the most prominent ceremony in Semang religion.

The native mythology reveals many contradictions and inconsistencies. According to one version, however, the moon, the mother of the stars, once deprived the sun, a female in human form, of her children by means of a trick. The vengeful sun occasionally assumes the form of a dragon and seeks to devour the moon, producing an eclipse, which the people dispel by a loud clamor. The rainbow is a great serpent, and the accompanying rain its sweat. The first man and woman, ignorant of how to acquire children, were instructed by a coconut monkey. Instead of a flood myth, the Semang preserve the tradition of a great fire, from which they escaped only with the greatest difficulty—not unscathed, however, for their hair was singed, and it has been frizzly ever since.

Except for an occasional white visitor or Chinese trader, the experience of the Semang with civilization has been confined to their contact with the Malays, who have regularly cheated them in trade, occasionally raided them for slaves, and slowly crowded them out of their lands. Today, thanks to British protection, their numbers show no marked decline, but "they are fast tending to become assimilated and absorbed, losing their language, their customs, their purity of blood and (worst loss of all) their natural truthfulness and honesty." Opium, the loss of their native arts, and their growing dependence on alien wares threaten to make them ere long a parasitic group. Their condition and prospects are aptly summed up by Sir Hugh Clifford in his *Song of the Last Semangs:*

> We suffer yet a little space
> Until we pass away,
> The relics of an ancient race
> That ne'er has had its day.

BIBLIOGRAPHY

ANNANDALE, N., and ROBINSON, H. C. *Fasciculi Malayenses.* London, 1903–04.
——. "Some Preliminary Results of an Expedition to the Malay Peninsula." *Journal of the Anthropological Institute of Great Britain and Ireland,* Vol. XXXII. London, 1902.

BROWN, A. R. *The Andaman Islanders.* Cambridge, 1922.

CLIFFORD, H. *In Court and Kampong.* London, 1897.

EARL, G. W. *Native Races of the Indian Archipelago—Papuans.* London, 1853.

EVANS, I. H. N. *Papers on the Ethnology and Archæology of the Malay Peninsula.* Cambridge, 1927.
——. "Schebesta on the Sacerdo-Therapy of the Semangs." *Journal of the Royal Anthropological Institute of Great Britain and Ireland,* Vol. LX. London, 1930.
——. *Studies in Religion, Folklore and Custom in British North Borneo and the Malay Peninsula.* Cambridge, 1923.

MARTIN, R. *Die Inlandstämme der Malayischen Halbinsel.* Jena, 1905.

*SCHEBESTA, P. *Among the Forest Dwarfs of Malaya.* Trans. by A. Chambers. London, 1928.
——. "The Bow and Arrow of the Semang." *Man,* Vol. XXVI. London, 1926.
——. "Gesellschaft und Familie bei den Semang auf Malakka." *Anthropos,* Vol. XXIII. Wien, 1928.
——. "Jenseitsglaube der Semang auf Malakka." *Festschrift Publication d'Hommage offerte au P. W. Schmidt.* Wien, 1928.

SCHEBESTA, P. "The Negritos of the Malay Peninsula." *Man*, Vol. XXVII. London, 1927.

——. "Über die Semang auf Malaka." *Anthropos*, Vols. XVIII–XIX. Wien, 1923–24.

SCHMIDT, W. "Die Forschungsexpedition von P. P. Schebesta." *Anthropos*, Vol. XX. Wien, 1925.

——. "Die Sprachen der Sakei und Semang auf Malacca und ihr Verhältnis zu den Mon-Khmer-Sprachen." *Bijdragen tot de Taal-, Land- en Volkenkunde van Nederlandsch-Indië*, Vol. LII. 's Gravenhage, 1901.

——. "Die Stellung der Pygmäenvölker in der Entwicklungsgeschichte des Menschen." *Studien und Forschungen zur Menschen- und Völkerkunde*, Vols. VI–VII. Stuttgart, 1910.

SKEAT, W. W. "The Wild Tribes of the Malay Peninsula." *Journal of the Anthropological Institute of Great Britain and Ireland*, Vol. XXXII. London, 1902.

*SKEAT, W. W., and BLAGDEN, C. O. *Pagan Races of the Malay Peninsula*. 2 vols. London, 1906.

STEVENS, H. V. "Materialen zur Kenntniss der wilden Stämme auf der Halbinsel Malaka." *Veröffentlichungen aus dem Königlichen Museum für Völkerkunde*, Vols. II–III. Berlin, 1892–94.

SWETTENHAM, F. A. "On the Native Races of the Straits Settlements and Malay States." *Journal of the Anthropological Institute of Great Britain and Ireland*, Vol. XVI. London, 1887.

WILKINSON, R. J. *Papers on Malay Subjects*, Supplement: "The Aboriginal Tribes." Kuala Lumpur, 1926.

WINSTEDT, R. O. *Malaya*. London, 1923.

CHAPTER V

THE TODAS OF SOUTHERN INDIA

IN the south of India, from 11° to 12° north of the equator and from 76° to 77° east of Greenwich, rise the Nilgiri Hills. Though individual peaks reach an altitude of nearly 9,000 feet, the Nilgiris form, in the main, an undulating table-land about 500 square miles in extent, ranging from 6,000 to 7,000 feet above sea level. The tropical climate of southern India is here greatly modified by the altitude. The mean annual temperature is only 58° F.; the thermometer rarely rises above 70°, and frosts occasionally occur on cold winter nights. The heavy precipitation of the monsoons nourishes the vegetation of the grassy prairie and forested valleys; from December to March, however, comes a dry season, during which the grass is parched. The plateau is singularly isolated from the rest of southern India. On every side the land falls away precipitously 3,000 to 5,000 feet to the plains below, and the steep slopes are covered with a dense, malarious, and almost impenetrable jungle where tigers, leopards, deer, and other animals abound.

The most interesting inhabitants of this plateau are the Todas, a pastoral tribe of buffalo herders. Their culture, though unique, reveals certain points of similarity with that of the Nairs and other peoples of Malabar, and this may indicate a common origin. Nevertheless, they have certainly lived in isolation in the Nilgiris for a very long time. They preserve no traditions about the prehistoric cairns which dot the hills, and their culture was already fully differentiated when they were first visited by a European, a Portuguese missionary, in 1602. Attracted by the salubrious climate, the Europeans in southern India began, about 1820, to retire to the Nilgiris for relief during the hot season. After 1850 they came in considerable numbers, founding summer colonies at Ootacamund and other towns. They introduced venereal disease, from which the natives have since suffered severely. Today, however, the population of the Todas—about 800— is again slowly increasing.

The Todas speak a Dravidian tongue, akin to the languages of their neighbors. They frequently employ archaic or secret words and expressions in their ceremonial and in the presence of strangers. Though they possess no written language, they are able to count into the thousands. Time is reckoned according to a calendar with twelve months of thirty days each and a week of seven days.

Racially, the Todas differ markedly from their neighbors. They are lighter in complexion—the men a rich brown and the women still lighter. Their hair is thick, black, and wavy. The men, in contrast to the other peoples of India, have thick coarse beards and extensive hair on the body. Tall in stature, the men average five feet seven inches, the women six inches less. Other physical characteristics include a narrow head (cephalic index 73 to 74), a long oval face, brown eyes, a prominent nose of medium breadth (nasal index 75), and moderately full lips. The men are athletic and robust. One man seventy years of age, for example, used to walk fifteen miles to market in the plains, returning the same day to the hills, an ascent of 3,000 feet, with a heavy sack of grain. The young women with their bright eyes and ringlets of raven hair are sometimes distinctly pretty (see Fig. 31), but they rapidly degenerate in appearance. One observer describes the Todas as a race of superb men and hideous women.

Four other tribes also inhabit the Nilgiri Hills. The Badagas, who number about 34,000, and the Kotas, with a population of 1,200, share the plateau with the Todas, while two wild tribes, the Kurumbas and Irulas, occupy the encircling jungle-clad slopes. The mutual relations of these five tribes present an interesting example of an intergroup division of labor. The Todas practice no agriculture and few industrial arts. They devote nearly their sole attention to their herds of buffaloes, supplying the other tribes with dairy products in return for various goods and services. The

FIG. 28. A TODA MAN.
From Rivers, *The Todas*

Badagas, a predominantly agricultural tribe, provide their neighbors with grain and other farm products, and act as middlemen in the trade with the peoples of the lowland. They pay an annual tribute of grain to the Todas, partly because the latter are considered the original owners of the land, partly from fear of Toda sorcery, and partly because it is immemorial custom. The Kotas, though they practice a little agriculture and possess a few buffaloes, are primarily an artisan tribe. They make and supply to the other tribes most of their pottery and ironware. They also provide the Todas with music and certain ceremonial objects, receiving in return the flesh of all sacrificed buffaloes as well as various dairy products. The Todas believe implicitly in their own superiority over all other peoples, and they regard the Kotas as definitely inferior. The Badagas, however, they treat in general as equals. The relations of these three tribes with the Kurumbas and Irulas are much less intimate, though the latter furnish certain forest products. Between all the tribes, however, complete peace prevails. War is absolutely unknown. The Todas, indeed, do not even possess weapons, save for degenerate clubs, bows, and arrows which survive in certain ceremonies.

The material culture of the Todas is surprisingly meager. Inasmuch as they neither till the ground, hunt, fish, nor wage war, they possess no tools or weapons for such purposes. They manufacture neither pottery nor textiles. They have knives and axes for cutting firewood, utensils of earthenware and bamboo for cooking and dairy operations, and brooms, sieves, and grain pounders for household purposes, but most of these articles they obtain from the Kotas. They generate fire by means of a simple fire-drill. Thorns serve them as needles, and leaves as dishes and drinking cups. Their fine arts are as undeveloped as their industrial processes. Decorative art is confined to simple adornment of the person and clothing. Occasional playing of the flute and the composition of songs for ceremonial events exhaust the musical attainments of the tribe. Their dances are rudimentary and confined to funerals. In general, the arts have been overshadowed by ceremonial.

The Todas clothe themselves in coarse cotton garments

obtained from the Hindus through the Badagas. Both sexes wear a loin cloth and a long loose mantle or cloak thrown over the shoulders. The latter garment has a capacious pocket and is frequently embroidered. The men also wear a perineal band supported by a string about the waist. Head and feet are commonly bare. The women wear their hair in long ringlets, the men in a thick mop cut evenly at a moderate length. Children have their heads shaved at the sides and

FIG. 29. TODA DWELLING.

top, leaving locks of hair before and behind. The women load themselves with ornaments of gold, silver, and brass—earrings, bracelets, armlets, necklaces, waist circlets. The men commonly wear silver rings and gold earrings, formerly also silver chains around the neck. Adult women are tattooed on the chest, shoulders, and upper arms. The men usually reveal raised scars on the left shoulder—the result of piercing with a hot stick as a magical cure for fatigue from milking. Circumcision is not practiced. The Todas paint the face very sparingly, the body not at all, but they smear themselves with ghee (the native butter), which soon becomes rancid and gives off an unpleasant odor.

Architecture is almost the only art at which individual Todas have become specialists. The ordinary dwelling resembles in shape a half of a barrel which has been split longitudinally. The side walls are merely a continuation of the curved roof; both are of thatch fastened with rattan to curved bamboo rafters. They project some distance beyond the end walls, which are constructed of solid planks. One end serves as the front of the dwelling. Here a tiny entrance with a sliding door gives access to the interior. The atmosphere inside is usually intolerably stuffy, since a fire is kept constantly burning in the fireplace with no provision for the escape of the smoke. Raised platforms of earth, smeared over with a thick layer of dry buffalo dung, serve as beds. A hole in the center of the floor, where the women pound grain, divides the house into two portions; the women confine their domestic activities to the rear, while the men carry on their dairy operations in front. A village consists of from one to six such huts, usually situated at a slight elevation near a wood and a stream, and surrounded by a stone wall with openings large enough to admit a man but not a buffalo.

With the exception of a few cats, the Todas possess no domesticated animals save their buffaloes. These animals, a particularly fine variety of the common water buffalo of India, are tended exclusively by males. They graze by day, watched by boys, and are penned up at night. They are driven from place to place at different seasons, partly to secure better pasturage and partly to fulfill certain ceremonial obligations. The cows are individually named and their pedigrees remembered—only in the female line, however, for no attention is paid to breeding and no importance is attached to paternity. The bulls are unnamed and held in comparatively low esteem. Male calves are usually sacrificed or given away to the Kotas; a few only are retained for breeding. The Todas distinguish two classes of buffaloes— sacred and ordinary animals. The ordinary buffaloes are tended by the boys and men of the village without special ritual, and their milk is churned in the dwelling house. The sacred buffaloes, however, are tended by special dairymen alone, their milk is churned in special dairy buildings, and their care is surrounded with an elaborate ritual. Moreover, they are subdivided into herds of varying degrees of sanctity, each with its own dairies, its own ritual, and its own class of dairymen.

The dairies associated with the sacred herds are usually situated at some distance from the villages, preferably adjacent to a separate water supply. Near each dairy is a circular inclosure for the buffaloes at night, a smaller pen for calves, and usually a small building for very young calves. The great majority of dairies resemble houses in architecture

FIG. 30. CHURN AND DAIRY UTENSILS OF THE TODAS.

except that they are surrounded by higher walls. A few very ancient and sacred dairies, however, are circular in shape with high peaked conical roofs. A partition divides the interior into two rooms. In the outermost, containing a fireplace and two beds, the dairyman sleeps and receives his friends. In the inner room, which he alone may enter, he performs the dairy operations and keeps, each in its special place, the various dairy utensils.

The principal dairy operations, milking and churning, are performed twice a day—in the early morning and late afternoon. The buffaloes are milked outside the dairy. In the bamboo milking vessel is placed a little whey from the previous churning, in order to cause a rapid coagulation of the milk, for the Todas make little use of fresh milk or cream. The milk coagulates before the cream is able to rise—the morning's milk by evening, the evening's milk by the next morning. It is then churned in an earthen pot by means of a stick rotated by a cord. Churning separates the coagulated milk into a liquid part, whey, and a solid part, which may be called "butter" although it differs from our butter in containing the casein as well as the fat of the milk. The "butter" is heated over the fire and clarified by the addition of grain, which sinks to the bottom of the vessel along with the proteid constituents of the milk, forming a deposit which is a staple article of the Toda diet. The remaining liquefied portion, containing the fat of the milk, forms ghee or clarified butter, another staple product.

The Todas subsist solely on dairy and vegetable products. Except in a single ceremony, they never eat the flesh of their buffaloes. Nor do they eat any other meat with the single and rare exception of the sambar deer. They make considerable use of wild berries, thistles, nettles, and bamboo shoots, and they obtain grain and vegetables from the Badagas either in the form of tribute or by purchase. Their favorite dishes include rice boiled in milk or whey, vegetable broth, rice and jaggery (crude sugar) boiled in water, and a kind of curry. Millet is roasted and pounded, mixed with whey and jaggery, rolled into large balls, and eaten with ghee or honey. Whey is the usual drink; there are no native intoxicating liquors or other indigenous narcotics or stimulants. The men do the cooking and eat before the women. The Todas take two principal meals a day; they break their fast between nine and ten o'clock in the morning and dine between seven and eight in the evening. They are modest about allowing others to observe them eating—from fear of the evil eye.

The tribe is divided into two endogamous divisions or moieties, which in some ways resemble castes, although there are no restrictions against their mutual intercourse.

They reveal minor divergences in dialect and ceremonial, but they chiefly differ in the fact that the Tarthar division owns all the higher sacred herds and dairies while the Teivali division alone furnishes the sacred dairymen who tend them. The Tarthar division, which is much the larger, considers itself superior. Each moiety is subdivided into a number of exogamous clans, which are territorial rather than totemic in nature. The Tarthar division contains twelve clans; the Teivali, six. The clan is further subdivided into families. Expenses incurred by the clan as a whole, notably for the repair of dairies, are equally distributed among its constituent families, irrespective of their size or wealth.

The ownership of property may be vested either in the individual, in the family, or in the clan. Individuals hold title to clothing, ornaments, household possessions, and the like, never to land. Buffaloes, whether sacred or ordinary, are usually the property of individuals or families, though the highest of the sacred buffaloes, the *ti* herds, are owned by the clan as a whole. Houses and the smaller villages belong to the family. Land and the chief villages with their dairies are the common property of the clan, whose members migrate from one village to another at different seasons. The inheritance of property is patrilineal, *i.e.*, in the male line, and it always follows legal descent, which does not always coincide with actual paternity. The legal sons of a man either share in common or distribute equally the money, ornaments, and household possessions which he leaves behind. Grandsons inherit the portion of a deceased son. Daughters receive a dowry from their parents, but inherit nothing. If the sons continue to live together, as is customary, they hold their inherited buffaloes in common. If they separate, however, the buffaloes are equally divided except that the eldest and youngest receive an extra animal each; odd buffaloes after such a division are either sold and the proceeds distributed or taken by one son who recompenses the others. Debts are also inherited. Sons must pay off the debts of their deceased father; in default of sons, the brothers must settle.

Each family has a head, who is responsible for the collection of its share in clan expenses. The clans possess informal headmen, who owe their positions to their personal qualities and lose them with sickness or old age. The tribe as a whole, however, has no chief. Its sole governmental institution is a council (*naim*) of five members. Seats in the council are privileges held by certain families in particular clans. One member is chosen from a Teivali clan, and three are similarly drawn from Tarthar clans. The fifth member is a Badaga, who usually sits, however, only in cases involving the relations of the two tribes. The council concerns itself chiefly with civil disputes between clans, families, or individuals, and in such cases a representative of each party sits with it. It also possesses wide powers in regulating ceremonial. A strong member frequently dominates the council either by the force of his personality or by the exercise of bribery or intimidation. The council has no voice in criminal cases. Indeed, crime seems to be absolutely non-existent. There is no recorded case of a theft or a murder by a Toda. On occasion, to be sure, a Kurumba is killed for sorcery, but this is regarded, not as murder, but as an act of self-defense. Certain acts which we consider crimes, *e.g.*, infanticide and adultery, are not so regarded by the Todas. Other acts, especially ritual offenses against the dairy, are viewed as sins rather than crimes. This striking respect for law simply reflects in one direction the extreme subservience of the people to ancient custom and tradition.

The Todas adhere to a classificatory system in reckoning kinship. Thus the term "father" includes not only one's actual or legal father, but also one's paternal uncles and all other males of the father's clan and generation, as well as the husbands of one's maternal aunts. "Mother" similarly embraces one's maternal aunts, other women of the same clan and generation as one's mother, and the wives of one's various "fathers." "Son" and "daughter" are equally inclusive terms. Differences of age play a rôle in the terms for brothers and sisters, those older than oneself, those of the same age, and those younger being distinguished. Otherwise, however, these terms are equally inclusive. "Elder brother," for example, includes all older men of one's own clan and generation. A cousin, therefore, will commonly be called "brother" or "sister." A special term (*matchuni*), however, is used for "cross-cousins," *i.e.*, the children of a brother and sister as opposed to the children of two brothers or of two sisters. A man should normally marry his cross-cousin, *i.e.*, the daughter either of his father's sister or of his mother's brother. Cross-cousins of opposite sex call one another "husband" and "wife," whether or not they are actually married, for they are potential spouses. The term "father-in-law" (*mun*) is applied also to a mother's brother and to the husband of a father's sister, for with cross-cousin marriage such persons are potential fathers-in-law. The terms for mother-, son-, and daughter-in-law have a similarly broad connotation. The Todas, though they follow a true classificatory system, have nevertheless advanced one step in the direction of a descriptive system. Thus the son of one's own sister is distinguished from the son of one's clan or classificatory "sister" by calling the former "*my* sister's son" and the latter "*our* sister's son."

This system of kinship affects social life in several ways. At certain ceremonies, notably funerals, kinsmen of various degrees have definite duties to perform. Again, kinship may involve taboos. Thus a man may not mention the name of his several "fathers-in-law" and "mothers-in-law." Moreover, relatives when they meet must observe definite forms of salutation. Though these are usually verbal formulas, a woman must salute an older male relative by kneeling and raising his foot to her forehead.

Descent is patrilineal. In other words, a child belongs to the clan of its father. To the Todas, however, fatherhood does not mean physical paternity but a legal relation established by a ceremony performed when a woman has reached the seventh month of pregnancy. The legal "father" of the child may or may not be the actual father. Indeed, he need not even be a husband of the woman, for if she is unmarried or her husband is unable to attend to the matter, another man may perform the ceremony and thereby become the "father." For the actual ceremony, the man and woman retire into the woods with certain relatives. The man cuts a niche in a tree, places in it a lighted lamp, fashions a crude imitation bow and arrow, promises the woman a calf, and presents her with the bow and arrow according to a definite ritual. She raises the toy weapons to her forehead and gazes at the lamp till it goes out. Then he cooks a meal; they eat together and pass the night in the woods. This ceremony must be performed during a woman's first pregnancy; thereafter it is performed only when it is desired to change the fatherhood of her children. Thus it happens that a man may become the "father" of several children after his death. But for a child to be born without benefit of a bow-giving ceremony constitutes one of the worst scandals of Toda society.

An expectant mother observes one other important rite. At about the fifth month of pregnancy she secludes herself for a month in a special hut at some distance from the village, submitting to certain ritual acts when entering and leaving. Childbirth itself, however, involves no special ceremonies, and any interested party may be present. A woman skilled in midwifery attends the mother, who kneels with her head on her husband's chest. Prayers and ritual acts facilitate a difficult delivery. The umbilical cord is cut with a knife, and the afterbirth buried. Unwanted children, especially girls, are suffocated at birth and buried like a stillborn child. The preponderance of a hundred males in a population of 800 reflects the prevalence of female infanticide, which is, however, declining today. If twins are born, one is killed, even if both are boys; if both are girls, they are both killed.

Shortly after childbirth, the woman retires once more to the seclusion hut, where, with ceremonies similar to those on her previous visit, she remains for approximately a month. Until a child is three months of age, its face is covered as a protection against the evil eye. Then, in a special ceremony, it is uncovered. Shortly thereafter, in another ceremony, the child is given a name and its head is shaved. The sexes receive different names, commonly derived from such things as prayer words, gods, hills, villages, dairies, buffalo pens, dairy vessels, and stones. Each individual also has a nickname, usually given by the Badagas with reference to some personal peculiarity. In addition to the current name taboos, the Todas show a certain reluctance about uttering their own names and an even greater reticence about their nicknames. A man may change his name in certain cases, *e.g.*, if illness or some other misfortune befalls him.

Children are born about three years apart on an average. They are suckled for two years or more, though after the naming ceremony mother's milk is commonly supplemented to an increasing extent by a gruel of boiled millet or rice in warm milk. Parents display much fondness for their offspring and look indulgently upon their games with wooden buffalo horns and little imitation buffalo pens. Neither adoption nor formal puberty rites prevail. In the case of boys, however, an analogous ceremony involving the piercing of the ears must be performed before a sacred dairy office may be held. It may take place, however, at any time from infancy to adulthood.

Todas are usually married during childhood, sometimes as early as two or three years of age. The father of a boy selects a suitable girl and arranges matters with her parents. The wedding takes place at the house of the bride with a simple ceremony involving the presentation of a loin cloth as a bridal gift. Thereafter the groom is expected to present

the bride twice a year with a loin cloth or, after she reaches
the age of ten, with a mantle. These garments, small and
cheap at first, gradually become larger and more valuable.
The family of the groom must contribute a buffalo—now
more commonly a sum of money—to the funeral of any
member of the bride's family who dies. The child-bride,
who continues to live at her own home, submits shortly
before puberty to defloration by a man of another clan. To
defer this ceremony until after puberty is a disgrace which
will stigmatize the girl the rest of her life. When she reaches
the age of fifteen or sixteen, she receives a dowry of clothing
and ornaments and is conducted by her husband to his
home, where she is inducted into his clan with a feast but no
ceremony. Either party may annul the marriage at this
time, the groom by payment of a single buffalo, the bride
by paying a heavy fine of five, ten, or even more buffaloes. In
either case the groom receives back any buffaloes previously
given as funeral gifts.

The Todas observe a number of restrictions with respect
to marriage. They never intermarry with non-Todas. The
orthodox union is that with a cross-cousin, but in any case
a man must marry a woman belonging to another clan in
his own division, for, as noted above, the divisions are
endogamous and the clans exogamous. Even though they
belong to proper clans, however, persons may not marry
if they fall within certain prohibited degrees of blood relationship. Thus a man, though he may and should marry
his cross-cousin, may not marry an ordinary or parallel
cousin, a cross-cousin of his parents, or a woman who would
be a cross-cousin of his children. These restrictions, it
should be noted, apply only to marriage, not to extramarital
relations.

Though monogamy is not uncommon, and sporadic cases
of polygyny occur, the prevailing and characteristic form of
marriage among the Todas is fraternal polyandry. When a
woman marries a man, she automatically becomes the wife

of his brothers, living or as yet unborn. They all live to-gether with little jealousy or friction. One brother gives the bow during the wife's first pregnancy and thus becomes the legal father of her children, though the others are also considered fathers. When one brother is with the woman, he places a staff and mantle outside the door of the hut as a warning to the rest not to enter. In rare instances the hus-bands are not brothers, but even in such cases they are usually clan brothers. If they live in different villages, the wife usually visits them in turn for a month at a time, but disputes not infrequently arise. One husband gives the bow at the first pregnancy, and the first two or three children belong to him and his clan; then another husband performs the ceremony, and so on. Toda polyandry is unquestionably connected with female infanticide and the resulting scarcity of women. Even with the decrease of infanticide, however, the custom does not seem to be dying out. What ordinarily happens is that a group of brothers takes two wives instead of one. Even where different brothers take individual wives, they clearly hold them in common.

A man may divorce his wife on the grounds that she is lazy or a fool, not, however, for barrenness or adultery. He pays her family a fine of one buffalo and receives in re-turn any buffaloes he has given as funeral contributions. It is a reproach to be a widow or a widower. If a woman sur-vives all her husbands, she may either return to her parental home with her children, live with her grown sons or a mar-ried daughter, or remarry. If she remarries, her new husband must make a payment of buffaloes to the children of his predecessor. The death of a woman, in a community prac-ticing child marriage and infanticide, is a serious matter. It leaves a man or several men without a wife and with no women available to marry. Toda custom provides for this situation by permitting widowers to purchase a wife from another man. They obtain the consent of the woman, her father, and her husband or husbands, and pay the latter a number of female buffaloes fixed by the council with reference to their ability to pay. The wife is then transferred with a feast and ceremony. The majority of cases coming before the council arise from this practice, especially today, when abuses have crept in and any man who desires a woman seeks to have her transferred to him, even without her consent or that of her husband.

Though members of the opposite divisions are forbidden to intermarry, a special form of union is permitted between them. Sometimes a Teivali man and a Tarthar woman, for example, live together as man and wife, their relation differing from an actual marriage only in the fact that their offspring are regarded as the legal children of the woman's legitimate husband or of some other man in her own division who has performed the bow-giving ceremony. More commonly, however, the man simply visits the woman from time to time as her recognized lover, after obtaining the consent of her husband or husbands and undergoing a ceremony in which he makes them handsome presents.

Great laxity prevails in sexual relations both before and after marriage. In addition to her various husbands and recognized lovers, a woman may have authorized relations with certain sacred dairymen and others, not to mention more casual unions which, though not socially sanctioned, are nevertheless not frowned upon. There is, in fact, little restriction of any kind upon sexual intercourse, even between members of the same clan. As Rivers says, "the Todas may almost be said to live in a condition of promiscuity." They possess no word for adultery, and even the concept itself is totally alien to them. "Instead of adultery being regarded as immoral," says the same classic authority, "immorality attaches rather to the man who grudges his wife to another."

Women occupy a definitely subordinate status in Toda society. With a few minor ceremonial exceptions they may not approach or have anything to do with the buffaloes and dairies. They are rigidly excluded from all political, religious, magical, and most ceremonial activities. They suffer at times, as when in the seclusion hut, from a stigma of uncleanness like that of a corpse. And they labor under other

FIG. 31. A TODA WOMAN.
From Rivers, *The Todas*

disabilities. For example, they must leave the village during certain ceremonies, and they may not use certain paths, especially those trodden by buffaloes. In spite of their distinct inferiority, however, they are not treated with cruelty or contempt, and they enjoy a considerable measure of personal freedom. Their low status may possibly be correlated with their slight contribution to the economic life of the tribe. The men, in addition to their political, religious, and ceremonial functions, do the herding, milking, churning, fuel gathering, building, trading, and cooking. In the absence of agriculture and important domestic arts, the female share in the division of labor by sex is confined to such comparatively minor activities as fetching water, mending and embroidering clothes, pounding and sifting grain, sweeping the floor, and cleaning the furniture and household utensils with dry buffalo dung. There can be little doubt, at least, that female infanticide and polyandry represent an adjustment to this unequal distribution of industrial activities between the sexes. It is not surprising, moreover, that the Toda women, in view of their circumscribed lives and interests, have been described as markedly less intelligent than the men.

Recreation finds little place in the life of the Todas. To be sure, they derive considerable amusement from some of their ceremonies, and they enjoy visiting, but true games are few and little indulged in. In one game, a boy or man tries to crawl through a narrow tunnel of stones before another, starting with a handicap, can touch his feet. Another game resembles tipcat; a pointed piece of wood is propped against a rock, struck with a stick by one person, and caught at a distance by another. The Todas also occasionally hold lifting and jumping contests, and they are fond of riddles, but they have no mechanical puzzles or string figures.

Sickness may have various causes, prominent among which are sin, sorcery, and the evil eye. It bodes ill, for example, to be told that one looks well or that one's buffalo gives much milk. Indigestion, a common effect of the evil eye, is cured by a special class of medicine men, who rub the belly of the patient, put salt on his cloak, stroke the salt with a thorn, and burn the salt and thorn with an incantation. The same specialists treat headache, snake bite, and other ailments by similar rites and formulas. When seriously ill and expected to die, the patient is dressed up in jewels and finery to await the end. Occasionally an individual who has unexpectedly recovered may be seen strutting about proudly in his funeral raiment.

The Todas hold two funeral ceremonies for their dead. In the case of children, the second takes place on the same day as the first. With adults, however, it is usually postponed for several months or a year, and is often held for several persons at the same time. Kinship ties play a prominent part in determining who shall perform certain acts in the funeral ritual and who shall make contributions of buffaloes, money, and other necessary accessories. The chief mourner is a man's brother or son, a woman's husband, or a child's father. At the funeral of an unmarried boy, a female cross-cousin plays the rôle of wife and widow, and the usual pregnancy ceremonies are always performed in connection with the funeral of a girl or a childless woman. The Kotas participate by furnishing music and certain ceremonial objects, receiving in return the flesh of the sacrificed animals.

The first funeral is held, in the case of men, either at a dairy or at a special hut symbolically called a "dairy"; in the case of females, at a hut which similarly represents a house and is later burned. Thither, on the appointed day, the corpse is brought on a wooden bier. There follows a series of elaborate rites, including especially a sacrifice of buffaloes and a ceremony of cremation. The slaughtered animals—now limited by the British Government to two at a funeral—are dispatched to provide the deceased with a source of livelihood in the next world. The buffaloes selected for the sacrifice, infuriated by goadings, are caught in an exciting contest by the young men of the division opposite to the deceased, who rush at them, seize them by the horns, hang on their necks, and bear them to the ground. As the captive animal, smeared with butter and decorated with a sacred bell, expires from a blow on the skull, the corpse is brought up to its head. Every one weeps and laments in characteristic Toda fashion

—in couples, forehead to forehead—but whether they mourn the deceased or the buffalo is not certain. The funeral pyre is lighted from a fire generated by friction. Before cremation, however, the corpse, the pocket of its mantle filled with food, money, ornaments, and other gifts, is swung thrice over the flames, then temporarily removed and the valuables thriftily extracted and redistributed to their donors. A lock of hair and a piece of the skull, rescued from the ashes, are wrapped in a bundle and kept in state in the chief village of the clan until the second funeral. Those who have attended the funeral, or have come into contact with the corpse or the relics, are rendered unclean. They refrain, especially if they are younger relatives of the deceased, from mentioning his name. The widow or widower, in addition, cuts his hair, covers his head, and observes a number of food taboos.

The second ceremony repeats many of the rites of the first, including an even more lavish sacrifice of buffaloes, and adds a number of new ones. Within a circle of stones, after an elaborate introductory ritual, the relics, anointed with butter, are burned along with certain vessels, implements, and other articles of a ceremonial nature. The ashes are buried and covered with a stone. A man encircles the spot three times, ringing a bell and shattering a new pot on the stone. All salute the stone, break their fast, and cut off a lock of hair as a token of mourning. At the time of the next new moon, certain ceremonies of purification are held to cleanse contaminated persons and places.

After the second funeral the soul of the deceased, which has hitherto haunted the earth as a malignant ghost, departs for Amnodr, the spirit world in the west where the sun shines while it is night on earth. Here the dead Todas lead a life much like that on earth. They tend their buffaloes and dairies—free, however, from rats and other destructive animals. Curiously enough, as they walk about, their legs gradually wear down, and when only knee-length stubs remain, they are reborn into the world as new individuals.

Of superior spirits or gods, the Todas believe in a vast number. Invisible and somewhat vaguely conceived, they are reputed formerly to have inhabited the Nilgiri Hills and later to have retired to the summits of the hills, where they now live with their spiritual buffaloes and dairies. They intervene in the lives of men to punish sins and inspire divination. The Toda gods are not totemic, though each clan has its patron divinity; they are not the ancestors of men, though a few are deified heroes; nor are they personifications of the forces of nature, for there is not even a sun god. The outstanding deity, though by no means a supreme being, is the goddess Teikirzi, the divine ruler of this world. She instituted the characteristic customs of the Todas, but did not create buffaloes and men. The latter task fell to her younger brother, Ön, who now lives in and rules over the realm of the dead. Ön brought forth from the earth 1,600 buffaloes, the ancestors of the sacred herds, and the first man made his appearance clinging to the tail of the last buffalo. From one of man's ribs, woman was created. This original pair reproduced so rapidly that within a week there were already a hundred Todas.

Though they pay scant attention to omens, the Todas have faith in divination. To ascertain the cause of a misfortune, such as sickness, the burning of a dairy, or the death, disease, or drying up of a buffalo, they consult a special class of diviners, who are quite distinct from the medicine men. These specialists, who usually operate in pairs, frequently work themselves into a semi-hypnotic frenzy, during which they speak an alien tongue and are thought to be directly possessed or inspired by the gods. In this state they are able to reveal the cause of the misfortune, which is invariably either sorcery or sin, and to indicate the remedy.

The power of sorcery is transmitted in certain families, and its practitioners are distinct alike from the medicine men, the diviners, and the dairyman-priests. A sorcerer usually exercises his magical powers only against persons who have deceived him or quarreled with him. If, for example, a man has given him an evasive or deceitful answer to a request for assistance, he obtains some human hair, binds five small stones together with the hair, wraps them up in a cloth, pronounces an incantation over them, and hides them secretly in the thatch of his enemy's house. When misfortune overtakes the victim, he resorts to a diviner and learns the identity of the sorcerer. He then goes to the latter with a present of food and grants the original request, whereupon the sorcerer utters a magical formula of recantation and removes the articles from the thatch. The hair employed need not belong to the victim; nevertheless, the Todas are careful to hide their hair and nail clippings. Other similar forms of sorcery prevail, and the Todas are feared by their neighbors for their proficiency at the black art. An exceptionally intimate association between magic and religion is revealed by the fact that both sorcerers and medicine men, instead of relying merely on "the belief in the efficacy of like producing like," make use of formulas which specifically invoke the gods and bear a marked resemblance to prayers.

A diviner may decide, however, that a particular misfortune is due, not to sorcery, but to sin. To the Todas, sins are ritual offenses against the sacred buffaloes and dairies, in which the gods have a lively interest. They include such acts as theft of milk from a dairy, entering a dairy after sexual intercourse in the daytime, and approaching a herd or a dairy after visiting a seclusion hut or a funeral, or even after chewing tobacco. But a man does nothing, however flagrant his sin, unless the gods manifest their displeasure. Only when and if a misfortune befalls him, does he appeal to the diviner, who then advises him to make a sin offering of a buffalo or a piece of cloth, depending on the gravity of the offense. He makes this offering, strangely enough, not to the gods or their representatives or the dairy, but to the other section of his own clan, each clan being divided into two sections for the sole purpose of satisfying this ceremonial requirement. A man may also make atonement by dedicating a buffalo to the gods. Instead of sacrificing or giving away the animal, however, he actually vows to do neither; he keeps it until it dies a natural death and meanwhile uses its milk.

Sacred days play an important part in Toda religion. Not only does every ceremony have its appropriate day, but each village observes once a week a special rest day, when certain activities are taboo. On these days, for example, women may not leave or enter the village and its inhabitants may not bathe, wash their clothes, clean the household furniture with dung, hold a feast or a funeral, or sell or otherwise dispose of any object in the village. The Tarthar clans, in addition, celebrate a special dairy day each week, with similar restrictions. In spite of the fact that these taboos are frequently evaded by subterfuges, the Toda rest days resemble in many respects an embryo Sabbath.

The outstanding characteristic of Toda religion, however, is the extraordinary emphasis placed on ritual. Worship has become formal; divorced from the ideas which originally inspired it, it survives, buttressed by the immense prestige of custom and tradition, in the form of an elaborate and often meaningless ceremonial. Ritual permeates every phase of the life of the tribe. We have found it in the ceremonies attending pregnancy, name-giving, marriage, and death. It reaches its highest development, however, in the conduct of the sacred dairies.

The dairy is the Toda temple. When a man visits a strange village, he first goes to its dairy, prostrates himself at the threshold, and utters a prayer. The sacred dairies fall into several classes, each associated with a particular grade of sacred buffaloes. They range in sanctity from the village dairies to the venerated *ti* dairies, the highest of all, and the elaborateness and complexity of their ritual varies with their sanctity.

Each class of dairy with its herds is tended by a special

FIG. 32. A SACRED TODA DAIRY AND DAIRYMAN
From Rivers, *The Todas*

class of dairymen, the priests of the Todas. The assumption of the office of dairyman involves elaborate ceremonies of initiation, varying in complexity with the sanctity of the dairy. Thus to become a *palol*, the sacred dairyman of a *ti*, a man must first pass a qualifying ceremony, in which, naked, he receives food from an old Tarthar woman who has never had intercourse with a man of her own clan, and then undergoes an ordination ceremony, lasting nine days, in which at various stages he drinks water from the leaves of a sacred tree and rubs his body with the bark—in accordance with a belief in sacred numbers—three times seven, seven times seven, and nine times seven times. Thus he acquires a high degree of ritual purity, which enables him to come into contact with sacred things. He must maintain this purity by keeping stringent rules of diet, sleeping, and dress, and by observing a variety of taboos. He must not, for example, cut his hair or nails, cross a bridge, attend a funeral, transact business in person with the outside world, or associate with a woman, even his own wife. He submits to these restrictions chiefly because of the profits he derives from the sale of the products of his dairy. If he serves his full term of office, eighteen years, he performs a ceremonial act which under any other circumstances would be considered highly immoral, namely, intercourse in the daytime with any Tarthar woman of his choice. None of the dairyman-priests exercises any governmental influence, nor are they ever consulted on mundane matters; their sanctity is purely ceremonial.

In the daily conduct of his dairy operations, the dairyman must follow a definite procedure, each minute detail of which is prescribed by custom. The daily routine of the *palol*, for example, begins at 5:00 A.M., when he rises. On stepping outdoors, he salutes the sun with his hand to his forehead. He washes his hands and face in a special vessel in front of the dairy. Then, taking water in his right hand, he pours it into his left hand and thence conveys it to his mouth, which he rinses. He ties up his hair in a prescribed manner, bows at the threshold of the dairy, and enters, reciting a formula. After transferring fire from the ordinary fireplace to a sacred fireplace, he doffs his cloak and dons a special loin cloth. Reciting a prayer, he kindles three special pieces of wood at the sacred fireplace and with them lights the lamp. Still praying, he touches with a particular bamboo stick the three special vessels containing the milk drawn the previous evening. Placing a special wand against the wall, he begins to churn the coagulated milk in the middle vessel. Soon he pauses to "feed" the sacred bell, *i.e.*, to smear milk on it, repeating a sacred formula three times as he does so. And so on through the day. Space is here lacking for more than a sampling of such minutiæ, but the same complex and elaborate detail characterizes all Toda ritual.

Among the prominent features of the dairy ritual are the important part played by special utensils, bells, lamps, and other sacred objects, and the rigid separation maintained between the vessels and other articles which come into direct contact with the milk and those which come into contact with the outside world or with the finished products of the churning. Underlying the ritual seems to be the idea that the dairyman is dealing with a sacred substance. The sanctity of the buffaloes, apparently much greater formerly than now, seems to have been transferred to their milk. If, as appears probable, the sacred animals were not originally milked, the ritual may well have been developed as a prophylactic against the evils to be expected from the profanation of a sacred substance, in short, as a means of removing the taboo.

Prayer plays a prominent rôle in the dairy ritual. Toda prayers contain no direct invocation of the gods. They consist of two parts: an enumeration of the sacred objects (*kwarzam*) for the sake of which they are uttered, and a recitation of the blessings prayed for. The latter portion, considered much the less important, is frequently omitted. Since the *kwarzam* are frequently unintelligible, prayer is in the process of being reduced to seemingly meaningless ritual words.

The daily ritual by no means exhausts the ceremonial of the sacred dairies. New vessels introduced into the dairy must be purified by an appropriate ritual. Salt is given to the buffaloes several times a year in a special ceremony. Elaborate ceremonies attend the seasonal migrations of the buffaloes from village to village, probably in order to counteract the evil involved in conducting the sacred animals through the profane world. The procession moves in a definite order, the vessels are transported on poles in prescribed positions, stops are made for prayers, and the new dairy is purified according to a special ritual. At a ceremony held when a calf is fifteen days old, the people partake of the milk of the sacred buffaloes, which is ordinarily taboo to them. This suggests a sacrament of communion. If an especially sacred pot, which is buried in the buffalo pen, is broken, stolen, or tampered with, or if a foreigner enters the dairy or a dairyman uses tobacco, an elaborate ceremony must be held, involving the consecration of a complete new set of dairy utensils, the ordination of a new dairyman, and the purification of the dairy. At a notable ceremony, held annually or oftener, a young calf without blemish is ceremonially sacrificed, dismembered, roasted, and eaten—the only occasion on which the Todas ever eat the flesh of the buffalo. The basic idea, as in the ritual eating of the totem animal among the Australians, seems to be that the sacrifice of one animal will promote the welfare and increase of the rest.

This overemphasis on ritual, thinks Rivers, indicates a state of degeneration in religion, in which the underlying ideas and beliefs have become atrophied, with the result that the worship originally based upon them has become formal and largely meaningless. "The study of the Toda religion makes it seem to me most probable that the Todas came to the Nilgiri Hills with a religion of a higher order than they possess at present, with a developed system of gods who were believed to direct and govern the affairs of men, and that by a long and slow process these gods have become unreal, the supplications of the people for their guidance and assistance have become mechanical, and worship has been transferred from gods, not to stocks and stones, but to bells and dairy vessels."

BIBLIOGRAPHY

BREEKS, J. W. *An Account of the Primitive Tribes and Monuments of the Nilagiris.* London, 1873.

HARKNESS, H. *A Description of a Singular Aboriginal Race Inhabiting the Summit of the Neilgherry Hills.* London, 1832.

KING, W. R. "The Aboriginal Tribes of the Nilgiri Hills." *Journal of Anthropology*, Vol. I. London, 1870.

MARSHALL, W. E. *A Phrenologist amongst the Todas.* London, 1873.

MODI, S. J. J. "A Few Notes on the Todas of the Nilgiris." *Journal of the Anthropological Society of Bombay*, Vol. VII. Bombay, 1904.

OPPERT, G. "Ueber die Toda und Kota in den Nilagiri oder den Blauen Bergen." *Zeitschrift für Ethnologie*, Vol. XXVIII. Berlin, 1896.

*RIVERS, W. H. R. *The Todas.* London, 1906.

SHORTT, J. "An Account of the Hill Tribes of the Neilgherries." *Transactions of the Ethnological Society of London*, New Series, Vol. VII. London, 1869.

THURSTON, E. "Anthropology of the Todas and Kotas of the Nilgiri Hills." *Madras Government Museum Bulletin*, Vol. I, No. 4. Madras, 1896.

——. *Castes and Tribes of Southern India.* 7 vols. Madras, 1909.

——. *Ethnographic Notes in Southern India.* Madras, 1906.

——. *Omens and Superstitions of Southern India.* London, 1912.

CHAPTER VI

THE KAZAKS OF CENTRAL ASIA

THE vast steppes of Central Asia, the hypothetical cradle of the human race, have from time immemorial harbored hordes of restless and warlike nomads. Typical of the modern adherents of this mode of life are the Kazaks—commonly but improperly called the Kirghiz-Kazaks—a nation of some three million people occupying an area of over a million square miles extending in a broad band from European Russia to the borders of China. The Kazaks, who must not be confused with the Russian Cossacks, have inhabited this general region for nearly two thousand years at least, if their identification with a people mentioned in early Chinese annals is correct. Their precise location, however, has shifted back and forth in their checkered history of wars and alliances with the Usbegs, Turkomans, Bashkirs, Kalmucks, Mongols, and other neighboring peoples. The Russian Empire, expanding eastward, gradually reduced the Kazaks to submission—a process which began in 1730 and required a century to complete. Today they form the autonomous republic of Kazakstan in the Union of Soviet Socialist Republics.

Racially, the Kazaks represent a typical Turkic stock with a strong admixture of Mongolian blood, and are closely akin to the Kara-Kirghiz, or Kirghiz proper, of the Tian Shan Mountains. Their great physical variability betrays their mixed origin. Thus a light Caucasoid complexion occasionally appears amid the commoner yellowish tints. Though sturdy in physique and robust in constitution, they attain only a moderate stature—less than five feet five inches in men. Their heads are decidedly round (average cephalic index 87), their faces broad with prominent cheek bones, and their noses short and low but not broad (nasal index 69). Their eyes frequently reveal the Mongolian fold over the inner corner. The hair, which is straight, black, and coarse, becomes gray late in life. Beard and body hair are scanty. Young children often have dark blue patches of pigment on the body, the so-called "Mongolian spots." The women possess more regular features than the men, and are often

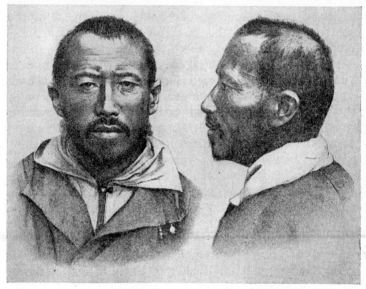

FIG. 33. A KAZAK MAN.
From Finsch, *Reise nach West-Sibirien*

attractive up to the age of twenty-five, but they rapidly degenerate in appearance. Both sexes show a tendency to put on fat, which is considered a mark of beauty. The sense of vision is exceptionally well developed; a Kazak can identify a horseman where a European can see only a distant cloud of dust.

The Kazaks speak a highly agglutinative language, belonging to the Kipchak branch of the Turkic division of the

Ural-Altaic linguistic stock, but they have enriched their vocabulary by extensive borrowings from Mongolian, Arabic, and Russian. From its clarity, precision, and free use of vivid images, their tongue has been called "the French of the steppes." The Uigur alphabet, introduced at an early date by the Nestorian Christians, was supplanted in the fifteenth century under Mohammedan influence by the Arabian alphabet. Few Kazaks, however, can write; the vast majority are illiterate. Their calendar, borrowed from China by way of the Mongols, divides the year into twelve solar months. Years, instead of being numbered, are grouped in cycles of twelve; the years of a cycle are named successively after animals—Mouse, Ox, Leopard, Hare, Fish, Serpent, Horse, Sheep, Ape, Fowl, Dog, and Hog. Asked for his age, a Kazak never tells the number of years; he simply replies, for example, "My year is that of the Horse," leaving the questioner to estimate from his appearance in which twelve-year cycle he was born.

The habitat of the Kazaks is a vast steppe, for the most part low, flat, and monotonous, but broken in places, especially in the south, by mountain ranges. It extends on the west nearly to the Volga River in Europe, on the east to the Tian Shan Mountains on the border of Chinese Turkestan, on the south nearly to Samarkand, and on the north to the vicinity of Omsk in Siberia. Rain is infrequent, especially in the summer, and the annual precipitation seldom exceeds ten or twelve inches. The few streams rarely reach the ocean; they usually dry up in desert sands, salt wastes, or brackish lakes and marshes. The vegetation consists mainly of grass, which in certain seasons is rank and abundant. There are no extensive forests; even individual trees are rare. The indigenous fauna includes the wolf, fox, bear, glutton, marmot, jerboa, deer, antelope, wild boar, leopard and other cats, various snakes, and geese, cranes, and other birds. Flies, mosquitoes, and other insect pests make life near the rivers intolerable in the summer. High winds sweep over the steppes, bringing sandstorms in summer and severe blizzards in winter. Extreme variability characterizes the climate. Though the mean annual temperature is about 37° F., the average for January is approximately zero and for July about 73° F., and the thermometer frequently falls far below zero in the winter and occasionally rises as high as 112° F. on hot summer days. Changes of more than fifty degrees in a single day are by no means unknown.

The Kazaks lead an almost exclusively pastoral life. They hunt to protect their animals, or for sport, rather than for food. They trap wolves and foxes in loosely built stone chambers which tumble down when the bait is touched. They ride after foxes with dogs, much after the manner of English squires, dispatching the animals with bow and arrow —today, of course, with firearms. Falconry is the favorite sport. Falcons are caught young, kept hooded in the home to accustom them to men, and trained to come when called for a reward of food. Perched on the arms of the mounted huntsmen, they are unhooded in the sight of their prey, returning to their masters when summoned. Fishing is unimportant, though occasionally a stream is dammed except for a narrow passage, where the fish are caught with spears, forks, nets, or baited hooks. The Kazaks harvest a minimum of hay as winter fodder for very young lambs and calves. Otherwise they practice no agriculture, save where the Russians have introduced the cultivation of wheat, millet, oats, and rye. They despise tillage and resort to it only when the loss of their cattle compels them to labor for hire on the lands of the rich.

The Kazak is primarily a nomadic herder. His whole existence centers about his domesticated animals; through them he adapts himself to his environment. They provide him with food, clothing, shelter, transportation, fuel, and utensils. Herds mean wealth, power, security. Anything that affects them adversely—inadequate protection against the rigors of the winter climate, a severe storm, lack of water, insufficient pasturage, disease, a hostile raid—injures their owner, and may even plunge him suddenly from affluence into poverty. It is small wonder, therefore, that a man, on meeting a friend, invariably inquires first as to the welfare of his herds, and only then about his family.

Dogs are kept for herding and hunting, cats for catching mice, donkeys as beasts of burden in the towns and oases, and yaks in the mountains, but the Kazaks derive their primary support from their herds of horses, sheep, goats, cattle, and camels. The small but spirited native horse takes first rank among domestic animals, usurping the usual rôle of the dog as the friend and constant companion of man. It possesses great endurance and can go several days without food. So intimate are rider and steed that to praise or criticize the latter is to flatter or insult the former. The horse represents the ideal of beauty; a bride is complimented by comparing her to a filly. Sheep, however, are more numerous, and furnish the main source of income. They also constitute the accepted standard of value. Goats rank next in numbers, but are somewhat less highly regarded. Cattle, though comparatively less important than the foregoing, are more profitable than horses and are increasing today. The camel, the dearest and least numerous of the five, is esteemed almost as a sacred animal. Though the one-humped dromedary occurs in the south, the two-humped Bactrian camel greatly predominates. Meek, obedient, and strong, the camel is nevertheless extremely sensitive; it quickly dies if overtaxed, plagued by flies or vermin, or forced to kneel on the bare snow in winter.

The needs of the various animals determine the annual migrations. The winter must be spent in a place with good pasturage, since all but the very young animals are compelled to fend for themselves, finding forage beneath the snow. Protection against the elements is another requisite. Terrific winter snowstorms frequently cause great loss; thus in 1827, in a particularly severe blizzard, one horde lost

10,000 camels, 30,000 cattle, 280,000 horses, and over a million sheep and goats. Forested stretches and protected valleys furnish the best winter abodes. Good sites are comparatively rare and are always private property. They have been a prime object of war and strife, and they really govern the density of population. In such locations the Kazaks inhabit permanent winter quarters from early November to the middle of April. Each family occupies a group of buildings surrounded by a wall of earth, reeds, and dung, and inclosing a court. The house itself, in its most typical form, is a sod hut about six feet high, with walls a foot thick, a flat roof of willow branches and reeds covered with turf, a floor of trampled earth, a low door, and one or two small windows with panes of bladder membrane. In these cold, cramped, smoky, vermin-infested quarters the family impatiently awaits the release of spring, passing the lagging hours in daily chores, handicrafts, conversation, and games. Stalls and storehouses of similar construction adjoin the dwelling, while reed sheds in the court furnish partial protection to the huddled animals.

Spring ushers in a season of abundance and gaiety. The kin-group inhabiting a winter site divides into a number of smaller units—*auls* or summer camps—which wander individually in search of pasturage for their herds. The length of stay in a particular place depends upon the season and the condition of the grass, and varies from two days to a week or more. Different *auls* compete for good sites. They do not wander aimlessly, however, but confine their roamings to recognized grazing grounds, the communal property of a larger group, the clan. An *aul* consists of from four to thirty yurts or felt tents, occupied perhaps by a single patriarch with his married sons and slaves and their families, perhaps by a number of households temporarily or permanently associated. The yurt, a light framework of wood over which strips of felt are stretched and secured by ropes, can be erected or dismantled in half an hour. The frame

consists of three parts firmly bound together by thongs or
cord—a circular and approximately vertical external wall of
wattle four or five feet high, a ring of wood at the center
supported by a pole, and roof slats inserted into holes in the
periphery of the central ring and sloping gently downward
to the framework of the wall, to which they are tied. The
finished yurt has the shape of a cylindrical dome. Wooden
double doors in a solid wooden frame, or sometimes mere
curtains of felt, form the entrance. Rush screens divide
the interior into compartments. The earth floor is beaten
hard and covered with carpets. A shallow pit near the center
serves as the fireplace. The central ring is left free for

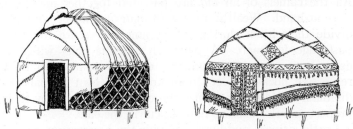

FIG. 34. KAZAK YURTS: A PLAIN ONE, SHOWING FRAMEWORK,
ON THE LEFT; A RICHLY DECORATED ONE ON THE RIGHT.

smoke to escape and light and air to enter; in inclement
weather it is closed by a felt. The yurt is well adapted to
both warm and cool weather as well as to a nomadic existence; it can be opened up to the breezes, closed against the
sun's rays, and its felt covers doubled for protection against
cold. The Kazaks regard their yurts with pride, and even
with a certain reverence, for they take oath upon them.

The various animals are herded differently. Horses live
in family herds consisting, on an average, of one stallion,
nine mares, and about thirty colts, fillies, and geldings.
They need no protection, for the stallions are fully capable
of guarding their herds from wolves and other dangers.
They do not range far afield, for the colts are tied by halters

to a picket line near the *aul*. Sheep and goats are herded together in large flocks, often belonging to several owners. They are hitched to a picket line at the *aul* during the night and driven out to water and pasture during the day. They are constantly guarded against straying and the depredations of wolves and leopards by mounted shepherds, usually boys, assisted by dogs. The shepherds arm themselves with long staffs, slings, and ropes which can be cracked like whips to scare away marauders. Cattle graze, unguarded, in herds of one bull to thirty or forty cows, returning at night to the vicinity of the *aul*, where the calves are tied to a picket line. Oxen and steers roam in separate herds at a distance. All the camels of an *aul* are pastured together and kept close at hand. Wealthy men with many animals commonly divide their herds during the summer to secure the best pasturage for each. A patriarch and his chief wife, for example, may wander hundreds of miles apart with their respective flocks. Every man knows his own animals individually, and can recognize those of his neighbors by their property marks, such as notches cut in the ears.

Cattle, camels, and horses provide the necessary means of transportation. Oxen, when used as beasts of burden, carry loads weighing about 350 lbs. on pack saddles. They are also ridden, especially by children and sheep herders, being guided by ropes attached to the ends of a nose plug. The camel, which is rarely ridden, is the principal pack animal. Loads of equal weight are tied securely over felt covers on either side of the tender humps. Properly loaded, a Bactrian camel can transport half a ton a distance of fifteen to twenty miles a day; a dromedary, nearly three-fourths of a ton. But the Kazak is primarily a horseman. He always keeps near his yurt a few geldings for riding, hobbled to prevent them from joining the herd. Only poor people ride mares. Women are as much at home in the saddle as men, and children learn to ride almost as soon as they can walk. The bridle is practically identical with our own. A piece of felt and a saddlecloth protect the back of the horse from the saddle, which is constructed of wood and includes a pointed pommel, a girth, leather leg guards, stirrups of iron or horn, a cantle with coat straps, and a cushion strapped on the seat. The horse is urged on by a quirt, never by spurs. The Kazaks usually ride at a walk or gallop; in trotting they rise in the stirrups and lean far forward. A Kazak migration is a festive sight. The women don their most gorgeous apparel, deck their horses with immense red saddlecloths, and carry their infants in their cradles on great red sacks over the pommels of their saddles. The men and children on their various mounts, the pack animals laden high with tents and household equipment, and the different herds and flocks kept in line by shepherds and dogs, stretch out in a column oftentimes several miles in length.

The Kazaks subsist almost entirely on the products of their herds. Cereals, vegetables, and fruits, as well as game and fish, find practically no place on their bill of fare, though the people do, to a limited extent, eat unleavened dough fried in mutton fat and other vegetable foods when obtainable. They spare their herds and, in the summer at least, eat comparatively little meat. The rich never eat beef, and the flesh of the camel is considered too tough for food, though thought to possess curative properties. At the onset of winter, old sheep and goats are slaughtered, occasionally also a barren cow, and the meat is cut in strips, salted, and stored for future use. The fat tail of the sheep is regarded as a special delicacy. In severe winters, when the animals must be slaughtered wholesale, the Kazaks gorge themselves on meat, eating two to four pounds a person per day. In the summer, however, sheep are killed only for feasts, for the entertainment of guests, and for sickness on the prescription of a shaman. The flesh of the horse, though highly prized, is rarely eaten. Only the rich can enjoy the supreme delicacy —the abdominal fat of a young mare.

The principal sustenance of the Kazaks, especially in the

summer, is derived from the milk of their various animals. Ewes, goats, and cows are milked twice a day, mares and camels oftener. From ewes' milk the women churn butter, prepare a sort of cottage cheese (*irimchik*), and make little round dry cheeses (*kurt*), which are stored away for the winter, when they are grated in warm water and drunk as a substitute for milk. Goats' milk is used in conjunction with that of ewes. Cows' milk yields butter, which, like that made from ewes' milk, is commonly salted and mixed with animal fat. *Airan*, a refreshing and popular drink, consists of sour cows' milk mixed with water or sweet milk. By all odds the favorite drink, however, is kumiss, a moderately intoxicating and highly nutritious beverage of fermented mares' or camels' milk. In the summer months the rich subsist almost wholly on kumiss, consuming it in enormous quantities. The Kazaks likewise drink beer, often flavored with salt, and brick tea, to which they add butter or *irimchik*. They eat and smoke opium, often to excess, but without the ill effects observable in their sedentary neighbors.

Their herds even furnish the Kazaks with fuel. Lacking firewood, they carefully collect the dung of their animals and store it in piles to dry. Over a slow fire of dung, lighted by flint and steel, they boil meat, prepare cheese, and make tea. They dine squatting around a low table, the women after or apart from the men. All eat from one platter, using their fingers instead of knives and forks. The hands are always washed before and after meals, and a napkin is provided to wipe off grease. It is etiquette to express thanks or satisfaction by a hearty belch.

The conditions of a nomadic existence demand that the material equipment of the household consist of unbreakable articles. Instead of basketry and pottery, therefore, the Kazaks use wood, metal, leather, and fabrics. Their wooden articles include plates and dishes, buckets for milking and carrying water, cradles, chests and trunks, saddles, and tent frames and doors. Though mostly bought at the bazaars,

they are in part manufactured by native wood workers, and
are often handsomely carved.   Bone and horn find comparatively little use in the handicrafts. The ubiquitous cast-
iron cauldron, for boiling meat, washing clothes, and bathing
babies, and the kitchen pots and basins of copper are purchased, but native smiths fashion iron knives, spearheads,

FIG. 35. INTERIOR OF A KAZAK YURT.
From Buschan, *Illustrierte Völkerkunde.* Courtesy of
Strecker und Schröder Verlagsbuchhandlung

shears, bits, and stirrups. Itinerant silversmiths make jewelry and saddle ornaments of silver, gold, and brass, and do
tasteful chased and inlay work. Skins, especially of sheep,
goats, and horses, are prepared in a mixture of meal and sour
milk and made into harness, clothing, and bags and bottles
for kumiss and milk. The Kazaks plait strips of horsehide
into whips and horsehair into ropes. From goats' hair they
make bands for their yurts and tassels and fringes for their

rugs. Camels' hair, collected in the spring when the animals molt, serves them for thread and for padding winter clothing. By means of the spindle and a primitive loom, they spin a little wool and occasionally weave narrow strips of woolen or camels' hair cloth, which they sew together for outer garments. With these exceptions, however, they make no true textile products, not even woven rugs. Their all-important fabric is felt, used not only for their yurts but also for rugs, hangings, bedding, clothing, saddlecloths, bags, and covers for trunks and other household possessions. To make felt, wool is spread in two layers on a straw mat, sprinkled

FIG. 36. KAZAK CHEST WITH DECORATIVE FELT COVER.

with water, rolled up with the mat, and tied. A number of people form in two parallel lines, pushing the roll back and forth between them with their feet until the wool is sufficiently pressed. Then the roll is undone, and the women, sitting in a circle, beat the fabric between the palms of their hands for two or three hours. The native felt is sometimes wonderfully light and beautiful, and is frequently embroidered with much skill and taste.

The products of the various handicrafts are decorated whenever possible. The Kazaks show a marked appreciation of line and color, and their decorative art consistently maintains a high standard. Designs differ, of course, but the predominant *motif* is a symmetrical double curved line, probably a conventionalized representation of a pair of ram's horns.

The native clothing of the Kazaks consists mainly of sheepskin and felt, but they obtain silk, cotton, and woolen

FIG. 37. A KAZAK WOMAN.
From Finsch, *Reise nach West-Sibirien*

goods today through trade. The ordinary costume of the men includes a cotton undergarment, a coarse shirt with a wide collar, great baggy leather breeches, high leather boots, and two or three outer robes of materials varying with the purse of the owner. The robe or caftan extends to the ankles, has long sleeves, and is restrained at the waist by a girdle;

for riding, its long tails are tucked into the breeches. The men cover the head with embroidered skullcaps, over which they wear conical felt hats with upturned brims or sheepskin hoods with the wool inside. In the winter they add felt stockings, leather gloves, fur ear protectors, and an outer cloak of sheepskin or fur. The women wear similar garments, except that the shirt is longer, the robes narrower at the waist, and the materials more gaily colored. They swathe the head and neck in loose folds of white cloth, for ancient custom demands that the hair be concealed, but they do not veil the face. The men shave their heads and remove body hair with tweezers, but grow scraggly beards on the chin. The women wear their hair shorn in the back and hanging in long braids in front. Before marriage they wear a score of fine braids; afterwards, two larger ones. They also pierce the ears, rouge the face, and color the finger nails yellow.

The Kazaks display their wealth on their persons. The rich wear magnificent robes of silk and velvet embroidered with gold and silver, stud their saddles, bridles, and belts with precious metals, and load their women with costly rings, armlets, necklaces, and earrings. They obtain these and other foreign articles by bartering their nomadic products—mainly through the mediation of the Sarts, for the Kazaks, though they control the caravan routes of Central Asia, do not themselves engage in commerce. They consequently have little use for money, and, instead of hoarding coins, usually melt them down into ornaments.

The patriarchal family forms the basis of the elaborate hierarchical social and political organization of the Kazaks. Not only wives and children but even adult sons, at least until they are well advanced in years, acknowledge the authority of the father. Inheritance, as well as descent, follows the male line, and a form of ultimogeniture prevails. As a man's herds increase beyond the limits of his winter quarters, and his eldest son attains his majority and marries, he buys for the latter another winter site and makes a division of his animals either orally or in writing in the presence of reliable witnesses. From time to time he provides for succeeding sons in similar fashion. If he dies, his property descends to the younger sons still living with him; those already provided for have no claims to the inheritance. The youngest son, even though married, continues to live with the father, and becomes his sole heir if all the rest have left. In any event he inherits the winter quarters. In default of sons, brothers inherit. Widows receive, in addition to their dowries, a portion of the estate or the right to enjoy it in common with the heirs. A woman's property goes to her children.

A number of related families form an *aul*, the unit of summer migrations. The patriarch of the largest and wealthiest family acts as headman. Several *auls*, possessing adjoining winter sites, are banded together by community of blood or for mutual protection into a sub-clan with a common crest, perhaps of totemic origin, which is used as a property mark and is inscribed on the monuments of deceased members. The power and importance of a sub-clan depends largely on the prestige and influence of its beg, who is less a chief than a judge, arbitrating disputes between individuals, families, and *auls*. The beg owes his position, not to election, but to usurpation of power or to general recognition, based on his wealth, the numerical strength of his kinsmen, his personality, and his reputation for learning, integrity, and justice. His authority varies with these personal factors; it is rarely absolute and may be purely nominal. Several related sub-clans form a clan (*sök*). The clans are historical groups, which have existed for centuries and owe their origin to common descent or migration or to military alliances. They are held together by a strong sense of group solidarity, involving joint responsibility for the crimes of their members as well as the duty of avenging injuries to the latter at the hands of outsiders. This solidarity finds expression in the proverb: "It is better to be a herder in one's own clan than a czar in an alien race." The clan has a common war cry, often the name of a famous chief or hero, and it owns communally the lands on which its members graze their herds.   The authority resides in the begs of the constituent sub-clans; it may be divided and dissipated among them, or concentrated in the hands of a single beg who in some way has usurped absolute power.

The clans are compounded into tribes and the tribes into hordes, three of which make up the Kazak nation: the Great or Elder Horde in the east and southeast, the Middle Horde in the center and north, and the Small or Younger Horde in the west, including the Inner Horde in European Russia between the Ural and Volga Rivers. The tribe and horde no longer have political significance. Formerly, however, they were ruled by great elective chiefs or khans. The relatives of the khans formed, and their descendants still form, an hereditary aristocracy enjoying certain privileges and a measure of prestige. They are known collectively as the "white bone" in contrast to the "black bone" or common people. Below the latter stood a slave caste, which survives, since the abolition of slavery in 1859, as a servile class of poor people, dependent upon and exploited by the wealthy cattle owners. The primary basis of class distinctions, however, is wealth in herds; a rich man through loss of his cattle may fall to the status of a hired laborer, unless a relative lends him a few animals with which to make a fresh start.

In spite of a strong sense of national unity, the Kazaks have never been able to weld their various elements into a unified state. The hordes not only have always been independent of one another, but have even failed individually to achieve a stable organization. Their khans rarely held more than nominal power, and lacked authority to command permanent obedience from their subjects. Only in times of war, when they could offer protection from hostile aggression or the prospect of booty in lands and herds, could they hold their people together. When such material advantages were no longer apparent, the constituent tribes and clans largely withdrew their support, and separated to pursue their nomadic livelihood independently. A new danger from without would give rise to new tribal alliances. Political institutions, therefore, were in a constant state of flux, with shifting allegiances and frequent realignments.

Before their pacification by the Russians, the Kazaks were a warlike and predatory people. They considered theft from a fellow clansman a crime, but regarded as honorable such activities as stealing cattle from other groups, attacking alien caravans, and sacking the towns of sedentary tillers. They resorted to arms whenever the unprotected condition of their neighbors offered opportunity for plunder, or a raid demanded revenge, or a bad winter decimated their herds, or increasing population made their winter quarters and grazing grounds inadequate. Their weapons, before the introduction of firearms, included the bow and arrow, a long slender lance, a formidable iron battle-ax, and a heavy whip with a lash an inch in diameter, a direct blow from which could kill a man. Their favorite tactics were ambushes and night attacks; they usually fled rather than engage in an open fight. If victorious, they were neither cruel nor vindictive; they preferred to capture and enslave their enemies rather than kill them.

Internal order is maintained by an unwritten common law (*adat*). Judges act by custom and conscience alone. When a cause of action arises, the litigants, in lieu of blood-vengeance, agree to refer the matter to a court of their own choosing and to abide by its decision. Either they both unite on one or two begs to settle the case, or each selects a beg, and a third man is chosen as arbiter. Civil and criminal law are not distinguished. Crimes are really torts, and can be settled out of court by compromise. Hence the criminal is not punished; he simply pays damages, which represent a sort of composition of the earlier *lex talionis*. Custom prescribes a graded schedule of damages, ranging from a wergild (*kun*) of 100 horses, 1,000 sheep, or 50 camels for homicide, through lesser payments in cattle for adultery, fraud, and serious personal injuries or assault, to a horse and a robe or skin for slander, breaking a finger or tooth, and minor assault. The full wergild must be paid for killing a man, one-half for a woman or slave, and one-third for a child under ten, the circumstances and intent being in no case considered. A man pays no penalty, however, for killing his child, slave, or adulterous wife. For cattle theft, a man must restore the stolen animals and pay twice their number in addition as damages. For rape of an unbetrothed girl he must marry the girl, give her father the usual bride-price, and pay him a fine of nine head of cattle.

The begs hold court very informally. The litigants and their witnesses squat before them and tell their stories. The rules of evidence are strict. The plaintiff must ordinarily substantiate his case by means of three witnesses, but women, children, servants, and persons of bad reputation cannot testify, and hearsay evidence is excluded. A relative may testify against a man but not for him. If, in spite of these handicaps, the plaintiff can prove his case, the court pronounces judgment, fixes the damages, and levies on the defendant a special fine, not exceeding one-tenth of the damages, as its own compensation. The plaintiff must execute the judgment himself. If the defendant cannot pay, his kinsmen must. If they refuse to pay, the plaintiff secures the aid of his clan or sub-clan and drives off by force the cattle of the nearest clansman of the defendant—frequently precipitating a feud. Usually, however, the plaintiff cannot prove his case, owing to the difficulty of producing enough qualified witnesses. In this event the court gives the defendant two alternatives. He may come to an amicable compromise with the plaintiff and pay the latter one-half the customary damages, or he may elect to have a kinsman take oath of his innocence. The kinsman, who is chosen by the plaintiff, is summoned to court. If he takes the oath, the defendant is acquitted; if he refuses, the latter is adjudged guilty. He is usually given a week or more to investigate the case and come to a decision, for if he swears falsely he assumes the guilt himself.

The Kazaks have universally won the respect and liking of travelers, who describe them as simple but self-respecting, honest though not always truthful, and curious but friendly, good-humored, and sociable. Perhaps their outstanding trait is their hospitality. They consider it an honor to conduct a stranger along his road, lend him fresh horses, or entertain him, and they accept no pay for such services. A host who harms or affronts a guest is dishonored, though once his visitor had departed he might, in former days, be among the first to waylay and rob him. Etiquette demands that a visitor approach a yurt from the rear and wait at some distance till the host comes out and invites him to enter. Inside, he greets the occupants, takes the seat of honor opposite the door, and is offered kumiss and tea. A sheep is brought into the yurt to be shown to the guest and blessed by him. It is then slaughtered, skinned, and boiled in the cauldron, while the neighbors gather to enjoy the feast. The host cuts the meat into small pieces, mixes them with fat and gravy, selects a choice morsel, which he places with his fingers in the mouth of the honored guest, and then similarly feeds the other visitors. Etiquette requires that each shall swallow his portion, however large, at a single gulp. After the meat, a bowl of broth is passed around, and kumiss is served. The guest of honor utters a benediction, and the diners retire to spend the evening in conversation, stories, games, and music.

The Kazaks know how to enjoy life. On every possible occasion—a visit, a birth, a wedding, a religious festival, even a funeral—they indulge in games and athletic contests. Their games include knucklebones, a kind of checkers played with pellets of dung, string figures, guessing games, forfeits, riddles, masquerades, and practical jokes. They enjoy wrestling and jumping contests, including a high-jump over a rope and a running broad-jump over the backs of three or four squatting comrades. Long horseraces for prizes are common. In one game, the youths and maidens pair off. The youth endeavors to catch the girl, who is mounted on a swift steed and is armed with a formidable whip with which to keep him off. If he succeeds, he has the right to touch her breasts. If she likes him, she readily yields, and romances sometimes begin in this way. In another popular game, twenty or thirty mounted men engage in a veritable scrimmage over the headless and legless body of a goat or calf. The one who succeeds in seizing the animal, throwing it across his saddle, and riding away from his pursuers while he skins it, wins the prize.

The native folklore, poetry, and music are inseparably intertwined. Animal fables, romantic and supernatural tales, droll stories, love lyrics, and epic narratives are usually couched in definite metrical forms, with rime and alliteration, and are not recited but sung to the accompaniment of a two-stringed guitar or the three-stringed balalaika. Other musical instruments—or rather toys—are the jew's-harp, the ocarina, and a crude reed flute. Contests in the improvisation of songs constitute a popular form of amusement. Itinerant minstrels, resembling the bards of Homeric times, travel from *aul* to *aul*, singing epic and lyric poems and songs composed for the occasion.

A child makes its bow to Kazak society with little ceremony. The mother works up to the last. The men absent themselves, and experienced female relatives offer their services. If delivery is difficult, they press the mother's body, sing exorcistic songs to drive away evil spirits, hold her hand over the fire, or prepare her a potion of water mixed with sand from a grave. The afterbirth and umbilical cord are buried. The mother rests for two or three days and then resumes her work. On the second day the infant is bathed and tied securely and permanently in a wooden cradle equipped with a specially constructed tube to drain off the excreta. At a feast a few days later the child receives its name, frequently taken from an object seen or an event happening at the time of birth. Parents welcome offspring; infanticide is unknown, and abortion is practiced only by unmarried girls. Contagious diseases and the rigors of the climate lead to a high, but not an excessive, infant mortality.

Mothers frequently suckle their children until the fourth or fifth year, though supplementary foods are added at an early age. They stretch their infants' ears to improve their hearing. Parents, especially fathers, devote much time to fondling and playing with their offspring, and they never discipline them except for an occasional light slap. Girls play with dolls—sticks decorated with rags. Boys engage in children's games, play with carved animal figures, and shoot birds with the sling or bow and arrow. As soon as they are able, children undertake light tasks—gathering fuel, fetching water, tending babies, holding sheep during milking, etc. They learn the economic duties of adult life more by observing and imitating than by formal education. Boys are circumcised between the ages of seven and twelve by Moslem mullahs, and both sexes attain their legal majority at fifteen.

Before a boy reaches the age of ten, as a rule, his father seeks a wife for him. Neither the boy nor the girl has much voice in the transaction. Sometimes, indeed, two men seal a pact of friendship by pledging their still unborn children in marriage. When the boy's father has selected a girl of suitable qualifications from another clan, for the Kazak clans are strictly exogamous, he sends matchmakers to her father to arrange the bride-price (*kalym*). Except where a brother and sister are married by exchange to a sister and a brother, marriage is always by purchase. The bride-price, payable in horses, cattle, sheep, and camels, varies with the means of the groom and the desirability of the bride, forty animals representing perhaps an average *kalym*. In return, the bride takes with her from her father's house a dowry, much inferior in value, consisting usually of a yurt, a riding horse or other animals, a chest of clothing, rugs, bedding, and other household articles. When the negotiations are settled, the groom's father rides with a few relatives to the home of the bride, where, with much feasting, hilarity,

and exchanging of gifts, the betrothal is formally sealed.

Marriage is deferred until the children attain their majority. Two wedding ceremonies are celebrated— one when the first instalment of the bride-price is paid, the second, sometimes several years later, when the balance is transferred. The first ceremony, held at the home of the bride, consists mainly of games, feasting, and revelry, in which neither the groom nor the bride participates. The groom remains in hiding in a special tent half a mile from the *aul*, a prisoner of the women, who minister to and make sport of him. The bride cowers, veiled, in the yurt of a friend. On the evening of the second day the friends of the groom attempt to remove her by force, and after a series of sham fights with her relatives finally suc-

FIG. 38. A KAZAK BRIDE.   ceed in carrying her, still resisting, to her father's yurt. Hither the groom, also, is conducted by his female guardians. The friends of the bride, bribed by the groom, leave the yurt but wait outside until the bride herself sends them away—a sign that she has come to an understanding with her captor. The groom spends the night with her but departs before dawn.

Until the second ceremony the groom is permitted to visit

his bride secretly from time to time, always coming at night, leaving before morning, and avoiding her parents. If he is too poor to pay the full bride-price, he occasionally enters into an agreement with her father to live with him and tend his flocks for a term of years. The parents of either party may annul the union before the second wedding—those of the bride by refunding the bride-price and paying a fine, and those of the groom by substituting another son and making an additional payment.

The second ceremony resembles the first, including a repetition of the mock abduction and ceremonial resistance. These and similar customs have been interpreted as survivals of actual wife-capture, and until recently, as a matter of fact, aristocratic Kazaks preferred to steal wives from the neighboring Kalmucks. After spending the night in a new yurt with his bride, the groom officially meets her father for the first time and receives his blessing. Then the bride, decked in her wedding finery and equipped with her dowry, accompanies her husband to his home and thereby comes for the first time under his authority. She is led, veiled, into her new yurt, where she greets the fire, takes the house-wife's place, and, after feasting and games, reveals her face to her new relatives in return for presents of cattle.

The law allows a man four wives, but only the wealthy can afford so many. "When he becomes rich," runs a native proverb, "a Sart builds a new house; a Kazak acquires wives." The women themselves often favor polygyny, for it lightens their tasks and makes possible a division of labor in the female sphere of economic activity. The first wife occupies a special position; she manages the household and apportions the work among the others. Though theoretically the property of her husband and occasionally ill-treated by him, the Kazak woman enjoys a higher status than does her sister among the neighboring sedentary tribes. She is neither veiled nor secluded in a harem. She converses with men and entertains guests in her husband's absence. She is free to visit her friends and to ride to market. She participates in feasts and games. In the division of labor by sex, while the men tend the flocks and herds, wage war, and manufacture all tools and utensils, the women milk the animals except the mares, make cheese and kumiss, cook, sew, embroider, make felt, rugs, and clothes, trade at the bazaars, and erect and dismantle the yurts. Thus they work considerably harder than the men, but they enjoy, in return, a position of honor in the household.

The Kazaks regard breaches of morality with leniency. The intimacy between the bride and groom before the final ceremony makes it comparatively easy for her to carry on clandestine love affairs with impunity. She must be circumspect, however, for the groom has the right to tear down her yurt and thus publicly disgrace her. Even in marriage, adultery by either party is not uncommon or particularly frowned upon, in spite of severe theoretical penalties.

Marriage, while regarded as a permanent union, may be terminated by divorce under certain circumstances. Specific grounds include disrespect and adultery on the part of the wife and impotence, non-support, and cruelty on the part of the husband, but mutual consent or the will of either party is usually sufficient. Divorce always involves the disposition of the bride-price and dowry as a bone of contention; the mode of settlement differs with the circumstances. The children, however, always remain with their father. If the husband dies, his widow usually marries his eldest surviving brother, though not compelled to do so. If she marries another, however, she forfeits her dowry, or else her second husband pays a bride-price to the brother of the first.

As might be expected from their outdoor life and their vitamin-rich milk diet, the Kazaks are an exceptionally healthy people. They treat their relatively rare cases of sickness by sweating, dung poultices, decoctions of herbs, cupping, and bloodletting, as well as by less rational therapeutic methods. They apply snake flesh to wounds, take pulverized birds' bones for broken limbs, and even employ exorcism. Thus the boys and girls gather about the yurt of a sick man and sing songs to drive away the evil spirits.

When a person dies, his body is washed, wrapped in winding sheets, and interred according to Moslem rites within thirty-six hours after death. The men alone accompany the corpse to the grave, which is dug three or four feet deep with a niche at the side. The body is deposited without gifts or personal possessions in the niche, and is covered with a cloth so that no earth may touch it. A stone cairn or monument serves the primary purpose of protecting the grave from beasts of prey. Formerly the favorite horse of the deceased was often interred with him. Today, however, the survivors merely cut off its mane and tail and saddle it backwards, though sometimes they also place the skull of a horse beside the grave. The female relatives of the deceased tear their hair, scratch their faces, and lament for seven days. The chief mourner—a man's wife, a woman's daughter, a child's mother—observes certain unimportant mourning rites for a year. On the seventh day the clansmen and neighbors for miles around are invited to a great funeral feast. During four days of horseraces, games, eating, and drinking the deceased is never mentioned. Similar feasts follow on the fortieth and hundredth days and on the anniversary.

As Mohammedans of the orthodox Sunnite sect, the Kazaks believe that the observance of circumcision, head shaving, prayers, ablutions, and alms-giving helps pave the road to paradise. They celebrate Abraham's offering of Isaac by a sacrifice of their best male horses, thought to enable the souls of dead sinners to ride through hell. They fast during the month of Ramadan in commemoration of the fast of the Prophet. Their faith prescribes strict abstinence at this time from all food and drink between the hours from early dawn to sunset, but they adapt themselves readily enough to this rule by spending the nights in eating and drinking and the days in sleeping. As might be inferred from this evasion, Islam sits comparatively lightly on the people. They have few mullahs and no priests or mosques. They seldom make pilgrimages to Mecca, nor do they display the characteristic Moslem fanaticism. They do not follow strictly the prescribed ablutions, prayers, and fasts. They even drink blood and eat animals which have died a natural death—abominations which distress their more pious neighbors. Finally, they still preserve marked traces of their former pagan beliefs and practices.

Numerous superstitions surround milking, cooking, spinning, and pitching the yurt. Sneezing establishes the truth of a statement previously made. Three is a lucky number. Prehistoric bronze spearheads are worn as talismans. The owl is a sacred bird and may not be shot. Children must not mention the wolf lest it come. Outspoken praise or blame arouses fear. The evil eye is especially dreaded in the case of blue-eyed and red-haired persons, and is counteracted by amulets or, in children, by drinking a mixture of urine, sand, and water.

Remnants of fire-worship seem to survive in the taboos against spitting on a flame and blowing out a light. Likewise a woman, on entering a new yurt and at the birth of her first child, prostrates herself before the fire and throws fat on the flames. Before partaking of their brick tea, the Kazaks throw small portions to the four winds, and they occasionally make sacrifices at springs and the banks of great rivers. In view of the scarcity of trees on the steppes, it is not surprising that they should often be regarded as sacred. Barren women sometimes sacrifice sheep at such places. When a man passes a sacred tree, he dismounts, places his saddle-cloth on the ground, kneels on it, recites a prayer, and then hangs on a branch a few hairs from his horse or a piece of cloth torn from his clothing. Such offerings are thought to insure happiness, health, and long life.

The Kazaks read omens from the twitching of the eyes, lips, and nose. They believe firmly in the interpretation of dreams, and change their plans to accord with them. To dream of meat, fat, or body lice, for instance, means wealth; of a bird of prey, marriage or children; of weeping, rain. It is unlucky to dream of a woman, camel, dog, or cow; lucky to dream of hunting, flying, seeing a snake, or beating one's wife. Divination is practiced in many forms. Fortune or misfortune is inferred from the position assumed by a thread strongly twisted and then released. By placing the shoulder-blade of a sheep in the fire a diviner can foretell the future from the cracks appearing upon it, and he can determine the sex of an unborn child by observing the entrails of slaughtered animals.

Strong survivals of the shamanism that prevails throughout northern Asia still linger among the Kazaks. The shaman (*baksa*), an itinerant practitioner, is an adept at sorcery, divination, medicine, and legerdemain. Singing, dancing, beating his tambourine, and shouting, he works himself into a state of utter frenzy, when he trembles, foams at the mouth, and mimics the actions and cries of animals. In this condition he can stab himself with a knife, swallow a sharp sword, or walk with naked feet on red-hot iron—without injury to himself. He summons friendly spirits to his aid, converses with them, and reveals the future. Or he beats the sick man with clubs and whips to drive out the demons that possess him. Finally, exhausted, he collapses in a cataleptic fit.

Such is the historic culture of the Kazaks, now doomed to rapid extinction, in all probability, through their acceptance of Communism, the opening up of the steppes by railroads, and the progressive extension of agriculture. Students of society will watch with interest the steps by which these individualistic nomads, with their strong emphasis upon private property in herds, adjust their lives and culture to a system of socialism.

BIBLIOGRAPHY

ATKINSON, T. W. *Oriental and Western Siberia.* New York, 1858.

CASTAGNÉ, J. "Magie et exorcisme chez les Kazak-Kirghizes et autres peuples turks orientaux." *Revue des Études Islamiques* Vol. IV. Paris, 1930.

CZAPLICKA, M. A. *Aboriginal Siberia.* Oxford, 1914.

——. *The Turks of Central Asia in History and at the Present Day.* Oxford, 1918.

FINSCH, O. *Reise nach West-Sibirien im Jahre 1876.* Berlin, 1879.

HELLWALD, F. VON. *Centralasien.* Second edition. Leipzig, 1880.

HOWORTH, H. H. *History of the Mongols.* 4 vols. London, 1876–1927.

HUNTINGTON, E. *The Pulse of Asia.* Boston, 1907.

JOCHELSON, W. *Peoples of Asiatic Russia.* New York, 1928.

*KARUTZ, R. *Unter Kirgisen und Turkmenen.* Leipzig, 1911.

KOSLOW, L. "Das Gewohnheitsrecht der Kirghisen." *Russische Revue,* Vol. XXI. St. Petersburg, 1882.

KUCZYNSKI, M. H. *Steppe und Mensch.* Leipzig, 1925.

LANSDELL, H. *Russian Central Asia.* 2 vols. London, 1885.

LEVCHINE, A. DE. *Description des hordes et des steppes des Kirghiz-Kazaks ou Kirghiz-Kaïssaks.* Trans. by F. de Pigny. Paris, 1840.

MEAKIN, A. M. B. *In Russian Turkestan.* London, 1903.

PALLAS, P. S. *Voyages de M. P. Pallas en différentes provinces de l'empire de Russie, et dans l'Asie septentrionale.* Trans. by Gauthier de la Peyronie. 5 vols. Paris, 1789–93.

*RADLOFF, W. *Aus Sibirien.* 2 vols. Leipzig, 1884.

SCHUYLER, E. *Turkestan.* 2 vols. London, 1876.

SPONVILLE, A. J. "Chez les Kirghis." *Bulletin de la Société de Géographie,* Cinquième Série, Vol. IX. Paris, 1865.

SYKES, E., and P. *Through Deserts and Oases in Central Asia.* London, 1920.

UJFALVY DE MEZÖ-KOVESD, C. E. DE. *Expédition scientifique française en Russie, en Sibérie et dans le Turkestan.* 6 vols. Paris, 1878–80.

VÁMBÉRY, A. *Sketches of Central Asia.* London, 1868.

——. *Travels in Central Asia.* New York, 1865.

ZALESKIE, B. *La vie des steppes Kirghizes.* Paris, 1865.

CHAPTER VII

THE AINUS OF NORTHERN JAPAN

WHEN the forefathers of the Japanese people reached Japan, some 2,500 years ago, they found the islands occupied by a race of primitive aborigines, the supposed ancestors of the Ainus of today. In a long series of wars the more civilized invaders gradually wrested the land from the natives, partly exterminating them, partly absorbing them, and partly driving them back toward the more inhospitable north. By the year 1000 A.D. the Japanese had obtained sole possession of the main island, Honshu, and had gained a foothold on the northern island, Yezo or Hokkaido. Thoroughly subdued, the Ainus laid down their arms and have now lived in peace with their conquerors for several centuries. The dwindling remnants of the race, numbering today about 17,000, inhabit Yezo, the southern half of Sakhalin or Karafuto, and a few of the Kurile Islands.

Racially, the Ainus present one of the most perplexing problems of anthropology, for they differ markedly in physical characteristics from all their neighbors in eastern and northeastern Asia. They are short in stature, the men averaging five feet two or three inches, the women four inches less. They possess sturdy bodies with massive bones, long arms, and comparatively large heads of medium breadth (cephalic index 76). Their eyes are brown or even hazel rather than black in color, horizontal rather than slanting, round rather than almond-shaped, and they almost never reveal the typical Mongolian fold. The face is broad, oval, and orthognathous, the lips rather thick, and the nose intermediate or mesorrhine (nasal index 82) with round nostrils and a depression at the root. The skin shows no trace of yellow. It is light brown or brunette—somewhat lighter than

163

that of the Japanese—and is frequently rosy over the cheek bones. The complexion, in short, resembles that of a tanned European. The hair of the head is thick, coarse, and usually black, though brown and auburn shades occur, and it shows a definite tendency to wave. Above all else, however, the Ainus are characterized by the hairiness of their bodies. The men, besides heavy beards and mustaches—they have invented a special implement to keep the latter out of their soup—have extremely hirsute bodies. Even the women have

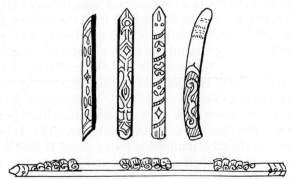

FIG. 39. AINU MUSTACHE-LIFTERS.

a coat of short, thick, dark hair on their legs, though not on the body. The view prevails today, after a long controversy characterized by numerous bizarre theories, that the Ainus are most closely akin to the Caucasian races of Europe, though separated from their cousins by thousands of miles of intervening Mongoloid peoples.

The language of the natives gives no clue to their origin, for it shows no relationship to any other known speech. In type it is neither isolating like the Chinese, nor agglutinative like the Japanese, Korean, and Tungus, but is incorporating or even polysynthetic like many American Indian languages. The elements of a sentence follow a definite order: subject, object, adverb, verb. Adjectives precede and prepositions follow their nouns. The vocabulary embraces about 14,000

words. The name "Ainu" means "man." No form of writing, not even picture-writing, exists. The numerical system
is vigesimal, *i.e.*, based on twenty rather than ten; eight
hundred is the highest number. Units of measurement are

FIG. 40. AINU MAN AND WOMAN.
Courtesy of the American Museum of Natural History

exceedingly simple; distance is reckoned in steps, length in
spans, quantity in handfuls, weight and area not at all.

The habitat of the Ainus lies between 42° and 50° north
latitude, and embraces some 40,000 square miles. The
islands, volcanic in origin, are mountainous and characterized by frequent earthquakes and a number of active volcanoes. Brackish lagoons parallel parts of the irregular coast.
Snow covers the ground for from five to seven months of the

year, but the summers, though short, are singularly hot. A heavy rainfall induces excessive humidity and fogginess in the warm season, and feeds the numerous lakes and short rivers. The rich soil supports dense forests of evergreen and deciduous trees, interspersed in places with an almost impenetrable undergrowth of scrub bamboo. Settlements are confined to the coast and the banks of the larger rivers. The waters teem with fish, while the land fauna includes the bear, deer, wolf, fox, marten, raccoon, otter, hare, and numerous birds.

The Ainus gather for food purposes about a hundred wild plants—fruits, berries, nuts, seeds, leaves, shoots, bulbs, roots, and fungi. Wild grapes, strawberries, raspberries, blueberries, crowberries, and mulberries are eaten raw. Mugwort, almost a staple, is collected in the spring, boiled, pulverized in a mortar, made into cakes, and dried in the sun for future consumption. Chestnuts are boiled, peeled, pounded into a paste, and eaten mixed with fish roe. Under Japanese influence the Ainus of Yezo have begun to cultivate a little millet and a few vegetables with primitive implements and methods. The only domesticated animal, except where the Japanese have introduced others, is the dog.

Hunting provides the Ainus with a considerable portion of their food. They use as their primary weapon the bow and arrow, the latter poisoned with a preparation of aconite and carried in a quiver slung over the shoulder. The arrow consists of three parts: a notched shaft of reed or bamboo equipped with feathers, a foreshaft of bone or wood, and a detachable barbed head of bamboo, bone, or Japanese iron (formerly also of stone). The men hunt deer with the aid of trained dogs, or else stalk them, decoying them within arrow range by imitating their cries on a special instrument. To kill a bear, an intrepid hunter, with his face and head bound up for protection, enters the den of the animal, jabs it with his knife, and drives it outside, where his comrades dispatch it with poisoned arrows. This animal, which compares favorably in size with a grizzly, is also caught in pitfalls. Both deer and bears are killed by traps so constructed that touching a string releases a bow and transfixes the animal with a poisoned arrow. Smaller traps of similar construction, as well as snares, are used to secure lesser game and birds.

Above all else, however, the Ainus subsist on products derived from the sea. They obtain crabs, lobsters, oysters, clams, mussels, and scallops along the shore. They occasionally surprise a turtle on the surface of the sea. They dam streams and build traps and weirs. In the winter they catch fish with hook and line through holes in the ice. They use nets in shallow water. At night they attract fish within reach of their spears by torches; in the daytime, by dragging along the bottom a decoy or bait made of iron, bone, and colored cloth. They go out in boats after fish of all kinds, and also after seals, walruses, and even whales, employing ingenious spears with reversible hooks and harpoons with two barbed, and sometimes poisoned, prongs. Salmon, which fill the rivers at certain seasons, are caught in various ways, and are prepared for future use by splitting them in half and smoking them over the hearth fire, drying them in the sun, or, in the winter, hanging them over poles to freeze. These resourceful fishermen even make use of their dogs, which they train to swim out to sea in two parallel columns 200 yards apart, to wheel at a cry and swim toward each other, and at another signal to swim shoreward in a crescent formation, driving the fish into shallow water by their splashing. On touching bottom, each dog seizes a fish and carries it to his master, receiving the head as a reward.

Though the Ainus occasionally roast fish on spits, they boil most of their food in an iron kettle over the hearth. Everything goes into the kettle together—vegetables, seaweed, fish, game, the flesh of surplus dogs, etc. Human flesh is never eaten, despite legends of former cannibalism. A light breakfast is taken at dawn, a heavy dinner in the evening, and other meals whenever some one feels hungry and food is at hand. The family, with guests, sits around the hearth in the center of the hut. The mistress ladles the stew out of the kettle as it hangs over the fire, and serves it in individual wooden cups. After eating, each person simply wipes out his cup with his index finger and licks the latter. The kettle is never cleaned; fresh ingredients are added to the remains from previous meals. The natives today smoke tobacco, manufacture millet beer—a sour, milky, and moderately alcoholic beverage—and are inordinately fond of Japanese *sake* or rice beer.

Although the evidence of archeology, history, and tradition shows that the Ainus formerly lived in semi-subterranean earth dwellings, they now inhabit square or rectangular thatched huts, grouped in small villages on the coasts and river banks. Construction begins with the roof. Rafters are lashed with fibers to a long ridgepole and to horizontal poles at the eaves. Then upright posts, six or seven feet high with forks at their upper ends, are driven into the ground, and the roof is lifted bodily upon them. Walls and roof are then thatched with reeds. In default of specialized housebuilders, both sexes participate in the erection of the dwelling. They celebrate its completion by a housewarming ceremony, with feasting, drinking, prayers, and libations. Near the house stands the family storehouse, a small structure built on posts for protection against rodents. The huts vary considerably in size, but they average about ten by twelve feet. They are usually oriented with a window at the sacred east end and a door on the west, leading into an inclosed porch or antechamber where the firewood, tools, and dogs are kept. A rectangular hearth, slightly depressed, occupies the center of the single room. Above it, on a wicker platform, fish, meat, and vegetables are smoked, dried, and stored. A measure of sanctity attaches both to the hearth and to the northeast corner of the room, which contains treasures, heirlooms, and certain sacred objects. Near the door stand the water buckets, tubs, and household utensils. Reed and grass mats

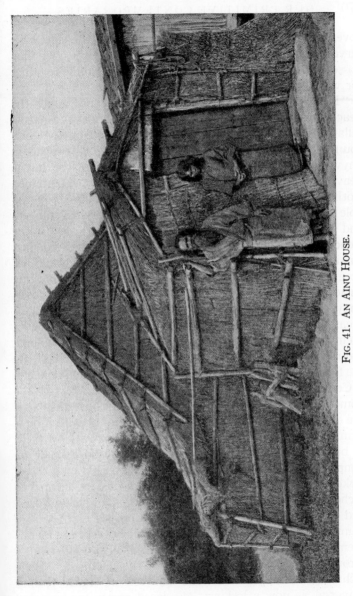

FIG. 41. AN AINU HOUSE.

From Hitchcock, *The Ainos of Yezo, Japan*. Courtesy of the Smithsonian Institution

cover the floor. Rude plank platforms along the side walls serve as beds. The occupants sleep in their clothes, for they possess no bedding, and on cold nights they huddle together for warmth.

"I poked my nose into several of the huts along the beach," writes a noted traveler of his first visit to a native village. "This was a mistake on my part, for in the Ainu country the nose is the last thing one ought to poke in anywhere." The atmosphere of the interior of the hut is heavy with the odor of soiled, sweaty, and fish-stained clothing, and with smoke, which can escape only through a hole in an angle of the roof. The smell of the drying, smoked, and half-decomposed fish in the rafters mingles with the stench from the fly-breeding refuse pile in the corner or just outside the door. The reek of unwashed bodies adds another note to this olfactory symphony. The Ainus consider bathing an admission of filthiness. "They do not regard themselves as dirty, and therefore dispense with such an 'uncleanly habit.' " Fleas, which infest the bunks and are tolerated because of their traditional divine origin, and snakes, which glide along the rafters and thatch in search of mice, further complicate the foreigner's problem of adapting himself to Ainu home life.

Contact with the Japanese has seriously affected the domestic arts of the Ainus. Flint and steel have displaced the older fire-drill, twirled between the palms or with a bow. Primitive means of lighting, however, still prevail—a piece of blazing birch bark held in a cleft stick, and a crude oil lamp consisting of a large mussel shell supported on a three-forked stick. The ancestors of the Ainus, according to archeological evidence, used stone knives, arrowheads, adzes, and hammers, but for two centuries iron has entirely supplanted stone. To be sure, the natives do not work in metals themselves, but they secure iron fishhooks, knife-blades, arrowheads, spear-points, etc., from the Japanese. Bone technic has disappeared for the same reason. Pottery, once universal, is now a lost art—displaced partly by imported ironware, partly by an intensive development of wood carving, made possible by the introduction of the iron knife. Plates, ladles, mortars, pestles, and many other articles are now carved out of wood. Buckets, dippers, and dishes of bark, with water-tight stitched seams, are still in common use. The women weave mats, bags, and nets, but few baskets. The fact that the greatest treasures of the household are old Japanese swords and lacquered drinking cups, both of alien manufacture, bears witness to the decay of the native arts and industries.

The Ainus prepare a kind of cloth from the inner bark of

FIG. 42. WOODEN AND BARK UTENSILS OF THE AINUS.

the mountain elm. After softening the bark in water, they separate it into long slender threads, which they wind in balls and weave on a primitive loom into a coarse yellow fabric. The cloth is brittle when dry but very strong when damp. In warm weather the children go about entirely naked, and even adults are scantily clad, especially indoors and when fishing. Both sexes wear as their principal garment an ankle-length coat or wrapper of bark cloth with wide sleeves and embroidered designs. The style shows strong Japanese influence. The patterns differ from village to village as well as by sex. A girdle of embroidered bark cloth, or of leather studded with brass ornaments, restrains the coat at the waist. In the winter, the skins or furs of birds, seals, bears, and other animals are sewed together into a short sleeveless tunic, worn over the coat or stitched to it. The women, in cold weather, wear undergarments of deerskin, or more commonly today of imported cotton cloth.

Both sexes formerly wore tailored skin trousers. They go barefoot in summer or don sandals of walnut bark; in winter they wear moccasins or boots of leather or salmon skin, stuffed with straw for warmth. Leggings of bark, plaited rushes, bark cloth, or skin protect the legs from insects or cold, according to the season. Two kinds of snowshoes are in use: one, of wood, resembles a short ski; the other consists of an oval wooden frame crossed by bearskin thongs. The women wear cheap metal ornaments of Japanese manufac-

FIG. 43. AINU MAN'S COAT.

ture—beads, rings, necklaces, bracelets, etc. Both sexes cut their hair just above the shoulders at the side and back, and pierce their ears for the insertion of metal earrings or strips of colored cloth. The women tattoo bluish-black designs on the forehead, arms, and hands, but they take special pride in marks surrounding the mouth and extending nearly to the ears. The latter marks give the appearance of a mustache and make the women look remarkably like men. The operation consists in gashing the skin with a knife, rubbing in soot, and wiping the wound with a cloth dipped in a decoction of bark. The tattooing requires several years to complete and is usually finished by the husband during the honeymoon.

FIG. 44. A TATTOOED AINU GIRL.
From Hitchcock, *The Ainos of Yezo, Japan.*
Courtesy of the Smithsonian Institution

The Ainus of Sakhalin harness their dogs to sledges, but those of Yezo transport burdens only on their own backs, supported by a band or tumpline across the forehead. On the rivers the natives use narrow dugout canoes about twenty-five feet in length, propelled, not by paddles, but by oars inserted in tholepins. They also build larger sea-going canoes of planks joined with twine and caulked with moss. The native anchor, which is of wood, has either one or two arms and is weighted with stones.

The Ainus show exceedingly little specialization by occupation. They possess no money or other native medium of exchange, but they have long carried on an extensive trade by barter with the Japanese and even with the neighboring peoples of the mainland of Asia. They exchange fish, furs, and stag horns for ironware, clothing, ornaments, rice, and *sake*.

On the social organization of the Ainus our information is very fragmentary. One author speaks vaguely of clans and totemism but denies the existence of exogamy. Several state that descent is reckoned primarily through the mother. The father, however, wields the authority in the family, although the maternal uncle is said to occupy oftentimes a position of influence or even dominance in the household. Property descends from father to son, except household articles and female apparel, which daughters inherit from their mothers. If a man has no sons, his possessions go to the husband of his eldest daughter. Though each village has its recognized fishing and hunting grounds, communism in property does not otherwise prevail. Each family owns its own canoe and garden plot, while individual ownership of weapons, utensils, and similar articles is indicated by property marks.

A chief, assisted by several subordinate officials, rules each village. He takes the lead in hunting, fishing, and warfare, presides at ceremonies, settles disputes, and judges crimes. He occupies a large hut, has several wives, and enjoys considerable prestige, but his authority is not absolute. A council of elders, which meets at his house, has the right to veto his decisions. Succession to the chiefship normally falls to a son or a brother, provided he possesses the necessary qualifications of courage, strength, and intelligence. Otherwise the council elects another man to the position. Women do not exercise political authority, though they are privileged to attend the council meetings.   Villages are practically independent.   Except for infrequent cases of intermarriage, the Ainus do not shift their residence.   A number of villages, however, may be loosely united into a district, with a paramount chief who functions in disputes between villages and in intertribal wars.

Serious crimes are extremely rare among the Ainus, and blood-revenge does not exist.   Individuals usually settle their personal quarrels by private compromise or retribution. Only when the offense is serious enough to arouse the village, does the community as a whole intervene.   In such a case the elders assemble at the home of the chief to hold a public trial.   In a wordy discussion, often lasting several days, the interested parties present their cases through chosen representatives.   The chief, with the advice and consent of the assembled elders, renders the judgment and fixes the penalty.   Frequently the suspected person must submit to an ordeal to determine his guilt.   Thus he may be required to thrust his arm into a kettle of boiling water, or to hold a hot stone in his hand.   If uninjured, he is innocent; otherwise he is guilty.   Or he may be ordered to drink a cup of water and throw the cup over his shoulder.   If it lights with the right side up, he is innocent; if not, he is guilty.   Punishment takes a comparatively mild form.   The Ainus never inflict the death penalty, for, curiously enough, they do not consider death a punishment.   In case of theft—theft, that is, from a fellow tribesman, for stealing from a foreigner is regarded as praiseworthy—the value of the stolen article must be returned by the culprit or his family.   In addition, the thief receives a flogging for the first offense; for the second, he may be ostracized from the community and have the tip of his nose cut off.   Adultery, like theft, is punished with fines and flogging. Occasionally, too, the adulterer is suspended by his hair with the tips of his toes just touching the ground. A murderer is maimed for life by having the tendons of his feet severed.

Until their pacification by the Japanese, the Ainus seem to have been a warlike people. Petty conflicts between villages and districts, caused in the main by encroachments on hunting and fishing grounds, were common, and the Ainus fought sanguinary battles with the Oroks and Gilyaks of Sakhalin as well as with the Japanese. The native weapons included the bow and arrow, a dagger six inches long, light leather armor, and a formidable war club of hard wood usually weighted with a stone and carried on the wrist by a thong. The sword and the spear are Japanese rather than aboriginal implements. The weapons of war, unlike those of the chase, were not poisoned. Archeologists have unearthed prehistoric native fortresses on the crowns of hills, defended by ditches and practically impregnable. The chief led his village into battle. Every able-bodied adult—women as well as men—engaged in the fray, and the women are said to have rendered very effective service, especially against the females of the opposing force. They even accompanied the men on night raids against enemy villages, in which the males were slaughtered and the females carried off to become the slaves or concubines of their captors.

A complicated etiquette surrounds social intercourse. On meeting a stranger, a man steps off the path to give him the right of way, and does not address him until spoken to. A woman, on encountering a man, uncovers her head, steps aside, conceals her mouth, and looks at the ground. The Ainus express affirmation, not by a nod, but by bringing both hands to the chest and waving them downward; negation, by passing the right hand back and forth across the chest. They never enter a house without announcing themselves and waiting for an invitation. Host and guest go through an elaborate ritual of salutation. Sitting cross-

AN AINU MAN, ACCORDING TO AN
OLD JAPANESE PRINT.

legged beside the hearth, they stroke the palms of their hands and their beards in a special way and make rumbling noises in their throats—sometimes for the better part of an hour—until they have exchanged the news and can relax into informality. The women of the house, when noticed, salute the visitor by drawing the index finger of the right hand up the left arm to the shoulder and thence across the upper lip, ending by stroking the hair behind the ear. If compelled to leave the hut, they walk out backwards, for it is impolite for a woman to turn her back on a man. Although extremely hospitable, the Ainus know how to inform a guest that he has overstayed his welcome. They invite all the neighbors and friends to a feast, called "the feast of being sent back, the mouth having been cooked for," and everybody bids the visitor a cordial good-bye.

The Ainus take life seriously. They never laugh, and rarely indulge in sports. In one game, a man leans forward and allows another to belabor his bare back with a war club wrapped in a cloth. The man who can stand the most blows takes the palm for courage. It is even said that sometimes the succession to the chiefship is decided in this way. Another game serves the practical purpose of training the eye for spearing fish. The men and boys, armed with imitation spears, line up in two groups and roll a hoop, six inches in diameter, back and forth between them. The members of the receiving side try to transfix the hoop with their spears as it passes. If they succeed, a man of the other party joins theirs. The game ends when all the players have been brought over to one side.

The æsthetic side of life is equally undeveloped. The Ainus know neither painting nor sculpture. Their decorative art is largely confined to carving conventionalized plant and animal designs on wooden articles—knife sheaths, plates, mustache-lifters, and the like. They possess no musical instruments except an occasional shaman's drum, a rare five-stringed guitar, and a bamboo jew's-harp, used only by children. They sing mainly to express joy or depression, to exorcise demons, and to facilitate the performance of monotonous economic tasks, such as rowing or pounding millet. Their dances consist largely of ungraceful movements of the arms and upper body, accompanied by clapping and imita-

FIG. 45. CARVED WOODEN PLATES
OF THE AINUS.

tive noises. Dancing is primarily for pleasure and is usually associated with drinking and bacchanalian songs. The native folklore, which is surprisingly rich, differs markedly from that of the Japanese. Ainu stories deal mostly with mythological subjects and the incredible deeds of animals, and they usually point a moral.

The Ainus greatly desire children and regard childlessness as a manifestation of divine displeasure. They never practice infanticide, except possibly to slay one of a pair of twins, and abortions are performed only by unmarried mothers. A pregnant woman observes certain taboos; she may not spin, or eat the flesh of birds or lobsters. She abstains from intercourse with her husband for two months before childbirth and for a month or two thereafter. She delivers her child in the hut, on a mat, in a squatting position. The men and children leave the house, and the mother is tended by experienced female relatives. If labor is difficult, the midwives assist by praying, pressing the abdomen of the patient, massaging her with seaweed or a dead bat, or bouncing her up and down on her feet. They cut the umbilical cord with a knife, bathe the infant in warm water, and wrap it up in a cloth. For a few days its head is molded, and on the sixth 'day a small feast is given in its honor. The mother rests quietly for six days; then, after a bath for purification, she is considered fit to resume her household labors. The father rests for twelve days, during the first six of which he observes numerous taboos and remains wrapped up near the hearth as though ill. The natives assert that, while the body and life of the child come from the mother, its spirit and intellect are derived from the father during these days of enforced rest.

Some time after birth, the child receives its name, which must never be that of another person, living or dead. The chief of the village acts as name-giver. In a brief ceremony he calls the child by the name he has chosen and makes it a small present. To the Ainus, "names are living beings, and, like the persons to whom they are given, they have separate personal identities." A wife may never pronounce her husband's name, for to do so would subtract something from his life. But he does not observe a similar taboo toward her. A person sometimes changes his name if he becomes ill or if he witnesses a particularly evil omen, such as an owl flying across the face of the moon.

Owing to a high infant mortality, families are rarely large, four children representing perhaps an average, and adoption is a common practice. Mothers frequently suckle their infants until the fourth or fifth year. In the hut, they suspend them from a beam in a wooden cradle near the hearth, and pay no attention to their crying. "Babies," runs a native saw, "are like talkative men and women; they must have their say." Outdoors, they are carried about on the backs of older children, sitting on a stick supported by a tumpline. Fathers teach their sons, and mothers their daughters, not only their respective economic duties, but also proper etiquette and religious customs and traditions. Above all, children must learn to obey their parents, to respect their older brothers, to honor old men, not to speak unless spoken to, and never to interrupt their elders. Puberty is celebrated with a feast and drinking bout.

Before marriage, both sexes enjoy complete freedom in sexual relations, and marriages frequently grow out of temporary or trial unions. The young people carry on their own courtship.   Strangely enough, they do not kiss, but bite, as a sign of affection. One traveler describes an amorous adventure with a native girl in the following words: "Loving and biting went together with her. She could not do the one without doing the other. As we sat on a stone in the semi-darkness she began by gently biting my fingers, without hurting me, as affectionate dogs often do to their masters; she then bit my arm, then my shoulder, and when she had worked herself into a passion she put her arms round my neck and bit my cheeks." Either the boy or the girl may propose, and their parents are powerless to prevent the match. Even in the case of infant betrothal, an old custom in which the children exchange clothing and homes, the betrothed couple can veto the decision of their elders when they reach the marriageable age, about sixteen for girls and nineteen for men. Marriage is rarely exogamous; it usually takes place between members of the same village and hence commonly between near relatives. A man is forbidden to marry only his mother, his sister, and the sister of his brother's wife; he may wed his cousin, his niece, and even occasionally, says one authority, his own daughter.

Though the young people court and propose, their parents arrange the wedding ceremony. The two fathers worship the divinity of the hearth with libations of *sake* and exchange an old Japanese sword. The bride prepares millet cakes, which she gives to the groom. He provides *sake*, which she pours into a cup; he sips a little, and passes the rest to her to finish. Presents are exchanged, and the ceremony ends in a feast with drinking and dancing. The young couple may reside with the parents of either, but they usually build themselves a new hut near the house of the bride's father. Shortly after the wedding the groom makes a spoon, a shuttle, a loom, and a knife sheath, and presents them to his bride. She makes and gives him a girdle, a necklace, a cap, and a pair of leggings. In this way they indicate satisfaction with their new status.

A man may take a second, and occasionally even a third wife. The first or "great wife" tyrannizes over the "small wives," although they live in separate huts. A marriage endures for only so long as suits the convenience of both parties. The wife unceremoniously leaves her husband if she ceases to like him or he fails to provide sufficient fish and game, and he sends her away, with a small gift to her parents, for disrespect, idleness, infidelity, barrenness, or incompatibility. In case of divorce, sons remain with their father and daughters go with their mother. A widow is supposed to marry the younger brother of her deceased husband, or else to remain single the rest of her life.

In the division of labor by sex, the men hunt, fish, and propitiate the gods; the women till the soil, gather fuel and all vegetable foods, clean and prepare fish, cook, tend the fire, draw water, make bark cloth and mats, spin, weave, make and mend clothes, and even assist the men in salmon fishing. Though they work long and hard, the women enjoy a comparatively high status. They labor under no disabilities at menstruation and are highly honored during pregnancy. They engage in war with the men and can make themselves heard in council meetings, but they have practically nothing to do with religious matters. Before marriage a woman is regarded as a man's equal; afterwards, she becomes subservient to her husband but retains the management of household affairs. A man fears to anger his wife lest she hide or burn his fetishes and thereby do him irreparable harm.

The Ainus sometimes treat disease in a seemingly rational manner. Thus they use scores of herbs in various preparations for medicinal purposes, they set broken limbs and bind them in rough splints, and they suck and wash wounds from poisoned arrows and treat them with powder scraped from a deer's horn. The great majority of remedies, however, are purely superstitious in character, e.g., eating an otter's heart for stomach ailments, and rubbing warts with a snake's cast-off skin. To the native mind, disease results, not from natural, but from supernatural causes, and must be treated accordingly. It is usually due to demoniacal possession, in which case it can be cured only by exorcising or propitiating the indwelling evil spirit. But it may also result from sorcery. The Ainus dispose carefully of their hair clippings, lest an enemy obtain them and work magic with them. One can injure another by cutting his garments, or kill him by securing his headdress, wrapping it up like a corpse, and burying it. If a man fashions an image of his enemy out of mugwort and buries it upside down with a curse, his victim will pine away as the image disintegrates. Similarly, one may fix an image of an enemy to a tree with nails through the heart and head, or set it adrift on a river in a miniature canoe of rotten wood. Magic is also employed for other purposes. To bring rain, for example, the ground is sprinkled with water, or a bowl, fitted out like a boat, is dragged around a garden. Practically without exception, however, prayers to the gods or spirits accompany these acts, so that magic, far from being independent, appears as a mere adjunct of religion.

When a person hovers at the point of death, the women sprinkle him with water to revive him, or hold his body tightly in the endeavor to prevent his soul from escaping. The Ainus do not fear death, and even look on with equanimity while their own funeral garments are being prepared. When death occurs, a blazing fire is lighted on the hearth, and messengers summon the friends and relatives to the funeral. The children of the deceased gash themselves on the forehead, and the widow or widower shaves his head with a sharp shell. The body is laid out beside the hearth in its best clothes, which are always cut or torn in places. By its side the relatives place a number of tools, weapons, utensils, trinkets, and similar articles, appropriate to the age and sex of the deceased and later to be buried with him. All of them are broken, chipped, torn, or otherwise damaged. Prayers and libations are offered to the household divinities. Then, after charging the corpse with messages to those who have gone before, and offering it food and drink, the survivors partake of a funeral repast.

Interment usually takes place on the following day. The corpse, rolled up in a mat, is carried to the grave on a pole by two men. The mourners follow in single file, carrying the mortuary articles. At a secret place, unknown to strangers, a grave is dug and the body buried with boards or mats to protect it from the earth. A small mound, a post, and a few broken utensils mark the site. After washing their hands and brushing their garments with grass, the mourners return to the village. Here they burn the hut of the deceased. Sometimes, for reasons of thrift, an old and infirm person is placed in a tiny shelter near the hut and fed till he dies, when the shelter is burned instead. The period of mourning lasts about a year, during which a widower remains unmarried and a widow wears a hood.

That man has a spiritual double, a soul, which survives after death, is proved by the fact that, as the Ainus themselves say, "the dead sometimes really show themselves to people in dreams." The ghosts of the dead go to an underworld, where they live precisely as do men on earth, though without death or sorrow. They return from time to time to haunt their graves or to help or injure the living, and are consequently propitiated on occasion by their survivors and never mentioned by name. They are invisible to men, though dogs can scent them and give evidence of their presence by howling. According to a curious complementary belief, the living can also visit the underworld, where they are invisible to the dead but not to their dogs.

But men are not alone in possessing souls. The Ainus also endow animals, plants, and even inanimate objects, not only with life, but with spiritual doubles or souls. They are, indeed, thoroughgoing animists. Whenever they kill game or take a good catch of fish, they offer thanks not only to the gods but also to the souls of the slain animals, which, if politely treated, may return to animate other bodies. The souls of things, like those of men, survive the destruction of their bodies. The object of burning the hut, tearing the clothes, and breaking the implements of a dead man is simply to "kill" these objects so that their souls may shelter, clothe, and serve the deceased in the hereafter.

Not content with investing all material objects with souls of their own, the Ainu, in addition, attributes to every natural phenomenon a presiding or indwelling divinity, an "owner" or "possessor." Every tree, every plant, every species of animal has its divine "owner"; every spring, stream, river, lake, and waterfall; every mountain, hill, and valley; every storm, cloud, and star; and likewise the sun, moon, sea, thunder, rain, and fire. Some are male, others female; some are good, others evil. The divinity of an elm tree must be propitiated before the bark can be removed. A hunter pursued by a bear clasps the nearest tree and prays to its presiding spirit for deliverance. The "owner" of the sun is a powerful goddess. But most important of all is the goddess of fire, who presides over the hearth in every household, gives warmth and supervises cooking, and witnesses all that happens. The fire, sacred to her, is saluted before and after meals and on rising in the morning, and is protected from profanation by taboos. Thus one must never spit or drop hair or nail parings into the fire, or point a sharp implement toward it.

Souls and spirits are believed to have, under certain conditions, the power to enter or "possess" alien bodies. Thus demons, ghosts, and even the souls of certain living men, it is thought, can temporarily animate the bodies of animals. Conversely, animal spirits can "possess" human bodies. Insanity, for example, is attributed to possession by the snake demon. Demoniacal possession is, of course, the stock explanation of disease. Sometimes the same phenomenon assumes a more benign form, as in what is known as "the call of the mountains." A man occasionally feels an irresistible impulse to flee to the hills, where he communes with the spirits and comes back exhausted after an orgy of "running wild, jumping, howling, and rolling."

Guardian, familiar, or tutelary spirits constitute another class of divinities. Each individual has his own guardian spirit, just as trees or rivers have their "owners." When a child is born, its father manufactures, with due formalities, a fetish of willow, which he sets up at the hut for the baby. The individual worships before this fetish all his life, and his prosperity depends upon its proper care. Shamans have their private familiar spirits, by whose aid they are enabled to work their wonders. Each hut possesses its tutelary divinity, the "Ancestral Governor of the House," who resides in the sacred northeast corner and is regarded as the husband of the goddess of the hearth.

Whether the Ainus believe in spiritual beings superior to souls, ghosts, "owners," demons, and guardian spirits, is debatable. A well-informed missionary, to be sure, insists strongly that they acknowledge a supreme being, the creator and preserver of the world, but no other authority reports this belief and one denies it categorically. The other outstanding candidate for godhood is Æoina, the first ancestor and culture hero of the Ainus, who first taught them how to hunt and fish, to make implements and worship their divinities.

The Ainus deal with their various supernatural beings in a number of different ways. They propitiate them on every possible occasion with libations of *sake* or millet beer, never, however, with food offerings. They scold them for not answering their prayers, and even threaten to make them no more libations. They seek to avoid mischievous or malevolent spirits. Thus, during a thunderstorm, when the thunder demon is abroad, the people cower beside the hearth and preserve silence. When a man sees a little whirlwind of dust approaching, he hides in a bush till it passes, and then expectorates. Ghosts are avoided by never mentioning the name of a dead person, by giving a wide berth to graves, and by washing the hands and face and beating the clothes when it has been necessary to visit a burial place. Sometimes a demon is punished. Thus a tree which has fallen on a man and killed him is chopped to pieces. Evil spirits may likewise be exorcised, *i.e.*, driven or frightened off. Thus the natives expel the demons causing disease by kneading and pummeling the body of the patient or by giving him nauseous doses to cause vomiting. During epidemics they set up sticks with notches containing evil-smelling substances such as garlic and putrefied fish. When a person dies from drowning, the men hold a wild dance near the place of death, brandishing their weapons and execrating the river demons.

One class—the shamans—specializes in dealing with spirits. The office of shaman is not hereditary; a practitioner receives a "call" in his youth and thereafter seeks solitude and communion with the spirits. Though usually of a nervous, sensitive, and impressionable temperament, shamans are neither epileptic nor insane. Neither are they charlatans. Women, as well as men, may follow the profession, but they are fewer in number and less powerful. Shamans receive payment for their services in material objects according to the gratitude of their clients, but they never become wealthy. They observe certain taboos, *e.g.*, against hunting, and make use of ceremonial paraphernalia consisting of a drum, a wooden wand, the skulls of birds and animals, and other fetishes. Each shaman enlists one or more familiar spirits to aid and inspire him. They may be either good or evil, but if the latter predominate he acquires a sinister reputation as a sorcerer and may come to an untimely end. The people call upon him comparatively rarely—usually only in emergencies such as sickness, theft, and poor hunting. Among their various functions, shamans diagnose and cure illness, detect crime and sorcery, control the weather, and practice divination.

When a sick person calls in a shaman, he sacrifices a dog to provide the familiar spirits with the blood they crave. A shamanistic performance bears a striking resemblance to a spiritualist séance. It is invariably held in the dark, under cover of which seeming miracles are wrought. Thus with practiced dexterity a shaman, his limbs bound up, can make—*i.e.*, cause a spirit to make—a drum sound at a distance. Waving his wand, beating his drum, praying, dancing, and making the cries of the animal spirits who serve him, he works himself into a state of ecstasy in which he becomes the mouthpiece of his divinity. He hypnotizes his audience into believing his pantomime and description of the combat between his familiar spirits and the demons he is seeking to exorcise. In the end, by sleight of hand, he produces a stone, stick, or other small object as evidence of success.

An outstanding characteristic of Ainu religion is its extensive use of a unique type of fetish, the *inao*—a willow wand, one to three feet long, whittled with a knife so that the shavings remain attached to the stick but curl up into either a single cluster at the top or several tufts at different places. These fetishes are set into the ground near the hearth, on the seashore, beside rivers and springs, at crossroads—in short in all places associated with divine beings. A large number of them are always to be found in a cluster, the "sacred hedge," several yards from the eastern end of each hut, along with the skulls of animals killed in hunting. Frequently they seem to be crude representations of the human figure. The large *inao* erected to the "Ancestral Governor of the House" in the sacred northeast corner of the hut, for example, has a slit for a mouth and a coal from the hearth for a heart. Permanent *inao* are renewed at least once a year, and temporary ones are set up on every important or critical occasion—sickness, the birth of a child, the building of a hut, the launching of a canoe, the start of a hunting or fishing expedition, etc. Indeed, the men spend a considerable portion of their lives in fashioning them. Although the Ainus invariably offer prayers and libations before the *inao*, they never invoke them but always address the divinities directly. The *inao* are neither gods nor offerings. It has been ingeniously suggested that they are mediators, artificial but indispensable, between men and their divinities. More probably, however, they simply represent

FIG. 46. AINU SACRED HEDGE.

a special form of fetish or idol, which the divine being makes his temporary or permanent abode.

Another notable religious practice of the Ainus is a sort of communion ceremony in which a captured bird or animal of certain species is worshiped and then reverently slain and eaten. Some authorities have interpreted this custom as a survival of totemism, of the ritual killing and eating of a totem animal that the species may prosper. The most striking example is the bear festival. When a hunter captures a bear cub, he takes it home and tames it. It plays with the children, sleeps with the father, and is suckled by the mother. When old enough to be dangerous, it is confined in a cage. At all times, however, it is treated with the utmost consideration. In the autumn when it is two or three years old its master sends out invitations to the festival. The guests assemble in gala costume. *Inao* are made and libations poured out to the household divinities. After quantities of *sake* have been consumed, the women and girls engage in a dance about the cage, while the men offer *sake* to the cub, tell him what an honor they are about to render him, and ask him not to be angry for they have treated him well and are now sending him back to his ancestors in the mountains. A young man opens the cage and leads the bear by a rope for a short promenade. The men shoot blunt arrows at the excited animal, while the women shout and clap. Then the young men seize the cub, thrust a piece of wood into its mouth, and strangle it between two poles. The men drain off the warm blood, which they drink and smear over their beards. They then skin the body and offer it food and drink. The flesh is boiled in a large cauldron and ceremoniously eaten by the family and guests, after which the head is placed on a pole, decorated with willow shavings, and set up at the "sacred hedge."

The Ainus are rapidly losing their native culture as a result of their contact with a higher civilization. Foreign goods are replacing native artifacts, and old customs are disappearing. The population is slowly declining from smallpox and other diseases, intemperate use of alcohol, and changed conditions of life. Firearms and game laws have seriously reduced the available supply of sea and land animals, and the natives are being forced to change from a meat to a vegetarian diet. Eventually, without doubt, the Ainus will be assimilated by and amalgamated with the Japanese people.

BIBLIOGRAPHY

BATCHELOR, J. *The Ainu and Their Folk-Lore.* London, 1901.
*——. *Ainu Life and Lore.* Tokyo, 1927.
——. *The Ainu of Japan.* New York, 1895.

BATCHELOR, J. "Ainu Words as Illustrative of Customs and Matters Pathological, Psychological and Religious." *Transactions of the Asiatic Society of Japan*, Vol. XXIV. Yokohama, 1895.

——. "Ainus." *Encyclopædia of Religion and Ethics*. Edited by J. Hastings. 12 vols. New York, 1908–22.

——. "Items of Ainu Folk-Lore." *Journal of American Folk-Lore*, Vol. VII. Boston, 1894.

——. "Notes on the Ainu." *Transactions of the Asiatic Society of Japan*, Vol. X. Yokohama, 1882.

BATCHELOR, J., and MIYABE, K. "Ainu Economic Plants." *Transactions of the Asiatic Society of Japan*, Vol. XXI. Yokohama, 1893.

BICKMORE, A. S. "The Ainos, or Hairy Men, of Saghalien and the Kurile Islands." *American Journal of Science and Arts*, Second Series, Vol. XLV. New Haven, 1868.

——. "The Ainos, or Hairy Men of Yesso." *American Journal of Science and Arts*, Second Series, Vol. XLV. New Haven, 1868.

BIRD, I. L. (MRS. J. F. BISHOP). *Unbeaten Tracks in Japan*. 2 vols. New York, 1881.

BUXTON, L. H. D. *The Peoples of Asia*. New York, 1925.

CZAPLICKA, M. A. *Aboriginal Siberia*. Oxford, 1914.

DIXON, J. M. "The Tsuishikari Ainos." *Transactions of the Asiatic Society of Japan*, Vol. XI. Yokohama, 1883.

DRÖBER, W. *Die Aïnos*. München, 1909.

GOODRICH, J. K. "Das Familienleben und die Religion der Ainu." *Ausland*, Vol. LXII. Stuttgart, 1889.

*HITCHCOCK, R. "The Ainos of Yezo, Japan." *Smithsonian Institution, Annual Report of the Board of Regents for the Year ending June 30, 1890*. Washington, 1891.

HOLLAND, S. C. "On the Ainos." *Journal of the Anthropological Institute of Great Britain and Ireland*, Vol. III. London, 1874.

HOWARD, B. D. *Life with Trans-Siberian Savages*. London, 1893.

JOCHELSON, W. *Peoples of Asiatic Russia*. New York, 1928.

KARUTZ, R. *Die Völker Nord- und Mittelasiens*. Stuttgart, 1925.

KINDAICHI, K. "The Ainu." *Proceedings of the Third Pan-Pacific Science Congress*, 1926, Vol. II. Tokyo, 1928.

KOGANEI, Y. "Ueber die Urbewohner von Japan." *Mittheilungen der Deutschen Gesellschaft für Natur- und Völkerkunde Ostasiens,* Vol. IX. Tokyo, 1903.

LANDOR, A. H. S. *Alone with the Hairy Ainu.* London, 1893.

MACRITCHIE, D. "The Aïnos." *Internationales Archiv für Ethnographie,* Vol. IV, Supplement. Leiden, 1892.

MONTANDON, G. "Résultats d'une enquête ethnologique chez les Aïnou." *Proceedings of the Third Pan-Pacific Science Congress,* 1926, Vol. II. Tokyo, 1928.

MUNRO, N. G. *Prehistoric Japan.* Yokohama, 1911.

PILSUDSKI, B. *Materials for the Study of the Ainu Language and Folklore.* Cracow, 1912.

——. "Der Schamanismus bei den Ainu-Stämmen von Sachalin." *Globus,* Vol. XCV. Braunschweig, 1909.

——. "Schwangerschaft, Entbindung und Fehlgeburt bei den Bewohnern der Insel Sachalin." *Anthropos,* Vol. V. Wien, 1910.

ST. JOHN, H. C. "The Ainos: Aborigines of Yeso." *Journal of the Anthropological Institute of Great Britain and Ireland,* Vol. II. London, 1873.

SCHEUBE, B. "Die Ainos." *Mittheilungen der Deutschen Gesellschaft für Natur- und Völkerkunde Ostasiens,* Vol. III. Yokohama, 1882.

——. "Le culte et la fête de l'ours chez les Ainos avec quelques observations sur les danses de ce peuple." Trans. *Revue d'Ethnographie,* Vol. I. Paris, 1882.

SCHRENCK, L. VON. *Reisen und Forschungen im Amur-Lande.* 4 vols. St. Petersburg, 1858–81.

SIEBOLD, H. VON. "Ethnologische Studien über die Aino auf der Insel Yesso." *Zeitschrift für Ethnologie,* 1881 Supplement. Berlin, 1881.

STERNBERG, L. "The Inau Cult of the Ainu." *Boas Anniversary Volume.* New York, 1906.

CHAPTER VIII

THE POLAR ESKIMOS

NORTHERNMOST of all the inhabitants of the earth, the Polar Eskimos occupy a narrow fringe of coast on the Hayes Peninsula in northwest Greenland, between Cape York on the south and Etah on the north. Less than a thousand miles from the Pole itself, this remote tribe of 271 persons (in 1926) is separated by hundreds of miles from its nearest neighbors, the Eskimos of West Greenland and those of North Baffin Land. Their physical characteristics reveal their membership in the Eskimo race, which inhabits the coasts and islands of Arctic America from eastern Greenland to northeastern Siberia, a distance of nearly 3,000 miles. Though muscular and well-proportioned, their bodies are short in stature, averaging five feet two inches for men and five inches less for women. Their high skulls reveal a large cranial capacity. Modern investigators describe the head as of medium breadth (cephalic index 77), though earlier measurements record a considerably lower, dolichocephalic index. The face is broad and oval, with prominent cheek bones (see Frontispiece). The nose is straight, rather long and narrow, and frequently aquiline (nasal index 73). The skin, though reddish or copper-colored on the cheeks, is a light yellowish brown on the covered parts of the body. "Mongolian spots" occur. The brown eyes, while not oblique, show distinct traces of the epicanthic or Mongolian fold. The heavy, coarse, black hair manifests a slight tendency to wave. Even extremely old persons have only a few gray hairs, and baldness is unknown. The scanty beard is always plucked out to prevent ice from forming on it in subzero weather.

The language belongs to the Eskimauan linguistic stock,

the various dialects of which differ so little that a Greenland Eskimo can make himself understood in Alaska. In type it is polysynthetic. By adding affixes to a stem, a whole sentence, including subordinate clauses, may be expressed in a single word. An example from the West Greenland dialect will illustrate the principle. "He wants to find some one who can build a large house" is rendered by the word *igdlorssualiortugssarsiumavoq*. With few exceptions only nouns and verbs are used; other parts of speech are incorporated in them by flection. The Polar Eskimos possess no written language, not even picture-writing. Their name for themselves is *Inuit*, meaning "men." They have words for only the first five numerals, but make shift to count as high as twenty. They divide the year into moons, but take little account of the passage of time.

Thule, as the habitat of the Polar Eskimos is called, lies between 76° and 79° north latitude, though archeological remains prove that the natives once ranged as far north as 81°. It is thus approximately as far within the Arctic Circle as Scotland is south of the latter. Existence in such an inhospitable region demands a highly perfected adjustment to geographical conditions. The culture of the people, consequently, cannot be understood without an adequate knowledge of their environment.

The coast of Thule is dotted with rocky islets, deeply indented with bays and fiords, and broken into small stretches of low foreland and beach by glaciers, precipitous cliffs, and high granite promontories. Its inhabitants are limited in their wanderings, on the north by the impassable Humboldt Glacier, on the east by the immense ice cap of the interior, which extends in places to the coast and is everywhere visible from eminences, on the south by the forbidding shores and glaciers of Melville Bay, and on the west by the waters of North Baffin Bay and Smith Sound. Along the coast in winter there forms an ice foot, where the sea ice freezes solidly to the shore in a band of varying width. Outside, the ice rises and falls with the tides, forming a boundary or break with the ice foot, where masses of ice are often washed up. Smooth ice, indispensable for sledging, forms permanently behind protecting islands and promontories, but strong winds and currents so agitate the open sea that the surface ice is constantly being broken up and open water prevails throughout most of the winter.

Four well-differentiated seasons characterize the climate of Thule. For four months, from about October 21st until February 21st, the sun never appears above the horizon, and snow and ice mantle land and sea. Midnight blackness does not, however, prevail all the winter, for the moon circles the sky for ten or twelve days each month, the stars give considerable light, and at times the sun lies just below the horizon, creating a gray twilight. On about February 21st the sun makes its appearance, and for two months of spring rises earlier and sets later each day, without, however, giving sufficient heat to melt the snow and ice. On about April 21st it rises but does not set, and for the four ensuing months circles the sky once every twenty-four hours. By the end of June it has generated enough heat to begin to break up the ice. For the last two months of summer the shores and bays are open, the snow has melted, and the soil is thawed out to the depth of a foot or two, leaving the ground exceedingly boggy. On about August 21st the sun sets again, and decreasing periods of daylight alternate with increasing periods of twilight for the two months of autumn. Ice begins to form in late August or early September and remains for the next ten months. Although summer descends very suddenly, the onset of winter is gradual. The temperature averages 34° F. in summer, 16° in the autumn, −11° in winter, and −7° in the spring. The climate during the short cool summer resembles that of Delaware in midwinter. The open sea exerts an ameliorating influence on the winter climate. The lowest recorded temperature at Etah, 42° F. below zero, is considerably higher than extreme winter temperatures in

Montana and North Dakota. Snow falls every month of the year, but especially in the spring and autumn. Rain occurs occasionally in the summer, and fogs hang over the water in winter, but the humidity is comparatively low, and clear days far outnumber cloudy ones.

The animal, bird, and plant life exceeds in abundance that of neighboring regions to the south, a fact which largely explains why Thule is inhabited while they are not. The land mammals include the polar bear, caribou, wolf, fox, and hare. The sea, besides salmon and other fish, harbors the whale, walrus, narwhal, beluga or white whale, and several varieties of seal. The feathered life embraces land birds, like the raven, hawk, owl, and ptarmigan, and an abundance of sea birds: large and small auks (murres and dovekies), eider ducks, brant geese, loons, fulmars, gulls, and terns. The birds fertilize the soil, producing a luxuriant summer vegetation of mosses, grass, and hardy perennials. There are no trees except a dwarf willow, and even driftwood is exceedingly scarce. So short is the growing season that flowers often bud before the snow has left the ground, and then burst suddenly into bloom. "Development," it has been said, "is almost explosive."

The climate renders agriculture impossible, and the environment produces practically no edible plants. The women, to be sure, gather and eat a few sourish leaves and sweet flower buds, but the vegetable food of the men is confined exclusively to the contents of the stomachs of slain caribou. The dog, the only domesticated animal, is eaten only in emergencies. Fish are not plentiful, and, although a few salmon are caught, fishing is a recent innovation and an unimportant source of subsistence. The Eskimos never collect shellfish along the shore; they eat them only when they find them in the storage paunch of a slain walrus. With these and a few other minor exceptions, all food is obtained by hunting. Although foxes, hares, musk oxen, and land birds appear occasionally on the native menu, and polar bears, caribou, and sea birds are even more important, sea mammals easily rank first among hunted animals. The Eskimos do not pursue large whales, but they secure quantities of flesh and blubber from carcasses washed ashore. The walrus, hunted nearly the year round, is the staple food animal. Seals come next in importance, and the narwhal and beluga rank not far behind. Surplus game is cached in depots, covered with heavy stones for protection from foxes; frozen, it keeps for months or even years.

The conditions of existence give rise to a nomadic mode of life. A family rarely remains in one settlement for more than a single year. Only by moving can it secure a change of diet and the necessary variety of skins for clothing and household uses. Each year, moreover, it follows a seasonal migration, determined by climatic conditions and the habits of the various game animals. In the late fall the Eskimos move into their permanent winter dwellings in preparation for the winter. During the colder months they live in small villages located in protected sites, where the ice is smooth and accessible by sledge, and near which good hunting grounds, a supply of fresh-water ice for drinking purposes, and passable overland routes are available.

For a period before the ice forms solidly, hunting languishes and the Eskimos live on their accumulated stores. If these fail, famine prevails. Occasionally, if the ice freezes rapidly, a number of narwhal or beluga are trapped in a fiord, providing the neighboring villages with abundant meat and blubber. From the time of the formation of solid ice until total darkness sets in—and even by moonlight thereafter in case of necessity—sea mammals are hunted by dog sledge. Walrus, beluga, and narwhal are caught at the margin of newly forming ice, and seals are obtained by two distinctive methods. If the ice is smooth and does not crackle under foot, the hunters, clad in noiseless bearskin shoes, scatter over the ice, looking and listening for seals at their breathing-holes. When one appears, the nearest hunter runs up silently, harpoons it as it lowers its head, and dispatches it with his lance when it comes up to breathe a second time. If the ice is rough or snow-covered, however, the wary animals cannot be caught in this way, and the hunters resort to the tedious *maupok* or waiting method. A man sits on a little three-legged stool beside a promising hole and waits patiently hour after hour, without a move or a sound, until a seal appears.

During midwinter the animals retreat or hibernate, and hunting is at a standstill. The men make sledge journeys by moonlight to bring in food from scattered depots. Occasionally, by torchlight, they kill a polar bear that ventures near the settlement in search of food. For the most part, however, they devote the winter months to visiting, feasting, dancing, and story-telling.

When daylight reappears, the hunters journey to the open water after walrus. After a heavy wind, the ice rapidly reforms and within twenty-four hours will support a sledge. A man waits beside a walrus hole, or hastens up when a new one is made, and thrusts his harpoon into the animal. Quickly withdrawing the shaft, he fixes its spiked end in the ice and braces it to hold the line against the struggling captive. When the animal reappears, it is dispatched with a lance, and its body, which may weigh over a ton, is hoisted onto the ice by an ingenious block-and-tackle arrangement. By cutting two or three holes in the surface of the ice and an equal number in the tough skin of the walrus, and by passing the harpoon line back and forth between them to distribute the weight and multiply the leverage, a hunter, even single-handed, can land his quarry. While the men are hunting walrus, the women spear salmon through holes in the ice with the aid of ivory decoys shaped like small fish, and the boys and old men catch hares in running nooses suspended from strings stretched across their runways, and trap foxes in stone cages with narrow entrances which are closed with a heavy stone when the bait is touched.

The springtime, likewise, is the season for the occasional

excursions southward to Melville Bay after polar bears and for the even less frequent expeditions across the ice of Smith Sound into Ellesmere Land after musk ox. A hunter tracks a bear by dog sledge. When his quarry is sighted, he releases his dogs, which are trained to surround the bear and hold it at bay until their master comes up and dispatches it with his lance. A hunter often pays for the valuable pelt with terrible wounds. In hunting musk ox, the dogs drive the clumsy animals onto rough ground, where a man easily evades their lunges and kills them with the lance.

With the onset of summer, the ice begins to break up in places, dispersing the walrus. The Eskimos now abandon their winter dwellings, live in their summer tents, and hunt

FIG. 47. POLAR ESKIMO SNOW GOGGLES AND FRAGMENT OF A BONE KNIFE.

seals. They take advantage of the fact that the mother seal, when calving, digs for her offspring a hole in a snowdrift, from which a passage leads down under the ice. On discovering such a "seal igloo," the hunter jumps on the mound till it caves in, and kills the baby with a kick on the head. He harpoons the mother if she is present; otherwise he awaits her return. By another method, known as *utok* hunting, a man approaches his watchful prey as it lies sunning on the surface of the ice. He crawls along on his stomach, imitating the movements of the seal by flapping his arms like flippers and moving his legs like a tail, until close enough to hurl his harpoon. *Utok* hunting in the glare of the snow and the oblique rays of the sun strains the eyes and easily causes snow blindness. But the Eskimos have adapted themselves to this situation by the invention of special snow goggles, with narrow slits which admit little light but allow remarkably clear vision.

Toward the end of May the ice becomes unsafe, and the Eskimos resort to the bird grounds. Birds, otherwise an unimportant item of subsistence, tide them over a critical season of the year, when sea mammals are unavailable. The women secure enormous numbers of dovekies or little auks with nets of sinew attached to long poles. When they have caught several hundred, they cache them in the rocks for winter consumption and move to another spot. The birds freeze in a solid mass, sour from the fermentation of the intestines, but the natives pry them out and eat them whole —bones, feathers, intestines, and everything except the bills and feet. A family can consume several hundred birds in a day. Dovekies are also stored between layers of blubber in sealskin bags; when thus treated, they are considered a great delicacy. The men catch murres or large auks in stronger nets among the cliffs and ledges. Eider ducks are snared in slip nooses. The men reserve the eggs of all three birds for themselves, eating them raw or half-hatched, caching them under stones, or making them into "sausages" by sucking out their contents, thoroughly masticating whites and yolks, and ejecting the mixture into casings of seal intestine to vary the monotonous winter diet. Gulls, ravens, etc., are caught to a much more limited extent. During the bird season the people keep no regular hours but work day and night. It is a time of intense life and animation.

The women and children stay at the bird grounds all summer. The men also remained in the days before they had boats, for the disappearance of the snow and ice made sledging and hunting impossible. Today, however, they possess *kayaks* or skin canoes, in which they venture out with harpoon and lance after walrus, seal, beluga, and narwhal. *Kayak* hunting lasts from the appearance of open water until the first thin ice begins to form.

With the close of the summer, families journey inland. The men hunt caribou with the bow and arrow, either by following a trail on the run or by diverting the animals into ambushes by lines stretched across their runways. The women spear salmon with two-pronged forks through holes in the ice of the inland lakes. Both caribou hunting and salmon fishing, however, are comparatively recent introductions. After gorging on meat and fish and storing the surplus in caches, the Eskimos return to the coast and prepare for the winter, thus completing their annual cycle.

FIG. 48. POLAR ESKIMO KAYAKS
Courtesy of the American Museum of Natural History

Although the Polar Eskimos boil much of their food in a pot over their blubber lamps, they eat great quantities of meat entirely raw. Only in this way do they obtain the necessary vitamins to avoid scurvy, for their vegetable diet is inadequate for this purpose, and cooking destroys the vitamins in meat. In eating, they stuff a long strip of flesh as far as possible into the mouth and cut it off at the lips with a knife. A hungry hunter can devour eight or ten pounds of meat at a sitting without the slightest inconvenience. Only by consuming enormous quantities of food can life, vigor, and efficiency be maintained under Arctic conditions. The natives laugh at the idea that a man can be satiated. "Dogs," they say, "can be stuffed till they are satisfied and can eat no more; but people—people can always eat!" They regard as special delicacies the skin of narwhal and beluga, the raw liver of walrus, and the marrow of the leg bones of musk ox and caribou. Only under the stress of direst necessity do they resort to cannibalism. They are fond of "high" meat, and often purposely allow their game to become partially decomposed. "When you have grown accustomed to the taste," says the explorer Rasmussen, "this 'issuangnerk,' as they call it, is really a very pleasant change from all the raw meat." Water, the only drink, must be melted from snow or ice over the blubber lamp throughout most of the year. It is much too valuable a commodity to be wasted in bathing.

The weapons of the chase are admirably adapted to their uses. The harpoon has a shaft of wood or narwhal tusk about four feet long. An ivory foreshaft is fixed to the shaft by a ball-and-socket joint, so that it becomes dislocated but not detached by the lateral pressure exerted by the struggling animal. The detachable ivory head has an iron point, a socket into which the foreshaft is inserted, one or two barbs of different shapes for different animals, and a hole in the side for the attachment of a long line. When the harpoon is thrown, the head becomes engaged in the animal, which is held by the line, while the shaft with the foreshaft comes loose and floats on the water. In *kayak* hunting an inflated sealskin is attached to the line as a float; sometimes also a drag, to impede the flight of the animal. The lance differs from the harpoon chiefly in its lack of a line and detachable head, and in its employment for killing rather than securing the quarry. It has an unbarbed iron point and sometimes a small bladder to keep it afloat if it breaks loose. The Polar Eskimos do not possess the spear-thrower, nor do they use bird darts. The bow, arrow, and quiver, like the *kayak*, are comparatively recent borrowings from other Eskimo tribes. The bow is composite, consisting

of three pieces of caribou antler bound together and strengthened by leather thongs.   The fish spear, which is likewise
modern, has a central spike of bone, iron, or ivory and two
outer barbed prongs.

In their snow- and icebound environment the dog sledge
furnishes the Polar Eskimos with their best, and formerly
their only, means of transportation.   The sledge is constructed of seal bones lashed with thongs, with runners of
small bits of driftwood bound together and shoes of narwhal
or walrus tusks.   Sometimes ice shoes are added by rubbing

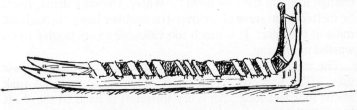

After Rasmussen

FIG. 49. POLAR ESKIMO SLEDGE.

on snow melted in warm urine.   At the rear of the sledge rise
two uprights, connected by a crosspiece and straps.   Five
dogs, more or less, are hitched to the sledge in fan formation,
each with a sealskin collar and a separate trace of rawhide.
They are guided by a long whip and the voice of the driver.
Gentle and amenable to training, loyal to their masters
and hostile to other teams, the "huskies" also display
marvelous endurance.   They can go several days without
food and can draw a loaded sledge at the rate of four or
five miles per hour for ten or twelve hours a day, in a pinch
for thirty-six hours at a stretch.

By comparison with the sledge, boats assume a decidedly
subordinate importance, and until seventy years ago were
entirely unknown.   Even today, the Polar Eskimos have
not adopted the *umiak*, or woman's boat, of the other
Eskimos.   Since it is too large to be transported on a
sledge, it would necessitate returning every summer to

the same place, and its advantages during the short season of open water would not compensate for the sacrifice of mobility. On the other hand, the *kayak* or man's boat, made of skins stretched over a wooden frame, propelled by a double paddle, and holding a single man with his hunting equipment, has proved valuable enough to establish itself.

The winter house, situated on the sloping beach just above

FIG. 50. A POLAR ESKIMO DOG TEAM.
Courtesy of the American Museum of Natural History

the ice foot, and accommodating one or two families, represents an almost perfect adjustment to the climate and the available building materials. The main part of the dwelling is pear-shaped, wider in front and narrower behind. In dimensions it rarely exceeds twelve by ten feet, with an internal height insufficient for an average man to stand erect. No wood, bone, or ice enters into its construction. Heavy stone walls support cantilever beams of stone, upon which rest flat slabs of slate. The whole is covered with earth and an outer layer of stones. This marvel of engineering is entered by a low semi-subterranean tunnel, ten feet long, lined and covered with stones and turf, and protected at the entrance by a wall of snow. The tunnel opens into the single room of the dwelling by a narrow door less than two feet in height. The floor, nearly level with the roof of the tunnel, is restricted in area, paved with stones, covered with grass and skins, and flanked by raised platforms on both sides and on the rear. In front, over the door, a window overlooks the sea. It consists of a skin, in which is inserted a square pane of animal membrane with a tiny peephole in the center. It is made fast and airtight by tucking the edges underneath the stones and turf of the roof and walls. Sealskins line the walls and ceiling, and from bone pegs hang nets, whips, harpoon lines, and clothing. The small platforms on either side of the floor hold food and household ar-

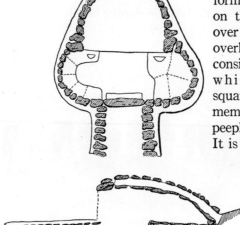

FIG. 51. THE WINTER HOUSE OF THE POLAR ESKIMOS: GROUND PLAN AND LONGITUDINAL AND TRANSVERSE CROSS-SECTIONS.

ticles. On each stands a blubber lamp, over which are suspended a cooking pot and a frame for drying clothes. The rear platform, covered with dry moss and bearskins, occupies at least half of the room. Here the members of the household sit and sleep, each in his special place, the house-wives at the sides within easy reach of the lamps. The problem of ventilation is admirably solved. The air enters through the tunnel in a quiet stream and spreads out over the floor, where the temperature is nearly always below the freezing point. It is not warmed until it reaches the level of the lamps, where it streams over the raised platforms. Here the temperature, though constant, is so high that the occupants regularly divest themselves of all clothing except their trousers, the men frequently even these. Under the roof the heat is stifling; the Eskimos therefore assume a

FIG. 52. THE SUMMER TENT OF THE POLAR ESKIMOS.

reclining position as the most comfortable. However warm the room may be, the air is always fresh and pure, for all fumes and odors escape through the peephole and a tiny opening in the roof.

The summer tent consists of a framework of wooden poles — formerly of narwhal tusks or whale bones—over which are stretched two layers of sealskin held to the ground at the lower edges by heavy stones. The interior arrangement resembles that of the winter dwelling. On journeys or hunting expeditions in cold weather the men build dome-shaped snow houses for temporary occupation. In warmer weather they seek shelter for a night in natural caves, abandoned winter dwellings, or other makeshift abodes.

In the manufacture of their household tools and utensils the Polar Eskimos use little wood on account of its scarcity. They fashion bags, drinking cups, water buckets, and dishes of sealskin with waterproof seams. For working in bone, horn, and ivory they employ a bow drill, consisting of an ivory shaft, an iron point, a bone mouthpiece, a skin thong, and a seal's rib for a bow. Their implements of these materials include needles and combs of ivory, scrapers and back-scratchers of bone, and spoons and hammers of horn.

After Kroeber

FIG. 53. A POLAR ESKIMO AX.

They have never made extensive use of the art of chipping stone, though they formerly made knives, axes, and scrapers of slate. From soft steatite or soapstone they carve rectangular cooking utensils and especially lamps. The native lamp is a shallow crescent-shaped vessel filled with melted blubber. The flame burns at one end on a wick of moss, which the housewife is constantly rearranging to keep a smooth steady flame and to regulate the heat. Fire is usually generated, when it cannot conveniently be borrowed from a neighbor, by means of sulphur pyrites, a piece of quartz, and tinder. Even at the time of their discovery the Polar Eskimos were using iron to a limited extent, though they did not mine or smelt it. From four large meteors in the vicinity they laboriously hammered off small flakes, which they used to tip their harpoons and inserted in bone or ivory backs to make rude knives (see Fig. 47).

For clothing the Eskimos use only the warm skins of the native animals, neatly tailored to fit the contours of the body and to permit free movement of the joints. Both sexes wear a shirt made from the skins of the dovekie and murre, feather side next the body. Though soft and warm, this garment cannot be kept free from lice. The natives employ a special instrument to remove these vermin, and, naturally, they eat what they catch. Over the shirt they wear a jacket or jumper with the hairy side outermost—of sealskin in summer, of fox, hare, or caribou skin in winter. Attached to it is a hood which can be drawn over the head.

FIG. 54. A FAMILY OF POLAR ESKIMOS.
Courtesy of the American Museum of Natural History

Married women have the jacket enlarged in back to carry their babies, and protect the head with a fur cap. The trousers of the men are of bearskin, and extend from the knees only to the upper part of the thighs, not to the hips as with us. The women wear abbreviated breeches or trunks, only a few inches wide, made of fox fur lined with bird skins. Consequently, while the boots of the men just reach the knees, those of the women extend far up the thighs and give the legs of the fair sex a grotesque elephant-like appearance. In both cases the boots are of sealskin, scraped to remove the hair and outer layer, stitched with waterproof seams, and provided with an extra sole of tough leather. Under the boots both sexes wear stockings of hare or caribou skin, and between the two layers of footwear they stuff dry grass for warmth and to absorb moisture. On the hands they wear short skin mittens, similarly stuffed with grass. For the sake of freedom of movement the various garments do not overlap at the joints. To protect these regions in cold weather, bearskin flaps or foxes' tails are frequently added. Children dress like adults. The treatment of skins and manufacture of clothing consume most of the women's time. The skin is removed from the animal whole with the hair on, scraped free of blubber with a knife, stretched on the ground with pegs to dry, chewed thoroughly on the inner side to soften it and remove the fat, dried again, scraped with a blunt instrument to make it flexible, cut according to the traditional pattern, and sewed with sinew thread. Leather tanned by the methods of civilization is stiff, cold as ice, and brittle as glass at sub-zero temperatures, but skins prepared by chewing remain warm, soft, and as pliable as chamois even at 50° below zero.

The severe struggle for existence centers the attention of the Polar Eskimos on practical matters. They wear few if any ornaments, not even the trinkets given them by explorers. Nor do they tattoo or mutilate the body in any way. The women bind their hair in a simple knot or chignon; the men wear theirs long and loose. Decorative art, confined largely to the ornamentation of weapons, is much less developed than among other Eskimo tribes. The natives do not draw or paint, though they occasionally carve figures of men and animals in bone or ivory. They find amusement in wrestling, boxing, pulling and lifting contests, playing with a stuffed sealskin ball, whirling a bull-roarer, and playing cat's cradle and a cup-and-pin game in which a bone, perforated with two holes, is tossed in the air and caught with a pointed stick. Their chief pleasure, however, especially during the total darkness of midwinter, is in visiting and feasting. Hospitality is never refused, and is taken so much for granted that it is never offered. After a feast, perhaps over the rotten carcass of a seal, the participants joke, tell stories, sing, and dance. The abundant native folklore includes animal fables, accounts of the creation, and tales about great shamans and supernaturally gifted hunters. The chief singers and dancers are the shamans, who usually perform in pairs, one man alternating with the other. They accompany their monotonous improvised melodies by beating on a drum of seal intestine stretched over a rude bone hoop—the only native musical instrument. They dance as they sing, bending the knees and swinging the body at the hips with the feet planted in one place. As they abandon themselves to the spirit of the dance, their songs grow louder and their movements more violent, until they reach a state of exaltation which they can sustain for hours.

As an adaptation to their environmental conditions, and as a means of insurance against the vicissitudes of life, the Polar Eskimos have developed a measure of communism with respect to food. The spoils of the chase are divided according to definite and complicated rules. The hunter who kills or first strikes an animal receives the best portion, the next man to throw his harpoon or touch the body receives the second choicest portion, and so on until all obtain a share. In times of famine, however, even these rules break down, and those with food share it with the needy. A hungry traveler may always help himself from another man's cache. The Eskimos do not recognize property rights of any kind in land or water. Even the winter house does not belong to the family which inhabits it. Once abandoned for the summer, it becomes free to any one, and, unless specifically reserved, is occupied the following autumn by the first family to take possession by putting it in order. In spite of these marked traces of communism, private property is by no means non-existent. In default of any specialization or division of labor other than by sex, and until recently of any trade or barter, every individual is a Jack-of-all-trades, making everything he needs and uses. And whatever he makes is his inalienable private property. He may lend such an article to another, but he cannot sell it or give it away, for the idea that property may be transferred has never dawned upon the natives. A man feels entitled at any time to demand back from another any tool or weapon which he himself has manufactured. The nomadic mode of life, however, forbids the accumulation of possessions. Prosperity is measured, if at all, only in terms of dogs. A man with a strong team can range farther, seek better hunting grounds, establish larger caches, bring home heavier loads, provide better for his wife and children, and entertain more lavishly than his less fortunate neighbors.

Kinship and comradeship form the cement of Eskimo society. The strong bond of kinship finds expression in sympathy and kindliness toward relatives and, by contrast, a sharply critical attitude toward persons and things not belonging to one's own family. The common interests and dangers of the chase, on the other hand, frequently engender in men of about the same age a sense of comradeship which leads them to hunt, travel, and live together. The only social unit larger than the family, however, is the village, an impermanent and shifting aggregation. There is no clan organization, no system of age-grades or secret societies. Artificial social distinctions do not exist. There is no chieftainship, no political organization of any sort. "The Polar Eskimo is his own master in everything he does, and he permits no interference from others."

Having no neighbors, the Polar Eskimos not only do not fight, but do not even know what war means. Internal peace is preserved by public opinion. The principal rule governing social life is: Thou shalt earn thine own living and not interfere with the livelihood of others. Disputes are sometimes settled by wrestling matches. Murder and other crimes, though occasional, are extremely rare. A man who offends against public opinion never receives a formal trial. The incensed victims, perhaps with the advice of a shaman, wreak private vengeance. Thus, in one case, a shaman who took a malicious delight in deceiving the people about the hunting, and in frightening them with false warnings of disaster, was invited on an expedition by two of the best men of the tribe, and secretly killed.

Though greatly desiring offspring, parents are sometimes forced by circumstances to destroy them, and women occasionally produce abortions by crude physical means. When a man dies, his widow strangles her small infant, since it has now no means of support, and when the mother of a suckling baby dies, the father buries the child with her, unless he has the good fortune to find another woman in the community who can nurse it. No special ceremony attends childbirth. The mother leaves the family dwelling shortly before the event, and retires to a special tent in summer or a snow house in winter, returning as soon as the infant is born. After delivery, she bathes herself and observes certain taboos regarding food and clothing. On the following day she begins to make herself new garments, for the old ones must be thrown away. In case of a miscarriage these taboos are enormously multiplied, and even affect the father to some extent. The newborn child is licked clean by its mother and is placed on her back under her jacket, whence it is removed only to be suckled. Even older children often have their faces, noses, and bodies cleaned in the same way, for water is too scarce and valuable. An infant is usually named after a person recently deceased, preferably a grandparent. Mothers suckle their young for five years, or even longer. Children play with dolls, puppies, and miniature sledges and weapons. They never suffer corporal punishment, though squalling babies are sometimes placed naked in a snowdrift, even at sub-zero temperatures, till they stop crying. Mothers instruct their daughters in their household duties. Boys learn from their fathers the use of weapons and the art of driving the dog sledge. At about twelve years of age they follow the hunters after seal and walrus.

The Polar Eskimos observe no special ceremonies at puberty, although a boy does not become a man and may not take a wife until he has slain a polar bear. Children and youths of both sexes are forbidden to eat narwhal, young seals, all small animals, viscera, and eggs. Release from these food taboos marks full maturity, and comes only when a young man has killed one of every kind of animal hunted and a woman has borne five children. The unmarried youths and girls form loose and shifting sexual unions, without responsibilities, and commonly live together in a special "young people's house" in each village. A casual union of this sort, when the couple find themselves suited to each other and their parents raise no objections, ripens into a permanent marriage.

Girls usually marry at about sixteen years of age, men not until they reach twenty. Though parents sometimes arrange marriages, the young people as a rule exercise almost complete freedom of choice. Practical, not emotional, considerations determine the selection of partners. A man seeks a wife who can work and bear children; a woman, a husband who can feed and clothe her and support her children and aged parents. A man who is physically or mentally incapable of earning a living cannot obtain a wife, but voluntary celibacy is unknown. An Eskimo criticized the explorer Rasmussen for not marrying: "But you should understand that it is not the right thing for a man to travel all over the country, as you are doing, young and unmarried. You will get a bad reputation, and expose yourself to be made game of. Seest thou, a bachelor is a man who is rejected because he is a poor provider."

The bride does not bring a dowry to her husband, nor do

her parents receive either gifts or bride-price. The wedding ceremony takes the form of a mock abduction. The bride, however willing, is compelled by public opinion to make a show of resistance, "kicking and screaming with might and main" as the groom carries her off by force to her new home. The young couple may reside with the parents of either, or in a separate dwelling, depending on the circumstances. Though polygyny is permitted, it is exceedingly rare, for the economic union of one man and one woman seems best adapted to the conditions of life.

Though marriage is dominated by practical considerations, affection usually develops from living together. A husband often displays signs of tenderness toward his wife. "He rubs his face against hers," writes Mrs. Peary, "and they sniffle at each other; this takes the place of kissing." On other occasions, however, he treats her with what we should call brutality, for the alleged reason that, "if affection is to be kept alive, the woman must feel occasionally that the man is strong." The status of woman is not high. She must observe rigid taboos during menstruation, and she is definitely subordinate to her husband. A barren wife is scorned, and may be discarded. On the other hand, a woman is indispensable to a man, especially for making and mending his clothing, and the Eskimos admit that "a man is what his wife makes of him." If he fails to provide for her, she may leave him for another. Thus she is not devoid of rights. "There is only one thing in which the woman is not allowed any voice whatever, and that is in sexual matters." Her husband can lend her to a friend for a night or longer without considering her wishes in the slightest, indeed without even consulting her, but she is severely condemned if she gives herself to another man without permission. The exchange of wives is a well-established custom. Two men may change houses for a single night, or a man may lend his homesick wife to a friend for a visit to her family, or the husband of a pregnant woman may borrow the wife of another man for an extended hunting expedition. A woman who refuses to be exchanged is punished. One Eskimo told Rasmussen that "he only beat his wife when she would not receive other men. She would have nothing to do with any one but him—and that was her only failing!"

Though a singularly healthy people, the Polar Eskimos are subject to a peculiar ailment known as Arctic hysteria. Attacks come on without warning, most commonly in late autumn; they last from a few minutes to half an hour, and subside as suddenly as they appear. In one reported case, a woman sat on the ground, staring in front of her, quite oblivious of her surroundings, swaying her body to and fro, moaning, screaming, and interjecting disconnected sentences, while her children and neighbors looked on indifferently as though nothing unusual were happening. Men, however, sometimes become violent, are seized with a lust for destruction, and must be restrained by force.

The aged and incapacitated, in times of scarcity, are left behind to shift for themselves—and perish. But the men usually die, as Peary expresses it, "with their boots on"—killed by a walrus or polar bear, drowned when a *kayak* or iceberg capsizes, dragged to death by the bight of a harpoon line, buried under an avalanche. When a death occurs, burial follows with all possible haste. The corpse is fully clothed, sewed in a sealskin winding sheet, and removed through the door of the house—through the window, if a woman—after which the dwelling is abandoned. The relatives, their nostrils plugged with straws, drag the body to the place of burial, where it is stretched out with its head away from the sea and covered with a cairn of stones. Beside the grave are placed the tools, implements, extra clothing—in short all the private property—of the deceased. A man's dog team is slaughtered at the cairn; in the case of a woman, a single dog is strangled, and likewise, of course, her infant child if she has one. Then the relatives gather to mourn and praise the deceased. For five days, no one in the village may hunt or fish, and all who have come into contact with the corpse remain indoors, abstain from all work, eat from separate utensils, and keep their clothes on day and night. At the expiration of this time they wash their hands and bodies to rid themselves of their uncleanness. For months. however, they wear their hoods indoors, manufacture nothing, and abstain from the flesh of the bear, fox, and seal. Nothing may ever be removed from a grave—at least without compensation.

Man, in the opinion of the Polar Eskimos, possesses two spiritual attributes, a name and a soul. A measure of vital power inheres in the name, so that an individual inherits the qualities of the person after whom he is named. After death the name leaves the corpse and enters into the body of a pregnant woman, to be reborn in her child. In the interim it exerts an evil influence and is never mentioned. The soul exists, like a shadow, as an appendage of the body, which it resembles, though it is smaller and is invisible to all except shamans. It may leave the body temporarily, causing illness, or permanently, causing death. The soul of a dead person, now a *tornguang* or ghost, restlessly haunts the corpse, arousing terror in the survivors, until its name has been assigned to a newborn infant by the shaman. Then it either wanders through the air or descends to an underworld beneath the sea. Ideas about the hereafter are vague and confusing, but it is clearly not a place where rewards and punishments are distributed. The ghosts of the dead can visit the living in dreams or in animal forms, and they can punish those whose acts have angered them. They are sometimes propitiated by food offerings.

The Polar Eskimos do not distinguish sharply between men and animals. Man is merely *primus inter pares*. Animals also possess souls, and these must be propitiated when they are slain, lest they return to take revenge. The soul of a dead bear is especially dangerous, and offerings of food, weapons, and other articles are consequently made to it.

The natives apparently do not differentiate clearly between the ghosts of the dead and the malicious spirits which reside in the sea, the cliffs, the dwelling, and all natural and man-made objects possessing names. All are called *tornguang*. The outstanding divinities—there is no supreme being—are Nerivik, a goddess residing in the underworld, and Torn-gaxssung, the oldest and most powerful of the *tornguang*. The Eskimos, like other men, resort to supernatural explanations when practical knowledge fails them. Thus a shaman, to the question why no polar bears had appeared that year, replied: "No bears have come because there is no ice, and there is no ice because there is too much wind, and there is too much wind because we mortals have offended the powers."

Magic plays a distinctly subsidiary rôle in the life of the Polar Eskimos. To be sure, they dislike others to obtain possession of their hair, but they seem not to use it for purposes of sorcery. Certain meaningless formulas, handed down from generation to generation, jealously guarded, and disclosed only when death draws near, are thought to possess a supernatural potency in preventing illness, escaping danger, and bringing success in hunting. They must be uttered in a low voice, but distinctly. If misused, they lose their power forever. The men frequently wear amulets, especially parts of animals not killed by human hands. When sewn in the clothing, these charms impart certain of the animal's qualities. Thus a piece of a fox's head imparts cunning. Sometimes the virtues of an old man are transferred to a child by smearing its lips with his spittle or placing some of his lice in its hair.

Though possessing no government, the Polar Eskimos have a highly developed shamanism. This is explained by the fact that their struggle for existence is directed, not against hostile tribes competing for the same hunting grounds, but "exclusively against nature and the misfortunes arising from the forces of nature." A shaman or *angakok* is usually also a respected hunter, but he exercises no secular leadership or authority. He operates, as a rule, only when called upon, though he may give warning of impending danger, and he is paid for his services. Shamans are very numerous; nearly every family has one, and every village several. A woman can become an *angakok*, though she is rarely as powerful or as dangerous as a man. The power of a shaman resides in his possession of a familiar spirit or *tornguang*, either a human ghost or an animal or nature spirit, to which he sings and prays, and which he can summon at any time to do his bidding. Through his *tornguang* he acquires control over life and death, sickness and health, the weather and game animals. To become a shaman one must receive a call, manifested, for example, by seeing or hearing a spirit while walking alone. After seeking advice from an older *angakok*, the candidate undergoes certain supernatural experiences, during which he converses with Torngaxssung, who gives him his familiar spirit and instructs him how to control it. A shaman has power to raise or calm a storm, to banish or summon seals, to ascend into the sky, to walk on the clouds or over the water, to descend into the underworld. His principal activity, however, is to control sickness. If disposed toward evil, he can injure or kill an enemy, for example, by stealing his soul and hiding it in a snowdrift. The victim sickens and dies unless another shaman aids him in finding his soul. To cure disease, an *angakok* addresses his familiar spirit in a special dialect of obsolete, metaphorical, and mutilated words, sings a spirit song accompanied by the drum, dances a wild hysterical dance, and commands the *tornguang* to recover the lost soul of the patient. During their performances, the shamans tremble, groan, and "work themselves up into a peculiar state of ecstasy, during which, with their closed eyes, long floating hair, and anguished expression, they sometimes produce an overwhelming effect on their auditors."

The Polar Eskimos seem, like the rest of their race, to have come originally from Asia, and to have migrated to their present home from the extreme north of Canada. But when first discovered, by John Ross in 1818, they had lived in isolation in Thule so long that they had forgotten their origin and believed themselves the only people in the world. Their surprise and terror at the sight of the white men and their ships is described by Ross, who tells how he "beheld the first man approach with every mark of fear and distrust, looking frequently behind to the other two, and beckoning them to come on, as if for support. They occasionally retreated, then advanced again, with cautious steps, in the attitude of listening, generally keeping one hand down by their knees, in readiness to pull out a knife which they had in their boots; in the other hand they held their whips with the lash coiled up; their sledges remained at a little distance, the fourth man being apparently stationed to keep them in readiness for escape." When addressed in the Eskimo language, they cried, "Go away, don't kill us." Only with difficulty were they finally conciliated. They displayed great curiosity about the ships, inquiring what kind of birds they were, and whether they came from the sun or the moon. A little terrier dog aroused their contempt—"it was too small for drawing a sledge"— but a live pig caused them to shrink back in terror, and when it chanced to grunt, to rush precipitately for safety.

During the next half-century the tribe was visited by several later expeditions and by occasional whalers, but about 1862 happened an event of outstanding importance. A group of Eskimos in North Baffin Land, learning of the existence of a people far to the north, set out to join them. After a migration which required several years, during which they suffered fearful hardships, a few survivors finally reached Thule, and were adopted into the tribe. The newcomers taught their hosts many arts of which they had previously been ignorant—the *kayak* and open-water hunting, the fish fork and salmon fishing, the bow and arrow and caribou hunting.

Peary's Arctic explorations between 1891 and 1909 wrought a further transformation in native culture. On his last two expeditions he was accompanied by seventy or eighty Polar Eskimos, in short by all the best young men of the tribe. Without their aid he could scarcely have reached the Pole, and he showed his gratitude by furnishing them with adequate supplies of wood, steel knives and files, and modern firearms, which they are now able to replenish from Danish trading posts. The tribe today is neither declining in numbers nor suffering any considerable infusion of alien blood, but it faces a new danger in the possibility that the use of firearms may decimate the fur-bearing animals, indispensable for food and clothing, and thus render uninhabitable the world's uttermost Arctic frontier.

BIBLIOGRAPHY

BESSELS, E. "Einige Worte über die Inuit (Eskimo) des Smith-Sundes, nebst Bemerkungen über Inuit-Schädel." *Archiv für Anthropologie*, Vol. VIII. Braunschweig, 1875.

——. "The Northernmost Inhabitants of the Earth." *American Naturalist*, Vol. XVIII. Philadelphia, 1884.

EKBLAW, W. E. "The Material Response of the Polar Eskimo to Their Far Arctic Environment." *Annals of the Association of American Geographers*, Vols. XVII–XVIII. Albany, 1927–28.

HAYES, I. I. *The Open Polar Sea.* New York, 1867.

HRDLIČKA, A. "Contribution to the Anthropology of Central and Smith Sound Eskimo." *Anthropological Papers of the American Museum of Natural History*, Vol. V. New York, 1910.

KANE, E. K. *Arctic Explorations in the Years 1853, '54, '55.* 2 vols. Philadelphia, 1856.

KROEBER, A. L. "The Eskimo of Smith Sound." *Bulletin of the American Museum of Natural History*, Vol. XII. New York, 1899.

MARKHAM, C. R. "The Arctic Highlanders." *Transactions of the Ethnological Society of London*, New Series, Vol. IV. London, 1866.

PEARY, J. D. (MRS. R. E.). *My Arctic Journal.* New York, 1893.

PEARY, R. E. *Nearest the Pole.* New York, 1907.

——. *Northward over the "Great Ice."* 2 vols. New York, 1898.

RASMUSSEN, K. *Greenland by the Polar Sea.* Trans. by A. and R. Kenney. London, 1921.

*——. *The People of the Polar North.* Edited by G. Herring. London, 1908.

RINK, H. "The Eskimo Tribes, Their Distribution and Characteristics, Especially in Regard to Language." *Meddelelser om Grønland*, Vol. XI. Kjøbenhavn, 1887.

ROSS, J. *A Voyage of Discovery.* London, 1819.

*STEENSBY, H. P. "Contributions to the Ethnology and Anthropogeography of the Polar Eskimos." *Meddelelser om Grønland*, Vol. XXXIV. Kjøbenhavn, 1910.

STEIN, R. "Geographische Nomenklatur bei den Eskimos des Smith-Sundes." *Petermanns Mitteilungen aus Justus Perthes' Geographischer Anstalt*, Vol. XLVIII. Gotha, 1902.

WEYER, E. M., JR. *The Eskimos.* New Haven, 1932.

WISSLER, C. "Archæology of the Polar Eskimo." *Anthropological Papers of the American Museum of Natural History*, Vol. XXII. New York, 1918.

CHAPTER IX

THE HAIDAS OF BRITISH COLUMBIA

FORTY miles off the northwest coast of British Columbia and an equal distance south of Prince of Wales Island in Alaska, between 52° and 54° north latitude and between 131° and 133° west longitude, lie the Queen Charlotte Islands, an archipelago of two large islands and numerous smaller ones, with a total area of nearly four thousand square miles. From the coast, deeply indented with fiords or inlets, the land rises gradually toward the interior, attaining an altitude of 3,500 feet in the mountains to the west. Inland lakes and swamps feed numerous streams and short rivers. Rain, heaviest in the autumn and lightest in midsummer, falls on considerably more than half the days of the year, and the heavy annual precipitation of sixty inches or more produces an excessive humidity. Owing to the high latitude the days are very short in winter and long in summer, but the warm Japanese Current renders the climate mild and equable. The temperature ranges between a monthly mean of 35° in January and 57° in August. The light winter frosts barely succeed in freezing the streams. Forests of hemlock, spruce, and cedar, with a few willows, alders, pines, and yews, clothe the interior, interspersed with a dense undergrowth of berry-bearing bushes. The abundant bird life includes wild ducks and geese, cranes, herons, grouse, eagles, ravens, and a hundred other species of land and sea fowl. Black bears, deer, otters, martens, and weasels are common, but the marine fauna is especially rich. Shellfish abound along the shores. Among sea mammals, whales of several species, porpoises, fur and hair seals, sea lions, and sea otters are found in considerable numbers. The coastal waters teem with halibut, cod, herring, and other fish. Salmon run in the rivers and streams during the summer months—sometimes in such myriads that they pack the surface of pools almost solidly.

The Haidas, the aboriginal inhabitants of these islands, as well as of the southern part of Prince of Wales Island in Alaska which they seized about two hundred years ago, are typical of the Indians of the northern Pacific coast both in race and in culture, in spite of bizarre theories of their descent from Aztec exiles or Japanese blown across the Pacific in junks. Powerfully built but graceful, the men average five feet seven inches in stature, the women five inches less. The Haidas have broad heads (cephalic index 81), brown eyes, broad faces with prominent cheek bones, and medium or mesorrhine noses (nasal index 74). Their black hair is thick, coarse, and straight on the head, but scanty on the face and body. Their complexions, though coppery in tone, are scarcely darker than in the average European, and rosy cheeks are common.

Culturally, the Haidas resemble most closely the neighboring Tlingits and Tsimshian, though they typify the whole northwestern coast area. Their language, the sole representative of the Skittagetan linguistic stock, reveals a distant relationship to that of the Tlingits and to the great Athapascan stock of the northern and western interior of Canada. Its grammar is characterized, amongst other things, by the extensive use of affixes, the differentiation of active and neutral verbs, and the classification of nouns by shape into such categories as long, round, and flat. The numerical system is vigesimal rather than decimal. The name "Haida" comes, through a corruption, from the native word for "people."

The Indians divide the year into twelve lunar months, each beginning on the second day of the new moon, when the satellite "looks three fingers wide." They also note the position of the sun. Each morning at dawn, when a ray from the rising sun enters a knot-hole in the eastern wall of the dwelling and alights on the opposite wall, they mark the spot with charcoal. The resulting line of marks is the native calendar. At each solstice the sun shines several days in succession at one end of the line and then starts back toward the other. The new year begins with the second day of the first new moon after the winter solstice. The natives know that the lunar year is shorter than the solar, and they ingeniously correct the discrepancy. If the new moon on which the first or the seventh month is due to begin appears before the sun has reached the solstice, an extra "moon" is intercalated, or rather the old month is doubled and made to extend over two moons.

The Haidas possess no domestic animal save the dog, and their agriculture, until recently, was confined to the cultivation of small plots of problematical tobacco. They gather clams, cockles, mussels, and crabs at ebb tide, and a quantity of birds' eggs in season. They collect and eat a variety of wild roots, herbs, and fruits. They dry certain edible seaweeds and press them into cakes for winter consumption. The inner bark of the alder and spruce is scraped from the tree with a stone implement, steamed, molded into cakes, and preserved for the winter. The women and children gather enormous quantities of huckleberries, cranberries, salal berries, salmonberries, strawberries, etc., which, dried and stored, constitute a major item of subsistence.

The natives trap a few birds and small animals. They lure deer into ambush by imitating their rutting call on a special whistle, and dispatch them with bows of cedar or yew and unfeathered arrows with wooden shafts, foreshafts of bone or wood, and barbed heads of shell or bone. Bears are sometimes treed by dogs and killed with arrows. More commonly they are caught in ingenious deadfalls or with nooses adjusted across a trail so that, when sprung, the animal is hoisted aloft and strangled. When a hunter secures a bear, he immediately removes, cooks, and eats the heart and tongue; cuts off the head, singes it over the fire, and throws it into the water; and sings a special song over each of the three parts. To omit these rites would seriously offend the Bear People, for whom the natives have the greatest respect.

But the Haidas derive most of their food from the sea. They hunt sea mammals—except the whale—for their skins and furs as well as for food. With the aid of screens they approach sea otters, seals, and sea lions in shallow water or on rocky ledges, and kill them with the bow and arrow. They also pursue them in canoes. A party of hunters, on sighting an animal, surrounds it with a circle of canoes, gradually closing in as it tires, until it can be shot with arrows, or harpooned, when it comes up to breathe. The native harpoon consists of a light cedar shaft, a detachable barbed head of bone, and a strong line equipped with a float or bladder. A wooden club is used to give the animal its quietus. Before hunting or war a man must purify himself by a month of strict continence, abstention from water, and ritual fasts, medicines, emetics, and baths.

It is as fishers, however, that the Haidas excel. They catch cod and dogfish with hook and line, as many as a hundred hooks being attached to a single line. They secure herring, which run near the surface in enormous shoals, by means of dip nets, open-mesh baskets, seines, and rakes. With the fish-rake, a piece of wood with a row of bone spikes, they beat the surface of the water, bringing up two or three fish at a time. Salmon and halibut, however, are the staple foods. The Haidas do not use hook and line for salmon. They catch them at the mouths of streams with dragnets, and in waterfalls or rapids with fish-spears or harpoons with detachable barbed heads of bone. They also employ weirs. Where the water is deep, they build a wicker fence across the stream, with openings at intervals leading into cylindrical basket traps. Where the water is shallow and swift, they construct two weirs a short distance apart; the salmon, leaping the first, are caught between the two, and can be secured at leisure with spears or dip nets. During the salmon season the

Indians desert their villages and move to the best sites on the rivers, where they dwell in insubstantial shacks and smoke their catch of fish in special smokehouses with plank walls and bark roofs.

Halibut, which are especially abundant from March to November though present throughout the year in certain localities, are caught only with hook and line. The fishermen anchor their canoes with stones and tend several lines at a time. Woven cords of vegetable fiber or knotted stems of the giant kelp serve as lines. To each is attached a wooden float carved in the shape of an aquatic bird and a stone sinker which can be released to lighten the weight in hauling up a fish. The hooks, baited preferably with octopus, are made in a variety of ingenious forms out of yew or other wood, steamed and bent to the proper shape and equipped with barbs of bone or shell. A fish, when caught, is hauled up, played for a while, drawn alongside, grappled, and dispatched with a blow from a special club. To land a halibut, which may weigh several hundred pounds, in a light fishing canoe requires no slight measure of skill.

The struggle for existence is never severe, and food is especially abundant during the summer, when the natives bend their energies to the accumulation of a reserve for the leaner winter months and for the lavish feasts and ceremonies occurring then. Great quantities of bark, berries, and fish are dried and stored away in boxes. The women, to whom falls the duty of preparing the staple halibut and salmon, cut off the heads of the fish, slit them down the back, remove the entrails, backbone, tail, and fins, slice the flesh into long strips, and hang these on frames to dry in the sun or to smoke over a slow fire. Shellfish are steamed, dried, and strung on skewers. Strips of deer fat are dried and smoked, cooked, and packed in boxes. Oil and grease, used as a sauce with bark cakes, dried fish, and practically everything else the natives eat, are obtained from herring, cod, surplus salmon, and sea mammals. The flesh, often partially putrefied, is boiled, and the oil or grease skimmed from the surface, strained, and stored in boxes. Not content with their own supply, the Haidas obtain from the mainland quantities of candlefish, a fish so oily that, when dried, it can be used as a candle by simply inserting a wick. The odor of rancid oil "permeates everything Indian and renders a visit to a lodge on the northwest coast somewhat of an ordeal."

The Haidas generate fire by rotating a stick of hard wood on a piece of dry cedar bark, and they cook most of their food. Fresh meat and fish are either broiled on sticks over the fire or boiled in wooden vessels or water-tight baskets with the aid of hot stones. Dried foods are soaked and boiled before eating, or simply dipped in grease. The special native delicacies include the flesh and blubber of seals, the putrefied heads of salmon and halibut, and fish roe. The latter is either removed from the fish or, in the case of herring spawn, collected on hemlock branches submerged in the sea. The Haidas eat it in several forms—boiled with herbs and berries and pressed into cakes, or pounded, mixed with water, and beaten to a creamy consistency, or in a decomposed condition after being buried in boxes on the beach. They possess no native alcoholic beverages, nor did they smoke until taught by the whites. They pounded their tobacco in mortars, pressed it into plugs, and chewed it mixed with lime from burnt clamshells.

The natives take three regular meals a day—a light breakfast of dried halibut and boiled seaweed at dawn, a hearty dinner shortly before noon, and a substantial supper at six or seven o'clock in the evening. Both sexes eat together, sitting cross-legged on the floor around a mat on which the food reposes in wooden platters. Each person has a large wooden or horn spoon with which he helps himself and eats. Before each meal the face and hands are carefully washed and the mouth rinsed out, and a drink of water follows every salty course. When guests are invited to dine, the hostess cooks and the host stands and serves but neither eats. Far more food is provided than can possibly be consumed, and all that remains, after the guests have left, is heaped on the dishes and sent to their homes. The dishes are returned, clean and sometimes containing presents, on the following day.

Except when temporarily away from home, the Haidas live in huge rectangular dwellings grouped into villages—

FIG. 55. A HAIDA HOUSE.

usually in a single row facing the beach a few feet above high-water mark. An average house measures about forty feet in depth by thirty in width, with a low roof sloping gently from a height of ten feet at the ridge to six feet at the eaves. On six, eight, or ten massive posts sunk deep in the ground rest heavy plates, frames, and purlins, supporting a roof of planks or bark. Perpendicular planks, split from cedar logs with wedges, form the walls. These substantial houses, the finest in the northwest, will last half a century. Their construction, however, is enormously expensive, requiring the coöperation of large numbers of men for months or even years and a vast outlay for their entertainment and payment. The most striking feature of the dwelling is the great "totem pole," which rises from the center of the front or gable end, sometimes to a height of sixty feet. An elliptical hole near

Photograph by the Author

FIG. 56. TOTEM POLES IN THE DESERTED HAIDA VILLAGE OF YAN.

the bottom often serves as the door of the house; above, elaborately carved and painted, are the totemic crests of the owner and his wife. Other poles, of a mortuary or commemorative character, are scattered throughout the village, which from a distance suggests a crowded harbor with its forest of masts.

Entering the door of a large house, one finds on either side of the entrance an inner post, carved and painted, beside which are kept the paddles, weapons, and fishing tackle. To the left, against the front wall of the house, is piled a supply of firewood. In the corresponding place to the right are stored the boxes of grease, berries, fish roe, and other moist foods. Along the side and rear walls stand the beds—raised plank platforms covered with mats and furs—and quantities of additional boxes, filled with dishes, blankets, clothing, dried fish and seaweed, etc. Mats with woven designs cover the floor, which, six feet from the walls, is often excavated in a series of steps to a shallow rectangular pit or cellar in the center. Here, on a hearth of clean sand, burns the fire, which helps to dispel the gloom of the interior, lighted otherwise only from the door and a smoke-hole in the roof.

In the art of canoe building few peoples have ever equalled the Haidas. Seven types of craft are distinguished: (1) the "half canoe," a low, flat dugout for use on inland streams; (2) the "small canoe," with a high bow and stern, for short trips on the open sea; (3) a special double-ended "sea otter canoe," designed to pass readily through a bed of kelp; (4) the "hunting canoe," with flaring gunwales and high projecting bow and stern, for deep-sea fishing and sealing; (5) the "big canoe," broader in the bow than the foregoing and much larger, used for war, trading, and ceremonial visits; (6) the "deer canoe," a second type of large vessel, with a prow carved to represent the nose and ears of a deer; and (7) the "head canoe," the third type of large craft, with undifferentiated ends shaved for some distance to the thinness of a plank, rendering it far more ornamental than seaworthy. Even the largest canoes, seventy feet in length, eight in beam, and capable of carrying thirty men and a load of three tons, are hollowed from a single log. When sufficiently shaped and excavated, the log is half filled with water, and hot stones are added. In this way the wood is softened so that the canoe can be widened in the beam by inserting stretchers or thwarts of gradually increasing size. The natives ordinarily propel and steer their vessels with paddles. When the wind is calm, however, they hoist square sails woven from cedar bark on masts inserted in the thwarts. They use the sails, which are water-tight, as temporary tents and as covers to protect the canoes from warping and cracking when hauled up on the beach.

What renders the houses and canoes of the Haidas so remarkable, however, is the primitive character of their implements. They chop down huge cedars, hew out planks so smooth that they appear sawed, and fashion their canoes with tools no better than wooden wedges and hafted axes,

FIG. 57. MODEL OF A HAIDA "BIG CANOE."

adzes, and hammers of polished basalt and jade. Other native stone implements include mortars and pestles, scrapers, and knives. From time immemorial the Haidas have made articles of beaten copper, a metal obtained from the mainland tribes by trade but little used for industrial purposes on account of its softness. From pieces of iron found attached to bits of driftwood on rare occasions, apparently even before white contact, the people of the west coast hammered knives, which were among the most valued of native possessions.

The Haidas have no pottery, but they make water-tight twined baskets in a variety of shapes from cedar bark and spruce root fibers, and ornament them with red and black bands. They import the horns of the mountain goat and sheep from the mainland, and fashion them by carving and steaming into elaborate and decorative dishes, ladles, and spoons. A ceremonial horn spoon (see Fig. 61) sometimes holds as much as two quarts. The Haidas utilize wood for utensils as well as for nearly every other industrial purpose. With stone knives for carving and dogfish skins for polishing, they fashion wooden dishes and plates in every conceivable shape and in sizes ranging from eight inches to six feet in length. They likewise make heavy rectangular boxes of cedar (see Fig. 61) in different sizes for the storage of everything from skins and valuables to oil and fish.

After Niblack

FIG. 58. A CHILKAT BLANKET.

For their textile arts the natives use spruce roots, wild hemp, and the outer bark of the cedar. After soaking them in water and beating them with sticks, they pick out the fibers, which they twist into thread between hand and thigh, and braid into fishing lines, ropes, and cordage. Besides making mats, they know how to weave vegetable fibers into fabrics on a frame with suspended warp. Their fine ceremonial blankets, however, woven from the wool of the mountain goat, are obtained by trade from the Chilkat Tlingits.

The native clothing consists partly of garments woven from vegetable fibers and partly of furs and skins, especially of the sea otter. Both sexes wear a shirt extending to the waist. The men assume a breechclout, the women a long skirt or petticoat. The outer garment for both sexes is a cloak, usually of fur for men and of tanned leather for women, thrown over the shoulders and fastened with thongs. In wet weather a circular raincoat of fiber cloth, with an opening in the center for the head, furnishes additional protection. Both sexes go barefoot, and usually bareheaded, though they sometimes don basketry hats in the shape of a truncated cone (see Fig. 61). Little girls wear only a petticoat, boys only an abbreviated shirt, and even adults are often very scantily clad. Garments for special occasions include ceremonial shirts and cloaks with woven or other designs, Chilkat blankets, turbans of shredded cedar bark stained red, and leggings of deerskin ornamented with puffins' beaks, which rattle with the movements of the wearer. One of the various types of ceremonial headdresses consists of a tall wooden cylinder, beautifully polished, carved, painted, and inlaid with shells and copper, with a tail of ermine skins behind and a fringe of sea lion whiskers on top. The down of eagles or other birds fills the crown and is scattered like snow in the movements of the dance. Outstanding among the objects of this class are the ceremonial masks, carved out of wood to represent animals, fish, or supernatural beings, painted with grotesque designs, and inlaid with abalone shell. By means of ingenious concealed mechanisms, the jaws are sometimes made to open and shut, and the eyes to roll.

After Niblack

Fig. 59. Haida Ceremonial Headdress.

The women wear their hair long, parted in the middle, and plaited in two braids down the back. The men wear theirs loose and cut off straight just below the shoulders. They also pluck out all facial hairs. Both sexes smear their hair with bear grease scented with aromatic herbs. For ornament they

FIG. 60. AN OLD HAIDA WOMAN WITH LABRET AND NOSE ORNAMENT.
Courtesy of the American Museum of Natural History

string together necklaces of shells, teeth, and objects of bone and copper, and, if of high rank, wear bracelets and armlets of bone. On ceremonial occasions they paint their faces with designs in blue, black, and vermilion. Men, and to a some-what lesser extent women, are tattooed with charcoal on the lower legs, forearms, and chest, and sometimes also on the fingers and back. Both sexes pierce the septum of the nose for the insertion of semicircular ornaments of bone, shell, wood, and copper. They likewise bore several holes in the rim of each ear for studs or earrings of shell, bone, or teeth. Women of rank wear an elongated wooden plug or labret in a slit in the lower lip. "It is as embarrassing to an Indian woman to be seen without her labret as for a European woman to be seen with uncovered bosom."

Decorative art—and the art of the Haidas is almost exclusively decorative—attains a development scarcely equalled anywhere else in the savage world. It is applied to practically every object of personal, social, ceremonial, religious, or industrial importance, and it always conforms to a single, characteristic style. Its subjects, with the rarest of exceptions, are animals—either the totemic crests of the owner's clan or mythological beings with animal characteristics. In highly conventionalized representations these animal forms appear everywhere: painted on the face, tattooed on the body, woven into fabrics, carved on utensils of horn and wood, emblazoned on ceremonial accessories, etched on articles and ornaments of copper, and carved and painted on canoes, house timbers, totem poles, and mortuary columns. The process of conventionalization has not led, as has happened so frequently elsewhere, to the development of geometrical patterns. The artist strives to make the animal recognizable for what it is. But he cannot be realistic, because he is compelled to adapt its body to the varying surfaces which he must cover. Hence he resorts to symbols. Thus a figure on a totem pole, though it looks like a human face, is shown to be a beaver by portraying its ears, its paws, its tail, and its large incisor teeth (see Fig. 63). But the artist does not content himself with depicting the symbols alone; he tries to bring as much of the body of the animal as possible into the decorative field by means of sections and distortions, at the same time preserving the nat-aral relation of the various parts. The native art thus represents a curious blend of realism and conventionalization.

The Haidas display little national consciousness and have no unified government. The tribe is divided into two exogamous matrilineal moieties or phratries, called respectively the Ravens and the Eagles. Divinities as well as men are

FIG. 61. EXAMPLES OF HAIDA DECORATIVE ART: BASKETRY HAT, WOODEN BOX, HORN SPOON, WOODEN BOWL, RATTLE, AND PADDLE.

classed as Ravens or Eagles, the most important being Ravens. Even the moieties, however, possess no governmental functions; they exist solely for the purpose of regulating marriage and descent. Between them a healthy rivalry prevails, but no hostility.

Each moiety is subdivided into some twenty matrilineal clans, the fundamental social and political units of the Haidas. A clan is merely a localized segment of a moiety; it consists of that particular branch of a moiety which now inhabits, or at some time in the past has inhabited, a single village, and it derives its name from that village, not from an animal or the like. Sometimes, from historical causes, several clans come to occupy one village, or one clan several villages, but this does not affect the traditional and sentimental association of a clan and one locality. Land, in so far as it is property, belongs to the clan, which enjoys recognized rights to definite hunting grounds, salmon streams, village and camping sites, unusually abundant berry patches, rocky islands where aquatic birds lay their eggs, and strips of beach where whales drift ashore. The chief holds these lands as trustee for the clan, but he can neither sell nor rent them, although in exceptional cases he may alienate them as an indemnity to settle a feud or as a dowry when his daughter marries another chief.

Even more important than its material possessions are the intangible privileges or prerogatives of a clan. It owns a fund of personal names and of ceremonial titles for houses and canoes, which no one outside the clan may use. Its members have the exclusive right to certain songs, dances, and ceremonies. More important still, they are privileged to employ certain totemic crests, for the most part representing animals, which, as we have seen, they tattoo on their bodies, display on their garments, and carve, paint, or inlay on all industrial and ceremonial objects. Crests are not true totems, however, for the animals they represent are not regarded as ancestors, nor are they worshiped or tabooed, nor do the clans bear their names. Although the crests usually differ in the two moieties, several clans in the same moiety frequently have the right to the same crest. Nearly all the Eagle clans, for instance, are entitled to the eagle crest. Furthermore, each clan, as a rule, possesses several crests. Thus one Eagle clan numbers among its crests the eagle, the beaver, the humming bird, the skate, and the sculpin. The raven crest, curiously enough, is usually owned not by Raven but by Eagle clans—a fact which puzzles the Haidas no less than it does the anthropologists. The crests seem to have, therefore, not a truly totemic but a genealogical significance. They indicate a person's descent, and thus resemble the quarterings of heraldry.

A clan comprises from one to a dozen separate households, the primary economic units of Haida society. Though a household may number thirty persons or more, it always occupies a single dwelling. A typical household includes the owner or house chief, his wife or wives, his young sons and unmarried daughters, a married daughter with her husband and children, a younger brother of the chief with his wife and children, an unmarried nephew (sister's son), a married nephew with his family, possibly some other poor relative, and a slave or two. With only the rarest exceptions the adult males of the household belong to one moiety, all the females to the other. For all practical purposes, however, the household is associated with the moiety and clan of its male owner.

Authority in the clan and in the household is vested in their respective chiefs. Any man who owns a dwelling, either through inheritance or by amassing sufficient wealth to erect one for himself, is a house chief. He directs the economic activities of his household, protects and cares for its members, exercises a mild paternal authority over them, and is treated with deference. The clan chief is always also a house chief, usually the richest and most powerful in the village. He holds his position by inheritance and cannot be deposed. His authority depends on his wealth, personality, and prestige. He can normally count on the support of his house chiefs, but he cannot command their obedience or punish insubordination. A discontented house chief, if influential enough, can desert the village with a band of followers and establish an independent sub-clan with himself as chief, but this is very exceptional. The clan chief, as trustee of the valuable clan lands, holds a powerful weapon. Where several clans inhabit a village, one of their chiefs may enjoy more prestige than the others, but this is due solely to his superior wealth or social status or to the number and strength of his followers. No chief wields any actual authority outside of his clan.

Chiefship, both in the household and in the clan, is hereditary in the female line. Property, privileges, and authority descend in a body to the next of kin—a younger brother, or in default thereof the eldest sister's eldest son. A woman inherits the chiefship only if there are no male heirs. An incumbent during his lifetime has the power to set aside the next of kin in favor of a junior heir, but he seldom does so unless the senior already holds an equally high position or is disqualified by reason of physical or mental incapacity, laziness, poverty, or low repute or standing. If a house chief has not selected his successor, the clan chief appoints him. If a clan chief fails to name his heir, all the men and women of the clan meet in a council at which the two, three, or four candidates next in line stand up and are voted upon. Unless disqualified for adequate reasons, however, the next of kin is always elected.

The Haida kinship terms reflect the organization into moieties and clans. Separate terms distinguish relatives through the father from similar relatives through the mother, e.g., *ye* for paternal and *qa* for maternal uncle, since they belong to different moieties. Within a clan, lineal and collateral relatives are grouped together; a mother's sister or female cousin, for example, is called "mother" (*au*). Differences in generation are often ignored; thus any woman of the father's clan may be addressed as "aunt" (*sqan*). The relationship associated with each kinship term involves a series of stereotyped patterns of social behavior, which prescribe precisely how the individuals must react toward each other both in general and in specific situations. Thus a young man obeys his maternal uncle, renders services for and expects favors from his male cross-cousin, avoids his mother-in-law, shows respect for his brother-in-law but jokes and plays on terms of the greatest intimacy with his sister-in-law, etc. The relationship of outstanding importance is that between a person and his *sqan*, *i.e.*, his paternal aunt or her daughter. At every crisis in his life—birth, marriage, death, etc.—his *sqan* plays a leading rôle and is compensated for her services with valuable gifts.

If the kinship system fixes the channels through which the social life of the people mainly flows, the dominant drive or incentive to activity is the desire to amass wealth. Tools

FIG. 62. HAIDA "COPPERS."

and weapons, canoes, household utensils, clothing, and orna-ments are all private property, and the economic activities of the household are directed toward the accumulation of as large a surplus as possible. The rare furs of the sea otter constituted the standard of value and the medium of ex-change until superseded, after contact with the whites, by the trade blankets of the Hudson Bay Company. Men and women assemble quantities of furs or blankets and store them away in boxes. Another conventional article of value is the so-called "copper," a thin shield of native copper hammered in a traditional pattern and imported from the Chilkat region where the metal abounds.

Slaves, obtained by war or purchase from distant Haida cians or from the mainland tribes, constitute an important

item of wealth. They do the drudgery and receive the leav-
ings of food. They may not marry or hold property. They
can be bought and sold, beaten, or killed, and their status
is hereditary. When sick they are neglected, and when dead
their bodies are dumped unceremoniously into the sea. A
clan which loses one of its members into slavery suffers
disgrace and humiliation, and usually bends every effort to
assembling and paying a ransom. The parents of the redeemed slave scrub his body thoroughly to remove the
stigma. So despised are slaves that they rarely attempt to
escape. Not only is a runaway not welcomed back by his
relatives, but all his clansmen are stigmatized as "slaves"
unless and until they wipe the slate clean by raising a princely
ransom.

Amongst themselves the Haidas very seldom engage in
trade. On rare occasions a man sells a slave or a canoe to
a neighbor. If a purchased slave dies within a month, the
price is refunded; within a year, half the price. A flourishing
trade prevails, however, with the mainland tribes. Every
year in June the Indians cross over to Port Simpson in the
Tsimshian territory to exchange their wares. Since the
Tsimshian are their inveterate foes, trade with them can
be carried on only under the protection of a kind of artificial
blood brotherhood. A Haida and a Tsimshian chief of
equivalent phratries entertain each other lavishly and exchange valuable gifts and ceremonial names. Thereafter
neither ever engages in war with the other, and the dwelling
of either is a sanctuary where the other can always find refuge.
A visiting chief makes immediately for the house of his
"brother" and then trades under his protection. The Haidas
exchange dried halibut, seaweed, mats, furs, and canoes
for supplies of grease, candlefish, berries, copper, horn, slaves,
and Chilkat blankets. They are expert traders, subjecting
every article to the closest scrutiny and beating down the
price for any defect. Owing to the abundance of sea otters
in their habitat, they are the wealthiest of all the tribes of

the region, and it is among them that we find the finest examples of northwestern arts and industries.

War frequently offers an easier road to wealth than do industry and trade, and the Haidas are the Vikings of the coast, the scourge of the surrounding tribes. They fight amongst themselves over real or fancied injuries, and they wage relentless war, partly for revenge but mainly for plunder, against the Tlingits, Tsimshian, and Bellabella. In retaliatory conflicts, as a rule, only single clans are engaged, but in important wars all the clans of both moieties in several adjoining villages commonly unite under the leadership of the chief with the strongest influence or the deepest grievance. Each house chief outfits a canoe. Chiefs, since they pay the expenses and assume the risks, receive most of the captives and booty. An expedition starts on a lucky day, after the usual purificatory preliminaries. The warriors paint their faces, don warlike attire, and exchange belts with their wives. Success depends largely on the conduct of the women at home, who sing and dance every day, eat and drink little, act with strict propriety, touch no property of the men, and sleep together in the same relative positions that their husbands occupy in the canoes.

The principal native weapons are the bow and arrow, long spears with bone heads, wooden war clubs, and—especially effective at close quarters—daggers with blades of stone, bone, or beaten copper, attached to the wrist by a thong. For defense, besides temporary fortifications with stockades at home, the Haidas employ wooden helmets and suits of armor. Over a jerkin or doublet consisting of several thicknesses of leather, the native warrior wears a cuirass of wooden slats woven together with twine. A shaman always accompanies an expedition to read omens and capture the souls of the enemy. On meeting a hostile canoe party, the warriors don helmets and armor and advance cautiously with taunting songs and menacing speeches in the enemy's language. To ward off arrows and spears, they skillfully heel the canoe and interpose the gunwale. Their bravery, however, is strictly proportionate to their superiority in numbers, and they much prefer tactics of ambush and surprise to a fair fight. The usual practice is to waylay a party peacefully returning from a fishing trip or to attack a village by night. Those who resist are slaughtered, those who submit are enslaved, and all movable property is carried off. The Haidas do not torture their captives, though they show no mercy, even to women and children, in the heat of battle. They cut off the heads of the slain enemies, carry them home on poles, and use them as trophies in a great victory dance. The rewards of a successful war in plunder, slaves, and ransoms are sometimes immense.

The profits of industry, trade, and war are accumulated only to be given away, for among the Haidas, unlike certain more civilized peoples, it is not the amassing of wealth but its distribution which confers prestige and distinction. Hospitality and liberality are the cardinal virtues of the natives. To maintain their social standing persons of wealth give frequent feasts. A feast resembles an ordinary invitation to dine except that it is much larger and more lavish and formal. Only members of the opposite moiety are invited. They are seated according to rank and are served by the younger clansmen and clanswomen of the host. The guests provide their own ceremonial dishes and spoons, which are returned to them later heaped with the remains of the banquet. But the outstanding social event, and the surest road to position and standing, is an extravagant distribution of property known as the "potlatch."

Before an heir succeeds to the position and inherits the house of a deceased chief he must validate his claim by giving a funeral potlatch. He invites the members of the opposite moiety, entertains them while they carve and erect a mortuary column to the deceased, and then makes a distribution of property to them. Far more important and spectacular, however, is the house-building potlatch. For perhaps a decade a man and his wife labor industriously to assemble the requisite property. A year before the ceremony the wife lends furs or blankets from the common store to various members of her clan, who return them at the potlatch with one hundred per cent interest. The host goes by canoe to all the surrounding villages to issue invitations to the men and women of the opposite moiety—opposite, that is, to his wife, not to himself, for she is the real donor of the potlatch and he only the collaborator. The guests are welcomed on their arrival with a big dance, and they remain the entire winter working for their hosts and being entertained by the clansmen of the hostess.

At occasional tobacco palavers the visitors are assigned specific tasks in the gathering of timbers, the carving of the totem pole, and the erection of the house. Feasts and dances enliven the nights and the intervals between labor. Several days are usually devoted to certain religious ceremonies in which the clansmen of the wife impersonate supernatural beings and engage in various pranks and mummeries. If possessed by the Dog-eating Spirit, for example, they dance with the carcass of a dog and eat it. These ceremonies have been borrowed, through the medium of slaves, from the Bellabella tribe of the mainland, among whom they are associated with secret societies, a feature not adopted by the Haidas. Following the completion of the house and the erection of the totem pole a special day is reserved for the tattooing of the children of the host and hostess and also of other children of the same moiety whose parents pay for the privilege.

The actual potlatch comes as the climax of the weeks or months of labor and festivities. The guests assemble in the new house, where they are seated according to rank. In the rear, concealed by a curtain of sails, lies an immense pile of furs, blankets, carved dishes, and other property. Parents now pay for the tattooing of their children and borrowers return their loans with interest, further augmenting the pile. As the curtain is thrown back, the host and hostess stand revealed in ceremonial attire. They confer privileged names upon their children and explain to the assembled multitude how they accumulated the property. Then the hostess, or her husband under her direction, calls out in turn the ceremonial names of the guests and the amount of property to be distributed to each, and her younger clansmen and clanswomen carry out her orders. Visitors of rank, to whom the most important tasks have been assigned, receive slaves, coppers, and other valuable gifts. Others receive amounts proportionate to their rank and the services they have performed. A small boy who has helped fetch water gets one blanket. Each person knows precisely what he is entitled to, and quarrels sometimes arise over real or fancied slights. At the very end of the distribution, the hostess turns to her husband, who of course belongs to the moiety of the recipients, and, in a spirit of comedy, presents him with a single last dilapidated blanket.

After giving away property worth, in our currency, thousands or even tens of thousands of dollars, the givers of a potlatch are left completely destitute of material possessions. If a man and his wife cannot afford quite so reckless an expenditure, they sometimes combine with the man's brother and his wife to give a potlatch jointly, or they give a sort of half-potlatch, involving the erection only of a totem pole, deferring the construction of the house until later. By so doing, however, they acquire considerably less prestige. At a superficial glance the potlatch looks like a mere senseless display of wealth, motivated by an exaggerated vanity. It is, however, nothing of the kind. It involves a definite *quid pro quo*. If the recipients gain in material goods, the donors acquire intangible values of at least equal importance. The host gets a dwelling and becomes thereby a house chief. The hostess gains prestige for her clan and social status for her children. The potlatch, indeed, is the dynamic factor in the most vital of all native institutions—the system of rank.

To avoid confusion, it is necessary to understand that two independent but interrelated systems of rank are operative in Haida society—first, rank as *position* or political rank and, second, rank as *status* or sociological rank. The former relates to chiefship alone; the latter to membership in a so-called "social class." Chiefship in both the clan and the household is, as we have seen, hereditary in the female line; status, on the other hand, is not hereditary at all. But the potlatch underlies both. No man can become a chief without giving a potlatch—either a funeral potlatch to validate an inherited position or a house-building potlatch to acquire a position through his own effort. Similarly no person can obtain social status without a potlatch. It is, however, not his own potlatches but those of his parents which confer status upon him. Thus a Haida cannot inherit status, nor can he acquire it for himself; he can only possess it if his parents have potlatched.

The Haidas proper, excluding their slaves, fall into two great classes—those possessing status and those lacking it, often rather inaccurately called "nobles" and "commoners" respectively. A so-called "commoner" is simply a person whose parents have given no potlatches; a "noble" is one whose parents have acquired status for him by a distribution of wealth. There are, moreover, many intricate gradations of status, all arising directly from the number and quality of the parents' potlatches. A person whose father and mother have given two house-building potlatches outranks another whose parents have but one to their credit; both outrank a person whose father has given only a funeral potlatch; and so on. Only a minority of the population lacks status altogether. The children of poor parents are commonly adopted by a wealthy relative, especially a paternal uncle, when he gives a house-building potlatch, and they acquire thereby the social standing they would otherwise lack.

Status affects social relations in many ways. "Nobles" rarely associate with "commoners," and may snub or insult them almost at will. Only a person with status can wear certain kinds of ornaments and occupy seats of honor at feasts and potlatches. And only such a person can inherit a chiefship; if the next of kin lacks status by reason of the remissness of his parents, he is always passed over in favor of another heir. Thus a chief is regularly also a "noble." But a "noble" is not necessarily a chief. Indeed, it is quite possible to enjoy a higher social status than any one else in the village and yet hold no chiefly position at all.

A person, of himself, can do little to affect his status. It, through his parents' liberality, he enjoys a high social standing, but is too lazy or shiftless to give a potlatch of his own, he loses the respect of the community but he does not thereby lose his status. His position resembles that of the "black sheep" of an aristocratic European family. On the other hand, a man who lacks status through the fault of his parents cannot achieve it for himself. He may show himself capable and industrious. He may accumulate great wealth and give lavish potlatches. By so doing he can confer status upon his children, making them the equals of any one in the village. He can even secure a measure of respect for himself and become technically a chief. But he can never escape the stigma of his low status. His situation is quite analogous to that of the *nouveau riche* in our society.

A Haida, instead of stating directly that So-and-so has never given a potlatch, will commonly resort to a circumlocution and say, "He never did anything for his children." The primary motive behind the potlatch thus stands revealed. It is not an exaggerated vanity or a senseless love of display, but rather the universal desire of parents everywhere to give their children a good start in life, to obtain for them a position of security and respect in society. Amongst ourselves a man and woman may save and sacrifice to send their children to college; Haida parents give a potlatch. Only the method is different; the motive is the same. Incidentally, the potlatch furnished the outstanding incentive to industry and thrift in

Haida society, and its elimination through the misguided zeal of missionaries and educators has perhaps been the most potent single factor in undermining the morale of the present generation of Indians.

In addition to the two major types of potlatch with their dual function of conferring sociological status and establishing or validating political position, there are two minor types which serve, not to confer status, but to uphold or justify it. A person of high standing who has made an unfortunate slip of the tongue in a public speech, or whose child has fallen into the water and been helped out by another, or who has suffered public humiliation in any way, gives what may be called a face-saving potlatch. He invites all members of the opposite moiety who witnessed the mishap, tears ten or more blankets into shreds, and distributes the pieces. No one thereafter may recall the incident. Similar but more spectacular is the vengeance potlatch, given by a man of high rank to avenge or extinguish an insult or an infringement upon his honor or property. He invites the opposite moiety, as in all potlatches. In the presence of his rival and a large audience he brings out valuable property and deliberately destroys it, for example, killing a slave, hacking to bits a treasured canoe or "copper," or tearing a quantity of blankets into shreds and distributing the pieces among the guests. His antagonist must immediately destroy an equal amount of property or suffer lifelong disgrace.

Distinctions in rank emerge clearly in the native system of justice. Theft and assault are regularly compounded by property damages, graded according to the status of the injured party. For murder, whether through violence or sorcery, the clansmen of the victim seek blood-vengeance. If they succeed in slaying the murderer or another member of his clan, this terminates the blood feud, to be sure, but it still leaves a balance to be settled one way or the other unless the two victims happen to be identical in rank. The clansmen of the inferior must make a payment of property strictly proportionate to the difference in status. To avoid retaliation, however, the murderer flees to the home of his house chief, where his entire clan also takes refuge. The injured clan, armed and hostile, gather in front of the dwelling. The chiefs of neutral clans try to mediate between the parties. Discovering what compensation the outraged clan will accept in lieu of blood-vengeance—an amount determined precisely by the status of the victim—they communicate the information to the beleaguered house chief. With his own property, and with contributions from his clansmen and from the murderer's father, he raises the necessary sum, which is transferred to the injured clan and is later used to give a funeral potlatch for the deceased. A general feast is held, and the incident is closed. If the murderer enjoys a bad reputation or his clan is too poor to make settlement, he must pay the penalty in person. He dons the war helmet of his paternal grandfather, walks out of the house, and falls riddled with arrows. His kinsmen show no signs of grief but make preparations for the feast and dance of reconciliation. If a man borrows a canoe or a weapon from a member of another clan, and is killed or hurt while using it, the owner is liable for damages as though the injury were intentional.

The Haidas prefer girl children to boys, since they will add numbers to the clan. They never practice abortion or infanticide, even in the case of weaklings, twins, and illegitimate children. During her pregnancy a woman must not lift heavy burdens, roll over in bed, look at an ugly object or a dying animal, or eat any sea food gathered at low tide. Her husband must not eat similar foods or trifle with other women. No one in the house may start out the door and then turn back, or the delivery will be difficult. Childbirth takes place in the house on a soft bed of mats and furs. The mother squats and grasps a stout pole driven into the floor. All the men and children of the household absent themselves. A paternal aunt ushers the child into the world, severs the umbilical cord with a knife—one used by the father for a boy or by the mother for a girl—and ties it with a string of cedar bark fiber. The rest of the cord, the afterbirth, and all soiled bedding and clothing are later burned. The aunt takes the newborn babe, cleans out its mouth with her finger, gives it a drink of warm water, greases its body, bathes it, and rubs it with powdered charcoal to prevent chafing. The mother remains very quiet for ten days, wearing a broad belt of cedar bark around her abdomen and avoiding all heavy foods. Then, after a bath, she resumes her normal duties. Owing to good care, few infants die at birth and the maternal mortality rate is lower than among civilized peoples. Mothers nurse their children for two years or more, and keep them in hollowed wooden cradles padded with soft moss and so constructed as to drain off the excreta.

The mother, after consultation with the father and grandparents, gives the child its name at a feast a few days after its birth. The name selected is usually that of some deceased ancestor of the same clan, although a boy may receive the name of his paternal grandfather whatever the clan of the latter. The soul of the ancestor is believed to be reincarnated in the child, and a seeress is usually consulted in choosing the name. If the child becomes sick, the shaman may decide that it has been wrongly named and that the ancestral soul is angry; the name is thereupon changed. The Haidas use personal names only for unmarried people; all others are spoken of as the father, mother, husband, or wife of So-and-so—a practice known as teknonymy. Besides their personal names, children receive honorary names at the house-building potlatch of their parents and the funeral potlatch of their paternal grandfather. Chiefs often possess additional ceremonial names, used only at potlatches, which they inherit from their predecessors in office, assume at their own house-building potlatches, or receive as gifts, *e.g.*, from friendly chiefs of the mainland tribes.

A girl lives with her parents until her marriage and usually even thereafter. A boy, however, leaves his parental home at about the age of ten and takes up his residence with his maternal uncle either permanently or until he becomes independent. He assists his uncle in all military and industrial enterprises, and the latter has sole charge of his education and discipline. In order to toughen the lad it is customary for the uncle, several times each winter, to send him out to swim in the icy sea water and to warm him on his emergence by lashing him on the back with brush.

Boys undergo no special ceremonies at puberty. A girl, however, is considered unclean at this period and is secluded for a month or more behind a curtain in the house. She smears her face with hemlock gum, wears a special hat to shield her eyes from the light, eats little food and drinks no water, and observes various other rites and taboos. Great care is taken to keep fishing, hunting, and gambling implements from contamination by too close proximity to her person. She is visited daily by her paternal aunts, who talk to her, cook and care for her, and receive from her all the toys, trinkets, and clothes of her girlhood. At the expiration of the period she bathes and dresses in new garments for a feast and dance given in her honor. The screen is removed, disclosing her to the assembled guests. Soon after making her *début*, she marries.

Young people of both sexes are permitted considerable sexual freedom before marriage, provided that they belong to opposite moieties. If the girl becomes pregnant, however, the boy must marry her. A young man may also have clandestine but semi-sanctioned affairs with the wife of his brother or maternal uncle, and a girl with her sister's husband. Property and rank figure prominently in arranging a match. The preferred marriage is between cross-cousins. A young man ordinarily weds a girl who stands to him in the relationship of father's sister's daughter, but if he is heir to a chiefship he usually marries a daughter of the maternal uncle whom he is to succeed. The mother of the youth, after consultation with her husband, brothers, and sisters, proposes marriage to the girl's mother, who discusses the matter with her husband and clansmen before coming to a decision. The wishes of both principals also receive consideration. An engagement usually lasts a year, during which time the youth lives with the parents of the girl and works for them but observes strict continence.

The wedding takes place at the home of the bride in the presence of the immediate relatives of both parties. The groom sits on a mat in the seat of honor behind the fireplace, and the bride is escorted to his side. After speeches by the men of both families, the mother and sisters of the groom exchange presents with the clanswomen of the bride, and the girl's father gives his new son-in-law a slave, a canoe, a "copper," or some other valuable present. At a feast following the wedding the clanswomen of the groom shower the bride with clothing, household utensils, and other practical gifts. The young couple live for an entire season in rotation at the homes of the groom's sisters, where they are lavishly entertained. They then take up their residence with the bride's father, unless he is dead or the groom is himself a house chief. A man scrupulously avoids his mother-in-law and shows great deference in the presence of the male relatives of his wife.

In the division of labor by sex the men hunt, fish, fell trees, fetch firewood, build houses and canoes, wage war, and make all tools, weapons, wooden utensils, musical instruments, ornaments, and ceremonial objects; the women snare birds, collect roots, berries, bark, seaweed, and shellfish, prepare and cook food, tan skins, and make thread, rope, mats, baskets, and all textile products and clothing. These economic spheres are not, however, rigidly distinct. The women often paddle the canoes when the men hunt sea otters, and a man does not disdain to help his wife in cooking, gathering berries, smoking salmon, or the like. Friendship, mutual respect, and a spirit of coöperation characterize the relation of husband and wife. They discuss all their plans together, but neither interferes with the activities of the other. The husband exercises at best but a mild authority, and he is ashamed to display even this in the presence of others. A woman holds property independently of her husband. She participates on a plane of equality with men in feasts, potlatches, religious ceremonies, and clan councils. She enjoys status in her own right and can be a shaman or in exceptional cases even a chief.

Polygyny, though comparatively rare, is permitted to men of high rank. The first wife always takes precedence over the others, but there is no distinction in the status of the children. Marriage does not create an exclusive sexual monopoly. Either party may have relations with a clansman of the other, and the injured spouse, though he may object, can take no action. But adultery—a *liaison* with any one else—gives adequate grounds for divorce. A husband can take personal vengeance against neither his adulterous wife nor her lover. The latter, nevertheless, must pay damages—not, however, to the husband, but to the wife's mother. In cases of separation, which are not uncommon, the children always remain with the mother. The relatives of both parties, however, try to patch things up; having arranged the marriage, they are humiliated if it fails.

Old people of both sexes enjoy great respect and are well cared for by their relatives, never abandoned or killed. In death "the soul flies away." The Haidas believe that every person possesses two souls. One, the shadow-soul, returns at some indefinite time after death to enter the body of a pregnant woman and animate her child; the quickening marks its appearance. It is with this soul that the idea of reincarnation is associated. The other soul leaves the body in sleep and experiences the adventures seen in dreams. If a person is suddenly startled, his dream-soul takes fright, flies away, and its owner sickens and dies. In death the dream-soul "drops down" to an underworld, where it is welcomed with a feast and dance by the spirits of those who have gone before. Here it lives a life much like that on earth. From time to time it returns to earth temporarily as a ghost, and may be seen or heard in a graveyard or a deserted village. The dream-souls of those who die by drowning become incarnated in killer-whales and inhabit special villages under the sea. The souls of those who are killed in war or feuds go to a third spirit world—a beautiful realm in the sky with eternal summer and an abundance of singing birds.

When a person lies at the point of death, his property is piled high about his bed, his friends come to condole with him, and a male cross-cousin is delegated to make his coffin—in his presence. When he dies, the women of his father's clan decorate his face with red stripes, clothe the body in ceremonial garments, and prop it up in a lifelike position on a box in the post of honor behind the fireplace, where it reposes in state for four days. On the same evening the clansmen of the deceased file past the corpse, singing a song of mourning and leaving gifts to help defray the funeral expenses. For four successive nights relays of male and female cross-cousins keep a vigil, during which they chew tobacco, exchange reminiscences, and sing mourning chants. Then the male cross-cousins place the corpse in a cedar chest or a special coffin, carry it out of the house through a hole in the side wall, and deposit it in the burial hut of the clan. No property is placed with or in the coffin, but all garments and other objects touched by the deceased during his last illness are removed and burned. After the funeral the clansmen of the deceased smear their cheeks with charcoal mixed with hemlock pitch, and the women also cut off the ends of their hair. The widow—or widower—goes into the bushes with a slave, who makes four rings out of brush, slips them over her head, and then places each over a separate tree stump with a prayer that she may live long. She then bathes in the mud of a small stream and washes the mud downward off her body with a similar prayer. The kinsmen

Photographs by the Author

FIG. 63 (*left*). BASE OF A HAIDA MORTUARY COLUMN AT SKIDEGATE, CARVED WITH THE BEAVER CREST.

FIG. 64 (*right*). CARVED FIGURE MARKING THE GRAVE OF A HAIDA SHAMAN ON A ROCKY ISLAND NEAR THE ANCIENT VILLAGE OF KIUSTA.

of the deceased then give a small feast to those who have performed the funeral duties. The corpse of a person dying away from home is brought back for burial unless it is too badly decomposed, in which case it is burned on the spot and the charred bones brought back.

A month or so after the funeral the next of kin to the deceased—usually a man's nephew or a woman's daughter—invites the opposite moiety to an important feast, which terminates the period of mourning. A little food is placed in the fire and some water sprinkled around it, to be conveyed thus to the spirit world. During the following winter the heir of a deceased chief, or the nearest kinsman of an important person other than a chief, hires the members of the opposite moiety to erect a mortuary column to the deceased. This may be hollowed out to receive the corpse, which is then transferred from the burial hut, or it may be a simple commemorative shaft ornamented with crests and perhaps a "copper." Feasts, dances, and ceremonies alternate with the work and culminate in the funeral potlatch, at which the heir distributes the property he has inherited—or, if insufficient, his own—and thereby validates his title to the name, position, house, and widow of the deceased.

The Haidas conceive of the earth as a circular expanse of ocean covered by a solid firmament, like an inverted bowl, to which the heavenly bodies are attached. On the surface of the sea float two island groups—the Queen Charlotte Islands and the mainland. A great divinity lives under the earth with his dog, who supports the islands on its back and causes earthquakes when it gets up to shake itself. When this happens, an old woman drives a yew wedge into the earth to peg it down, and tells the dog to be quiet or it will spill the grease which she has put out for it in a clamshell on the floor. The Haidas account for the creation of the world and of man in an elaborate cycle of myths, in which a mythical Raven plays the leading rôle. A very popular legend relates how the Raven stole the moon. Another tells of a great flood.   Others recount historical events heavily disguised with supernatural embellishments.

The natives people their universe with supernatural beings. Spirits or gods inhabit the sea, earth, air, heavenly bodies, fire, mountains, cliffs, rocks, reefs, lakes, streams, swamps, and trees.   Dominant among them is a great sky god, who disposes over life and death and approaches the stature of a supreme being.   Other important nature spirits include a great sea deity, a Thunderbird who produces thunder by flapping its wings, a goddess of fire who resides under every hearth, and the Creek-Women, one of whom lives at the source of each stream and presides over all the fish in it. Animals, birds, and fish present a dual aspect.   From one point of view they are mere animals to be hunted; from another they represent the embodiment of supernatural beings, who may help or injure men and who can assume human forms on occasion.   As might be expected of a people whose lives are so closely bound up with the sea, the Haidas assign first rank to the divinities incarnate in fish and sea mammals.   The Killer-Whales, in whom are incarnated the souls of men who have died by drowning, are the most powerful of these Ocean-People; they control the principal sources of food, receive more attention and sacrifices than any other beings, and figure prominently in art and mythology.   The Land Otters and the Bear People are also important.   Other divinities include the Gyagit, a class of ghostly bogies with spiny faces and hairy bodies, and the Property-Woman, who will answer any prayer for riches if one can but capture her baby.

Supernatural beings receive comparatively little cult attention, none at all in the case of the Raven and other prominent mythological figures.   To appease the Killer-Whales, a man caught at sea in a storm places a flicker feather, a bit of deer tallow, or a pinch of tobacco on his paddle and lowers it gently into the water, or pours a cup of fresh water into the sea.   The spiritual masters of harbors and islands receive similar offerings, and a hunter, out of deference to the spirit of a mountain, may drop a feather, some grease, or a few berries into his campfire. Except for these insignificant rites, sacrifice does not exist—unless we include an old custom of the northern Haidas, who, in erecting a totem pole, used formerly to place a slave in the hole and crush him to death. The natives do not worship idols; their totem poles have merely a heraldic significance. Intercourse with divine beings, as well as success in war, hunting, and magic, is promoted by ritual purity, attained through fasting, abstinence from water, continence, bathing, and purging the stomach of its contents by alternate draughts of salt and fresh water.

In each village certain persons stand in particularly close rapport with the supernatural beings. Besides a class of seeresses, old women who possess the power of prophesy through dreams, there are the shamans proper or medicine men, who can summon to their aid at any time their familiar spirits, i.e., those spirits, usually of animals, with whom they have established communion. The shaman, who may be of either sex, leads a life in most respects like that of an ordinary individual. He distinguishes himself from his fellows, however, by abstaining from seaweed and whale blubber and by never combing, washing, or. cutting his hair lest, like Samson, he lose his power. He is also buried in a separate place and in a special way—on a low platform raised above the ground on four posts and covered with a roof. In his professional capacity he wears a Chilkat blanket about his loins, a curved bone through the septum of his nose, and a necklace of small bone objects carved to represent the animal forms of his familiar spirits. His paraphernalia also include rattles, a baton, and a hollow bone tube. Shamans possess considerable medical knowledge and are credited with miraculous vision and the power of levitation. They practice and counteract sorcery, influence the weather, and secure the souls of salmon and force them up the rivers when they are reluctant to come. But they function chiefly in the treatment of sickness, when they receive payment according to the wealth of the patient. Shamans never assist each other. On the contrary, they display the keenest rivalry and hatred. One will always depreciate another and try to kill or injure him by sorcery. A certain shaman, for example, "saw" a rival in a distant village hurl an invisible rope at his head; his clansmen arrived just in time to grasp his legs as he was being pulled into the air, but they could not bring him to earth until they had taken his knife and cut the imaginary rope above his head.

The office of medicine man usually descends from maternal uncle to nephew, or from mother to daughter. Of the several possible heirs, one is revealed as the proper successor by his physical peculiarities, his nervousness, or his unusual dreams. To him the older shaman teaches his secrets and transmits his paraphernalia. The candidate must purify himself, however, by long fasts, continence, medicines, and the usual salt water emetics. He gets his first familiar spirit by dreaming of some animal, and as he increases in skill he acquires other and stronger supernatural helpers. Some of the most powerful medicine men, however, do not inherit their position. Marked from birth by some evidence of exceptional gifts, they steal a bone from an old shaman's grave, make an expedition by canoe, point and jab the bone at every animal they encounter, and then, while it is paralyzed, cut a thin slice from its tongue and release it with a prayer to lend them its power. The greatest of all medicine men is one who has thus obtained a piece of a land otter's tongue.

Although the shaman is usually well versed in herbal lore, many medicines are common knowledge, and some are the secret possessions of individual families. The Haidas use a variety of ointments, poultices, and laxatives. They consider sweat baths efficacious for many ailments. They apply heat to swellings, or lance them and dress the wounds with soft vegetable matter and spruce pitch. They even cauterize the nerves of aching teeth with a sharp piece of flint. Some of their methods seem less sensible, *e.g.*, beating a rheumatic limb with nettles or burning shredded cedar bark on the flesh. To set a broken bone, they remove the splinters and bind tightly about the limb a putty-like mash made by crushing two crows, feathers and all, in a mortar. The medicine man is called in, as a rule, only when a patient does not respond to ordinary treatment and sorcery is suspected. After the usual purification, the shaman arrives at the sick man's house, where the whole village has assembled. He breathes on the patient and acts as though trying to blow the cause of the ailment, like a feather, out through the smoke-hole. With one hand on the patient he walks slowly around the bed shaking his rattle. Then, while a slave beats a drum and his clansmen sing four ritual chants, he fingers a bone on his necklace and invokes the appropriate spirit, who shortly arrives and takes possession of him. In this state he imitates the animal cry of his spirit and speaks the language of the region whence it comes—perhaps Tlingit or Tsimshian—even though he may be ignorant thereof at other times. Finally, with the aid of his supernatural helpers he prescribes the proper treatment and reveals, often vaguely, the identity of the sorcerer whose hostile magic has caused the ailment. The shaman's function throughout, indeed, is rather that of detective than of physician.

The strong influence of magic among the Haidas compensates for the comparative superficiality of their religion in the stricter sense. One need not be a shaman to practice magic. An ordinary person can make the wind blow in a desired direction by erecting a drift log on the beach and building a fire on one side of the base so that the log will topple over like a forest tree uprooted by the wind. If born on a fine day, he can control the weather, for example, by going outdoors at night and proclaiming aloud the advent of bright weather while a slave on the roof brandishes a blazing torch. A man can make a love charm by performing certain rites over a piece of hemlock gum, a favorite cosmetic, and leaving it where his sweetheart will find and use it. Black magic or sorcery is invariably worked with exuviæ of the victim—a lock of his hair, a nail paring, a drop of spittle, a piece of food left by him, or a little dirt or a bit of clothing that has been in contact with his body. If the sorcerer places such an object beside a corpse, his enemy sickens and dies. If he buries it in the ground, his victim suffers a lingering death as it rots. The natives know several ways of protecting themselves against sorcery. If, for example, a man makes an image of himself out of spruce gum mixed with dirt scraped from his skin and places it in a little waterfall, magic will henceforth flow over him like water over the effigy.

Sorcery is always inspired by a mouse, which enters a man as he lies sleeping, takes possession of him, and bends him to its will. Ordinarily the mouse is not malicious, but it takes affront at the slightest injury or slur against its owner and compels the latter, even against his will, to take revenge. It secures the necessary exuviæ and directs the magical operations. When the victim falls ill, and ordinary remedies fail, a relative may attempt to discover the sorcerer. He catches a mouse and retires into the bushes for four days of purificatory rites. Then he takes the animal gently in his hands and repeats slowly the names of everybody in the village. At the name of the culprit the mouse nods its head. If it refuses to do so, it is killed or blinded in one eye, and ere long the sorcerer similarly dies or becomes blind and the patient recovers. If, however, it nods its head, it is set free and the sorcerer is forced to recant. In other cases the shaman is called in to disclose the identity of the evildoer with the help of his familiar spirit. If, as is often the case, he vaguely hints that a slave is guilty, all the slaves of the village are bound hand and foot and plunged into deep water; he who floats high harbors the mouse. Threatened with death if he refuses, a detected sorcerer fetches his "poison" from its hiding place and burns it or throws it into the sea. Should the retraction come too late and the victim die, the culprit, if a slave, is immediately killed; if a freeman, he is treated as an ordinary murderer. If the victim recovers, however, the sorcerer goes scot-free for not he but the mouse is to blame. Nevertheless the community needs protection in the future. Hence the sorcerer, if a slave, is ducked in the sea until the mouse comes out and is killed; otherwise he goes into the bushes and lies on his back while his friends place sand on his stomach and build a fire on the sand until the guilty rodent emerges.

Although possibly seen by a Spanish expedition under De Fonte in 1640, the Haidas had their first real contact with the whites when visited by Pérez and Bodega in 1774 and 1775. Within a few years British and American traders began to come in considerable numbers, and they soon stripped the natives of their valuable sea otter furs. Smallpox, introduced by the whites, has ravaged the islands in successive waves. Pulmonary diseases, bad whiskey, and venereal infections, spread by the prostitution of native women in the coast cities, have also contributed to the reduction of the population from over 8,000 in 1841 to approximately a tenth of that number today. For the last twenty years, however, the population has been slowly increasing, aided perhaps by the infusion of white blood, which now flows in the veins of more than half of the natives. The Indians are segregated on allotted lands or reservations. Missions of the Church of England and the Methodist and Presbyterian denominations have weaned them from their aboriginal beliefs. War, slavery, and most of the native arts and industries have disappeared, although fishing is still the primary source of livelihood. From earliest times the Haidas have been notable for their readiness to borrow the customs and ideas of their neighbors, and they have not found it difficult to adapt themselves to a new materialistic civilization.

BIBLIOGRAPHY

ADAM, L. "Stammesorganisation und Häuptlingstum der Haida und Tsimshian." *Zeitschrift für Vergleichende Rechtswissenschaft*, Vol. XXX. Stuttgart, 1913.

BANCROFT, H. H. *The Native Races of the Pacific States of North America.* 5 vols. New York, 1875–76.

BOAS, F. "The Decorative Art of the Indians of the North Pacific Coast." *Bulletin of the American Museum of Natural History*, Vol. IX. New York, 1897.

——. "First General Report on the Indians of British Columbia." *British Association for the Advancement of Science, Report of the Fifty-ninth Meeting.* London, 1890.

BOAS, F., and FARRAND, L. "Physical Characteristics of the Tribes of British Columbia." *British Association for the Advancement of Science, Report of the Sixty-eighth Meeting.* London, 1899.

CHAMBERLAIN, A. F. "Haida." *Encyclopædia of Religion and Ethics.* Edited by J. Hastings. 12 vols. New York, 1908–22.

COLLISON, W. H. *In the Wake of the War Canoe.* London, 1915.

CURTIS, E. S. *The North American Indian*, Vol. XI. Seattle, 1916.

DAWSON, G. M. "The Haidas." *Harper's New Monthly Magazine*, Vol. LXV. New York, 1882.

——. "Report on the Queen Charlotte Islands." *Geological Survey of Canada, Report of Progress for 1878–79.* Montreal, 1880.

DEANS, J. "A Little Known Civilization." *American Antiquarian*, Vol. XVII. Chicago, 1895.

DURLACH, T. M. *The Relationship Systems of the Tlingit, Haida and Tsimshian.* New York, 1928.

GODDARD, P. E. *Indians of the Northwest Coast.* New York, 1924.

HARRISON, C. *Ancient Warriors of the North Pacific.* London, 1925.

HODGE, F. W. (editor). "Handbook of American Indians North of Mexico." *Smithsonian Institution, Bureau of American Ethnology, Bulletin 30.* 2 vols. Washington, 1907–10.

KROEBER, A. L. "Tribes of the Pacific Coast of North America." *Proceedings of the Second Pan-American Scientific Congress*, Section I, Vol. I. Washington, 1917.

MACKENZIE, A. "Descriptive Notes on Certain Implements, Weapons, etc., from Graham Island, Queen Charlotte Islands, B. C." *Proceedings and Transactions of the Royal Society of Canada*, Vol. IX. Montreal, 1892.

MURDOCK, G. P. "The Kinship System of the Haida." To be published in *American Anthropologist*, New Series, Vol. XXXVI. Menasha, 1934.

NEWCOMBE, C. F. "The Haida Indians." *Congrès International des Américanistes*, XVe Session, Vol. I. Quebec, 1907.

NIBLACK, A. P. "The Coast Indians of Southern Alaska and Northern British Columbia." *Smithsonian Institution, Annual Report of the Board of Regents for the Year Ending June 30, 1888.* Washington, 1890.

SAPIR, E. "The Social Organization of the West Coast Tribes." *Transactions of the Royal Society of Canada*, Third Series, Vol. IX. Toronto, 1916.

SWAN, J. G. "The Haidah Indians of Queen Charlotte's Islands, British Columbia." *Smithsonian Contributions to Knowledge*, Vol. XXI. Washington, 1876.

*SWANTON, J. R. "Contributions to the Ethnology of the Haida." *Memoirs of the American Museum of Natural History*, Vol. VIII. Leiden, 1909.

——. "Haida, an Illustrative Sketch." *Handbook of American Indian Languages.* Edited by F. Boas. *Bureau of American Ethnology, Bulletin 40*, Part 1. Washington, 1910.

——. "The Haida Calendar." *American Anthropologist*, New Series, Vol. V. Lancaster, 1903.

——. "Haida Texts and Myths." *Smithsonian Institution, Bureau of American Ethnology, Bulletin 29.* Washington, 1905.

——. "Haida Texts—Masset Dialect." *Memoirs of the American Museum of Natural History*, Vol. XIV. Leiden, 1908.

——. "Social Organization of the Haida." *Proceedings of the International Congress of Americanists*, Thirteenth Session. Easton, 1905.

WOLDT, A. *Capitain Jacobsens Reise an der Nordwestküste Amerikas, 1881–1883.* Leipzig, 1884.

CHAPTER X

THE CROWS OF THE WESTERN PLAINS

THE Indian of fiction and popular fancy, so far as he is not a pure figment of the imagination, has been drawn, in the main, from the natives of the great plains which stretch from the Mississippi River to the Rocky Mountains and from Canada nearly to Mexico. Of these Plains Indians, the Crow tribe may be taken as representative. Until gathered into reservations, the Crows ranged over a territory of some 100,000 square miles, between 43° and 48° north latitude and between 104° and 112° west longitude, in northern Wyoming and in Montana south and east of the Missouri River. This region, which includes the present Yellowstone National Park, is unrivaled in natural beauty. Its topography runs the gamut from level prairie to the majestic peaks of the Rockies. The eternal snow of the summits feeds numerous rivers and streams, swelling them to torrential proportions with the spring thaw in late May and early June. Evergreen and deciduous forests clothe the lower slopes of the mountains, carpet the fertile valleys, and fringe the streams. Edible plants and berry-bearing bushes are found in abundance. Before the coming of the white man, the country teemed with game—mountain sheep and grizzly bears in the mountains, deer and elk in the valleys, antelope on the prairie, beavers and waterfowl along the streams, and—most important of all—the bison or "buffalo" which roamed the grassy plains in immense herds.

Physically, the Crows are characterized by light reddish brown complexions, tall stature (the men averaging five feet eight inches), straight black hair, scanty beards, broad heads (cephalic index 81), dark brown or black eyes, and prominent leptorrhine noses. The women appear as strong as the men;

FIG. 65. A CROW WARRIOR.
Courtesy of the Staatliches Museum für Völkerkunde, Berlin

with no apparent exertion they can ride all day and night or carry a quarter of a buffalo. In physique, as in culture, the Crows resemble the other Indians of the Plains.

The natives call themselves *Apsaroke*, of which "Crows" is a somewhat inaccurate translation. Their language reveals a close affinity with that of the Hidatsa tribe. Though not mutually intelligible, the two form a distinct subfamily of the widespread Siouan linguistic stock. The evidence of tradition, and to some extent of culture, bears out that of language in indicating that the Crows originated by fission from the Hidatsa not many centuries ago, when they abandoned agriculture and permanent villages to take up a nomadic mode of life. They possess no writing, except in the germinal form of pictographic representations of military exploits. Extensive use is made of smoke signals for communication, and a highly developed sign language enables the Crows to carry on long and animated conversations with Indians of alien tribe and speech. The first snowfall in the autumn and the disappearance of the ice in the spring divide the year into two recognized seasons. Years are called "winters" and are identified and remembered by their outstanding events. The Crows employ a decimal system of numeration. "They do not usually count higher than a thousand, as they say honest people have no use for larger numerals."

The only native domesticated animal of the Plains Indians —popular opinion to the contrary notwithstanding—is the dog. The dogs of the Crows carry their masters' moccasins on the warpath and transport their household possessions by means of the travois, a primitive vehicle consisting of two poles strapped to the animal and dragging along the ground behind. Having no boats, the Crows are forced to wade or swim across rivers, towing their property on improvised rafts of driftwood, lodge poles, and buffalo skins. The horse, though inseparable from the Indian in the popular mind, was unknown in the New World until brought over by the

Spaniards. Once introduced, however, it spread—and with it the saddle, stirrups, quirt, and lariat—with such rapidity that it reached the Crows as early as about 1650. By the time the tribe was first seen by a white man, nearly a century later, the alien steed had supplanted the dog in transportation, and even the children were accomplished equestrians. The horse vastly increased the mobility of the Indians in hunting and warfare. So perfectly was it adapted to their needs that it intensified rather than modified their native mode of life.

The Crows practice no agriculture except to cultivate a little tobacco each year for ceremonial purposes. They make little or no use of the fish which abound in the rivers. The women, or parties of girls with their sweethearts, gather wild fruits and berries, collect edible plants, and dig wild turnips and other roots. But the people subsist mainly on the products of the chase and lead the life of nomadic hunters. They pass the long tedious winter in some protected spot near the bank of a stream. During the summer they move frequently, following the bison herds. A Crow migration is a festive occasion. Scouts ride far in advance to warn of enemies. Police guard the flanks. The chiefs and old men lead the procession. The various families follow with their horses, dogs, and household possessions, the women dressed in their finest apparel. A moving column sometimes extends for several miles.

The principal weapon of the chase is the bow and arrow. The latter consists of a feathered wooden shaft and a head of bone, horn, or chipped flint. The Crows carry their arrows in skin quivers and value them highly; ten good arrows will buy a horse. The bow is of wood or horn, three feet long, and equipped with a sinew string and a wristguard of rawhide. The finest specimens are made of fresh elkhorns, softened in a hot spring and cut into strips, which are straightened, shaped, riveted together, and reënforced with sinew. Although individual hunters occasionally stalk deer in a disguise of buckskin and horns, the commonest and most productive method is the communal drive. Sometimes the hunters drive a herd of buffalo, antelope, deer, or elk between two lines of shouting men and women converging toward a precipice, over which the frightened animals plunge to their death. Sometimes they impound a herd in a valley with steep cliffs on three sides, erecting a strong fence across the entrance, or drive the animals between converging rock piles or lines of men into artificial corrals, where they can be slaughtered at leisure. If mounted, the hunters may also surround a herd in a narrowing circle until the animals become massed and fall easy victims to their arrows.

The Crows subsist mainly on meat, especially that of the buffalo. Nevertheless they taboo as food the flesh of dogs, muskrats, moles, rats, mice, frogs, snakes, turtles, owls, and fish. They either boil their meat in rawhide vessels with the aid of hot stones, or bake it in the ashes, or roast it in holes, or broil it over the fire. Though able to generate fire with a simple drill and tinder of dry buffalo dung, they often carry a burning "buffalo chip" on a stick from one camp to another to save themselves the trouble. They preserve buffalo meat by cutting it into strips, drying it on frames in the sun, browning it over the fire, pounding it into a powder, and stuffing it, often mixed with dried fruits or berries, into cleaned intestines or skin bags, which are sealed with melted fat. This "pemmican" is a highly nutritious and concentrated food, and has been widely adopted by white trappers and explorers. In the spring the natives enjoy a special delicacy called "cottonwood ice cream," the frothy gelatinous sap obtained by peeling off the outer bark of the tree and scraping the exposed surface.

The Crows sometimes inhabit rude log cabins in winter, and men on the warpath occupy temporary windbreaks of sticks interlaced with bark and roofed with foliage. But the characteristic shelter is a conical skin tent, described as the most beautiful of Plains Indian tipis and "the stateliest dwelling ever nomad used." A Crow tipi stands twenty-five feet high and will accommodate as many as twenty persons. Against a framework of four main poles of fir or pine, sloping inward and meeting at the apex, lean about twenty other poles, arranged in a circle. Over them is stretched a cover of buffalo skins, dressed as white as linen and sparingly deco-

rated with paint and quills. The cover is fastened to the ground with pegs or stones, and an aperture with an adjustable flap is left at the top for the escape of smoke. From the ends of the poles, which project far above the apex, fly streamers of red leather. A fire burns in the center of the floor, and clothing, weapons, and implements hang from the poles. At the rear is the place of

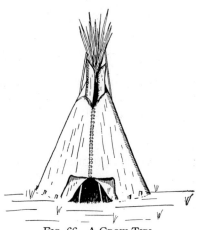

FIG. 66. A CROW TIPI.

honor. The occupants recline or sleep on soft skins and furs placed on the bare ground.

The Crows manufacture neither basketry nor pottery. They make cooking utensils of soapstone and buffalo hide, bags and pouches of skin, cups and bowls of wood, and spoons, cups, and small dishes from the horns of the buffalo and mountain sheep. The paunch and pericardium of the buffalo serve as water vessels. The native tools include hafted stone hammers and mauls, wedges of horn, mortars and pestles of stone, awls and scrapers of bone, knives of chipped flint, and drills made from the prongs of elk antlers. Fragile articles find no place in the nomad household.

The Crows clothe themselves entirely in skins, obtained from the mountain sheep, antelope, deer, elk, and buffalo.

They render these hides soft and pliable by treating them with a mixture of vegetable substances and buffalo brains, and by repeated scraping, pounding, and rubbing. The men wear a breechclout, leggings extending to the hip, a fringed shirt ornamented with trophies and decorative bands on the sleeves and over the shoulders, and a buffalo robe with the hair inside. The women wear knee-length leggings, a small buffalo robe, and a sleeveless dress extending to the feet, studded with elk teeth, and provided with cape-like shoulder pieces falling loosely over the arms. Both sexes protect the feet with moccasins cut from a single piece of leather. On special occasions the men don their war bonnets; otherwise the head is bare. Children go about practically naked. The men wear their full clothing only in winter; in the heat of the summer they lay aside everything but breechclout and moccasins. Adult women and adolescent girls, however, may not with propriety expose any part of the body except face and hands—save only at the morning bath in the river, a custom which both sexes and all ages observe every day of the year.

For ornament the Crows wear earrings of bone and shell, and necklaces of bear claws and bone discs. The men paint their faces for war, and sometimes tattoo designs on the chest with the aid of porcupine quills and powdered charcoal. The women tattoo a narrow line on the chin, a dot on the nose, and a small circle on the forehead. Great attention is paid to the care of the hair, especially by the men, who dress their wives' hair as well as their own. The women wear their hair parted in the middle with the line of demarcation painted red. The men strive to cultivate long locks, and, when possible, let them trail on the ground on special occasions. They oil them with bear grease, perfume them with sweet-smelling herbs, rub them glossy with cactus pith, and supplement them with other hair if too short. Parted in the center, these tresses hang down loosely at the sides and back. They are gathered out of the way in a knot in front of each ear, or are matted together with a band of pitch around the head, or are simply carried in a bundle in the arms or the folds of the robe.

The native decorative art consists principally of geometrical designs—combinations of triangles, diamonds, rectangles,

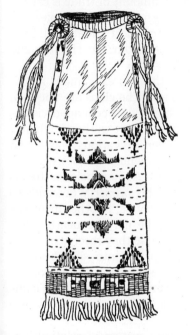

After Lowie

FIG. 67. QUILL-WORK BAG AND CRADLE OF THE CROWS.

and the like—incised or painted on articles of rawhide or embroidered with dyed porcupine quills on bags, clothing, and riding gear. The work, though attractive, reveals little individuality and a minimum of symbolism. Realistic art is confined to painted representations of military exploits and scenes of religious significance on robes and the interiors of the tipis.

In the division of labor by sex, the men hunt, fight, and

make weapons, while the women gather firewood, fruits, berries, and roots, cook, prepare skins and clothing, embroider with quills, and make, erect, and dismantle the tipis. A certain degree of specialization by occupation has likewise developed, notably in the manufacture of bows and arrows and in quill embroidery. A limited amount of trade is carried on with the surrounding tribes. Corn, beans, and squash are occasionally obtained from the agricultural Hidatsa, elkhorn bows from the Shoshoni, and pipes from the Hidatsa and Dakotas.

The Crow tribe is divided into thirteen exogamous matrilineal clans, each with its own chief. The clans are not local groups; all are represented in each of the three main divisions of the tribe. Clansmen camp and feast together, exchange presents on visits, aid one another in various ways, and avenge the murder of their fellow members. Descent and inheritance follow the female line. A man belongs to his mother's clan, not his father's, and his property descends to his brothers and sisters or, if none survive, to other members of his own clan. On his deathbed he may bequeath a few articles to his wife or son, but otherwise they receive nothing. The clans are linked, mostly in pairs, into six phratries. Thus the Sore-lip and Greasy-inside-the-mouth clans form a phratry. Closer relations exist between these linked clans than between others, and in some instances they may not intermarry.

The Crows follow a classificatory system of relationship, and their kinship terms often have an exceedingly wide application. Thus a man addresses as "father" (*axe*), not only his own father, but also the latter's brothers, maternal uncles, sisters' husbands and sons, and fellow clansmen irrespective of age. Terms commonly differ according to the sex of the relative, and sometimes also according to the sex of the person speaking. Generations are frequently disregarded. Thus a mother's brother is classed as an elder brother, and a sister's son as a younger brother. Cross-cousins are regarded neither as cousins nor as brothers and sisters; a mother's brother's son is called "son," and a father's sister's son is called "father."

This kinship system prescribes very definite social attitudes. A mutual taboo of avoidance exists between a man and his parents-in-law. He may, for example, neither look at nor speak to his mother-in-law, nor even mention a word that occurs in her name. Similar taboos prevail between a man and his wife's brother's wife and his daughter's husband. Brother and sister maintain an attitude of great respect, do not converse freely, and are never seen alone together after childhood. Brothers-in-law, though they live on terms of great friendship, likewise maintain an attitude of respect, and never use obscenity in the presence of one another. A "joking relationship" exists between persons whose fathers belong to the same clan or phratry. They may, with entire impunity, play practical jokes on one another or even put each other to shame in public for infractions of tribal custom. Between a man and his sister-in-law there prevails a relationship of excessive familiarity. They may joke together without regard to the ordinary rules of propriety. He may even raise her dress, exposing her in public, and she can retaliate in kind.

The clan organization serves an important function in the regulation of marriage. Exogamy is the rule, marriage within the clan being regarded as highly improper. Girls usually marry before they attain puberty; indeed, they are ridiculed if they do not. A young man, on the other hand, must wait until he is twenty-five, unless he has previously distinguished himself in war. In the meantime, however, he has plenty of opportunities for philandering. The young men frequently accompany their sweethearts on expeditions after roots, berries, and lodge poles, or take them along on buffalo hunts to care for their spare horses. These *liaisons* often ripen into permanent unions without further ceremony; the girl simply accompanies her lover to his parents' tipi. Sometimes a man makes a woman a fine present and induces her to elope with him. The Crows often marry women captured from hostile tribes, and under certain circumstances the stealing of women is permitted even within the tribe. The approved mode of marriage, however, is by purchase. The man presents meat to the girl's mother and makes valuable gifts such as horses, to her brothers. The bride usually joins the camp group of her husband and receives presents from his clanswomen. The purchase of a woman gives a man the right to marry her younger sisters without additional payment, for the Crows are polygynous. All the wives of a man live together, whether or not they are sisters.

Marriages are easily terminated. A woman may desert a husband whom she dislikes, and a man may send away his wife for infidelity or incompatibility, or even for being "cranky." A man, it is said, even subjects himself to ridicule if he lives too long with one woman, and it is considered positively disgraceful to take back a divorced wife. When the parents separate, the younger children go with their mother; the girls remain with her, but the boys return to their father when older. A man generally marries the younger sister of his divorced wife, and a widow frequently weds the brother of her deceased husband. In theory, a double standard of morality prevails. Public opinion condones, and even expects, a measure of irregularity in the conduct of the men, but it sets up before the women a high ideal of virtue. Nevertheless practice conflicts with theory. In spite of outward observance of the rules of propriety, sexual laxity is widely prevalent, and despite severe theoretical penalties for infidelity, a woman may even become notorious for her immorality without losing social standing.

Women perform most of the menial labor. They are subject to the will of their husbands. They are considered unclean at menstruation, when they must observe certain taboos and undergo purificatory rites. But they are by no means mere chattels. They enjoy property rights quite independent of their husbands, and they participate in religious and ceremonial activities. True romantic love is not uncommon. Lovers serenade their mistresses with flutes at night, and they may grieve for days over a rebuff. Husbands often become deeply attached to their wives, although custom forbids them to show jealousy in any way.

At childbirth a woman is attended by specialized obstetricians, of either sex, who are liberally paid for their services. She kneels and grasps two upright sticks with her hands, while her attendants exert pressure on her abdomen. The newborn baby is rubbed with grease and red paint, dusted with powdered clay and "buffalo chips" to prevent chafing, and wrapped in a soft skin. If it is a girl, its umbilical cord is preserved in a bag and is tied to her cradle, later to the back of her dress. Two days after birth the mother pierces the infant's ears with an awl for the insertion of earrings. Women rock their babies to sleep and sing them lullabies. The infant, when six months old, is strapped to a cradle, a tapering skin-covered board, by means of three decorated flaps with strings (see Fig. 67). Parents rarely punish their offspring, and never beat them. If a child cries too long, they put it on its back and pour water down its nose. Before long the words "Bring the water!" suffice to quiet it.

When a child is four days old, its father chooses, and pays, some person of prominence to give it a name, which is commonly descriptive of some valorous deed of the namer. The godparent lifts up the child four times, a little higher each time, to make it grow. If the infant is sickly, its name is changed. Men frequently assume new names, either by purchase or in commemoration of some creditable exploit. Nicknames are freely bestowed, and sometimes supersede the true names. Those given men are commonly obscene in character; those bestowed on women are usually derived from some ridiculous performance of which the woman herself, or more often one of her father's clanswomen, has been guilty.

Adoption is a very prevalent practice, especially among

relatives. At a little ceremony, which includes a feast, a dance, and a distribution of presents, the foster father sprinkles the head of the child with water. Fathers teach their sons to ride, to swim, and to use the bow and arrow. Mothers and grandmothers instruct girls in their household duties at an early age. In general, however, children grow up with a minimum of formal education. They learn largely through unconscious imitation of their elders, even in their games. Thus they "play house," "get married," and "hunt buffaloes," sometimes using real bison calves captured and kept as pets. Boyhood friendships sometimes last into adult years, when such comrades exchange presents in the manner customary among relatives. Neither sex undergoes any special ceremonies at puberty.

The Crows esteem liberality as a major virtue, and despise miserliness. A man is expected to give meat to any one who comes up as he is butchering a slain animal. Visitors are hospitably received, given the seat of honor in the rear of the tipi, and served immediately with pemmican or other food, no matter what time of day. Guests may take home with them any food that remains, and sometimes even ask for containers in which to carry it away. Good-humored raillery characterizes social intercourse. The Indians affect a modesty about their personal achievements and quickly take offense if one puts on airs. They are particularly averse to brawls between tribesmen, considering a resort to blows debasing. "The white people," they scornfully aver, "all want to be prize-fighters."

Existence is comparatively easy, and the Crows find plenty of time for games and sports. They spin tops, play dice games, slide on the ice, coast down hill on toboggans made of buffalo ribs and rawhide, engage in foot races and archery contests, throw darts at rolling hoops, and play a kind of shinny, in which the men are often pitted against the women. They are very fond of gambling, especially on a guessing game played with two elk teeth or marked bones.

The men divide into two sides, each of which encourages its players with songs, drum beating, and magical performances. Two men hide the teeth in their hands, and a member of the opposite side guesses where they are. For a wrong guess, a side surrenders a tally stick. When it loses all its counters, it loses the wager.

When a person dies, his clansmen paint the body, array it in its finest apparel, wrap it in part of a tipi cover, and

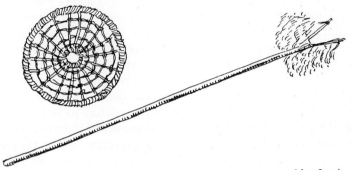

After Lowie

FIG. 68. HOOP AND DART GAME OF THE CROWS.

remove it through the side of the tent, never through the door. Led by drummers, the mourners march in a funeral procession to the place of burial, where, amid singing, dancing, and yelling, they chop off a finger joint, gash their legs, tear strips of flesh from their arms, and pierce the scalp with knives till their bodies are covered with blood. The women also crop their hair short, but the men sacrifice only a few of their treasured locks. The corpse is then deposited on a burial scaffold elevated on four poles, or in the fork of a tree, with its head oriented toward the west. The scaffold of a great chief is sometimes erected in his tipi, which is then abandoned. Occasionally the survivors kill the favorite horse of the deceased and bury it near his body. When the corpse has become decomposed, the bones are commonly removed and deposited in a cave or rock crevice. The relatives give away most of their property, absent themselves from camp for two months, erect a new tipi on their return, and remain in mourning for an entire season. If the deceased was slain in battle, the whole camp mourns. If no enemy was killed in the encounter, the relatives stay in the hills, living in miserable shelters, fasting, mourning, and crying for vengeance, until a member of the hostile tribe has been slain in revenge.

The soul or "shadow" of the deceased leaves the body and journeys to a spirit world in the west. The Crows exhibit little interest in the hereafter, though they seem to consider it a pleasant place where people live much as they do on earth. The dead can return and injure the living, *e.g.*, producing insanity. They are therefore feared, and to compare a person to a ghost is a grave insult. Relatives use different names in speaking of one who has passed away, and it is impolite to mention the deceased in their presence. Ghosts are not always malevolent, however. Some people possess the power of communicating with them and thus prophesying the future or discovering the fate of lost persons and property.

Of superior beings, the Crows believe in a host of spirits inhabiting animals, trees, stones, rivers, stars, and other natural phenomena. Many of them, especially those in bird or animal forms, appear to men in visions and become, as it were, their guardian or tutelary spirits, assuring them success in life. Although no priestly caste exists to arrange these supernatural beings into a hierarchy and to standardize their characteristics, some have risen to greater prominence than others. This is the case, for example, with the Moon, the Thunder, and a benevolent mythical Dwarf. Higher even than these, however, stand the Sun and Old Man Coyote, two great deities who are not always clearly distinguished. Old Man Coyote figures especially prominently in mythology and folklore—in the tales recited by old people around the fire on winter evenings. Sometimes he appears as the creator of the earth, of man, and of the animals, and as the great culture-hero who taught the Crows all their arts and tribal institutions. At other times he assumes the contradictory rôle of a cheap trickster, participating in all sorts of comic adventures. The Sun, on the other hand, comes to the fore in actual religious practices. Though his character is vaguely defined, he usually appears as a dignified, benevolent, and powerful deity—virtually a supreme being.

Prayers and sacrifices, though also made to other supernatural beings, are addressed preëminently to the Sun. Warriors, before starting on an expedition, offer eagle feathers or fox hides to this deity in a ceremony at sunrise. The skins of albino buffaloes are dedicated to him with an appropriate ritual. Though steam baths certainly serve a purificatory function, the erection of a sweat-lodge is regarded primarily as an offering to the Sun.

The mainspring of native religion, however, is revelation. The spirits appear to men in dreams and visions, revealing information of practical value. The importance of visions scarcely admits of exaggeration. They are the source of all songs, art forms, and sacred ceremonies. They govern the conduct of hunting, warfare, and other communal activities. Through them alone can one attain wealth, prestige, success. All seek them, but not every one receives them. They color the whole life of the tribe. Visions come, unsolicited, to a few gifted individuals in dreams or at other times. The great majority, however, must court them deliberately by propitiating the spirits through self-torture. The seeker usually retires, after purification by bathing and sexual continence, to a lonely peak where he fasts. thirsts, and undergoes other hardships for four days. Very frequently he subjects himself to additional physical tortures. He may cut out a piece of flesh or chop off a finger joint. He may pierce his shoulder with an arrow, insert a stick, and tie a horse to it. Or he may fasten a rope to a flap of skin cut in his chest or back, and run around a pole or drag the skull of a bear or buffalo about, until the flesh gives way or he collapses from exhaustion. That persons in such an over-wrought state should see visions is scarcely surprising. Later events, of course, sometimes prove the revelation to have been deceptive or false, but there is no way of determining this fact in advance. The virtue of a vision can only be established by the pragmatic test of success. Faith, however, is infinite and uncritical.

The shamans or medicine men do not form a distinct class. They differ only in degree, not in kind, from other visionaries. They are simply men or women who have received important visions and have convincingly demonstrated the supernatural powers thus acquired. They are commonly thought to be invulnerable, or at least to possess extraordinary ability to recuperate from wounds. Most of them are adept at legerdemain. They can produce rabbits, even without a hat, and can convert a piece of bark into tobacco or meat. As their visions vary, so their powers and functions differ. Some specialize in prophesy and divination. Others, skilled in charming deer and buffaloes, direct hunting drives. Still others have special medicines for war, and are much sought after by young men ambitious to distinguish themselves. All have some acquaintance with magic. For example, a shaman may draw a picture of his enemy on a river bank; when the water rises and obliterates the image, the victim dies. To cause blindness, he may put a coal in the eye of the image. Rival shamans frequently engage in contests, in which each strives to demonstrate the superiority of his supernatural powers. If the affair is amicable, they seek merely to outdo each other in sleight of hand. Sometimes, however, they battle in grim earnest, bringing to bear all their gifts of sorcery to blind, paralyze, or impoverish the opponent and to cause his failure or death on the warpath.

Magic does not pervade the intellectual atmosphere of the Crows, as it does among some savage peoples. It remains distinctly subordinate to activities inspired by revelations

Even charms are not truly magical but are obtained from spirits through visions. Nor is disease explained by sorcery. It is attributed either to the malevolent act of a ghost or to the violation of a taboo. Few taboos apply to the tribe as a whole; in most cases they are based on specific visionary instructions and apply only to the recipient. Here, as elsewhere, the Crow religion reveals its essentially individualistic character. Certain herb specialists and wound-doctors, as well as true shamans, devote themselves to the curing of disease. Their methods, being based largely on visions, differ widely, with much specialization as a consequence. The commoner modes of treatment, however, include decoctions of herbs, hot applications, poultices, kneading, lancing, bleeding, blowing on the affected part, and sucking out the alleged cause through a pipestem.

Various sacred objects or "medicines" figure prominently in the religious life of the tribe. A stuffed bird, the tooth of a dead shaman, a weasel skin stuffed with buffalo hair—in short any object revealed in a vision as sacred—may be a medicine. Certain classes deserve special mention. Painted tipis, ornamented according to visionary instructions, belong to important medicine men and play a rôle in ceremonial. Sacred shields, decorated with revealed designs, furnish supernatural protection in battle. Stones which chance to resemble the head of an animal are adopted as medicines and receive offerings and supplications. Medicine bundles convey immunity in war; a typical example includes an arrow, several horse tails, a bunch of feathers, and the skin of a buffalo calf painted with horse tracks. If a man achieves striking success, thereby proving the potency of his medicine, he may make reproductions of it and sell them to persons anxious to share his fortune. With the fourth replica, however, his property right lapses.

Four, the sacred number of the Indians, reappears repeatedly in their ceremonial. Though ritual does not dominate the life of the Crows, it finds expression in a number of minor ceremonies and a few major ones.   It clusters particularly about the cultivation of tobacco, a privilege confined to the members of a Tobacco Society. The songs, regalia, and ritual of this society have originated in visions, and vary somewhat in the different chapters.   Initiation into the order involves heavy fees to the members, and takes place at a special adoption lodge in a ceremony characterized by songs, dances, smoking a communal pipe, a sweat bath, scourging, and prayers. In May, after the seed has been mixed according to a revealed ritual, the members of the society, painted and arrayed in their finest, form a ceremonial procession to the field and plant their tobacco amid singing, dancing, and feasting. During the growing season they observe certain taboos, and after the harvest they dance in the adoption lodge with the newly gathered tobacco. The lodge, the mode of painting, and the right to mix the seed are the private property of individual members of the society; for their use the owners receive handsome fees.

The most spectacular native ceremony is the Sun Dance, held every few years when a man who has lost a near relative at the hands of a hostile tribe decides to show the excess of his grief by vowing revenge in this manner. Returning to camp after a period of severe mourning, he notifies the chief to preserve the tongues of all buffaloes caught on the next hunt. He then chooses a medicine man, the owner of a particularly potent medicine bundle containing a doll, to act as master of ceremonies. The mourner abstains from food and drink for several days, during which dances are held, the buffalo tongues are distributed, a tree symbolizing an enemy is cut down, and a special lodge is erected—all according to an elaborate ritual. Warriors enter the lodge in search of visions; many suspend themselves from the poles by thongs passed through incisions in the breast and shoulder, or mortify the flesh in other ways. On the last day of the ceremony, the mourner dances to the beat of the drum with a whistle in his mouth, until he collapses from exhaustion and is dragged to his bed. Here he remains until he receives a vision of a vanquished enemy, when the warriors begin preparations for an expedition of revenge.

The traditional enemies of the Crows are the Blackfeet and Dakotas, though from time to time they have fought with practically all the surrounding tribes, the Arapaho, Cheyennes, Shoshoni, Flatheads, and Nez Percés. Though revenge sometimes precipitates a conflict, the dominant motive in war is individual ambition for honor and glory. Personal prestige among the Crows depends primarily on martial exploits. Age, intelligence, and skill count for little by comparison. The warrior strives for deeds that will bring him credit and advance his social standing. Such deeds, however, must comply with a rigid conventional standard. It is honorable, of course, to slay an enemy, and it is pleasant to bring back a scalp as a trophy. But the deeds that really count, the exploits that enhance a man's prestige and bring him glory, are four in number: leading a successful war party, capturing an enemy's bow, driving off a horse tethered in a hostile camp, and "counting coup." The fourth —and in some respects the greatest—of these consists in being the first to touch an enemy. The warrior may count coup with his hand, his spear, or a special coup-stick, and he may score in this way on a fallen foe, on a living and armed warrior, or even on a defenseless woman. The second person to touch the victim also receives some credit; the third and fourth, a little. A man who has performed each of these four meritorious feats at least once becomes automatically a chief. A dispute over the credit for an exploit is settled by an oath invoking the Sun; the contestant who first suffers a misfortune thereafter is branded as a liar. Men frequently amuse themselves in friendly contests over military honors. They divide into two groups, often along clan lines, and spokesmen for each side enumerate the meritorious deeds of their partisans until one side emerges triumphant.

Any man may organize a war party. But he must first have a vision, or else purchase medicine and receive the details of a vision from a war shaman. When he announces his intention and his revelation, all who are greedy for honors flock to his standard and make ready their weapons— bows and arrows, spears tipped with the prongs of elk antlers, hafted stone war clubs, and circular shields of buffalo hide. Scouts, smeared with gray clay to look like wolves and wearing the skins of these animals, explore the terrain in advance. The captain, *i.e.*, the visionary or organizer, commands the main party. He wears a magpie tail as the symbol of leadership and is absolved from the menial tasks incidental

After Lowie

FIG. 69. A CROW WAR CLUB.

to the expedition. His medicine is carried at the head of the party by another man. The warriors sometimes amuse themselves around the campfire at night by calling off the names of the women who have been their mistresses. If the husband of such a woman is present, he assumes an air of indifference, though he may discard his faithless wife on his return.

When the party approaches the destination specified in the vision, the captain unwraps his medicine, offers it incense, and sings a song against the enemy. When the scouts sight a hostile party they return with the news. After advancing to survey the situation, the warriors usually place themselves in ambush along the enemy's line of march, and fall upon them when they approach. Rarely, however, do they pursue their advantage to the utmost, for when one foe has been brought down, they all make a mad rush to count coup on his fallen body. In theory all plunder belongs to the captain, but in practice he always divides it. The victors occasionally treat their wounded foes with great cruelty, and they customarily take the scalps of the slain. Captive women become the property of their captors, who either marry them or give them to other men. Even male prisoners, especially young boys, are often adopted into the tribe. The returning warriors blacken their faces in token of victory and mark their shirts with emblems of their coups. The women go forth to meet them and escort them into camp with a dance. Fathers sing in praise of the exploits of their sons. The jubilant warriors assemble for a victory dance, beating drums, singing songs, telling stories of the encounter, and praising those who have counted coup. If a single Crow has been killed, however, no celebration is held. A messenger signals the sad news to the camp. The war party remains in the hills for ten days to mourn, then sets out on another expedition without returning home.

Military honors directly affect government. The men who have to their credit at least one of each of the four meritorious martial exploits, hold the rank of chiefs and constitute an informal advisory council. In each camp, one of them acts as head chief. He holds his office, not by election, but by virtue of his recognized precedence over the rest in the accumulation of war honors. The head chief has little real authority except on a buffalo hunt and other occasions demanding concerted action. In particular he determines when camp shall be moved, and where, and assigns the positions of the various lodges. He is expected to be liberal with food, and returning hunters frequently leave a supply of meat for this purpose at his tipi. A man of distinction in each camp holds the office of herald, and makes all announcements of general interest.

Primitive and informal methods predominate in the preservation of law and order. If two men become enraged, a pipe is thrust between them; to disobey this command to desist means instant death. Murder leads to blood-revenge unless the criminal or his clansmen pay an indemnity to the clan of the slain man. In case of adultery, the injured hus·band has the right to destroy or appropriate the property of the male offender, and he may punish his wife by beating her severely, gashing her face and head with a knife, or even allowing his clansmen to exercise marital rights with her. Rarely, however, does he exercise his privilege, and often he does not even discard his wayward spouse. Ridicule serves as a powerful regulative weapon, for no punishment is more real and severe to a Crow than to be made the laughing stock of his people. Derisive songs are sung in public at the expense of the perpetrator of an injustice. A man who has violated a tribal custom becomes the butt of gibes and jeers from his "joking relatives." If he has married a woman of his own clan, for example, they taunt him with marrying his sister, and remark scornfully that he has no brother-in-law save his own rump. They may even cut off a lock of his hair—a terrible humiliation, which many would rather die than suffer.

Important regulative functions are exercised by certain clubs or societies, partly military and partly social in character. Membership depends, not on age or clan affiliations, but on election. When a member dies, the society invites a relative to fill the vacancy. Upon the officers, elected annually, devolve hazardous duties on the battlefield. The four staff-bearers in each society, for example, must plant their staffs in the ground at the beginning of an engagement and remain with them till the end, even at the risk of death. Each spring the head chief appoints one of the societies to act as the camp police force for the ensuing year. They enforce the rules of the camp, restrain war parties from setting out at an inopportune time, prevent the premature startling of a herd on a buffalo hunt, and punish offenders. Between the two most famous clubs, the Foxes and the Lumpwoods, an intense rivalry prevails during the summer

season. Every spring the members of either society are
entitled to kidnap any of the wives of their rivals with whom
they have been on terms of intimacy. A despoiled husband
may neither resist nor show resentment, nor under any
circumstances take his wife back again. The abducting
society leads the woman to one of their lodges and celebrates with songs and dances. On the following day they
dress as for war, parade with their captive before the eyes
of their opponents, and hold another dance. The woman is
then placed in the custody of her lover, to be abandoned
as a rule after a brief period. When all the wives eligible
for capture have been stolen, the two societies go on the
warpath, where they continue their rivalry. If a Fox, for
example, counts coup first, his club-mates are privileged to
steal and adapt the Lumpwood songs.

The Crows, though they despise the whites, have rarely
molested them, except occasionally to plunder them. At
times they have even aided them, as when they acted as
scouts for Custer's expedition. Though visited as early as
1742, they did not feel the pressure of our westward expansion for a century thereafter. By a series of treaties with
the United States in 1868 and the following years, they
relinquished all their lands except a reservation of some two
million acres in southern Montana, where they have since
been confined. They have never troubled the government,
except in 1890, when a medicine man named Wraps-up-
his-tail, chafing under alien restraint and asserting supernatural powers as the result of a vision, led a few Crows
in a very minor and abortive uprising. The population,
never more than 7,000, has been reduced by new diseases,
the excessive use of alcohol, and changed life conditions to
about 1,800 at present. It is no longer decreasing, but
extensive intermarriage with the whites has diminished the
proportion of full-blooded Indians to only a little more
than half. The native culture has suffered especially from
the disappearance of the buffalo, which has deprived the

Crows, not only of their primary food supply, but also of their principal source of clothing, shelter, fuel, and utensils. They have turned largely to the raising of horses and cattle, though a few have taken up agriculture. The tribe is comparatively prosperous today, owning land and other property valued in excess of $10,000,000. Catholic and Protestant missionaries have converted the great majority to Christianity, and many of the children receive an education at mission schools. Over ten per cent of the Crows have become full American citizens, and in another generation the tribe will probably have merged with the general population.

BIBLIOGRAPHY

BUSHNELL, D. I., JR. "Burials of the Algonquian, Siouan, and Caddoan Tribes West of the Mississippi." *Smithsonian Institution, Bureau of American Ethnology, Bulletin 83*. Washington, 1927.

——. "Villages of the Algonquian, Siouan, and Caddoan Tribes West of the Mississippi." *Smithsonian Institution, Bureau of American Ethnology, Bulletin 77*. Washington, 1922.

CAMPBELL, W. S. "The Tipis of the Crow Indians." *American Anthropologist, New Series, Vol. XXIX*. Menasha, 1927.

CATLIN, G. *Illustrations of the Manners, Customs, and Conditions of the North American Indians*. Sixth edition. 2 vols. London, 1848.

CURTIS, E. S. *The North American Indian*, Vol. IV. Seattle, 1909.

DONALDSON, T. "The George Catlin Indian Gallery in the U. S. National Museum." *Smithsonian Institution, Annual Report of the Board of Regents to July, 1885*, Part 2. Washington, 1886.

GOLDENWEISER, A. A. "Remarks on the Social Organization of the Crow Indians." *American Anthropologist, New Series, Vol. XV*. Lancaster, 1914.

GRINNELL, G. B. "Coup and Scalp among the Plains Indians." *American Anthropologist, New Series, Vol. XII*. Lancaster, 1910.

HAYDEN, F. V. *Contributions to the Ethnography and Philology of the Indian Tribes of the Missouri Valley*. Philadelphia, 1862.

HODGE, F. W. (editor). "Handbook of American Indians North of Mexico." *Smithsonian Institution, Bureau of American Ethnology, Bulletin 30.* 2 vols. Washington, 1907–10.

LINDERMAN, F. B. *American.* New York, 1930.

——. *Red Mother.* New York, 1932.

LOWIE, R. H. "Crow Indian Art." *Anthropological Papers of the American Museum of Natural History,* Vol. XXI. New York, 1922.

——. "The Kinship Systems of the Crow and Hidatsa." *Proceedings of the Nineteenth International Congress of Americanists.* Washington. 1917.

*——. "The Material Culture of the Crow Indians." *Anthropological Papers of the American Museum of Natural History,* Vol. XXI. New York, 1922.

——. "Military Societies of the Crow Indians." *Anthropological Papers of the American Museum of Natural History,* Vol. XI. New York, 1913.

——. "Minor Ceremonies of the Crow Indians." *Anthropological Papers of the American Museum of Natural History,* Vol. XXI. New York, 1924.

——. "Myths and Traditions of the Crow Indians." *Anthropological Papers of the American Museum of Natural History,* Vol. XXV. New York, 1918.

——. "Notes on the Social Organization and Customs of the Mandan, Hidatsa, and Crow Indians." *Anthropological Papers of the American Museum of Natural History,* Vol. XXI. New York, 1917.

*——. "The Religion of the Crow Indians." *Anthropological Papers of the American Museum of Natural History,* Vol. XXV. New York, 1922.

*——. "Social Life of the Crow Indians." *Anthropological Papers of the American Museum of Natural History,* Vol. IX. New York, 1912.

——. "Some Problems in the Ethnology of the Crow and Village Indians." *American Anthropologist,* New Series, Vol. XIV. Lancaster, 1912.

——. "The Sun Dance of the Crow Indians." *Anthropological Papers of the American Museum of Natural History,* Vol. XVI. New York, 1915.

LOWIE, R. H.   "The Tobacco Society of the Crow Indians." *Anthropological Papers of the American Museum of Natural History*, Vol. XXI. New York, 1919.

MARQUIS, T. B. *Memoirs of a White Crow Indian*. New York, 1928.

SIMMS, S. C. "Traditions of the Crows." *Field Columbian Museum, Anthropological Series*, Vol. II. Chicago, 1903.

SULLIVAN, L. R. "Anthropometry of the Siouan Tribes." *Anthropological Papers of the American Museum of Natural History*, Vol. XXIII. New York, 1920.

WIED-NEUWIED, Maximilian zu. *Travels in the Interior of North America*. Trans. by H. E. Lloyd. London, 1843.

WISSLER, C. "The Influence of the Horse in the Development of Plains Culture." *American Anthropologist*, New Series, Vol. XVI. Lancaster, 1914.

——. *North American Indians of the Plains*. New York, 1912.

CHAPTER XI

THE IROQUOIS OF NORTHERN NEW YORK

WHEN first discovered by Europeans, the Iroquois Indians or "Five Nations" occupied the lake region and Mohawk valley of northern New York, a fertile territory extending from the Hudson River on the east to the Genesee River on the west and from the Adirondack Mountains on the north to approximately the present boundary of Pennsylvania on the south. The climate of this region is temperate and is characterized by four definite seasons, including a comparatively mild winter and a summer sufficiently long and warm to be ideal for agriculture. An abundant rainfall feeds innumerable springs, streams, and lakes, and nourishes a varied flora. Forests of pine, spruce, hemlock, cedar, ash, elm, oak, maple, chestnut, and hickory clothe the hills and fertile valleys. Fish abound in the lakes and streams, and the bird life is rich and varied. The native mammals include the bear, deer, moose, wolf, fox, cougar, lynx, raccoon, otter, porcupine, opossum, beaver, skunk, badger, hare, and squirrel. In former times even the bison was not unknown.

The Iroquois reveal physical characteristics fairly typical of the Indians in general: tall stature (nearly five feet eight inches in men), light coppery brown skins, straight black hair, scanty beards, black eyes, prominent cheek bones, and heads of medium breadth (cephalic index 79). In language they belong to the Iroquoian linguistic stock, as do the neighboring Hurons on the north, the Neutrals and Eries on the west, and the Conestoga on the south. To the northeast, east, and southeast, however, lie tribes of alien speech, the Algonquian Adirondacks, Mahicans, and Delawares. Other Iroquoian peoples, notably the Tuscaroras and Cherokees, inhabit North Carolina and adjoining regions of Virginia,

Tennessee, Georgia, and South Carolina. Before the dawn of history, the various Iroquoian tribes dispersed to their later homes from a common center not far from the mouth of the Ohio River. About the year 1570, weakened by wars with the Algonquian peoples and their own kinsmen, five of these tribes united for mutual protection and formed the famous League of the Iroquois. These five tribes were, from east to west, the Mohawks, Oneidas, Onondagas, Cayugas, and Senecas. They constitute the Iroquois proper, the other tribes of kindred speech remaining outside the League.

By the time of their discovery, in 1609, the Iroquois had advanced to a position of cultural leadership among the Indians of northeastern North America, and they retain to the present day the shell of their aboriginal civilization. We are here interested, however, not in the shell but in the substance, that is, in the native culture as it existed when the white man first arrived.

The Iroquois, since their language lacks labial consonants, "can talk with their pipe in their teeth." In addition to the singular and plural, they distinguish a dual number. Where we use the one pronoun "we," they employ four distinct words, meaning respectively "thou and I," "he and I," "ye and I," and "they and I." Adjectives usually coalesce with their nouns to form a single word. The vocabulary, indeed, is predominantly polysyllabic. Though unacquainted with the art of writing, the Iroquois use pictographs and mnemonic aids. They describe military exploits on posts by means of animal figures and other symbols, and they keep records with the aid of tally sticks and wampum. A string of wampum—shell beads—accompanies every important agreement, communication, or transaction of any kind, and alone gives it validity. Certain civil officials are charged with the duty of keeping the wampum and remembering the terms of the treaties and agreements with which the various strings are associated. Once a year, in public assembly, they bring forth these primitive records, one by one, and solemnly repeat the exact meaning of each. The Iroquois possess a decimal system of numeration, and can count into the hundreds of thousands.

Nature furnishes many food products obtainable without specialized implements. Thus the natives gather and eat mushrooms and a variety of edible leaves and shoots. From the bark of the maple and from pond lily roots, wild parsnips, and groundnuts, dried and pulverized, they make a kind of bread. In the autumn they collect quantities of walnuts, hickory nuts, butternuts, hazelnuts, beechnuts, chestnuts, and acorns, and utilize them as ingredients in many of their dishes. They also gather wild grapes, cherries, and plums, and wild strawberries, raspberries, blackberries, gooseberries, cranberries, and huckleberries, which they dry, press into cakes, and mix with other foods. They tap the maple tree with the aid of bark funnels and buckets. The sap, when fresh, is a favorite beverage; boiled and condensed into maple syrup and sugar, it is used extensively as a condiment. The eggs of the quail, partridge, wild duck, and other birds are collected and eaten, preferably when just ready to hatch. Frogs, turtles and their eggs, crayfish, and clams likewise find a place on the native menu. Ants, eaten raw, are highly esteemed for their acid flavor. Poor people even gather deer excrement and make from it a kind of soup.

The Iroquois devote the late autumn and early winter to hunting, and carry on only desultory trapping at other seasons. A taboo on the flesh of pregnant animals operates as a sort of game law to protect females at certain times of the year. Before setting out to hunt, the men commonly fast, bathe, and offer sacrifices, and they rely on charms and dreams to bring them success. The women often accompany them to prepare and bring home the game. The principal weapon of the chase is the bow and arrow. The native arrow is about three feet long, tipped with a head of bone, horn, or chipped chert, equipped with feathers twisted so as to cause rotation in flight, and carried in a deerskin quiver slung across the back. The bow, nearly four feet in length, is capable of projecting an arrow with sufficient velocity and force easily to penetrate a human skull; even to draw back the string of this powerful weapon requires considerable muscular strength and long practice. Hunters usually stalk their quarry singly or in small parties. They pursue bears until they tire them out; in winter they easily overtake them on snowshoes. Occasionally a large party of hunters fires the woods and drives a herd of deer between two converging fences of brushwood, at the mouth of which they are shot from ambush. Deer are also caught in nooses fixed to bent saplings, and bears are secured in deadfalls so constructed that, when sprung, a heavy timber falls and pins the animal to the ground. There are similar traps for smaller mammals. The Indians hunt pigeons at night with torches and sticks, they catch quails and other birds in snares and in nets made from bark fiber, and they shoot all manner of feathered game with a long blowgun and slender pointed darts.

In the spring, when fishing is especially productive, the natives resort to the streams and lakes to catch salmon, sturgeon, trout, and eels. They angle with unbarbed bone hooks. They employ traps, open-mesh baskets, dip nets, seines with stone sinkers, and spears either with or without points of stone and bone. They shoot fish with the bow and arrow. They drive them into weirs by dragging a grapevine, stretched across a stream, along the bottom. The favorite fishing implement, however, is a harpoon with a barbed bone head loosely attached to a socketed shaft by means of a thong and toggle. The men go out at night in their canoes, carrying a fire blazing on a bed of bark and gravel, and harpoon the eels attracted by the light.

The primary source of subsistence, however, is agriculture, an art at which the Iroquois surpass all their neighbors. Sometimes several hundred acres of tilled land surround a single village. Of maize or Indian corn, the staple crop, several varieties are known—flint and starchy corns as well as sweet corn and popcorn. In the same fields with the maize, and usually in the same hills, the Iroquois plant beans, squashes, and pumpkins. They cultivate tobacco, melons, and sunflowers in separate plots. Tracts of land are cleared by burning them over, or by felling the trees with the alternate use of fire and stone axes. For preparing the soil and removing weeds, the Indians use only a primitive hoe—either a simple wooden pick, a piece of an antler, the shoulder blade of a deer, or a sharpened tortoise shell attached to a stick. Before planting, they invariably soak the seeds in herb concoctions or "medicines," which, though superstitious in purpose, actually serve to promote germination. They make several holes in each hill with a digging stick, drop in the seeds, and cover them up. Furry and feathered thieves are caught in snares and traps or are frightened away from the growing crops with whistles blown by the wind. When the grain is ripe, the ears are picked, stripped with a husking pin, and braided into bunches by means of a few husks left for the purpose. The Iroquois understand the principles of transplanting and selection. Each year they save for seed the ears which seem superior with regard to size, color, flavor, and early maturity. On the other hand, they plant their fields every year to the same crops, and use no fertilizers. As a result, the land becomes exhausted in ten or twelve years, and the whole village must move to a new site.

The Iroquois store venison and other meats, cured by drying and smoking, in underground pits lined with skins and covered with earth. They cut squashes and pumpkins into strips, dry them, and preserve them in similar caches lined with bark. Maize is parched or dried and stored in bark barrels or hung in bunches in the dwellings. Parched corn, pounded into a fine meal with maple sugar, makes a very compact and nutritive food for hunters and warriors. To prepare corn meal, the maize is shelled by hand, crushed in a wooden mortar, and sifted through a basket sieve. The women do the cooking over a fire of hardwood, generated by means of a pump drill. Meat and fish are usually boiled in earthen pots or broiled on spits. Beans, squashes, and pump-kins are boiled, baked, and mashed. The recipes involving maize, numbering nearly fifty, include green corn boiled on the cob, roasted ears, popcorn popped in the open fire, un-leavened corn bread, dumplings, puddings, hominy and mush, succotash, and soups of all kinds. Many of these dishes, as well as the vegetables from which they are pre-pared, have been borrowed outright by the white man. The native succotash consists of green corn cut from the cob and boiled with beans, pumpkins, or other vegetables in season. The corn bread, to which nuts, beans, and dried berries are often added, is sometimes baked in hot ashes or on a flat stone, but is usually boiled in a pot of water. One kind, often carried in traveling, has become known as "johnnycake," from "journey cake." Soups are prepared from green, dried, and parched corn, boiled with game, vegetables, berries, and nuts, and flavored with maple sugar and the oil extracted from sunflower seeds. Similar ingredients are added to hominy, although nothing is thought to impart quite so delicate a flavor as a decomposed fish.

The Indians take only one regular cooked meal a day, at ten or eleven o'clock in the morning; at other times people simply help themselves to soup or to cold hominy whenever they feel hungry. The men eat first and by themselves, the women and children afterwards. The diners either stand or sit, and use dishes and ladles of bark or wood. Food dropped on the ground is left for the ghosts of the dead. The Iroquois make no intoxicating liquor from maize. Their favorite beverage is maple sap, occasionally fermented, but they also drink broths, the juice of corn stalks, water flavored with maple sugar and berry juices, and "teas" brewed from hem-lock twigs, birch bark, sassafras roots, etc. They smoke tobacco, mixed with sumac leaves, in stone and earthenware pipes. They chew, not tobacco, but spruce gum, the bark of the basswood and slippery elm, and a spongy tissue obtained from the teats of female deer.

The dog, the only domesticated animal of the Iroquois, is used for food but not for transportation. The natives carry all burdens on their own backs. With the aid of a tumpline or burden strap across the forehead, they transport maize in baskets, and fuel, game, and household effects in a wooden frame. Trained runners, capable of traversing as much as a hundred miles a day, convey intelligence from village to village and from tribe to tribe over beaten trails through the forests. In the winter the Indians travel on snowshoes and use sleds to a limited extent. On the lakes and rivers they employ canoes made from a single strip of elm bark reënforced with ribs and rim of ash. Owing to the scarcity of suitable birch trees in their environment, they rarely make birchbark canoes, but their heavier and clumsier vessels are sometimes large enough to hold twenty men or a cargo of two tons or more.

Hunters and warriors erect temporary shelters of bark on a framework of three poles. At home, however, the Iroquois occupy large communal houses grouped irregularly in villages of from three hundred to three thousand inhabitants. In most cases a village is situated beside a lake, stream, or spring, and is surrounded, for purposes of defense, by a trench and a high palisade of stakes surmounted by a platform from which stones and weapons can be hurled at an approaching enemy. The "long house," the characteristic Iroquois dwelling, is a substantial rectangular building twenty to thirty feet in breadth, approximately the same in height, and from fifty to one hundred and fifty—in one recorded case, three hundred—feet in length. A framework of upright poles, beams, and rafters supports a rounded or arched roof with holes for the escape of smoke. Flattened slabs of dried bark are laid like clapboards on the side and end walls, and like shingles on the roof. Throughout the length of the house runs a corridor, with fires at intervals of about twenty feet. Each fire serves two of the numerous related families which inhabit the dwelling. Each individual family occupies an apartment at one side of a fire. A platform of bark, about twelve feet long by six feet in width, raised a foot or two from the ground, and covered with mats and skins, serves the family as a seat by day and a bed by night. Along the wall, above the platform, is a shelf for tools, utensils, and clothing, and between the beds of adjoining apartments are storage spaces for barrels of maize and the like. At each end of the dwelling a door of bark or

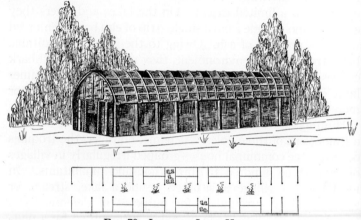

FIG. 70. IROQUOIS LONG HOUSE.

skins leads outside through a small lobby reserved for firewood and an exterior porch where the men congregate in summer. To accommodate additional families, the inmates tear down the end walls and add extra apartments. The houses, though cool in summer and comfortable in winter, are infested with vermin and are often unsavory with the odor of dried or smoking fish.

The Iroquois possess no metals, and they display a marked distaste for working in stone. To be sure, they manufacture arrowheads, hammers, and rude knives of chipped chert, and very occasionally a mortar and pestle, chisel, or scraper of polished stone. Their most important stone implement, however, is a polished ax or celt, shaped like a wedge, and secured in a hole in a wooden handle. Sometimes a young sapling is split and a celt inserted; when the growing tree has clasped the stone securely, it is cut off and fashioned into a handle. But the natives use other materials than stone whenever possible. From bone and horn they manufacture needles, awls, punches, knives, and combs. Clamshells serve them as

FIG. 71. REPRESENTATIVE IROQUOIS UTENSILS: EARTHEN POT, BARK TRAY, BARK BARREL, AND WOODEN MORTAR AND PESTLE.

rude knives and spoons. They make scrapers and paddles of wood, and from maple knots they carve dishes, bowls, and spoons, the latter often provided with handles sculptured to represent animals. For pounding maize they use a pestle of hardwood and a mortar excavated from a block of oak. From bark, which they prefer even to wood, they manufacture a variety of ladles, bowls, dishes, trays, tubs, barrels, and other household articles. Cooking utensils and pipes are made of pottery. The native potter mixes clay with pulverized rock, fashions it into a long rope, coils the rope roughly into the shape of a pot, smoothes out the coils by hand, dries the vessel in the sun, and bakes it in a slow fire. Iroquois pots rarely deviate from a single standardized pattern with a rounded bottom. a constricted neck, and a flaring rim decorated with conventional incised designs of dots and lines. The earthenware pipes, on the other hand, display great æsthetic freedom and originality in the ornamentation of their graceful bowls with geometric designs and in their realistic representation of human and animal figures. They are, indeed, the finest aboriginal pipes north of Mexico.

The textile arts show a moderate development. From splints of ash wood, as well as from rushes and corn husks, the Iroquois weave baskets for numerous purposes. They twist the fibers of bark and wild hemp into thread between the palm of the hand and the bare thigh. They braid cordage of various sizes, weave bags and fishing nets, and plait mats of rushes, bark, and corn husks. Their finest textile product, however, is the tumpline or burden strap, woven by hand with a warp of heavy cords and a woof of fine threads or animal hair, and beautifully embroidered with dyed porcupine quills. The Iroquois do not make cloth. For clothing and bags they use only skins, prepared by scraping, soaking in a mixture containing animal brains, stretching, drying, and smoking.

Most of the native garments are made of deerskin ornamented with quill embroidery and fringes of human hair. The men wear a breechcloth, a leather belt, a short sleeveless tunic, a kilt or short petticoat extending to the knees, leggings, moccasins, and an outer robe of fur. The female costume lacks the breechcloth and includes a somewhat longer kilt, but is similar in other respects. In warm weather, however, the men frequently dispense with everything but the breechcloth, and the women retain only the kilt. For traveling in winter they sometimes add separate sleeves, tied to the shoulders with thongs. The commonest ornaments are necklaces of perforated shells, rude stone or bone beads, and animal teeth. On ceremonial occasions the men wear knee rattles of deer hoofs and an elaborate headdress consisting of a frame of splints surmounted by a tuft of small feathers and by a single long eagle feather inclining backwards. They shave their heads for war, leaving only a small scalp-lock on top for the convenience of a victorious enemy.

The Iroquois carry on a certain amount of trade with the surrounding tribes, exchanging their surplus grain and manufactures for skins, wampum, and birchbark canoes. Specialization by occupation is but slightly developed, although old men and those incapable of hunting and fighting devote themselves to the making of bows and arrows, nets, and wooden utensils. On the other hand, a rigid division of labor by sex prevails. The men hunt, fish, wage war, make weapons, build houses and palisades, make canoes, paddles, and snowshoes, manufacture bark and wooden utensils, and assist the women in clearing the land and harvesting the crops. Practically the entire burden of the agriculture falls on the women, who, in addition, cook, keep house, care for the children, gather roots, berries, fruits, nuts, and firewood, smoke and dry fish and game, make baskets and pottery, weave, carry burdens, do the quill embroidery, and make clothing and wampum. Coöperation plays a prominent rôle in the economic activities of both sexes. Thus the men combine to hunt, fish, and build houses. The women unite at planting time under an elderly matron, and work on the various fields in rotation under her direction. At harvest time they coöperate in similar fashion, and they husk the maize at communal "husking bees."

The women work long and hard, and associate very little with the men. A menstruating woman is considered unclean and dangerous. She must not engage in agricultural operations, or come in contact with food and medicines, or touch the implements belonging to the men. Facts like these led one early observer to call the Iroquois woman "the inferior, the dependent, and the servant of man." Nothing could be farther from the truth. A husband has no authority over his wife. One woman, urged by her spouse to do something against her will, replied: "I am my own mistress, I do what I choose; and do thou what thou choosest." The wife enjoys strictly independent property rights. She alone exercises authority over the children. She is the mistress of the apartment in the long house occupied by the family. The husband always goes to live with his wife, and he is present in the home only on sufferance. "No matter how many children, or whatever goods he might have in the house, he might at any time be ordered to pick up his blanket and budge; and after such orders it would not be healthful for him to disobey." When he leaves, he can take nothing with him except his clothing, weapons, and pipe, for the house and all its utensils and furniture, stores of food, and land belong exclusively to the women. From these and other social, political, and religious rights, the native women may be said to enjoy a status at least equal, if not superior, to that of the men. Indeed, of all the peoples of the earth, the Iroquois approach most closely to that hypothetical form of society known as the "matriarchate."

The unit of society is not the individual or the family but the household or—perhaps more accurately—the maternal lineage. Its core consists of a body of adult women who occupy together a single long house and who trace their descent in the female line from a common ancestress. Children, both own and adopted, belong to the household or lineage of their mother. A man, when he marries, takes up his residence in his wife's household, but he acquires no rights there and does not forfeit his membership in his mother's group. The authority in the long house rests in the hands, not of a man, but of an old woman, a chieftainess or chief matron, who is normally the grandmother, mother, maternal aunt, or elder sister of the other women. She supervises the domestic economy and exercises important political functions, assisted by a council composed of all the women of child-bearing age. Each household worships a tutelary divinity, whose cult is tended by a special priestess or medicine woman, and whose animal fetish or "totem" is frequently painted on the gable end of the house.

Within the household, property is communal. Individuals, in general, own little more than what they can carry on their persons, and this property is inherited in the female line. The possessions of a woman descend to her children or her sisters; those of a man, to his brothers or his sisters' children, never to his wife or his own offspring. But the implements and utensils of domestic use, the accumulated stores of food, and even such things as war trophies and medicines, belong to the household in common, or rather to its adult female members. Food, for example, though cooked at the separate hearths, is pooled and distributed by the chief matron among the various families. Agricultural lands are likewise the communal property of the household, although special fields are usually reserved for the village as a whole, to furnish food for festivals and similar general purposes. Households differ in wealth, but such differences are slight and mostly temporary, for communistic practice exerts a leveling influence. "A whole village must be without corn before any individual can be obliged to endure starvation."

A number of households or lineages, united by blood and a common totem, constitute a clan, a kin-group characterized by exogamy, matrilineal descent, and the duty of aiding its members, redressing their injuries, and avenging their death. Each clan has a body of chiefs or officers and a council on which both sexes are represented. The Iroquois clans for the most part bear animal names, *e.g.*, Bear, Turtle, Snipe, Eel, but they are not strictly totemic since they do not worship their eponymous animals, taboo them as food, or regard them as ancestors. The number of clans varies from tribe to tribe, but eight may be regarded as typical. Normally, the clans of a tribe are divided into two moieties or phratries. In the Seneca tribe, for example, the Bear,

Wolf, Turtle, and Beaver clans constitute the first moiety; the Deer, Snipe, Heron, and Hawk, the second. The Mohawk and Oneida tribes are exceptional in possessing but three clans each and in lacking phratries. The moiety has no officers other than those of the constituent clans. It functions as a social and ceremonial rather than as a political unit. Thus the members of one moiety conduct funerals for those of the other, oppose them in games of skill and chance, and intermarry with them according to exogamous rules.

The tribe is a political unit, with a definite territory, a common dialect, and a council of chiefs representing the various clans. Hunting and fishing grounds and all natural monopolies are tribal property, available to all. Though enjoying local autonomy and a considerable measure of political independence, the five Iroquois tribes have banded together, like the states in the United States, to form a federal union on a basis of mutual equality—the celebrated League of the Iroquois. This confederacy has as its primary purpose the preservation of peace among its members by the prohibition of internal warfare and by the substitution of atonement for blood-revenge. Its great founders, Dekanawida and Hiawatha, were even animated by the ideal of ultimately bringing all peoples into the union, of expanding the League of the Iroquois into a League of Nations. Following this ideal, the "Five Nations," at subsequent periods in their history, have admitted other tribes into their federation, notably the Tuscaroras in 1715. But the League is more than a union of tribes; it is also a confederacy of clans. The Bear, Wolf, and Turtle clans occur in all five tribes, and the others in several. Thus clan ties cross tribal lines and help to cement the union. War between the Senecas and Cayugas, for example, would involve strife among brothers, for it would set Bear against Bear, Wolf against Wolf, etc. The League may thus be likened to a firmly woven fabric, in which the tribes form the warp and the clans the woof.

The supreme executive, legislative, and judicial authority is vested in a council of fifty great peace chiefs or sachems. The council exists primarily to maintain internal peace and order, although it also conducts foreign relations—declaring war, making treaties, entertaining embassies, etc. Far from exercising arbitrary powers, it is highly susceptible to public opinion. It assembles once each year in regular session at Onondaga, which is virtually the national capital, and it meets in extraordinary session whenever a public emergency arises. Any body of chiefs, warriors, or women may bring up a matter for discussion, submitting it first to a tribal council, which, if it considers the question of sufficient importance, has power to convoke a special session of the federal council. A messenger is sent out to each of the other tribes, bearing a string of wampum and a tally stick with notches to indicate the date of assembly.

A council provides the people with their principal opportunity for social intercourse, and they sometimes journey for hundreds of miles to listen to the oratory, exchange tales of military exploits, and participate in the games, feasts, and dances which always accompany a meeting. The debate is conducted around a council fire with uniform dignity and decorum. The interested parties present their cases to the sachems through spokesmen. The latter enjoy high repute, for oratory and arms are the two outstanding paths to fame and distinction among the Iroquois. The sachems must reach a unanimous decision, for the concept of majority rule is unknown. They vote, however, not as a body but by classes and tribes. The Seneca sachems, for example, are divided into four classes, the members of which meet separately, thresh out their differences, and arrive at a unanimous vote. Each class then appoints one sachem to meet with the representatives of the other three classes. They in turn reach an agreement and select one of their number to represent the Seneca tribe in conferences with delegates similarly chosen by the Cayugas, Onondagas,

Oneidas, and Mohawks. The unanimous decision of these five sachems is announced as the decision of the League. So strong are public opinion and the influences which can be brought to bear on an obdurate sachem under this method of voting, that the council rarely fails to reach an agreement. If unanimity is found impossible, however, the matter must perforce be dropped.

The five tribes do not enjoy equal representation on the council. The Senecas, for instance, have only eight sachems, while the Onondagas have fourteen. But this inequality matters little in view of the requirement of unanimity. Special respect and deference are accorded to one of the Onondaga sachems, although he is in no way a king or executive head of the League. Another Onondaga sachem holds the hereditary office of Keeper of the Wampum and has charge of the preservation of laws and treaties. The sachems are *ex officio* members of the councils of their respective tribes. They wear no distinguishing costume or badge of office. They exercise powers and functions of an exclusively civil or peaceful character; if they go to war, they must temporarily divest themselves of their authority and fight as common warriors. Each sachem has an assistant, who stands behind him on ceremonial occasions, acts as his messenger, keeps a check on his activities, and often succeeds him.

Succession follows the female line. Each sachemship is hereditary in a particular privileged household or lineage— not merely in a particular clan, although most of the clans in each tribe have at least one sachem. Within the household, however, the office is elective. No one possesses a special right to become the next sachem, although a younger brother or a sister's son is usually chosen in preference to a more distant kinsman. If an infant is elected, a guardian or regent, sometimes a woman, discharges the duties of the office until he reaches maturity. The nominating power is vested exclusively in the women. The chief matron, after consultation with a few other old women, selects a candidate from among her sons and grandsons, and calls together all the child-bearing women of the household in a council to which the other members of the clan are invited. When the council has ratified her choice, as it seldom fails to do, she notifies the chiefs of the other clans of the moiety and of the opposite moiety. Separate moiety councils confirm the candidate, and the tribe sends out messengers with wampum to summon the federal council into extraordinary session. At this so-called "condoling council," the sachems mourn their deceased colleague with appropriate civil rites and instal or "raise up" his successor. The new sachem drops his own name and assumes the hereditary title of his office, *i.e.*, the name of the original sachem whose place he is taking. Peace and order characterize the whole election process.

The federal council has the power to refuse confirmation and also to depose unworthy sachems, and it thus exercises sufficient control over its membership for its own protection, while the people find insurance against oppression and misgovernment through the power of recall. If a sachem loses the respect and confidence of his constituents, the chief matron of his household, after twice warning him, initiates impeachment proceedings against him at a clan council. His deposition then follows by the same steps as his election. Although women cannot hold the office of sachem, they exercise so large a measure of influence and control through their powers of nomination and deposition, that the tribal and federal councils may be said really to consist of their representatives.

Besides the sachems and assistant sachems, the Iroquois have a special class of lesser or "pine-tree" chiefs, similarly nominated and confirmed. These chiefs hold office for life, but their positions are not hereditary. They act as advisers and counselors to the sachems, and possess great influence in the tribes and clans. Women, as well as men, are occasionally honored with a "pine-tree" title. The office provides a means of recognizing and rewarding able warriors and orators, and of allaying discontent, without altering the constitution of the League.

The various councils meet as courts without juries to try criminal cases. They follow precedent and established rules of procedure in listening to the evidence and pronouncing sentence. Death is the penalty for witchcraft. The lash of public indignation suffices in the case of theft. For adultery, the woman alone is punished—by a public whipping—for she is "supposed to be the only offender." For flagrant or persistent disregard of the public welfare, a clan or tribal council may pronounce the sentence of outlawry. In case of murder or accidental homicide, the moieties of the murderer and his victim meet separately in council to determine the question of guilt and to arrange for atonement. To avoid blood-revenge, the kinsmen of the criminal send strings of wampum to the clansmen of the victim. The indemnity for slaying a woman is double that for killing a man.

Although the League occasionally engages in a general war and unites its forces under a single supreme war chieftain, it ordinarily leaves military operations entirely to private enterprise. The Iroquois are theoretically at war with all peoples with whom they are not definitely allied, and any man who thirsts for personal glory and adventure, and who can enlist a band of followers, may take to the warpath. After a feast, a war dance, and rites of divination, the party sets out. Scouts move well in advance, while the main body marches in single file, carefully covering up its tracks with leaves. The weapons of war include the bow and arrow, a knife of stone or bone, a tomahawk or stone ax, a war club weighted at one end with a knot of wood or a ball of stone, a sword-shaped club equipped with a sharp spike of horn, a shield of wood or bark, and a suit of armor consisting of reeds or wooden rods woven together with thongs or fiber threads. The tomahawk is the symbol of war. To raise it is to open hostilities, while to "bury the hatchet" is to conclude peace. The Iroquois prefer tactics of surprise and stratagem. They commonly fight in the woods, each warrior seeking shelter behind the nearest rock or tree. Sometimes, however, they make concerted attacks on fortified towns, trying to ignite the houses with flaming arrows and to burn or hew down the palisades under cover of a testudo of planks. They remove the scalps of slain enemies, stretch them on hoops, scrape them clean, and dry

After Morgan and Beauchamp
FIG. 72. IROQUOIS WAR CLUBS.

them over the fire. Oftentimes they take the entire head. They return home with their wounded comrades strapped in burden frames on their backs, and are welcomed with speeches and a war dance.

The Iroquois never exchange prisoners; they either kill or adopt them. Each household that has lost a warrior has the right to select a captive to replace him. Then others choose from among the remaining prisoners those whom for any reason they desire to adopt. Death by torture is the fate of the rest. The Iroquois frequently tie captives of either sex to a stake, bite off their fingers, tear out their nails, gash them with knives, and burn them to death over a slow fire. Sometimes they even eat the body, or at least the heart, "to acquire the bravery or other virtues of an enemy." The captives chosen for adoption are forced to "run the gantlet," *i.e.*, to run, unarmed and with bare backs, between two

FIG. 73. AN IROQUOIS WARRIOR.
From an exhibit in the American Museum of Natural History. Courtesy of the Museum

310

parallel lines of men, women, and children, who strike them with thorn branches as they pass. To fall means instant death. If they survive, they receive new names and are adopted into the various households. For some time, however, they live under a cloud of suspicion and are compelled to do menial work in the fields and elsewhere as virtual slaves, though they may later attain full tribal status and even aspire to the rank of chief. Besides determining the fate of prisoners, the women exert a strong influence on military matters in other ways. A chief matron can forbid the men of her household to go to war, and the sachems often take advantage of this fact to prevent a rupture with another tribe. On the other hand, a woman has the power to send the clansmen of her husband to war; by presenting them with a string of wampum, she places them under the obligation of securing a captive to compensate her for the loss of her son or husband.

Iroquois women have little difficulty in childbirth, and usually work up to the last. A few experienced women render the necessary assistance. The infant is wrapped in a skin and lashed to a cradle, a tapering board with a foot piece and an arching bow or hoop. The mother carries the cradle on her back by means of a tumpline, or, when working, hangs it on the limb of a tree to swing in the breeze. Shortly after birth, she gives the child its first name, selected from a list belonging exclusively to the clan. Since the name must be one not borne by any other living person, it must be publicly announced and confirmed on some occasion when the entire clan is assembled. A new name is taken upon reaching maturity, on assuming office, and at other times, the change always being formally announced at a council meeting. A mother nurses her child for two or three years, gradually supplementing its fare with corn soup and gruel. If she dies during this period, the infant is killed. Fathers have no authority over their children and take little interest in them. Their care devolves entirely on the mother, who rarely disciplines them except occasionally to dash water in their faces.

A girl is isolated during her first menstruation and is subjected to severe tasks and special food taboos. Any dreams she has at this time, it is thought, will come true. A boy at the age of puberty must remain in seclusion for a year in a hut in the forest, where he is tended by an old man or woman. He must undergo numerous tests of endurance and fortitude such as bathing in icy water and gashing his shin with a stone every morning. His future depends very largely upon his behavior during this period of trial.

Girls frequently marry at as early as fifteen years of age, men usually not until they have become proficient hunters. Marriage is based, not on love or affection, but on economic considerations. Indeed, although young people are allowed a considerable measure of prenuptial freedom, they have no voice in the selection of their life partners. Marriages are arranged for them—not by their fathers but by their mothers, and often even without their knowledge. The mother of a young man selects an industrious and promising girl, belonging, of course, to a clan in the opposite moiety, approaches her mother, and negotiates a match by an exchange of presents. The wedding ceremony consists of a feast, for which the bride makes corn bread and the groom provides venison or bear meat. The husband then goes to live with his bride and submits to the domestic authority of the chief matron of her household, for whom he is expected to furnish game as long as he remains. He is not fully accepted, however, until the birth of his first child. Strict monogamy prevails, although a man may contract a temporary union with an unattached girl for the duration of a hunting expedition, if his wife refuses to accompany him. Both sexes enjoy equal rights of divorce, and marriages are easily and frequently terminated, usually for economic causes. The two mothers, however, exert themselves to preserve harmony and settle differences, for ruptures reflect discredit on them.

The Iroquois cherish and care for their aged and incapacitated, and kill or abandon them only under pressure of dire necessity. When a person dies, the survivors array the body in its finest apparel and paint its face. Members of the opposite moiety bear the corpse to the burial ground of the clan, inter it in a circular pit lined and covered with timbers, and erect a post or other memorial to mark the site. In lieu of earth burial, the Iroquois sometimes expose the body on a bark scaffold or secure it to the limb of a tree. Beside the corpse the survivors deposit the implements and utensils of the deceased, a pipe and some tobacco, and a little food. They build a fire on the grave, and often release a captive bird to bear away the departing soul. After a period of mourning, lasting from ten days to a year, the friends and relatives assemble for a feast, at which the property of the deceased is distributed.

In death the soul, an incorporeal shadow-like double, ceases to animate the body and becomes a ghost. It haunts the grave by day and wanders abroad at night in search of food, manifesting its presence by moaning, squeaking, and whistling noises. To appease its hunger and prevent possible visitations, the survivors continue for some time to set aside for it a regular portion of food. Ghosts cause sickness and other misfortunes, and they often crave human flesh. They are consequently feared, and men take the precaution of never mentioning the name of a deceased person. At the end of the mourning period, however, the ghost quits the grave and journeys to a spirit land in the west, where game is fat and plentiful and huckleberries grow as large as one's fist. The souls of children and of weak and decrepit persons, lacking the strength for the journey, remain on earth as inoffensive ghosts, eking out a miserable livelihood from the scraps of food left over at mealtimes.

Five great deities dominate the Iroquois pantheon. Ataentsic, grandmother of the gods and divinity of death, presides over the realm of the dead. Her grandson Taronhaiwagon, the holder of the heavens, the creator of men and animals, and the benevolent national god of the Iroquois, personifies the creative and reproductive forces of nature and manifests his will to men in dreams. Opposed to him stands his brother, the evil Tawiskaron, patron of the destructive forces of nature and the noxious forms of life. Heno, the benevolent god of thunder, brings rain and ripens the crops and fruits when propitiated with burnt offerings of tobacco. The mighty Agreskwe, sun god and patron of war and the chase, receives the first fruits of hunting and fishing, and occasionally also the flesh of a captive as a human sacrifice. Somewhat below these powerful beings stand the beneficent patrons of agriculture, the Earth Mother and the Three Sisters or spirits of the maize, the bean, and the squash. Hideous Flying Heads, malevolent demons without bodies or limbs, haunt the forests and send plague and pestilence. The lesser supernatural beings almost defy enumeration. They include, amongst others, a race of mischievous Pygmies or fairies, a contrasting race of Stone Giants, great Horned Serpents and other monsters, local divinities, spirits of fire and water, of the winds and heavenly bodies, and of plants and animals, the great spiritual prototypes or "elder brothers" of each animal species, demons of disease and crop failure, evil spirits who inspire witches and sorcerers, deified heroes like Hiawatha, tutelary divinities of households and clans, and individual guardian spirits.

The Iroquois place great faith in dreams. As manifestations of the will of Taronhaiwagon, or as revelations to the soul as it wanders abroad during sleep, they must be obeyed at all costs, once they are interpreted. Sachems have even been known to resign their offices as the result of dreams, and hunters acquire charms and learn the haunts of game through similar revelations. Individuals receive their guardian spirits through dreams, usually after a period of seclusion and rigorous fasting. If a youth dreams of a muskrat, for example, the spirit of that animal becomes his tutelary genius, and thenceforth he wears the skin of a muskrat as his personal "medicine." Although they possess no true idols, the

Iroquois hold sacred such things as albino animals, the places where powerful spirits are reputed to dwell, and a variety of charms and medicines.

A class of shamans or medicine men claims to possess supernatural power (*orenda*). With the aid of their familiar spirits and their pouches of charms and medicines, they control the weather, work exuvial magic with the hair of an enemy, and prophesy the future from dreams. They also cure disease by such seemingly rational means as bleeding, bonesetting, and prescribing herb decoctions, lotions, emetics, and steam baths. Where illness is due to hostile magic, they hold a shamanistic séance with rattles, songs, and dances, and by feats of jugglery remove from the patient's body the stick, stone, or other alleged cause of the complaint.

In the treatment of disease by spiritual means, however, as well as in most other religious and magical functions, the shamans yield precedence to a number of secret societies or "medicine lodges." Each society is organized to propitiate a particular class of supernatural beings, and traces its origin to some legendary founder who became lost in the woods, discovered animal or other spirits engaged in their rites, was captured, forgiven, and adopted, and finally returned to his people laden with mystical lore. Each society has its own songs and dances, an elaborate ritual, special officers to fill the various rôles, and characteristic properties such as charms, fans, masks, drums, flutes, whistles, and gourd, bark, and tortoise-shell rattles. The False Faces, who enjoy undisputed preëminence among the medicine societies, know how to appease by their rites the malevolent Flying Heads. The Bear Society offers sacrifices of tobacco to the spirits of the bears, and the Society of the Three Sisters tends the cult of the spirits of the maize, bean, and squash. The Pygmy Society propitiates the "little people" with night dances and songs in which the spirit members join. The primary function of most of these organizations, however, is the curing of disease. The Otter Society exorcises illnesses caused by killing water animals without offering proper invocations and sacrifices of tobacco to their spirits. The Chanters for the Dead give feasts to allay sickness and misfortune brought

FIG. 74. DANCE OF THE IROQUOIS FALSE FACE SOCIETY.
From a painting by A. A. Jansson. Courtesy of the American Museum of Natural History

by restless ghosts. The Eagle Society can even restore the aged and dying to health. Certain of the societies employ special exorcistic methods in addition to their charms and secret rites. Thus the Otters sprinkle water on their patients with corn husks, the Bears blow on the body, and the False Faces strew hot ashes on the head. A person becomes a member of a society either by dreaming of the necessity of joining or by falling ill and calling for its services. There is little discrimination on the basis of sex; indeed the chief officer is in most cases a woman.

Native religious ideas find their other main channel of expression in a series of annual public festivals, character-ized by sacrifices, thanksgiving, dances, feasts, and games. A special priesthood, the Keepers of the Faith, is charged with the supervision of these ceremonies. Each clan in the tribe nominates six Keepers of the Faith, three men and three women, who are confirmed by the tribal council and given new names. The women enjoy equal authority with the men, as in all religious matters. Festivals, marked by prayers, offerings, and thanksgiving to the Three Sisters, accompany the planting, cultivation, and harvesting of the crops, and special ceremonies are held when the maple sap begins to flow and when the strawberries, huckleberries, beans, and maize successively ripen.

The gala occasion of the year, however, is the New Year festival, which usually occurs in February and lasts five days with two or three additional days of dancing and games. It begins with the extinguishing of the fires in every cabin and the scattering of the ashes, after which the Keepers of the Faith generate new fire with a pump drill. Then fol-low several days of mad tumult, during which the people rush wildly from house to house, often in masquerade. Boys try to steal food. Persons who have had dreams ask others to interpret them. The women of the Otter Society sprinkle water on passers-by, and the False Faces, in masks, strew ashes over people to exorcise the demons of disease. The festivities culminate in the sacrifice of a white dog, perhaps as a scapegoat to expiate the sins of the people. On the first day of the festival the animal is strangled and decorated with paint, feathers, and wampum by two young men who have attained a state of ritual purity. On the final day, people who have sins to confess deposit offerings on the body, which is then carried on a bark litter in a procession to an altar and is burned with speeches, songs, prayers, and sacrifices of tobacco.

Dances and games follow every important festival and council meeting. Of the numerous native dances, some communal and others the private property of the medicine societies, the majority are characterized by lifting the heel and striking the ground with great force and rapidity to the accompaniment of vocal music or the beating of drums and rattles. Moieties and villages compete with one another in foot races, archery contests, throwing the javelin at rolling hoops, and lacrosse. The latter game, which the white man has borrowed, is played in much the same way as with us. The players undergo a rigorous course of training and diet, and the onlookers lay large wagers under the supervision of the officials. The moieties also compete at snow-snake, in which sticks are thrown so as to glide along the surface of the snow, and at snow-boat, in which small wooden boats are made to slide down iced trenches on the side of a hill. A point is scored for each snake or boat which outdistances all those of the opponents. A popular gambling game, of which there are many variants, consists in throwing six elkhorn buttons or plum pits, each blackened on one side, in a wooden bowl. If the dice turn up all black or all white, the thrower scores five points; if five of a color, one point; otherwise he loses his turn. This game also has ritual significance and is an essential feature of most ceremonies.

A strong spirit of hospitality pervades the social life of the Iroquois. They throw open their houses to strangers and entertain them as long as they care to stay. A friendly white man receives similar treatment. "We dry him if he is wet," explained one Indian, "we warm him if he is cold, and give him meat and drink that he may allay his hunger and thirst; and we spread soft furs for him to rest and sleep on. We demand nothing in return. But if I go into a white man's house at Albany, and ask for victuals and drink, they say, 'Where is your money?' And if I have none, they say, '*Get out, you Indian dog.*'"

The first experience of the Iroquois with this ungracious alien race came in 1609, in an encounter with the French under Champlain. Close contact, however, did not begin until 1615, when the Dutch opened a trading post at Albany. From the Dutch the Iroquois received firearms in exchange for furs. Armed with this new weapon, in the use of which they soon became expert, they rapidly conquered and subjugated their neighbors, the Hurons, Neutrals, Eries, Adirondacks, and Delawares, and then extended their conquests to the south and west. By the year 1700 they had reduced to subjection all the tribes from New England to Lake Michigan and from the Ottawa River to Tennessee, and had founded the most powerful Indian empire ever established north of Mexico. The American Revolution, however, brought their political independence to an end. Most of the tribes favored and fought with the British, although the opposition of the Oneidas prevented unanimous action by the League. At the end of the war many migrated to Canada, where two-thirds of the nation reside today. By 1797 those who remained had ceded their lands to the whites, except for a few reservations in New York, which their descendants still inhabit. The population of the nation, probably never more than 16,000, suffered heavily, in spite of wholesale adoptions of captives, from the constant warfare which followed contact with the Europeans, and from whiskey, smallpox, and venereal disease obtained from them. For the past century or more, however, it has been steadily gaining, until today the Iroquois number slightly more than ever before in their history.

Probably no other Indian nation has so seriously affected the course of American history. The Dutch cultivated relations of extreme cordiality with the Five Nations, and the English, after taking over their possessions in 1664, took pains to follow in their footsteps. Each new governor renewed the "covenant chain" with the sachems. Trade and friendly intercourse increased "until councils with the Iroquois became nearly as frequent as sessions of the provincial legislature." The French, on the other hand, alienated the Iroquois from the first. Champlain, in 1609, defeated a band of Mohawks, and in the following years he incited the Hurons and Adirondacks to attack the League. He aroused a hatred and resentment which never cooled. For nearly a century the Iroquois waged almost ceaseless war with the French. They intercepted their valuable fur trade. They blocked the direct route to the west through the Great Lakes. They repeatedly ravaged their territories and at times even threatened their very existence in Canada. In 1688, for example, they descended on Montreal Island and killed or captured nearly a thousand of their enemies. French attempts at retaliation proved as abortive as those at conciliation, for the Indians simply abandoned their villages and retired into the forests. The Iroquois not only formed a sturdy barrier protecting the New England colonies from French aggression; they also repeatedly rendered invaluable assistance to the colonists in their struggles with the hostile Algonquian tribes. In addition to military aid, the Iroquois enriched the English through the fur trade. Their unvarying friendship and support, perhaps more than any other single factor, determined that the English rather than the French should dominate North America.

BIBLIOGRAPHY

BARTRAM, J. *Observations on the Inhabitants, Climate, Soil, Rivers, Productions, Animals, and Other Matters Worthy of Notice.* London, 1751.

BEAUCHAMP, W. M. "Aboriginal Chipped Stone Implements of New York." *New York State Museum, Bulletin 16.* Albany, 1897.

———. "Aboriginal Use of Wood in New York." *New York State Museum, Bulletin 89.* Albany, 1905.

BEAUCHAMP, W. M. "Civil, Religious and Mourning Councils and Ceremonies of Adoption of the New York Indians." *New York State Museum, Bulletin 113.* Albany, 1907.

——. "Earthenware of the New York Aborigines." *New York State Museum, Bulletin 22.* Albany, 1898.

——. "A History of the New York Iroquois." *New York State Museum, Bulletin 78.* Albany, 1905.

——. "Horn and Bone Implements of the New York Indians." *New York State Museum, Bulletin 50.* Albany, 1902.

——. *Iroquois Folk Lore.* Syracuse, 1922.

——. "Iroquois Women." *Journal of American Folk-Lore,* Vol. XIII. Boston, 1900.

——. "Polished Stone Articles Used by the New York Aborigines." *New York State Museum, Bulletin 18.* Albany, 1897.

——. "Wampum and Shell Articles Used by the New York Indians." *New York State Museum, Bulletin 41.* Albany, 1901.

CARR, L. "On the Social and Political Position of Woman among the Huron-Iroquois Tribes." *Reports of the Peabody Museum of American Archæology and Ethnology,* Vol. III. Cambridge, 1887.

CHADWICK, E. M. *The People of the Longhouse.* Toronto, 1897.

CLARK, J. V. H. *Onondaga.* 2 vols. Syracuse, 1849.

COLDEN, C. *The History of the Five Indian Nations of Canada.* New edition. 2 vols. New York, 1922.

CONVERSE, H. M. "The Seneca New-Year Ceremony and Other Customs." *Indian Notes,* Vol. VII. New York, 1930.

CURTIN, J., and HEWITT, J. N. B. "Seneca Fiction, Legends, and Myths." *Thirty-second Annual Report of the Bureau of American Ethnology.* Washington, 1918.

GOLDENWEISER, A. A. *Early Civilization.* New York, 1922.

——. "On Iroquois Work, 1912." *Canada Geological Survey, Summary Report for the Calendar Year 1912.* Ottawa, 1914.

GRAY, L. H. "Iroquois." *Encyclopædia of Religion and Ethics.* Edited by J. Hastings. 12 vols. New York, 1908–22.

HALE, H. *The Iroquois Book of Rites.* Philadelphia, 1883.

——. "The Iroquois Sacrifice of the White Dog." *American Antiquarian and Oriental Journal.* Vol. VII. Chicago, 1885.

HEWITT, J. N. B. "A Constitutional League of Peace in the Stone Age of America." *Smithsonian Institution, Annual Report of the Board of Regents for the Year Ending June 30, 1918*. Washington, 1920.

——. "The Iroquoian Concept of the Soul." *Journal of American Folk-Lore*, Vol. VIII. Boston, 1895.

——. "Iroquoian Cosmology." *Twenty-first Annual Report of the Bureau of American Ethnology*. Washington, 1903.

——. "Orenda and a Definition of Religion." *American Anthropologist*, New Series, Vol. IV. New York, 1902.

HODGE, F. W. (editor). "Handbook of American Indians North of Mexico." *Smithsonian Institution, Bureau of American Ethnology, Bulletin 30*. 2 vols. Washington, 1907–10.

LAFITAU, J. F. *Mœurs des sauvages amériquains, comparées aux mœurs des premiers temps*. 2 vols. Paris, 1724.

LOSKIEL, G. H. *History of the Mission of the United Brethren among the Indians of North America*. Trans. London, 1794.

MORGAN, L. H. *Ancient Society*. New York, 1877.

——. "Government and Institutions of the Iroquois." Edited by A. C. Parker. *Researches and Transactions of the New York State Archeological Association*, Vol. VII. Rochester, 1928.

——. "Houses and House-life of the American Aborigines." *Contributions to North American Ethnology*, Vol. IV. Washington, 1881.

*——. *League of the Ho-Dé-No-Sau-Nee or Iroquois*. Edited by H. M. Lloyd. 2 vols. New York, 1901.

PALMER, R. A. "The North American Indians." *Smithsonian Scientific Series*, Vol. IV. Washington, 1929.

PARKER, A. C. "The Archeological History of New York." *New York State Museum, Bulletins 235–236*. Albany, 1920.

——. "The Code of Handsome Lake, the Seneca Prophet." *New York State Museum, Bulletin 163*. Albany, 1913.

——. "The Constitution of the Five Nations." *New York State Museum, Bulletin 184*. Albany, 1916.

——. "Iroquois Uses of Maize and Other Food Plants." *New York State Museum, Bulletin 144*. Albany, 1910.

——. "The Origin of the Iroquois as Suggested by their Archeology." *American Anthropologist*, New Series, Vol. XVIII. Lancaster, 1916.

PARKER, A. C.   "Secret Medicine Societies of the Seneca."
American Anthropologist, New Series, Vol. XI. Lancaster,
1909.

SEAVER, J. E. *Life of Mary Jemison.* Fourth edition. New York,
1856.

SKINNER, A. "Notes on Iroquois Archeology." *Indian Notes and
Monographs.* New York, 1921.

——.   "Some Seneca Masks and Their Uses."   *Indian Notes*,
Vol. II. New York, 1925.

SMITH, E. A. "Myths of the Iroquois." *Second Annual Report of
the Bureau of Ethnology.* Washington, 1883.

STITES, S. H. *Economics of the Iroquois.* Lancaster, 1905.

THWAITES, R. G. (editor). *The Jesuit Relations and Allied Docu-
ments.* 74 vols. Cleveland, 1896–1901.

WAUGH, F. W. "Iroquois Foods and Food Preparation." *Canada
Department of Mines, Geological Survey, Memoir 86.* Ottawa,
1916.

CHAPTER XII

THE HOPI OF ARIZONA

THE Indians of the southwestern United States and north-ern Mexico fall into three well-defined groups. The Apache and Navaho lead a nomadic existence based primarily on hunting. The Mohave, Papago, Pima, Yuma, and many other tribes inhabit permanent villages and till the soil intensively. The most advanced and interesting group, however, is that of the Pueblo Indians—the Tewa, the Keres, the Zuñi, and the Hopi. The prehistory of the Pueblo peoples has been reconstructed with striking success by American archeologists. About four thousand years ago maize was introduced into this region from the south, and a few low hunting and collecting tribes in northern Arizona and south-ern Utah gave up their nomadic habits and became tillers of the soil. These Basket-Makers, as they are called from their excellent basketry, lived in houses in the open, but stored their grain and buried their dead in dry caves. They gradually advanced in culture, learning, for example, how to make pottery. Shortly before our era a new brachycephalic people began to appear among the long-headed Basket-Makers, bringing the bow and arrow, which supplanted the earlier spear-thrower. These forerunners of the modern Pueblo tribes inhabited scattered circular pit-dwellings at first, rectangular masonry houses somewhat later. They extended their habitat in all directions until it included most of Utah and New Mexico, half of Arizona, and parts of Colorado and Nevada. By about 500 A.D., however, they began to suffer inroads from nomadic warrior tribes, and were forced to abandon much of their territory and to gather together for protection in large cliff dwellings and pueblos of stone and adobe. In spite of notable cultural advances, they continued to decline in numbers and in area, until in 1540 the Spanish discoverers found less than 20,000 of them in sixty-six scattered pueblos in northeastern Arizona and western New Mexico.

Perhaps the least changed and most representative of the modern Pueblo nations is the Hopi or Moki, a people of heterogeneous origin inhabiting the six villages of Walpi, Sichomovi, Mishongnovi, Shongopovi, Shipaulovi, and Oraibi in northeastern Arizona. Their speech belongs to the Shoshonean linguistic stock, which embraces the Ute, Comanche, Shoshoni, and other languages of the Plains and California, and which is usually grouped with the distantly related Nahuatlan or Aztecan tongues of Mexico into a single Uto-Aztecan stock. The Hopi possess neither a sign language nor writing, although they use pictographs to a limited extent. With a dearth of abstract terms, they make free use of metaphorical expressions. They reckon time by "sleeps" and "moons" and follow an elaborate ceremonial calendar accurately correlated with the position of the sun.

The Hopi reveal typical Indian racial characteristics in their reddish-brown skins, high cheek bones, broad faces, and straight black hair. They are for the most part brachycephalic, the back of the head being flattened from infancy as a result of tight lashing to the cradle. Albinism prevails to an exceptional degree; five or six persons in every thousand are thus afflicted. Adult males average five feet four and one-half inches in stature, females five inches less. From differences in training and economic duties the native man is said to resemble a race horse in type; the woman, a draft horse.

The Hopi pueblos with the surrounding territory, once known as the province of Tusayan, form today a reservation of nearly four thousand square miles, situated between 110° and 111° west longitude and between 35° 30′ and 36° 30′ north latitude. The region is an arid plateau 6,500 feet in elevation, a sandy rolling waste which processes of erosion have gashed with gullies, washes, and canyons and studded with fantastic buttes and flat-topped mesas. On three of

FIG. 75. A HOPI CHIEF.
Courtesy of the American Museum of Natural History

the latter, rising with precipitous rocky walls four hundred feet above the plain, the six native villages are strategically located. Color as well as contrast characterizes the landscape, for the sand, rocks, and vegetation display a diversity of pastel shades. Day after day, in an atmosphere of crystalline clearness, the bright sun traverses an incredibly blue sky flecked with fleecy clouds. Precipitation scarcely averages ten inches per annum. Winter snows store a certain amount of moisture deep in the ground, and nourish a few springs. Rain, confined almost entirely to midsummer, falls torrentially in occasional violent thunderstorms, converting the dry washes momentarily into rivers, but sinking almost immediately into the sand. In the spring, windstorms of indescribable intensity, charged with sharp particles of sand, tear growing plants to shreds. The climate is dry, temperate, and exceedingly healthful. Cool nights alternate with hot days in summer. Frosts begin in late September, but the winters are far from severe. The indigenous vegetation includes sage, yucca, greasewood, cactus, and other plants adapted to semi-desert conditions. A few cottonwoods grow in the beds of the washes, and junipers, piñons, and scrub oaks flourish in places, but there are no forests except on the slopes of the distant ranges. Grass and flowers spring up as if by magic after a rain, make the most of the temporary supply of moisture, then relapse into endurance until another season. The native fauna includes the bear, deer, antelope, cougar, wildcat, badger, wolf, fox, and coyote, but game animals, other than rabbits, rats, and prairie dogs, are so scarce as to be practically negligible as a source of food.

In view of the paucity of wild plants and animals, mere hunters or collectors could scarcely make a living in this arid environment. But the soil is fertile, and by careful utilization of the scanty sources of water the Hopi are able to support themselves by agriculture. They raise beans, squashes, pumpkins, sunflowers, and cotton, but their principal crop is maize, of which they possess numerous varieties. Through centuries of selection they have produced small, hardy, deep-rooted, early-maturing types adapted to the arid conditions. They plant in May and harvest in September. Choosing the least unfavorable spots—in protected gullies, near springs, etc.—they plant a dozen kernels to a hill in hills six feet or more apart, after clearing the surface of brush. They insert the seeds in holes a foot deep, made with a pointed stick or dibble, and depend on the moisture surviving from the winter snows for their germination and on summer thunderstorms for their growth. Lacking permanent watercourses, the Hopi do not practice irrigation, but they guard their fields against birds, clear away weeds with wooden hoes, dig ditches to prevent damage from sudden floods, and build windbreaks of brush and stones for protection against winds and drifting sands. Despite all their care and ingenuity, however, they not infrequently suffer a partial or total crop failure. For this reason they providently set aside a portion of each year's crop as a reserve against famine.

The Hopi supplement their agricultural products, especially in lean years, with piñon nuts, juniper berries, mesquite beans, prickly pears, and many other wild seeds, roots, leaves, and fruits. They gather wild tobacco, and utilize in some way—in medicine, ceremonial, or the domestic arts if not for food—nearly every wild plant in their environment. Flesh figures but slightly on the native menu. The dog is not eaten. The turkey, the only other native domesticated animal, is kept, curiously enough, not for food but for its feathers. The environment furnishes no fish. Hunting, in general, assumes the character of a religious ritual rather than an economic enterprise. Large animals—when available—are killed in communal drives with small bows of oak strung with sinew and arrows feathered with hawk plumes and tipped with chipped flint or obsidian. Individual hunters sometimes stalk antelopes with the head of an animal as a decoy. Bands of men, after elaborate ceremonial preparations, beat the brush for rabbits in narrowing circles, dispatching the animals with boomerangs, flat curved throwing sticks which rotate in the air and execute gyrations after striking but do not return to the thrower. During a heavy

rain the men catch prairie dogs by diverting rivulets into
their burrows and killing the half-drowned rodents with
sticks when they emerge. Foxes and coyotes are trapped
in deadfalls—flat stones insecurely supported by pegs to
which bait is tied. Birds are captured in nooses. Every
spring parties of men scale the cliffs with ropes and take
young eagles from their nests. The birds are kept in captivity
and carefully fed until July, when, with much ceremony,
they are strangled for their valuable feathers and buried
with high honors in special eagle cemeteries. Adult eagles
are caught in circular tow-
ers erected on eminences.
A man, after lashing a rabbit near an opening in the
roof, patiently lies in wait
until an eagle swoops down
for the bait, when he seizes
the bird by its legs with his
bare hands, drags it inside,

After Hough

FIG. 76. HOPI THROWING STICKS.

and strangles it. Hunting methods are devised, with few
exceptions, to avoid shedding the blood of the quarry, for
animals taken ceremonially—and the chase is primarily
ceremonial—must not be mutilated in any way.

The Hopi like their predominantly vegetarian fare well
cooked. *Piki*, their characteristic food, is a grayish paper-
thin bread made by mixing corn meal batter with wood
ashes as a leaven, spreading it thinly over a hot polished
stone, and rolling it as it bakes into crisp cylinders, which
in color and texture resemble nothing so much as the material of a hornets' nest. To make *pikami*, another favorite
dish, the women masticate corn meal thoroughly, allow the
resulting paste to ferment from the action of the saliva, and
bake it into a pudding. Recipes involving maize number
more than fifty, including mush, hominy, succotash, boiled
corn, roasted ears, dumplings, puddings, and cakes. The
pièce de résistance of a meal is usually a stew concocted from

maize, vegetables, wild herbs, oily seeds, and game when available. Harmless vegetable dyes are frequently used to impart brilliant colors to *piki* and other foods. In the morning and evening, when hot meals are served, the family sits on the floor around a pot of stew or mush. Each member, after throwing aside a little food as an offering to the super-

FIG. 77. SCENE AT THE HOPI PUEBLO OF WALPI.
Courtesy of the American Museum of Natural History

natural beings, dips his forefinger or a piece of *piki* into the common bowl, fishes around, and deposits his catch in his mouth with a resounding smack. The Hopi have never invented an intoxicating liquor. They smoke tobacco in straight pipes on ceremonial occasions, but prefer cigarettes with corn-husk wrappings for secular enjoyment.

For protection against their marauding neighbors, the Hopi have built their pueblos or villages on the flat summits of mesas, accessible only by steep trails ascending, often by

steps carved in solid rock, through breaks in the cliffs.
They live, not in single dwellings, but in great terraced
apartment houses two stories or more in height, irregularly
grouped into streets and plazas. Each individual family
occupies a single room, with perhaps a lower interior room
for the storage of food. The walls, about twenty inches
thick and seven feet high, are made of stone cemented and
plastered with adobe mud and coated on the inside with white
gypsum. Several stout beams, resting on the walls, support
the flat roof, which consists of successive layers of poles,
brush, grass, dried mud, and trampled earth. The floor is
simply the roof of the lower story smoothly plastered with
mud. Doors connect apartments on the same level and give
access to the upper terraces, but, for the sake of defense,
there are none in the outer walls of the lower story. Nor are
there any windows save the merest chinks. One can enter a
Hopi home only by climbing an outside ladder and descending through a hatchway in the roof. Each pueblo has several
kivas or subterranean chambers, used by the men as clubs,
workshops, and council rooms, but especially as the scene of
their secret religious ceremonies.

In one corner of the living room stands a mud fireplace,
where the cooking is done. A wicker hood, plastered with
mud, conducts the smoke into a chimney of bottomless pots
stacked in a column. Several large water jars occupy another
corner. There is no furniture save occasionally a low bench
along a wall; blankets or skins spread on the floor serve as
beds. At one end of the room stands a three-compartment
metate or mill, at which the women of the household spend
several hours each day. It consists of three slanting slabs of
stone, graded in surface from rough to fine, on which corn is
successively ground with a mealing stone until it is reduced to
a very fine flour. Other household implements include a
pump drill with a stone point, bone awls, horn spoons, hafted
obsidian knives, and stone mortars and pestles, hammers,
axes, and mauls. Metals are not worked. Gourds serve a

variety of purposes, but utensils of wood and skin are rare. The Hopi make earthenware jars, vases, bowls, dippers, and dishes of diversified texture and pattern. The potter molds the clay into a rope, coils it spirally into the desired shape, presses and smooths the surface, applies a wash of white clay, polishes the vessel with a smooth stone, paints it, and fires it in a kiln heated with lignite. Twined, twilled, and

FIG. 78. A LARGE HOPI POT.
Courtesy of the American Museum of Natural History

coiled baskets are made in various forms—carrying baskets, mats, sieves, bowls, and the especially characteristic flat trays or plaques for corn meal. Symbolic and often highly conventionalized designs, representing birds, clouds, and the like, are applied with the aid of vegetable dyes. A high authority describes the native wicker baskets as "the most artistic to be found in the world."

The textile arts fall exclusively within the province of the men, who make all the clothing for the women as well as

for themselves. They spin thread by hand from cotton and
yucca fibers and manufacture a strong cord from human hair.
On a true loom, suspended from a beam in the living room or
kiva, they weave blankets, kilts, belts, and sashes, sometimes

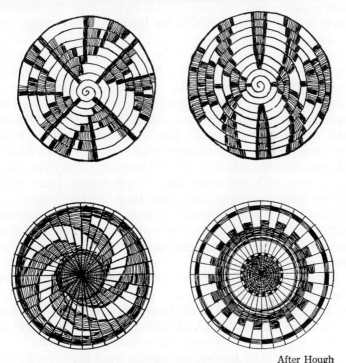

After Hough

FIG. 79. REPRESENTATIVE DESIGNS OF HOPI COILED AND WICKER
BASKET TRAYS.

embellishing them with tassels and embroidery. The fineness
of the native fabrics excited the admiration of the early
Spanish explorers. The men likewise weave thick blankets
from strips of rabbit fur. These garments, though warmer
than dressed skins, form an "excellent harborage for fleas
and other vermin."

The costume of the men consists of a cotton loin cloth, a

poncho or shirt of undyed cotton cloth with loose sleeves
and a hole for the head, a kilt of the same material held at
the waist by a woven belt, long cotton leggings, deerskin
moccasins or woven sandals of yucca leaves, and, in emergencies, a rabbit-skin robe over the shoulders. When the weather
permits, however, they doff all but the loin cloth, and children
under twelve wear nothing at all. The women, on the other
hand, never dispense with their single article of everyday
apparel—a sleeveless dress or robe of undyed cotton extending just below the knees. This garment is little more than a
blanket passed around the body under the left arm, tied or
sewed over the right shoulder, overlapping at the right side,
and restrained by a belt. The women, in addition, wear
moccasins and leggings on ceremonial occasions and a cotton
blanket over the shoulders in cold weather. The Hopi daub
their faces with red ocher and, in ceremonies, paint their
bodies with vegetable dyes, but they neither tattoo nor
scarify. They wear necklaces of shells, stone beads, berries,
and seeds, and rawhide anklets with quill embroidery. Unmarried girls display tasteful earrings of turquoise set in
gum on wooden tablets.

Both sexes take great pains with their hair. The men part
theirs in the center, cut it off evenly at the front and sides
on the level of the ear lobes, keep it out of the eyes with a
head band, gather it in back into a bunch at the nape of
the neck, and insert a white eagle feather on the left side.
Women part their hair in the middle from the brow to the
nape of the neck. Unmarried girls then do it up into an
immense whorl over each ear—supposedly symbolic of the
squash blossom—while matrons tie it tightly in two pendant
braids, symbolizing the ripened fruit of the squash. "Neither
men nor women dress their own hair; women comb the men's
hair and one another's, though sometimes a lover or bride-
groom undertakes the part of hairdresser for his beloved."

In the division of labor by sex the men spin, weave, make
all clothing, hunt, gather fuel and building materials, carry

on all agricultural operations, tend the domestic and captive animals, make ceremonial objects, and assume charge of religious and governmental functions. The women collect seeds, roots, and herbs, prepare and cook the food, tend the children, make baskets and pottery and gather the materials for these handicrafts, build and repair the houses, and carry on barter. Their most arduous tasks, however, are grinding corn at the metate and carrying water in pots up the mesa from the springs at the foot. Occasionally a woman specializes as a potter or a man in the manufacture of moccasins, and wares are exchanged, at least in modern times, at embryonic markets. The Hopi engage in a fairly extensive trade with the Havasupai, Apache, Zuñi, and other surrounding tribes, giving agricultural and textile products in return for mescal and piñon nuts, red ocher and shell beads, baskets and tanned deerskins.

The Hopi are organized into a large number of exogamous matrilineal clans, which are loosely linked together into twelve phratries, likewise exogamous. Basically, the clan consists of a group of families united by descent in the female line, although occasionally it includes several unrelated lineages. The great majority of clans bear plant or animal names, *e.g.*, Bear, Snake, Reed, and Mustard. Certain clans, like the Butterfly and Coyote, refrain, at least at times, from killing their eponymous animals, though others, like the Bear and Rabbit, observe no such taboos. Another trace of totemism exists in the vague feeling that the eponymous being exercises a tutelary supervision over the clansmen. Many clans possess totemic fetishes. The Bear clan, for instance, is said to own a small effigy of a bear, and the Butterfly clan a winged idol of cottonwood bark. These sacred objects are left in the custody of one particular family, which also furnishes the clan as a rule with its male head or chief and its female head, called "our oldest mother." The various religious fraternities commonly bear the same names as the clans, though their membership is not identical. Nevertheless, the clan chief is customarily the chief priest of the fraternity, and the clan members are regarded as at least potential participants in the ceremonies conducted by the fraternity. The clan enjoys a communal property right in certain shrines, springs, and ceremonial objects, in the *kiva* used by the fraternity of the same name, and, curiously enough, also in the wild eagles nesting in certain definitely delimited territories at a distance from the pueblo.

The cultivated land is owned by the clans and parceled out amongst the individual families. Though tilled by the husband, a plot is actually held by the wife, who likewise owns its produce, the house itself, and all the household utensils and furnishings. House and land descend from mother to daughter; in default of daughters or other near female matrilineal relatives, a son inherits. If a man acquires property in this way, or by reducing untilled land to cultivation, it passes at his death to his daughter, and thus out of the clan. In spite of the mother's property rights, the father is the head of the household, though he shares his authority over the children with their maternal uncle. Although they adhere to a classificatory system of relationship, the Hopi seldom employ kinship terms as terms of address; they prefer teknonymous usage. Thus a husband addresses his spouse, neither by name nor as "wife," but simply as "mother of So-and-so" (their child).

The Hopi possess neither a federal government nor a supreme chief. Each pueblo is politically independent, although on rare occasions of great public calamity the chiefs of the different villages meet for discussion and prayer. Within the pueblo, authority is vested in a council of hereditary clan chiefs, who are exempt from ordinary economic activities. Since they are also the heads of the religious fraternities, the government is in large measure theocratic. Succession to office, like descent and inheritance, follows the female line; a chief is succeeded by a younger brother or a sister's son, never by a son. Certain members of the council hold special offices. A Village Chief, who in certain pueblos, at least, is the head of the Bear clan, directs all communal activities and exercises a right of veto over all proposals coming before the council. A Crier Chief makes public the decisions of the council and announces impending cere- monies. A House Chief assists the Village Chief, supervises the affairs of the pueblo, brings matters of common interest before the council, and each day at dawn offers a prayer to the sun for the health and welfare of all. A War Chief holds the military command and likewise a veto privilege in the council. He also acts as a police officer with power to stop quarrels, using force if necessary. The council exercises judicial as well as administrative and legislative functions. It settles all disputes and possibly punishes crimes, though infractions of the law are so few—murder is unknown, and adultery and theft are exceedingly rare—that it is difficult to say how they are dealt with. In all probability, however, punishment takes the form mainly of public ridicule, loss of prestige, and social ostracism.

Though naturally peace-loving—their very name signifies "peaceful ones"—the Hopi are frequently compelled in self- defense to take to the warpath against the neighboring Navaho, Apache, and Ute. Marauding bands of these no- madic tribes descend periodically on the sedentary villagers, plundering their fields, burning their crops, cutting off de- tached hunting parties, and stealing women. The Hopi maintain themselves only by the impregnable strength of their settlements, by ceaseless vigilance, and by prompt defensive and retaliatory measures. A patrol guards the pueblo day and night. The War Chief enjoys full authority in military matters. A private war party can go out only with his permission. If he leads a retaliatory expedition in person, he can call for support on every member of the War- rior Society, composed chiefly of those who have taken the scalp of an enemy, and he must not return until he has defeated the enemy or met his death. Before setting out, he makes offerings to the images of the war gods in his house. Scouts bring information about the enemy, and a surprise attack, preferably in bad weather, is planned. The Hopi fight principally with wooden clubs, sinew-backed bows, and reed arrows tipped with flint or obsidian and carried in skin quivers. They possess neither slings nor spear-throwers, and they employ spears, stone axes, and rawhide shields only in a subordinate capacity. They spare neither the women, the children, nor the aged of a defeated enemy. The returning warriors remain for twenty days in the *kiva*, making offerings, dancing, and undergoing ceremonial ablutions. On the twentieth day a great dance is held around a pole to which the captured scalps are fastened, after which the trophies are thrown into a fissure in the cliffs. Every warrior who has taken a scalp must, until the day of his death, meet every evening at the home of the War Chief and wait till all the village is in bed, when one man is delegated to throw sacred meal on the scalps in the fissure. So arduous is this nightly vigil that men in recent times have hesitated to take scalps, and the Warrior Society has declined in numbers.

The natives are fond of games of all sorts. Children play with stilts, pea-shooters, and tops spun with whips. Adults cast reed dice, throw feathered corncob darts at a ring, and play "cup and ball," a game in which the object is to guess under which of four wooden cups a pebble is concealed. They engage in archery contests and impromptu wrestling bouts, and play shinny with oak clubs and a buckskin ball. But long distance running is the great national accomplishment. The swiftest runners are honored, and a foot race forms an integral part of nearly every religious ceremony. Messages are carried great distances in an incredibly short time. Rabbits are easily outrun and caught. One old man of the Oraibi pueblo, who owned a small patch of cotton forty miles from his home, used regularly to run out to this field in the morning, cultivate his crop, and run

back the same day. It is small wonder that Hopi runners
in recent years have won numerous marathon races from
professionally trained white athletes.

Painting and sculpture are poorly developed among the
Hopi, and decorative art is symbolic rather than æsthetic in
purpose. The fine arts are overshadowed by religious ceremonial; or rather they have been absorbed by it, for the
dance, the drama, and dry painting with colored sands
achieve, in connection with ceremonial, a degree of æsthetic
and technical excellence probably unrivaled among primitive
peoples. Music, too, though there are songs of love, of war,
of work, and of play, finds its highest development under
religious auspices. The native instruments include flutes
with five stops, bone whistles, bull-roarers, rattles of all
kinds, drums made from hollow cottonwood logs, and "horse-
fiddles" consisting of a notched stick laid over the open
mouth of a pot or a gourd and rasped with a rod. Ceremonial songs accompanied by the flute create an especially
pleasing impression. "In general effect the music is minor,
but frequently major motives of great beauty spring out of
dead-level monotonous minors."

Every married woman desires "a quiver full of children."
Occasionally, however, an abortion is produced by a tight
bandage or manual pressure on the abdomen. An expectant
mother goes about her household duties till the last and
rests only a day or two after childbirth, for confinement is
usually easy. She delivers herself of her child in a kneeling
position on a bed of sand. Her only attendant, her mother,
absents herself at the critical moment from motives of delicacy, but returns, when summoned, to tie and cut the
umbilical cord and dispose of the afterbirth. The paternal
grandmother is now called, and takes full charge of the
infant. She washes it with warm water and suds, rubs its
body with wood ashes, wraps it in warm cloths, and deposits
it in a basket with an ear of corn by its side. For twenty days
the mother is ritually unclean. She remains in a darkened

room, for the sun must not shine on her. She abstains from meat and salt, and drinks only warm water or juniper tea. She submits, every fourth or fifth day, to a ritual head-washing with amole suds.

On the twentieth day after childbirth an important cere-mony takes place. The relatives on both sides assemble before dawn, bringing presents for the child. The mother's impurity is removed by the paternal grandmother, who washes her head with suds, bathes her limbs, and prepares her a ritual steam bath, after which she sweeps the room and sprinkles the floor. The same old woman then bathes the baby, rubs it with corn meal, and gives it a name. Each of the other clanswomen of the father similarly christens the child. Some one of these various names usually survives, but since they all have some reference to the totem of the name-giver's clan, a child invariably bears a name char-acteristic, not of his own (his mother's) clan, but of his father's. The recipient of all these names is now introduced for the first time to its cradle, a wicker board with a collaps-ible bow of withes, to which it is lashed securely with a long band of cloth. Meanwhile the father has gone to the edge of the mesa to watch for and announce the sunrise. The women then go forth and stand in the dawn, clad in clean white garments, "a picturesque group of sun-worshippers." The paternal grandmother holds the child in her arms, draws back the blanket from its face, utters a short prayer, and throws an offering of meal toward the sun. A feast closes the ceremony.

A child remains in its cradle, even at night and while being nursed, until it is able to walk. It is removed four or five times a day, however, to renew its diaper of absorbent frayed cedar bark. Mothers sometimes suckle their infants for as long as five years, although they give them supplementary foods at an early age. Indeed, a high infant mortality results from eating green corn and unripe melons. Parents display great fondness for their offspring, and are able to win respect

FIG. 80. HOPI MOTHER AND CHILD.
Courtesy of the American Museum of Natural History

and obedience without resorting to corporal punishment. The play of childhood is largely a preparation for life. Boys chase rabbits, pretend to wage war and defend the pueblo, and practice with miniature bows and arrows. They can shoot at a mark almost before they can walk. Small girls play house, amuse themselves with toy metates and cradles, fashion crude little baskets, and learn pottery technic by making mud effigies. They play, not with secular dolls, but with actual religious images given them after ceremonies, and thus acquire a respect for sacred things. Industry is inculcated from earliest years, and children, as soon as they are able, assist their elders in gathering foods and materials, fetching water, watching the fields, etc. Girls of six carry their younger brothers and sisters on their backs, and in a few years begin to grind corn. The maternal uncle rather than the father assumes responsibility for a child's religious, ceremonial, and ethical instruction.

The development of physical hardiness is stressed in education. In cold weather, for instance, the elders usurp the places near the fire, while the children shiver in the background to accustom themselves to cold. A boy may be stopped in the middle of a meal and bidden to eat no more; thus, he is told, he will learn endurance to hunger which will stand him in good stead in the future. At about eight years of age, boys join the men in their daily morning plunge in the spring at the foot of the mesa; in the winter they even break the ice for this purpose. Women bathe in the house, but much less frequently owing to the scarcity of water. A joking relationship exists between children and their classificatory "grandfathers." Old men tease their grandsons, dashing them with cold water or rolling them in the snow "to make them grow strong." The boys retaliate when older. Thus a lad of sixteen or seventeen may seize his aged grandparent and toss him into a snowdrift.

At seven or eight years of age, all boys and some girls are initiated into the Kachina (or another) fraternity at the

Powamu ceremony. After a flogging with yucca whips by the *kachinas*, masked dancers impersonating spirits, they receive new names and learn for the first time that the *kachinas* are not genuine divine beings but merely impersonations. Subsequently they may be initiated into other fraternities, in each case receiving a new name. A special relationship exists through life between a novice and his sponsor, who, though unrelated, is called "father" or "mother." A girl is sent at puberty to the house of a paternal aunt, where she remains for four days in seclusion behind a curtain, grinding corn for her aunt, eating no meat or salt, and scratching her head only with a special forked stick. On the fourth day, after a ceremonial head-washing, she returns home, and shortly thereafter she marries.

The Hopi regard marriage as the only natural state, and a bachelor or spinster is a rare phenomenon. The women invariably ask a stranger whether he is married, "and if the answer is negative, they express condolence and sympathy." Chastity prevails among the unmarried, but unchastity is condoned if marriage follows. Young people exercise great freedom in their choice of mates, subject, however, to the approval of their maternal relatives and to the social rule of exogamy with respect to clan and phratry. The girl usually takes the initiative in proposing, and she announces the betrothal by combing the young man's hair in public. Marriage, though it involves an exchange of presents, is not a transaction of purchase.

The wedding takes place in the autumn or winter, when economic activities slacken, at a time appointed by the youth's maternal uncles. The bride's mother, bearing a tray of meal as a present, escorts her daughter to the home of the groom and leaves her there to grind corn for three days behind a curtain. On the third day she returns and arranges her daughter's hair in the two braids of a matron. In the evening the bride's relatives arrive with quantities of meal, from which the groom's kinswomen bake *piki*, while his clansmen provide meat, for the wedding feast on the morrow. Before dawn the next day the bride and groom have their heads washed in a bowl of yucca suds by their respective mothers-in-law. Now man and wife, they go to the edge of the mesa and offer meal and a prayer to the rising sun. The wedding breakfast follows, and the guests depart. Sometimes, it is said, the clanswomen of the groom's father, pretending to be angry because his son has brought home a strange woman, visit his house and pelt him with mud. The bride lives for several weeks with her parents-in-law, while the groom's male kinsmen spin cotton and weave her bridal costume: two cotton blankets, a white sash with a long fringe, and a pair each of moccasins and leggings. When these garments are completed, she dons them and departs, followed by her husband, for her mother's house, where they reside until they can build a separate apartment. During the first year of her married life the bride must grind nearly a ton of corn meal in compensation for the presents she has received.

The native women enjoy a comparatively high and secure status. To be sure, they are forbidden to enter the *kivas* except to repair them or to engage in ceremonies conducted exclusively by their own sex, but otherwise they labor under no important disabilities. They have no rivals, for marriage is strictly monogamous and adultery is severely frowned upon. They possess such preponderant property rights that a husband "is even frequently regarded as an outsider in his wife's home." Finally, they enjoy an equal right in divorce, which, though comparatively rare, may be accomplished without formality at the will of either party. The husband simply packs up his possessions and leaves the house. The wife may inform her spouse that his presence is no longer welcome, "or in his absence she may simply but eloquently pile his effects outside the door."

Shamans of both sexes employ various methods of treating disease. Those who specialize in the cure of a particular class of ailments are frequently organized into a fraternity.

The Yaya order of "fire priests," for example, heals fevers and inflammations by means of fire and its products, ashes and soot. A special class of herb doctors applies divers vegetal remedies, not, however, according to their actual or supposed medicinal qualities, but according to the magical principle that "like cures like." Thus they restore hair with the hairy seeds of the clematis, treat a prickly sensation in the throat with a decoction from thistles, and set fractured bones with splints from trees struck by lightning. Though not themselves capable of sorcery, some shamans possess the power to cure ailments caused by sorcerers. They blow on the patient, massage his body, employ mental concentration, and by an act of legerdemain pretend to extract a stone or an arrowhead from the affected part.

The aged, though respected and humanely treated, are not relieved of economic duties. They contribute their utmost until the end, and die "tottering along the trail." The Hopi regard death with fear and abhorrence, and refer to it only by circumlocution. For this reason a dying person is usually attended only by a few immediate relatives. The paternal kinsmen prepare the remains for immediate burial. They wash and dress the hair, paint the chin and cheeks black, place a mask over the face, clothe the body in its best garments, decorate it with ceremonial and symbolic feather objects, and wrap it tightly in a mat or blanket. In a graveyard near the foot of the mesa, a clansman of the deceased digs a circular pit just large enough to accommodate the body in a sitting position with the legs drawn up under the chin. He carries the corpse to the grave and inters it with its face to the east, while the relatives deposit trinkets and ceremonial objects beside it and in the earth above it. The site is marked by a heap of stones and by insignia representing the fraternal affiliations of the deceased. A gourd of water and a dish of food are placed on the ground. Though coyotes may eat the material food, the ghost of the departed consumes its spirit, for to the Hopi all things, including the inanimate, have "breath bodies" or souls. To prevent the return of the deceased, the mourners on their way back to the village draw lines across the trail with a piece of charcoal. On the following day they wash their heads, and for four days they visit the grave with food and ceremonial offerings.

The body of a child, *i.e.*, of a person not yet initiated into a religious fraternity, is not buried in this way, but is simply deposited in a rock crevice at the edge of the mesa, and meal is scattered along the path back to the house. The explanation lies in the belief that its soul returns to the parental home to be reincarnated in the next child born there. When the mother hears a creaking noise in the house, she offers the little ghost a pinch of meal. The "breath body" of an adult, however, lingers with the corpse for four days and then journeys to the "Skeleton House" in the underworld. Here the dead live much as do the living, except that the seasons of the year are reversed; they plant and reap, adhere to their clan organization, and conduct their religious ceremonies. The ghosts of the dead become metamorphosed into *kachinas*, or ancestral spirits of their respective clans, who form the basis of the Hopi hierarchy. Each year the *kachinas* return to earth for about six months. Their arrival is celebrated in a series of important midwinter ceremonies, and their departure in the great Niman festival in July. During their sojourn they participate, impersonated by masked men, in a variety of colorful Kachina pageants and dances, and are besought to use their supernatural powers to bring rain and ripen the crops and to intercede with the higher gods for similar favors.

But the basis of the Hopi religion is not a simple "ancestor worship." A *kachina* represents, not an individual ancestor, but rather "a generalized mythical conception which cannot be accurately identified, and is quite unlike the ancestor among the natives of the Old World." It is really an anthropomorphic totemic ancestor of a clan, which at the same time worships zoömorphic totemic culture heroes, besides being commonly named after and traditionally descended from a particular animal. The Snake clan, for example, regards snakes as its kin and venerates a Snake Youth and a Snake Maid as its totemic clan ancestors. The *kachina*, therefore, belongs to a cycle of totemic clan beliefs. But clan totemism has evolved among the Hopi into a number of cults conducted by religious fraternities or priesthoods, each with its own insignia, paraphernalia, and ceremonies. To be sure, these organizations no longer correspond in membership to the clans. Nevertheless, in most cases a fraternity still bears the name of a particular clan and recruits from it the majority of its members, particularly the chief priest.

As a result of the heterogeneous origins of the tribe, and of extensive borrowings, diverse alien elements have been grafted on this totemic foundation, so that the final product is susceptible to varied interpretations. Shall the native religion be classed as "serpent worship" in view of the veneration of Palulukon, the Great Plumed Serpent, an important god who frequents springs, controls the waters of the earth, and is associated with a legend of former human sacrifice; or as "fire worship" from the prominence of the Yaya fraternity of "fire priests," from the elaborate annual ceremonies of generating new fire, and from the cult of Masawu, the terrible God of Fire and of Death; or as "sun worship" in consideration of the conspicuous rôle of Tawa, the Sun God, to whom prayers and sacrifices of corn meal are offered in every ceremony, at each of the great crises of life, and in a special rite every morning in the life of an individual; or as "nature worship" because every heavenly body, meteorological phenomenon, and natural object is endowed with its spirit or god, and because the deities of highest rank are Sotukunani, the Sky God, in varied forms, and an Earth Goddess under a number of different names?

No particularistic explanation, however, seems sufficient to account for this composite religion. The facts best accord with the view that the primitive totemic beliefs and practices have evolved into the present cults, by internal growth, external accretion, and blending of diverse elements, under the dominating influence of the environment. An agricultural people inhabiting a cool and arid region needs, above all things, warmth and rain for the growth of its crops. It is understandable, consequently, that the Hopi should worship a Sky God who brings rain, an Earth Goddess who nourishes the seed, and a Sun God who matures the crops, as well as a special Corn Mother and a God of Growth or Germination. Moreover, the essential summer rains fall only in sudden torrential thunderstorms at irregular and unpredictable intervals; sometimes they fail entirely, or an unseasonable frost or severe windstorm blights the crops. Thus man's very existence depends upon an element of chance which manifests itself in ways so violent and seemingly arbitrary that they suggest the agency of supernatural powers as capricious as they are mighty. It is but natural, therefore, that the Hopi should bend every effort to control these unseen powers through propitiation and coercion. To this end they have developed an elaborate and time-consuming ritual, which furnishes perhaps the best example on record of a pseudo-adaptation to environment through the instrumentality of religion.

Although an element of propitiation may inhere in the ritual itself, especially in its dramatic and spectacular aspects, and perhaps also in the fasting, head-washing, sexual continence, and other forms of lustration and abnegation commonly associated with it, the motive of conciliation emerges most plainly in sacrifice. The simplest form of offering consists merely in adding a stick or a stone to the irregular piles at certain sacred places. The Indians sacrifice neither animals nor human beings to their divinities, but food offerings, especially of sacred corn meal, figure prominently in their religious ritual. They also manufacture various sacrificial objects of turkey or eagle feathers, notably their *pahos* or plumed "prayer-sticks," short sticks to which are usually tied small packets of sacred meal wrapped in corn husks in addition to the indispensable feathers. A supplication to a divine being most commonly takes the form of setting up a *paho*, scattering a pinch of corn meal, and uttering a silent prayer. This is done, as part of every ceremony, at all the sacred spots where divinities reside, especially at springs and shrines. A native shrine ranges from a mere cleft in the rocks to an elaborate structure in the center of the pueblo plaza, but the commonest form is a ring of stones for the reception of offerings. In every case it harbors a fetish, usually a rude natural stone of peculiar or suggestive shape. Superior fetishes, true idols, are found on the altars in the *kivas*. With these should perhaps be classed the studiously carved statuettes or dolls, representing *kachinas*, manufactured for the great ceremonies in which these beings participate, and later distributed among the small girls. Similar in significance and

FIG. 81. HOPI PRAYER-STICK.

execution are the elaborate masks and helmets of wood, rawhide, and basketry employed in the impersonation of animals, spirits, and gods. Upon their ceremonial paraphernalia the Hopi expend "an immense amount of inventive ability, mechanical skill, and artistic labor." In one ceremony, for example, huge mechanical serpents emerge from jars, screens, or holes in the altar and struggle realistically with one another and even with the actors.

Imitative magic likewise pervades the native ritual. The rites are coercitive as well as propitiatory. By utilizing the principle that "like produces like," man compels the powers that control natural phenomena to do his bidding. Symbolism plays an important rôle in this connection. Symbols of the sun, of rain clouds, and of fertility and growth decorate the altars and dominate the sand paintings. The designs on masks, *pahos*, and all ceremonial equipment possess an esoteric significance. "Take any one of the great Hopi ceremonies, analyze the paraphernalia worn by the men, dissect the various components of the altar and sand painting, examine the offerings made to the springs and those placed upon the shrines, and in everything and everywhere we see prayers for rain."

Ritual permeates every aspect of native society. Hunting, art, and recreation are primarily ceremonial. Rites surround planting and harvesting, and attend every crisis in the life of the individual or of the community. Remove the strands of religious ceremony from the fabric of Hopi society, and only a shell would remain. But ritual reaches its fullest development in an imposing series of regular annual ceremonies. The more elaborate of these, in the years when they are given *in extenso*, consume nine days, eight of which are spent by the priests in their *kivas* making and arranging paraphernalia and conducting secret rituals, while the ninth is devoted to a public performance or "dance." Since, however, they are preceded at a considerable interval by a formal "smoke talk" and a public announcement and are followed by three or four days of purification, a complete performance really extends over a period of approximately twenty days. The ceremonies fall into two distinct groups: the unmasked or nine-day ceremonies of the summer and autumn, characterized by altars, sand paintings, ceremonial foot races, and extensive sacrifices; and the masked or Kachina ceremonies, in which men in masks and costumes impersonate—and in theory temporarily become—ancestors and gods. Of the latter group, some are elaborate, consume nine or five days, and recur at regular periods each year; others, the "Kachina dances," are abbreviated and variable, original each year as to costume and acting, and characterized by gaiety and buffoonery. The ceremonies in general combine drama with religion, and provide the Hopi with "the best round of free theatrical entertainments enjoyed by any people in the world."

Considerations of space prevent a detailed description of even the most important ceremonies; they permit only a brief synopsis of the ceremonial calendar:

SOYALUNA or Winter Solstice Ceremony: December; nine days; celebrates advent of *kachinas* of Cloud clan; masked impersonations; dramatic representations of Sky God impregnating Earth Goddess, and of Sun God being forced back into his northward path.

MOMCITA or War Dance: December; five days; rain-making and fertility imagery conspicuous by their absence; stone fetishes of War Gods, Puukonhoya and Palunhoya, invoked for military success; public dance by Warrior Society.

PAMURTI: January; five days; celebrates advent of Badger and Mustard *kachinas;* masked impersonations; dance dramatizing return of sun.

POWAMU or Bean Planting Ceremony: February; nine days; celebrates advent of ancestors of Kachina clan; masked impersonations; dolls; beans planted in *kivas*, forced to grow in super-heated rooms, and distributed; consecration of fields for planting; initiation of children by flogging.

PALULUKONTI: March; five days; masked impersonations; a mystery play featuring the Great Plumed Serpent; grotesque mechanical serpent effigies; corn sprouted in *kivas*.

KACHINA DANCES: April to June; successive one-day performances in varied masks and costumes, impersonating *kachinas;* frenzied rhythmic dances, with clowns furnishing comic relief.

NIMAN: July; nine days; celebrates departure of *kachinas* for the underworld; masked impersonations; presents to children.

TCUATIKIBI or Snake Ceremony: August; biennial, in odd years in eastern pueblos and in even years in western pueblos; nine days; a spectacular rain-making drama.

LELENTI or Flute Ceremony: August; biennial, alternating with Snake Ceremony; nine days; rain-making symbolism prominent; vocal and instrumental music; public rite at spring.

LAGON or Basket Dance: September; biennial, in even years; nine days; ceremonial foot race and public dance with basket trays by priestesses of a women's society.

OWAKUL or Harvest Dance: October; biennial, in odd years; nine days; a basket dance by members of a women's society impersonating divinities of germination and growth.

MARAU or Tablet Dance: October; biennial, in odd years; nine days; public dance by members of a women's society bearing wooden tablets instead of baskets.

WUWUCHIM or New Fire Ceremony: November; nine days; four fraternities participate; generation of sacred new fire with a pump drill; dancing with phallic symbols and obscene songs as rites of imitative magic to promote fertility; initiation of novices every fourth year after vigils, fasting, and ordeals; a foot race of twenty-five miles and a ceremonial rabbit hunt.

In addition to these major ceremonies, the Hopi celebrate numerous minor ones, including a Buffalo Dance, a Children's Dance, a Butterfly Dance, and abbreviated winter performances of all the summer festivals to synchronize with the ceremonies in the underworld, where the seasons are reversed. Thus throughout the year one rite has scarcely ended before the next begins.

The details of a single ceremony will suffice to illustrate the complexity of the native ritual. For this purpose the *Tcuatikibi* or Snake Ceremony may be selected, for, although neither the most important nor the most elaborate on the calendar, it is the most spectacular and famous. It combines worship of the totemic ancestors of the Snake clan with ritual pleas for rain. Preparations begin the preceding winter, when *pahos* are manufactured and offered to the divinities of the cardinal directions. On the first day of the ceremony proper, the members of the Snake and Antelope fraternities assemble in their respective *kivas*. The rites in the Antelope *kiva* center about a beautiful colored sand mosaic representing lightning, clouds, and falling rain. From the third to the sixth day the Snake priests, their bodies stripped to the loin cloth and painted, deposit *pahos* at the springs and shrines, and scour the country in all directions for snakes, beating the sagebrush and thrusting their hands fearlessly into holes. On finding a snake, they strew it with sacred meal, stroke it gently with a feather whip, seize it by the neck, and deposit it in a pouch, which is returned to the *kiva* in the evening. The seventh day is devoted to the preparation of paraphernalia and medicines, and to chants and prayers, and the eighth to the ceremonial foot race and public dance of the Antelope society. At dawn on the ninth or final day, two Snake priests circumambulate the village with bull-roarers and curious lightning-frames of crossed sticks so constructed that they can be projected and returned in imitation of lightning. The morning race of the Snake society follows. The priests now assemble in the *kiva* to wash the snakes by way of purification for the coming dance. One man, dressed as a warrior, plunges his hand into a bag of miscellaneous serpents, brings out a handful, dips them in a bowl of medicine water and yucca suds, and drops them on a field of sand, where the priests herd them to dry. Here they are left for two hours, while the boys toy with them, "permitting them to crawl over and under their feet, handling them, using them as playthings, paying no more attention to the rattlesnakes than to the smallest harmless whip-snakes."

For the final act of the ceremony, the public dance, the Snake priests array themselves in ceremonial kilts, ornaments, and rattles, let their hair hang free, and smear their faces and bare bodies with black, white, and brown paint. Then, while the Antelope priests dance, sing, and shake gourd rattles, they circle the plaza and advance in trios to a cottonwood bower. Here one member of each trio receives a snake and holds it in his mouth or wraps it around his neck as he dances, while the second member strokes it with a feather whip. After completing the circuit of the plaza four times, the dancer drops the reptile, which is immediately seized by the third member of the trio. When all the snakes have been thus handled, they are deposited in a charmed circle and sprinkled with meal by the women. At a signal, the priests rush wildly forward, seize as many of the reptiles as they can hold, dash down the trails to the plain, and release them at specified shrines. Four days of purification and festivity follow, during which rain seldom fails to fall in answer to the rites and prayers. Why the performers so rarely suffer from snake bite in this ceremony remains something of a mystery. The fangs are not removed, nor are the reptiles stupefied. Careful handling and herding with others of their kind furnish a partial explanation. The Snake priests themselves, though mortally afraid of rattlesnakes at other times, are sustained by a firm conviction that they enjoy complete immunity during the ceremony—an immunity which they attribute to their totemic relationship to the serpents.

The first white men to visit the Hopi were the Spaniards under Tovar and Padilla in 1540. Contact remained casual until 1629, when the Spaniards established missions among them. These met with little success, for the natives resented the demands of the priests for labor and female companions, and, in 1680, when the fathers forbade the planting of *pahos*, they rose in open revolt and slew every Spaniard in the country. An attempt to reëstablish a mission in 1700 was equally unsuccessful, and the Hopi preserved their comparative isolation for two centuries longer, indeed, for some years after the establishment of their reservation in 1882. Wars and recurrent famines have reduced the population from nearly 5,000 to perhaps one-third of that number today. From the Spaniards the Hopi received horses, sheep, cattle, and goats, and of late they have become more or less pastoral. Iron implements, glass beads, new food plants, and other alien importations have also greatly modified their material culture. Peace prevails today, and many families have deserted the pueblos to live in modern houses near their fields. The native ceremonial, however, has altered but little; the Hopi neither want nor need "the stern religion of the missionary, which will not guarantee rain."

BIBLIOGRAPHY

BOURKE, J. G. *The Snake-Dance of the Moquis of Arizona.* London, 1884.

COOLIDGE, M. R. *The Rain-Makers.* Boston, 1929.

CRANE, L. *Indians of the Enchanted Desert.* Boston, 1925.

*CURTIS, E. S. *The North American Indian,* Vol. XII. Seattle, 1922.

CUSHING, F. H., FEWKES, J. W., and PARSONS, E. C. "Contributions to Hopi History." *American Anthropologist,* New Series, Vol. XXIV. Menasha, 1922.

DORSEY, G. A. *Indians of the Southwest.* Chicago, 1903.

DORSEY, G. A., and VOTH, H. R. "The Mishongnovi Ceremonies of the Snake and Antelope Fraternities." *Field Columbian Museum, Anthropological Series,* Vol. III. Chicago, 1902.

——. "The Oraibi Soyal Ceremony." *Field Columbian Museum, Anthropological Series,* Vol. III. Chicago, 1901.

EICKHOFF, H. "Die Kultur der Pueblos in Arizona und New Mexico." *Studien und Forschungen zur Menschen- und Völkerkunde,* Vol. IV. Stuttgart, 1908.

FEWKES, J. W. "Ancestor Worship of the Hopi Indians." *Smithsonian Institution, Annual Report of the Board of Regents for the Year Ending June 30, 1921,* Part 1. Washington, 1922.

——. "Fire Worship of the Hopi Indians." *Smithsonian Institution, Annual Report of the Board of Regents for the Year Ending June 30, 1920,* Part 1. Washington, 1922.

——. "The Growth of the Hopi Ritual." *Journal of American Folk-Lore,* Vol. XI. Boston, 1898.

——. "Hopi Basket Dances." *Journal of American Folk-Lore,* Vol. XII. Boston, 1899.

——. "Hopi Katcinas." *Twenty-first Annual Report of the Bureau of American Ethnology.* Washington, 1903.

——. "Hopi Shrines near the East Mesa, Arizona." *American Anthropologist,* New Series, Vol. VIII. Lancaster, 1906.

FEWKES, J. W. "Minor Hopi Festivals." *American Anthropologist*, New Series, Vol. IV. New York, 1902.

——. "Notes on Tusayan Snake and Flute Ceremonies." *Nineteenth Annual Report of the Bureau of American Ethnology*, Part 2. Washington, 1900.

——. "Property-Right in Eagles among the Hopi." *American Anthropologist*, New Series, Vol. II. New York, 1900.

——. "The Sacrificial Element in Hopi Worship." *Journal of American Folk-Lore*, Vol. X. Boston, 1897.

——. "Sky-God Impersonations in Hopi Worship." *Journal of American Folk-Lore*, Vol. XV. Boston, 1902.

——. "Sun Worship of the Hopi Indians." *Smithsonian Institution, Annual Report of the Board of Regents for the Year Ending June 30, 1918*. Washington, 1920.

——. "Tusayan Katcinas." *Fifteenth Annual Report of the Bureau of Ethnology*. Washington, 1897.

——. "The Tusayan Ritual: a Study of the Influence of Environment on Aboriginal Cults." *Smithsonian Institution, Annual Report of the Board of Regents to July, 1895*, Part 1. Washington, 1896.

——. "Tusayan Snake Ceremonies." *Sixteenth Annual Report of the Bureau of American Ethnology*. Washington, 1897.

——. "The Use of Idols in Hopi Worship." *Smithsonian Institution, Annual Report of the Board of Regents for the Year Ending June 30, 1922*, Part 1. Washington, 1924.

FEWKES, J. W., STEPHEN, A. M., and OWENS, J. G. "The Snake Ceremonials at Walpi." *Journal of American Ethnology and Archæology*, Vol. IV. Boston, 1894.

FORDE, C. D. "Hopi Agriculture and Land Ownership." *Journal of the Royal Anthropological Institute of Great Britain and Ireland*, Vol. LXI. London, 1931.

GODDARD, P. E. *Indians of the Southwest*. New York, 1913.

GRAY, L. H. "Hopi." *Encyclopædia of Religion and Ethics*. Edited by J. Hastings. 12 vols. New York, 1908–22.

HODGE, F. W. (editor). "Handbook of American Indians North of Mexico." *Smithsonian Institution, Bureau of American Ethnology, Bulletin 30*. 2 vols. Washington, 1907–10.

HOUGH, W. "The Hopi in Relation to Their Plant Environment." *American Anthropologist*, Vol. X. Washington, 1897.

HOUGH, W. "The Hopi Indian Collection in the United States National Museum." *Proceedings of the United States National Museum*, Vol. LIV. Washington, 1919.

*——. *The Hopi Indians*. Cedar Rapids, 1915.

HRDLIČKA, A. "Physiological and Medical Observations among the Indians of Southwestern United States and Northern Mexico." *Smithsonian Institution, Bureau of American Ethnology, Bulletin 34*. Washington, 1908.

JAMES, G. W. *The Indians of the Painted Desert Region*. Boston, 1903.

KIDDER, A. V. *An Introduction to the Study of Southwestern Archæology*. New Haven, 1924.

LOWIE, R. H. "Hopi Kinship." *Anthropological Papers of the American Museum of Natural History*, Vol. XXX. New York, 1929.

——. "Notes on Hopi Clans." *Anthropological Papers of the American Museum of Natural History*, Vol. XXX. New York, 1929.

MINDELEFF, C. "Localization of Tusayan Clans." *Nineteenth Annual Report of the Bureau of American Ethnology*, Part 2. Washington, 1900.

MINDELEFF, V. "A Study of Pueblo Architecture: Tusayan and Cibola." *Eighth Annual Report of the Bureau of Ethnology*. Washington, 1891.

OWENS, J. G. "Natal Ceremonies of the Hopi Indians." *Journal of American Ethnology and Archæology*, Vol. II. Boston, 1892.

RENAUD, E. B. "Evolution of Population and Dwelling in the Indian Southwest." *Social Forces*, Vol. VII. Chapel Hill, 1928.

SPENCER, F. C. *Education of the Pueblo Child*. New York, 1899.

STRONG, W. D. "An Analysis of Southwestern Society." *American Anthropologist*, New Series, Vol. XXIX. Menasha, 1917.

VOTH, H. R. "Brief Miscellaneous Hopi Papers." *Field Museum of Natural History, Anthropological Series*, Vol. XI. Chicago, 1912.

——. "Hopi Proper Names." *Field Columbian Museum, Anthropological Series*, Vol. VI. Chicago, 1905.

——. "The Oraibi Marau Ceremony." *Field Museum of Natural History, Anthropological Series*, Vol. XI. Chicago, 1912.

VOTH, H. R. "Oraibi Marriage Customs." *American Anthropologist*, New Series, Vol. II. New York, 1900.

——. "Oraibi Natal Customs and Ceremonies." *Field Columbian Museum, Anthropological Series*, Vol. VI. Chicago, 1905.

——. "The Oraibi Oaqol Ceremony." *Field Columbian Museum, Anthropological Series*, Vol. VI. Chicago, 1903.

——. "The Oraibi Powamu Ceremony." *Field Columbian Museum, Anthropological Series*, Vol. III. Chicago, 1901.

——. "The Oraibi Summer Snake Ceremony." *Field Columbian Museum, Anthropological Series*, Vol. III. Chicago, 1903.

CHAPTER XIII

THE AZTECS OF MEXICO

BY about 4000 B.C., the nomadic Indians of southern Mexico and the adjacent regions of Central America had laid the corner stone of a new and original civilization with the invention of pottery and textiles and the domestication and cultivation of the maize plant. Several centuries before the dawn of our era, the leading tribe, the Mayas, had perfected a hieroglyphic system of writing, a numerical system with a symbol for zero, and a calendar more accurate than any then existing in the Old World. By 200 A.D. the Maya civilization, with its intensive agriculture and its developed arts, sciences, and religion, was in full flower. Its inexplicable decline about 600, its rebirth in a new home, Yucatan, four centuries later, and its second and final decline after 1200 concern us here far less than its spread north and west into Mexico. The Zapotecs of Oaxaca, in particular, had developed a high derivative culture perhaps as early as 300 A.D. From the far north there now came a series of invasions by the various tribes of the barbarous Nahua nation, allied in language and possibly in culture to the Shoshonean tribes of the western United States. The first Nahuan immigrants, the Toltecs, established themselves in the valley of Mexico in the seventh century, absorbed the elements of Maya culture from the Zapotecs, and, with significant contributions of their own, built an urbane civilization at Tula and other cities. After flourishing for four centuries, they were overwhelmed by later Nahuan invaders—the Chichimecs, Acolhuas, Tepanecs, and other tribes—yielding their culture to the newcomers.

The last of the Nahuan tribes, the Aztecs, arrived in the valley of Mexico in the thirteenth century. Weak in numbers and low in culture, they wandered from place to place, subject first to the Acolhuas and then to the Tepanecs. At last, in 1325, they settled permanently on a marshy island in Lake Tezcuco and founded there the city of Tenochtitlan or Mexico. In 1376 they elected their first king. Protected by their inhospitable and inaccessible location, they gradually advanced in civilization and numbers. Under their fourth monarch, Itzcoatl (1427–1440), they succeeded, with the aid of neighboring cities, in throwing off the Tepanec yoke, and then founded a powerful tripartite confederacy with the Acolhua city of Tezcuco and the Tepanec city of Tlacopan. The allies, led by the Aztecs, embarked on a career of conquest. Warring against the other Nahuan peoples and against the Otomi on the north, the Huaxtecs and Totonacs on the east, the Zapotecs and Mixtecs on the south, and the Tarascans on the west, they gradually built up a loose empire extending from coast to coast and reaching from 18° to 21° north latitude on the Atlantic side and from 14° to 19° on the Pacific. Within this region, however, certain cities and tribes, like the Nahuan Tlaxcaltecs and the Tarascans, retained their independence, and others were only nominally tributary.

During the reign of the ninth Aztec king, Montezuma II, the Spaniards arrived. Grijalva skirted the eastern coast in 1518, and in the following year Cortez landed with 450 men to conquer the country. Every reader of Prescott is familiar with the dramatic story of the march to Mexico, the imprisonment of Montezuma, the massacre of native worshipers at the great temple, the bloody retreat of the Spaniards on *la noche triste* (June 30, 1520), their return, the siege and systematic destruction of the city, and the capitulation on August 13, 1521, of the last broken remnant of a warlike people.

Typical Indians in their physical characteristics, the Aztecs had complexions of a light copper color, an average stature of not quite five feet three inches for men and five inches

FIG. 82. A NAHUA WOMAN OF TODAY, DESCENDANT OF THE AZTECS.
Courtesy of the American Museum of Natural History

less for women, heads of medium breadth (cephalic index 79), intensely dark brown eyes, mesorrhine noses (nasal index 80), regular teeth, coarse, straight, black hair, and scanty beards and body hair.

The Aztec language, still spoken by nearly a million Mexicans, belongs to the Nahuatlan branch of the Uto-Aztecan linguistic stock. Of its rich vocabulary of some 27,000 words, a number have found their way into English, *e.g.*, avocado, chili, chocolate, cocoa, copal, ocelot, and tomato. A language of the incorporative type, it is able to weld ten or more individual words into a unified whole, so that a single word may be equivalent to an entire sentence. Thus the full name of King Montezuma means "when-the-chief-is-angry-he-shoots-to-heaven." For recording historical events, calendrical and astronomical knowledge, religious ritual, land titles, and tribute receipts, the Aztecs employed a partially pictographic and partially hieroglyphic form of writing. They represented material objects by pictures, numbers by conventional symbols, and names by rebuses. On the rebus principle, for example, the name of King Itzcoatl was shown by the picture of a snake (*coatl*) bristling with stone knives (*itztli*). From the few books which have survived the bonfires of a fanatic Christian clergy, we know that the Mexican scribes wrote in colors with a feather brush on deerskin parchment, fine cloth, or a paper manufactured from agave fibers, and that they folded the pages in zigzag fashion like a series of picture postcards and bound the backs with boards.

In counting, the Aztecs employed a quinary-vigesimal system, *i.e.*, one based, not on tens, but primarily on twenties and secondarily on fives. Thus the word for five meant "a hand taken"; for ten, "two hands"; and for twenty, "a complete count" (meaning, probably, all the fingers and toes of a man). In writing, 1 was represented by a dot, 5 by a bar, 20 by a flag, 400 by a tree, and 8,000 by an incense pouch. To write the number 8,888, for example, one would draw a pouch, two trees, four flags, a bar, and three dots.

The geographical backbone of Mexico consists of two converging mountain ranges, the eastern and western Sierra Madre, whose snow-clad and often volcanic peaks culminate in Mt. Orizaba, with an altitude of over 18,000 feet. Along either coast stretches a narrow strip of lowlands, the so-called *tierra caliente*, characterized by a tropical climate, fauna, and flora. Farther inland, on the outer slopes of the mountains between 3,000 and 6,000 feet above sea level, lies a subtropical zone, the *tierra templada*. A plateau 7,500 feet in elevation occupies the region between the two ranges and constitutes a third or temperate zone, the *tierra fria*. Here, in the fertile valley of Mexico, rich in mineral deposits, lived the Aztecs. The temperature of this region varies comparatively little from the annual mean of 63° F. The summers are cool. Snow is rare and frosts infrequent in winter, though chill winds are not uncommon. Irregular violent storms bring rain from June until October, when a dry season of eight months commences. The annual precipitation does not exceed twenty-five inches, and the few streams drain mostly into five brackish highland lakes, of which the largest is Lake Tezcuco. Forests of pine and oak clothe the mountain sides, and cactus and other desert plants the more arid places. The native fauna includes the bear, puma, jaguar, ocelot, deer, wolf, coyote, and countless lesser mammals, birds, reptiles, fishes, and insects.

The ancient inhabitants of this country derived their subsistence chiefly from maize, which they cultivated in fields watered by irrigation canals and protected by hedges of agave or walls of stone and adobe. They allowed exhausted lands to lie fallow for a few years and then burned them over, but otherwise they used no fertilizer. After preparing the ground with a wooden mattock, they planted the seed in parallel rows in holes made with a pointed stick. They heaped up the earth about each plant, kept the fields well weeded, and drove birds away with slings. The harvested grain they stored in wooden granaries and ground into corn meal on metates. Though the ears were sometimes boiled or roasted, maize was usually eaten in the form of unleavened cakes (*tortillas*) of various sorts, especially a thin bread baked on a hot plate, and balls of dough wrapped in leaves and steamed. Another popular dish was a maize porridge, made by boiling corn meal in water, straining off the liquor, and boiling it down into a gruel.

In addition to maize, the Aztecs or their subjects cultivated a wide variety of plants and trees for food and other purposes: kidney beans, squashes, gourds, chia, sweet potatoes, red peppers, cacao, vanilla, tobacco, cotton, guavas, avocados, Indian figs, and pineapples. The most universally useful native plant, however, was the agave or maguey. Its thorns served as needles and its trunk as a building material; its roots were edible; its leaves provided thatch for houses and fibers for cloth and paper; and its sap yielded a sweet syrup and an alcoholic beverage. Persons who could afford to do so maintained gardens of fragrant flowers and medicinal herbs, with fountains, pools for fish, and walks bordered by rows of ornamental trees.

Fish, caught in the lakes and streams with hook and line, tridents, nets, and weirs, supplemented the native plant foods. Certain marsh flies, pounded, rolled into balls, and boiled, were eaten with relish. Other delicacies included a kind of caviar made from the eggs of the same flies, and a sort of cheese prepared from the curdled ooze which formed at certain times on the surface of the lakes. Meat was little used, although venison, wild fowl, and other game found a place on the tables of the rich. A little hunting was done with the bow and arrow, a blowgun shooting pellets, a sling, darts, nets, and snares, but the chase was mainly either a noble sport or a means of supplying the temples, by communal drives, with animals for sacrifice. The principal domesticated animals were the turkey, prized for its meat and feathers, and the dog, fattened for food but not used for transportation. The Aztecs also raised bees for their honey and wax, and carefully cultivated the cochineal insect on plantations of cactus for the sake of the rich crimson dye which it yielded. They kept geese, ducks, and quails in a semi-domesticated state, and the kings and wealthy nobles even maintained game preserves, menageries of wild animals, and aviaries of tropical birds.

A variety of condiments provided seasoning for the native dishes: vanilla, honey, syrup from the sap of the maize and agave, salt made by the evaporation of brackish water in pots or shallow trenches, and especially the red or chili pepper, which was made into a sauce for *tortillas* and nearly every other food. From cacao, the Aztecs prepared a delicious frothy chocolate, frequently seasoned with vanilla, honey, or pepper. They brewed a variety of fermented liquors from maize sap, chia seeds, and fruit juices, but their favorite alcoholic beverage was pulque, made from the sap of the agave. They chewed tobacco or smoked it, mixed with powdered charcoal and fragrant herbs, in hollow reeds or in the form of cigars. To induce religious ecstasy or visions they ate peyote, a kind of cactus, and unmarried girls are said to have been addicted to the use of a chewing gum of resin or bitumen.

For cooking, eating, and other household purposes the Aztecs used earthenware dishes, bowls, cups, pitchers, and vases, supplemented to a limited extent by gourd vessels, woven wicker baskets, and utensils of wood and tortoise shell. Lacking the potter's wheel, the artisans worked entirely by hand—modeling directly from a lump of clay, building by the coil method, or using a basketry mold. They applied colored slips and designs, and added handles, legs, and decorations in relief, before firing. In addition to the common ware—thin, unglazed vessels of orange-colored clay with geometric designs in black—they manufactured utensils of other types, occasionally glazed, and clay figurines and musical instruments.   The finest pottery, however, was obtained by trade from the natives of Cholula.

In the art of stone-working few peoples have equaled the ancient Mexicans.   They manufactured very serviceable stone axes, adzes, and chisels, laboriously grinding the material into shape wth the aid of emery and water, and giving the surface a fine polish with bamboo.   From obsidian, an exceedingly hard and sharp volcanic rock, they obtained, by

After Saville

FIG. 83. AN AZTEC OBSIDIAN MIRROR IN A GILDED WOODEN FRAME.

pressure chipping, long slender flakes which served excellently as knives, razors, and points for weapons. Axes and adzes were supplied with wooden handles, but a lump of resin ordinarily sufficed for knives and razors.   Mexican monumental sculpture—stone images, "calendar stones," and bas-reliefs on temple walls—impresses the modern artist as rather stiff and conventional, but the art of the lapidary arouses enthusiasm. The native jeweler set gems in gold, did tasteful inlay work with semi-precious stones, and with infinite labor worked obsidian into beautiful polished mirrors and masks. He reached the climax of his art, however, in his incomparable stone mosaics. To wooden masks and helmets, to the handles of ceremonial knives, even to human skulls, he applied, on a

matrix of resin, stones of the most gorgeous and varied colors
—amethyst, crystal, and jade; turquoise, jasper, and jet;
pyrites, pearls, and shells—achieving effects and combinations of striking beauty.

Though still living primarily in the stone age, the Aztecs
worked copper, silver, and gold with considerable skill.
Copper was mined by applying fire to the ore and driving
wedges into the resulting cracks, and was hammered or cast
into ax and adze blades, chisels, needles, mirrors, and bells.

After Saville

FIG. 84. MEXICAN GOLD ORNAMENTS FROM OAXACA.

But in smelting this metal—done in a clay crucible over a
charcoal fire fanned by a blowpipe—tin was never intentionally added to produce bronze. Gold, curiously termed "excrement of the gods," was obtained by mining or by washing
river sands, was worked by the same methods as copper, and
was used mainly for ornaments and ceremonial objects. The
native goldsmiths hammered the metal into thin foils for
plating articles of baser materials, and into wires with which
they did fine filigree work. They also cast the metal by the
cire-perdue method. On a core of clay and charcoal, incised
with the desired design, the artist built up a wax model of the
object to be cast, and covered core and model with a shell of
charcoal and clay. When the whole was fired, the wax melted
away, leaving a hollow earthenware mold. Molten gold was
then poured in, the mold broken, and the article cleaned and
polished. The admiration with which the Spanish conquerors

beheld such products of the goldsmith's art as miniature birds with movable heads, wings, and legs, and fish with scales alternately of gold and silver, was exceeded only by the cupidity with which they seized them and consigned them to the melting pot.

From cotton and agave fibers the Aztecs spun thread, using a pottery spindle whorl, and wove textiles on a simple horizontal loom. They decorated their fabrics with embroidery and with vegetable and mineral dyes, which they commonly applied to the cloth with pottery stamps in geometrical

After Spinden

FIG. 85. AZTEC
BLANKET DESIGN.

designs. Occasionally they interwove rabbit fur with cotton to produce rich warm fabrics, but their featherwork surpassed all other textiles. In addition to coarser work with turkey feathers, they utilized the gay plumage of the parrot, toucan, humming bird, scarlet tanager, and other tropical birds to manufacture mantles and ornaments for warriors, priests, and the idols of the gods. To a base of cloth they attached, either by threads or by paste, a layer of coarser plumes, and to this an outer layer of the finest feathers. The designs, applied with the aid of stencils, were mainly symbolical or indicative of rank. The brilliance of the feathers themselves, the patterned masses of color outlined in black, the iridescent hues and harmonious combinations, produced effects gorgeous beyond description.

On ordinary occasions the men wore a girdle and a knee-length mantle knotted over the right shoulder; the women, a sleeveless tunic and a skirt extending from waist to calf. Leather sandals with embroidered straps completed the costume of both sexes. The women wore their hair long and loose, and painted their faces yellow with stamped designs of birds and monkeys in red. Tattooing and circumcision were not practiced, but the ears, lower lip, and nasal septum were commonly pierced and the teeth occasionally filed. For adornment, especially in war and on ceremonial occasions, the people wore headdresses, earrings, nose plugs, lip pendants, bracelets, necklaces, anklets, feather ornaments, and other jewels or trinkets of the most diverse patterns and materials. But ornament and clothing, to the Aztecs, served primarily, not an æsthetic purpose, in gratifying individual tastes, but a practical one in distinguishing gradations of rank and social status. Poor and undistinguished persons were forbidden, under drastic penalties, to wear garments of fine cotton and ornaments of precious stones and metals, whereas brave warriors and high officials were privileged to assume styles in clothing, hairdressing, and jewelry graded strictly according to their achievements and station.

The common people inhabited rectangular one-room huts of adobe or wattle smeared with mud, the roof flat and thatched with agave leaves, the floor often raised above the marshy ground on piles. Granaries, a raised building for fowls, and a bathhouse surrounded the dwelling. Pine torches lighted the interior, for windows were rare. The entrance was protected, not by a door, but by suspended reeds with shards and other objects attached to give warning of intruders. In the center of the room a fire burned on a stone hearth. A single family occupied the dwelling, eating on mats spread on the floor, and sleeping on mud or wooden beds covered with rushes, mats, skins, mantles, or sheets. The wealthy and noble could afford carved wooden furniture—chairs, tables, screens, chests—as well as more pretentious dwellings. They lived in large houses or palaces, built around rectangular courts, with plastered floors, flat battlemented roofs, and walls of stone faced with white stucco. Owing to ignorance of the arch, the masonry was massive and the rooms small, but pleasing columns and colonnades were not uncommon. Completely dominating the architecture of the Mexican city, however, were the great temple pyramids, sometimes over a hundred feet in height. The pyramids themselves, of earth or rubble faced with sculptured masonry, with their flat tops and stepped or terraced sides, served merely as platforms for the comparatively insignificant altars and temples which surmounted them. From the summits, perpetual fires cast a ghostly illumination over the city at night.

The island city of Tenochtitlan or Mexico, the true home of the Aztecs, was connected with the mainland by a number of long artificial causeways, pierced by sluices and protected by

FIG. 86. THE GREAT AZTEC TEMPLE, ACCORDING TO A RECONSTRUCTION.
Courtesy of the American Museum of Natural History

drawbridges. Over one of them a double aqueduct of stone and cement brought the inhabitants a constant supply of fresh water. The city itself was intersected by narrow paved streets and a network of canals. In the absence of any beasts of burden, all travel was either by water or by foot. Dugout canoes and bamboo rafts brought produce into the city by lake and canal, and, on land, porters carried goods on their backs with the aid of a tumpline around the forehead. Important persons were sometimes transported in litters. A system of narrow but well-kept roads covered the country, spanning streams and ravines by stone or wooden bridges and rivers by suspension bridges of vines. At posts, situated every few miles along the main highways, were stationed trained couriers. Running in relays, they are said to have borne news and messages with incredible speed and to have supplied the table of Montezuma daily with fresh fish from the Gulf of Mexico.

In the division of labor by sex, the women cared for the house, prepared and cooked the food, made and laundered the clothing, performed the lighter agricultural tasks, and engaged to a certain extent in trade. The men did the heavy agricultural labor, engaged in war and governmental activities, and monopolized the specialized trades. The latter were exceedingly numerous: carpentry, wood carving, masonry, stonecutting, metal-working, weaving, tanning, fishing, floriculture, the manufacture of pottery, basketry, mats, weapons, jewelry, and featherwork, etc. It was common, but not compulsory, for a son to follow his father's occupation. One economic class, the *pochteca* or itinerant merchants, occupied a unique position and enjoyed special privileges. It formed practically a closed guild, with hereditary membership and its own insignia, officials, gods, ceremonies, and system of justice. United in strong armed bands with retinues of porters to transport their goods, these lordly merchants traveled throughout the realm and far beyond its borders, exchanging their wares for the products of other tribes. Acting at the same time as spies, they secured information of military and political importance for the government at home. They thus formed the advance guard of Aztec imperialism, for any injury to a merchant was seized upon as a pretext for a war of conquest.

Along with their high development of specialization by occupation and locality, the Aztecs engaged extensively in trade. Although retail shops and middlemen were unknown, local markets sold provisions, and a great market was held every fifth day in the suburb of Tlaltelolco. Here the various artisans and producers assembled with their goods from miles around, and throngs of purchasers appeared. Each ware had its assigned place, and special officials kept order, supervised weights and measures, and tried disputes. Although barter was extensively practiced, certain articles found general acceptance as media of exchange, notably sacks of cacao beans, small squares of cotton cloth, copper ax blades, and quills of gold dust. In addition to transactions for cash, the Aztecs extended credit and made loans on security though without interest. For failure to pay a debt or repay a loan, the penalty was enslavement.

An organization into twenty exogamous non-totemic clans (*calpulli*), united by descent in the male line, formed the basis of Aztec society. Localized in separate districts in the city of Mexico, the several clans, each with its own temple and cult, council house and officials, tilled their lands and carried on their other economic activities. Each married male member had the right to receive from the clan a plot of land for the support of his family. He could use his plot as he saw fit or rent it to a fellow clansman if unable, on account of incapacity or the conflict of official duties, to cultivate it himself. At his death he could transmit it to his eldest son—or, in default of sons, to a younger brother or nephew—and even, by a deathbed disposition, disinherit a senior heir in favor of a junior. Nevertheless, the land was not his private property, for he could not sell it, and it reverted to the clan if his line became extinct or if he abandoned it or left it untilled for two years. The undistributed lands of the clan formed a fund from which younger sons were allotted plots as they came of age and married. Portions were cultivated in common for the support of officials, temples, and warriors. The landholders or family heads formed a council, which administered the affairs of the clan and exercised civil and criminal jurisdiction in cases involving clan members. A headman (*calpullec*) presided over the council, distributed the lands and kept a written record of all holdings, settled property disputes, and administered the public stores. He was elected by the council—nearly

always, however, from among the sons of the predecessor—
and, in return for his services, was relieved from the duty
of tilling his own land. A war chief (*achcacautli*) led the
forces of the clan in battle, instructed the youth in military
exercises, and served as a chief of police in preserving order
and executing justice. A third elective official, the *tlatoani*
or "speaker," represented the clan in the tribal council.

Above the ordinary clansmen, or commoners, stood a
class of honorary lords or knights (*tecutin*), constituting,
with various gradations, a non-hereditary order of merit.
The rank was conferred for life upon men conspicuous for
prowess in war, for sagacity in office, for meritorious public
service as in the case of itinerant merchants, and for exceptional piety as manifested by long periods of fasting,
self-torture, and penitential exercises. Such men enjoyed
special privileges, especially freedom from all but nominal
taxes and the right to wear fine cotton clothing, ornaments
of gold and precious stones, and various special emblems
and insignia of rank. Universally honored and esteemed,
they were preferred above all others for responsible offices.

The conquests of the Aztecs and the resulting prosperity
tended in several ways to elevate the class of lords and to
differentiate them more and more sharply from the common
people. As military leaders and public officials, they received the lion's share of the rich tribute which poured in
from the subject provinces. Marked inequalities in the
distribution of wealth began to develop—inequalities made
possible by the recognition of private property in movables
and perpetuated by the law permitting the inheritance of
such property. Since power inevitably accrues to power,
the son of a wealthy lord was almost as certain to acquire
in some way the rank of his father as he was to inherit a
share of the property. Even the principle of the communal
ownership of land began to waver. Great tracts of conquered
territory were distributed to deserving lords in reward for
their services, and large landed estates thus arose. To be

sure, these awards were usually only for life. The land could not be alienated or inherited; at the death of the lord it passed to his successor in office, not to his heir. In other cases, however, though it could not be alienated, it could be inherited, reverting to the state only if the family became extinct. But even in the former case, the heir received the land if he succeeded to his father's office—an event of increasingly frequent occurrence. Thus, with virtual, if not actual, private property in landed estates and virtual inheritance of rank, the Aztecs may be said to have hovered on the verge of an hereditary feudal aristocracy.

Below the common clansmen in the social scale stood two unprivileged classes—a propertyless proletariat and a class of slaves. The proletariat, consisting partly of expropriated aliens and partly of persons who had forfeited their clan membership for refusal to marry or to till their lands, earned their livelihood either as porters or as virtual serfs tilling the lands of the lords under heavy burdens of taxes and services. Slaves were recruited from several sources: debtors, especially gamblers and spendthrifts, forced into slavery for inability to meet their obligations, criminals of certain types, youths and girls delivered by subject peoples as part of their tribute, members of the proletariat voluntarily selling themselves into slavery, and children sold by parents in dire distress. In the last case, the contract frequently specified that a younger child might be substituted when the older attained marriageable age. On the whole, slavery assumed a very mild form. The master owned, not the person of the slave, but only a right to his services. He could not kill or mistreat him. He could not even sell him without the slave's consent, and then only by a formal contract with four witnesses. The slave retained the right to marry, to raise a family, and to accumulate property of his own, and his children were free, *i.e.*, not slaves but members of the proletariat. Finally, he might secure redemption from his status in several ways: by marrying his master or mistress, by accumulating sufficient property to pay back his purchase price or indebtedness, or by successful flight to an asylum in the royal residence.

The freemen with their clan affiliations, however, were overwhelmingly preponderant in numbers and formed the backbone of the state. The twenty clans were grouped into four phratries or major tribal subdivisions, each with its temple, its armory, and its leader or captain-general. These officials were among the most powerful lords of the realm. They advised and assisted the king, led the forces of their phratries in war, and were responsible for the execution of justice. Their offices, like all others, were at least theoretically elective and non-hereditary. The Aztec tribe, strictly speaking, inhabited only the city of Mexico and its immediate environs. The league with the Acolhuas of Tezcuco and the Tepanecs of Tlacopan was merely a military alliance. Each of the allies retained its own laws and government, and could make conquests and have tributaries of its own. Any of the members, however, could call upon the others for assistance, in which case the Aztec king assumed the military leadership, and the tribute from the conquered peoples was distributed two-fifths to Mexico, two-fifths to Tezcuco, and one-fifth to Tlacopan. The Aztecs, as the most warlike of the three tribes, became the dominant member of the league, with by far the greatest number of conquests to their credit, but their so-called "empire" was merely a loose aggregation of subject and allied peoples variously related to them.

Within the tribe, a council of twenty "speakers," representing the clans, administered the ordinary affairs of state, declared war and made peace, and deliberated and decided disputes between clans or between members of different clans. Matters of exceptional moment, such as legal cases of unusual difficulty and the election of a new king, were referred to a great council, which met every eighty days and which included—besides the speakers—the headmen and war leaders of the clans, the captains-general of the phratries, other high officials, and the ranking priests. At the *tecpan* or great plaza in the center of the city, near the temples of the tribal gods and the houses of the priests, stood the tribal buildings— council house, royal residence, arsenals, and warehouses— maintained by special officials in return for the life use of certain tribal domains.

The Aztec king, the *tlacatecutli* or "chief of men," was elected by the great council from the members of a single royal lineage according to a fairly definite rule of succession. Primogeniture did not prevail here as it did in other instances. Instead, the succession commonly fell to a younger brother of the deceased king, or, if no brothers survived, then to a nephew in an elder branch of the family, *i.e.*, to the son of an earlier monarch. The newly elected ruler, in the rôle of a penitent, offered incense at the temples of the gods and was formally invested with the insignia of his office, notably a diadem of turquoise mosaic set in gold. As the first important act of his reign, he led his troops in a military campaign to secure victims for a coronation sacrifice. The Aztec king was, first and foremost, the supreme war chief of the tribe and the confederacy. Besides commanding the army in the field, he had charge of the collection of tribute, supervising a corps of tax collectors stationed in the subject cities. He exercised summary judicial powers, like a court-martial, in war and in emergencies. He acted as the tribal representative in receiving foreign embassies and delegates from the allied and subject tribes, and in entertaining them and the nobles of the court and council at a daily banquet. It is obvious from the foregoing that the supreme authority was vested, not in the king, but in the council. Nevertheless, in the later reigns, fortified by the prestige gained in a succession of victorious wars, the Mexican rulers were able to add to their original functions such influence in legislation and administration that they approached, even though they never quite attained, the stature of absolute monarchs in the European sense. They surrounded themselves with magnificent appointments and an elaborate court ceremonial until even the Spaniards marveled at their luxury and splendor.

By the side of the king stood an extremely important official, known by the curious name of *ciuacoatl* or "Snake-Woman." The man—for it was a man, never a woman—who filled this position ranked nominally as the equal of the king and was entitled to wear the same insignia and receive the same honors. The office derived its prestige from Tlacaellel, its incumbent during the Tepanec wars, the great national hero whose military genius had laid the foundations of Aztec supremacy. In later times, the Snake-Woman commanded the Mexican contingent in wars where the king led the combined confederate forces; he had charge of housing and distributing the tribute, after the agents of the king had collected it; and he presided over the tribal council and thus stood, as a sort of chief justice, at the head of the judicial system.

The criminal law of the Aztecs reveals many advanced features. Unwritten custom had given way to codified statutes. The interests of the whole community had in many respects subordinated those of the clan and the individual. Such primitive legal traits as blood-revenge, responsibility for the crime of a kinsman, and punishment for injuries accidentally inflicted, had completely disappeared, preparing the way for a consideration of personal and subjective factors. Weight, for example, was given to the age and intent of the wrongdoer, heavier penalties were exacted for repeated offenses, and accessories to a crime were punished as well as the principals. The interest of the state in prevention and punishment had entirely superseded private composition and self-help. Partly for this reason, perhaps, the penalties were exceedingly severe. Corporal punishment survived only in exceptional cases, *e.g.*, cutting off the lips for slander and perjury. Fines were never exacted, although confiscation of property accompanied other penalties in aggravated crimes such as treason. Enslavement was not an uncommon punishment; a thief, for example, became the slave of his victim if he could not make restitution. Imprisonment was not a regular mode of punishment but merely a means either of coercing debtors or of temporarily detaining persons condemned to death. Not infrequently a criminal was subjected to public ridicule or disgrace; a procuress, for instance, was exposed on a pillory and had her hair singed off. For the great majority of offenses, however, the death penalty was exacted—not only for murder and for crimes against the state, religion, and sex, but also for such seemingly inoffensive acts as the remarriage of divorced persons to each other, unnecessary delay by a judge in deciding a case, wearing clothing of the opposite sex, and harvesting maize before it ripened. The mode of death differed widely. Although hanging was the commonest form, nobles and warriors were beheaded, strangling was employed where secrecy was desired, and flogging to death and tearing limb from limb prevailed in other instances. Adultery seems to have inspired a gruesome ingenuity in this respect, for it was variously punished by drowning, stoning to death, burning at the stake, impaling with a spear or arrow, and grinding the head between two stones.

In one respect, however, the code seems harsher than it actually was. Certain crimes, among them adultery, were at the same time sins against some particular god. The sinner could expiate his guilt by confessing his act to the priest of the god concerned, and by offering sacrifices and doing penance, thereby freeing himself at the same time from liability in the temporal courts. The severe penalties of the code, consequently, applied only to sinners who refused to confess and to those who sinned a second time, for absolution could be granted only once in life. The ancient Mexicans were well acquainted with sumptuary laws. For a commoner to build a stone house or to wear cotton clothing or ornaments of gold and precious stones, constituted a capital offense.

The law similarly prohibited drunkenness, although it did not penalize temperate drinking. For appearing intoxicated in public, except at certain religious festivals, a youth was punished by death; an adult had his hair shorn and his house razed, and for a second offense received a death sentence. A person over seventy years of age, however, was privileged to tipple to his heart's content.

The life of the Aztecs, in nearly every aspect, centered upon war. Exploitation by arms formed the basis of their economic prosperity. Their social hierarchy was rooted in military honors and rewards. Education consisted largely of martial drill. War even permeated the religion. A god of war headed the pantheon, death in battle gave access to the highest paradise, and the temples dripped with the blood of sacrificed captives. Small wonder, therefore, that the Aztecs called themselves "idle" when no war was in progress. Every able-bodied man was liable for military service, for there was no standing army. The military organization paralleled that of the state. The phratries became regiments, and the clans companies, each with its proper commander and its special banner and badge. A system of graded honors, based on the number of prisoners taken and the mode of their capture, divided the warriors into various ranks with distinctive insignia and privileges. The outstanding braves were rewarded with the command of squads of twenty men and with membership in one of the military orders of knighthood, the Eagles and Ocelots.

Although slings, spears, and clubs figured to some extent in warfare, the characteristic native weapons were the following: a plain bow with a string of hair or sinew; arrows of hard wood, pointed with bone, flint, or obsidian, and equipped with feathers and sometimes with multiple prongs, but never poisoned; darts with a cane shaft, a point either hardened by fire or tipped like an arrow, and an attached cord for retrieving the missile; a spear-thrower (*atlatl*) with a hook at the end for the propulsion of darts; and a flat wooden sword with obsidian flakes set in resin along the edges—an instrument so sharp that wielders have actually been known to decapitate a horse with a single blow. For defense, warriors carried, on the left arm, a circular shield of canes interwoven with cotton and covered with feathers. Although common soldiers went naked except for a girdle, distinguished warriors wore a corselet of quilted cotton, over an inch in thickness and strong enough to resist an arrow, and likewise a wooden helmet shaped like the head of a ferocious animal. Great lords wore, instead of cotton armor, a cuirass of plates of gold, and over this a mantle of featherwork. Nobles frequently dressed as gods; the king, for example, assumed in battle the garb and attributes of the god Xipe.

In the absence of a good cause, such as a revolt or an outrage to a merchant, the Aztecs readily fabricated a pretext for precipitating hostilities. Sometimes ambassadors, with diplomatic immunity, visited the enemy chief with a demand to submit and pay tribute; if refused. they presented him with weapons, chalk, and feathers as a formal declaration of war. Summoned to arms by a drum, the warriors assembled at the phratry armories to receive their weapons. On a propitious day, after appropriate sacrifices, the expedition sallied forth, led by priests with the idols of the gods. Porters carried the tents and baggage, tributary tribes along the line of march furnished provisions and reënforcements, and scouts explored the terrain in advance. The troops maintained excellent discipline, the death penalty awaiting any who deserted, disobeyed orders, or looted the countryside. The first engagement took place on neutral ground on the enemy's border. When the priests had generated new fire, the men advanced in a furious mass attack with shouts and trumpet blasts. The battle soon resolved itself into a series of personal combats. The loss of life was slight, for each side sought primarily, not to slay, but to capture its enemies and to rescue its own wounded—a circumstance which greatly aided the Spaniards. If the first attack failed. a favorite ruse was to pretend flight in order to lure the foe into an ambuscade. In case the enemy were put to rout, a race ensued with their city as the objective. If, upon reaching it, the Aztecs found their opponents already securely ensconced behind the walls and ramparts, they usually retired, attempting a siege only when victory seemed certain and imminent. If they succeeded in reducing the city, they imposed a heavy tribute in kind and stationed a tax collector to supervise its payment, but they left its institutions, laws, and government unchanged. Prisoners were never released or exchanged, for their capture was the primary object of war. They bore the tribute and spoils back to Mexico, where they awaited their turn on the sacrificial stone.

The life of the day began, in an Aztec household, with a libation to the god of fire. After a few hours of work, the family assembled for a breakfast of maize gruel. The principal meal—and the only cooked one—was taken shortly after midday, followed by a smoke and a siesta. The sexes always ate separately, the men first and the women later. For the ablutions which were scrupulously observed both before and after meals, finger bowls and napkins were served, but spoons and forks were unknown. In their social intercourse the Aztecs obeyed an elaborate etiquette, especially in the matter of visits, the offering of condolences and congratulations, and the exchange of presents. For amusement, they engaged in foot races, gambled with dice or lots, and played a game called *patolli*, resembling our pachisi. Acrobats and jugglers furnished entertainment at the courts of the nobles, and a game of ball with strong religious or mystical associations was played on courts in the temple grounds.

The dance, in ancient Mexico, fulfilled a religious rather than a social function. It consisted of rhythmic movements of the limbs or body by masses of people in unison. At some ceremonies one sex danced alone, at others both together. Myths and legends were dramatized in the dance, but a primitive secular drama also existed. On an open terrace in the market place, actors performed as buffoons, imitated animals, and even presented ballets. The native musicians had at their disposal a variety of instruments: reed flutes; flageolets of wood, bone, or clay with three or four finger stops; huge conches serving as war trumpets; earthenware whistles in fanciful shapes, oftentimes with loose balls inside to produce a rolling sound; small bells of copper used as the Spaniards use castanets; wooden kettledrums covered with a taut skin and struck with rubber-tipped drumsticks; large cylindrical drums or gongs of hollow wood, sometimes with an H-shaped incision in the side to produce two tongues of different note; resounding metal discs suspended by cords; gourd and pottery rattles; and serrated bones rasped with a stick. With few exceptions, these instruments served only to give signals, beat time for dances, and drown the groans of the victims at sacrificial ceremonies. Vocal music was rather better; specially trained temple choirs, for example, chanted hymns at religious festivals. Poetry of a superior order was composed by the priests and sung to a musical accompaniment. Varied in meter but without rime, rich in metaphor and in archaic and impromptu words, it frequently reveals a strain of philosophic melancholy, as a brief excerpt will show. "All the earth is a grave, and naught escapes it. . . . That which was yesterday is not today; and let not that which is today trust to live tomorrow."

The Aztecs regarded motherhood as the feminine equivalent of war. They likened a newborn child to a captive taken in battle, and accorded to women dying in childbirth the same honor as to warriors slain in action. The parents of a prospective mother gave a feast when she announced the good news. Throughout her pregnancy a woman took care not to lift heavy burdens, stand in the hot sun, or eat anything that might harm the child. She also observed a number of less rational taboos; for example, she must not sleep in the daytime, or go outdoors at night, or look at any red object. The father, too, wore amulets and remained indoors at night.

Abortion, produced by an herb decoction, was forbidden on pain of death, unless to save the life of the mother. Infanticide was similarly prohibited, except that one of a pair of twins was invariably killed. As the hour of confinement approached, the attendant midwife gave the mother a sweat bath and a massage to promote ease of delivery. At the moment of birth she raised the battle cry of the warriors to announce that the mother had taken a "captive." She then severed the umbilical cord and lighted a fire which was kept burning for four days. The mother, after a purificatory bath, received visits, congratulations, and gifts from her friends and relatives.

Shortly after the birth of a child its parents consulted a soothsayer to learn its fate. At dawn on the fourth day, unless postponed until a more propitious date, a baptismal ceremony was held in the courtyard of the house. The midwife took the child in her arms and with speeches appropriate to the occasion presented it to the gods, sprinkled its lips, breast, head, and body with water, and passed it four times over the fire. It was next presented with miniature weapons if a boy, or with tiny weaving implements if a girl, and was then given a name—usually that of the day of its birth. At another ceremony, held at the temple several months later, it received a second name, and honorary titles might be added subsequently for bravery in battle or the like. Mothers carried their infants on their backs in wicker cradles and nursed them for three years or longer, during which time they observed certain dietary taboos. At a ceremony held every fourth year, all children born since the last occasion were taken to the temple to have their ears pierced; a cotton thread was inserted, to be replaced later by earrings.

The early education of children lay in the hands of their parents. Fathers taught their handicrafts to their sons, and mothers instructed their daughters in the domestic arts. Parents were wont to preach long moral homilies in the effort to instil industry, honesty, moderation, and filial piety, and they did not hesitate to enforce these virtues with such punishments as flogging, binding, pricking with agave thorns, holding over a fire containing pepper, and exposure naked in the rays of the noonday sun. Daughters, though ordinarily educated at home, sometimes entered temple convents for a few years or until marriage. The sons of commoners, from the age of fifteen until their marriage, attended a clan school (*telpochcalli*), where they received military training and instruction in singing, dancing, and rhetoric under the *achcacautli* or war chief of the clan. They lived and worked at school, although allowed to return home occasionally to aid their parents. Strict discipline prevailed, with the single exception that the youths were permitted to keep concubines or associate with prostitutes. The sons of nobles attended a central priestly seminary, the *calmecac*. Living under monastic rules, involving chastity and mortification of the flesh, they studied writing, astronomy, history, and religion until the time came to decide between remaining as priests and leaving for private life or public service.

When an Aztec reached the proper age—from twenty to twenty-two for boys and from sixteen to eighteen for girls—it became his social duty to marry. A measure of freedom in the selection of partners was left to the parties concerned, but the parents made all the arrangements and their consent was required. Incest taboos almost identical with our own forbade marriage between near kin in either the male or the female line, and, in addition, exogamous restrictions prevented unions within the clan. Before undertaking negotiations, the father of the youth consulted an astrologer to ascertain whether the fates of the couple were in harmony. If he received a favorable reply, he sent two elderly clanswomen with gifts to lay a proposal before the girl's father. Custom demanded that the suit be promptly rejected. Two days later the matchmakers returned. This time matters progressed, and the question of property was thoroughly discussed. To be sure, no bride-price was involved, but a woman always brought a dowry into marriage, and her suitor contributed an approximate equivalent in the form of gifts. The negotiations having been settled, a favorable day was fixed for the wedding.

On the evening of the appointed day the bride was conducted with music and torches to her future home. The groom met her in front of his house and, after an offering of incense, led her inside by the hand and sat beside her on a mat near the hearth. A priest, after the inevitable moral homily, united them in marriage by tying together the corners of their mantles. The bride then circumambulated the hearth seven times, and offered incense and exchanged presents with the groom. At the wedding supper, which followed, the newly married couple fed dainty morsels to one another. While the company drank and danced, they retired to the bridal chamber, where they remained in seclusion for four days—fasting, offering prayers and sacrifices, and drawing blood from their ears and tongues. Not until the fourth night did they consummate their union. On the following day, after a bath and a visit to the temple, they kept open house and showered their guests with generous gifts.

Polygyny prevailed extensively among the upper classes, and to some extent even among the commoners. The first wife, however, took precedence over the secondary wives, who were wedded by an abbreviated ceremony, and her children alone were entitled to succeed their father. In addition to their actual wives of both descriptions, men occasionally took concubines, who enjoyed no legal status at all. Sometimes, in a sort of trial marriage, a man took a girl as his concubine under a contract to marry her when and if she gave birth to a child. Divorce, though strongly disapproved of, was obtainable by decree of a special court for sufficient grounds—by a husband for sterility, quarrelsomeness, laziness, or neglect of duty in his spouse, and by a wife for ill-treatment, non-support, or failure to attend to the education of the children. The guilty party forfeited half of his property to the other. Sons followed their father, and daughters their mother. A divorced woman might return to her home and remarry as she chose. A widow, on the other hand, never returned to her clan; she married the brother of her deceased husband or, if none survived, then one of his clansmen.

Women, though subordinate to their husbands, were by no means without rights. They could hold property, make contracts, and go to court. In the matter of sexual morality, however, a marked double standard prevailed. Chastity was insisted upon in unmarried girls, while boys, as we have seen, could associate with mistresses or prostitutes. Even married men could do likewise with impunity, for a wife had no claim to fidelity in her husband. Only an illicit relation involving a married woman counted as adultery.

The treatment of disease was the function of a special class of physicians or medicine men, who, says an ancient chronicler, "were so far better than those in Europe that they did not protract the cure, in order to increase the pay." These practitioners set fractured bones, sewed wounds with hairs, prescribed bloodletting and sweat baths, and applied their knowledge of herbs in the preparation of various infusions, purgatives, emetics, and ointments. They depended heavily, however, on magic, astrology, and exorcism in making their diagnosis and cure. Very commonly, for example, they would smoke and mutter spells over a patient, massage and suck the affected part, and extract some small object like a worm or a stone knife as the pretended cause of the ailment. A sick child was sometimes hung up by the heels and its head shaken. Another way to get rid of an affliction was to make a dog out of dough and place it in the road; the first passer-by would then carry the disease away with him.

Not the character of a person's life but the manner of his death determined the nature of his funeral and his fate in the hereafter. The souls of those who died in undistinguished ways—through accident, sickness, or old age—after lingering for four days near their bodies, departed for an underworld. On their journey they encountered a succession of terrible dangers; they had to pass between two mountains which threatened to crush them, evade a giant snake and a monstrous crocodile, traverse eight deserts and eight hills replete with terrors, resist a wind full of sharp knives, and finally swim a great river. After four years they reached Mictlan, the subterranean home of the dead, a dark and dreary region but not a place of punishment. The body of such a person was dressed in clothing befitting his rank, decked with ornaments, and wrapped up in a bundle with his knees against his breast and his arms fast to his sides. The funeral attendants sprinkled his head with water and placed beside him a vessel of water and a number of balls of paper, each one a passport to surmount some danger on the journey to the underworld. On the fourth day after death the body was placed on a funeral pile and burned with incense, a little food, a few weapons or implements, the body of a red dog to ferry the deceased across the river to Mictlan, and even, in the case of important people, a number of slaves and concubines as a grave escort. The survivors collected the ashes in a vase, inclosed a small jewel to serve as a "heart," and buried the vase in some convenient place. Here they returned with offerings of food and drink on the twentieth and eightieth days and on the annual festival of the dead for four years.

Persons who died from drowning, lightning, dropsy, or leprosy were not cremated but buried, and their souls went to Tlalocan, the terrestrial paradise of the rain god Tlaloc, a delightful region with perpetual summer and an abundance of food and drink. An even more glorious fate awaited warriors slain in battle, the victims of human sacrifice, and women dying in childbirth. Martyrs to motherhood were buried at a temple, and their bodies were carefully guarded lest some sorcerer steal an arm or some warrior a finger as an amulet. Warriors, too, were buried, if their bodies were recovered; otherwise a wooden effigy was placed in the temple, burned on the fourth day, and the ashes buried. These fortunate souls went to the heavenly abode of the sun. The warriors greeted the luminary every morning at dawn, accompanied it to the zenith, where they met the women who had died in childbirth, and then descended to earth to spend the rest of the day as humming birds amid the flowers. The women escorted the sun to the western horizon, whence they visited the earth in the form of moths.

The religion of the Aztecs was a composite of heterogeneous elements. Basically a typical agrarian cult with elaborate rites of imitative magic calculated to produce rain and promote the growth of crops, it nevertheless also incorporated many traits of primitive shamanism, nature worship, and euhemerism. Into this amalgam entered a number of fetishistic components—the veneration of obsidian, of animals such as the jaguar, serpent, and humming bird, and of heavenly bodies, notably the sun. A warrior people with a savage nomadic past had naturally added traits of conspicuous cruelty and barbarism. Finally, an organized priesthood had united the various elements into a system, constructed an imposing speculative theology, and invested the barbaric rites with symbolic and mystical meanings.

In addition to hosts of lesser beings—nature spirits, tutelary divinities of households, clans, and occupational groups, and individual guardian spirits—the Aztecs worshiped hundreds of true gods. As a result of numerous borrowings from neighboring tribes, and of theological speculation, considerable confusion prevailed; a single god often appeared under different names and in different forms, and several deities frequently shared the same attributes. In this "pantheon or pandemonium," no one being stood out as supreme or even dominant. Four, however, overshadowed the rest. Uitzilopochtli or "Humming-bird-on-the-left" was the special tribal divinity of the Aztecs, the terrible war god or

Mars of Mexico, with subsidiary solar and agrarian characteristics. Tezcatlipoca or "Smoking Mirror" was the powerful god of the Nahuan tribes in general, the Mexican Jupiter. Omniscient and all-seeing, he judged and punished sinners and humbled the proud. Eternally young, he personified the breath of life, presided over feasts and banquets, and patronized the military schools. But, with his black face, limbs, and body, he also presented darker aspects—as the god of night and of fate, as the patron of sorcerers and black magic, and even, on occasion, as the malevolent enemy of mankind. Tlaloc, great god of rain, of water, of thunder, and of mountains, the Mexican Neptune, shared with Uitzilopochtli the great temple pyramid in the center of the city. Quetzalcoatl, the "Plumed Serpent," was to the Aztecs the god of wind and air, and the special divinity of the priesthood. Ultimately derived from the Maya Kukulcan, he appears in legend as the great king, priest, and culture hero of the Toltecs, the inventor of the calendar and all priestly arts and sciences. According to the prevailing myth, he had once ruled over an empire of peace and plenty but had succumbed to temptation through a plot of his enemies. Losing his throne, he departed toward the east and, according to one version, vanished into the ocean on a raft of serpents. The Mexicans expected his return with a Messianic confidence, and at first mistook Cortez for him— to the very considerable advantage of the Spaniards.

Of the remaining deities only a few of the most prominent can be enumerated here: Centeotl and Chicomecoatl, god and goddess of maize; Coatlicue, mother of Uitzilopochtli; Ilamatecutli, a very old star and maize goddess; Mictlantecutli, lord of death and the underworld; Mixcoatl, god of the morning star and of the chase; Ometecutli and Omeciuatl, the ancestral creative pair, cultless creatures of priestly speculation; Tlazolteotl, "goddess of ordure," patroness of sexual sin, confession, and purification; Toci, mother of the gods, earth divinity, mistress of the harvest. and patroness of weaving and medicine; Tonatiuh, powerful and blood-thirsty sun god, lord of warriors, of sacrificial victims, and of women dying in childbirth; Uixtociuatl, goddess of salt; Xilonen, mistress of the young maize ear; Xipe, warlike agrarian god, clad always in the skin of a flayed human victim as a symbol of the renewal of vegetation; and Xiuhtecutli, "lord of turquoise," oldest of the gods, the great divinity of fire and the hearth.

The cults of these various deities were tended by a class of priests, recruited for the most part from the younger sons of the nobility. The novices received their education in the *calmecac* or priestly seminary along with their brothers, but remained after the latter had left for war or public life. Living under the strictest discipline, they began with menial tasks in the service of the gods and gradually advanced to more important duties, receiving instruction meanwhile in the sacred writings, calendrical lore, ritual, chants, and ascetic practices. The priests of inferior rank lived with the novices in the *calmecac* and performed subordinate sacerdotal functions. Those of superior grade bore distinctive titles and specialized in the service of individual gods or in particular activities such as divination, sacrifice, music, or ceremonial. At the apex of the ecclesiastical hierarchy, elected for their merits from the ranks of the superior clergy, stood two high priests, of whom one served Uitzilopochtli and the other Tlaloc, although both bore the honorary title of Quetzalcoatl. They advised the king and council on matters of war and public policy. Priestesses received a similar education, but could not aspire to high station. Priests wore black cotton mantles, painted their bodies black, and never cut their hair, which hung long, loose, and frequently matted with blood. Four times a day and thrice each night they drew blood and offered incense to the sun. They underwent various prescribed fasts, vigils, and forms of self-torture. Although sometimes married, they commonly took vows of chastity. For the slightest infraction of their ascetic regulations they performed severe penitential rites. In other respects, however, they lived in ease and often in luxury, supported by large landed estates, rich contributions of tribute, and a continuous stream of sacrificial donations. The social services which they rendered in return included, besides their strictly religious functions, the education of the young and the cultivation of the sciences and fine arts, in which they enjoyed a complete monopoly.

Allied and sometimes identical with the temple priests were several classes of religious functionaries who resembled more closely the shamans of primitive peoples. The mid-wives and the medicine men or physicians have already been mentioned. Another class specialized in magic. Some could assume the form of owls, influence the hearts of women, rob houses by rendering themselves invisible with the arm of a woman who had died in childbirth, or inflict injuries on their enemies by introducing foreign objects into their bodies or by working magic with a kind of paper effigy. Other sorcerers, among them the priests of Tlaloc, used magic for good rather than evil purposes. Highly esteemed for the extreme asceticism of their lives and credited with miraculous knowledge and the power of levitation, they foretold the weather, brought rain, warned against plagues, and combated the evil sorcerers. A class of jugglers, laying no claim to supernatural powers, employed suggestion and sleight of hand to conjure up springs filled with fishes, to roast maize on a cloth without the aid of fire, to dismember themselves and then piece together their severed limbs, etc. Finally, a class of diviners or soothsayers foretold the outcome of a disease or the success of an enterprise by reading knots, observing reflections in a bowl of water, or casting lots with beans or maize kernels. They also detected thieves by assembling the suspects in a circle and producing from a basket a snake which crawled toward the culprit. By all means the most influential of the soothsayers, however, were those versed in astrology.

The calendar exerted a dominating influence on the life and religion of the Aztecs. Their basis of time reckoning was the *cempoualli*, an artificial "month" of twenty days, divided into four "weeks" of five days each. A day was identified by a number and a sign. The numbers ran from one to thirteen and were then repeated. The signs, of which there are twenty, likewise ran in rotation and were repeated each month. Thus the days of the first month were called successively: 1 alligator, 2 wind, 3 house, 4 lizard, 5 snake, 6 death, 7 deer, 8 rabbit, 9 water, 10 dog, 11 monkey, 12 grass, 13 reed, 1 ocelot, 2 eagle, 3 vulture, 4 motion, 5 flint, 6 rain, and 7 flower. The second month began with 8 alligator, and so on. After two hundred and sixty days, or thirteen months, the day known as "1 alligator" reappeared, and the cycle was repeated. This period of 260 days constituted the astrological year, called *tonalamatl* or "book of days." The Aztecs also recognized an actual or civil year of 365 days, divided into eighteen 20-day months plus five extra days. On these five supernumerary days, which they regarded as ill-omened, they rested, avoided quarrels, and took no action of importance. They did not intercalate or correct for leap year, so their calendar gradually fell behind. They also reckoned a number of longer cycles, notably one of fifty-two years. At the expiration of this period of time, during which precisely seventy-three 260-day astrological years had likewise elapsed, the same number and sign of the *tonalamatl* again fell on the initial day of the civil year.

This peculiar calendar became the basis of an elaborate system of astrology. A special god ruled each of the 260 days of the *tonalamatl*. Moreover, thirteen "lords of the day," and likewise nine "lords of the night," governed the same days in rotation. Furthermore, special divinities presided over each of the 5-day weeks, each of the 20-day months, and each of several longer periods. And, finally, the thirteen day numbers were variously regarded as lucky, unlucky, or indifferent. Through the various combinations of these calendrical periods with their different gods and characteristics, there was brought to bear on any given day a diversity of supernatural influences. It was the function of the astrologers, steeped in such lore, to study these influences and the manner in which they supplemented or counteracted each other, and thus to pronounce whether a particular day was favorable or unfavorable for a particular enterprise. No action of moment was ever taken without their advice. They likewise read the horoscopes of children, for the influences affecting the day of one's birth determined and unalterably fixed one's fate. Every act of life, including sins, was foreordained. This belief accounts in part for that pessimistic fatalism which constituted one of the outstanding traits of Aztec character.

But the calendrical and astrological system formed only a part of the vast body of esoteric pseudo-knowledge to the study and elaboration of which the priests devoted so much of their attention. Numbers were invested with characters and mystical meanings. An elaborate mythology divided the history of the world into five ages or "suns," each coming to an end in some great calamity—a future earthquake in the case of the present age. The priestly cosmology placed Mexico at the center of the earth and described in detail the thirteen heavens above and the nine hells below. Each of the four cardinal directions, to which were sometimes added the zenith, nadir, and middle, was associated with certain colors, gods, day signs, and the like. All this priestly schematism and symbolism, however, made comparatively little impression on the popular mind, which found its chief satisfaction in the objective, especially the dramatic, aspects of the cult.

Among the practical cult activities, although fasting, prayer, and confession had their place, by far the most important was sacrifice. Men offered to the gods whatever they themselves valued—food, clothing, flowers, jewelry, etc. In particular, they devoted to them the firstfruits of the field and harvest, of hunting and fishing, of the handicrafts and all other activities. These products flowed in abundance into the temples, where, even after the gods had abstracted the spiritual essence, the priests managed to thrive on the material substance. Among animal sacrifices the commonest were quails, which were decapitated in quantities to Uitzilopochtli. Incense, especially copal mixed with tobacco, was burned to the gods in pottery censers on every possible occasion. But by far the most acceptable—the indispensable—offering was human blood. On a plentiful supply of this life-giving fluid the gods depended to keep them young and vigorous. Without it they would grow old and feeble, unable to perform their tasks of bringing rain and ripening the crops. For penance, to attain ritual purity, and on many special

From the Codex Laud

FIG. 87. HUMAN SACRIFICE, ACCORDING TO AN OLD AZTEC MANUSCRIPT.

occasions, the people pierced their tongues and ear lobes, sometimes also their limbs and sex organs, with an agave thorn and offered the blood to the gods. The priests performed this act at least seven times daily, their ears being torn to shreds as a result. To assist them in the operation they even bored holes through their tongues and kept a thread inserted.

It was through human sacrifice, however, that man could provide the gods most abundantly with the refreshment they craved. Hence war—to replenish the supply of victims—became to the Aztecs a religious duty. Sometimes the captive was shot with arrows, or burned on a pyre, or decapitated and flayed, or slain in a gladiatorial combat, but in general these methods were but minor variations of, or preliminaries to, the usual procedure. In full view of multitudes of devout spectators, the victim solemnly ascended the steps of the pyramid and was seized at the summit by five priests. While these bent his body over backwards on a convex sacrificial stone and held his head and limbs, a sixth priest, distinguished by a scarlet mantle, with a deft stroke made an incision under the ribs, inserted his hand, and tore out the palpitating heart. This he held aloft to the sun and then tossed into a basin of copal so placed that the odor ascended into the nostrils of the idol. The priests now smeared the lips of the idol with blood, cut off the head of the victim, and tossed the body down the steps of the pyramid. The honored donor or captor of the sacrifice removed the corpse to his home, where he had the arms, legs, and thighs cooked and served in a ceremonial banquet to his kinsmen and friends. Female captives and slaves, though sacrificed less often than men, were usually flayed after the ceremony and their skins worn by the priests. The rain god, Tlaloc, demanded frequent offerings of children, who were either sold by poor or donated by devout parents. If they wept as they went to the slaughter, it was regarded as a good omen—a sign of rain. As to the extent of human sacrifice, perhaps the most modest estimate fixes the number of victims each year, in the city of Mexico alone, at 2,500, while Cortez reports counting 136,000 skulls in the collection at the great temple.

Our abhorrence of these barbarous practices tends to make us overlook their true meaning and to blind us to the fact that they represent a genuine expression of the religious impulse. To the Aztec they were not gruesome. The victim, far from being brutally treated, was fêted, honored, and accorded the most reverent care, for he represented the god to whom he was sacrificed. Nay more, for the time being he *was* the god. As a rule he went willingly to the slaughter, conscious of the honor that was his, uplifted by a truly religious ecstasy, confident of the glorious fate that awaited him in the hereafter. Even the cannibalistic sequel, far from being a gross orgy of savage gluttony, was to the Aztec a rare spiritual experience. In consuming the flesh of the human representative of his divinity, he was uniting himself with the divinity. What the devout Christian does when, in the sacrament of the Eucharist, he partakes figuratively of the body and blood of his God, the Aztec still did in a strictly literal sense, inspired, moreover, by an identical emotion and conception.

Sacrifices, human and otherwise, did not take place, however, as isolated and independent acts of worship. On the contrary, they formed an integral part of a complex and elaborate system of ceremonies and provided merely the most spectacular acts in a series of religious dramas. These rites fell into three classes: the fixed ceremonies, eighteen in number, culminating on the last day of each of the months of the civil or true year; the movable ceremonies, brief and comparatively minor festivals occurring on definite days in the *tonalamatl;* and the occasional ceremonies, held at long intervals when one of the major cycles in the calendrical system terminated. Of the last type, the most interesting was the ceremony which took place at the expiration of the 52-year cycle. On the last day of the old cycle, the people repaired their houses, discarded their old utensils, renewed their household fetishes, and put out all fires. At sundown, a procession of all the priests of all the temples filed slowly and silently out of the city and ascended a neighboring mountain. Here, at midnight, a priest generated new fire with a drill on the breast of a selected captive. Meanwhile the people breathlessly awaited the appearance of the flame, for, according to tradition, failure to generate it would betoken the immediate end of the present age and the destruction of the human race. When the fire flared up, the heart of the victim was torn out and his body consumed in the flames, the rejoicing people gashed themselves to offer blood sacrifices of thanksgiving, and the boys and men raced with brands of the new fire to relight the hearths of houses and temples for another fifty-two years.

The most important ceremonies, however, were those of the fixed type. Diverse as to detail, they nevertheless presented many points of similarity. Although they commonly lasted several days or even weeks, they invariably terminated with a spectacular drama on the final day of the month. Preceded by a period of fasting and preparation, they opened with solemn processions bringing from field and forest materials to decorate the temples and altars, were characterized by endless dances and processions, and closed with an orgy of permitted drinking. Considerations of space make possible here only the briefest synopsis of the ceremonial calendar:

ATLCAUALCO: Feb. 2; paper flags on poles erected in houses and sacred places and carried in processions; children sacrificed to Tlaloc.

TLACAXIPEUALIZTLI: Feb. 22; war captives of both sexes and all ages sacrificed, flayed, and eaten on first day of month; their skins worn for twenty days by persons afflicted with skin diseases; gladiatorial sacrifice in which a selected captive, armed with a wooden sword and tied to the center of a circular stone, sought to withstand four fully armed warriors, and was showered with honors if he succeeded; dances by wearers of skins; final sacrifice of the firstfruits of flowers to Xipe, and dance by priests disguised as vegetables.

TOZOZTONTLI: March 14; spring flower festival; wearers of skins doffed them on first day at the temple of Xipe; a virgin sacrificed to Coatlicue; children offered to Tlaloc; flowers and snakes sacrificed to Centeotl and Chicomecoatl.

UEITOZOZTLI: April 3; bloodletting by youths; occasional child sacrifices to Tlaloc; houses and temples decorated with young maize plants; seed corn blessed by priests of Chicomecoatl; mock combat before her altar.

TOXCATL: April 23; sacrifice of quails to Uitzilopochtli; public exhibition and decoration of the image of Tezcatlipoca; sacrifice of a youth to the same god.

ETZALQUALIZTLI: May 13; a great rain ceremony; ceremonial bath in lake by priests, imitating birds; reeds gathered and made into mats, on which specially prepared cakes were offered to the gods; slaves and captives sacrificed to Tlaloc; their hearts deposited in the lake with rich gifts.

TECUILUITONTLI: June 2; ball games on temple courts; a woman with an escort of male captives sacrificed to Uixtociuatl.

UEITECUILUITL: June 22; torchlight dance by nobles; great distributions of food to the poor; a woman decapitated on the back of a priest as a sacrifice to Xilonen.

TLAXOCHIMACO: July 12; a flower festival without human victims; sacrifices to the ghosts of dead children; a final dance by warriors and their mistresses at the temple of Uitzilopochtli.

XOCOUETZI: Aug. 1; great festival in honor of the dead; a contest among the young people to obtain the insignia and a dough image of Xiuhtecutli erected on a tall pole; gruesome sacrifices to the fire god, in which the victims were cast into a huge brazier, roasted alive, and dragged out with hooks just in time to tear out their hearts before they ceased beating.

OCHPANIZTLI: Aug. 21; the "broom feast"; houses and streets swept, and temples and idols refurbished; a woman, told that she was to marry a rich lord, was suddenly seized by a priest, sacrificed to Toci, and flayed; a priest, wearing her skin, slaughtered four captives at the temple of Uitzilopochtli; a race by the warriors to deposit a mask made from the skin on the border of the hostile state of Tlaxcala, where a battle usually occurred with the lurking enemy; military honors distributed by the king.

TEOTLECO: Sept. 10; celebration of the return of the gods to earth; night vigil by the priests around a circle of corn meal, watching for the footprint of Tezcatlipoca, who always led the rest; final dance around a great fire; living victims tossed into the flames.

TEPEILUITL: Sept. 30; dough images of Tlaloc made and sacrificed to; snake effigies carried in processions; a man and four women sacrificed to Tlaloc.

QUECHOLLI: Oct. 20; weapons manufactured; arrows offered to Uitzilopochtli; a great communal hunt in the mountains; victims, trussed up like captive deer, sacrificed to Mixcoatl.

PANQUETZALIZTLI: Nov. 9; wholesale slaughter of slaves and captives to Uitzilopochtli; a dough image of the god, kneaded with the blood of the victims, distributed among the people and eaten in a communion ceremony; a great gladiatorial combat between warriors and prisoners, dramatizing the myth of Uitzilopochtli.

ATEMOZTLI: Nov. 29; dough images of Tlaloc made, sacrificed, and eaten; no human sacrifices.

TITITL: Dec. 19; a woman impersonating Ilamatecutli sacrificed, decapitated, and her head carried by a priest throughout the festival; masked dances in honor of the goddess.

IZCALLI: Jan. 8; ceremonial kindling of new fire for the coming year; land and water animals captured by children and cast into the flames; children encouraged to become intoxicated with pulque; every fourth year only, human sacrifices to Xiuhtecutli and piercing of children's ears.

So inadequate a conception does the foregoing outline give of the richness and complexity of the Aztec ritual in detail, that it seems well to append, as an example of the latter, a fuller account of the outstanding episode in the Toxcatl ceremony. A captive youth, selected for his bravery, physical perfection, and musical accomplishments, was chosen a year in advance to impersonate Tezcatlipoca. Clad in costly garments and wreathed with flowers, he lived in regal splendor at the temple of the god with four priests and four warriors as attendants. Enjoying the freedom of the city, he wandered as he listed. Wherever he went, people prostrated themselves before him, showered him with flowers, and offered incense and sacrifices to him. Even the king bowed before the incarnation of the god. A month before the ceremony he was married to four beautiful maidens, who bore the names of goddesses. For twenty days his brides ministered to his every desire, the great lords vied in giving feasts and dances in his honor, and every joy of earth was placed at his disposal. On the morning of the twentieth day, however, he boarded a canoe, bade farewell to his brides, and was rowed across Lake Tezcuco. Accompanied only by his eight attendants, he followed a desert trail to a small ruined temple. Stripped of his costly raiment and jewels, and clad only in a necklace of flutes, he slowly ascended the pyramid, breaking a flute at each step. Exactly at midnight, as his successor was being chosen and acclaimed in Mexico, his heart was wrenched out ard offered to the god whom he had impersonated.

BIBLIOGRAPHY

BANCROFT, H. H. *The Native Races of the Pacific States of North America.* 5 vols. New York, 1875-76.

BANDELIER, A. F. "On the Art of War and Mode of Warfare of the Ancient Mexicans." *Reports of the Peabody Museum of American Archæology and Ethnology*, Vol. II. Cambridge, 1877.

——. "On the Distribution and Tenure of Lands, and the Customs with Respect to Inheritance, among the Ancient Mexicans." *Reports of the Peabody Museum of American Archæology and Ethnology*, Vol. II. Cambridge, 1878.

——. "On the Social Organization and Mode of Government of the Ancient Mexicans." *Reports of the Peabody Museum of American Archæology and Ethnology*, Vol. II. Cambridge, 1880.

BEUCHAT, H. *Manuel d'archéologie américaine.* Paris, 1912.

BIART, L. *The Aztecs.* Trans. by J. L. Garner. Chicago, 1900.

BRINTON, D. G. *Ancient Nahuatl Poetry.* Philadelphia, 1887.

——. *Nagualism.* Philadelphia, 1894.

CLAVIGERO, F. S. *History of Mexico.* Trans. by C. Cullen. Second edition. 3 vols. London, 1807.

DANZEL, T. W. "Mexiko." 2 vols. *Kulturen der Erde*, Vols. XI–XII. Hagen, 1922.

GENIN, A. "Notes on the Dances, Music, and Songs of the Ancient and Modern Mexicans." Trans. *Smithsonian Institution, Annual Report of the Board of Regents for the Year Ending June 30, 1920*, Part 1. Washington, 1922.

HAEBLER, K. *Die Religion des mittleren Amerika.* Münster, 1899.

HÖLTKER, G. "Die Familie bei den Azteken in Altmexiko." *Anthropos*, Vol. XXV. Wien, 1930.

JOYCE, T. A. *Maya and Mexican Art.* London, 1927.

——. *Mexican Archæology.* London, 1914.

LEHMANN, W. "Ergebnisse und Aufgaben der mexikanistischen Forschung." *Archiv für Anthropologie*, Vol. XXXIV. Braunschweig, 1907.

MORGAN, L. H. *Ancient Society.* New York, 1877.

NUTTALL, Z. "The Gardens of Ancient Mexico." *Smithsonian Institution, Annual Report of the Board of Regents for the Year Ending June 30, 1923*, Part 1. Washington, 1925.

PAYNE, E. J. *History of the New World Called America.* 2 vols. Oxford, 1892–99.

PHILLIPS, G. B. "The Metal Industry of the Aztecs." *American Anthropologist*, New Series, Vol. XXVII. Menasha, 1925.

PRESCOTT, W. H. *The Conquest of Mexico.* Edited by T. A. Joyce. 2 vols. New York, 1922.

PREUSS, K. T. "Der Ursprung der Menschenopfer in Mexiko." *Globus*, Vol. LXXXVI. Braunschweig, 1904.

RADIN, P. "The Sources and Authenticity of the History of the Ancient Mexicans." *University of California Publications in American Archæology and Ethnology*, Vol. XVII. Berkeley, 1920.

SAHAGUN, B. DE. *Historia general de las cosas de Nueva España.* 3 vols. Mexico, 1829.

SAVILLE, M. H. "The Goldsmith's Art in Ancient Mexico." *Indian Notes and Monographs.* New York, 1920.

——. "The Wood-Carver's Art in Ancient Mexico." *Contributions from the Museum of the American Indian, Heye Foundation*, Vol. IX. New York, 1925.

SELER, E. "Altmexikanische Studien." *Veröffentlichungen aus dem Königlichen Museum für Völkerkunde*, Vol. VI. Berlin, 1899.

——. "Ancient Mexican Feather Ornaments." *Smithsonian Institution, Bureau of American Ethnology, Bulletin 28.* Washington, 1904.

——. *Gesammelte Abhandlungen zur amerikanischen Sprach- und Alterthumskunde.* 4 vols. Berlin, 1902–15.

——. "The Mexican Chronology." *Smithsonian Institution, Bureau of American Ethnology, Bulletin 28.* Washington, 1904.

——. "Mexicans (Ancient)." *Encyclopædia of Religion and Ethics*, Vol. VIII. Edited by J. Hastings. New York, 1916.

SPENCE, L. *The Civilization of Ancient Mexico.* Cambridge, 1912.

SPENCE, L. *The Gods of Mexico.* London, 1923.

SPENCER, H. *Descriptive Sociology.* New York, n.d.

SPINDEN, H. J. *Ancient Civilizations of Mexico and Central America.* Second edition. New York, 1922.

STARR, F. "The Physical Characters of the Indians of Southern Mexico." *Decennial Publications of the University of Chicago,* Vol. IV. Chicago, 1903.

STEFFEN, M. *Die Landwirtschaft bei den altamerikanischen Kulturvölkern.* Leipzig, 1882.

THOMAS, C. "Numeral Systems of Mexico and Central America." *Nineteenth Annual Report of the Bureau of American Ethnology,* Part 2. Washington, 1900.

*THOMPSON, J. E. *Mexico before Cortez.* New York, 1933. (This excellent book, published too recently to have been available in writing the chapter, is here listed for reference and recommendation only.)

TOY, C. H. "Mexican Human Sacrifice." *Journal of American Folk-Lore,* Vol. XXVIII. Boston, 1905.

TOZZER, A. M. "The Domain of the Aztecs and Their Relation to the Prehistoric Cultures of Mexico." *Holmes Anniversary Volume.* Washington, 1916.

TYLOR, E. B. *Anahuac.* London, 1861.

WATERMAN, T. T. "Bandelier's Contribution to the Study of Ancient Mexican Social Organization." *University of California Publications in American Archæology and Ethnology,* Vol. XII. Berkeley, 1917.

WINTZER, H. M. "Das Recht Altmexikos." *Zeitschrift für Vergleichende Rechtswissenschaft,* Vol. XLV. Stuttgart, 1930.

WISSLER, C. *The American Indian.* Second edition. New York, 1922.

CHAPTER XIV

THE INCAS OF PERU

In the Andean highlands and along the Pacific coast of South America, between the River Ancasmayo (2° north latitude) and the River Maule (35° south latitude), the Spanish adventurers discovered—and destroyed—one of the mightiest empires and most unique civilizations known to human history. More than ten million Indians, occupying a territory 2,500 miles in length from north to south and 300 miles in average breadth—a region comprising the modern republics of Ecuador and Peru, northern Chile, western Bolivia, and northwestern Argentina—had been welded into a political and cultural unit by the arms and statecraft of the Inca dynasty. Only a knowledge of the geography of the region can give an adequate conception of the magnitude of this achievement.

The Andes, next to the Himalayas the loftiest mountains in the world, parallel the Pacific coast in two majestic ranges, the Eastern and the Maritime Cordilleras, forming a gigantic avenue lined with snow-capped peaks and volcanoes. The precipitous eastern slope of the Eastern Cordillera constitutes a zone of impenetrable tropical forest. The trade winds from the South Atlantic, still vapor-laden after crossing the thousands of miles of low Amazonian jungle, are chilled in rising and bathe the slope with constant torrential rains. Sufficient moisture remains to produce an annual precipitation of from twenty-five to forty inches in the inter-Andean plateau, but the winds are completely parched as well as chilled when they descend the Maritime Cordillera into the narrow coastal zone. The Pacific contributes dampness and fog but no rain, for the Humboldt Current from the Antarctic makes the ocean colder than the land. As a result the coastal zone.

which averages less than 100 miles in width, is, except in the far north, a desert of windblown sand, utterly without rain save for an occasional destructive cloudburst in an exceptional year, with a monotonous damp climate and a mean annual temperature of from 65° to 75° F., and with no vegetation except a few cacti, stunted trees, and fugitive plants. Marine fauna and birds are abundant, but the land supports only a few rodents, armadillos, and reptiles. The monotony of this barren coastal strip is broken, at intervals of about thirty miles on the average, by bands of green—ribbons of vegetation which mark the courses of short, and often intermittent, rivers fed by the melting snows on the western slope of the Maritime Cordillera. Only in the fertile, but isolated, valleys of the permanent streams is man able to live and thrive.

Between the two ranges of the Andes lies a plateau, 12,000 feet in average elevation, from 100 to 200 miles in breadth, and extending for more than two thousand miles from north to south. It is broken up, however, into large *hoyas* or drainage basins by a third range, the Central Cordillera, in Peru, by three great transverse ridges or "knots"—the Nudo de Loja, Nudo de Pasco, and Nudo de Vilcañota in northern, central, and southern Peru respectively—and by innumerable ramifying spurs and ridges. The southernmost basin, the *hoya* of Titicaca in Bolivia, centers on Lake Titicaca, which drains southward into a series of salt swamps, where the water evaporates. In Peru are found five great *hoyas*, drained by the Urubamba, Apurimac, Mantaro, Marañón, and Huallaga. These rivers, shallow, clear, and swift, flow through their respective basins in a general northerly direction, pass to the east through mighty gateways or *pongos* in the Eastern Cordillera, and plunge rapidly to the swampy lowlands to join the sluggish Amazon or its upper tributaries. In Ecuador, numerous smaller *hoyas* drain southward and eastward into the Amazon. The countless snowclad peaks ranging from 18,000 to 23,000 feet in altitude, the wild labyrinthine gorges, the valleys sometimes a mile in depth and inaccessible from above, the land riven by earthquakes and seared by lava flows, all conspire to produce scenery of breathless grandeur. Although rich in mineral resources, the country supports only a meager mammalian fauna, including deer, pumas, hares, guanacos, vicuñas, and rodents. Waterfowl, however, abound in the lakes and streams. The climate ranges from semi-tropical in the deepest valleys to frigid in the mountains. The temperature varies little in any season from the annual mean of about 50° F., but its range at different altitudes and at different hours of the day may be immense. Rain, confined to the summer months, is lightest in the valleys. The plateau is treeless except for occasional clumps of gnarled evergreens and for thickets of reeds and bushes along the streams. Grass-covered slopes alternate with rocky wastes, swampy moors, and stretches of desert. The scanty vegetation never succeeds in moderating the monotonous gray of the landscape. "It is never winter here, never spring, never summer; it is a land of eternal autumn."

Lacking in navigable rivers, poor in fauna and flora, surrounded by desert and jungle, its few habitable regions isolated from one another by barren wastes and mountain barriers insurmountable save by a few passes three miles or more in height—an environment theoretically more unfavorable for the development of civilization could scarcely be imagined. Yet civilization did arise here. As a result of migrations and of acculturation from Central America an archaic agricultural civilization was diffused over the highland and coastal zones, superseding an earlier hunting and fishing culture. By the beginning of our era, regional specialization had produced distinctive elaborations of the common heritage in three widely separated parts of the area. Along the northern coast of Peru the Yuncas had developed a civilization characterized by an intensive agriculture, an elaborate system of irrigation, large and well-built cities, the use of gold, silver, and copper, superb textiles, and massive stepped pyramids and artificial hills of adobe brick. What especially distinguishes this so-called Chimu civilization is its pottery, on which, in reddish-brown colors over a cream-tinted slip, are depicted with amazing realism the most varied scenes of domestic and court life, of hunting, fishing, war, and industry, and even landscapes and individual portraits. A parallel

FIG. 88. CHIMU PORTRAIT VESSEL FROM CHICAMA, PERU.
Courtesy of the Göteborgs Museum

development on the southern coast of Peru gave rise to the Nazca culture, with a ceramic art noted for the wealth and brilliance of its colors and for its highly conventionalized representations of such mythical beings as the Spotted Cat, the Bird Demon, and the Centipede God. At Tiahuanaco, on Lake Titicaca in the Bolivian highlands, the Colla tribe created an independent civilization renowned for its massive megalithic architecture. Huge blocks of stone, frequently weighing many tons, were sculptured in polygonal shapes and individually fitted to their neighbors with a precision almost incredible for a people totally ignorant of iron tools. The decorative art of this region is characterized by the severity of its lines and by its conventionalized treatment of animals, men, and the creator god Viracocha.

Between 500 and 600 A.D. the Tiahuanaco culture was spread, apparently by conquest, throughout the plateau. It even eclipsed temporarily the indigenous civilizations on the coast. After three centuries of dominance, however, it

After Means and Mead

FIG. 89. PERUVIAN POTTERY: AN EARLY NAZCA VASE AND A DOUBLE WHISTLING JAR.

suddenly collapsed through some unknown cataclysm, and was succeeded by a period of disorder. On the coast a renaissance of the Chimu and Nazca cultures set in after 1100, but anarchic conditions continued to prevail on the plateau. Small warring tribes under petty chiefs or *sinchis* maintained a precarious economic and political existence. The Incas, though their origin is shrouded in myth, seem to have been a typical tribe of this sort, inhabiting one of the small mountain valleys tributary to the Urubamba River, with their principal seat at Cuzco. Here, about the year 1100, their chieftain and first historical ruler, Sinchi Rocca, established hegemony over a small group of tribes and laid the foundation of the later empire. His immediate successors consolidated their position in the same region by further conquests, and expanded southward until they had brought the entire Titicaca basin under their control. The seventh

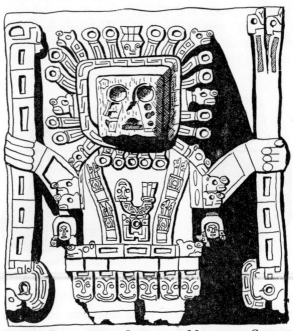

FIG. 90. DETAIL FROM A SCULPTURED MONOLITHIC GATE AT TIAHUANACO.

monarch, Viracocha (c. 1347–1400), succeeded in conquering the Chancas, a powerful rival confederation in the Apurimac basin northwest of Cuzco, and thus opened a path to the north, which was followed by his successors, the great conquerors Pachacutec and Tupac Yupanqui. The tenth ruler, Huayna Capac (c. 1485–1525), brought the empire to its maximum extent. It was in the closing years of his reign that the Inca realm was first seen by a European, one Alejo

Garcia, a Portuguese adventurer who accompanied a horde of Guarani savages on a raid from Paraguay to the vicinity of Sucre.

The Inca tribe with their immediate neighbors belonged to the great Quichua nation. Physically, if we may judge by measurements on the Indians of the same region today, they were characterized by an olive-brown complexion, short stature (about five feet two inches for adult males), comparatively short legs and long arms, heads of moderate breadth (cephalic index 80), black or deep brown eyes, mesorrhine noses (nasal index 82), abundant, straight, black hair, and scanty beards.

The Quichua language, an agglutinative tongue with a sentence structure in which adjectives precede the nouns they modify and the object precedes both the verb and the subject, was spoken by the Inca tribe and later became the official language of the empire. A number of its words have even found their way into English, *e.g.*, alpaca, coca, condor, guano, llama, pampa, puma, and quinine. Although they recorded historical traditions in paintings, and made relief maps of cities and provinces in clay, the Incas possessed no form of true writing. The Peruvian *quipu*—a thick cord from which hung a fringe of colored and knotted strings—was used only as a means of enumeration or as an aid to memory. The colors of the strings represented classes of objects, and the number and position of the knots indicated numbers in the current decimal system of numeration. A special class of learned men, versed in the use of the *quipu*, were thus enabled to keep accurate accounts of tribute payments and the like, even in figures running into the millions. For the measurement of gold and other valuables a balance-beam scale was employed—an instrument consisting of a horizontal beam of bone or wood with a shifting fulcrum, two suspended pans of wood, metal, or netting, and a set of fixed weights of stone or metal. The Peruvian year began with the winter solstice, was divided into twelve months of thirty days each, and

ended with five supernumerary days. The native astron-
omers were able to calculate equinoxes and solstices with
precision by observing the shadows cast by stone pillars and
the position of the rising and setting sun with reference to
groups of stone towers to the east and west of Cuzco.

Life in Peru from time immemorial had centered in the
ayllu or clan, an ex-
ogamous kin-group
acknowledging the
authority of a chief,
joint responsibility
for the acts of its
members, and the
duty of avenging
injuries to them.
Each clan traced its
descent — through
the female line in
most cases though
not universally—
from a common to-
temic ancestor, and
found an additional
bond of union in the
communal cult of
this tutelary being.
Typical among the
totems were the condor, the puma, serpents, fishes, rivers,
mountains, and celestial bodies. Each clan laid claim to a
definite territory (*marca*) and inhabited, as a rule, a single
village adjacent to a fortified place of refuge. The village consisted, on the average, of about a hundred irregularly clustered houses, each occupied by an individual family.

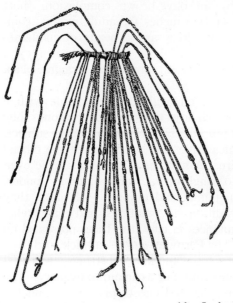

After Locke

FIG. 91. A PERUVIAN QUIPU.

The typical dwelling in the highlands was a one-story
rectangular structure of stone or clay, with a floor of trodden
earth, a gabled roof of thatch, and a narrow door protected

by a mat. Sometimes a rude partition set off a recess for cooking or sleeping from the main living room. On the coast were found rather more commodious huts of sun-dried brick or mud and wattle. But everywhere the interiors were dark and ill-ventilated from the lack of windows and chimneys, and squalid with vermin and animals. A crude niche in the wall harbored the household fetishes. Others contained such utensils as gourds, baskets, earthen pots, wooden spoons, stone mortars, and various tools of metal or polished stone. Implements and clothing hung from pegs, beams, or suspended cords. Except for a stone metate and a stove of clay or stone resembling our kitchen ranges in construction, no furniture was in evidence. The people squatted on pelts or rush mats on the floor and slept on piles of skins, mats, or coarse textiles.

The house and its contents, together with the adjacent garden plot and a small stable and storehouse, belonged to the family. Outside the village, however, all land was the collective property of the clan. Its members enjoyed equal rights to game, wood, and pasturage on the communal forest and meadow, and they tilled in common a portion of the agricultural land for the support of the cult, the chief, and the aged and incapacitated. The major portion of the cultivated land, however, was not communally tilled but was periodically divided into equal strips and distributed among the individual families to exploit for their own profit and at their own risk. Frequent redistributions prevented the growth of marked inequalities.

The family worked as an economic unit under the leadership of the father, who exercised the authority in the household even where descent was matrilineal. The men broke the ground with a crude spade—a stick of hard wood flattened at the lower end and equipped with a crosspiece for the foot. The women and children followed to remove the stones and break the clods. The crops were planted and harvested with a pointed digging stick and weeded with a stone hoe.

Extensive irrigation and drainage canals regulated the moisture, and artificial fertilization was practiced with human
and animal manure in the highlands and with guano and
fish on the coast.

Maize constituted in most regions the mainstay of existence. Though its kernels were sometimes ground and made
into bread, it was more often boiled or roasted and eaten in
the ear. Over large areas on the plateau, where maize cannot
ripen on account of the altitude, it was replaced as the staple
by another grain, quinoa, eaten most commonly in the form
of a porridge. The so-called "Irish" potato, which is really
a native of Peru, assumed economic importance everywhere.
It was commonly reduced to a flour (*chuño*) by exposing it
alternately to frost by night and to the sun by day, and
was then made into a thin insipid gruel (*chupe*) by adding
hot water, salt, and pepper. The inhabitants of the coast
cultivated a variety of additional food plants: lima and
kidney beans, squash, sweet potatoes, manioc, tomatoes,
chili peppers, the avocado, guava, and other fruits, etc.
The highlanders added peanuts and the tuberous oca. Agave
and cotton, the principal textile plants, grew in the warmer
regions. The eastern forests contributed coca, the source of
our cocaine; by chewing the dried leaves of this shrub, mixed
with lime, the natives were able to go long periods without
food and to endure excessive exertion without fatigue. Tobacco, though cultivated to some extent, was used only for
medicinal purposes, when it was taken in the form of snuff.
The Peruvians manufactured a very intoxicating liquor from
maize kernels, which they sprouted in water, mashed, and
allowed to ferment. They also prepared milder beverages
from quinoa, the sap of the agave, and the leaves of certain
plants. But their national drink was *chicha*, the fermented
product of maize kernels chewed by the women and mixed
with brackish water.

Meat supplemented only to a limited extent the predominantly vegetarian fare of the Peruvians. Game birds

were caught with nets, snares, and blunt arrows. Hunting yielded only rodents and opossums with an occasional larger animal, a deer or a guanaco. The coastal tribes caught fish in small nets, by hook and line, or with barbed spears. All the smaller domesticated animals—dog, guinea pig, and muscovy duck—were eaten. The llama and alpaca, the only large animals ever domesticated by an American Indian tribe, were too valuable for other purposes to be used very often for food. Even when this was done, however, their flesh, like that of the wild guanaco and deer, was rarely eaten fresh, but was usually cut into strips, salted, and dried in the sun, yielding a product called *charqui* (whence our "jerked" meat).

The llama and alpaca formed the basis of economic life in the regions too high or too arid for productive agriculture. They grazed on the grassy uplands in large herds, each the communal property of a clan. The llama, although never ridden or yoked to a plow or vehicle, served as a beast of burden. It can go several days without water and will carry a load of a hundred pounds on a daily journey of twelve or thirteen miles, but it balks stubbornly if tired or overloaded. Hence a pack train must necessarily include a number of spare animals. The llama also supplied the Peruvians with wool, which was inferior in quality, however, to that of the smaller and weaker alpaca. Every year the clan herds were brought to the village to be shorn, and the wool was equally distributed among the several households.

The women devoted their spare moments to the spinning of cotton and woolen thread. From a distaff held in the left hand or under the armpit they drew the material bit by bit, moistening it with saliva and rolling it between the fingers. A wooden spindle with a whorl, rotating steadily at the right side or in a bowl, imparted an even twist to the thread. The product was then woven into fabrics on a true loom. The warp threads passed back and forth between two horizontal beams and were stretched by staking the latter to the ground or by fastening one beam to a wall and attaching the other by a belt to the body of the weaver. A thick rod was inserted through the warp so as to pass under each alternate thread and over the others, leaving an aperture or shed through which the weft thread could be passed on the spindle. By lifting the heddle, a light rod attached by loops to the lower warp threads, the shed was reversed and the weft passed back again. After each reversal the weft was pressed tight with a smooth piece of bone. In this manner the women wove the various cotton and woolen fabrics from which the native clothing was made.

The garments of the men included the *huara* or breechclout, a strip of cloth passed between the legs and supported in front and back by a string around the waist; the *uncu*, an untailored and sleeveless shirt or tunic with a slit for the head and the side seams left open at the top corners for the arms; and the *yacolla*, a narrow mantle drawn over the shoulders and knotted on the chest. Women wore the *anacu*, an ankle-length tunic consisting of a large piece of cloth wrapped around the body under the arms with its edges pulled up over the shoulders and fastened with pins; the *chumpi*, a broad and graceful sash or girdle wound several times around the waist over the tunic; and the *lliclla*, a shoulder mantle secured at the breast with a pin. Both sexes, when necessary, wore sandals (*usata*) with soles of agave fiber or untanned leather and latchets of wool or thongs.

Clothing, shelter, and food, in spite of certain regional differences, varied little within any particular clan. The chief alone towered above the common level of the clansmen, from whom he was distinguished by a higher standard of living, exemption from labor in the fields, and the possession in many instances of private property in land and herds. He held his position variously by seniority, by election, by appointment from his predecessor, or by hereditary succession in either the male or the female line, and his power ran

the gamut from purely personal influence to military despot-
ism. Although sometimes politically autonomous, clans frequently became combined into larger units or tribes through
ties of common descent, the need of mutual protection, the
exchange of women under conditions of exogamy, or the
necessity of joint action in the construction and regulation
of irrigation projects. In such cases one clan leader became
the tribal chief while the others constituted a tribal council.
In a like manner tribes were sometimes further compounded
into confederacies, *e.g.*, those of the Collas in Bolivia and
the Chancas in highland Peru, and even into feudal states,
such as Quitu in Ecuador and Chimu on the coast.

The Inca empire followed this typical evolution from
clan to state. It went, however, a long step farther. The
eighth ruler, Pachacutec, transformed the irregularly organized feudal state, which he inherited, into a symmetrical
hierarchy of groups and officials pyramided strictly according to a decimal system, and he initiated therewith a regulated system of production, distribution, and consumption
which bore most of the earmarks of what we have come to
know as state socialism. And he accomplished this feat of
statecraft with a minimum of violence to existing institutions.

The clan, the most vital institution in Peruvian life, was
not destroyed. On the contrary, it was absorbed, virtually
intact, into the imperial system, and became, indeed, the
very corner stone of that system. It was merely standardized.
The Incas classified all males into ten age-grades on the
basis, principally, of their capacity to work. Boys and youths
under twenty-five years of age, as well as men over fifty,
were held liable at the most for lighter tasks. The system
took into account only the eighth age-grade, the so-called
purics, men in the prime of life, between twenty-five and
fifty years of age. Each *puric* was a married man, a householder, and a laborer for the state as well as for himself.
The clan, as standardized, comprised one hundred *purics*,
its average number even in pre-Inca times, and means were

employed to keep it always as close as possible to this figure. Hence it now received the name of *pachaca* or "century." The former clan chief, instead of being deposed, was ai lowed to remain in office; he was absorbed into the official hierarchy as a "centurion." The century likewise retained the old clan lands. Its new artificial character even invested the latter with a new significance; common territory tended to supplant community of blood as the primary bond of association.

The century was subdivided into ten "decuries" (*chunca*) of ten *purics* each. One member of each decury was appointed "decurion" or foreman over the rest, and a superior decurion was placed in charge of five decuries. In similar fashion ten centuries united in two groups of five to form a "phratry" (*huaranca*). Ten phratries constituted a "tribe" (*hunu*), which therefore numbered about 10,000 *purics*. The tribe and phratry corresponded, as a rule, to the earlier political confederations, and the former chiefs and petty kings usually remained in office although sometimes subject to the advice and control of resident Inca delegates. Four tribes formed a *guaman* or "province," over each of which presided a *tucuiricuc* or "governor," an official with highly important civil, judicial, and military functions. The provinces of the empire were in turn grouped into four "quarters" (*suyu*), each ruled by a viceroy (*capac*). These powerful officials resided at court and formed a sort of imperial council which advised the monarch and probably exercised a certain measure of limitation on his power. The ruler himself appointed the viceroys and governors. Local customs of succession determined the occupancy of the lesser posts, except that disloyal, incapable, and corrupt officials could be removed by their superiors. In this administrative pyramid a steady stream of reports flowed upward "through official channels," and a stream of orders flowed downward; there was no contact between functionaries of equal rank. A corps of secret agents, quite outside the hierarchy, circulated incognito through every corner of the empire to observe conditions, hear complaints, and spy upon officials. They reported their findings in person to the monarch.

At the apex of this pyramid stood the divine ruler, the Sapa Inca * himself, directing the operations of the vast administrative machine with an authority not far from absolute. His subjects revered him as a god on earth, the son of the Sun, and approached his person only with uncovered feet and a symbolic burden on the shoulders. As the insignia of his high office he carried a mace and wore a plumed headdress and a multi-colored fillet with a red fringe over the forehead. He wore clothing of the finest wool, dined only from vessels of gold and silver, and never used the same garment or utensil a second time. Although provided with numerous concubines, he had one legitimate wife, the Coya, who, at least in later times, was necessarily his own eldest sister. The first son of this union, if sufficiently capable, succeeded to the throne. One result of such a brother-sister marriage was that the monarch's son was at the same time his nephew. The arrangement thus possessed manifest advantages in an empire where patrilineal rules of succession prevailed in some regions and matrilineal principles in others. A ruler began his duties with a long and rigorous fast and a personal tour of inspection to acquaint himself with all parts of his domain. He actively cultivated the arts and sciences, and associated with the savants. The long line of Inca emperors reveals only one man of mediocre talents; all the rest displayed exceptional energy, resourcefulness, tolerance, and magnanimity in the conduct of affairs. Certainly no dynasty with a higher average order of capacity has graced a throne in the whole of human history.

The Inca tribe, whose conquests established and then extended the empire, became transformed with the passage of time into a dominant aristocratic class, the Incas proper

* To avoid confusion the simple title "Inca" is preferably reserved for the members of the dominant tribe or caste in the empire.

or *orejones*—"big ears"—as the Spaniards called them from their characteristic practice of piercing the ears for an ornamental plug and enlarging the hole until the lobes hung nearly to the shoulders. The members of this class, bound to the sovereign by ties of blood and common interest, filled all the more responsible civil, military, and ecclesiastical positions. When not on active duty in the provinces, however, they resided at Cuzco.

A step beneath the Incas on the social scale stood the Curacas or provincial nobility, from whose ranks came most of the lesser officials, the heads of centuries, phratries, and tribes. In accordance with the cardinal Incaic principle of altering local institutions as little as possible, the chieftains of vanquished peoples were fitted into posts in the administrative hierarchy commensurate with their former positions, being removed only if they displayed irreconcilable hostility. The sovereign sought to win them over to active support of the imperial system by exemptions from local restraints, by generous gifts of property, servants, and wives, and by grants of Incaic privileges in reward for faithful service. He further secured their fidelity by requiring their sons to reside at Cuzco—not only to serve as hostages but also to receive the education of an Inca youth and thereby become imbued with the culture and attitude of the ruling class. By measures such as these the Curacas were gradually assimilated to the Incas, and the line of cleavage between conquerors and conquered was largely erased.

Between nobles and commoners, on the other hand, the line of demarcation grew correspondingly sharper and more rigid. The great mass of common people by their economic activities—mainly agricultural and pastoral—not only maintained themselves but also produced a surplus sufficient to support the classes which rendered only intangible services to the state: the officials, nobles, and priests. Such a surplus was assured, in part, by a body of sumptuary laws regulating and rigidly restricting the standard of living of the masses.

They could wear only the coarser garments of llama wool, the finer fabrics of alpaca and vicuña wool being reserved for the nobility. Forbidden to them, also, were the choicer food delicacies, the more intoxicating beverages, and coca. They might wear wisps of straw or wool in their ears, or small pendants of wood or clay, but not larger earrings of dearer materials. They could adorn themselves with neither gems, feathers, nor the gold and silver rings, arm bands, anklets, and breast ornaments of the upper classes. And, finally, they had no share in such other prerogatives of the Incas and Curacas as the right to hold landed estates, receive an education, and practice polygyny.

The industrial life of the clan and village remained comparatively unchanged under the Inca régime. The conquering tribe divided all the cultivated land of the empire into three parts. The first and much the smallest portion belonged to the cult and was concentrated in the vicinity of the temples which its produce supported. The second portion, the property of the crown or state, consisted partially, perhaps, of lands confiscated from conquered chieftains but mainly of waste regions reclaimed for agriculture through the irrigation construction and other engineering accomplishments of the conquerors. A small fraction of the state domain fell, through grants from the sovereign for outstanding services, into the hands of individual nobles, sometimes, apparently, as estates held for life only and sometimes, probably, as hereditary but inalienable and indivisible private property. The third and largest portion of the tilled land belonged to the centuries, which the conquering Incas were careful not to dispossess of their old clan holdings. Each century likewise owned communally its stretch of pasture and woodland, although the more extensive forests and grazing grounds were state property. The arable land was divided into strips of equal size, called *tupus*, each just large enough to support a married but childless couple. Some were tilled in common for the maintenance of the widowed and incapacitated; the rest were allotted annually, under the direction of the centurion, to the *purics* or heads of families, each of whom received one *tupu* for himself and wife, an additional strip for each male child, and half a strip for each daughter. On marrying, a son took over one *tupu* from his father, but a daughter's share reverted to the common fund. Each family cultivated its own plot and enjoyed undisputed possession of everything it raised. Hence the economic organization of the clan or century was not, strictly speaking, socialistic or communistic, as some authorities have maintained. On the contrary, it followed the familiar pattern of agrarian collectivism, typified, for instance, by the Russian *mir*.

The agrarian community, however, became the basis of a truly socialistic superstructure. Instead of allowing free rein to personal interest and competition to achieve an automatic equilibrium of economic forces, the Incas substituted a rationally planned economy in which demand and supply were artificially regulated. The sumptuary laws stabilized and limited the demand, while the supply was cared for by a nationalized system of production superimposed upon the clan economy.

The first task was the support of the economically unproductive classes—the administrative hierarchy, the nobility, the army, and the priesthood. This was not accomplished, as we might expect, through taxation. Only in a few very exceptional cases did the state impose levies in goods or products upon its subjects. On the contrary, it followed the principle of the *corvée*, namely, that tribute should take the form of personal services. Every able-bodied householder or *puric*, besides cultivating his own plot of ground to support his family and coöperating with his clansmen in tilling the undistributed lands of the century to provide for its less fortunate members, was expected to devote a portion of his time and labor to the service of the state. This contribution took the form, primarily, of labor on the lands of the crown and the cult. Each century was held responsible for a definite acreage, and each decury for an equal tenth thereof. The decurion divided his section into narrow parallel strips, taking one himself and assigning the others to his men. The workers, dressed in their best and making a holiday out of the occasion, advanced in a line along their respective rows, singing as they went. They were fed, entertained, and provided with seed and other necessities at public expense. The products contributed to the support of the official and ecclesiastical hierarchies.

The pastoral economy paralleled the agricultural. In the highlands each *puric* possessed a pair or two of llamas and had the right to use their wool and to kill their offspring for food. Small herds were owned communally by the centuries and privately by the Curacas. The crown and the cult, however, possessed enormous herds of llamas and alpacas, often numbering thousands. The *purics*, as part of their labor obligation to the state, took turns in tending the animals and performed assigned tasks at the periodic shearings and slaughters. The wool, hides, and meat, of course, flowed into the warehouses of the cult and the state.

Although clansmen were privileged to secure small game on the woodland belonging to the century, the hunting of the larger wild animals was a state monopoly. Once a year each *tucuiricuc* or governor assembled the *purics* under his jurisdiction on one of the national forests in his province for a great communal drive. Surrounding a wide territory, the men advanced with a deafening din, penning their quarry in an ever narrowing circle. All beasts of prey—pumas, bears, foxes, wildcats—they slew on sight with arrows, darts, and clubs. In the case of deer, they killed only a portion of the males, sparing all the does and the best bucks lest the supply become depleted. The guanaco and vicuña, wild cousins of the llama and alpaca, were captured alive with the bola—a cord of twisted rawhide weighted at the ends with stones. When thrown, this weapon wrapped itself around the legs of the animal, bringing it to the ground. The victims were shorn and then released, except for a certain proportion of the males selected for slaughter. The hunters feasted on part of the meat. The remainder, together with the hides and fleeces, belonged to the state.

Mining, too, was nationalized. The Peruvians obtained gold by panning river gravels. They extracted silver and copper ores with hammer and chisel, either in pits or in short galleries following outcropping veins. They likewise mined mercury to a limited extent, exploited salt deposits, and were adept at quarrying enormous blocks of stone for building purposes. Miners were drafted for a term of one month a year and in this way performed their labor obligation to the state, which, of course, owned the product.

An important part of the tribute obligation of the *puric* consisted in labor in the construction of public works. As soon as a new province was conquered, for example, a complete census of its population, land, and resources was taken, the monarch with his council laid plans for the construction of needed roads, fortresses, irrigation systems, etc., and an army of engineers and drafted laborers was put at work. Mountain slopes were reclaimed for agriculture by terracing them with rows of stone retaining walls like gigantic steps. Swamps were drained and arid lands brought under cultivation by digging irrigation canals. The latter were ten feet in width, five or six feet deep, and as much as sixty miles in length. They were carried over valleys on aqueducts, provided with reservoirs, feeders, and sluices, and sometimes covered with stone slabs to prevent excessive evaporation. The lands thus reclaimed became the property of the state, which could thus afford to leave the clan holdings intact.

Similar levies built the Cyclopean fortresses, temples, and palaces for which Peru is famous. Great blocks of stone, sometimes measuring thousands of cubic feet, were fitted to each other, by grinding with wet sand, so accurately that a knife blade could not be inserted between them. No mortar was used, although the joints were sometimes filled with gold or silver. In the later Inca buildings the stones were laid in mathematically regular courses. In spite of their imposing size—walls hundreds of feet in length were common—these edifices had plain exteriors, unrelieved by columns, cornices, or windows. Architecture reached its highest development in Cuzco, a city of perhaps 200,000 inhabitants, with five squares and narrow but regular paved streets meeting at right angles. Adjoining the Huatanay River, which bisected

Courtesy of Hiram Bingham

FIG. 92. DETAIL OF THE WALL OF THE SACSAHUAMAN FORTRESS, CUZCO.

the town, stood the temples and the palaces of the emperors and nobles. The latter were usually surrounded by walls and gardens, built around a central court, and even provided with running water piped from hot and cold springs in the mountains. The city centered about the great Temple of the Sun but was dominated by the impregnable fortress of Sacsahuaman which guarded the approach on the north with its three parallel walls three hundred feet in length and its ingenious system of reëntrant angles for defense.

Drafted labor likewise built and maintained the roads,

being maintained while at work, as in all similar cases, at public expense. Two main highways traversed the empire from north to south, one along the coast, the other in the highlands. Numerous transverse and secondary roads formed a giant network converging on Cuzco. The roads, being primarily footpaths, were narrow, but nevertheless remarkably straight; wherever possible they surmounted natural obstacles instead of circling them. In the mountains they were paved or hewn out of solid rock; on the coast they ran between low walls or rows of posts or shady fruit trees. They crossed marshes on causeways, small streams on stone culverts or wooden bridges, broad rivers on reed pontoons or by means of cable-drawn rafts or ferries. Gorges were spanned either by a single rope from which was slung a moving basket or by marvelous suspension bridges consisting of two or more giant cables moored to masonry piers, covered with a floor of wattle, and lashed to two smaller ropes which served as handrails. The Inca highways remained unequaled in the world, even by the Roman roads, until a century ago.

At intervals of every two or three miles stood post houses, where two or more couriers, apparently recruited from youths between the ages of twenty and twenty five, were always in attendance. When a runner from the next station approached, a fresh courier would run alongside him to learn the message or receive the burden or *quipu* and then dash off for the next post without slackening of pace. The speed records over long distances attained in this way are almost incredible, *e.g.*, ten days between Quito and Cuzco (1,300 miles). Even greater rapidity of communication was achieved by smoke signals, used only in cases of rebellion. By touching off successively the pyres kept ever in readiness at all post stations, it was possible to inform the emperor at Cuzco in a few hours of an insurrection two thousand miles away, and an army could thus be mobilized and on the march before specific news arrived. Every twelve to eighteen miles along the roads stood an inn with accommodations for travelers and a cluster of twenty to fifty small rectangular storehouses stocked with food, clothing, and arms.

The rigid decimal organization of Peruvian society, which appears so arbitrary at first glance, becomes comprehensible when we regard it as an adjustment to the system of tribute by labor in lieu of taxes. Lacking a written language and a knowledge of mathematics adequate for dealing with large figures except with the aid of the *quipu*, which lends itself to computation only in terms of decimals, the Incas could devise only one equitable way of levying drafts of labor, namely, by fixing a quota for a large group, assigning one-tenth of the quota to each constituent sub-group, and so on. Thus, if 1,000 men were needed from a particular tribe for the construction of an irrigation canal, each phratry would have to furnish 100, each century ten, and each decury one. If, however, the units had varied in size, *e.g.*, if some centuries had had fifty *purics* while others had two hundred, the smaller units would have contributed disproportionately and the tribute burden would have been inequitably distributed. It was imperative, therefore, to maintain the various units at approximately their standard size.

Once a year each decurion reported to his superior the number of births and deaths in his ten families. These figures were transmitted through official channels to the *tucuiricuc* or provincial governor, who had them compiled by an accountant, reported the total to the emperor, and turned over the records to the official *quipu* keepers at Cuzco. On the basis of these statistics the state imposed a permanent levy upon every group which appreciably exceeded its ideal population. The surplus thus drawn off was, in part, formed into *mitimaes* or colonies, which were granted special privileges and exemptions, and were transported to settle underpopulated areas, to man military outposts, to introduce Incaic culture to backward regions, or to replace rebellious tribes removed to safer sections. From the surplus not absorbed in *mitimaes* were recruited two anomalous classes in Inca society: the *yanacuna* and the *acllacuna*.

The *yanacuna* consisted of men levied as youths for the personal service of the monarch. He employed them as palace attendants, devoted them to the temples for similar services, used them as porters in the army, presented them to officials as domestic servants or as serfs to till private estates, assigned them minor administrative posts such as the supervision of warehouses, or trained them in specialized handicrafts. They lost their clan rights and also all duties except to their masters, but their status, though hereditary, was scarcely that of slaves. They fared, on the whole, rather better than the *purics*. Being in a position to gain the confidence and favor of their masters, they were frequently rewarded with rich gifts and even with landed estates and official positions, to which the commoner could never aspire.

The *acllacuna*, sometimes called Virgins of the Sun by a superficial analogy with the Roman Vestal Virgins, formed the second anomalous class. Selected at the age of eight or nine from overpopulous centuries, they lived in convents under the supervision of matrons. Some, at the age of fourteen, took vows of chastity and became priestesses. The majority, however, at the will of the emperor, became imperial concubines, married *yanacuna*, or were bestowed upon favored nobles as secondary wives. The *acllacuna*, too, lost their clan membership, yet acquired an enhanced social status.

These special classes, though never very large, seem nevertheless to have filled an important place in the Inca economy. Besides rendering personal service in palace and temple, they carried on the specialized arts and crafts. Except for them, a division of labor in production, other than by sex, scarcely existed in Peru. Each clan, indeed each family, was practically self-sufficient economically. Every woman could spin, weave, and make mats, baskets, pottery, and clothing. Every man could hunt, fight, make weapons, till the soil, herd llamas, and perform his share in the construction of public works. Every one was conversant with all save a few luxury arts, such as metal-working and fine weaving, and these were carried on by the classes in question.

Yanacuna smiths worked with gold, silver, and copper, not with iron. They smelted copper in pottery crucibles over a fire, blowing through long tubes to provide a blast. To smelt silver, which requires a much higher temperature, they built furnaces on the summits of hills, where strong winds furnished the blast. They apparently understood how to make bronze by mixing copper and tin in the ore. They cast or hammered such implements as knives, axes, chisels, hoes, spades, needles, and tweezers. They plated copper vessels with silver and silver ones with gold by applying the precious metal as a leaf and then hammering it. They produced a gold plate on copper objects by the use of an amalgam of gold and mercury. With a copper hammer and a stone anvil they beat the precious metals into exceedingly delicate threads for the ornamentation of textiles.

After Mead

FIG. 93. BRONZE AND COPPER KNIVES FROM PERU.

Perhaps nothing better reveals their skill and artistry than their ability to fashion golden butterflies with wings one-tenth of a millimeter in thickness, so light and so well balanced that when thrown they soared like toy airplanes before falling. The precious metals and their products poured into Cuzco, a veritable El Dorado where even the palace walls were often decorated with golden friezes on the exterior and panels of gold and silver on the interior. The Temple of the Sun had a golden garden, where trees and plants, fruits and flowers, birds and insects were all of gold, and where grazed a herd of golden llamas under a life-sized golden shepherd.

The *acllacuna,* working in the convents under the direction of expert matrons, wove the fine fabrics of vicuña wool and supplied the ruler, the higher officials, and the temples with their rich garments. In skill and technic in the textile arts the ancient Peruvians have had no equals in human history. They wove plain webs, double-faced cloths, gauze and voile, knitted and crocheted fabrics, featherwork, tapestries, fine

FIG. 94. INCA FIGURE OF AN ALPACA IN SILVER.
Courtesy of the American Museum of Natural History

cloths interwoven with gold and silver threads—employing, in short, every technic save twilling known to the Old World in addition to some peculiar to themselves. They dyed the threads with cochineal, indigo, yellow ocher, etc., after rendering them receptive to the colors by immersion in mineral mordants. They wove strands of different hues to produce fabrics with stripes, geometric designs, and conventionalized patterns of plants and animals. They embellished the finished products with embroidery, with fringes and tassels, and with painted and stamped designs. They practiced tie-dyeing, and utilized the plumage of tropical birds in fashioning magnificent feather garments and headdresses. But it was in their tapestries that they reached the climax of their art. Employing methods identical with those used in the famous Gobelin and Beauvais tapestries, they nevertheless, in harmony of colors, fastness of dyes, and perfection of technic, far surpassed the finest products of Europe.

The collectivistic economy of the clan or century provided automatically for most of the needs of the masses. The superimposed régime of the state restricted popular consumption by sumptuary laws. It assured a surplus production of manufactured goods through the special classes of *yanacuna* and *acllacuna*, and of raw materials through the general requirement of labor on the lands, in the mines, and with the herds belonging to the state. What marks it indelibly as socialistic, however, is its system of distribution. It achieved an equilibrium of production and consumption, not through the free interchange of goods, but through state-supervised periodic distributions of the surplus production. In this system the warehouses strategically located in clusters along the highways played a vital part. Into them flowed a steady stream of raw and finished products from the crown and cult lands, the state herds, the mines, the organized game drives, and the specialized handicrafts. From them the state drew: (1) means of subsistence and luxuries for the ruling and official classes, the priesthood, their servants, and the artisans, (2) food and military stores for armies on the march, (3) raw materials for manufacture into finished goods, (4) support for *purics* engaged in public work, (5) supplies to relieve regions stricken with famine or crop failure, and (6) consumption goods for the masses in all cases where the latter could not supply themselves. Since the warehouses contained reserves of food sufficient to support the entire population for several years, and corresponding quantities of other articles, the system provided adequate insurance against privation. The supervisors made periodic reports, which were tabulated and preserved in the archives at Cuzco. Thus the authorities always knew the exact status and location of the reserves, and could order their transfer by porter or llama train from well-stocked regions to those with a shortage. The people received distributions of staples, such as seeds, meat, wool, cotton, and copper implements, periodically, and of other articles whenever the statistics revealed a surplus above necessary reserves. Distributions, like levies, took place by successive allotments to tribe, phratry, century, etc.; each family thus received the same as its neighbor, irrespective of its individual needs. Under this system economic life pursued an even course undisturbed by the boom periods and depressions which result from leaving the adjustment of production and consumption to automatic forces.

Travel and transportation were public functions. No one used the roads except couriers, officials, soldiers, colonists, authorized pilgrims, and porters. Nevertheless a heavy traffic existed in the interchange of regional products. Into the highland warehouses flowed cotton, pepper, fruits, and fish from the coast, and wood, coca, feathers, and dyestuffs from the eastern forests; in return they shipped out wool, meat, potatoes, and metals. But this movement of goods did not take place by private trade, which was confined within very narrow limits. At local markets, held thrice a month, families exchanged—by barter, for there was no money—the surplus products of their garden plots and unneeded articles received from the state. These markets served principally to adjust the inequalities resulting from the rule-of-thumb system of distribution. The limited range of private property, the sumptuary laws, and the state's participation in the circulation of goods effectually prevented the development of trade on a broader basis. Even foreign commerce, as in Soviet Russia, was a government monopoly.

Inca socialism, absurdly idealized by some writers and as unjustly dismissed as a fiction by others, emerges from a survey of the facts, not as the product of a utopian dream, but as a natural adaptation to a special set of conditions. To the conquerors it assured power, position, and luxury; to the conquered, economic security, the essential preservation of local institutions, and probably an enhanced standard of living. Pragmatic rather than dogmatic, it sought, for example, not to extirpate commerce and private property on principle but rather to limit them on practical grounds. Socialism, linked with democracy in Marxian theory, was consistent in Peru with monarchy and aristocracy. The Inca system exerted a leveling influence, creating a uniform standard of living throughout the empire. If it thus realized the ideal of equality, it was equality only within a given social class. It subordinated the individual to the state, regimented and controlled his life from birth to death, and left little scope for personal initiative and ambition. On the other hand, it achieved an exceptional degree of law and order; it prevented the waste of natural resources, e.g., in timber and game; it placed public interest before profit, e.g., by prohibition or strict regulation of dangerous occupations like pearl fishing and mercury mining; and it eliminated entirely the hazards of poverty and involuntary unemployment. In general, it displayed many but not all of the virtues for which socialism has been exalted and many but not all of the defects with which it has been charged. Let us not forget, in this connection, that it was a working system and not a theory.

The Incas altered but slightly the customary laws prevalent in the various parts of the empire, merely superimposing upon them a body of regularized rules designed to guarantee the stability of the state and its fiscal and social system. The centurion adjusted disputes and punished wrongs in all cases where local custom and the local community alone were involved, as the clan chief had done before him. The support of the state strengthened his position, but his jurisdiction was restricted to cases not involving the death penalty. These cases and all those involving two or more communities fell within the province of the higher officials in the administrative system, notably the provincial governors. The ecclesiastical hierarchy had jurisdiction over priests and over crimes against religion. The monarch himself or his council of viceroys tried serious offenses such as treason as well as all crimes committed by Incas and Curacas. Thus there was no independent judiciary unless we count the inspectors appointed by and responsible to the emperor.

The state rigidly prohibited private vengeance and self-help. Judges held court publicly and were compelled to render a judgment within five days. No appeals were allowed, although the monarch reserved to himself the right of pardon. In default of witnesses the court could resort to torture to force a confession, or to divination or an ordeal to determine the guilt or innocence of the accused. Judgments followed established precedents wherever possible.

The imperial code differed from the common law of the clans in its primarily criminal rather than civil character and in its preventive rather than punitive and compensatory purpose. It concerned itself with acts which directly or indirectly threatened the established order, such as treason, lese majesty, official misconduct, evasion or embezzlement of tribute, the violation of sumptuary and game laws, and attacks upon life, property, and morality. Since it sought not to punish these acts but to prevent their occurrence, it imposed penalties that were always severe and often ferocious. Fines were unknown and imprisonment rare. Petty thieves and minor sex offenders were flogged or scourged. Other lesser criminals were sentenced to forced labor in the unhealthy mines and coca plantations. But the death penalty was inflicted for murder, sorcery, adultery, incest, arson, theft from the state, and most other crimes. Hanging was the favorite mode of execution, although beheading, burning, quartering, and hurling over a cliff were preferred for certain offenses. These punishments coupled with rigor-

THE INCAS OF PERU 433

ous enforcement resulted in an exceedingly low crime rate. The common law often graded penalties according to objective damage rather than subjective guilt, but the imperial law took such factors as intent, age, knowledge, and provocation into consideration. Two special provisions are not without interest. For the crime of a child its father was held equally responsible and received the same punishment. For theft motivated by distress or need rather than by malice or greed, not the thief but the official who had failed to provide for him was punished.

The army consisted of one-tenth of the adult male population selected in rotation and organized decimally into units paralleling those of the state. During their term of service, if not actually engaged in war, the soldiers rested from their other labors in behalf of the state and engaged in military exercises under their leaders. Fortresses manned by *mitimaes* with special privileges guarded all paths of access to the empire as a defense against marauding neighbors. But the majority of wars were aggressive and imperialistic. The Incas always tried—frequently with success—to induce their enemies by propaganda, presents, and other peaceful means to join the empire voluntarily. They resorted to war only when diplomacy had failed. Conquests were carefully planned. Spies studied the country. Bribes purchased the neutrality of the enemy's neighbors and allies. Each advance was thoroughly consolidated by road building, economic organization, etc., before undertaking the next. Armies on the march never lived off the country. They derived all supplies from the warehouses along the route and from accompanying trains of llamas and porters. The penalty for pillage, even of a single ear of maize, was death.

The principal weapons were slings for hurling stones, bows and arrows, spear-throwers for propelling darts, lances tipped with bone or copper, battle-axes of bronze, and clubs with star-shaped heads of stone or copper wielded with both hands. For protection the warriors wore padded wooden helmets and jackets of quilted cotton, and carried square or circular wooden shields sometimes large enough to cover twenty men. The slingers and archers opened battle; shock troops then closed in for hand-to-hand combat with axes and clubs. With victory assured, all violence ceased. Prisoners were freed. The vanquished chieftains received rich gifts and were assigned appropriate places in the administrative hierarchy. The idols of the region were transported to

After Mead
FIG. 95. INCA BATTLE-AX
AND WAR CLUBS.

Cuzco to serve as hostages for the good behavior of their worshipers. The rare magnanimity of the Incas toward conquered peoples sprang probably, not from humanitarian motives, but from enlightened self-interest.

Among the fine arts music perhaps ranked first. The Peruvians used skin drums stretched over wooden hoops or hollow cylinders, bronze gongs, copper bells, gourd rattles, bone flutes, trumpets and resonator whistles of terra cotta, conches with copper mouthpieces, and panpipes consisting of a series of reeds or hollow tubes of graduated length and pitch. They employed the five-toned or pentatonic scale. They composed hymns, love songs, and epic poems commemorating the deeds of their ancestors. An embryonic drama existed in the dances and mimes held at court.

Parents greatly desired children for the economic assistance they could render, and infanticide was consequently very rare. An expectant mother—and the father as well—abstained from certain foods. She bore her child in private, usually with no aid from a midwife. After bathing herself and the infant in a neighboring stream, she swaddled it tightly, placed it in a cradle, and went about her ordinary tasks. The umbilical cord was carefully preserved, and a portion was given to the child to chew whenever it fell ill. To toughen the baby its mother gave it a cold bath every morning but did not otherwise remove it from the cradle, over which she even leaned to suckle it. To conform to the prevailing ideal of beauty she bound its head between two boards. When a child reached two years of age and was weaned, its relatives assembled for a feast lasting several days. Its hair and nails were cut for the first time by an uncle, who used a stone knife and carefully preserved the clippings. It received a name, usually that of an ancestor, animal, or natural object, and was then showered with gifts.

Formal education was reserved for youths of the Inca and Curaca classes, and its purpose was to train them for public life. They studied at Cuzco, where the *amautas* or learned men of the empire—those versed in mathematics, the natural sciences, history, law, statecraft, engineering, theology, music, and poetry—were grouped together in a college. Under the tutelage of these men they pursued a varied curriculum for four years, specializing the first year on language, the second on theology and religious ritual, the third on the lore of the *quipu*, and the fourth on history.

Girls at puberty, after a three-day fast, underwent a ceremony in which they donned new garments and a pair of white sandals, had their loose tresses plaited into a braid, and received presents and a new name which they bore throughout life. At a similar ceremony boys of fifteen or sixteen assumed the breechclout and a permanent name. In the case of youths of the Inca class these rites coincided with the completion of their formal education and were elaborated into one of the principal festivals on the ritual calendar, that of Capac Raymi. After a six-day fast, they competed in a four-mile foot race from the sacred hill of Huanacauri to the fortress of Sacsahuaman. Then, dividing into two parties, they fought a sham battle; despite the use of blunt weapons, casualties frequently occurred. Contests with sling, bow, lance, and spear-thrower and severe tests of fortitude, endurance, and self-control followed.   Each candidate then had to demonstrate his ability to make a bow, a sling, and a pair of sandals. No one who failed in these tests could aspire to high office, even though he were the monarch's own son. Next, in an impressive ceremony, the emperor in person ritually pierced their ears with a golden bodkin, and other high officials invested them with the breechclout, a pair of sandals, and the insignia of rank. And finally each received from his nearest kinsman a new name and a shield, a sling, an ax, and a club.

Marriage, like most Peruvian institutions, reveals the superimposition of unified imperial regulations upon a basis of diverse local customs. The clan exogamy of pre-Inca times gradually gave way, under the influence of the imperial system, to local endogamy. The artificial constitution of the century paved the way. In his choice of a wife, a man was confined to his local community, within which, however, he was compelled to observe certain prohibitions against the marriage of near relatives. Parents exercised considerable authority in the selection of mates, and a union without their consent was invalid. Marriage was obligatory at the age fixed by law—eighteen to twenty for girls, twenty-four to twenty-five for men—and recalcitrant celibates were wedded against their will by official edict. To arrange a match a man gave small gifts—costlier ones in the case of nobles—to the local centurion and to the father of the girl. A Peruvian could take only one wife himself, but he might receive *acllacuna* as secondary wives by gift of the sovereign in recompense for services. Among commoners monogamy was universal by economic necessity. Polygyny prevailed only in the noble classes, the recipients of the monarch's largess, and was thus definitely a badge of rank. In the case of the emperor, who had hundreds of concubines, it was a political necessity; he needed a large body of near relatives to whom he could intrust the more responsible civil, military, and ecclesiastical positions. In every instance, however, including the empress, the first or legitimate wife took precedence over the rest and could not be deposed.

There were two wedding ceremonies—one public and the other private. Once a year all the betrothed boys and girls of the Inca class assembled on a square in Cuzco, and the emperor in person united the hands of each couple in matrimony. His personal representatives performed the same ceremony for the Curacas and commoners in the various provincial towns. After this public rite, the groom led the bride in a procession of relatives to the house of her father, who handed her over to him. He knelt before her and placed a sandal of wool upon her right foot. He then led her to the house which the village authorities were always obliged to provide for a newly married couple. Here she presented him with a shirt, a fillet, and a breast ornament, which he donned forthwith. The relatives then showered them with gifts and advice. Bride and groom each received, as a wedding present from the state, two complete outfits of new clothing, one for ordinary wear and a finer one for festive occasions. The distribution of *acllacuna* as secondary wives took place at the same public ceremony, but it did not involve other formalities. A marriage, once contracted, was indissoluble; no divorce was allowed. Widows received support from the community and rarely remarried; secondary wives, however, were inherited by the brother or sons of the deceased husband.

The Peruvians attributed disease either to sin and consequent punishment or to possession by evil spirits. The proper procedure in the former case was confession and atonement; in the latter, exorcism after a propitiatory sacrifice. Therapeutic practices such as massage, bleeding, and the use of purgatives were primarily exorcistic in purpose, though more rational motives doubtless underlay bonesetting and the use of poultices and salves for sprains and wounds. If quinine was used as a febrifuge in pre-Columbian times, as some authorities maintain, the custom was not widespread.

The *amautas* practiced trepanation of the skull for fractures from club blows and also probably for less adequate reasons. They scraped the surface of the bone with a stone knife, incised a square, circular, or irregular segment, forcibly pried out the button, and rasped the edges smooth. Their workmanship was crude and bungling. A study of twenty-four skulls showed that only eight of the victims had recovered sufficiently for new bone to form, although six others may have lived a short time.

The Peruvians mummified their dead. Although they occasionally removed the viscera, preservation was due primarily to the dryness of the climate. The body, arranged in a sitting position with its knees against its chest, was swathed in successive layers of cloth and then wrapped tightly in a reed mat. The coastal tribes, with additional padding and wrapping, produced a more elaborate mummy-pack. The body, thus prepared, was deposited, on the coast in a single grave or a multiple burial chamber, on the plateau in a rock crevice or a natural cave faced with masonry. Beside it were placed food, drink, and the personal belongings of the deceased—a man's weapons, a woman's weaving implements, a child's playthings. The mummies of the emperors and their consorts were preserved in the Temple of the Sun at Cuzco, whence they were brought forth at stated intervals for important festivals and processions. The wives and attendants of a deceased monarch frequently immolated themselves voluntarily at his funeral that they might accompany him to the next world. The residence of a dead ruler was left intact with all its furniture, its staff of servants, and landed estates to support them; the successor erected and equipped a new palace. Widows and other near relatives blackened their faces, cut their hair, wore black mantles, and fasted for five days. Offerings of food and drink were left from time to time at all places of burial, so that the departed souls might consume their spiritual essence and in return offer protection to the survivors.

On the basis of this simple cult of the dead the Peruvians elaborated a complex of animistic, fetishistic, and totemistic beliefs and practices which constituted their religion. The ghost of a deceased person, after lingering for a while in the vicinity of the corpse, was commonly thought to take up its residence in some animate or inanimate object of nature. Things thus occupied or "possessed" by spirits were called *huacas, i.e.*, fetishes, and included such objects as mummies, tombs and other burial places, caves, the house where a monarch had died, animals and birds in whose bodies human souls had become reincarnated, etc. Through similar associations all outstanding geographical features—hills, cliffs, rivers, lakes, springs, etc.—received homage as *huacas;* the "nature worship" of Peru had its roots in animistic beliefs. Even the celestial bodies were fetishes; the souls of deceased monarchs, for example, took up their residence in the sun.

In addition to things directly and obviously associated with the dead, the *huacas* included a wide variety of objects and phenomena which, through the possession of extraordinary or mysterious qualities, raised the presumption of a similar spiritual association, *e.g.*, a pebble of peculiar shape, an albino animal, a freak or monstrosity, a stone that had crushed a man. Every person cherished one such object, called his *huauqui* or "brother," as the abode of his personal guardian spirit. The legends surrounding *huacas* of this type demonstrate that the underlying idea was animistic and fetishistic rather than a diffuse notion of mysterious impersonal power. A rock of peculiar formation, for example, was commonly explained by a story of some ancestor who had died at that spot and been transformed into stone.

Each clan worshiped a common ancestor (*pacarina*) as its tutelary spirit and carried on a communal cult in his honor. His fetish—be it puma, condor, or serpent, a hill, lake, or celestial body—became the totem of the clan. Thus Peruvian totemism had its roots in ancestor worship and fetishism. From the fact that *pacarina* and totem were not always clearly differentiated, at least in language, it became customary to call the fetish objects "ancestors" and to assert that men were descended from stones, caves, mountains, or the like. This quite natural confusion, however, does not obscure the essential facts.

Households, too, had their guardian spirits—beings analogous to the *lares* of ancient Rome—whose fetishes, usually small stones of peculiar shape, were kept in niches in the walls.   These fetishes, together with various ceremonial paraphernalia, were inherited from father to son and thus constituted one of the few forms of private property. Images designed to promote fertility in crops and herds likewise figured prominently in the domestic cult, notably dolls called *zaramama* (corn mother) fashioned of maize stalks, etc., and figurines in the shape of llamas with backs hollowed for the reception of offerings.

The conquering Incas did not attempt to destroy or supplant the local clan and household cults. They merely superimposed upon them, and demanded nominal recognition of, their own cult, which became that of the state. To distinguish, perhaps, the imperial cult from those of the conquered peoples, the Incas emphasized celestial rather than animal and geographical fetishes. Their great deities were Inti, Illapa, and Quilla—respectively Sun, Thunder, and Moon. They did not, however, worship these phenomena themselves, but only the gods who inhabited or actuated them. The sun, for instance, was merely one of the fetishes of Inti, others being the hawk, the serpent, and certain stones. Hence a rock sacred to the sun god might be called confusingly a "sun-stone" or simply "sun." The Incas, regarding the sun as their peculiar totem, were but following the usual practice when they dubbed themselves "sons of the Sun." Other gods of national importance were Mamacocha, the Sea, mother of waters, prominent on the coast; Pachamama or Earth Mother, great goddess of fertility and vegetation; and Viracocha, creator, maintainer of order in the universe, and vaguely conceived supreme being of philosophical speculation.

The priests who served the various cults, though sometimes hereditary, were usually appointed by their superiors in the ecclesiastical hierarchy, oftentimes because of some personal peculiarity such as epilepsy, birth during a thunderstorm, or recovery after being struck by lightning. The higher priests received support from the cult lands, but the lower clergy, who served only for brief terms in rotation and otherwise lived the life of ordinary citizens, were merely relieved of their tribute obligation to the state. The priests of the imperial cult were organized according to a decimal system under a sort of pontifex maximus, the Villac Umu, who was the uncle or brother of the sovereign. He resided at the great Temple of the Sun in Cuzco, lived an exemplary life hedged in by restrictions, and enjoyed a prestige and power second only to that of the monarch. The higher clergy of the state cult were all members of the ruling class. Even in the provincial temples of the Sun an Inca priest always presided over the lesser clergy, who were drawn from local Curaca families. In conjunction with each state temple stood a convent where, secluded from the world, lived the *acllacuna*. These novices, in addition to their economic function in the manufacture of fine textiles, kept the temple in order, maintained the sacred fire, and prepared the sacrificial foods and drinks. With them, but distinct from them, lived the daughters of the nobility, who thus received an education in religion and the domestic arts. The *acllacuna* who were not distributed as concubines remained as matrons, of whom one had supervision over each ten novices. Each convent was in charge of a head priestess, who was regarded as the wife of the Sun, and who lived a life of great piety and exaggerated chastity.

Lesser priests served the local *huacas* and transmitted to the people the revelations of their divinities. Intoxicating themselves with alcoholic liquors or the fumes of narcotic herbs, they engaged in frenzied dances until they fell into a trance and gave voice to their oracular utterances. Pilgrims flocked in thousands to consult the famous oracles at Rimac and Pachacamac. Various classes of soothsayers, stationed in the vestibules of the temples, foretold the future from dreams, the twitching of muscles, the flight of birds, the position of the stars, the shape of a column of smoke, the number of maize kernels in a random heap, the pattern of the blood vessels on the inflated lungs of a sacrificed llama, or the distribution of a spider's legs knocked off by a blow with a stick. A class of ascetic eunuchs isolated themselves from their fellows and submitted to a rigorous discipline marked by prolonged fasts and mortification of the flesh. There were also unauthorized practitioners of the black art who worked magic with the hair or effigies of their enemies or cast sleep upon them by spells and then sucked their lifeblood or devoured their souls.

Sin, according to Peruvian belief, brought misfortune not only upon the sinner himself but upon his whole community. Hence, just as sickness proved guilt in the individual, so a drought or similar public calamity betrayed the existence of sin in the community. Either situation called for confession and atonement—private in the one case, public in the other. The sinner appeared before a local priest or diviner, confessed his fault, listened to some good moral advice, and received instructions as to the appropriate penance. He spat upon a bundle of grass, threw it into a river, bathed, and then fasted or mortified the flesh as prescribed by the priest. Fasting in Peru was a ritual matter consisting merely in abstention from salt, pepper, and sex relations.

Of all cult acts, however, sacrifice was by far the most important. Everything that man cherished he shared with his gods: shells, feathers, precious gems and metals, dogs and guinea pigs, wild animals captured in the chase, the first fruits of the harvest, etc. Coca and *chicha* were sprinkled on the fields at planting and harvest times as an offering to the

Earth Mother. Quantities of fine garments manufactured from the wool of the herds belonging to the cult were burned at all the great festivals. A white llama was sacrificed each morning at the Temple of the Sun in Cuzco, and from a hundred to several thousand at the major ceremonies. A priest seized the victim, turned its eyes toward the *huaca*, slashed its throat, tore out its heart and lungs, and sprinkled the blood on the image of the god. It was firmly believed that if the sacrifices were neglected or improperly performed the sun would not shine, the rain would not fall, the crops would not ripen, and the flocks would not multiply.

Human sacrifice, common in pre-Inca times, declined greatly under the imperial régime though it was never entirely abandoned. It survived only in extremely critical occasions, *e.g.*, war, pestilence, earthquakes, or the sickness, death, or accession of a monarch. The victims, with the exception of persons voluntarily immolating themselves at the death of the emperor, were children. The girls were selected from among the *acllacuna* in the convents; whether the boys came from the drafts of *yanacuna*, while probable, is not certain. They usually met their death by strangulation although other methods were sometimes employed. In all cases, however, the *huacas* were smeared with their blood. The victims were not numerous—rarely more than one of each sex. The Incas seem to have attempted—with considerable success—to substitute other sacrifices for those of human beings. The llama, for instance, made an admirable vicarious sacrifice. Other examples were the burnt offerings of wooden figures clad in woolen garments and the metal heart immured in the foundation of a new palace or public building.

The imperial cult found expression in a series of elaborate ceremonies distributed throughout the solar year. Of these the most important were Intip Raymi, the great sun festival at the winter solstice in June; Situa, the purificatory ceremony at the spring equinox in September; and Capac Raymi, the summer solstice festival in December, with its initiation rites as described above. For Intip Raymi the Incas and Curacas flocked to Cuzco from all the provinces and assembled at dawn on the great square before the Temple of the Sun. As the first rays of light appeared over the eastern horizon they prostrated themselves and saluted the rising sun with a kiss. The emperor rose first, offered a golden goblet of liquor to his celestial father, and poured its contents into a conduit which conveyed the libation directly to the image of the god in the temple. Taking a second goblet, he sipped from it and passed it around among the Incas present. The members of the ruling class entered the temple in a solemn procession and deposited gifts of gold and silver at the feet of the god. A priest then sacrificed a black llama and inspected its lungs for omens. If these were unfavorable, he sacrificed a second and then a third. If the auguries were still unpropitious, the ceremony terminated amid gloomy forebodings for the ensuing year. But if the omens were favorable, there followed a holocaust of llamas, a general feast upon their roasted flesh, and nine days of orgiastic festivity.

For the Situa ceremony, which was associated with the cult of the Moon and was designed to exorcise all sickness and other evils, the important *huacas* from the provinces were brought to Cuzco and all dogs, strangers, cripples, and unlucky persons were sent out of the city. The people assembled at night on the great plaza, where four hundred chosen warriors formed a square, one hundred facing in each of the cardinal directions. When the moon rose, the priests shouted, "Go forth, all evils!" The warriors, taking up the refrain, rushed from the city along the various roads. The people shook their mantles as they passed and then followed them. When the crowds reached the rivers they bathed in their waters that all diseases might be carried down to the sea. Next they brandished straw torches to drive away other evils. A special maize pudding, mixed with the blood of sacrificed llamas, was smeared on the faces of the citizens, on the lintels of their doors, and on the idols, mummies, and other *huacas*, then washed off and the remnants cast into the river. The banished persons returned to the city for a final series of parades, sacrifices, feasts, dances, and games.

The fame of the Inca empire and its fabulous riches spread as far as Panama, where Balboa in 1513 learned of its existence. Fired by the lust for gold, Pizarro in 1526 formed a pact with other adventurers for the conquest of the kingdom. He visited the port of Tumbez in 1527, but returned to Spain for assistance in men and money. When he arrived a second time in 1531 he found the empire racked by a civil war. Huayna Capac had violated the customary law of succession by dividing his empire upon his death. To his legitimate son, Huascar, he willed Cuzco and the bulk of the empire, but he left the kingdom of Quitu to Atahualpa, his son by a daughter of the royal line of that province. Dissension involved the heirs in a war, in which Atahualpa defeated and captured his rival and made himself ruler over the entire realm. Pizarro, advancing with a force of 183 hardy adventurers, was welcomed by the partisans of the vanquished monarch. Atahualpa, to safeguard his position, had Huascar executed, and then moved with his army to meet the invader. Pizarro, with a gesture of almost incredible bravado, rode into the imperial camp to pay his respects to the emperor, and when the latter returned the compliment, he seized him by an act of calculated treachery. Helpless without their leader and fearful of injuring him, the Indians were paralyzed. Pizarro agreed to release the emperor if he would fill a chamber twenty-two feet in length and seventeen feet wide solidly with gold to a depth of nine feet. When this seemingly impossible ransom was actually produced in a few hours, Pizarro made good his word by murdering his prisoner. After a feeble resistance, the empire fell like a ripe fruit into the lap of the Spaniards. Its very strength was its weakness. The Spaniards simply put themselves in the place of the monarch at the head of the centralized administration, and the system continued to function automatically under them.

The conquerors soon fell out amongst themselves over the spoils, and ere long all their outstanding leaders had been either executed or assassinated. Internal chaos disrupted the imperial system. Wars, epidemics, excessive levies of forced labor in the mines, and the devastation of entire regions through failure to maintain the canals and aqueducts caused wholesale depopulation. The last shadowy Sapa Inca was beheaded in 1571. The traditional learning, art, and science disappeared with the elimination of the noble classes. A new taste for idleness and luxury spread through the population. The Inquisition, introduced from Spain, took its toll of heretics burned at the stake. Efforts of enlightened administrators to revive the old system failed because discipline and morale had vanished. The clan with its agrarian collectivism still survives, though it is steadily retreating before the encroachments of wealthy landed proprietors and the church with their enormous estates, and peonage is taking its place. Neither dictatorships nor abortive attempts to apply European notions of democracy have succeeded in raising the Indians from the poverty, alcoholism, idleness, and inertia into which they have been plunged and which make their condition today, despite certain compensations, definitely less enviable than under their ancient rulers.

BIBLIOGRAPHY

ACOSTA, J. DE. *The Natural and Moral History of the Indies.* Trans. by C. R. Markham. 2 vols. London, 1880.

BAESSLER, A. *Altperuanische Metallgeräte.* Berlin, 1906.

——. *Peruanische Mumien.* Berlin, 1906.

*BAUDIN, L. "L'empire socialiste des Inka." *Travaux et Memoires de l'Institut d'Ethnologie*, Vol. V. Paris, 1928.

BEUCHAT, H. *Manuel d'archéologie américaine.* Paris, 1912.

BINGHAM, H. *Inca Land.* Boston, 1922.

——. "The Inca Peoples and Their Culture." *Proceedings of the Second Pan-American Scientific Congress*, Vol. I. Washington, 1917.

BOLLAERT, W. *Antiquarian, Ethnological and Other Researches in New Granada, Ecuador, Peru and Chile.* London, 1860.

BUSCHAN, G. "Die Inka und ihre Kultur im alten Peru." *La Cultura Latino-Americana,* Vol. I. Cöthen, 1918.

CARRIÓN CACHOT, R. "La mujer y el niño en el antiguo Perú." *Inca,* Vol. I. Lima, 1923.

CIEZA DE LEON, P. DE. *The Seventeen Years Travels of Peter de Cieza through the Mighty Kingdom of Peru.* Trans. by J. Stevens. London, 1709.

CRAWFORD, M. D. C. "Peruvian Fabrics." *Anthropological Papers of the American Museum of Natural History,* Vol. XII. New York, 1916.

——. "Peruvian Textiles." *Anthropological Papers of the American Museum of Natural History,* Vol. XII. New York, 1915.

CUNOW, H. *Die soziale Verfassung des Inkareichs.* Stuttgart, 1896.

EATON, G. F. "Food Animals of the Peruvian Highlands." *Congrès International des Américanistes,* XXIe Session, Part 2. Göteborg, 1925.

ENOCK, C. R. *Peru.* London, 1920.

——. *The Secret of the Pacific.* London, 1912.

FERRIS, H. B. "The Indians of Cuzco and the Apurimac." *Memoirs of the American Anthropological Association,* Vol. III. Lancaster, 1916.

GARCILASSO DE LA VEGA. *First Part of the Royal Commentaries of the Yncas.* Trans. by C. R. Markham. 2 vols. London, 1869–71.

HARDY, O. "The Indians of the Department of Cuzco." *American Anthropologist,* New Series, Vol. XXI. Lancaster, 1919.

*JOYCE, T. A. *South American Archæology.* London, 1912.

KARSTEN, R. *The Civilization of the South American Indians.* New York, 1926.

KROEBER, A. L. "Coast and Highland in Prehistoric Peru." *American Anthropologist,* New Series, Vol. XXIX. Menasha, 1927.

LATCHAM, R. E. "The Totemism of the Ancient Andean Peoples." *Journal of the Royal Anthropological Institute of Great Britain and Ireland,* Vol. LVII. London, 1927.

LEHMANN, W., and DOERING, H. *The Art of Old Peru.* London, 1924.

LOCKE, L. L. *The Ancient Quipu or Peruvian Knot Record.* New York, 1923.

MARKHAM, C. R. "Andeans." *Encyclopædia of Religion and Ethics*, Vol. I. Edited by J. Hastings. New York, 1908.

——. *Contributions towards a Grammar and Dictionary of Quichua.* London, 1892.

——. *A History of Peru.* Chicago, 1892.

——. "The Inca Civilization in Peru." *Narrative and Critical History of America*, Vol. I. Edited by J. Winsor. Boston, 1889.

——. *The Incas of Peru.* London, 1910.

——. "On the Geographical Positions of the Tribes Which Formed the Empire of the Yncas." *Journal of the Royal Geographical Society*, Vol. XLI. London, 1871.

MEAD, C. W. "Conventionalized Figures in Ancient Peruvian Art." *Anthropological Papers of the American Museum of Natural History*, Vol. XII. New York, 1916.

——. "The Musical Instruments of the Inca." *Anthropological Papers of the American Museum of Natural History*, Vol. XV. New York, 1924.

——. *Old Civilizations of Inca Land.* New York, 1924.

——. "Prehistoric Bronze in South America." *Anthropological Papers of the American Museum of Natural History*, Vol. XII. New York, 1915.

——. "Prehistoric Mining in Western South America." *Natural History*, Vol. XXI. New York, 1921.

——. "Technique of Some South American Feather-Work." *Anthropological Papers of the American Museum of Natural History*, Vol. I. New York, 1907.

*MEANS, P. A. *Ancient Civilizations of the Andes.* New York, 1931.

——. "Indian Legislation in Peru." *Hispanic American Historical Review*, Vol. III. Baltimore, 1920.

MONTELL, G. *Dress and Ornaments in Ancient Peru.* Göteborg, 1929.

MUÑIZ, M. A., and McGEE, W J. "Primitive Trephining in Peru." *Sixteenth Annual Report of the Bureau of American Ethnology.* Washington, 1897.

MURDOCK, G. P. "The Organization of Inca Society." *Scientific Monthly*, Vol. XXXVIII. New York, 1934.

NORDENSKIÖLD, E. *Calculations with Years and Months in the Peruvian Quipus.* Göteborg, 1925.

——. *The Copper and Bronze Ages in South America.* Göteborg, 1921.

——. "The Guarani Invasion of the Inca Empire in the Sixteenth Century." *Geographical Review,* Vol. IV. New York, 1917.

ONDEGARDO, P. DE. "Report." *Narratives of the Rites and Laws of the Yncas.* Trans. by C. R. Markham. London, 1873.

ORCHARD, W. C. "Peruvian Gold and Gold Plating." *Indian Notes,* Vol. VII. New York, 1930.

PRESCOTT, W. H. *History of the Conquest of Peru.* 2 vols. New York, 1847.

RIVET, P. "Les éléments constitutifs des civilisations du nord-ouest et de l'ouest sud-américain." *Congrès International des Américanistes,* XXIe Session, Part 2. Göteborg, 1925.

SARMIENTO DE GAMBOA, P. *History of the Incas.* Trans. by C. R. Markham. London, 1907.

SAVILLE, M. H. "Balance-Beam Scales in Ancient Peru." *Indian Notes,* Vol. II. New York, 1925.

SCHMIDT, M. *Kunst und Kultur von Peru.* Berlin, 1929.

SPENCER, H. *Descriptive Sociology.* New York, n.d.

SQUIER, E. G. *Peru.* New York, 1877.

STEFFEN, M. *Die Landwirtschaft bei den altamerikanischen Kulturvölkern.* Leipzig, 1883.

TELLO, J. C. *Antiguo Peru.* Lima, 1929.

TRIMBORN, H. "Familien- und Erbrecht in präkolumbischen Peru." *Zeitschrift für Vergleichende Rechtswissenschaft,* Vol. XLII. Stuttgart, 1927.

——. "Die Gliederung der Staende im Inka-Reich." *Journal de la Société des Américanistes de Paris,* Vol. XIX. Paris, 1927.

——. "Der Kollectivismus der Inkas in Peru." *Anthropos,* Vols. XVIII–XX. Wien, 1923–25.

——. "Kulturhistorische Analyse der altperuanischen Soziologie." *Atti del XXII Congresso Internazionale degli Americanisti,* Vol. II. Roma, 1928.

——. "Die kulturhistorische Stellung der Lamazucht in der Wirtschaft der peruanischen Erntevölker." *Anthropos,* Vol. XXIII. Wien, 1928.

TRIMBORN, H. "Straftat und Sühne in Alt-Peru." *Zeitschrift für Ethnologie,* Vol. LVII. Berlin, 1925.

TSCHUDI, J. J. VON. "Das Lama in seinen Beziehungen zum alt-peruanischen Volksleben." *Zeitschrift für Ethnologie,* Vol. XVII. Berlin, 1885.

WISSLER, C. *The American Indian.* Second edition. New York, 1922.

WITTMACK, L. "Die Nutzpflanzen der alten Peruaner." *Congrès International des Américanistes,* VIIe Session. Berlin, 1890.

CHAPTER XV

THE WITOTOS OF NORTHWESTERN AMAZONIA

IF primitive man survives anywhere today under conditions unaffected by modern civilization, it is in the remoter parts of the Amazonian jungle. Typical of the culture of this comparatively unknown area is the Witoto tribe, which lives just beyond the borders of Brazil in the debatable country between the Yapura and Putumayo Rivers (73° to 75° west longitude, 0° to 2° south latitude)—a region claimed by Colombia and Peru but administered by neither. The flooded Amazonian lowlands here begin to rise imperceptibly toward the Andes, and rapids occasionally appear in the otherwise sluggish streams, but the altitude is still only a few hundred feet above sea level. Dew falls like rain at night, and torrential downpours occur daily in the early morning and mid-afternoon. Despite the dampness, the heat is not excessive. Fresh breezes, frequent thunderstorms, and heavy evaporation moderate the temperature, which rarely reaches 90° F. and occasionally falls as low as 70°.

The heavy alluvial soil—a layer of decayed vegetable matter so deep that stones are practically unknown—nourishes a luxuriant tropical vegetation. Twenty thousand species of plants, trees, and parasitic vines struggle for the light, and only here and there is the turquoise sky visible through the massed foliage. A traveler who leaves the rivers must literally cut his way through the interlaced tangle of roots, underbrush, and creepers and run the constant risk of transfixing his hand or foot on a concealed thorn or being crushed by a falling tree. The streams teem with fish, frogs, and alligators, and aquatic birds throng on the banks. Poisonous snakes abound, but fortunately do not attack man

451

unless inadvertently stepped upon. Among the mammals only the jaguar is dangerous. Far worse are the insects—mosquitoes, biting flies, vicious wasps and bees, burrowing ticks, and the stinging ants which crawl over one's feet or shower down on one's face and neck when a bush is shaken. Added to the physical hazards of the jungle there are, for the outsider at least, the mental ones—the oppressive sense of restriction, the monotonous sameness of sight and sound, and the haunting dread of losing one's way and succumbing alone to slow starvation.

The Witotos, of whom some fifteen or twenty thousand inhabit this inhospitable environment, conform in general to the American Indian physical type. They attain only a moderate stature—five feet four inches for men and four feet eight inches for women. Their skins are copper-brown in color; their heads medium or mesocephalic (cephalic index 77); their hair coarse, straight, black, and abundant except on the body; their eyes not infrequently Mongoloid; their noses broad or platyrrhine (nasal index 91); their lips medium in breadth; their hips slender; and their feet large and flat with prehensile toes adapted for picking objects from the ground. In figure the women at least are described as lithe, graceful, and well proportioned.

The tribal name is derived from the hostile Umaua tribe, in whose dialect it means "enemy." The Witoto language, despite borrowings in vocabulary, belongs to a distinct linguistic stock. Its grammar prescribes that personal pronouns be prefixed to nouns to form the possessive and suffixed to verbs of which they are the subject, e.g., "we-house" for "our house," and "hear-I" for "I hear." It is spoken slowly with a melodious intonation. The Witotos possess no form of writing, not even mnemonic marks or picture-writing, nor do they have a sign or gesture language. But they do employ a sort of primitive wireless telegraphy, sending messages from tribe to tribe in code on great signal drums. They count as high as twenty on the fingers and toes, reckon time by the height of the sun and the phases of the moon, and employ natural measures like a hand full and a foot long.

Since food, while not exactly scarce, is difficult to obtain in the jungle, the Witotos are omnivorous. They collect wild fruits and nuts and the tender shoots of the cabbage palm by climbing trees with the aid of a circling rope or liana. They catch rats, mice, frogs, lizards, and snakes, and eat their flesh with much relish. When they find turtles asleep on sand banks in the rivers they secure them by flipping them on their backs. They also eat the eggs of these reptiles but never those of birds. They gather honey from hollow trees after smoking out the wild bees. They are voracious eaters of clay, probably because of some deficiency in their diet. They do not despise even insects, for they consume with avidity the grubs of wasps and bees and larvæ extracted from the bark of trees. Head lice are considered a particular delicacy. It is an honor and a treat to allow one's friend to comb one's hair and eat the "bag."

Since they possess no domesticated animals save a few dogs and an occasional pet, the Witotos depend largely upon hunting for their supply of meat food. They secure large game, such as deer and tapirs, with light spears of cane equipped with barbs and poisoned points. Having no bows and arrows, they rely upon the blowgun for birds and the smaller mammals—pacas, capybaras, peccaries, sloths, ant bears, and monkeys. This weapon, which varies from eight to fourteen feet in length, is made in two sections. Two pieces of chonta palm are carefully trimmed and grooved with a paca tooth, fitted together with nicety, wrapped from end to end with strips of tough bark, coated with resinous gum, and provided with a mouthpiece of vegetable ivory. The bore is polished with a cord dipped in gum and sand. In a bamboo quiver slung from the neck is carried a supply of darts, each about nine inches long, made from the rib of a palm leaf, tufted at the base with a wad of silk-cotton, and provided with a poisoned tip filed so that it breaks off in the wound. The poison used is the celebrated curare, made by a secret process from the sap of the *Strychnos toxifera* boiled until thick with pounded ants, peppers, and other poisonous ingredients, and its effect is almost instantaneous. With a puff of breath a hunter can project a dart with accuracy at distances up to fifty yards. The larger animals are sometimes caught in great nets a thousand feet or more in length stretched among the trees. Traps of various sorts are also used: simple snares for parrots and other birds, running nooses adjusted along branches frequented by monkeys, deadfalls set in forest runs, and concealed pits with sharpened stakes fixed upright at the bottom.

The natives supplement game with fish, which they catch in fine-meshed dip nets of palm fiber, in narrow basketry traps, with special spears pointed with two-edged bamboo blades, and with fiber lines and hooks of wood or thorn baited with grubs. They secure the best results, however, with a poison prepared from the crushed roots of a jungle bush. When a basket of this material is dipped into a stream, the poison diffuses through the water and shortly kills the fish, which float to the surface and are easily collected. This method does not render the flesh unfit for food.

A primitive form of agriculture gives a measure of stability to the food quest. Each family owns a small plantation hidden in the jungle often several miles from the dwelling. The men clear the forest, felling the larger trees with fire and the smaller ones with stone axes. From this point the women take charge of all agricultural operations. They burn the dry branches and underbrush, prepare the ground with wedge-shaped wooden staves, plant the seeds and cuttings, keep back the encroaching jungle plants by incessant weeding, and harvest the crops. The cultivated plants include maize, yams, sweet potatoes, peanuts, peppers, plantains, pineapples, coca, and tobacco.

The staple product, however, is manioc, a large fleshy tuber containing a deadly poison, hydrocyanic acid. The roots are cleaned, scraped with a wooden knife, cut into sections, and soaked for twenty-four hours in a bowl with a piece of decayed manioc to promote fermentation. They are then grated into a large wooden trough on an oval bamboo plank studded with short palm spines. A long pliable web of palm fiber is wound spirally around the mass of grated pulp, much as a roll puttee is adjusted to the leg, and the web is twisted with a stick tied to one end until the pressure wrings out the poisonous juice. The damp flour is then dried in an open pan, rubbed finer between the hands, and sifted through a basket sieve. From this flour, kneaded with water and placed in a clay platter over the fire, the women prepare the leathery, half-baked, unleavened, native cassava bread.

The characteristic Indian dish is the "pepper pot," a miscellaneous stew highly seasoned with peppers which is kept constantly simmering over the fire. It never gives out, for new ingredients are added daily—a monkey and a few parrots today, the blood, brains, liver, and intestines of some larger animal tomorrow, and so on. Authorities differ as to whether the Witotos understand the generation of fire. It is a fact, nevertheless, that a man rarely ventures into the bush without a smoldering piece of resinous bark which he can blow into a flame when necessary, and that in the house a fire is kept constantly alight at the juncture of three logs which point outward at angles of 120°. Here rests the ubiquitous pot with its fiery contents. At dawn, after a bath in the river, every one partakes of a sparing breakfast, consisting of a piece of cold cassava bread and a dip in the pepper pot. Then the men disperse to hunt and fish, the women to work in the fields, and all return just before sundown for an evening bath and the principal meal of the day. The Indians store nothing for the future; they gorge wastefully in times of plenty and endure hunger philosophically when food is scarce.

Although they make no intoxicating beverages, the Witotos drink vast quantities of unfermented drinks prepared from manioc and various fruit juices. The narcotics, tobacco and coca, take the place of intoxicants. Both, however, are taboo to women. Tobacco is never smoked. The leaves are dried, soaked, pounded in a mortar, and made into a stiff black liquid by adding cassava starch. On every ceremonial occasion, as well as at other times, the men insert a stick through the hole of a shell containing the liquid and lick off the drops that adhere to it. The coca shrub requires careful cultivation. Its leaves, which contain cocaine as their active principle, are picked, toasted, pulverized in a mortar, and mixed with baked clay, cassava flour, and lime from burnt palm leaves. A man, carrying a plug of this mixture in his cheek, can go without food, drink, and sleep for several days and perform marvelous feats of endurance.

For the sake of security the Witotos build their houses well away from the rivers and conceal the approaching paths in every possible way. In the center of a large clearing in the jungle, framed against a background of magnificent palms, stands a single communal dwelling, perhaps seventy feet in length, sixty in width, and thirty in height on the average. Four tall poles, surmounted by a superstructure of beams, plates, purlins, and rafters of hard wood lashed together with cords or lianas, support a thatched roof which slopes from the central ridgepole nearly to the ground. The side walls are only three feet high. The end walls are extended by porticoes and the corners are rounded, so that the ground plan of the building is nearly oval. Roof and walls consist of overlapping layers of palm leaves set in split bamboos to a thickness of over a foot, and are absolutely waterproof. A doorway protected by a mat of leaves gives access at either end. The lack of any windows or chimney renders the interior dark, smoky, and hot but affords protection against insects. Although spiders, scorpions, and even bats find refuge in the thatch, the rain and ants prevent any accumulation of filth or unpleasant odors. The center of the interior is left free as a common meeting and dancing place. The rear is reserved for the chief. The other families of the clan find quarters along the walls, although many of them also possess temporary shelters on their own plantations.

Each family has its separate fire, adjacent to which is one hammock for the father, a second for the mother, and often a third, making a triangle with the others, for such of the children as do not sleep on the bare earth. The hammocks, which are manufactured very simply by tying cross-strings back and forth between two heavier cords, are slung from

After Tessmann

FIG. 96. COMMUNAL DWELLING OF THE WITOTOS.

the wall and house poles or special posts. An occasional unworked block of wood, serving as a stool, completes the inventory of furniture. The few possessions of the family—provisions, implements, and utensils—are stored in the rafters overhead or on the floor. The Witotos work neither metals, stone, nor leather. Their stone axes, hafted to wooden handles with fiber lashings set in pitch, are all heirlooms and do not therefore constitute an exception. Animal teeth serve as awls and scrapers, but most of the native implements are of wood: cassava graters, ironwood knives, mortars hollowed from tree trunks, double-ended pestles of heavy wood, combs with teeth of palm spines fixed in resin to two sticks, wooden platters and troughs, and simple utensils of bark, leaves, and the shells of wild fruits and nuts. The women make crude undecorated cooking pots, building them up by the coil method and baking them in hot ashes. Both sexes fashion impromptu baskets from twigs and palm leaves for any need of the moment, and superior articles, *e.g.*, large carrying baskets, sieves, and fish traps, are made of plaited bark fiber and cane. The natives also twist vegetable fibers against the thigh to make cords, from which, using their fingers alone, they fashion hammocks, game and fish nets, knotted pouches, cassava squeezers, tumplines, and ornamental ligatures. To

After Tessman

FIG. 97. WITOTO LEG LIGATURE, FISH TRAP, AND CARRYING BASKET.

a very limited extent they use bark cloth, prepared from the inner bark of a tree by soaking in water and beating with a wooden mallet.

For clothing the men wear only a simple breechclout of bark cloth, but they will never remove this garment in the presence of any person, of either sex. Modesty assumes a different form with the women, who go about in the costume of Eve without the slightest embarrassment, and whose scorn of concealment even impels them to leave a triangular opening in the front of the broad girdles which they sometimes don on festive occasions. The paucity of clothing—even the feet are unshod—finds compensation in a wealth of ornament. Both sexes decorate the limbs with tight bands or ligatures, delicately woven from fine fiber threads with tasteful geometric designs. The men wear one such band on each upper arm, the women one just below each knee and another above the ankle so that the calf bulges ab-

normally between them.   A dance brings out other ornaments: feather headdresses, fillets, garters with tassels and
tinkling nuts, and necklaces of shells, teeth, bone discs,
colored seeds, etc.   A man's necklace of teeth, in particular,
gives evidence of his rank and his skill in war and the chase.
Jaguar teeth, for example, distinguish the chief, and a string
of human teeth reveals the successful warrior.   Bracelets
made from the skin of an iguana's tail are thought to possess
magical properties.   For ceremonial occasions the women
paint the thighs and body with attractive curvilinear or
geometric designs in red, black, and white.   Both sexes remove all facial and body hair, even the eyebrows and lashes,
by applying a rubber latex which is pulled off after it has
dried.   The men let their hair grow long, and bind it into a
pigtail with a strip of red bark cloth; the women trim their
locks with a knife or singe them.   Both sexes pierce the ear
lobes and insert wooden plugs often decorated with tufts
of feathers.   They likewise pierce the septum and sometimes
also the alæ of the nose for the reception of pins, plugs, or
feathers.

The women carry water in vessels balanced on their heads
and bring home the products of the fields on their backs in
large baskets supported by a tumpline across the forehead.
The rivers, however, provide the main avenues of travel
and transportation.   To cross a stream the native provides
himself with a temporary canoe by carving out the soft
pulp of the bulging stem of a certain variety of palm.   To
make a permanent canoe, the trunk of a tree is hollowed out
to a length of twenty feet—first with stone axes and then
with fire—and is stretched while hot to a width of eighteen
inches.   The elongated paddles are carved from solid pieces
of wood.   Canoes belong to the community as a whole, rather
than to individuals.   Private property, indeed, scarcely
extends beyond personal ornaments and implements.

Certain tribes in this region specialize to a limited extent
in different products.   Thus the Witotos make the best

FIG. 98. WITOTO WOMEN PAINTED FOR A DANCE.
From Tessmann, *Die Indianer Nordost-Perus.* Courtesy of Friederichsen, De Gruyter & Co.

baskets, the Boro the best blowpipes, the Carajone the most efficient poisons, and the Menimehe the finest pottery. These products pass from tribe to tribe through informal private barter and interchange of gifts, but there is no organized trade—no markets, middlemen, or recognized medium of exchange.

The Witoto tribe is a linguistic rather than a political unit. It is divided into some hundred and fifty independent and often hostile clans, which number from fifty to several hundred members each. The clans are patrilineal and exogamous but non-totemic, despite the fact that the overwhelming majority are named after animals, birds, trees, plants, or the like. Each clan has its own communal dwelling, its chief, and its recognized hunting and fishing territories which it jealously guards against encroachment. The chief acknowledges no higher authority, for the clans seldom unite, even temporarily, into larger groups. His authority depends upon his personal influence and the power of his rival, the shaman. He assumes the leadership in war and the chase, acts as master of ceremonies at festivals, and presides over council meetings, but he has no power to command or to punish, nor can he dispose of the property or plantations of others. He has the largest apartment in the communal dwelling and owns the clearing on which it stands, but he is shown no outward signs of respect. When he dies, he is usually succeeded by his eldest son, or by a brother in default of sons, but the clan council has the power to set aside the heir in favor of a more capable man.

The council consists of all the adult males of the clan. A definite ritual governs its meetings. The man who brings a matter up for discussion makes a long speech and, on closing, dips a stick into the tobacco pot, licks it, and passes it around the circle of squatting elders. All who agree with him likewise lick the stick. Those who disagree speak in their turn. A majority vote eventually decides the issue. The council also meets as a court of law, and rarely indeed does it deviate from established custom. A marked dualism of ethics prevails. To rob a fellow clansman is a serious offense and is severely punished; the injured party can hack off the head of the culprit or at least give him a sound beating. But to rob, or even to slay, the member of another clan or tribe is no crime at all. It may even be a praiseworthy act. Aggression of this sort leads, of course, to retaliation. The entire clan becomes responsible and may be plunged into a feud. Murder in particular demands the death of the murderer or a relative in order to appease the ghost of the deceased.

The Indians live in chronic fear of their neighbors, whether of the same or an alien tribe. The surest road to safety lies in the extermination of the enemy; hence every death, every accident, every encroachment, is sufficient to precipitate a war. According to a plan elaborated at a tobacco palaver, the warriors stealthily approach the house of the enemy clan, preferably on a night when their foes lie asleep exhausted after a revel. Success depends upon avoiding the pitfalls with poisoned stakes which stud the paths, and upon preserving absolute silence. With a sudden furious rush the attackers fall upon the defenseless enemy with heavy poisoned spears and murderous double-edged swords of hard wood. All who do not flee are slain or borne home as prisoners, but the dead are not mutilated.

Captive children under seven years of age are spared. They become the property of the chief, and grow up practically as members of his family. A boy becomes free at puberty, but until his marriage he gives the chief half of all the game he secures. The girls are married off. These slaves—if the term can be appropriately applied to them—are kindly treated and seldom try to run away.

All other captives are kept a day or two without food or water until a victory feast can be arranged. Then they are decapitated with a wooden sword, dissected, and portions of their legs, arms, and heads distributed among the warriors. Each recipient fixes his piece of flesh to a stick and places it in a pot over the fire where it is seasoned with peppers and cooked by the old women. While the pot boils, the entire clan, adorned with paint and finery, dances to the sound of drums, singing a wild song of victory and carrying the gory heads aloft on staves. The cannibal repast follows. The parts not eaten—trunk, viscera, brains, etc.—are cast into the river or thrown to the dogs amid jeers and insults. The male genitals are reserved for the chief's wife, the only woman who shares in the feast. The captor of each victim makes the upper arm bones into flutes, uses the bones of the forearm to stir the ceremonial liquor, and makes the teeth into a necklace. The skull, cleaned by ants, is erected on a pole as a trophy or suspended from the rafters of the house.

The orgy often lasts for several days. The men, drunk with victory and excitement, lurch to the great troughs of liquor, stir the contents with an arm bone of the victim, quaff deep drafts, and stagger back to rejoin the wild dance. Sometimes one captive is reserved for a particularly gruesome rite, in which his heart, liver, kidneys, and marrow are eaten only partly cooked and mixed with tobacco juice. The motives underlying cannibalism are partly the desire to incorporate in oneself the qualities of the victim and partly the thrifty disinclination to waste good meat when animal food is so scarce, but the main reason is revenge, the wish to wreak upon an enemy the supreme insult.

A prospective mother abstains from certain foods, especially meat, which are considered harmful to the child, and during the last month of pregnancy eats nothing except fruits, cassava, and small bony fish. When labor is imminent, she retires into the bush, usually unaccompanied, makes a small clearing, and prepares a bed of leaves. Delivery is rarely difficult. The mother ties the umbilical cord with a fiber string, then bites or cuts it off, and buries it along with the afterbirth. Then she bathes the infant in the nearest stream, smears its body with rubber milk, and returns to the house. Deformed and illegitimate children and the second of a pair of twins are usually left in the bush to die or else submerged a little too long in the river. If the mother dies, and no other woman will adopt the baby, it is abandoned in the forest or buried alive in the grave of its parent. The mother presents the newborn child to the father and on the following day resumes her usual labors in the fields, returning only at night to suckle the infant. The father, however, rests for a week or more in his hammock, observing certain dietary regulations and receiving congratulatory visits from his friends. His couvade—as this simulation by the father of the mother's rôle in childbed is called—endures until the infant's navel has healed, during which time he must not eat meat, hunt, or even touch his weapons.

Eight days after birth the child receives its name, commonly that of the paternal grandfather or a deceased elder brother in the case of a boy. Men usually bear the names of animals, birds, or masculine activities or implements; women, those of plants, flowers, or feminine interests or artifacts. The Witotos use kinship terms in conversation instead of personal names, for fear of the magical power associated with the use of the latter. The mother resumes care of the child when its navel is healed, and carries it wherever she goes, either seated astride her hip or suspended in a sling of bark cloth on her back. She nurses it for between two and three years, and it is not an uncommon sight to see a child stop playing, toddle up to its mother, suckle a while, and then run back to its playmates. When her baby gets its teeth, a woman sometimes milks herself into a cup fashioned from a leaf and lets it drink from this. Throughout lactation the parents abstain from sexual relations. Thus children are spaced nearly three years apart as a minimum. Because of this custom, coupled with the high rate of infant mortality, families of more than three or four children are rare.

Fathers do not play with their sons although they make toy spears, swords, and blowguns for them. Girls imitate the activities of their mothers. Children learn by observation, and nothing is concealed from them. Their games, indeed, exhibit elements that we should class as obscene. Parents show considerable affection for their offspring, punishing them rarely and never severely. Neither parental authority nor filial piety is strongly developed. At about five years of age boys assume the breechclout, which they make for themselves. Neither sex is permitted to eat meat until the age of puberty, which comes rather later among the Witotos than with ourselves. A youth at this age learns the ways of hunting, enters the clan council, receives a pouch of coca from the chief, and licks tobacco with the warriors, whose ranks he now joins. Girls at puberty retire to secret lodges in the bush, where they remain until their marriage is arranged. Here the wise old women of the clan guard them and instruct them in the ceremonial songs and dances and the duties of womanhood.

Chastity is expected in the unmarried, especially in girls, but it is not always strictly observed. A wayward girl, if discovered, is beaten. Marriage means independence. A single youth has no one to raise manioc and tobacco for him, to cook his food and prepare his drinks, or to remove thorns and burrowing ticks from his feet. And only through marriage can a girl escape the restraints of her seclusion lodge and food taboos and secure a desirable sleeping place beside the fire in the communal dwelling. Infant betrothals sometimes occur, but otherwise the young man takes the initiative and does not require the consent of his parents. He must, however, select a bride from a friendly clan, and he must observe carefully the exogamous restrictions, which prevent the choice of a girl from his own clan or one who is a close relative on his mother's side. He first clears a plot of ground in the jungle and builds a shelter there—as a test of his ability to support a family. Next he obtains the consent of the chief of the girl's clan, presenting evidences of his industry with gifts of coca and tobacco. He then discusses the matter with the father of his intended bride. He neither pays a bride-price nor receives a dowry, although he usually works for his prospective parents-in-law for a time or makes them small presents. The girl has the right—one that is seldom exercised—to decline the offer. If she acquiesces, the groom licks tobacco with her father and the union is thereby concluded without further ceremony. Consummation is deferred for two weeks, when the bride takes up her residence permanently with her husband's clan.

Monogamy is the rule. Even chiefs rarely have more than one wife, although the captive and unattached women of the tribe, who come under his protection and till his fields, may also serve him as concubines. The marriage tie is firm, but adultery is not unknown. The wife enjoys a reasonably high status. Women, to be sure, may not eat certain foods, use coca or tobacco, or participate in certain ceremonies, and they must submit to the authority of their husbands. Nevertheless, they hold property of their own, their advice is not infrequently sought, and their share in the division of labor is not disproportionate. While they perform most of the agricultural labor, tend the children, cook, and make pottery, baskets, and hammocks, their husbands hunt, fish, clear the land, climb trees for fruits, cut wood, build the houses, make canoes, weapons, and all wooden implements, and prepare the poisons and ceremonial drinks. A husband seldom ill-treats his spouse, for to do so earns him the scorn of the clan. Moreover, she possesses a singularly effective defensive weapon. She needs only to tear off his breechclout in the presence of his clansmen to expose him to the worst possible humiliation and disgrace. He runs into the forest in shame and can only return when he has made himself a new garment. She follows him and places one or two stinging ants on the most sensitive parts of his body, which causes intense pain, swelling, and fever. After this the couple become reconciled.

A woman's rights extend to divorce. A husband can send his wife away for infidelity, laziness, insubordination, or childlessness, but unless he can justify his action at a tobacco palaver he becomes the target of ridicule, finds it impossible to secure another wife, and in effect suffers social ostracism. A woman can secure a divorce much more easily. She simply runs away. It is not she but her husband who is blamed—on the theory that a woman who forfeits her male protector and throws herself defenseless upon a hostile environment must have been cruelly ill-used. Unless he can convince a skeptical council of his innocence, he loses all prestige and influence in the clan. When a man dies, his widow, after her period of mourning is over, has the choice of remaining in the house under the protection of his brother or the chief, returning to her own clan, marrying again, or becoming an informal village prostitute.

The reigning law of the jungle is the survival of the fittest, and there are no sentimentalists to oppose its corollary, the elimination of the unfit. Hence all who cannot pay their own way in society—the aged, the infirm, and the incurably sick—unless they have something of great value to offer in their wisdom or experience, are removed from society. They are not, to be sure, killed outright; they are simply abandoned in the bush to die.

The Witotos attribute sickness to possession by an evil spirit sent by a hostile sorcerer. The cure, which logically consists in the exorcism of the spirit, is the primary function of the medicine man or shaman. Each clan has one of these practitioners, always a male, whose prestige and authority often exceed those of the chief. The office is partly hereditary, descending usually to the eldest son but sometimes to a junior son or another member of the clan. An essential prerequisite for the position is hairiness. The neophyte begins as a boy, observing special food taboos, accompanying the old shaman everywhere, learning his trade secrets, and finally undergoing an initiation with ordeals. The medicine man engages in the ordinary activities of the clan, but distinguishes himself from others by his peculiar food habits, his refusal to depilate, his solitary wanderings in the jungle, and his bizarre attire. His paraphernalia include a rattle, some small magic stones, a jaguar skin, the claws of a condor, and similar objects. He is a skilled conjurer, ventriloquist, and maker of poisons, and is credited with the power of conversing with spirits and assuming the form of a jaguar. Though he can divine the future, warn of impending attacks, and work black magic, his chief function is the cure of disease. When he succeeds, he receives presents for his services. When he fails, he has an impregnable defense: a rival sorcerer used stronger magic.

A shaman lances ulcers, sets fractured bones in splints, applies poultices, and prescribes emetics, narcotics, and herb infusions. That his percentage of cures is large, however, is due less to the efficacy of his remedies than to the implicit faith of his patients. In refractory cases he resorts to extreme methods. In the darkened house at night, stimulated by coca and tobacco, he works himself into a state of wild exaltation, shaking his rattle, beating the floor, and uttering intermittent shrieks and howls, until he summons the spirits with whom he is to converse. Their presence is made manifest to the onlookers by the cries of animals and birds which seem to stream in from all sides—by virtue of his ventriloquistic powers. Eventually, having diagnosed the ailment with supernatural assistance, he collapses with exhaustion. On recovering, a half-hour later, he commences his treatment. He breathes on his hands, massages and blows on the affected part, sucks it and spits out a black liquid, and finally produces some object, such as a thorn or a stick, as the material embodiment of the offending spirit.

Death, when not obviously due to a natural cause such as drowning or snakebite, is attributed solely to the machinations of a hostile sorcerer. Burial takes place on the day of death. A shallow grave is dug in the floor of the house beneath the fireplace and is lined with leaves. Here the body is deposited in a sitting position, wrapped in a hammock, with all of its ornaments, weapons, and utensils beside it. A fire is lighted on the grave and kept burning for several days. All who have participated in the funeral purify themselves with a bath. When the chief dies, the survivors burn the house, abandon the spot, and build another dwelling elsewhere. A widow always severs and burns the ligatures above her calves in token of mourning and sometimes also crops her hair short, but a widower manifests no signs of grief.

Men but not animals have souls—exact but insubstantial replicas of the body. The soul leaves the body through the mouth, permanently in death, temporarily in the trances of the shaman and in sleep, when it experiences the adventures recorded in dreams. A sneeze, it is thought, registers a thwarted attempt to escape. After death the soul lingers near the house until burial has taken place, and then journeys to a spirit world in the sky. Life there is an idealized reflection of that on earth; game is always plentiful and the women beautiful and amenable. The ghosts of the dead receive no cult. Occasionally they return to earth and wander abroad at night, converse with their descendants, or even injure their enemies. But the soul is not, strictly speaking, immortal; it lives only so long as it is remembered.

The Witotos endow all natural objects, animate and inanimate, with spirits. Some, like those of fruit-bearing trees, are good. Others are evil. A water spirit finds embodiment in the anaconda. Jaguar spirits are thought to eat little children. When a child is lost and the shaman, through divination, accuses a jaguar, a great hunt is organized. If a jaguar is slain, its flesh, taboo at other times, is eaten at a feast of revenge suggestive of a cannibalistic orgy. Hosts of demons reside in the earth and come forth at night on mischief bent. It is they who cause sickness and everything that is amiss in the world. A great creator god, Moma (father), made the world, raised the heavens, created plants and animals, and gave men their ceremonies and institutions. He lives under the earth, renews vegetation each year, and cares for the growing crops. In the blue vault of heaven dwells Husinyamui, great god of the sky, the sun, and fire, and the patron of war and cannibalism. Passively benevolent but remote, he figures but slightly in the thoughts and activities of the people.

The Indians wear amulets for protection against evil spirits and they heed omens and portents, but they have no cult in the strict sense, *i.e.*, they offer the supernatural beings neither prayer nor sacrifice. Nevertheless, they do observe certain religious ceremonies, and it is primarily in connection with these, moreover, that both their æsthetic and their recreational impulses find expression.

Dances, whether ceremonial or impromptu, provide the natives with their principal social entertainment. Several days are spent in preparing food and drinks. The signal drums sound invitations to friendly clans. The women paint; the men don their finest ornaments. All assemble after dark in the center of the house, where torches sputter and flare and cast weird shadows. The men, carrying staves with rattles and often wearing hooded masks of bark cloth, form a circle or crescent with interlocked arms. The women dance inside the circle, or outside with their left hands on the shoulders of the men. The dancers accentuate the rhythm by stamping in unison on the ground until the earth shakes with the swing of the movement. A typical dance step is: forward with the right foot, forward with the left, stamp with the right, backward with the right, backward with the left, toe the ground with the right, and repeat. Comic relief at a dance is frequently afforded by a man with a grievance, who dresses himself in a ridiculous costume to gain attention and airs his complaint aloud hour after hour. No one appears to notice him, but the chief takes cognizance and, if the matter is important, brings it up at the next tobacco palaver.

Songs, speeches, and rounds of feasting and drinking alternate with the dancing. One man leads with a solo, and the rest respond in chorus with high falsetto voices. The melodies are simple, rarely more than a single phrase endlessly repeated. The words are largely traditional and are often so archaic as to have no remembered meaning. Their import is partly religious but also strongly sexual. Although the dances themselves exhibit not the slightest suggestion of obscenity, the accompanying songs fairly reek with erotic innuendoes. Instrumental music serves the primary purpose, not of accompanying the dance, but simply of swelling the volume of sound. The Witotos possess flutes of bamboo and

After Whiffen

FIG. 99. WITOTO PANPIPES AND GOURD RATTLE.

of human arm bones, and panpipes consisting of three reeds of different lengths bound together with palm fibers. Their principal instruments, however, are the great signal drums, of which a pair usually hangs suspended from the rafters of the house. They are hollowed out of logs with the aid of fire, and have a longitudinal slit on top terminating in two larger holes near the ends. Owing to differences in the thickness of the sides, one drum, "the female," gives lower tones than the other, "the male," and the two sides of each drum give different notes. Hence the operator, who stands between them and beats with a rubber-tipped stick, commands a scale of four notes. In addition to their uses in communication, these drums serve to beat time or augment the uproar at dances.

Among the ceremonies which combine songs and dances with religious fervor and recreation is the *uike* or ball festival. The festivities last for days, the nights being devoted to dancing and the afternoons to a game in which a large rubber ball is bounced back and forth with the knees alone from one side to the other. Another important ceremony is the *jadiko* or log festival, held each year at harvest time. Several months in advance a large tree is felled, trimmed, carried to the clearing, and carved or painted with the image of a

FIG. 100. SIGNAL DRUMS OF THE WITOTOS.
From Tessmann, *Die Indianer Nordost-Perus.* Courtesy of Friederichsen, De Gruyter & Co.

woman at one end, an alligator at the other, and a snake in the middle. It is then set on a cross-log like a seesaw and kept in position by four upright stakes. On the afternoon of the ceremony six men masked as trees, jaguars, and birds attack the house with poles and axes and seek to uproot the crops in the fields. The clansmen buy them off with gifts of food. The dance begins in the evening and lasts until the next afternoon. The women form a circle around the log. The men dance on top of it, stamping in unison so that it alternately rises and then strikes the earth with a thunderous boom. Religious songs of thanksgiving accompany the dance. When the ceremony is over, the men hack the image of the woman to pieces and burn the remnants in their several fireplaces.

The white man has known vaguely of the Witotos for centuries, but he paid no attention to them until the advent of the automobile sent him into the jungle to gather wild rubber. Then he discovered not only that these Indians were the most intelligent and adaptable tribe in the area but also that they could be enslaved and exploited to his financial advantage. The barbaric methods by which he gained his ends remained hidden from the world until an American engineer, Hardenburg, in an article published in 1909, presented the indictment: "that the peaceful Indians were put to work at rubber-gathering without payment, without food, in nakedness; that their women were stolen, ravished, and murdered; that the Indians were flogged until their bones were laid bare when they failed to bring in a sufficient quota of rubber or attempted to escape, were left to die with their wounds festering with maggots, and their bodies were used as food for the agents' dogs; that flogging of men, women, and children was the least of the tortures employed; that the Indians were mutilated in the stocks, cut to pieces with machetes, crucified head downwards, their limbs lopped off, target-shooting for diversion was practiced upon them, and that they were soused in petroleum and burned alive, both men and women." The "Putumayo atrocities" soon acquired a notoriety paralleled only by those of the Belgian Congo. The British Government, since those mainly implicated were its subjects, felt impelled to send a consular agent, Sir Roger Casement, to investigate the situation. In his report he stated that "the condition of things fully warrants the worst charges" and that for the twelve years from 1900 to 1911 the Putumayo output of four thousand tons of rubber cost thirty thousand native lives. Thus was civilization brought to the wilderness.

BIBLIOGRAPHY

CLAES, F. "Chez les Indiens Huitotos et Correguajes." *Bulletin de la Société Royale Belge de Géographie,* Vols. LV–LVI. Bruxelles, 1931–32.

FARABEE, W. C. "Indian Tribes of Eastern Peru." *Papers of the Peabody Museum of American Archæology and Ethnology,* Vol. X. Cambridge, 1922.

HARDENBURG, W. C. "The Indians of the Putumayo, Upper Amazon." *Man,* Vol. X. London, 1910.

——. *The Putumayo.* London, 1912.

KOCH-GRUNBERG, T. "Die Indianerstämme am oberen Rio Negro und Yapurá und ihre sprachliche Zugehörigkeit." *Zeitschrift für Ethnologie,* Vol. XXXVIII. Berlin, 1906.

——. "Les Indiens Ouitotos." *Journal de la Société des Américanistes de Paris,* Nouvelle Série, Vol. III. Paris, 1906.

PREUSS, K. T. "Bericht über meine archäologischen und ethnologischen Forschungsreisen in Kolumbien." *Zeitschrift für Ethnologie,* Vols. LII–LIII. Berlin, 1920–21.

——. *Religion und Mythologie der Uitoto.* 2 vols. Göttingen, 1921–23.

SCHMIDT, H. "Die Uitóto-Indianer." Edited by T. Koch-Grünberg. *Journal de la Société des Américanistes de Paris,* Nouvelle Série, Vol. VII. Paris, 1910.

TESSMANN, G. *Die Indianer Nordost Perus.* Hamburg, 1930.

*WHIFFEN, T. *The North-West Amazons.* London, 1915.

——. "A Short Account of the Indians of the Issa-Japura District." *Folk-Lore,* Vol. XXIV. London, 1913.

WOODROFFE, J. F. *The Upper Reaches of the Amazon.* New York, 1914.

CHAPTER XVI

THE NAMA HOTTENTOTS OF SOUTHWEST AFRICA

WHEN the Dutch, in 1652, settled Table Bay, the present Cape Town, they found Africa south of the Tropic of Capricorn inhabited by three distinct groups of aborigines. In the Kalahari Desert and other inhospitable and isolated parts of the interior dwelt the Bushmen, a race of primitive hunters and collectors. To the east lived various agricultural and comparatively civilized tribes forming the southernmost extension of the great Bantu nation. In the south and west the Dutch encountered a race of nomadic herders, the Hottentots, of which the best-known branch, the Nama or Namaqua, still inhabits the southern two-fifths of the mandated Territory of Southwest Africa.

The skin of the Nama is a light brownish-yellow in color, scarcely darker than in European races, but it shows an excessive tendency to wrinkle. Hair is very scanty on the body and face; on the head it is short, black, and exceedingly kinky, being gathered into small isolated spirals or "peppercorns." In stature the men average five feet three inches, the women four inches less. The head is long and narrow (cephalic index 73); the forehead low; the face flat and triangular; the ears small with weak lobes; the eyes brown in color and reduced to narrow oblique slits by the remarkable fullness of the upper lids; the cheek bones high and prominent; the nose short, flat, and extremely broad (nasal index 100); the nostrils large, round, and directed forward; the lips protruding but not thick; the chin pointed and receding. The hands and feet are surprisingly dainty in appearance, being smaller and narrower than in Europeans. The women often display two very unusual characteristics: the so-called "Hottentot apron," consisting of an abnormal elongation of the labia

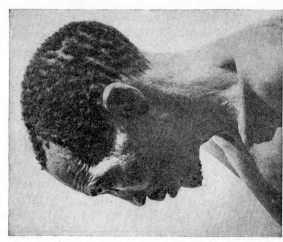

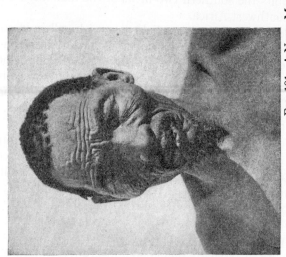

FIG. 101. A NAMA MAN OF FORTY-FIVE YEARS.
From Schultze, *Zur Kenntnis des Körpers der Hottentotten und Buschmänner.*
Courtesy of Verlag von Gustav Fischer, Jena

minora, and "steatopygia" or an exaggerated development of the buttocks. The latter, which is considered a mark of beauty, sometimes attains almost incredible proportions, so that the girth at the hips actually approximates the total stature.

The Hottentot language, like the Bushman, is characterized by its peculiar consonantal "clicks," of which there are four: dental (/), alveolar (≠), cerebral (!), and lateral (//). The meaning of a syllable varies with its tone, whether high, medium, low, rising, or falling. The grammatical features of the language include sex gender, dual as well as plural number, extensive use of auxiliary particles, and modification of the usually monosyllabic roots by free use of suffixes. The vocabulary is rich in concrete but poor in abstract terms. The Hottentots call themselves *Khoi-khoin* or "men of men." "Nama" is the name of a traditional ancestor. "Hottentot" comes from a contemptuous Boer word for "stammerer" applied to the natives in reference to their clicks. The Nama employ a decimal system of numeration and reckon time by moons and seasons.

The Hottentots, although slightly taller, lighter, and more dolichocephalic than the Bushmen, resemble them closely in racial characteristics. They differ from them chiefly in culture, especially in the possession of domesticated animals. The native cattle belong to the large, long-horned type found in the Eastern Horn of Africa, and thus point to an origin in that direction. The Hottentot language reveals a basic similarity to Bushman in grammar and vocabulary, differing principally in having sex gender and a dual number. In these respects it shows an affinity with the Hamitic tongues of northeastern Africa. The Sandawe language of Tanganyika has clicks, similar roots, and grammatical resemblances to Hottentot. Archeology likewise points to the northeast as the place of origin of the Hottentots. With these clues we can reconstruct the probable history of the people. At a remote time, when Rhodesian man and other prehistoric races had disappeared, the Bushmen apparently occupied most of

FIG. 102. A YOUNG NAMA WOMAN, SHOWING STEATOPYGIA.
From Schultze, *Zur Kenntnis des Körpers der Hottentotten und Buschmänner*. Courtesy of Verlag von Gustav Fischer, Jena

Africa south of the equator. Somewhere in the lake region of central Africa, or even farther to the northeast, a branch of the Bushmen came into close contact with an early Hamitic immigrant stock presumably tinged slightly with Negro blood, mixed to some extent with the newcomers, and borrowed their cattle and elements of their language. Certain of these pastoral Bushmen, the ancestors of the Hottentots, migrated to the southwest, following the best grazing lands and driving the true Bushmen back into the poorer sections. At a considerably later time the warlike and agricultural Bantus, a Negro race with some Hamitic admixture, began to advance southward with irresistible force and numbers, driving out or exterminating the Bushmen and Hottentots. When the Dutch arrived, and halted this advance, they found the earlier races confined to the southwestern extremity of the continent.

The habitat of the Nama comprises an area of over 100,000 square miles, bounded roughly by the Tropic of Capricorn on the north, the Kalahari Desert on the east, the 30th degree of south latitude on the south, and the Atlantic Ocean on the west. A range of sandstone mountains, 4,500 feet in average elevation, closely parallels the sea and separates a narrow coastal strip of desolate shifting sand dunes from the great interior plateau which stretches eastward to the Kalahari. The undulating plains of the plateau are intersected by two main watercourses, the Konkip and the Great Fish Rivers, which traverse the country from north to south. The climate is dry and invigorating. The temperature averages about 63° F. for the year, but freezing weather often prevails in winter. The annual precipitation is less than ten inches—on the coast but a fraction of an inch. Rain falls only during the summer months, when it comes in sudden heavy thunderstorms which convert the dry watercourses temporarily into raging torrents. Only the Orange River in the south carries water throughout the year. During the dry season the lesser streams shrivel to chains of pools, where a granite bottom prevents seepage or a deep gorge retards evaporation.

Life in this environment depends primarily upon the amount and distribution of surface water, which, except immediately after a rain, is confined to the stream beds—in pools, occasional springs, and water-holes dug in the moist sand. Animals and men congregate near the watercourses in the dry season and disperse with the rains. Acacias and other trees and shrubs line the streams. The unwatered hills and plains, though often "roasted like a burnt loaf under the scorching rays of a cloudless sky," are transformed by a few showers into a sea of waving grass providing admirable pasturage for months. The uncertainty of rain, however, makes life precarious. The native fauna is amazingly abundant and varied: the elephant, rhinoceros, and hippopotamus; the lion, leopard, hyena, jackal, and lesser carnivores; the giraffe, buffalo, zebra, and quagga; innumerable species of antelope, including the eland, koodoo, gnu, gemsbok, hartebeest, springbok, duiker, and steinbok; monkeys, porcupines, rabbits, and mice; the ostrich, bustard, and numerous other birds; crocodiles, lizards, and snakes, including the puff adder, cobra, and other venomous species; scorpions and spiders; and extraordinary numbers of locusts, ants, termites, bees, wasps, and other insects.

The scarcity of water makes agriculture impossible, but the Hottentots utilize to the full the meager food plants of their environment—roots, bulbs, leaves, seeds, and a melon-like fruit. They ransack ant-hills for their stores of grass seeds. They catch and eat mice, lizards, snails, caterpillars, beetles, locusts, ants, termites, and body lice. On the Orange and Great Fish Rivers and along the coast they make considerable use of fish, which they secure with simple wooden spears, hooks of bone or animal teeth, nets of bark fiber, weirs, and basket traps.

The abundance of game is favorable to hunting. For rabbits and other small animals the natives use the knob-

Kerrie, a short knobbed throwing club, which they can hurl a hundred feet with surprising accuracy. They also employ a crude bow with a sinew string and feathered arrows with triangular iron points fastened to a bone foreshaft, which in turn is inserted into a main shaft of reed. The arrows are carried in quivers of bark or hide, and their tips are commonly smeared with a vegetable poison. But the principal weapon of the chase is the spear, a long wooden shaft equipped with a narrow iron point. The Hottentots secure hares, dassies, and the lesser antelopes in running nooses; jackals, hyenas, and small mammals in stone deadfalls; elephants, zebras, elands, and other large game in concealed pitfalls with sharp stakes fixed in the bottom. A hunter may wait in ambush at a water-hole, near the nest of an ostrich, or beside the hole of a burrowing animal. Or he may stalk his game to leeward under cover of shrubs, gullies, or his own grazing herds. Not infrequently he simply outruns an animal, following it in the blazing sun until the hot sand burns its footpads and causes it to lag behind within range of a poisoned arrow. A number of hunters may drive a wild herd into a valley from which a high fence blocks escape except through gaps provided with pitfalls. Elephants, rhinoceroses, and other big game are surrounded by large parties armed with spears. When the wounded animal charges an assailant, others hurl spears from behind; turning against its new enemy, it is again attacked from the rear; it is thus held at bay until it falls exhausted from its wounds.

The grass which supports the abundant game animals likewise nourishes herds of cattle and flocks of hairy fat-tailed sheep. The Hottentots also possess dogs, which they use in hunting and herding, and in comparatively recent times they have acquired goats from their Bantu neighbors. Calves and sheep graze by day under the protection of shepherds and are penned up at night in special inclosures of thorn bushes or stone. Cows, after the morning milking, are driven out to pasture unattended and return to their calves in the evening.   The oxen require little care and range farther afield, returning only for water every second or third day.   Young bulls not needed for breeding are gelded, and a feast is celebrated over the exuviæ.   Oxen are trained to carry burdens and to be ridden.   As pack animals they carry the dwellings and household utensils on the march.   They are ridden with a sheepskin in place of a saddle and are guided by thongs attached to the ends of a stick passed through the cartilage of the nose.   The Hottentots even train their oxen to charge the ranks of the enemy in battle.

The women and girls milk the cows and ewes every morning and evening after the calves and lambs have sucked. Contrary to Bantu custom, the men concern themselves very little with dairy operations.   In the summer, milk forms almost the sole means of subsistence.   It is drunk fresh, either warm or cool, or thickened and soured by the addition of chewed leaves or acacia sap.   Sheeps' milk, however, is taboo to adult men.   To make butter, milk is poured into a calabash, which is closed with a stopper and is rolled back and forth for three hours on a skin in the hot sun or near the fire.   The buttermilk is drunk as a beverage, and the butter is eaten fresh or used for frying vegetables or greasing skins.

The Nama seldom slaughter their cattle or sheep except on festive or ceremonial occasions, although they eat those that die a natural death.   They obtain their supply of meat principally through hunting.   Flesh not immediately required for food may be cut into thin strips, salted, and dried in the open air.   Otherwise it is always cooked, either by boiling in a clay pot, roasting on a spit over the fire, or baking in the ashes.   The Hottentots do not care especially for broths, but they are very fond of fat and sometimes even drink it warm in liquid form.   They observe a taboo on the flesh of carnivorous animals and adult males, in addition, never eat the hare.

Every one takes breakfast in the morning after the cows have been milked and driven to pasture, but circumstances govern the time for other meals. The women cook the food on a fire generated with a simple fire-drill, and the two sexes eat separately. Whenever a man brings home game, the whole camp gathers at his hut and eats until the meat is entirely consumed. Hospitality assumes such proportions in the daily life of the Hottentots that many writers have incorrectly called them communistic. They possess one alcoholic beverage, a sort of mead, made by diluting wild honey with water and adding certain roots to promote fermentation. They also prepare infusions from several narcotic seeds and legumes. Even before receiving tobacco from the whites they smoked, especially on ceremonial occasions, certain narcotic herbs, notably a kind of hemp or hashish which induces a state of dreamy insensibility but has injurious effects.

The Hottentots dwell in light, portable, dome-shaped huts. The men, to whom falls the task of erecting them, plant twenty or more flexible acacia poles vertically in the ground in a circle ten to fifteen feet in diameter. They then bend the tops inward and fasten them together with cords or thongs where they meet or cross. Over this framework, which averages about eight feet in height, they bind rush mats, first around the sides, then across the top. Low door-ways in the front and rear are curtained with special mats, which can be rolled up when desired. The mats are exceedingly well made; the women dry the rushes in the sun, bore them with a fine awl, and sew them together with bast thread. The huts are warm in the winter, when an inner lining of skins is added; cool in summer, when the heat contracts the rushes and permits the air to circulate freely; and dry during a storm, when the rushes swell and become impervious to rain. They are likewise admirably suited to a nomadic life, for they can be dismantled in a short time. The mats and poles are rolled or tied into bundles, packed on the backs of oxen, and transported to the next camp. The huts of a camp or kraal are arranged in a circle inside a high fence of thorn bushes and facing an open space in the center which serves as a fold for the stock at night.

The floor of the hut is smeared with a mixture of cow dung and blood. A fire burns on an excavated hearth in the center, and around it the members of the family sleep on skins or mats in little holes or depressions. Near the rear door, in a net supported on four poles, rest objects which must be kept out of reach of the dogs. The household utensils include

calabashes and ostrich eggshells, carved wooden spoons, mortars, pestles, dishes, bowls, and milk pails, cosmetic boxes made from tortoise shells and the horns of animals, skin and netted bags, baskets and sieves woven from flexible reeds and twigs, and round-bottomed earthenware

Fig. 103. Hut of the Nama Hottentots.

vessels for storing liquids and cooking. The pots are provided with ears for suspension by cords, but are unglazed and are decorated only with rows of incised dots and lines around the neck. Women are the potters. They obtain the clay from termite hills, model it into the desired shape on a flat stone, smooth the vessel inside and out with their hands, dry it in the sun, and fire it in a hole in the ground until it is thoroughly baked.

The Nama use few stone implements. They employ sharp pieces of quartz for making incisions on the body and flat stones for grinding herbs and minerals, and they also possess stone hammers and anvils. From time immemorial, however, they have made tools and weapons of iron and ornaments of copper. They smelt the ores in clay crucibles placed over a fire built on a hearth of cow dung. They provide the necessary draft by means of skin bellows with horn nozzles which they insert under the hearth and operate vigorously until the ore has melted. The molten metal is then poured into molds of dung, where it cools into small bars which are

After Schultze

FIG. 104. NAMA UTENSILS: WOODEN DISH, BASKET SIEVE, WOODEN MILK BOWL, GOURD CHURN, WOODEN MILK PAIL, AND CLAY POT.

hammered into knives, arrow- and spearheads, and divers ornaments.

The principal native industry, however, is the preparation of skins. Entire hides of calves and small antelopes are turned inside out, cleaned of adhering bits of flesh, dried, and used without further treatment as containers for water and milk, all the openings, of course, being sewn up except one which serves as a spout. For pillows, bags, and certain garments the hair is removed after exposure for several days to the sun and fire, and the fleshy side is rubbed with fat. Floor rugs, superior bags, and most garments require tanning. After drying a fresh skin and then softening it with certain plant juices, the workman beats it with a club, scrapes off the fleshy particles with sand and a rubbing stone, smears the outer surface with fat, tans the skin with the inner bark of an acacia tree, steeps it in red lye made from the same bark, stretches it smooth, and dries it in the sun. The finished product is soft, water-tight, and dyed a beautiful red on the inside. Ox and antelope hides are sliced spirally into thongs. Thread and cord are made from the inner bark of an acacia by removing, soaking, and chewing the fibers and twisting them between palm and thigh. Animal sinews, however, are preferred in sewing skins.

The clothing of both sexes consists of a leather thong around the waist and, depending therefrom, an apron of skin in front and another behind. The men wear a ridiculously small pouch-shaped piece of fur in front, and in the rear a large triangular skin, which is narrower at the top and is lifted in sitting down. The rear apron of the women, though also triangular, tapers downward to a point at the knees, the other two corners being tied around the waist. The apron in front is smaller and is slit into thin strips at the bottom to form a decorative fringe, frequently ornamented with beads or shells. Only in cold or wet weather does either sex don an upper garment—a robe or "kaross" of sewn sheep, lynx, or jackal skins fastened over the shoulders with a thong. The women carefully conceal their hair with a cap of zebra skin, but the men go bareheaded except in bad weather. On the march both sexes wear leather sandals.

For ornament the men wear anklets of copper and ivory; the women, rings and armlets of iron or copper, anklets of dried rawhide, and necklaces of shells, teeth, or perforated sections of ostrich eggshells. Both sexes dangle small trinkets from the kinks of their hair. The ear lobes and sometimes the nasal septum are pierced for the reception of ornaments. Scarification and the removal of finger joints are prevalent but reflect magical and ceremonial rather than decorative motives. Owing to the scarcity of water the Hottentots rarely bathe. They devote great pains, however, to the care and beautification of the skin. The usual toilet consists in smearing the body completely with moist cow dung, allowing it to dry slightly, and then scraping it off with the palm of the hand. Fat is rubbed into the skin to make it smooth and glossy. On festive occasions the women decorate the forehead, cheeks, and chin with dots of red paint made by mixing fat with a pulverized red mineral. Both sexes, but more especially the women, make great use of sweet-smelling powders prepared from a wide variety of aromatic roots, herbs, and shrubs. A supply of *buchu*, as these cosmetics are called, is always carried on the person in a small leather pouch or more commonly in a tortoise-shell vanity box suspended from a strap encircling the waist. It is smeared over the body, or at least under the armpits and on the neck, on all occasions. A woman spends a considerable portion of her time in grinding *buchu*, and large sums are paid for the choicer and rarer varieties.

A division of labor, except for that between the sexes, does not exist. There are no specialized artisans, not even smiths. The Hottentots carry on a little barter informally amongst themselves and exchange cattle with the Herero and other neighboring Bantu tribes for metal implements and ornaments and with the Bushmen for ostrich eggs, feathers, etc. But there are no native merchants, middlemen, or markets.

A person owns a well which he has dug, although he may not refuse others permission to use it. Likewise a man who discovers a hive of wild bees can establish title to it by placing a few broken twigs in front of it, and in one limited region families enjoy hereditary rights to certain bushes and their fruits. With these exceptions, however, the land with all that pertains to it is communal property. On the other hand, huts, clothing, implements, utensils, and live stock are privately owned. Every person knows, for example, which cattle in the family herd are his personal property. Ownership does not, however, involve full rights of disposition, for before private property can be alienated the family of the owner must give its consent. Theft is a serious offense, and debts are recognized as binding obligations. It is only in their extreme hospitality and liberality with respect to food that the Hottentots give the deceptive appearance of "communism." A man who needs food can even help himself to an animal from another's flock in the absence of the owner and without his permission, but he must inform him later and recompense him or the act will be considered as theft. Behind this liberality lies the idea of reciprocity and a clear recognition of private property. "A Hottentot shares his food with others because he has the right to dispose of it, not because they have an equally legitimate claim to it."

Wealth, of course, consists primarily in herds and flocks. A person can acquire cattle and sheep in various ways. Shortly after his birth his parents set aside a few animals for him, and at his marriage he receives others. If he is especially skilled at handicrafts, he may barter weapons and utensils for cattle. He may add to his stock by raiding, or he may tend the herds of a wealthy man for a share of the increase. Finally, he may inherit property. When a man dies, all his live stock, except animals specifically allocated during his lifetime to his daughters and younger sons, is inherited by his eldest son, who becomes the head of the family and must support the widow and arrange the marriage of the daughters. The rest of a man's property—weapons, ornaments, and the like—is equally divided amongst all the children of both sexes.

The Nama are divided into twelve territorial groups or tribes. Seven of these are indigenous in Southwest Africa and are known collectively as the "Great Namaqua," the other five being "Little Namaqua" tribes who have emigrated in historical times from south of the Orange River.

The tribes bear the names sometimes of their traditional ancestors, sometimes of some special feature of their culture or geographical environment. Each tribe has a recognized chief and lays claim, not to a definite territory, but to a number of important pools or water-holes in the vicinity of which it leads its migratory life. All its members have free access to water and pasturage. Others may use the water-holes but must obtain permission if they plan to remain for any considerable period.

A Nama tribe is subdivided into an indefinite number of exogamous and patrilineal but non-totemic clans, the strongest social units in Hottentot society. Each clan has its own chief and bears the name of its earliest known ancestor. A clan may contain several distinct patrilineal lineages, but they all consider themselves related by a bond of common blood. The members of a clan owe one another the obligation of mutual protection, and they usually live together.

The family is the basic economic unit. It manufactures most of the artifacts that it uses. It migrates with its flocks and herds often independently of other families. And its members—man, wife, and unmarried children—occupy a single hut. A wealthy family usually has a few servants, who receive subsistence in return for their labor. In most cases they are war captives or rescued fugitives, especially of the Bergdama tribe. They are not slaves, for they cannot be sold, and they are free to leave if they wish. Although, amongst other tasks, they tend the flocks of their masters, they are to be distinguished from the hired herdsmen who receive a share of the increase for their services.

The Hottentots follow a kinship system of the classificatory type, and a definite pattern of behavior is associated with each relationship. Between "brother" and "sister"—in the wider or classificatory sense, of course—there prevails an exaggerated respect which practically amounts to avoidance. After the period of infancy has passed, they may not address each other directly or be in a hut alone together. If a brother uses bad language in the presence of his sister, she can demand a sheep from him with which to purify herself. If he gets into a fight, she has the power to step in and stop it. The worst native curse is a suggestion of incest with one's sister, and to take oath upon one's sister establishes the most sacred of obligations. If a man violates such an oath, his sister can confiscate his finest cattle and sheep. The relationship between maternal uncle and nephew is one of great tolerance on the one side and license on the other. A nephew may do as he likes in his uncle's house and may even help himself, without permission, to the finest animals in his uncle's herd. The uncle, to be sure, may seize an equal number from his nephew's herd, but he may take only ugly or misformed animals. Between cross-cousins of opposite sex there prevails a joking relationship involving free speech, horseplay, and sexual intimacy.

Two men, usually of distant clans or tribes, can establish an artificial bond of brotherhood by a ceremony of slaughtering a sheep and eating or drinking from the same utensil. Each acquires thereby a right to the property and wife of the other and an obligation to entertain, protect, and avenge the other. Two women or a man and a woman may enter into a similar pact. The relationship aims primarily at mutual aid in economic matters, but it also frequently involves sexual or even homosexual relations.

The Nama lay great stress upon relative age. The terms for brother and sister always distinguish those older and those younger than the speaker, and a paternal uncle is called "big father" or "young father" depending upon his age relative to that of the parent. In an encampment the huts are arranged in a definite order based on the principle of seniority. On the extreme right, facing the center, stand the huts of the clan chief and his descendants, immediately to the left are those of the next eldest clan "brother," and so on. Within each family cluster, the hut of the eldest son stands on the right, then those of the younger sons in order of age, then that of the father himself, and on the left the huts of secondary wives, widowed sisters, recently married daughters, and servants.

Political authority rests largely in the hands of the older men. A clan chief possesses an influence dependent largely upon his personality, but he can do little without the advice and consent of a council consisting of the adult males of the clan. He leads the clan in war and presides over the council. As a rule he is wealthier than other men and possesses a larger hut, but he receives no tribute save occasional presents, commands no personal services from his subordinates, and wears no insignia of office other than a kaross of leopard or lynx skins. Nor does any special etiquette or ceremonial set him apart from his fellows. The office is hereditary in the male line; a chief is succeeded by his eldest son or in default of sons by his eldest surviving brother or brother's son, never by a woman. If the heir is a minor, his paternal uncle acts as regent. A chief may abdicate voluntarily in favor of his heir, but he cannot be deposed.

The tribal chief is simply the headman of the senior clan in the tribe. The other clan chiefs form a tribal council, which discusses questions of war and peace, disputes between clans, and the like. In the council the voice of the tribal chief carries no more weight than that of another man unless it is supported by greater personal influence. The chief leads the tribe in war, conducts peace negotiations, presides at council meetings, and acts as trustee over the tribal lands. Loyalty to the clan, however, is far stronger than that to the larger group. A tribal chief, indeed, is powerless to stop a blood feud between two of his clans. If political cohesion is weak even within the tribe, it is non-existent outside. Never have the Hottentots succeeded in uniting against a common enemy, even in an extreme crisis. The enemy has always been able to play off one tribe against another to his own advantage. Under European influence the authority of the chief has increased considerably, and a number of subordinate officials have come into being, but the council still remains the power behind the throne.

The council also acts as a court of law. The clan elders try petty disputes and minor offenses, but serious crimes and disputes involving different clans or their members come within the jurisdiction of the tribal council. No distinction is made between civil and criminal cases. The plaintiff or complainant must deliver an animal or two to the judges to feed them during the sitting of the court; if he wins the case he recovers them later from the defendant. The litigants present their cases with the evidence. The councilors, after a cross-examination of principals and witnesses, confer privately and attempt to arrive at a unanimous decision. If they fail to agree, they may resort to divination. Or they may decide upon a regulated duel between the litigants, either with or without weapons, the victor winning the case. If the councilors agree, their verdict is executed immediately. For theft, the punishment consists of a flogging and a twofold restitution of the stolen property; for assault, a fine and the support of the victim and his family until his recovery; for slander, a flogging; for incest, rape, or repeated minor offenses, the death penalty in most cases. Accidental injuries are not regarded as crimes, but unsuccessful attempts are punished. Murder imposes the duty of blood-vengeance upon the next of kin of the victim—the eldest son or brother—and frequently plunges two clans into a prolonged blood feud.

Jealousy, petty quarrels, and shifting alliances characterize intertribal relations. A cattle raid, the abduction of a woman, or an unwarranted encroachment upon the territory of another tribe converts latent antagonism into open warfare. Frequently the injured group, before initiating hostilities, sends a messenger to the enemy with a statement of grievances and a demand for compensation. If this is refused, all the men of the tribe assemble under the leadership of the chief. Those who have never killed an enemy drink the blood of a slaughtered animal, and if the omens are favorable the party sets out. The Hottentots prefer tactics of surprise, *e.g.*, an ambush at a water-hole or a sudden descent upon an enemy camp. If they find the foe prepared, however, they may engage in a pitched battle, first at a distance with arrows, then hand to hand with spears and knobkerries. For defense they employ large shields of doubled cowhide. Sometimes, at an opportune moment, they bring up their fighting oxen and stampede them into the ranks of the enemy. A single battle ends the war. The victors withdraw with the captured women, children, and cattle, allowing the vanquished to bury their dead and sue for peace. Captives, though often retained as servants, are not mistreated, and atrocities are very infrequent. The returning warriors are considered unclean and must undergo elaborate purification ceremonies.

The Nama welcome children, especially boys since they increase the strength of the clan, and they scorn a barren woman. Nevertheless they occasionally practice abortion either by means of tight bandages or by certain decoctions. A pregnant woman has her abdomen carefully massaged several times a week. Her husband must satisfy her whims for special foods. If she wishes to impart to her child the swiftness, strength, or ferocity of a lion or leopard, she drinks the blood and eats the flesh of these animals.

A woman returns to the home of her own mother to bear her child. When labor approaches, all men leave the hut. A few female relatives and an old woman skilled in midwifery assist at the delivery. The mother assumes a special position on her left side with her shoulders and back supported on the knee of an attendant. The midwife ties the umbilical cord with a sinew or string, cuts it, and later buries the remainder of the cord and the afterbirth. She cleans the child with moist cow dung, never with water, rubs its body with fat and *buchu*, smears its nose, forehead, and temples with a salve of burnt ostrich eggshells and fat, and wraps it in a clean skin. Its mother must not suckle it for three days, during which time it is fed animal milk or is nursed by another woman. Although the Nama do not practice infanticide today, there is strong evidence that they once buried or exposed deformed children, those whose mothers died in childbirth, and one of a pair of twins unless both were boys.

Childbirth renders a woman unclean. She remains in seclusion in her hut, warmly wrapped, beside a fire at which no food may be cooked, and she carefully refrains from touching cold water. Her isolation terminates with a feast when the child's umbilical cord drops off. Before she can resume her normal activities, however, the midwife must introduce her to cold water in a special rite held at the nearest spring or water-hole, and both she and her husband must cleanse their bodies with cow dung and smear themselves with fat and *buchu.* At the next thunderstorm the baby is taken out into the rain to drench its skin.

A mother usually bestows a pet name upon her child, but its real name is determined by a simple rule. A son always bears the name of his mother, with a distinguishing masculine ending, and a daughter similarly takes her father's name. Consequently all the brothers of a family—or all the sisters —have the same name. They are differentiated only by the addition of a special descriptive adjective such as "big," "dark," "tall," or "young."

A child is not weaned until it is three or four years of age. The mother carries it slung in a lambskin on her back, and to nurse it simply tosses her breast back over her shoulder. Almost as soon as it can stand it begins to fend for itself, learning from its mother how to dig roots and bulbs, using miniature weapons to hunt mice, lizards, and birds, milking the cow which the father, if rich enough, always gives to his child, etc. Girls follow their mothers and gradually undertake the various household tasks. Boys soon begin to tend the flocks. Children of about the same age form into gangs with elected chiefs on the model of the political system of their elders. The gang organization directs all games, settles all disputes, imposes fines for disobedience to parents, etc. Adults, instead of disciplining their children themselves, leave the regulation of their conduct and activities to the gang.

A boy or a girl at puberty is considered unclean (*!nau*) and must undergo elaborate purification rites. The notion of uncleanness plays a very prominent part in Hottentot life. Not only puberty but also childbirth, the death of a spouse, remarriage, certain diseases, and the slaying of an enemy or a big game animal render a person unclean. In this state he is himself in danger, especially from cold water and raw meat, and he is a source of danger to other people and to animals and inanimate objects. The fire on his hearth, the clothing he wears, and the utensils he touches all become contaminated and dangerous. Likewise all persons who come into contact with him become unclean unless they have themselves safely survived the same crisis and have been rendered immune by the attendant rites. Consequently an unclean person is carefully segregated and placed under the care of an immune guardian. To remove the pollution, he must undergo a ritual cleansing, participate in a common meal with persons who have come unscathed through the same dangers, and be introduced by his guardian once more to normal contacts with the external world. In some cases he must also submit to a special rite of immunization, in which a concoction containing dirt from the body of an immune person is rubbed into incisions in his skin.

When a girl first menstruates, she is isolated for a fortnight in a segment of the hut screened off with mats, where she is tended by an old woman. She must not touch cold water, speak above a whisper, or leave the hut except at night. Her relatives slaughter a heifer and other female animals for a feast in which the girl, her guardian, and other women who have already passed through the ceremony participate. No man or boy and no immature, sterile, pregnant, or menstruating woman may be present. On the final day the guardian cleanses the girl with moist cow dung, removes and keeps her girlhood garments, and dresses her in a complete set of new clothing. She then slaughters a ewe, cooks it on the hearth fire, and shares the food with other old women past the age of child-bearing. After removing the impure ashes and coals from the hearth, she kindles a new fire. The hut is now free from pollution, and friends and relatives enter with presents. The girl, now safely past the crisis, is thought to possess power to confer fertility, and with this object in view she smears the testicles of the boys and youths with scented powder. Every one joins in a feast and then in a dance, which lasts throughout the night. In the morning, the old woman accompanies the girl to the kraal, where she helps her to milk a cow, and then to the spring, where she sprinkles her with water. The girl scatters *buchu* on all male animals and growing plants which she encounters, and is now free to resume her daily tasks. In the next thunderstorm, however, she must run naked in the pouring rain.

A boy, before he can marry and before he can leave the company of women to eat and associate with the men, must pass through a similar series of rites. He too is isolated behind mats in the hut, where he is cared for by an old man. His guardian cleanses his skin of the accumulated dirt and grease of his boyhood, urinates over him, and smears his body with the blood and fat of a specially slaughtered animal. The old man also makes a row of small incisions on the lad's chest and rubs ashes into the wounds to leave permanent scars. Meanwhile cattle are slaughtered in preparation for a feast at which the initiate eats in the company of the older men who have already passed through the ceremony. The boy remains in seclusion until his wounds heal, while his guardian lectures him on the importance of respecting age, refraining from eating the flesh of the hare, observing the moral canons of the tribe, and so on. Finally, the old man takes him to the spring and splashes water on his face.

The first time a young man kills, or receives the credit for killing, an elephant, rhinoceros, buffalo, or hippopotamus he undergoes a similar ceremony. He plunges his spear into the carcass, directs how the meat shall be cut up, drapes the entrails over his head, and smears his face with streaks of soot. He then participates in a feast with the men who have previously passed through the ceremony. The fire at which the flesh is cooked is used for no other purpose, and is later extinguished. On his return to the camp, the youth breaks the leg of a sheep on the bundle of hunting spears, slaughters a sheep, and drapes the entrails over the spears. His chest and abdomen are then scarified. After a short period of isolation he resumes his normal tasks and is privileged henceforth to wear a bracelet of beads strung on a rhinoceros sinew and to share in all similar feasts in the future.

The unmarried of both sexes are allowed considerable liberty in sexual matters, except that incest between classificatory brothers and sisters is rigorously prohibited. If a girl becomes pregnant, however, her lover must marry her. A young man has complete freedom in choosing a wife, but he may not marry a woman of his own clan or one who bears the same name. His parents send emissaries to obtain the consent of the girl's mother, who always refuses at first and only yields after a prolonged show of reluctance. But the girl herself must indicate her willingness. The youth visits her house at night and lies down beside her. She gets up and moves to another part of the hut, but he remains in her bed until dawn, when he leaves without a word. On the following night he returns. If he finds her in the same place, he knows that his suit is favored and that he has only to persist. For several nights in succession the girl moves away, as before, but eventually she remains with him and the union is consummated. The youth then stays until full daylight, when he presents a girdle of ostrich eggshell beads to his future mother-in-law, exchanges karosses with the girl, and receives a gift of *buchu* from her.

The wedding is celebrated on the same day. The groom

provides several cattle, some to be slaughtered for the feast, some as presents to his parents-in-law, who later turn over to him a few animals as a dowry for the bride. He then goes out to hunt game for the feast. Meanwhile a shaman slaughters a cow and joins the bride and her married female friends in eating the flesh. In the evening the general feast is held. The two sexes eat apart, as usual, but the groom joins the women, although he uses a separate utensil and is served a special portion. The guests spend the night in singing and dancing, while the bridal couple retire into the hut which has been given the bride as a dowry and has been erected near that of her parents. Here the groom resides, working for his parents-in-law, until the birth of his first child, when he usually returns with his family to his father's camp.

A wealthy and influential man may, in exceptional cases, take a second or even a third wife. Secondary wives live in separate huts and yield precedence to the first wife, whose children enjoy preferred rights of inheritance. Sometimes, if his wife has borne him no sons, a man takes a concubine to provide himself with an heir. A man regards his sisters-in-law, especially if they are unmarried or widowed, practically as secondary wives, but he behaves toward his mother-in-law with great deference and a measure of avoidance.

The women labor much harder than the men, whom observers unite in describing as lazy. The men leave the herding largely to boys and servants and spend most of their time hunting, although they also prepare skins and work in wood and metals. The women milk the animals, fetch water and firewood, gather roots and berries, cook the meals, look after the hut, and make the mats, clothing, pottery, and *buchu*. Nevertheless a woman is far from being a mere servant or chattel of her husband. In public life, to be sure, she is subordinate, but in the household she reigns supreme. She owns the hut with its contents and can even forbid her husband to enter. She has her own cattle, which he is powerless to slaughter or sell. The education of the children rests in her hands. She controls the provisions and apportions them to the members of the family according to their age and status. If her husband so much as takes a drink of milk without her permission, his female relatives impose upon him a fine of sheep or cattle and assign them to the wife.

Adultery may cause a temporary separation, but cruelty is the only ground for divorce, and it must be proved to the satisfaction of the council. A widow usually marries the brother of her deceased husband, but sometimes she returns to her own clan with her youngest child. The remarriage of a widow or a widower renders the bridal couple unclean. After the wedding ceremony they retire into their hut. Here an old woman, herself a remarried widow, gashes them both with a quartz flake, mixes their blood with some dirt scraped from her arm and the blood of a slaughtered sheep, and rubs the mixture into their wounds. The mutton, which in the meantime has been cooking over the fire, is now eaten by the couple, their guardian, and other persons who have passed through the same ceremony. The couple remain in seclusion until their wounds have healed, when the old woman cleanses them with cow dung, dresses them in a complete outfit of new clothing, and then introduces them ceremonially to the objects and activities of everyday life.

The Nama attribute different diseases to different causes, and treat them accordingly. Certain ailments are thought to be due to the displacement of the internal organs, which "have weird ways of wandering about the body." The proper treatment is massage, to restore the organs to their normal position. Diseases of another class—paralysis, fevers, cancer, and varicose veins—are called by the native term for "death." They render the patient unclean and dangerous, requiring his isolation, and can be cured only by a person who has had such a disease and has recovered. The healer, in his treatment, rubs dirt from his own body into incisions in the skin of the patient, shares a meal with him, cleanses him with a mixture of fat, milk, and cow dung, and introduces him ceremonially to water at the end of the isolation period. Other diseases are attributed to sorcery or the malevolence of ghosts and can be cured only by a shaman or "witch doctor" who has established friendly relations with the ghosts and has thus acquired immunity. He pretends to extract a foreign body from the affected part and then transfers his immunity by gashing the skin of the patient and rubbing into the wound some of his own dirt and sweat mixed with a magical concoction which he keeps in his medicine horn. Other ailments are recognized to have natural causes and are treated by rational or pseudo-rational methods such as purgatives and emetics, herbal decoctions, dung poultices, and applications of skin from a living animal. Broken limbs are set in splints. For localized pains the universal treatment is bleeding—either by opening a vein with the aid of a ligature or by cutting the skin and applying suction with a horn cup. A person bitten by a snake either applies to the wound a poultice made from the crushed body of the snake that bit him, or makes cuts around the wound and draws blood by cupping, or he calls in a special "snake doctor." The latter is a man who has immunized himself by swallowing or injecting into his skin various snake venoms in minute but gradually increasing doses, and who can transfer his immunity by rubbing his sweat into incisions in his patient's skin.

Age carries great prestige in Hottentot society. The aged are treated with respect and affection, and are cared for in every way. Nevertheless, in cases of extreme poverty or suspicion of witchcraft, an old man or woman is sometimes placed in a small hut with a few provisions and left behind to die. Although the Nama recognize that death may result from natural causes, they attribute it in many cases to sorcery, the ill will of the ghosts of the dead, or the violation of certain ritual precautions, e.g., the contact of an unclean person with cold water. A native myth explains the origin of death. The Moon, it is said, once sent the louse to promise immortality to men: "As I die and dying live, so you also shall die and dying live." The hare overtook the louse on its way, and promised to deliver the message. He forgot it, however, and gave the wrong version: "As I die and dying perish, etc." The Moon in anger struck the hare on its lip, which has been split ever since.

As soon as any one dies, an old woman wraps the corpse in skins after folding the hands across the chest and bending the head between the knees. The relatives spend the day and night wailing and lamenting outside the hut. On the following day three or four men carry the corpse out through a special opening in the back of the hut and transport it to a grave dug in some secluded spot. Here, after being strewn with *buchu*, it is lowered into a niche in the side of the grave, where it is protected by brush and stones from contact with the earth. The mourners cast handfuls of soil into the grave until it is filled, erect a mound of stones to mark the spot, and sprinkle water and *buchu* over the mound. On their return, all except near relatives rinse their hands in cold water. The hut is moved to another part of the camp and its site sprinkled with water. The survivors slaughter animals for the funeral feast. The flesh is boiled in one pot, to be eaten by the near relatives. The entrails are cooked in another vessel, to be consumed by the other members of the camp. The blood is collected in a third pot. When it boils, it is stirred with a red-hot iron, and the immediate relatives lean over it, covering their heads with skins, until the steam induces a profuse perspiration. The contents are then consumed by the elders who officiate at the feast. A widow is unclean after her husband's death and must remain for a period in isolation, tended by an elderly woman who has previously passed through the ceremony as a widow. At the expiration of the seclusion period her guardian cleanses her with moist cow dung, rubs her body with *buchu*, shaves the top of her head, changes her garments, and, after a purificatory meal and a renewal of the fire, introduces her ceremonially to the activities of normal life. A widower observes the same rites with minor variations.

The Hottentots have no definite conception of a spirit world. They believe that the soul of a deceased person follows the body into the grave, from which it can emerge as a ghost to assume temporarily the form of a jackal, or to animate a whirlwind, or to visit its relatives in their dreams. Whenever a native passes a grave, he throws a stone or a twig on the mound, which thus increases in size with the passage of time. If he omits this rite, or disturbs a grave or its skeleton, he incurs the anger of the ghost— a serious matter, since ghosts are largely responsible for sickness and death. The spirits of the dead are not uniformly malevolent, however, for people often visit the graves of their ancestors to pray for health, fertility, success in hunting, or the increase of their stock.

The cult of the dead and of ancestors forms the basis of the native religion. The Moon, to be sure, figures prominently in mythology, and the new and full moons are always greeted with songs, dances, and prayers. But the Nama worship no other nature spirits. Besides the Moon, only three supernatural beings rise above the ordinary ghosts of the dead in importance, and all three are regarded as traditional ancestors or heroes. Heitsi Eibib is reputed to have been a great magician in olden times. Born of a virgin impregnated by chewing a certain kind of grass, he lived a remarkable life, committing incest with his mother, killing monsters, and performing countless miracles. He died and was buried many times, but always came to life again. His "graves" dot the countryside—huge mounds upon which every passer-by casts a stone or makes an offering with a prayer for success in hunting. The second ancestral spirit bears the name //Gaunab, which means simply "ghost," and he may be merely a personification of the ghosts of the dead in general. Like them he brings sickness, death, and other evils to man, and is universally feared. In mythology, however, he figures as the antagonist of Tsui //Goab, the third and greatest of the traditional heroes of the Hottentots. During his lifetime Tsui //Goab was a powerful chief and warrior, who, after many battles, finally overcame //Gaunab. According to one account he made the stones from which the ancestors of the Hottentots sprang. He now lives in the clouds and speaks with the voice of the thunder. He brings rain and causes the grass to grow and the herds to multiply. The people invoke his aid in song and ceremony. Thus he has become, in essence, the god of rain and of the fructifying forces of nature.

The Nama have great faith in omens—the flight of birds and movements of animals, dreams, meteorological phenomena, twitchings of the body, etc. The chameleon and the mantis bring good luck; a hare crossing a hunter's path augurs ill success. The natives wear all sorts of amulets as well as trophies from slaughtered animals. A person born with a caul is credited with power to foresee the future and to tell fortunes. Certain men are skilled at divination, and others possess the ability to bring rain by sprinkling a burning fire with their urine. Still more influential are the medicine men or witch doctors, who have established rapport with the ghosts of the dead. They always possess a horn filled with a mixture of fat, various strange vegetable ingredients, and the pulverized flesh and bones of bats, lizards, and other small animals. They use the concoction in making love magic and curing disease. Sometimes, however, a medicine man employs his powers for evil instead of good. If he is suspected of sorcery, his fellows duck him and his medicine horn in the nearest pool. The cold water destroys his power, which resides in his medicines and in the grease and dirt on his body, and leaves him again an ordinary man.

The outstanding event in the religious life of the Nama is the great annual rain ceremony, held in November or December when the old men judge that the summer rains are due. The entire tribe gathers on the bank of a watercourse. Each family brings a supply of milk and, if it can afford to do so, a pregnant cow or ewe. The animals are slaughtered and cut up very carefully to preserve the uteri intact. The flesh is cooked and served at a general feast. Later the old men build a special fire on the bank and dig a channel down to the bed of the stream. Then they hold the uteri of the slaughtered animals over the flame and pierce them with sticks, so that the fluid flows through the fire into the trench. Others pour milk and fat on the fire until the liquids flow copiously down the channel and dense clouds of smoke rise on high. Every one now joins in a great tribal dance with prayers to Tsui //Goab for rain and plentiful grass and food. The smoke representing rain clouds, the drenching of the fire, the flowing liquids, the uteri symbolic of fertility—all stamp the ceremony as a rite of imitative magic designed to bring rain and abundance.

The Hottentots make no rock paintings such as those for which the neighboring Bushmen are celebrated, and their decorative art is confined to crude incised designs on ornaments, implements, and pottery. They find their chief artistic expression, as well as their principal recreation, in music and dancing, in which they display an unusual mimetic talent, fertility of imagination, and feeling for rhythm. They sing cradle songs to their babies, didactic songs to their children, love lyrics to their sweethearts, derisive chants to their enemies, hymns to their gods, and songs in praise of great exploits in war and the chase. The native musical instruments include a horn trumpet used only in war, a crude stringed implement resembling a guitar, a drum or "rommel pot" consisting of a skin tightly stretched over the mouth of a pot or calabash, and musical bows both with and without a sounding box.. The most remarkable instrument, however, is the *!goura,* a special form of the musical bow in which one end of the string, instead of being fastened directly to the stave, is attached to it by means of a flexible quill. The player holds the quill between his lips and makes it vibrate with his breath. The *!goura* thus combines in unique fashion the qualities of a stringed and a wind instrument. The oldest and most popular instrument, however, is the reed pipe, which has a long barrel like a flute and a grass stopper which can be adjusted for the desired pitch. A Nama orchestra consists of at least nine musicians, each with a pipe or set of pipes tuned to a note different from but harmonizing with the others.

The natives dance to the accompaniment of music and song. Every one participates, even blind old crones and mothers with infants on their backs. The dancers enact in pantomime the actions of animals, scenes of war or the chase, and historical incidents. In the favorite "reed dance," the men form a ring and hop up and down with jerky movements as they blow their pipes, while the women clap their hands, sing the songs, and dance in an outer ring with short steps and outthrust waggling buttocks. A reed dance is held on every ceremonial or festive occasion, *e.g.*, to entertain visitors, to celebrate the emergence of an unclean person from isolation, and to welcome the appearance of the Pleiades or the new or full moon. The Portuguese poet Camoëns, in the *Lusiad*, his immortal epic of the voyage of Vasco da Gama, has described the Hottentot reed dance:

> By turns the husbands and the brides prolong
> The various measures of the rural song.
> Now, to the dance the rustic reeds resound,
> The dancer's heels light quivering beat the ground.

The Hottentots first met the white man in 1497, when the Portuguese under Vasco da Gama encountered them at St. Helena Bay, but contact was slight until 1652, when the Dutch made their permanent settlement at Table Bay. The Nama were the last of the Hottentots to come under European rule when, in 1884, Southwest Africa was annexed by Germany, but indirectly they felt the alien influence much earlier. Alcohol, tuberculosis, and venereal disease were introduced, and smallpox swept the land in several severe epidemics. Pressure from the Dutch and English forced some of the southern tribes into Great Namaqualand and led to serious internal strife. Conflicts with the Herero, pressing down from the north, and a disastrous war with the Germans in 1905 made further heavy inroads on the population. Perhaps 20,000 Nama survive today, but the majority probably have an admixture of white blood. The indigenous culture is hopelessly in decay. European implements, ornaments, and clothing have replaced those of native manufacture. In the realm of material culture only the hut has survived relatively unmodified. Christian missions have largely obliterated the native religion. The nomadic life has been profoundly affected by the almost complete disappearance of cattle and by the introduction of the horse and, to some extent, of agriculture. Most of the Nama today lead a parasitic or dependent life as servants in the employ of Europeans.

BIBLIOGRAPHY

ANDERSSON, C. J. *Lake Ngami.* New York, 1857.

BLEEK, W. H. I. *Reynard the Fox in South Africa.* London, 1864.

DORNAN, S. S. *Pygmies and Bushmen of the Kalahari.* London, 1925.

FRANÇOIS, H. VON. *Nama und Damara.* Magdeburg, 1895.

FRITSCH, G. *Die Eingeborenen Süd-Afrika's ethnographisch und anatomisch beschrieben.* Breslau, 1872.

HAHN, T. "Beiträge zur Kunde der Hottentotten." *Jahresbericht des Vereins für Erdkunde zu Dresden,* Vols. VI–VII. Dresden, 1870.

——. "Die Nama-Hottentoten." *Globus,* Vol. XII. Braunschweig, 1867.

——. *Tsuni-// Goam, the Supreme Being of the Khoi-Khoi.* London, 1881.

HARTLAND, E. S. "Hottentots." *Encyclopædia of Religion and Ethics,* Vol. VI. Edited by J. Hastings. New York, 1914.

HOERNLÉ, A. W. "Certain Rites of Transition and the Conception of !nau among the Hottentots." *Harvard African Studies*, Vol. II. Cambridge, 1918.

——. "The Expression of the Social Value of Water among the Naman of South-West Africa." *South African Journal of Science*, Vol. XX. Johannesburg, 1923.

——. "The Social Organization of the Nama Hottentots of Southwest Africa." *American Anthropologist*, New Series, Vol. XXVII. Menasha, 1925.

KOHLER, J. "Das Recht der Hottentotten." *Zeitschrift für Vergleichende Rechtswissenschaft*, Vol. XV. Stuttgart, 1902.

KOLB, P. *Beschreibung des Vorgebürges der Guten Hoffnung, und der darauf wohnenden Hottentotten*. Trans. Frankfurt, 1745.

*SCHAPERA, I. *The Khoisan Peoples of South Africa*. London, 1930.

SCHINZ, H. *Deutsch-Südwest-Afrika*. Oldenburg, 1891.

SCHMIDT, M. "Die Nama, Bergdama und Namib-Buschleute." *Das Eingeborenenrecht*, Vol. II. Edited by E. Schultz-Ewerth and L. Adam. Stuttgart, 1930.

*SCHULTZE, L. *Aus Namaland und Kalahari*. Jena, 1907.

——. "Zur Kenntnis des Körpers der Hottentotten und Buschmänner." *Denkschriften der Medizinisch-Naturwissenschaftlichen Gesellschaft zu Jena*, Vol. XVII. Jena, 1928.

STOW, G. W. *The Native Races of South Africa*. London, 1905.

VEDDER, H. "The Nama." *The Native Tribes of South West Africa*. Cape Town, 1928.

WANDRER, C. "Die Khoi-Khoin oder Naman." *Rechtsverhältnisse von eingeborenen Völkern in Afrika und Ozeanien*. Edited by S. R. Steinmetz. Berlin, 1903.

CHAPTER XVII

THE GANDA OF UGANDA

In east central Africa, northwest of Lake Victoria, lies the native kingdom of Buganda, now a province in the Uganda Protectorate. The equator bisects the kingdom, which extends from 31° to 33° east longitude and is approximately bounded by the first degrees of north and south latitude. The natives, who still number nearly a million, belong mainly to the Ganda tribe, often styled the Baganda or Waganda.* The Ganda are members of the Bantu branch of the Negro race, which occupies most of Africa south of the fifth degree of north latitude. Like the other Bantus, they represent a fundamentally negroid stock with a certain admixture of Hamitic blood. In color the Ganda are a dark chocolate brown. The men attain an average stature of nearly five feet six inches, the women some four inches less. The head is narrow or dolichocephalic (cephalic index 73); the hair thick, coarse, black, and woolly or kinky; the beard moderate; the face oval and regular; the nose relatively broad although not quite platyrrhine (nasal index 83); the mouth small; and the lips comparatively thick. In general, the features are not unprepossessing, even according to European standards.

The native language belongs to the great Bantu linguistic stock. Agglutinative in type, it makes extensive use of prefixes to denote grammatical changes in verbs, nouns, and other parts of speech. Thus from the root "-ganda," which is said to mean "brother," different prefixes give rise to the words *Muganda* (a member of the tribe), *Baganda* (the tribe collectively), *Buganda* (the country), and *Luganda* (the

* The well-established practice of dropping the prefixes in Bantu tribal names is here followed. Cf. W. Wanger, "Afrikanische Völkernamen in europäischen Sprachen," *Africa*, II, 414 (London, 1929).

language). Nouns fall into ten classes, and other parts of speech are inflected to agree with them, so that a single prefix or its derivative particle keeps recurring throughout a sentence. The Ganda possess no written language, but they are able to send messages by drums, several hundred different beats or rhythms being recognized as conveying as many distinct meanings. They employ a decimal system of numeration which runs well into the millions. The natives use natural measures such as the span, the cubit, and the handful. They reckon time by the phases of the moon. Six lunar months make up the native year, which is thus only half the length of ours; on the equator, of course, the winter months do not differ from those of the summer.

The combined evidence of native tradition, culture, and physical characteristics seems to indicate that Uganda was inhabited, some three thousand years ago, by agricultural peoples of negroid stock and Bantu language. Then from the northeast came incursions of pastoral Hamitic peoples superficially influenced by contact with ancient Egyptian civilization. These invaders, akin probably to the Gallas of modern Abyssinia, conquered the aboriginal tillers, established a series of petty states in what is now Uganda, and spread into the adjoining regions of Tanganyika and the Congo. According to tradition, they reached Buganda perhaps five hundred years ago and founded the present dynasty of that kingdom. Although they probably introduced the complex political institutions of the Ganda and certain innovations in material culture and ceremonial, they do not seem to have affected the basic agricultural economy as they did, for example, in the kingdom of Kitara or Bunyoro to the northwest. The rulers have intermarried with the aborigines until they are now scarcely distinguishable from them in race. Only in the widely scattered tribe or caste of herders, the Hima, have the Hamitic invaders preserved a comparatively pure strain, and even the Hima speak a Bantu language.

Lake Victoria, next to Lake Superior the largest body of fresh water in the world, is subject to sudden, heavy storms and rough seas, but a fringe of islands off the shore of Buganda leaves a protected channel favorable to navigation. The lake empties northward over the Ripon Falls, giving birth to the Nile River, which forms the northeastern boundary of the kingdom. The surface of the lake is 4,300 feet above sea level. The country consists of a succession of low rounded hills covered with grass or cultivated lands and separated by broad marshy valleys inadequately drained by sluggish streams flowing toward the Nile. These swamps are invariably choked with papyrus and other aquatic plants and are frequently fringed with tropical forests. A fertile soil and an annual rainfall of about sixty inches support a luxuriant evergreen vegetation. Rain occurs, often in sudden destructive thunderstorms, almost every month of the year, but it reaches one maximum from March to May and another from September to November. There are thus two planting seasons and two crops each year, giving rise to the native six-month calendar. The temperature rarely exceeds 85° F. in the shade. The nights are refreshingly cool, with the temperature sometimes falling below 60°. The native fauna is amazingly rich and varied; it includes the elephant, buffalo, rhinoceros, and hippopotamus, the lion, leopard, serval, hyena, and lynx, the zebra, jackal, wart hog, and otter, twelve species of antelope, the chimpanzee and several kinds of monkeys, the crocodile, python, puff adder, and other reptiles, fish and crabs, countless species of aquatic and jungle birds, and hordes of locusts, ants, termites, mosquitoes, and other insects.

Fish forms an important item of diet near the lake, and is bartered with the inland people for agricultural products. The Ganda use spears to a limited extent along the shore and at Ripon Falls. They employ long dragnets knotted from papyrus stems. They fish from canoes, especially for bait, with light cane rods, lines of aloe fiber, and sharpened but unbarbed iron hooks. Long night lines with many hooks are moored with heavy stones and marked by wooden floats. Conical basket traps with funnel-shaped openings leading into one or more wicker chambers are set from canoes by means of floats and weighted lines. Fishermen obtain "medicines" from the temples, devote a portion of their catch to the gods, and, while their lines and traps are out, abstain from meat, salt, and relations with their wives.

The Ganda hunt to obtain meat as a supplement to their predominantly vegetarian fare. They secure antelopes and other small game with spears, in snares, traps, and pitfalls, and by driving the animals into long nets stretched among the trees. A species of large rat, highly prized as food, is captured alive with long sticks studded with wooden spikes. Larger animals are attacked by a special class of professional huntsmen. These men spear elephants from trees or stalk and surround them with the aid of dogs, employing a spear with a six-inch, leaf-shaped iron blade fixed in a wooden shaft by means of an iron shank. They also construct concealed pitfalls with sharpened and notched stakes in the bottom, and over a path they suspend weighted spears which are sprung when an animal passing underneath kicks a rope. To capture the buffalo they fasten a wreath of thorny creepers to a tree with a stout rope and arrange it over a concealed hole in a trail; an animal putting its foot through the wreath is inextricably caught. They spear the hippopotamus from canoes with two-pronged harpoons attached by long lines to wooden floats. Lions and leopards are slain in great communal drives initiated by the king, to whom their skins belong. Thousands of men surround an area, close in with shouts and beating drums, and dispatch the animals with clubs. Hunters of big game, before setting out, always offer a meat sacrifice to the god of the chase, and on their return they devote to him a portion of each animal killed. The man who inflicts the fatal wound keeps the horns as a trophy. The spirit of a slain buffalo must be propitiated by a ceremony in which its head is ritually eaten and its skull is placed with prayers in a specially constructed shrine.

The domestic animals of the Ganda include cattle, sheep, goats, fowls, hunting dogs, and a few wretched cats. Each family keeps a certain number of fowls, used especially for feasts on ceremonial occasions such as a visit from the husband's male relatives, the return of a son or husband from war, the birth of twins, and ceremonies of reconciliation and blood brotherhood. The Ganda possess few sheep, partly because of a superstitious fear of incurring the enmity of their souls in killing them. Mutton is taboo to women, as are the flesh and eggs of fowls. Chiefs own large flocks of goats, which are tended by commoners in return for a third of the kids. Each peasant has at least one or two of his own— for the payment of fines and other exactions. They are herded by boys and are tied up at night in a special shed or oftentimes in the house itself.

In contrast to many neighboring tribes, whose vast herds constitute their principal possessions, the Ganda own comparatively few cattle and display a marked aversion to herding or otherwise coming into contact with them. They leave them entirely in charge of herdsmen of the Hima tribe, who graze them by day and pen them up in kraals of thorny bushes at night. The king and chiefs alone possess large herds; if a peasant owns a cow, he usually places it in the herd of a friendly chief. Only bulls and barren cows are slaughtered for food, although animals dying a natural death are eaten. On the whole, however, beef is an insignificant item in the native diet. The herdsmen are extremely fond of fresh blood and frequently open an artery in a cow's neck to satisfy their craving. The cows yield very little milk, which is thus a luxury even for the upper classes. Only children drink it fresh; adults prefer it curdled or clotted. A complicated series of taboos surrounds the use of milk. It must not, for example, be drunk with certain other foods; several hours must intervene. It must never be boiled except at a ceremony four days after a cow has calved. These and other similar taboos, though vitally important to the Hima, affect the average Ganda but slightly. Butter, used in cooking and for greasing the body, is churned in large gourds by the wives of the herdsmen. No woman or girl, however, may engage in herding or milking.

The Ganda make their living primarily from the soil. Every freeman obtains a plot of ground from the chief to whom he owes taxes and services, and he allots a portion to each of his wives. He is allowed to bring as much land as he wishes under cultivation. The men clear the land of brush and trees but leave all other agricultural operations to the women. Once the ground is cleared, however, the work is light, despite the fact that the only implement is the hoe— a heart-shaped iron blade lashed to a short wooden handle. The Ganda cultivate sweet potatoes, gourds, sesame for its oil, millet for beer rather than for food, sugar cane for its juice only, coffee, and a kind of fig tree from which bark cloth is made. They also raise small quantities of maize, beans, yams, groundnuts, tomatoes, spinach, manioc, and other plants, most of which have been introduced into Africa either from Asia by the Arabs or from America by the Portuguese.

But the staple food crop, and almost the only one which the Ganda consider worth growing, is the banana or plantain. This fruit, of which the natives possess about two hundred varieties, is propagated by dividing the roots. The plants are set out in rows three yards apart and bear the second year. Each tree yields one bunch of fruit, weighing as much as a hundred pounds, then dies from the roots and sends up a new stem. The women place the dead leaves and stems around the roots, where they serve to check the weeds, conserve the moisture in the ground, and fertilize the soil. Unlike the other crops, which are seasonal, the banana produces continuously the year around. A woman with a good garden can support three or four men. In addition to the use of the banana for food, its juice is made into beverages, its fibers into cordage, its fleshy stem into sponges, its leaves are used as receptacles, and the ashes of its peel are decocted into lye for the manufacture of soap. A grove, moreover, is a symphony of color, with the rich green foliage, the glossy black stems, the yellow fruit, and the white flowers sheathed in huge purple spathes.

The Ganda only occasionally eat ripe bananas, either raw, baked, or boiled; they usually cut the fruit before it ripens and prepare it by steaming. In a special cookhouse a large pot is supported on three stones over a wood fire, which is generated by a simple fire-drill when it cannot be obtained elsewhere. The women, who do the cooking, put a little water and some shredded banana-leaf fibers in the bottom of the pot, fill the vessel with peeled fruit wrapped in green banana leaves, and allow the food to steam for two or three hours over a slow fire. The fruit is then mashed in the leaves and served. This banana "stodge" is very nourishing; thousands of natives eat little else. Accompanying it as a relish there is often a thick gravy of fish or meat or else cakes baked from pounded sesame seeds. Vegetables, meat, and fish are usually wrapped separately in banana leaves and cooked in the same pot with the bananas, but methods of broiling, baking, boiling, and frying are also known. Other favorite dishes include groundnuts fried with salt, animal blood cooked with the intestines, fried locusts and white ants, and cakes made by mashing and frying a kind of gnat which hatches in billions in the lake during the rainy season.

Salt, a great luxury, is imported from neighboring countries except for a very poor grade extracted from the ashes of marsh grass. The natives often drink unfermented banana wine, but the national beverage is *mwenge*, a mildly intoxicating banana beer. The men place ripe bananas in large wooden troughs, tread on them to express the juice, add millet flour and water, leave the mixture to ferment for three days, and then strain it into gourd bottles. It is made when needed and is drunk as soon as it is ready through richly decorated tubes. Coffee beans are plucked green, boiled in the husk, dried, and often roasted to render them crisp. The Ganda do not use them for beverage purposes but chew them; every one carries a few beans in a small box or basket to offer to friends whom he meets.

The Ganda rise before dawn, dress, warm themselves before the fire, and, after a ceremony to dispel evil influences from the household, break their fast at about seven o'clock. They devote the morning to work; no one except slaves or very poor people does any labor after the noonday meal. The family reassembles after sunset for the third meal of the day, and then sits around the fire drinking and conversing until eight or nine o'clock, when every one retires for the night. The Ganda are cleanly in their personal habits. They bathe daily, brush their teeth with fibrous sticks, and rinse their hands before and after meals. Among the lower classes the men, women, and children commonly eat together, and even a chief, unless he has guests, usually invites one or more of his wives to dine with him. At meals the people sit cross-legged on the floor around a neatly arranged cover of banana leaves, upon which the steaming food is placed in a wicker basket. Each person is served with a little mound of banana mash and some meat or fish if there is any. A few common receptacles contain gravy and extra vegetables. Each person rolls his "stodge" into little pellets, dips them with his fingers into the gravy bowl, and transfers them daintily to his mouth. He wipes his fingers on a flat sponge made from the pith of banana stems, the sap of which serves admirably to remove grease and dirt. Coffee berries and beer are served after the meal. A guest compliments his host by eating heartily and belching loudly.

A Ganda dwelling rarely stands alone. It forms but one unit in a cluster of buildings—cookhouse, fetish hut, privy, storehouses, and huts for slaves, servants, and wives—all of which, together with the owner's banana groves, are surrounded by a high fence of neatly plaited reeds. In a large establishment the whole inclosure or compound is divided into a number of courtyards, each with its fence. The dwell-

From Roscoe, *The Baganda*

FIG. 105. A GANDA DWELLING.

ing itself has the shape of a huge beehive, fifteen to twenty feet in height, with a circular ground plan as much as thirty feet in diameter. Rows of pillars, graded in height and forked at the top, support the conical framework of the roof. This consists of longitudinal rods meeting at the apex and secured every fifteen inches by horizontal rings of grass, which increase in size from the top to the point where the roof merges with the nearly perpendicular external wall. A thick layer of carefully trimmed grass thatch extends from the peak of the roof to the ground, except in front where the roof projects forward, much like the visor of a cap, and the thatch is shaved to a smooth edge at a height of about six feet, forming a covered porch or veranda. The door and the interior walls are neatly constructed of strips of glistening yellow canes. A partition often divides the interior into a sleeping and a living room, each with a rectangular fireplace. The floor, which is raised a foot above the ground, is of earth trodden and beaten perfectly smooth and level, smeared with clay and cow dung, and carpeted with fragrant grass. The occupants spread mats or rugs for visitors, since they have no stools or other furniture. The beds are merely raised platforms of beaten earth covered with hides or bark cloth. Loose articles are stored away in baskets or in bundles neatly wrapped in banana leaves. Everything is clean and in perfect order.

The household utensils include bowls and ladles carved from hard wood, gourd bottles and drinking vessels often ornamented with pleasing burnt patterns, and earthen cooking pots, water jugs, serving bowls, and vase-shaped milk containers. The manufacture of pottery is a specialized craft, transmitted from father to son. Potters either model their vessels from a lump of clay by hand with the aid of a wooden spatula or else build them up by the coiling method. After drying the pots in the sun, they fire them in a hole in the ground, using dry grass, reeds, and wood as fuel. To impart a permanent black finish, they suspend a pot over a smoky fire and then polish it with bark cloth. Different colors are obtained by the use of red and white clays. Ornamentation consists of designs impressed on the damp clay with plaited cords and of incised dots, lines, bands, rings, spirals, and checker patterns. The Ganda also make wicker carrying baskets and fish traps, excellent coiled serving trays, and small ornamental coffee baskets with patterns in red and black.

The native smiths smelt iron and also work with imported copper and brass. They fill a pit with dried papyrus stems, covered with alternate layers of charcoal and iron ore, and build a wall of clay around the edge. Several boys, each working a pair of bellows with the nozzle inserted into holes in the wall of the furnace, provide a steady blast to the accompaniment of a chant. The bellows consists of two earthen pots covered with pliable skins in the center of which

After Stuhlmann

FIG. 106. GANDA POTTERY.

a hollow stick is inserted; the boy holds a stick in each hand and works them alternately up and down, closing the end of the stick with his thumb as he presses down. After seven or eight hours, when the ore is smelted, the walls of the furnace are broken down and the fire extinguished. The smiths, working with cleft tongs of green wood and stone hammers and anvils, beat the iron into fishhooks, needles, ornamental rings, chains, bells, and blades for knives, hoes, spears, and axes.

The Ganda dress the skins of wild animals and of cattle for the manufacture of rugs, sandals, drum tops, straps, and thongs. The hide is stretched in the sun to dry, scraped to an even thickness with a knife, rubbed with a flat stone to obtain a smooth grain, and liberally treated with butter. From banana, aloe, and other fibers the natives twist thread and string between palm and thigh, and from string they plait three-, six-, and nine-ply cordage and rope. They make simple floor mats from reeds lashed together with papyrus stems, but they weave no true textiles. The only native fabric is a kind of bark cloth made from the inner bark of a species of fig tree, scores of which are planted in every compound. After a tree is stripped it is smeared with cow dung and wrapped with banana leaves, so that it recovers and bears again the next year. The men, who make the garments and bedding for their wives and children as well as for themselves, scrape the bark, beat it to the thickness of stout paper with circular grooved mallets of wood, patch the holes cleverly with trimmings from the edges, and dry it in the sun. The exposed side turns a dark reddish brown. Bark cloth is often dyed black, or painted, or ornamented with lozenge-shaped patterns stamped in colors.

Boys wear a narrow strip of bark cloth passed between the legs and supported in front and in back by a waist-string. Girls go naked until puberty except for a ring of banana fiber and lizard skin around the waist. Adults, however, must be fully clad or suffer severe fines. In this as in other matters of surface morality the Ganda are excessively Puritanical. Women, to be sure, go entirely nude in the privacy of the home, but in public they wear a long bark cloth wrapped around the body under the arms and restrained at the waist by a girdle of the same material. For a man to expose any portion of his body from neck to ankles is considered highly improper; at all times he must wear a breech-clout, a bark cloth toga knotted over the left shoulder, and a belt or girdle. At one time, according to native tradition, the Ganda wore only scanty garments of dressed skin, and of late they have largely adopted white cotton mantles in place of bark cloth. On the feet they wear hide sandals, turned up at the edges like a boat, tastefully ornamented with colored designs, and fastened over the instep with strips of otter fur. Elaborate headdresses and outer robes of antelope skin are often worn at court. Both sexes shave the head periodically, and hair is removed from the body though not from the face. In striking contrast to most African peoples, the Ganda do not scarify, circumcise, file the teeth, or mutilate the body in any way. The men wear few ornaments—at most a wire bracelet and a few amulets on a neck string. The women, however, display necklaces of colored seeds or beads and bracelets and anklets of iron, brass, and ivory.

In addition to small dugouts and crude rafts, used in shallow and inland waters, the Ganda construct splendid plank canoes sometimes fifty feet in length and capable of carrying sixty men. They split the planks from solid logs

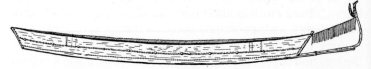

After Kollmann

FIG. 107. PLANK CANOE OF THE GANDA.

with wedges and hew them smooth with adzes. A long slender keel, hollowed from a log with fire and adze, forms the base of the canoe. Along either rim, tilted slightly upward, is lashed a long plank, and to the upper edge of this a second, almost vertical plank. The joints, caulked with plantain fiber and further protected by slender rods inside and out, are securely stitched with fine wattles, which encircle the protecting rods and pass through holes burned in the edges of the planks with a red-hot iron at intervals of two or three inches. Transverse poles, serving as thwarts and seats, are fixed in notches in the side planks, and give rigidity to the craft. In the bow a pole, attached to the keel, projects forward and then curves upward above the water line; it is surmounted by a pair of antelope horns, from which a string with an ornamental fringe of shredded papyrus extends back to the prow. The entire canoe is painted with red clay. It is propelled, not by sails, but by paddles of solid wood with

heart-shaped blades. Before a canoe is launched it is chris-
tened with the blood of a sacrificed animal, and its spirit
is provided with a little shrine on the shore.

For transportation on land the Ganda never use their
domesticated animals; they employ human porters, who carry
burdens slung from poles over their shoulders. A network
of excellent roads covers the country, connecting the residence of the king with those of his principal chiefs, and the
latter with those of their sub-chiefs. The roads, which often
exceed twelve feet in breadth, run as straight as possible.
They pass through miles of cool banana groves, ascend steep
hills instead of avoiding them, span streams on log bridges,
and cross marshes on long causeways constructed by heaping
mud and sand on papyrus stalks between two rows of piles
and rough basketwork.

In the division of labor by sex, the women till the soil,
cook, make mats and baskets, and carry burdens, while
the men clear the land, hunt, fish, fetch firewood, brew
beer, and make bark cloth. Men, too, are the specialized
artisans: smiths, carpenters, canoe builders, leather workers,
drum makers, potters, house thatchers, and floor makers.
The distribution of goods is effected through a system of
markets, where vendors offer for sale all the native fruits
and vegetables, cattle, sheep, goats, fowls, meat, fish, eggs,
beer, firewood, salt, sugar cane, coffee, pottery, bark cloth,
rope, baskets, iron implements, and ornaments. The ordinary
currency consists of cowrie shells, which are pierced and
threaded in strings of a hundred each. The real standard
of value, however, is the cow, which is worth about 2,500 cowries. A fowl costs ten cowries or more; a goat, about five
hundred cowries; a male slave, a cow or two; a female slave,
several times as much. Over each market the king appoints
an official, who keeps order, settles disputes, levies fines, and
collects a tax of ten per cent on all sales.

There are only three hereditary social classes in Buganda:
royalty, freemen, and slaves. The slave class is recruited in

the main from war captives, although Ganda children are sometimes sold or pawned by their parents. Masters have the power to sell and even kill their slaves, but as a rule they treat them almost as members of the family. A slave woman commonly enters the harem of her master, and she acquires a free status if she bears him a child. Freemen hold plots of land either from their chiefs or from the king himself.

FIG. 108. VENDORS OF BANANA BEER IN A GANDA MARKET.
From Ansorge, *Under the African Sun.* Courtesy of
William Heinemann, Ltd.

There is no permanent upper or middle class. The king, in his appointments to office and in his selection of wives, does not discriminate against persons of lowly birth in favor of the families of chiefs. He may even be himself the son of a peasant mother.

The Ganda are divided into thirty-six exogamous totemic clans, six of which have merged with others and practically lost their identity. Each clan (*kika*) traces its descent in the male line from a common ancestor, whose name is always borne by the clan chief. It has a fund of names reserved for its own members, a distinctive drum beat, and two totems, from the more important of which it obtains its name. The great majority of totems are mammals, although a few are birds, insects, plants, etc. No one may either kill or eat the totems of his clan, although he does not object to outsiders doing so. A Ganda observes the totemic taboos of his father's clan, ignoring, except during childhood, those of his mother's. Amongst royalty, however, totems descend in the female line; a prince takes the totems of his mother and is considered a member of her clan. Kings, consequently, may and do belong to different clans. The members of certain clans, however, are ineligible to the throne; if one of their women is taken to wife by the king, all her sons are killed at birth.

Land in Buganda belongs exclusively to the king, who parcels it out among his officials and favorites to hold during his pleasure or until his death, when all estates revert to the crown for redistribution by the new monarch. The sole exception to this rule is the burial grounds of the several clans. Every plot of land on which three successive generations of clansmen have been buried, together with the surrounding plantations, becomes the freehold property of the clan, exempt from royal interference. Each clan has several such estates, on many of which there stands a temple to an ancestral divinity of the clan, with priests to carry on his cult. The clan itself is divided and subdivided into smaller groups or "sub-clans," each associated with one of the freehold burial grounds and each with a petty chief to administer the estate. Succession to the chiefship, although always confined to the same sub-clan, is not hereditary in the strict sense. When the chief of a clan or of one of its constituent divisions dies, all the surviving chiefs of the clan meet and elect a successor, who may or may not be the son of the deceased. A similar rule governs the inheritance of property. The eldest son never inherits. The heir may be a younger son or a collateral relative, but the decision rests in the hands of the entire sub-clan.

A close bond of kinship and common interest unites the members of a clan. All clansmen of the same generation address and regard one another as brothers and sisters. When a man needs assistance to pay a fine, purchase a wife, or the like, he turns to his clansmen, and if he is appointed to an office he surrounds himself with kinsmen, whose own interests are best served by serving his. The typical native community, therefore, is not a village but a cluster of cultivated plots occupied by related families centering about the estate or compound of a chief or official of the same clan. If two men take an oath of fidelity before witnesses, smear two coffee beans with blood from incisions in the abdomen, and exchange and eat the beans, they not only become blood brothers thereby but they also unite their clans in a bond of friendship which endures as long as both men live.

The clans of the Ganda are doubtless much older than the state, but the latter has integrated the earlier with the later organization in a number of interesting ways. In particular, it has assigned to the clans definite prerogatives, offices, and functions in the political framework. The Lion and Leopard clans, for instance, are exempted from forced labor in the royal compound on the ground that they are related to the king; the members of the royal family, incidentally, respect the lion and leopard totems as well as those of their respective maternal clans. The important office of *Mugema*, or Custodian of the Royal Tombs, is hereditary in the Monkey clan. The king's guard comes from the Rat clan, his carriers from the Buffalo clan, his gatekeepers from the Mushroom clan, his drummers from the Hippopotamus clan, etc. The Otter clan provides the king with a wife whose function it is to make the royal bed, and other clans provide wives, attendants, and officials with other functions.

The king of Buganda is theoretically an absolute monarch, who can appoint and depose any official and requisition cattle, food, women, or anything else he wants. In practice he usually listens to the counsel of his advisers, but his power, nevertheless, is immense. An aura of sanctity surrounds his person. No one may see him eat; the wife who serves him turns her back, and the remains of his food are thrown to his dogs lest human hands come in contact with them. He may not walk outside his compound; he rides astride the shoulders of special carriers, and any one who touches their sanctified shoulders is severely fined. It is a capital offense for an unauthorized person to touch the rug upon which the king sits, or for any one to sneeze in his presence. The Ganda, ever punctilious in matters of etiquette and noted for their polished manners, display a cringing servility at court. For the slightest royal favor, or in flattering acclaim of every royal act, they fall flat on their faces and beat the ground with their hands, feet, and both cheeks. The king exercises his power arbitrarily. For the most trifling offense or at a mere whim he may condemn to death even a powerful chief or a favorite wife. If his food displeases him, he summons the cook and transfixes him with a spear. If he dreams of any one, he orders that person's death on grounds of meditated treason. Some monarchs, indeed, have kept their courts drenched with the blood of daily unjustified executions.

The royal residence is built on a hill near Lake Victoria in the center of an oval compound a mile long and half a mile in breadth. Between it and the main entrance lie the huts and courtyards of hundreds of guards, retainers, and slaves, and on the roads outside the inclosure are clustered the compounds of the great chiefs and officials. Within the royal compound paths lead from the residence to several private gates and to the lake, where canoes remain constantly in readiness should flight become necessary. Behind the residence and on either side lie the banana groves and huts of the king's wives and their slaves, grouped into courtyards with a principal wife in charge of each.

Although the king never submits to the wedding ceremony, he has hundreds of wives, obtained through inheritance, levies of tribute or taxes, and gifts from chiefs and officials seeking favors. Whenever one dies, her clan must provide a successor and substitute. One, chosen by the king's paternal grandmother, cuts his hair and finger nails and stores them in a special hut. Another, the wife given to the king by his father, holds the title of "chief wife," takes precedence over all other women in the royal compound, and has charge of the king's fetishes and amulets. By far the most important, however, is the *Lubaga* or Queen-Sister, who is chosen for this office from among the sisters or half-sisters of the monarch. She shares the coronation ceremonies with the king and receives a royal funeral if she dies in office. She lives in a separate compound adjoining that of the king. She has her own estates, independent of his control, throughout the country, her own officials, who bear the same titles as those of the king, and her own court with power over life and death. She visits the king daily, but bears him no children. After his death she becomes the custodian of his temple. Of at least equal importance is the *Namasole* or Queen-Mother, the king's own mother or a substitute if she is dead. Like the Queen-Sister but unlike the king's ordinary wives, the Queen-Mother has her own independent estates, officials, and court, travels only on the shoulders of carriers, and receives outward tokens of respect similar to those shown the king himself.

The foremost state officials are the *Katikiro* or Grand Vizier and the *Kimbugwe* or Keeper of the Royal Umbilical Cord. The Grand Vizier maintains a large establishment near the royal compound and has other estates throughout the kingdom. He consults with the king daily, advising him on matters of state. All administrative questions and all appealed cases at law come before him for decision, and are carried to the king only if his verdict is contested. The *Kimbugwe* has charge of the important royal fetishes, notably the king's umbilical cord or "twin," which he guards in a special temple. Every month at the new moon, the Keeper of the Royal Umbilical Cord carries the "twin" to the king for an inspection, then exposes it to the rays of the moon, anoints it with butter, and restores it to its place in the temple. Like the Grand Vizier, he has a large compound in the capital and estates in the country, and is exempt from taxes and services. He alone has free access to the king's person; all lesser chiefs must first apply to the Grand Vizier.

Next in rank to these two ministers are ten great chiefs or earls (*Basaza*), the governors of the ten districts into which the kingdom is divided. The earls receive their offices and landed estates from the king, who consults with his ministers and usually appoints a clansman of the former chief, and they automatically lose their positions when he dies. Each earl keeps up one establishment in the capital and another in his district, and has a steward in each place to represent him in his absence. His official duties include the maintenance of a road from his country seat to the capital, the construction and repair of a certain number of buildings in the royal compound, the provisioning of the king's household one month in every ten, and the civil and judicial administration of his district. Some of these officials have important additional functions. The *Kago* or earl of Kyadondo, the district in which the capital is situated, takes precedence over the others in council, supervises the servants in the royal compound, and substitutes for the king whenever the latter has mourning or other taboos to perform which would require his seclusion for considerable periods. The *Kasuju*, or earl of Busuju, has charge of all princes and princesses of royal blood, manages their estates, and is one of the three electors—the others being the two ministers—who choose a successor when the throne becomes vacant. The *Mugema* or earl of Busiro, the district where the kings are always buried, is the custodian of the royal tombs; his office, unlike most others, is hereditary, and, unlike all others, it does not terminate with the death of the king.

In each district, sub-chiefs or barons of six different grades hold estates of varying size. Many of them, *e.g.*, the *Gabunga* or Admiral of the Canoe Fleet, also fill state offices of considerable importance. The barons are appointed by the king, usually with the advice of the earl of the district, and they are responsible to the king alone. The earl cannot depose a baron, interfere with the administration of his estate, or command his assistance except on state work. Each baron must maintain a road from his estate to the country residence of his earl, and must furnish a contingent of troops in case of war. The barons also have establishments in the capital, where they spend much of their time. The earls and barons form a great council (*Lukiko*), which meets almost daily with the king in a large hall in the royal compound to discuss state business and hear cases appealed from the lower courts. Beer is always available in an adjoining building, and the councilors are free to leave the hall for refreshments at any time. Below the barons there is a class of petty officials (*Batongole*) who receive small estates from the king and serve him as guards, secret police, executioners, etc. Finally, there are various offices in the royal compound which are hereditary in particular clans. The Colobus Monkey clan, for example, always supplies the chief butler, the royal potter, and the guardian of the king's well. Indeed, "there is hardly a man in Uganda who does not hold an office of some kind."

Whenever the royal treasury becomes depleted, the king and his ministers set a date for the collection of taxes. For each of the ten districts six tax collectors are appointed— one each by the king, the Queen-Sister, the Queen-Mother, the Grand Vizier, the Keeper of the Royal Umbilical Cord, and the earl of the district. The collectors visit each baron, ascertain the number of houses in the district, and fix the tax to be exacted from each chief and peasant—usually after bargaining and bribery. After two months, allowed for the collection or manufacture of the levied cattle, goats, cowries, hoes, and bark cloths, the imposts are delivered to the earl and then to the Grand Vizier. The king gets half of the total; the rest is divided between his mother, his sister, and the two ministers, with each earl and baron receiving a share of the amount obtained from his own people. The Queen-Sister, Queen-Mother, Grand Vizier, and Keeper of the Royal Umbilical Cord have, in addition, the whole amount collected from their own estates, which are exempt from the state tax. From time to time the king orders a census of the population, on the basis of which he requires each chief to supply a number of boys and girls for service in his own compound and those of his sister, his mother, and his ministers. For the construction of all public works the king and Grand Vizier appoint overseers, who call upon the chiefs for drafts of laborers. Before a man can begin work, although he receives no compensation for it, he must pay his overseer a hundred cowries, a pot of beer, and a goat or fowl, and he is fined for any delay. If he is unable to pay, he can only escape going hopelessly into debt by pawning his wife or child as a virtual slave until he can redeem them.

Succession to the throne is patrilineal; the heir must be the son either of the reigning or of a former monarch. The sons of the reigning king are called "princes of the drums," the drum being the native symbol of office and authority. Shortly after they are weaned the king takes them from their mothers and sends them to the earl *Kasuju*, who provides each with an estate and a guardian. When they come of age, their father provides them with wives. The eldest son, who is ineligible to succeed, takes the title of *Kiwewa* and is responsible to the *Kasuju* for his brothers. The king's brothers, who are called "peasant princes," receive smaller estates. As the rejected candidates for the throne, they are likely to scheme with their adherents for a rebellion. It is customary, therefore, for the Queen-Mother, as soon as she and her son take office, to gather all or most of the eligible but rejected princes into a strongly guarded stockade and leave them there without food or water until they die of thirst and starvation.

A woman cannot succeed to the throne. The eldest daughter of the king receives the title of *Nasolo* and is responsible to the *Kasuju* for her sisters. Some of the princesses enter the temples; the others receive landed estates. Princesses are held in great honor. Even the highest chiefs kneel in addressing them, whereas in all other cases women kneel to men. No princess, however, may marry or have children on penalty of death. This fact, coupled with their prestige and their complete liberty of movement, results in a degree of sexual license which amounts practically to promiscuity. If a princess has an illegitimate child, it is secretly put to death. "There can be no doubt that the object of this stringent law was to end the old and regular law of succession through the female line, when the sister's son inherited the throne."

When the king dies, the fact is kept secret for several days. The *Kasuju* summons all the princes to the capital, and confers with the Grand Vizier and the Keeper of the Royal Umbilical Cord over the succession. If the electors disagree, they resort to arms to settle the issue. If they reach an accord, the king's death is announced by extinguishing the sacred fire at the main entrance to the royal compound and strangling its custodian, and by beating a special drum, which is relayed throughout the kingdom. The sound plunges the entire country not only into mourning but also into anarchy, for all law and order are bound up with the monarch. The weak hide their possessions; the strong ravage the countryside. When the princes are assembled, the *Kasuju* makes known the new king, and the Grand Vizier challenges any disappointed candidate and his supporters to a test of arms. The new Queen-Mother is then brought forward, the new Queen-Sister selected, and some of the more important new officials appointed.

The body of the deceased king, as soon as his successor

has draped it with a royal bark cloth, is taken by the *Mugema* or Custodian of the Royal Tombs to his district of Busiro. Here it is mummified by removing the viscera and washing them in beer, squeezing out the fluids with sponges, rubbing the corpse with butter, restoring the viscera, and wrapping the body in bark cloth. The bodyguard and widows of the deceased monarch, who perform these offices, drink the liquid by-products of the process. The new king, after a complicated series of ceremonies called "eating the country," retires to a temporary residence in the vicinity and mourns until the embalming is completed—a period of about six months. The mummy is then carried in solemn procession to its tomb, a large building surrounded by fences, and is deposited inside on a raised platform. The people press forward with offerings of bark cloth until the tomb is stuffed full, when the supporting posts of the porch are cut and the doorway thus closed. Four of the closest personal attendants of the late king, four of his widows, and hundreds of slaves and captives are clubbed to death and their bodies left in the inclosure where they fall. Other widows remain to cultivate the banana groves and make the inclosure their permanent home. The king then participates in a ceremonial hunt, has his head shaved, and declares the period of mourning at an end.

The coronation follows. The king and the Queen-Sister take the oath of office and are invested with the robes of their position, the royal fetishes are displayed and the royal drums beaten, and the king and his consort receive the homage of the multitudes. Two men, captured on the highway, are blindfolded and brought before the ruler, who wounds one of them with an arrow. He is carried on a raid to the border of Kitara, maimed, and left there to die along with a cow, a goat, a dog, and a fowl, all similarly treated. The other is conducted to a place of sacrifice, where eight men are slaughtered and disemboweled in his presence and their intestines draped around his neck; he receives the title of *Kawonawo* and is placed henceforth in charge of the king's wives. The earls now build a new royal compound under the direction of the king, who moves in as soon as it is completed and fills it with levies of servants and with wives—the childless widows of his father and women presented to him by the various chiefs.

Six months after the funeral, the Custodian of the Royal Tombs and other officials visit the mausoleum, remove the

From Roscoe, *The Baganda*

FIG. 109. ROYAL RELICS: UMBILICAL CORD AND JAWBONE OF A GANDA KING IN THEIR DECORATIVE WRAPPINGS.

head of the mummy, and clean it. One man drinks beer and milk from the skull, and becomes henceforth the medium through whom the ghost of the dead king speaks to his people. The skull is replaced in the tomb, which is sealed forever. The jawbone, however, is cleaned in a nest of ants, washed, wrapped in skins and bark cloth, and deposited in a temple in the old royal compound. Here, under the former Queen-Sister, reside all the widows who have borne children to the dead monarch, as well as all the officials of the old régime. The old Grand Vizier has charge of the jawbone, while the old Keeper of the Royal Umbilical Cord still guards the selfsame fetish. The widows and officials serve their departed master as long as they live, and when they die they are replaced, for the temple is a permanent institution. Once only during his reign does the king visit the temple of his father. On his return through the assembled crowds he gives a signal, and hundreds of onlookers are seized and sacrificed to the deified ghost of the royal parent.

No individual may take into his own hands the redressing of an injury or the punishment of a crime. He must resort to the regular courts, of which each baron and earl presides over one. The plaintiff or complainant, before his case can be heard, must pay the court a goat, a bark cloth, and twenty cowries, and the defendant or accused must pay a similar fee. The loser in a baron's court can appeal his case successively, with increasing fees, to the courts of the earl, the Grand Vizier, and the king. The winner recovers his fee and a fine from the loser. The judge profits through a portion of the fees and fines and through bribes from the litigants. Tortures are employed to extract confessions, and an ordeal by poison, administered by a priest or medicine man, decides close cases and disputed judgments. For murder, incest, and adultery the penalty is death, usually by beheading or strangling, sometimes by bleeding, dismembering, or burning. In addition, the property of a murderer is confiscated to the clansmen of the victim, and that of an adulterer to the injured husband. If a murderer escapes, one of his clansmen is seized and held as hostage or virtual slave. A man may kill a slave or a wife without punishment, except that in the latter case the relatives of the wife may recover a fine if they can prove her innocence to the satisfaction of the court. Accidental homicide is distinguished from murder and is punished only by a fine, raised by the clansmen of the culprit and paid to the clansmen of the deceased. Even a murderer or an adulterer can often escape the extreme penalty by paying a heavy fine, but in this case he is usually mutilated. The Ganda have no prisons, although a criminal may be confined temporarily in stocks—heavy logs with holes to secure the feet. Petty offenders are flogged or put in the stocks. A thief or burglar is killed if caught in the act; otherwise he is mutilated. "One meets a considerable number of people minus nose or ears, the loss of which is considered a great disgrace, not so much for the fault which has been committed, but for having been found out."

The Ganda wage war nearly every year with Kitara and other neighboring states, chiefly for captives and plunder. When a war god advises an expedition, the king consults with the Grand Vizier and the Keeper of the Royal Umbilical Cord and appoints a general. A war drum summons peasants to their chiefs and chiefs to their superiors. All take an oath of allegiance to their leaders and proceed to the frontier by different routes so as not to impoverish the country, off which they live. Warriors wear an apron, a cloak, and a girdle of skin, and in some cases elaborate helmets or headdresses. They are armed with knobbed clubs, spears with long wooden shafts and ten-inch iron blades, small knives, and convex oval shields of wood covered with wickerwork. Only the Hima use the bow and arrow. A wife accompanies each chief to cook for him and nurse him if wounded. Peasant wives, however, remain at home, observe strict chastity, and fulfill certain ceremonial requirements. After the first contact with the enemy, a captured animal is ceremonially eaten by the general and his chiefs, who, to insure the success of the expedition, must then "jump over their wives"—the native euphemism or ceremonial substitute for sexual intercourse. Detachments are sent out to raid and pillage the country, but the Ganda do not hesitate to engage the main body of the enemy in a pitched battle. These engagements, directed by the general with drum signals, are often extremely sanguinary, for the war drums and fetishes of the gods, which always accompany the army, must be defended to the last man. Moreover, the rewards of bravery are great, and the penalty for cowardice is death or utter disgrace and confiscation of property. The spoils of a successful campaign are brought back to the capital and distributed—half to the king, his ministers, the Queen-Mother, and Queen-Sister, half to the brave warriors and distinguished leaders, and, of course, a thank offering to the war god. Every man who has killed an enemy wears a grass crown and receives public congratulations, rewards in women and cattle, and often promotion to a chiefship.

The Ganda enjoy wrestling, kicking bouts, and other games, but the national pastime is *mweso*, a game played on a board containing thirty-two holes with counters that are moved according to intricate mathematical calculations. They are also very fond of dancing to a musical accompaniment. The two sexes dance separately and execute various figures, including an exhausting shuffle dance and others characterized by erotic suggestions. The Ganda possess soft, clear, melodious voices of considerable range, and they sing, either as solos or in chorus, a variety of love songs, war chants, dirges, and epic narratives. The native musical instruments include drums, gourd rattles, reed flutes, horns, whistles, harps, and xylophones. The harp, which is played with the fingers, consists of an oval wooden sounding box covered with skin and a long curved arm to which eight strings of animal gut are attached by pegs which can be turned to tune the instrument. The xylophone, played by two performers with drumsticks, has from twelve to twenty slabs of hard resonant wood laid across two banana stems and separated by pegs. The dancing drums are long hollow cylinders of wood, open at one end and covered with a python skin at the other, carried under the arm, and struck with the fingers. The great ceremonial drums, of which the king has ninety-three and each chief, clan, and temple at least one, range from one to five feet in height; they are hollowed out of wood in the shape of a kettledrum, covered with skins, and ornamented with decorated thongs. Each has a fetish inside, and many receive animal or even human sacrifices when the skin is renewed. The king has an orchestra of forty or fifty musicians under a special conductor.

After Roscoe

FIG. 110. GANDA DRUMS.

A pregnant woman must not come into contact with a man or his belongings and for this reason is segregated, if possible, in a special house. She must eat no salt, meat from a goat's head, baked foods, sugar cane, or certain vegetables, and she must avoid sickly children, wild animals, and spots where suicides are buried. As her confinement approaches, she relaxes her labors in house and garden and is massaged with butter. In childbirth she kneels and grasps a banana tree in the courtyard or a post in the seclusion hut. One midwife supports her by the shoulders; another receives the child from behind. A difficult or abnormal delivery is considered proof of adultery. A midwife cuts the umbilical cord with a reed, cleans out the child's mouth with her finger, and blows up its nose to start respiration. The afterbirth, which is regarded as the stillborn twin of the live baby, is buried according to special clan rites among the banana trees, and the remainder of the umbilical cord is carefully preserved. The first-born child of a chief's wife, if a son, is strangled at birth, lest it grow up and kill or supplant its father. The birth of twins, though a cause for great rejoicing, involves the father in an incredibly elaborate series of taboos, feasts, exchanges of presents, and prescribed rites toward the god Mukasa, a ceremonial "little father," his wife, his father, and the king, one small part of which consists in going to war with a ball made from his hair and nail parings, killing an enemy, and cramming the ball into the mouth of his victim. Every third child of a woman belongs to her clan unless redeemed by the father or his clansmen. The mother remains in seclusion for nine days, when a series of purification rites are held, and continues to live apart from her husband, except amongst peasants, until the child is weaned.

A baby is bathed daily and is carried by its mother or nurse astride her hips or slung in a bark cloth on her back. It cannot play on the floor until three months of age, when its paternal grandmother places it there with certain special rites. It receives its name in an important ceremony, which establishes its legitimacy and clan membership. Several mothers with their unnamed children assemble at the house of the clan chief. The paternal grandmothers take the preserved umbilical cords of the children and place them in a waterproof basket containing beer, milk, and water. If they float, the children are legitimate, and the clan chief accepts them into the clan by baptizing them with the mixture, jumping over the feet of their mothers, and telling the children that he is their father. If an umbilical cord sinks, the child is disowned and its mother flogged. On the following day, the paternal grandfather of each child, or his representative, recites the names of the deceased ancestors of the clan. When the child laughs, it is given the name last mentioned, and the soul of the ancestor is considered to have entered into its body. It bears this name throughout its life. unless sickness gives cause for changing it, but a second name is used on all save the most critical occasions. After this ceremony the child's head is shaved for the first time, and the clippings are buried beside the afterbirth. As soon as it is weaned, at about two years of age, a child is sent away from home to be brought up in the family of a paternal uncle, elder brother, or other male clansman. It is taught strict obedience and respect for its elders and is subjected to strict discipline. A boy tends goats and runs errands. If he shows himself bright and alert, he may gain a place in the household of a chief, with many opportunities for advancement. A girl learns to cook and cultivate, to make mats and baskets, and otherwise to prepare herself for her life work. She is isolated during her first menstruation, and is fed and cared for by her female relatives. Her father and her foster father celebrate her recovery by jumping over their respective wives.

A girl marries at about fourteen years of age, a youth at sixteen if he has sufficient property. Although wives may be obtained by inheritance, by gift from a superior or a subordinate, or by capture from the enemy in wartime, the most usual and honorable mode of marriage is by purchase. The qualities most desired in a wife are industry, skill, and obedience. Having found a girl to his liking a youth proposes marriage to her elder brother and paternal uncle, who, rather than her parents, have the authority to arrange her marriage. If they agree, he brings them several gourds of beer and swears before witnesses to be a good husband. The girl is given an opportunity to cancel the match; she signifies her consent, and seals the engagement, if she serves the beer. The clansmen of the bride now fix the bride-price, which consists of 2,500 cowries and an amount in cows or goats, beer, and bark cloth commensurate with the means of the groom. In any case it is a large sum, which may require several months for a poor man to assemble. In the meantime the girl is anointed with butter to beautify her skin, is fed well to make her plump, and is visited by her future sister-in-law, who bathes her and examines her critically for any physical defect.

The wedding takes place as soon as the bride-price is paid. The bride, veiled in bark cloth and loaded with borrowed ornaments, is carried from her home after dark in a torch-light procession headed by her brother. Halfway to the house of the groom she is met by a similar procession headed by the groom's sister, who receives her with a promise of good treatment and escorts her to her new home. The relatives of the bride depart, leaving only one girl to attend her. Weeping and wearing an air of dejection, the bride refuses to enter the house until the groom comes out and pays her a few cowries. Inside, she refuses to sit down and later to eat until similarly bribed. Consummation of the union is deferred till the third night. On the following morning the groom sends to the bride's relatives a bark cloth with the tokens of her virginity—or else with a hole punctured in the center. For a month or more the bride remains veiled and secluded, under the care of her girl attendant. Then she and her husband, in the presence of four witnesses, swear to respect and be faithful to each other. If either is dissatisfied, he can annul the union at this time. The girl attendant now returns home with the bridal ornaments and is welcomed under the pretense that she is the bride herself. The young wife lays aside her veil, receives congratulatory visits, cooks her first meal for her husband and his guests, and demonstrates her agricultural skill by hoeing the garden of her mother-in-law. She then receives from her husband a plot of her own, a set of gardening and household implements, and perhaps a servant or slave to assist her. The young couple move into a house of their own—preferably under some chief at a considerable distance from the families of both.

Polygyny flourishes almost universally in Buganda. The king has many hundred wives, and even a petty chief has ten or more. A peasant bends every effort to secure at least one wife to support him by her agriculture and to bear him children to carry on his cult after his death. In view of the high bride-price and the natural desire of a woman's clansmen to obtain as large a sum as possible, peasants can often afford only one wife, although many possess two, three, or even more. Such extensive polygyny could not exist, of course, without a great preponderance of women. As a result of male infanticide in the families of chiefs, arbitrary executions of men, the slaughter of princes, the heavy male losses in war, the numerous sacrifices of men to the gods, and the enormous number of captured women, adult females exceed males in the population by a ratio of approximately three to one. If a man has more than one wife, he provides each with a house and garden of her own, and she visits his hut when invited and takes her turn in cooking for and serving him. The first wife takes precedence over the rest and has charge of the household fetishes. The second wife, who must always be selected from the clan of the husband's paternal grandmother, has the duty of shaving his head and trimming his nails.

In the regulation of sexual morality the Ganda display an almost Victorian prudishness. They never refer directly to sexual matters, but resort to circumlocutions. They are shocked at the nudity of the body, especially in males. They observe their exogamous regulations strictly and show a horror of incest. They set great store on chastity and punish adultery with ferocity. Between cross-cousins of opposite sex, and between a man and his mother-in-law, they interpose rigorous taboos of avoidance. The native morality, however, lies largely on the surface. A man with a large harem places his trust, not in the moral code, but in gatekeepers to watch his wives and in guards to escort them when they leave his compound. Despite the severe penalty for adultery—or perhaps because of it—intrigues are rife; circumvention of the guards becomes almost a game, the danger serving chiefly to add zest to the adventure. In the case of widows and the unmarried, unchastity is winked at unless it results in children, when it is severely punished. The sexual laxity prevalent among princesses extends also to the Queen-Sister and Queen-Mother. "Of these two women it is commonly said all Uganda is their husband."

A man can divorce his wife whenever he wishes. He does so chiefly for barrenness, which not only is a great misfortune in itself but also renders the wife a positive danger to the fruitfulness of the gardens. As a rule, however, he simply neglects her, so that she becomes a mere drudge and virtual slave. A wife cannot divorce her husband; she can only run away to her relatives. To get her back he must explain his conduct to the men of her clan, give them a goat and a pot of beer, and, if proved in the wrong, make his wife a present and promise to reform. If she runs away repeatedly, he usually lets her stay and demands the return of the bride-price from her clansmen, thereby leaving her free to marry again.

The Ganda attribute sickness and death in most cases, not to natural causes, but to hostile magic, the violation of taboos, or the malevolent act of a ghost. When a person falls ill, he summons a medicine man to diagnose the cause and prescribe the remedy. The medicine men (*basawo*), of whom each clan has several, receive a fee of nine cowries— nine being the sacred number—in advance and full payment only if and when the patient recovers. They either ascertain the cause by divination or send the patient to a temple for an oracle. One method of divination is to throw nine coffee beans, cowries, or strips of buffalo hide and observe how they fall. Another is to force a fowl to swallow some of the patient's saliva, then cut it open and count the number of spots on the entrails, or to make the sick man spit into a pot of water with dust floating on the surface and then count the number of masses into which the dust and saliva gather. An odd number is always a good omen, whereas an even number bodes ill.

Having learned the cause of the complaint, the medicine man may prescribe massage, sweat baths, cupping with a horn, blistering with a hot iron, or the internal or external use of various herbal remedies. The native practitioners are also adept at setting broken limbs in splints, and they have even been known to cure men partially disemboweled from spear wounds by washing the protruding intestines, forcing them gently back into the abdomen, and keeping them in place with a piece of a gourd. They make and sell a variety of amulets with power both to avert and to cure disease. If the illness is due to sorcery, the medicine man may resort to counter-magic. The Ganda practice exuvial magic with the hair, nail parings, and spittle of an enemy or with objects which he has touched. Magic in most cases involves the use of incantations invoking the aid of a friendly ghost or god. After such incantations the sorcerer may place a branch from a tree near the house of his enemy, who sickens and dies as the leaves wither, or he may scatter the boiled flesh of a corpse in his enemy's banana grove, so that any one who eats the fruit will perish. A medicine man sometimes employs magical means to transfer the disease to an animal, e.g., by rubbing the patient's body with herbs, tying these to the animal, and then slaughtering the beast or driving it into the wilderness. He may even transfer the affliction to a human victim by rubbing a clay effigy over his patient and burying it in the road, where it will infect the first passer-by.

If the illness is due to the anger of a neglected ghost, the medicine man may recommend that propitiatory offerings be made at its grave. If the malicious ghost of a paternal aunt is haunting the house, he may seek to capture it in a horn and then drown it in the nearest river. If a ghost, incited perhaps by hostile magic or angered at the violation of some taboo, has taken possession of the patient, manifesting itself possibly in delirium or fits, the medicine man may exorcise it by making the sick man inhale the smoke of certain herbs. Another exorcistic rite consists in splitting a banana tree in the garden and sprinkling it with the blood of a sacrificed animal; the patient is directed to crawl through the crack, divest himself of his garments, and run into the house without looking backward; the shaman runs in the opposite direction carrying the meat of the animal and the discarded clothing, which constitute his fee, and also the split tree, which he throws on waste land to be consumed by the next grass fire.

When remedies fail and the patient lies at the point of death, his friends and relatives fill the house. No one dares to absent himself without cause, lest he be suspected of sorcery or arouse the anger of the ghost-to-be. When death occurs, all leave the house save the widows, who wail frantically, beat their breasts, laud the deceased, and throw themselves in a frenzy on the corpse. "These same women may be found shortly after talking cheerfully with friends outside the hut." The chief wife of a deceased man, who has charge of his funeral ceremonies, closes the eyes of the corpse, crosses the arms over the chest, straightens the legs, ties the great toes together, washes the body, covers it with a bark cloth, and has it placed on a low platform of banana stems with a pot of butter and some sponges by its side. When the relatives are assembled, they file past the bier, and each in turn rubs a little butter on the forehead of the corpse and wipes his finger on a sponge. The eldest son then blows a few seeds over one of the childless widows, who immediately ceases to mourn and becomes his wife. The body, wrapped in bark cloth, is carried feet foremost to the clan burial ground, where it is deposited on a bed of bark cloth in a grave dug by the clansmen of the deceased. A grandson of the latter steps into the grave, cuts the cloth over the face of the corpse, and tosses the knife to one of the childless widows, who thereupon becomes his wife. A mound of earth, sometimes thatched, is raised over the grave, and a small shrine is erected at the head to receive offerings of beer, bark cloth, live animals, etc.

After the funeral the participants cleanse their hands with sponges but do not disperse. For from one to six months the widows and clansmen of the deceased live in houses near the grave segregated from the rest of the world and from each other. During this period they wear old clothes and girdles of withered banana leaves, let their nails and hair grow, and observe strict continence. The widows tend the grave. The clansmen visit it every morning to mourn vociferously for a few hours and then lounge about during the rest of the day. At the conclusion of the mourning period all the relatives assemble at the house of the deceased for a feast and dance. The central pillar of the hut is cut down to symbolize the departure of the mainstay of the family. The clan chief announces the chosen heir and presents him with the shield and spear of the deceased. A sister of the heir is brought forward and seated by his side as his titular consort. She inspects the estate and presides over the feast with him, but does not actually become his wife. Mourning now ceases, and the clansmen disperse to their homes. The childless widows become the wives of the heir, but those who have borne children to the deceased continue to live at the grave and to care for it and its animals and gardens until at least two years have passed and the ghost has become reincarnated.

A woman is buried near the residence of her husband, not on the lands of her clan unless she is unmarried. Her brother conducts the funeral, and a sister who is appointed as wife to the widower in her stead is the sole mourner. A similar but even simpler ceremony is held for a child. Peasants receive the same funeral as chiefs, albeit somewhat abbreviated. Slaves are buried without ceremonies but with some care, lest their ghosts prove troublesome. Only the king, his mother, and his sister-wife are embalmed. Princesses, who are officially treated as men during their lives, receive also a masculine burial.

In death the soul (*mwoyo*) leaves the body and becomes a

ghost (*muzimu*). It first makes a visit to Walumbe, the god of death, at the site of his temple, to render an account of its life, and then returns to its grave where it resides in the shrine. Ghosts are invisible; it is they who cause the winds. They suffer hunger, cold, and pain, as do the living, and they can even die a second death by fire or drowning. Although most of them are well disposed toward their descendants, they display their wrath at any neglect, and the ghost of a paternal aunt is uniformly malevolent. In times of sickness and trouble, offerings of beer, bark cloth, and female animals are made at the shrine. Animals as well as men have souls, and hunters, for example, always propitiate the ghost of a slain buffalo. Two years or more after the death of its mortal body, the ghost becomes reincarnated in the child who receives its name. Its worship then ceases, and its grave is left to decay.

The Ganda endow the objects of nature with spirits. They build shrines near wells for the resident water spirits. Before felling a tree or crossing a river they propitiate the divinities of the tree or stream. They regard certain hills with fear because of the spirits dwelling there, and a person fleeing thence from the wrath of the king is inviolable. But the supernatural beings who figure most prominently in the native religion, with the possible exception of the ghosts of the dead, are the gods. All the gods, according to traditional mythology at least, once lived as human beings; they are the deified ghosts of heroes. The deities fall into three classes: clan gods, former kings, and national gods. Each clan worships one deified ancestor, who is provided with a temple and priests, and who is besought for aid by the members of the clan alone. The deified ghosts of former kings receive a cult of full divinity, and are consulted especially by the reigning monarch. The national gods receive homage from king and people alike. It is they who uphold the throne and the state. The king supports their temples with generous contributions, but if their priests displease him he may plunder their estates—a sacrilege which no other person can commit with impunity.

Among the more prominent national gods are Katonda, the "father of the gods," who created the world and then left it to his descendants to run, and who therefore receives a cult of only very modest proportions; Gulu, god of heaven; Musisi, who resides in the center of the earth and causes earthquakes; Musoke, rainbow god and patron of fishermen; Kitaka, earth deity; Walumbe, the divinity of death; Kaumpuli, god of the plague, whom his priests keep imprisoned in a hole in the earth; Kibuka and Nende, powerful gods of war; Dungu, divinity of the chase; Nagawonyi, goddess of rain and growing crops, who receives the first-fruits of the harvest; and Nabuzana, patroness of child-bearing women, with midwives as her priestesses. Above all the rest of the gods, however, towers Mukasa, who has been called the Neptune of Buganda. As god of the lake, he provides fish and controls storms. As god of fertility, he sends twins, children to childless women, and increase of crops and herds. The king consults him at every crisis and deluges his temples with sacrifices.

Each god has one or more temples—large houses situated on the summits of hills and surrounded by cultivated estates. The more important deities usually have one main temple, accessible only to the king and high officials, and several smaller ones scattered throughout the country for the common people. The servitors of the temples do not include the medicine men, who form an independent class. In each temple resides a medium, a man or woman chosen for some exhibition of supernatural power, who mediates between god and man. He communicates a message or a request to the god, and smokes a sacred pipe and gazes steadily into the fire until the deity "seizes him by the head," when he becomes frenzied, foams at the mouth, and utters rapid incoherent phrases intelligible only to the priests. A temple has from one to four priests, whose offices are usually hereditary within particular clans. They live near the temple and keep it in order, receive petitioners and their sacrifices, refer them to the medium, and interpret to them the utterances of the latter. Their persons are sacred, and they enhance their prestige with the people by performing miracles, *e.g.*, licking a red-hot iron without injury. Instead of priests, some of the national gods are served by priestesses, who are frequently princesses of royal blood, and the temples of former kings, of course, are maintained by their widows or the successors appointed by the clans of the latter. In addition to the medium and the priests or priestesses, most temples have a corps of virgins, young girls devoted by parents whose prayers or vows for offspring have been answered. They keep the temple and its grounds in order, guard the fire, and watch lest visitors infringe the taboos. They must leave at puberty, for no menstruating woman may enter a temple.

Fetishes, *i.e.*, objects in which ghosts or gods are thought to reside, figure prominently in Ganda religion. A very common type consists of an animal horn which a powerful medicine man has filled with herbs, clay, and other "medicines," such as portions of the hearts of lions, buffaloes, and crocodiles. It is in fetishes of this type, for example, that the gods of war go forth into battle. Other fetishes are carved or modeled in human form or in disc, crescent, and innumerable other shapes from wood, herbs, roots, clay, etc. Many of them are worn as amulets. Each has a single virtue; it protects against a particular disease, against the wrath of the king, or against seizure as a sacrificial victim, or it insures fertility, success in hunting, or the like. When not in use, a man's amulets and fetishes are kept in a special shrine and receive daily offerings of beer from his chief wife. A royal ghost clings to his jawbone, while his umbilical cord is the fetish of his "twin," *i.e.*, the ghost of his afterbirth. One of the king's fetishes is a gourd in which the wind spirit is imprisoned. Another very important one is a phallic effigy of a snake fashioned out of rope and clay. Even a living animal can be a fetish. In the temple of the python god, for instance, a live python is kept. It has a special bed and a stool on which to rest its head, and it receives periodic offerings of fresh milk, fowls, and goats.

Every month, at the new moon, the Ganda observe seven days of rest and festivity, during which all agricultural labor ceases and only the necessary cooking is done. Priests expose their fetishes to the moonbeams, and the Keeper of the Royal Umbilical Cord takes the "twin" to the king for the monthly inspection. Once every fifty native years the war god Nende is displayed to the people in a great ceremony lasting nine days, and there are annual festivals at some of the temples. In general, however, the Ganda do not fit their worship into a ceremonial calendar; they offer prayers and sacrifices when the need or occasion arises. Whatever men value constitutes an acceptable offering to the gods: slaves, women, cattle, goats, fowls, cowries, beer, bark cloth, etc. The slaves and women become servants of the temples, and the animals, though sometimes slaughtered, more often roam the temple precincts alive. Men, and occasionally women, are also slain in spectacular human sacrifices to the ghosts of former kings, to the war gods and certain other deities, and even to wells and drums. To avert a calamity, such as a plague, a man with some physical defect is chosen as a scapegoat, sent to the border of the kingdom, and there maimed and left to die. In most cases, however, the victims are war captives, condemned criminals, persons who have incurred the wrath of the king, or men seized upon the highways by order of the gods. As a rule, several hundred are slaughtered at one time. The executions are held at special sacrificial places, of which there are thirteen in the kingdom. Special usages prevail at each place. At one, the prisoners are clubbed or beaten to death and their bodies abandoned to the beasts and birds of prey. At another, their arms and legs are broken and they are placed on the beach for crocodiles to devour. At a third, princes of royal blood are starved to death. There are also numerous special sacrifices. Thus, in a ceremony designed to prolong the life of the king, a chief of the Lungfish clan gives one of his own sons to be beaten to death by the royal bodyguard; from the skin of the victim a whip is made for the king, and from the muscles of his back, a pair of anklets. At a commemorative feast, the musicians, on departing, leave a drum behind; the first bystander to call attention to the seeming oversight is slain and his arm bones made into a pair of drumsticks.

The very existence of the kingdom of Buganda remained unknown to the outside world for centuries after the coast of Africa had been fully explored and exploited. Not until 1850 was the country seen by an alien—a Baluch soldier who had fled from Zanzibar to escape his creditors. The first Arab traders arrived in 1852. Ten years later came the first European, the explorer Speke, who reported to an incredulous world his strange experiences at the court of King Mutesa and his discovery of Lake Victoria and the source of the Nile. Speke's claims were not substantiated until 1875, when Stanley reached Buganda on his circumnavigation of Lake Victoria. In response to a famous letter by Stanley advocating the evangelization of the country, an English mission was founded in 1877 and a French mission two years later. For a decade following the death of King Mutesa in 1884 the country was racked by intrigues and civil wars between the Protestant, Catholic, and Moslem factions. Peace came only with the establishment of Uganda as a British protectorate in 1894. The completion of a railroad from the coast, in 1902, finally brought isolation to an end and made Buganda economically as well as politically a part of the western world. The natives have made great strides in education, and Stanley's dream of evangelization has been fully realized, but the sudden introduction of monogamy has brought with it a train of evils which even the missionaries now recognize and deplore.

BIBLIOGRAPHY

ANSORGE, W. J. *Under the African Sun.* New York, 1899.

ASHE, R. P. *Two Kings of Uganda.* London, 1889.

BASKERVILLE, G. K. "Die Waganda." *Rechtsverhältnisse von eingeborenen Völkern in Afrika und Ozeanien.* Edited by S. R. Steinmetz. Berlin, 1903.

CUNNINGHAM, J. F. *Uganda and Its Peoples.* London, 1905.

FELKIN, R. W. "Notes on the Waganda Tribe of Central Africa." *Proceedings of the Royal Society of Edinburgh,* Vol. XIII. Edinburgh, 1886.

HARTLAND, E. S. "On the Evidential Value of the Historical Traditions of the Baganda and Bushongo." *Folk-Lore,* Vol. XXV. London, 1914.

JOHNSTON, H. H. *The Uganda Protectorate.* Second edition. 2 vols. New York, 1904.

KOLLMANN, P. *The Victoria Nyanza.* Translated. London, 1899.

LUGARD, F. D. *Story of the Uganda Protectorate.* London, 1900.

*ROSCOE, J. *The Baganda.* London, 1911.

——. "Further Notes on the Manners and Customs of the Baganda." *Journal of the Anthropological Institute of Great Britain and Ireland,* Vol. XXXII. London, 1902.

——. "The Negro-Hamitic People of Uganda." *Scottish Geographical Magazine,* Vol. XXXIX. Edinburgh, 1923.

—— "Notes on the Manners and Customs of the Baganda." *Journal of the Anthropological Institute of Great Britain and Ireland,* Vol. XXXI. London, 1901.

——. *Twenty-Five Years in East Africa.* Cambridge, 1921.

——. "Worship of the Dead as Practiced by Some African Tribes." *Harvard African Studies,* Vol. I. Cambridge, 1917.

SPEKE, J. H. *Journal of the Discovery of the Source of the Nile.* Second edition. Edinburgh, 1864.

STANLEY, H. M. *Through the Dark Continent.* New York, 1879.

STUHLMANN, F. *Mit Emin Pascha ins Herz von Afrika.* Berlin, 1894.

WEISS, M. *Die Völkerstämme im Norden Deutsch-Ostafrikas.* Berlin, 1910.

WILSON, C. T., and FELKIN, R. W. *Uganda and the Egyptian Sudan.* 2 vols. London, 1882.

CHAPTER XVIII

THE DAHOMEANS OF WEST AFRICA

THE Guinea Coast of West Africa from Nigeria on the east to Senegal on the west, together with the adjacent hinterland, is the home of the true Negro. In the heart of this region, bisected by the second degree of east longitude, lies Dahomey, a once powerful Negro kingdom now incorporated in the much larger French colony of the same name. The Dahomeans inhabit a strip of territory approximately forty miles wide extending from the Atlantic Ocean on the south about 120 miles into the interior. Typical representatives of the Negro race, they possess dark brown skins, comparatively narrow heads (cephalic index 75), black kinky hair, prognathous faces, platyrrhine noses (nasal index c. 94), full everted lips, long arms, and a slender but sturdy physique. Their stature is reported as five feet four inches for men and five feet two inches for women, but these averages increase somewhat toward the interior. The women possess fine figures and are said to retain their youthful comeliness for a remarkably long time.

Dahomey, although it faces the sea, is singularly inaccessible. Approaching the coast from the south, one encounters first a strong ocean current which runs parallel to the shore from west to east. Besides rendering navigation hazardous, this current creates, in conjunction with the tides, a shifting reef of sand two or three hundred yards from the beach and barely covered by the surface of the water. Vessels must anchor outside the reef and communicate with the shore by means of flat-bottomed native boats manned by strong paddlers, who display amazing skill in passing through the tremendous surf which breaks over the reef. Hordes of lurking sharks reap their reward when a boat capsizes.

551

The shore itself does not belong to the mainland, but forms part of an uninhabited sandy bar, from a few yards to a mile or more in width, separated from the land by an almost continuous lagoon of very brackish water. The lagoon rarely exceeds five feet in depth and is usually much shallower. Normally it attains a breadth of one or two miles, but in periods of heavy precipitation it inundates large stretches of the low and monotonously flat coast of the mainland. A belt of marshy land, the great Lama Swamp, separates the broad coastal lowlands from the next zone, a level elevated plain or low plateau, which in turn gives way abruptly to a chain of low mountains and a tract of wild country inhabited by the semi-independent Mahi tribe. The Dahomeans occupy the intermediate zone or plateau, where their capital, Abomey, is situated.

The rivers, of which there are very few—the Weme on the east being the most important—constitute the sole exception to the rule that all geographical features in Dahomey run east and west. Away from the rivers there is no good drinking water; the people depend on muddy and often polluted wells. The vegetation is luxuriant, especially near the coast, where mangroves clothe the swamps and the shores of the lagoons. Coconut, oil, and fan palms thrive on somewhat higher land. The interior plateau is covered with grass interspersed with small groves of trees. Fish, crocodiles, and shellfish abound in the lagoons, and the land fauna includes the elephant and buffalo, many species of antelope, the leopard, hyena, and wildcat, the chimpanzee and several kinds of monkeys, the porcupine and numerous rodents, the kite, raven, vulture, and other birds, the python and many lesser snakes, the scorpion and tarantula, and vast numbers of mosquitoes, ants, termites, and other insects.

The climate is excessively hot, damp, enervating, and unhealthy. Dysentery, fevers, and other tropical diseases are pandemic. The country has been called "the white man's graveyard," since Europeans rarely survive more than three years of uninterrupted residence. Even horses and dogs imported from Europe commonly die within a few months. Despite the cooling effect of thunderstorms and the prevailing sea breezes, the temperature attains an annual mean of nearly 80° F., and the heat is aggravated by an excessive humidity. The year is divided into four seasons: the "great rains" from April to July, a short dry period during August and September, the "little rains" in October and November, and the long dry season from December to March. In January the prevailing winds from the sea yield to the "harmattan," a parched wind which drives down intermittently from the northeast laden with dust from the Sahara. So intensely dry is the harmattan that it reduces the temperature ten degrees through accelerated evaporation, shrivels foliage, causes the skin to chap and peel, disintegrates leather, and makes woodwork warp and crack with loud explosions.

In language, dialectic differences distinguish the Dahomeans proper, or Fon, from the people of the coastal zone. Both, however, speak languages of the Ewe group, closely akin to the dialects of Togoland on the west and more distantly related to the languages of the Gold Coast and of Nigeria. A system of very precise tonal distinctions is characteristic of Fon. Thus the word *to*, according to its pitch, may mean either "father," "mountain," "ear," or "lagoon." The language reveals a rather simple isolating type of structure, most of its words being ultimately derived from monosyllabic verbal roots consisting of a consonant and a vowel. Many adjectives, for example, are formed from verbs by reduplication. The Dahomeans use a quinary-vigesimal system of numeration, but for large numbers they often prefer terms derived from the cowrie system of currency. Forty shells are threaded on a string, and fifty strings make a *hoto* or "head" of cowries. Thus a native will usually say *hoto* instead of using the numeral for two thousand.

The history of Dahomey is inextricably associated with

that of the slave trade, which played so vital—and so often overlooked—a part in the colonial expansion of Europe. The first step in the process which eventually brought most of the world under European domination was taken by the Portuguese in 1415, when they captured Ceuta across the Strait of Gibraltar in Morocco. Under the inspired leadership of Prince Henry the Navigator, the Portuguese undertook to explore the unknown western coast of Africa. Their greatest discovery came, however, in 1441, when they brought back two natives from Rio de Oro; within five years they had taken to Portugal more than a thousand slaves. Successive expeditions advanced ever farther southward, and within a few years after the death of Prince Henry in 1460 the entire Guinea Coast had been explored. The discovery and settlement of America gave an immense impetus to the slave trade. Negroes were being imported into Haiti in considerable numbers within ten years of the first voyage of Columbus, and a cargo of slaves was landed at Jamestown the same year that the Pilgrims disembarked at Plymouth. That portion of the Guinea Coast which includes Dahomey was found the easiest in which to obtain slaves and thus received the name of the Slave Coast, which it still bears. The Portuguese were trading here in the sixteenth century, and other nations, attracted by the profits, soon followed them—especially the Dutch, the French, and the greatest slavers of all, the English. By the end of the following century all four of these nations had established forts or "factories" at Whydah on the Dahomean coast, making this port probably the leading slave mart in Africa. When one realizes that for every Negro landed in America approximately ten others perished either on shipboard or in slave raids at home, one begins to understand how significantly the slave trade must have influenced native history and institutions.

Early in the seventeenth century the Alladahonu dynasty, the founders and rulers of the kingdom of Dahomey, established a small state with its capital at Abomey. Two other little kingdoms, Ardrah and Whydah, blocked the path to the coast and absorbed most of the profits of the slave trade. King Agadja (1708–28) resolved to conquer them. He subdued Ardrah in 1724 and Whydah in 1727, thereby increasing his realm fourfold in size and gaining for himself a virtual monopoly of the European trade on the Slave Coast. Further territorial expansion and annual slave raids against the surrounding tribes characterized the succeeding reigns, until under King Gezo (1818–58) Dahomey reached the height of its power, with a population conservatively estimated at 250,000. Firearms, gunpowder, liquors, tobacco, cloth, and other European goods poured into the country in exchange for a steady stream of slaves. During the nineteenth century, however, the slave trade began to decline as the nations of Europe, led by Denmark, one by one prohibited it, and as the nations of America abolished slavery itself. Deprived thus of the lifeblood of its commerce and of the main support of its political and military institutions, Dahomey too suffered a decline, accelerated by three disastrous campaigns against the natives of Abeokuta. The French seized their opportunity, acquired rights on the coast by treaty, established a protectorate in 1882 over Porto Novo, a petty state previously tributary to Dahomey, and in 1890 fought an indecisive war with the latter. In 1892 the French definitely undertook to reduce Dahomey by force of arms. After a bitterly fought campaign they destroyed Abomey, captured and exiled King Behanzin, and annexed the entire kingdom.

The Dahomeans have hunted the elephant for its ivory until it has become extinct in their territory. They also pursue the buffalo, which roams in small herds on the grassy plains, taking great care to appease the soul of a slaughtered animal in a special ceremony. Firearms have largely superseded the spear and the bow with poisoned arrows as weapons of the chase. Game is sometimes driven into ambush by means of grass fires. Small antelopes, porcupines, and edible rodents are captured in snares and pitfalls. A hunter lies in wait to spear the manatee, an herbivorous aquatic mammal which visits the river banks at night to feed on the grass; a float attached by a long rope to the shaft of the barbed spear reveals the location of the animal in the morning, and it is secured from a boat. Once each year the king assembles his followers for an important communal hunt.

The towns on the lagoons support themselves primarily by fishing. The inhabitants dry the fish in the sun or preserve them by smoking over a fire, and they carry on a flourishing trade in sea products with the inland people. The native fishermen employ spears and dip nets in shallow water. On the lagoons they set long seines from boats and haul them ashore with the catch. Cylindrical basket traps with funnel-shaped openings and vegetable poisons which blind or stupefy the fish are also used. Europeans have introduced the hook and line.

Although far indeed from being a herding people, the Dahomeans possess a fair number and variety of domesticated animals. The native dogs vie with the protected vultures as scavengers of the villages. A few cattle are raised but no use is made of their milk. Near the coast cattle do not thrive but sheep and goats are fairly numerous. The native sheep are small and have hair rather than wool. In Dahomey, as one writer expresses it, the rôles of men and sheep are reversed, for the sheep have the hair and the men the wool. Pigs range freely in considerable numbers and are fed just enough to keep them in the neighborhood. Every yard has a clay shelter for poultry, which are exceedingly plentiful and furnish the Dahomeans with their principal meat food. In addition to ordinary fowls, which are scarcely larger than pigeons, the natives possess numbers of guinea fowl and a few pigeons, ducks, and turkeys.

Agriculture, however, forms the basis of the Dahomean

economy. Every man, whatever his occupation, has his fields, although he leaves their cultivation, except the clearing of new land, mainly to the women of the family. As a result of foreign trade the natives have adopted many alien food plants, especially of American origin. The staple food crops are maize, yams, and manioc, but the oil palm is also of great economic importance. Other cultivated plants include millet, Guinea corn, sweet potatoes, beans, onions, okra, peppers, gourds, peanuts, bananas, oranges, limes, guavas, cashews, and papaws. Pineapples, tomatoes, cotton, and coconut palms grow freely with little or no cultivation. Before the rainy season begins, the natives fire the stubble from the previous harvest and loosen the soil with an iron hoe lashed with thongs to a wooden handle. Climatic conditions enable them to reap two rich harvests each year. Since they use no fertilizers and do not rotate their crops, they must clear new land whenever their fields become exhausted.

The Dahomeans prepare the grains and vegetables upon which they mainly subsist according to a variety of recipes, of which the most universal is *akasan*—corn meal soaked in water until it begins to ferment, boiled to the consistency of porridge, allowed to harden until it resembles blanc mange, molded into balls the size of an orange, and wrapped in banana leaves. This native substitute for bread is rather sour but very nutritious. Another dish is the Creole *kalalu*, which consists of smoked fish cooked in palm oil and highly seasoned with peppers and other herbs. Fresh fish, fowls, and the flesh of wild and domesticated animals, including even monkeys, rodents, and lizards, are roasted, boiled, fried in palm oil, and made into savory stews and ragouts. When the fruit of the oil palm is crushed in troughs, mixed with water, and heated in vessels over a fire, there rises to the surface a reddish oil which constitutes not only an important export commodity but also, when further refined, an essential ingredient in most native dishes. The Dahomeans season their food with peppers and with an impure salt which they collect at low tide on the muddy shores of the lagoons, where it forms like hoar frost in consequence of rapid evaporation.

The cooking is done, except when it rains, in the open air in a corner of the court, where a pot is supported over the fire on three stones or balls of earth. Sometimes there is also a crude oven, consisting of an earthen vessel embedded on its side in sun-dried clay. The Dahomeans do not, however, prepare all their meals at home; they often buy their viands, cooked and ready to eat, at the markets. They take a light breakfast, snatch a little food during the day, and eat a hearty meal just before retiring for the night—to induce sleep, since a person who "lies awake and counts the rafters" will shortly die. Wives serve their husbands and do not eat until their masters have finished. A host tastes the food before serving his guests—as a demonstration that it is not poisoned. Mats are placed on the floor, and the diners sit in a circle around the bowls or gourds containing the food. Each person takes a ball of *akasan* in his right hand, breaks off a piece, dips it into the sauce, seizes a piece of meat, fish, or ragout between the morsel and his thumb, and swallows the whole. When the food is consumed, drinks are served—water, palm wine, maize or millet beer, or imported liquors. After the meal each person scrupulously washes his hands, rinses his mouth, and brushes his teeth with the frayed end of a small stick.

The Dahomeans rarely live in isolated homesteads. For the most part they dwell in villages consisting of houses scattered irregularly along narrow streets radiating from a central plaza or market place. The unit of residence is not the dwelling of an individual family but rather a compound or cluster of houses centering on a court and inclosed by a wattle fence or a mud wall. Here, in separate buildings, reside the several wives of the owner with their children, the married sons and younger brothers of the owner with their families, and the household slaves. In addition, the compound contains storehouses, pens or stalls for animals, a fetish hut, and sometimes a cookhouse or a bathhouse. The rectangular walls of the dwelling are made, sometimes of reddish mud smeared over wattle, more often of sun-dried mud alone, laid in four tiers or courses. A gabled roof of lashed poles and neatly trimmed thatch covers the house and

Courtesy of Melville J. Herskovits

Fig. 111. Houses within a Dahomean Compound.

protects the walls from disintegration during the rains. A single rectangular doorway admits light and air to the interior, which is often divided into several rooms. In front, the roof usually projects considerably beyond the wall and is supported by a row of wooden pillars, forming a pleasant veranda. Here, on a clay bench which runs along the wall on either side of the doorway, the master entertains his guests and the family spends its leisure time.

The most characteristic piece of Dahomean furniture is

the stool. Those of important men are handsomely carved from a single block of wood, often in the form of an animal. Women own tiny stools, only a few inches high, which they carry wherever they go. Sometimes a house contains a low bamboo bedstead or two, but most of the natives sleep on the floor on mats made from reeds. The household utensils include gourds, baskets, pots, a wooden mortar and pestle, and a stone mill or metate. Gourds are made in almost any desired shape and size—from small drinking cups and bowls to huge tubs or barrels—by binding the growing fruit. The native pots are so well made that when tapped they give forth a clear metallic ring. They are modeled by hand, polished with a smooth stone, incised with simple geometric designs, dried in the sun, wrapped in moist grass, and baked in a brush fire. Ordinary pots, such as those used for cooking, are red in color, but the large water jars and the small flat sauce dishes are often given a black finish by smearing them with a mixture of soot and palm oil and firing them a second time.

After Hajdukiewicz de Pomian
FIG. 112. A CARVED STOOL
FROM DAHOMEY.

Lamps, made by inserting a cotton wick in a shallow earthen dish containing oil, illuminate the houses at night.

The native smith smelts iron ore in a large clay crucible so placed in the center of a cylindrical earthen furnace that the flames from a wood fire, aided by a constant blast from the bellows, envelop its sides. An enormous expenditure of fuel and labor produces insignificant results, and iron is today largely imported from Europe. The equipment of a native forge comprises a stone anvil, a hafted iron hammer, a granite whetstone, a crude pair of tongs, and a bellows consisting of two earthen pots covered with skins which are worked up and down with sticks. With these implements and a charcoal fire the smith manufactures ax and hoe blades, knives, chisels, hammers, nails, chains, bells, ornaments, swords, daggers, arrowheads, and spear points. Some individuals display considerable skill and artistry in making ornaments and cult objects from imported copper and brass.

Although unacquainted with tanning, the Dahomeans prepare the skins of goats and other animals by drying them in

Courtesy of Melville J. Herskovits
FIG. 113. A DAHOMEAN SMITH IN FRONT OF HIS FORGE.

the sun and scraping, beating, and greasing the inner surface to render them pliable. The hair is usually not removed. The products include thongs, bags and pouches, quivers, cartridge boxes, knife and sword sheaths, drum skins, and strings for bows and musical instruments. From wild cotton, raffia, and other fibers the natives spin thread, make nets and cordage, and weave cloth. In spinning, the worker takes the fibers from a bundle at the end of a distaff and twists them into thread with his fingers, meanwhile rotating at his side a spindle weighted with a clay whorl. A simple loom is used in weaving. The warp threads run over a wooden cylinder and are weighted at the end with a stone. By means of a heddle, often operated by the toes, the alternate threads of the warp can be lowered so that the weft may be drawn through the shed on a shuttle and beaten into place. The resulting cloth is very narrow, often less than six inches in breadth. To make a garment or a hammock, therefore, it is necessary to sew many strips edge to edge. The labor involved is tremendous, and this fact has favored the importation of European fabrics.

Children in Dahomey usually go naked. Adults of both sexes wear a narrow loin cloth passed between the legs and tucked in front and in back through a waist-string or a zone of beads. They also wrap a cloth around the hips, forming a sort of kilt which extends from waist to calf. This completes the everyday costume. On special occasions or as a protection against cold the men don a knee-length mantle draped over the shoulders like a Roman toga, and the women wear a similar garment drawn over the breasts and under the arms. The feet are unclad. On the head men of rank commonly wear a skull cap and women a bright-colored cloth. Both sexes wear rings, armlets, and anklets of metal and necklaces and girdles of beads. They practice scarification and assume peculiar styles of coiffure in connection with the religious cults. The natives are cleanly in their personal habits. They make soap from palm oil boiled with banana ashes, and bathe once a day when water is available. After the bath, women rub the body with unguents to make the skin glisten.

For navigating the rivers and lagoons the Dahomeans employ crude dugout canoes hewn from a single log by fire and ax, but the boats which brave the surf in transporting goods and slaves between Whydah and the European ships are manned by more skillful boatmen from the Gold Coast. The towns and villages are connected either by roads or by meandering paths. All travel and transportation by land are done on foot, the domestic animals being used only for food. The king maintains a regular courier service between Abomey and Whydah, with runners stationed at post houses in all intermediate towns. Travelers must carry the carved wooden staff of a chief as a passport or they will be stopped at a post house and severely punished. Porters transport all burdens on their heads. For loads heavier than sixty or seventy pounds they use a sledge-shaped carrying frame, which they steady with one hand while they support themselves with a staff in the other. Distinguished persons are carried in hammocks slung from a long pole which is balanced

After Hajdukiewicz de Pomian
FIG. 114. DAHOMEAN CARRYING FRAME.

at either end on the head of a porter. An awning fastened to the pole wards off the rays of the sun. With four or six bearers working in relays and maintaining a steady trot, it is possible to travel thus at a rate of four or five miles an hour.

Trade in Dahomey, except for the export of slaves and palm oil in exchange for European goods, takes place largely in markets, of which there is at least one in every village. In each market, police preserve order and a presiding official exacts a toll from vendors. Cross streets divide the larger markets into sections, each devoted to a special class of wares. The commodities sold include water, palm oil, amulets, imported goods, raw and cooked provisions of all kinds, and the products of all the native handicrafts. They are displayed in low thatched booths raised on clay platforms a foot above the paths, which are flooded during the rains. Purchases are effected either through barter or by means of the cowrie currency. Haggling is universal, and the women, who carry on almost all the native trade, convert a market into a perfect bedlam with their yells, oaths, and curses.

The vendors of similar products often organize into voluntary associations to regulate the price of their wares. Specialized artisans, notably male smiths and weavers and female potters, are organized into hereditary guilds. Non-secret societies for mutual aid, with an insurance character, offer their members protection against sudden burdensome demands on their financial resources, *e.g.*, the expenses of a funeral. Coöperation plays a dominant rôle in Dahomean economic life. It finds its major expression, perhaps, in the *dokpwe*, an organization of all the men of a local community. Over the *dokpwe* is a chief, who, unlike most other officials, inherits his position instead of being appointed by the king. If a man who has a field to clear falls ill, the *dokpwe* is summoned by its chief and performs the task without charge. A man with an important obligation toward his father-in-law to fulfill can secure the assistance of the *dokpwe* by entertaining the members on the day appointed for the work and by paying a small fee to the chief. These communal activities assume the form of recreation rather than of labor, for they are made the occasion for music, dancing, feasting, gaiety, and competitive tests of speed and skill.

The fundamental unit of Dahomean society is the totemic clan (*henu*), of which there are approximately forty. Its members trace their descent from a traditional common ancestor or founder, the *tohwiyo*, who is worshiped as the god of the clan and is usually represented in mythology as the son of a human parent and a supernatural totem animal or plant, from which the clan derives its name. The food taboos of the clan embrace the totem and objects associated with it. Thus the members of the Leopard clan, which includes the royal family, are forbidden to eat the flesh of the leopard or, by extension, of any other spotted animal. Descent in the clan, with a few exceptions, follows the paternal line.

Each clan has a chief, who is always its eldest living male member irrespective of ability, family, wealth, or reputation. Under no circumstances can he be deposed, although if he is completely senile the second in age may act in his name. The chief is, as it were, the high priest of the clan. Through him the ancestors continue to control the clan affairs. Since he can summon their spirits to enforce his decrees, his authority is tremendous, even though he does not possess the power of life and death, which is reserved to the king. He holds in trust the communal property of the clan—in agricultural lands and palm groves—and enjoys their usufruct although he may not alienate them. He can levy drafts of labor to till these common lands as well as to repair his dwelling and maintain the ancestral tombs. He must be consulted by the parents in all marriages, and the customary wedding gifts pass through his hands. His subordinates approach him only with uncovered head and bare torso, and they kneel before him touching their foreheads to the dust. Wherever he goes, he is followed by a large retinue and receives tokens of homage and respect. The oldest living women of the clan enjoy a similar prestige. No one dares offend them because of their intimate relationship with the dead and their power to influence them.

Those members of a clan who inhabit a particular village or local community constitute a sub-clan, a group with minor legal and ceremonial functions. A more important social unit—the primary one in native economic life—is the household, the group of families inhabiting a compound. The head of the household owns the cluster of dwellings in which his wives, his children, and the families of his married sons and younger brothers reside, as well as the fields they till, the animals they tend, the implements they use, and the slaves who assist them, and he exercises a patriarchal authority over the entire group. He bears the name of the original founder of the group and governs the household and administers its property as his representative. Every man who accumulates property, erects a dwelling, and establishes a new household within the clan has accomplished a work which should stand forever in his memory. Hence the primary obligation of every successor is to perpetuate intact the property, name, and household of the ancestral founder.

The head of a household is normally succeeded by his first-born son from a regularly contracted marriage. If the eldest son lacks character or intelligence, or if an oracle shows his fate to be unfavorable, he may be passed over in favor of a younger son. The household head, however, must announce such a disinheritance during his lifetime, if not publicly to his relatives then at least privately to his best friend. If the heir is too young to take possession, the property and widows of the deceased are held in trust for him by an older male relative until he comes of age. In default of eligible sons, a younger brother inherits, and if there are no surviving brothers, then a nephew, a brother's son. If a man dies without male heirs, his eldest sister— it is alleged—receives his property in trust and transmits it, with his name, to one of her own sons. In similar fashion a daughter may carry on the line. If there are no eligible near relatives of either sex, the clan elders assemble and select a suitable person to administer the property and perpetuate the name. Not infrequently, of course, the heir is already the head of an independent household, with a name which he must transmit to posterity. He is not permitted to merge the two estates. He holds the second one in trust, enjoying its usufruct, and the first son borne to him by a widow inherited from the deceased is regarded as the son of the latter, assumes his name, and on his maturity takes over the house and property.

A unique feature of Dahomean social organization is the institutionalization of friendship. Every man and woman, in addition to his ordinary or informal friends, must have a recognized "best friend" of his own sex, and usually has also a second-best friend and a third friend. In his best friend, chosen at about the age of puberty, a Dahomean reposes absolute confidence, recounting to him all his thoughts and actions, his problems and his secrets, even his crimes and moral lapses. If a man and a woman plan a *liaison* or an elopement, their best friends aid and shelter them. When a man commits a crime and flees from justice, his best friend is seized and tortured—not in any expectation of extracting information, but simply because the fugitive, on discovering that his friend is imprisoned, will out of loyalty surrender himself voluntarily. When a man dies, his best friend goes to his home to announce the son chosen by the deceased to be his heir—a choice sometimes unknown to the immediate family or even contrary to their expectation. During the funeral ceremonies the best friend has functions of the utmost importance to perform. So imperative is it to have a best friend that when this person dies the second-best friend steps into his position, the third friend becomes the second, and a new third friend is selected.

Slavery * has existed in Dahomey from time immemorial. The owner of a slave has the right to sell him, hire him out for wages, or pledge him as security for a debt. He may flog him for disobedience, but under no circumstances has he the right to inflict the death penalty. Slaves own no property; the fruits of their labor in the house and in the fields belong to their masters. The status is not hereditary, for the law provides that no one born on Dahomean soil may be made a slave. The child of a slave, to be sure, belongs to the master—not, however, as a chattel, but as a member of his family and clan. If a man has no near relatives, he may

---

* Slavery, like human sacrifice and all other customs associated directly with the monarchy, disappeared with incoming French control. In most other respects, however, Dahomean culture still survives essentially as herein described.

even adopt a male slave or the son of a slave as his heir. The European slave trade has given a tremendous impetus to slavery, and grafted certain harsher features upon the more moderate native institution. The opportunities for profit have led the kings, for example, to sell disloyal subjects into slavery and to engage in an annual war or raid for slaves.

The children of the king's own slaves, and of those given by him to his wives, relatives, and officials, are not completely emancipated but constitute a special class of serfs and hereditary servants. Some are assigned to the estates associated with official and honorary positions. They and their descendants are bound to the land, which they are compelled to cultivate, but they retain part of the fruits of their labor and are free to marry and to acquire and own property. Another group consists of young girls assigned to the wives and female relatives of the king as domestic servants. They are given in marriage by their mistresses, who retain their daughters for similar services but allow their sons to remain with their fathers as fully privileged freemen.

The commoners or freemen constitute the great bulk of the population. Those among them who gain the confidence of the king, through services, ability, or intrigue, receive appointments as state officials or are elevated to the rank of "caboceers" with accompanying grants of land, slaves, titles, and insignia. Unlike the official positions, which are rarely hereditary, the rank and property of caboceers descend by primogeniture from father to son or, in the case of women, from mother to daughter. A caboceer owes partial allegiance to his clan chief, but unlike the latter he can be deposed for a civil or religious transgression.

Above the commoners stands a princely class, consisting of the direct descendants of all the kings who have ruled over Dahomey. As a result of extensive royal polygyny, as well as of the fact that princely status descends through daughters as well as through sons, this class is very numerous, constituting approximately one-tenth of the total population. Commoners, even those holding the highest public offices, accord to members of the princely class at least the outward tokens of extreme respect and deference. Princes disdain manual labor, which they leave wherever possible to their slaves. Princesses, too, lead loose and idle lives and are happiest when making a display of their wealth at public festivals. The king rarely appoints a prince to a position of civil authority, for to do so would invite intrigue and revolt. With common men in high positions, however, he is assured of the gratitude and loyalty of their clans, and he knows that in case of revolt, pride of family will keep the princes from flocking to a commoner's banner. He keeps his relatives at Abomey in a state of "gilded domesticity," lulled by gifts of wives, slaves, and estates and by empty titles which carry with them honor but no power.

The Dahomean king is an absolute monarch. In theory he owns all the land, the people themselves, and their possessions. When he legislates, levies troops and taxes, dispossesses or moves a family, or issues orders, he is acting as master, not as the holder of a metaphysical sovereignty. Only prudence and self-interest limit his actions. The power of the monarchy makes itself felt in every aspect of social life. The king fortifies his prestige with a resplendent court, a retinue of armed guards, a series of special prerogatives, and an elaborate ceremonial. No one may watch him eat or drink, or be seated in his presence. Whoever approaches him must salute by prostrating himself, rubbing forehead, cheeks, and lips on the earth, clapping his hands thrice, making three peculiar fillips with the little finger, and finally throwing handfuls of dust over his head and shoulders.

The monarch lives in a walled palace in the center of Abomey. The buildings, which are of typical native construction, cover an area of nearly a hundred acres. Each king adds to the residence of his predecessors, who are buried in the palace grounds. The population of the palace—

over 8,000—is almost exclusively feminine, and includes the wives of the king, the "Amazons," representatives of the mothers of deceased monarchs, and the female slaves and servants of all these women. The royal wives fall into two classes: the ordinary wives, who prepare and serve the king's meals, and the "leopard wives," only about forty in number, who enjoy certain special privileges and have nothing to do save attend their master. In a sense the kingship is dual. The monarch rules Abomey as king; he governs the rest of the country from a palace outside the capital as "king of the bush." This mythical bush king has his own wives, guards, and officials. In theory it is he who engages in commerce, selling slaves and palm oil, while the king, with hands unsullied by trade, merely buys, spends, and distributes largess.

The throne is hereditary in the male line, by a qualified primogeniture. The successor must be a son by a wife of common origin, for the laxity of conduct among princesses, even when they are royal wives, is such as to cast doubt on the legitimacy of their children. Moreover, the heir must be the son of one of the wives given to the king as a prince by his father, other marriages being, as it were, morganatic. The eldest son of such a marriage normally succeeds to the throne, unless he bears a dishonored name, or is discovered through divination to be ill-fated, or is judged by the king to be lacking in character or ability. Having chosen his heir, the monarch presents him to his family and to the high officials, confides to him certain secret traditions, provides him with a palace, lands, wives, and slaves, and authorizes him to receive certain royal honors. At a coronation ceremony three days after the death of the king, the new monarch appears before the assembled people and announces the name by which he is to be known, and thereafter he assumes new honorific names to commemorate victories and other important events.

At the head of the administrative system stand two great

ministers. The first of these is the *Mingan* or Royal Executioner, who takes his station at the right hand of the king and, though a commoner, marries the eldest daughter of his sovereign. His original functions, the execution of criminals and the judicial and religious duties associated therewith, have expanded with time until he has become virtually a prime minister. His official residence contains the tombs of his predecessors, a charnel house with the skulls of all his victims, and a prison from which he derives a considerable revenue. He instals all local chiefs in office and has jurisdiction over them. He is the king's chief adviser and acts as regent during the three days between the death of the ruler and the coronation of his successor. The second outstanding official is the *Mehu* or Family Minister, who stands at the left of the king and marries his second daughter. He bears the same relation to the princely class that the Royal Executioner bears to the commoners of the kingdom. Though a commoner himself, he has charge of the princes and princesses from birth until death, choosing their names, arranging their marriages, supervising their funerals, judging their crimes, and, when necessary, secretly imprisoning or executing them. He is also master of all public ceremonies and has general surveillance over the conquered provinces.

The other important officials include: the *Yevogan* or viceroy of Whydah and the coastal region, a sort of foreign minister who has charge of all relations with Europeans; the *Adjaho* or chief gatekeeper, who has supervision over the officials and inmates of the royal palace and heads the secret police and espionage system; the *Gau* or commander-in-chief of the army; the *Posu* or second ranking general; the *Tokpo* or minister of the interior, who, with a corps of assistants, supervises markets, agricultural operations, the collection of taxes, and the surveying of land grants; the *Sogan* or overseer of the king's slaves; the *Tononun* or chief eunuch, who has charge of the king's personal attendants and his harem, and who is killed at the death of his master; and the *Benazon* or royal treasurer, who keeps and guards the king's cowries, cloth, war munitions, and other stores.

Each of the ministers and high officials has a lieutenant or assistant, a man of princely rank who has no real authority and no function save perhaps to watch the conduct of his principal. These honorary posts, unlike the others, are often hereditary. For each male official of state there is also a corresponding female functionary within the royal palace. A female official is called the "mother" of her male counterpart and takes precedence over him at court. This parallelism is carried so far that the *Tononun* or chief eunuch is even matched by a *Yavedo* or "chief eunuchess."

For administrative purposes the kingdom is divided into some twelve districts, each under a chief with fiscal and magisterial functions. A district, in turn, comprises a number of villages, and each of these has its chief with similar but lesser powers. Every chief and official possesses, as insignia of his rank and authority, a staff of office, a carved wooden stool of appropriate height, a pipe with a wooden case and a goatskin tobacco pouch, and an umbrella with emblazoned devices indicative of his rank and his military exploits. Secret agents circulate through the country, spying upon all officials and upon each other. The innumerable petty functionaries include village war captains, royal attendants, palace guards, town police, and court musicians, bards, and jesters.

To facilitate the levying of taxes and troops, the king orders an annual census and keeps full statistics of the population in a special building at the palace. Every year, just before the annual mobilization of the army, the head of each sub-clan gives his village chief a small sack containing a pebble for each male in his group over thirteen years of age. The village chief forwards these sacks through his district chief and the Royal Executioner to the king, who thus acquires an exact record of all adult males in his kingdom. To enumerate the women, each warrior is asked the number of his wives and his unmarried daughters over thirteen years of age, on the pretext that they will be recompensed if he dies in battle, and the heads of the sub-clans forward pebbles for the wives and daughters of men remaining at home. Births and deaths are reported several times a year, and special officials are charged with enumerating slaves, war

FIG. 115. A DAHOMEAN CHIEF AND THREE OF HIS WIVES.
Courtesy of Melville J. Herskovits, the International Institute of African Languages and Cultures, and the Oxford University Press

captives, and deaths in battle. The census archives contain fifteen boxes of pebbles—one for adult males, one for adult females, and one for the children of each age-group up to thirteen years, with separate compartments for the sexes. Each annual tabulation is made a matter of permanent record by keeping a sack of pebbles for all adult men, a second for women, a third for boys, a fourth for girls, and others showing the number of deaths and war captives. Thus the king always knows whether the population is increasing or declining, and can govern his actions accordingly.

The various officials and minor functionaries derive their principal support from the land grants, slaves, and presents which they receive from the king. The large revenues required by the monarch to maintain a reputation for conspicuous generosity, and to keep up his domestic and military establishments, are obtained from various sources. A percentage is assessed on all the palm oil produced, and vendors at the markets pay a sales tax on all transactions. Collectors stationed at post houses and at the entrance to every village impose fixed tolls on all transported goods save wood and water. The king is in theory the heir of his subjects, and as such he levies certain inheritance dues. The entire property of persons convicted of serious crimes reverts to the king, who, it is said, does not hesitate to trump up charges against a man careless enough to boast of his wealth. War, however, is the most productive source of revenue. A successful campaign fills the royal treasury with plunder and yields slaves which the king can distribute as gifts, sell to the European traders, or place in detention camps to raise food for the palace and palm oil for export.

The laws of Dahomey consist partly of ancient customs, partly of decrees promulgated by the king, after consultation with his ministers, at a general assembly of chiefs and people. Private vengeance is rigidly repressed. The local chiefs have jurisdiction over all civil cases and minor criminal offenses. Since gifts to a judge are considered entirely natural and proper, bribery not infrequently influences the decision of the court. If the accused pleads not guilty, he is often subjected to an ordeal, *e.g.*, drinking poison, licking a red-hot iron, pulling a seed out of boiling oil with his fingers, or washing his body with water containing crushed cowrie shells— an act supposed to make the skin of a guilty man break out with sores. If the accused comes unscathed through the ordeal, he is innocent. Appeal can be taken from an unfavorable judgment to the king's court, to which all serious offenses are referred in the first instance. The king, sitting between his two great ministers in a public gathering before the palace gate, accuses the prisoner and sums up the evidence. If the criminal confesses, he is sentenced at once. Otherwise he furnishes a cock for a special ordeal. A priest, after suitable invocations, opens the beak of the cock and forces it to swallow a preparation of pulverized bark and water. The death of the cock proves the guilt of the accused.

For theft, the usual punishment is a flogging or fine and the restitution of the stolen goods. For adultery, which includes illicit relations with a betrothed girl, the man is imprisoned, while the woman receives only corporal punishment. Adultery with a wife of the king, however, involves the death penalty, unless the woman is of princely rank. Murder and other serious crimes are also punished by death. Motive is ignored; accidental homicide is classed as murder. Prisoners condemned to death are usually decapitated by the Royal Executioner at an imposing annual ceremony. A person of wealth or high rank can often escape the death penalty by paying compensation to the family of his victim. A few of the highest officials have prisons. In that of the Family Minister, for example, only princes are incarcerated. Life sentences are served at a remote detention camp, where the prisoners cultivate the king's lands. When a chief commits a serious crime, his house is destroyed, his property confiscated, and his family deprived of their liberty and their clan rights. His sons are enrolled in the army, and his wives and daughters are sold in marriage to the highest bidder.

All able-bodied men must take arms under their local military chiefs when war is declared. Poorly equipped and inadequately trained for the most part, they constitute only an auxiliary force. The real military strength of Dahomey resides in its standing army, which is organized into a right wing, a center, and a left wing. The two wings, commanded respectively by the *Gau* and the *Posu*, are composed largely of the palace guards, the court attendants, the sons of chiefs, and certain classes of criminals. These men are organized into regiments, each with its officers and distinctive uniform. But the shock troops of the army, the best disciplined and most redoubtable warriors, are those of the center, a body composed of about 2,500 female soldiers—the far-famed Dahomean "Amazons."

From among the marriageable girls of his dominion, the king selects a certain proportion to grace his harem, and from the rest two special officials choose the most promising as soldiers. The Amazons are officially called "wives" of the king, and they live in a special quarter of the palace, but they do not actually form a part of the harem. Like the other palace women, however, they are strictly segregated from all contact with men, even at public ceremonies. They go armed at all times and accompany the king's wives or their slaves whenever these women leave the palace grounds. All men who encounter a contingent of the king's women on the road, scamper into the bushes or out of sight as though for their lives. Not all Amazons are virgins; married women convicted of crime are often inducted into the corps in lieu of other punishment. Amazon officials, corresponding, as we have seen, to all the male administrative offices of state, govern the female population of the palace. From the point of view of their arms, the Amazons are divided into five branches: the musketeers or main body; the blunderbuss women or veterans, called upon only in emergencies; the elephant huntresses, the most daring warriors of all and equally renowned for their exploits in the chase; the razor women, a small group armed with huge razor-shaped knives specially designed for decapitating enemy chiefs; and the archeresses, a body of young girls prominent only in parades. These various elements are distributed among the three battalions into which the Amazon corps is divided. Each unit has its own uniform, headdress, and officers. The Amazons keep their persons neat and their weapons in good order. They execute rigorous practice maneuvers such as charging through hedges of thorns which cruelly lacerate their bodies. In battle they display a fearlessness, determination, and ferocity, the like of which their French conquerors admit having encountered nowhere else in Africa.

The Dahomeans engage in a war or glorified slave raid once a year, toward the end of the long dry season. Mobilization takes place in connection with tax gathering, the census, and the assembling of the populace for the Annual Custom, a series of spectacular religious and patriotic ceremonies. The warriors provide their own food and equipment, but the king furnishes their weapons—especially firearms, which have largely replaced the earlier bow, spear, and battle-ax. A few scouts, who have previously explored the enemy country in the guise of merchants, lead the way. They follow the regular paths in disguise and seize all stragglers whom they encounter. The troops, however, avoid the roads and villages, cutting their way through the brush. They preserve absolute silence and build no campfires, for everything depends upon the element of surprise. They invest an enemy village under cover of night and advance with a furious rush before dawn. No one escapes. All who resist are killed, as well as those who are useless as slaves. The rest are taken captive. Cattle and all movable property are carried off and the village is burned, unless it seems possible to incorporate the region into the kingdom. The king distributes some of the captives to his followers as slaves, places others in detention camps to till his fields, and sells the rest to the European traders. The conquered chiefs, however, he reserves for human sacrifice, and keeps their cleaned and polished skulls as trophies. At important ceremonies these skulls are borne by slaves in processions or even used by the king as drinking cups.

The Dahomeans display considerable talent in the fine arts. Their wood carving, especially their staffs, stools, and statuettes, strikes a responsive chord in modern artists.

The clay walls of the royal palace are adorned with sculptured bas-reliefs. The native musical instruments include horns, tongueless bells fixed to handles and struck with an iron rod, large drums hollowed from a log and covered with

a goatskin, smaller gourd drums of hour-glass shape yielding different notes as the thongs at the waist are pressed or relaxed, and gourd rattles containing shells or pebbles and covered with a netting to which snake vertebræ are attached. Vocal music is much superior to instrumental. The people are passionately fond of dancing, which

FIG. 116. DAHOMEAN BAS-RELIEF REPRESENTING A EUROPEAN SHIP.

is accompanied either by singing or by an orchestra. Adults amuse their children with animal fables and entertain one another with more sophisticated tales and historical narrations. The exceedingly numerous and popular native proverbs often suggest our own, *e.g.:* "One tree does not make a forest"; "Clothes are men"; "No one chases two birds"; "Distant firewood is good firewood."

A pregnant woman avoids certain foods and acts on the advice of a diviner, wears around her body cords decorated with cowries and amulets, and refrains from intercourse with her husband. Prayers and sacrifices are offered for a safe delivery. When labor approaches, all males leave the house, and the expectant mother, who until now has gone about her household duties as usual, kneels on the floor attended by an old woman. The newborn child is placed on a mat near the fire where it lies until the afterbirth has been suitably buried and the mother has performed her toilet. Then the midwife bathes it and smears its navel with a mixture of palm oil and ashes. When the umbilical cord drops off, it is buried at the foot of a palm tree, which the child protects and respects throughout his life. Abnormal infants are often drowned at birth, but twins are welcomed and their arrival is celebrated with a special ceremony. For three months the mother pays particular attention to personal hygiene, bathes only in warm water, and receives from her husband a plentiful supply of soap, fuel, and food. She carries the child in a cloth on her back until it is able to walk. Throughout the period of lactation, which lasts two years or longer, she abstains from sexual relations.

A child receives a temporary name from some phenomenon associated with the circumstances or date of his birth. When he is three months of age, his parents summon a diviner who determines his "spirit father," *i.e.*, the ancestral ghost who will act toward him throughout life as his guardian spirit. He bears henceforth the name of this ancestor, unless he comes to be known by a nickname or an honorary or official title. Girls are scarified at seven or eight years of age. A boy shortly before his twentieth year is circumcised in company with a group of youths of his own age. The specialist who performs the latter operation keeps the youths in his own house until they have recovered, when he shaves their heads and sends them home. Circumcision not infrequently results in infection or even death, and to it is attributed every fault committed within the next three years. When a girl reaches puberty she is isolated from the opposite sex for five or seven days and receives visits and presents from her female relatives and friends. When she emerges from her chamber, her father gives her a white mantle and a new mat and sends her to the market on a ceremonial errand. After puberty, girls no longer play freely with boys of their own age. They form into groups to receive specific instruction in sexual matters from an older woman. The boys acquire their knowledge informally from girls or married women with whom they begin to have casual affairs at the age of sixteen or seventeen.

The initiative in marriage usually comes from the side of the girl, *i.e.*, from her father, who consults with the members of his household, his clan chief, and a diviner before arranging a match for her. There are two primary types of marriage, each with several variants. Clan exogamy prevails in both cases, but in one the children come under the authority of the father, in the other not. In the first type, the prospective groom makes a preliminary present of cowries, cloth, and grain to the father of his bride-to-be. This seals the betrothal, and is frequently arranged during the infancy of the principals. It obligates the man to participate in the funeral rites following the death of any near relative of the girl, and to perform each year some major task, such as roofing a house or clearing a field, for his future father-in-law as long as the latter lives. The girl, when of age, may repudiate the match, in which case her *fiancé* is reimbursed for all his expenses in money and services. Otherwise he makes a second present to her father, a sort of bride-price which includes as its essential element the precise sum in cowries that was paid to the midwife who brought her into the world. This signifies that the bride has belonged to the groom's family, as it were, from birth. At the same time the groom makes a third present, consisting of goats, fowls, palm oil, vegetables, and liquor which are sacrificed to the bride's clan ancestors. As a result of this series of transactions the bride goes to live with her husband and submits to his authority, while her children, even though born out of wedlock, belong to his household and clan. A variant of this type of marriage is common in the poorer rural districts. Two families effect a simple exchange of girls. In this way the respective gifts and obligations cancel one another, and both sides escape an onerous burden.

Marriages of the second type do not transfer paternal power over the children to the father and his clan. When a household is depleted in numbers, its head allows one or more of his daughters to arrange such a union. The repayment of the midwife's fee is significantly omitted from the ceremonies, and a gift of a cloth substituted. The woman remains at her own home, where her husband visits her from time to time. The children belong to her, although it is customary to release a few of them to the father. The marriages of princesses, though they involve more elaborate ceremonies, necessarily fall into this category, for otherwise the children might lose their princely status. Another variant is the so-called "free union," where a man and a woman simply agree to live together without bride-price or other obligations. Either can dissolve the union at any time, but the wife always keeps the children. Women of the hereditary servile class are given in marriage by their mistresses to poor men in return for a few unimportant presents. Their daughters inherit their mothers' status as domestic servants, although sons are usually permitted to remain with their fathers.

In marriages of either type the husband gives his wife a new name and by this act publicly ratifies the union. The wedding ceremony varies in detail with the mode of marriage, but the form associated with the first type of union may be regarded as typical. On the appointed day the groom sends a messenger in the early morning to ask for his bride. Her parents affect reluctance, and wait until a second and a third messenger arrive, the latter at sunset. Then an escort of friends and relatives conducts the bride to her future home, where, after an exchange of courtesies, the two families sit down to a banquet. Feasting and drinking continue until midnight, when the groom retires to the nuptial chamber. An older matron brings the bride to him, joins their hands, and retires. Virginity is expected in a bride who has been betrothed since girlhood. If the young wife is found wanting in this respect, her whole family is put to shame and may even be required to return the bride-price and compensate the groom for all the expenses he has incurred. If, however, she proves chaste, the husband the next morning proudly exhibits to his kinsmen the cover of the nuptial couch with its "tokens of virginity," and a young female relative of the bride carries the latter's discolored loin cloth home in triumph to her family. After a few days with her husband, the young wife returns to her parents for a brief visit, and then settles down permanently to married life.

The female population of Dahomey considerably exceeds the male. Women, moreover, perform most of the agricultural labor. Under these conditions polygyny becomes almost inevitable. A man has as many wives as he can pay for. Although commoners can rarely afford more than three, chiefs and princes have as many as twenty, and the king's harem numbers several hundred. Each wife lives with her children and slaves in a separate dwelling in the husband's compound. The first wife manages the joint household, but her children do not enjoy any preferred rights of succession. A good husband is careful to treat all of his spouses alike. He lives and dines for four days with each in turn, except those who are pregnant or nursing. Despite a natural rivalry and competition for favors, there is little apparent jealousy.

The Dahomean woman, even where marriage makes her dependent, is by no means a mere chattel. Her husband has no control over her property, which passes with death to her own children, and to which she can add by skillful trading in the markets. There has even come into existence in this way a class of "free" women, whose freedom extends to sexual as well as economic matters. Women also possess rights of divorce. In marriages of the second main type, either party can terminate the union with little formality. Marriages which give the father control over the children are much more stable. But even here the wife can obtain a divorce if the husband fails to perform his ceremonial duties toward her ancestors, or neglects his annual services to her father, or commits adultery with the wife of one of her near relatives. The husband, however, has no right to initiate a divorce. If he wishes to terminate the union, he can only neglect his spouse, insult her relatives, and resort to petty annoyances in order to force her to take action. A council of her kinsmen then assembles, reviews the evidence, and pronounces the divorce, which usually involves the return of the bride-price and other presents.

When a Dahomean dies, his widows and children yield temporarily to a frenzy of despair in which they throw them-

Courtesy of Melville J. Herskovits
FIG. 117. SCENE AT A DAHOMEAN FUNERAL: SACRIFICE OF A COCK TO THE DEAD.

selves on the floor and beat their heads against the wall. The best friend of the deceased is summoned and tries to quiet them. After the chief of the *dokpwe* or men's communal organization has performed a sort of coroner's inquest, the best friend, the eldest son, and the oldest woman of the family prepare the corpse for burial. They bathe and anoint the body, shave the head, cut the nails, stuff the nose and ears with cotton, wrap cloths about the head and loins, and place the corpse in a roll of mats or in a coffin. For three days the immediate relatives abstain from food and bathing, smear their foreheads with clay, and mourn vociferously to the accompaniment of dirges, drums, and gunfire. The best friend, sons, sons-in-law, and other relatives bring lavish presents of cloth, cowries, food, and drink. On the evening of the third day, six members of the *dokpwe* wrap the corpse in a shroud and bear it to the grave, which is dug in the floor of the house or of the ancestral residence of the deceased. Amid a din of wailing the body is lowered into the grave with ropes and covered with cloths. Beside it are placed certain mortuary articles and the hair and nail clippings of the deceased. After the interment the mourners disperse, to reassemble several days later for an elaborate series of additional rites: processions, dances, ritual songs, a pretended search for the deceased, animal sacrifices over the grave by the best friend and eldest son, and various ritual performances by the *dokpwe* chief and other participants. In one ceremony, for example, the oldest woman of the family recites obscene verses at the tomb, utters a curse upon any one who looks at her, disrobes, runs naked to a crossroad, digs a hole, performs over it certain intimate purificatory ablutions, resumes her clothing, imitates the crowing of a cock, and cries: "The day has come!" When the rites are completed, the widows and children shave themselves and take a bath for purification. The funeral must be as costly as the family can afford, even though it results in destitution.

With every individual the Dahomean associates a number of spiritual attributes. The spirit of an ancestor, desiring to perpetuate his name, finds some clay to fashion a new body and acts toward the new individual throughout life as a guardian spirit (*djoto*), receiving annual offerings from his protégé and interceding with the gods in his behalf. The personal soul (*se-medon*), which actually forms the body from the clay obtained by the guardian spirit, resides in the head and governs the thinking processes. It is associated with the voice or breath and is thought to leave the body temporarily in sleep and to undergo the experiences perceived in dreams. A personal "serpent" (*dan*), representing the principle of life and movement, brings the body to earth and is identified with the umbilical cord. It resides in the navel or abdomen, and, if well treated and propitiated, brings to its owner riches taken from other men who have neglected their "serpents." A wealthy man often builds a permanent shrine for his "serpent." A "divine spark" (*se-lidon*), a bit of the goddess Mawu which is thought to reside in every human being, gives man his intuitive powers. Every person, finally, has his individual "fate" (*kpoli*), which he acquires from a diviner and which he propitiates thrice a year or oftener with sacrifices.

In death, these spiritual attributes disperse. The guardian spirit finds other protégés until it has returned to earth sixteen times. The "serpent," if enshrined, becomes identified with the "serpent" of the clan, the *henudan;* otherwise it rises from the body as a gaseous emanation and seeks a home in the mountains, where it may cause men trouble. The "divine spark" returns to the goddess Mawu. The soul becomes a "shadow" or ghost (*ye*) and hovers over the earth to plague human beings until it receives a complete funeral ceremony. It then goes to the goddess Mawu to render an account of its life, accompanied by the "divine spark" which bears witness if it testifies falsely. After crossing three rivers it finally reaches the land of the dead in the west, where it continues to live much as on earth, engaging in the same activities and enjoying the same material pleasures.

Unless the funeral ceremony is properly performed within three years after death, however, the ghost can never gain entrance to the spirit world. It wanders homelessly about, harassing its neglectful descendants, and eventually becomes the spirit of a tree or other natural object. These cultless ghosts are the agents of native sorcery. To secure their aid in working magic, it is necessary to possess a charm or fetish (*gbo*). Men obtain fetishes, sometimes from a god, sometimes from the *tohosu* or spirits of children who are drowned at birth because of certain abnormalities and become thereafter the spirits of rivers, but most frequently from Azizan, a monkey-like forest spirit. The native fetishes include medicines for internal and external use, amulets to be worn on the body, and objects of wood, metal, and other materials to be set up in the house, buried in the fields, etc. Each is accompanied by a spirit to make it operative and a formula regulating its use, defining its powers, and prescribing the foods which it craves and detests. A fetish always has a specific virtue. It protects a house, temple, market, or field; it prevents sickness or accidents; it preserves hunters, children, or pregnant women; it brings success in love or in courts of law; it kills an enemy or turns his own magic against him. In the eyes of the natives, vaccination is simply the white man's charm against smallpox.

To prevent their dead from becoming malevolent ghosts and the agents of sorcery, the Dahomeans make every effort to give them an adequate funeral. In the case of persons dying far from home, as in war, they bring the hair and nail clippings back and bury them with the usual rites. The bodies of those who die of smallpox or by a stroke of lightning, disposed of by the priests in a special or irregular fashion, are ransomed by their relatives within three years and properly buried. Ancestor worship forms the core of Dahomean religion. In a clearing in front of every compound stands a small square building with altars where the various ancestral spirits receive regular cult offerings.

Every Dahomean who receives a proper burial becomes eventually a god. At intervals of several years each clan deifies its recent dead in a complex and esoteric ceremony. These deified ancestors or clan divinities (*tovodun*) receive periodic sacrifices and are consulted before every important undertaking. Above them stands a higher class of divinities, the *nesuxwe*, which includes all the dead of princely rank and all who have held office, great or small, under the kings. Each clan also worships its *tohosu* or ghosts of abnormal children killed at birth, and includes in its pantheon a divinity called Dambada Hwedo, a collective personification of all the unknown dead of the clan—those who lived in the remote past and those who have migrated elsewhere, notably the descendants of Dahomeans shipped as slaves to America. At the head of the pantheon stands the *tohwiyo*, the founder and god of the clan, who has a shrine in each compound and a special temple where his bones are thought to lie. He punishes, with death if necessary, all offenses against the welfare of the clan, and must give his assent before a woman can marry, and come under the power of, a man of another clan.

Once a year each clan holds an elaborate ceremony or "custom" in honor of all its ancestors. The clan chief fixes the date after divination, notifies all members and all men who have married into the clan, receives the contributions which each is bound to give, and presides over the actual ceremonies. The rites include litanies, dances in which the more important ancestral spirits are impersonated, copious libations of water and intoxicating liquors, offerings of cooked foods, and lavish sacrifices of fowls, sheep, goats, and bullocks. Each ancestor is summoned by name, the unknown dead being invited under the name of Dambada Hwedo; to overlook even a single ancestor might result in disastrous consequences. All who have contributed presents are likewise mentioned by name, that they may share in the prosperity which the ancestors, pleased with such liberal offerings of the foods they crave, are expected to bring. Pride and rivalry increase the lavishness of these periodic ceremonies, which constitute the chief drain on the productive activities of the Dahomeans and also their principal stimulus to labor.

In the yearly ceremony of the royal clan—the "Annual Custom"—native extravagance reaches its climax. It is held at Abomey during the long dry season in conjunction with the annual census and tax gathering, the mobilization of troops for war, the promulgation of laws, the hearing of appeals and punishment of criminals, the distribution of rewards and promotions in rank, and the weddings of princesses to high officials.   A great concourse of people, especially those of princely rank, assembles for a month of barbaric pageantry, characterized by music and dances, feasts, speeches, military exercises, and endless parades of officials, priests, soldiers, Amazons, and princesses.   In a particularly spectacular ceremony, the women of the palace march in a procession bearing vast quantities of costly fabrics which they arrange in an enormous mound upon which the king himself executes a series of dances.   The members of the royal clan offer extravagant libations and animal sacrifices to all their ancestral divinities, but especially to the kings from whom they are descended, and to their gifts the monarch himself adds nearly a hundred human victims.

Except for enemy chieftains and a few aged war captives worthless as slaves, human sacrifice is largely confined to criminals condemned to death.   It is thus both a method of execution and a means of providing the spirits of former kings with a suitable body of retainers in the other world. A few victims are dispatched by blows on the head to notify the deceased monarchs that the Annual Custom is at hand, and near the close of the festivities the king spends a night or more at the grave of each of his predecessors, offering them food and drink, animal sacrifices, and two human victims each.   The most spectacular exhibition, however, takes place on the great plaza before the royal palace.   The Royal Executioner and representatives of all his predecessors in office stand in the midst of a surging mob at the foot of a high platform of branches.   From the platform men toss cowries to the mob, who scramble madly to secure them, and hurl fowls, sheep, goats, and cattle to the ground, where the executioners behead them with cutlasses, plunge their hands into the gory throats, and smear themselves with the blood. A cat, a hawk, and a crocodile meet a similar fate. Finally a score of human victims are thrown after the animals and decapitated on the spot, their nude bodies, "mutilated with a curved knife out of respect for the king's wives," being later suspended from gallows or scaffolds on the plaza. Exceeding even the Annual Custom in splendor and bloodshed is the Grand Custom, held after the death of a ruler. On this occasion, in addition to quantities of other sacrifices, several hundred human victims are slaughtered, including wives, eunuchs, and a suitable following of soldiers, Amazons, and musicians in addition to the more usual criminals and war captives. With a single minor exception in connection with one of the religious cults, human sacrifice is a prerogative of the king. Even in ordinary times he sacrifices a criminal or two whenever he wishes to convey a message to his royal ancestors, *e.g.*, to announce the arrival of a white man, the marriage of a princess, or the institution of a new dance. The total number of victims ranges from a few hundred in ordinary years to nearly a thousand in years of a Grand Custom. Human sacrifice is inspired, not by cruelty, but by the monarch's wish to provide the spirits of his predecessors with the things they crave—wives and attendants as well as food. "It is a touching instance of the king's filial piety, deplorably mistaken, but perfectly sincere."

Rivaling the ancestral divinities in their importance in the religious life of Dahomey, stands a class of great or public gods, who support and nourish the kingdom. They are organized, on the model of human governments, into three great hierarchies or pantheons, those of the Sky, of the Earth, and of Thunder. The most important among them is Mawu, the Moon Goddess, who presides over the Sky pantheon with her husband Lisa, the Sun God. She is the parent of most of the other gods, to whom she assigned their respective domains, and she alone possesses the power of creation. Nevertheless, she is regarded neither as a supreme being nor as the creator of the universe. The Sky pantheon includes numerous lesser deities, the sons and daughters of Mawu, of whom the most prominent is Gu, the god of metals and war, the giver of tools and weapons. The gods of the Earth pantheon, with one exception, are males, and they thus differ radically from the fertility goddesses of Mediterranean antiquity. At their head stands Sagbata, the first-born of Mawu and Lisa, usually conceived as a pair of twins from whose mating sprang the other members of the pantheon. Sagbata, as Earth God, brings abundance of crops, especially of the staple grains, and he punishes offenses by causing these grains to erupt on the skins of evil-doers. Thus he has become, in one aspect, the god of smallpox and other skin diseases. As the great king of the earth, Sagbata inspires fear and jealousy in the Dahomean monarchs, especially since at least four of the latter have died of smallpox, and on various occasions priests and priestesses of the Earth cult have been transported into slavery. At the head of the third or Thunder pantheon stands Xevioso, the second son of Mawu, from whom he received control over thunder, rain, fire, and the sea. This pantheon includes Agbe, the god of the sea, and numerous lesser deities who preside over waves, rivers, thunder, and rain in their various aspects.

Each pantheon has its own cult and its own group of adherents, who form, as it were, a sect. The ordinary Dahomean pays little attention to the great gods unless he belongs to one of these cult-groups, and even then he professes little knowledge of or interest in the gods, mythology, and ritual of the other sects. In other words, like the average Christian, he belongs to a "church." The sects correspond to the secret societies of other parts of West Africa. The Dahomean kings, fearful lest such organizations provide a cloak for subversive movements, have discouraged their development, and have subjected even the sects to state regulation through a supervisor appointed by themselves. The sects enjoy equal status; though the Sky cult has a somewhat more elaborate ritual, it yields to the Earth and Thunder cults in the number of adherents. Persons of princely rank never join these cults; they worship only the gods and ancestors of the royal clan. In numbers and in ceremonialism, however, the cult of this clan ranks almost as a fourth sect.

Each sect has numerous temples—circular huts of mud and thatch containing, on a raised clay platform, an image of one of the gods of the particular pantheon. There are more than one hundred temples in Abomey and its environs, including twenty to Sagbata alone. The establishment of a temple involves elaborate sacrifices and a complicated series of rites for the installation of its god or *vodun* (whence the "voodoo" of the American Negroes). If done at the request of the king, a man and a woman are sacrificed. With each temple there is associated a chief priest, a number of assistants drawn from the older cult members who are conversant with the intricacies of the ritual, a body of fully initiated lay members called "wives" of the god, and a number of novices undergoing initiation and living in a sort of convent on the temple grounds. Ceremonies fall into three categories: secret rites performed by the priest alone, others held inside the temple walls in the presence of the initiates, and public spectacles. In details of language and liturgy, in forms of invocation and sacrifice, in types of songs and dances, and in dress and paraphernalia, the ceremonies of the various sects naturally differ considerably, but they all conform to a single general pattern.

Membership in a sect may be acquired in either of two principal ways—by inheritance or in fulfillment of vows. When an initiate dies, his place is reserved for another member of his clan, who is often inducted with an abbreviated ritual. In the other case, a family desirous of children or troubled by sickness resorts to divination for supernatural aid or protection and vows a child to the temple of the indicated god. When the child grows up, he is placed in charge of the priest and is secluded in the convent for seven months or longer, during which time he learns a sacred language and the rites and taboos of the cult. Among the countless ceremonies which mark the various stages of his initiation, the most important are those in which he is "killed" by the god and resuscitated after his family has confessed his sins; cicatrized with the marks peculiar to the cult; ritually bound to the god; ceremonially shorn and his hair deposited where it can be used for magic if he violates his obligations; subjected to ordeals in which he takes food out of a pot of boiling oil with his hands and steps on glowing coals; possessed by the god, whose spirit enters his head and inspires him to perform a frenzied dance; and finally ransomed by his family for a large sum of money. The initiate, who bears henceforth a new name, now returns to his home, where he spends several months relearning his native language. Once a person is initiated, worship consists mainly in observing the taboos and participating in the ceremonies of his cult. Individuals, of course, derive different satisfactions from membership in a sect. Some take pleasure in wearing the finery of a cult member. Others enjoy their enhanced social status. Still others experience a feeling of spiritual exaltation or a mystical sense of oneness with their god.

A belief in fate or destiny (*fa*) permeates Dahomean life. Before embarking on any undertaking, making any decision, or engaging in any rite, a man consults destiny through divination. As a result, there has come into being a very numerous class of diviners (*bokonon*), men who have spent years in acquiring a vast fund of esoteric knowledge. They are organized into guilds and receive generous fees for their services. A diviner operates by taking sixteen palm kernels in his right hand, dropping either one or two kernels into his left hand with a rapid motion, making a single or a double mark on a board sprinkled with white clay, and repeating the performance until he has made sixteen casts. The resulting set of lines on the board is called a *du*. The possible combinations or *du* are, of course, exceedingly numerous, and over each of them rules a great god or a lesser divinity, with whom an elaborate mythology is associated. The diviner must know intimately several hundred such mythologies, for his counsel is based on the relationship borne by the mythology of the *du* registered on the board to that of the *du* identified with the individual "fate" or *kpoli* of the applicant. A man learns his "fate" and the *du* associated with it only when he has grown to adulthood and has acquired status in the community as a married man and a father. Since the acquisition of this knowledge involves considerable expense, he usually postpones the ceremony until a succession of unfortunate events has convinced him of its necessity. Every boy at puberty, however, obtains a "partial fate," and, with rare exceptions, this is all that a woman ever acquires.

Although destiny determines who shall live and die, prosper and suffer adversity, its decrees do not execute themselves. The goddess Mawu issues the orders, designates which deity or pantheon shall carry them out, and sends her youngest son, Legba, to deliver the instructions. Legba, the messenger of the gods, is mischievous but not malevolent, hasty in anger but forgiving, gross but clever. He is a celestial trickster who delights in outwitting his brothers. Charged with delivering the decrees of fate and of Mawu to the gods who execute them, he may nevertheless fail to do so, or even distort the message. If the order he bears means death or misfortune to a favorite of his, a person who has offered him liberal sacrifices, he is quite likely to forget it, or else to designate as the victim another person, one who has displeased him. It is wise, therefore, to cultivate his favor. Although he belongs to none of the pantheons, Legba has a cult in every household and a shrine at the entrance to every village and temple. A rude phallic image of the god, modeled of clay and surrounded by a circle of knobbed clubs planted upright in the ground, stands in a little hut just outside of every compound—outside, because Legba is not to be trusted where there are women. On low mounds of earth beside the shrine each member of the household deposits daily offerings of food. Genial and very human despite his coarseness, Legba offers the native a means of circumventing fate. His intervention explains in part why the Dahomean, unlike certain other African peoples, is not oppressed or terrorized by the multitudes of supernatural powers that surround him.

BIBLIOGRAPHY

BÉRAUD. "Note sur le Dahomé." *Bulletin de la Société de Géographie*, 5ᵉ Série, Vol. XII. Paris, 1866.

BURTON, R. F. *A Mission to Gelele, King of Dahome.* 2 vols. London, 1864.

——. "Notes on Certain Matters Connected with the Dahoman." *Memoirs Read before the Anthropological Society of London*, Vol. I. London, 1865.

——. "The Present State of Dahome." *Transactions of the Ethnological Society of London*, New Series, Vol III. London, 1865.

DUNCAN, J. *Travels in Western Africa in 1845 and 1846.* Second edition. 3 vols. London, 1847.

ELLIS, A. B. *The Ewe-Speaking Peoples of the Slave Coast of West Africa.* London, 1890.

FOÀ, E. *Le Dahomey.* Paris, 1895.

FORBES, F. E. *Dahomey and the Dahomans.* 2 vols. London, 1851.

HAJDUKIEWICZ DE POMIAN, A. "Dahome, land och folk." *Ymer*, Vol. XV. Stockholm, 1896.

HÄRTTER, G. "Der Fischfang im Eveheland." *Zeitschrift für Ethnologie*, Vol. XXXVIII. Berlin, 1906.

HERSKOVITS, M. J. "Population Statistics in the Kingdom of Dahomey." *Human Biology*, Vol. IV. Baltimore, 1932.

——. "Some Aspects of Dahomean Ethnology." *Africa*, Vol. V. London, 1932.

HERSKOVITS, M. J., and F. S. "A Footnote to the History of Negro Slaving." *Opportunity*, Vol. XI. New York, 1933.

*——. "An Outline of Dahomean Religious Belief." *Memoirs of the American Anthropological Association*, No. 41. Menasha, 1933.

KLOSE, H. "Industrie und Gewerbe in Togo." *Globus*, Vol. LXXXV. Braunschweig, 1904.

LAFITTE, I. *Le Dahomé.* Tours, 1873.

*LE HERISSÉ, A. *L'ancien royaume du Dahomey.* Paris, 1911.

REPIN. "Voyage au Dahomey." *Le Tour du Monde,* Vol. **IV.** Paris, 1863.

SKERTCHLY, J. A. *Dahomey as It Is.* London, 1874.

SPIETH, J. *Die Ewe-Stämme.* Berlin, 1906.

INDEX

Abandonment, of dwelling after a death, 40, 102, 278, 469; of the aged and infirm, 10, 100, 214, 312–13, 467, 500.

Abortion, 7–8, 34, 67, 118–19, 121, 123, 155, 178, 211, 248, 311, 383, 434, 463–4, 494, 523, 530, 537, 540, 579.

Abstinence, sexual. *See* Continence.

Acculturation. *See* Contact with civilization.

Acllacuna, 426–9, 436–7, 441, 443.

Administrative system, 415–17, 570–2.

Adoption, of captives, 285, 309–11, 462; of children, 69, 119, 179, 245, 275–6, 538.

Adornment. *See* Ornaments.

Adultery, 9–10, 39, 75, 94, 97–8, 122, 151–2, 158, 175–6, 213, 252, 274, 286, 378, 386, 432, 466, 499, 533, 549, 575.

Adze, 24, 55, 170, 230, 366–7, 520.

Agave, 364–5, 368, 412.

Age at marriage, 38, 73, 98, 119, 155, 212, 273, 312, 384, 436, 538.

Aged, the, 10, 35, 39–40, 76, 100, 179, 214, 252, 312–13, 345, 467, 500.

Age-grades, 9, 415.

Agriculture, 50, 138, 166, 223, 267, 294–5, 327–8, 363–4, 405, 411–12, 419–21, 454, 513–14, 556–7; lack of, 4, 23, 88–9, 108, 138, 195, 480.

Alcoholic liquors, 13–15, 26, 114, 144, 168, 226, 196, 330, 365, 412, 455, 483, 514–15, 558.

Aleatory element, 348.

Alpaca, 413, 421.

Amazons, 576–7.

Amulets, 12, 101, 160, 216, 387–8, 470, 503, 520, 542, 547, 586.

Ancestor worship, 346–7, 439, 502, 545, 586–9.

Animals, domesticated, 4, 23, 50, 89, 112–13, 138–44, 166, 195, 223, 266–7, 297, 328, 364–5, 413, 421, 453, 477, 481–2, 512, 556; propitiation of, 183–4, 188–9, 215, 223–4, 511–12, 555; sacrifice of, 128–9, 159, 317–18, 394, 397, 399, 442–3, 504, 536, 546, 584, 587–9; souls of, 183–4, 215, 545, 555; spirits of, 79–81, 184, 256, 278, 314, 346–7, 388, 469.

Animism, 101, 183, 215, 345–6, 439, 469.

Anointing, of the body, 13, 56, 111, 487, 562.

Aqueducts, 370, 422–3.

Architecture, 113, 203–5, 369–70, 407, 422–3. *See* Dwellings.

Arctic hysteria, 214.

Armor, 176, 241, 308, 380, 434.

Army, 433, 575–7. *See* War.

Art, decorative, 92–3, 110, 146–7, 177, 208, 234–5, 271, 300, 332–3, 339, 350, 365, 368, 406–8, 428–9, 504, 517, 519, 560; pictorial, 13, 271, 339, 504; plastic, 365, 578. *See* Fine arts.

Artifacts. *See* Material culture.

Asceticism, 390–1, 441–2.

Astrology, 391–3.

Atonement, 104, 128–9, 378, 437, 442.

Authority, domestic, 75–6, 157, 181, 252, 274, 302–3, 312, 336, 411, 466, 498–9, 565; paternal, 94, 148, 174, 252, 311, 336, 411, 565, 580–1; political, 59–60, 94, 149–50, 174, 237–8, 285, 414–15, 461, 491, 524–8, 565, 569.

Avoidance, of relatives, 9, 30, 98,

597

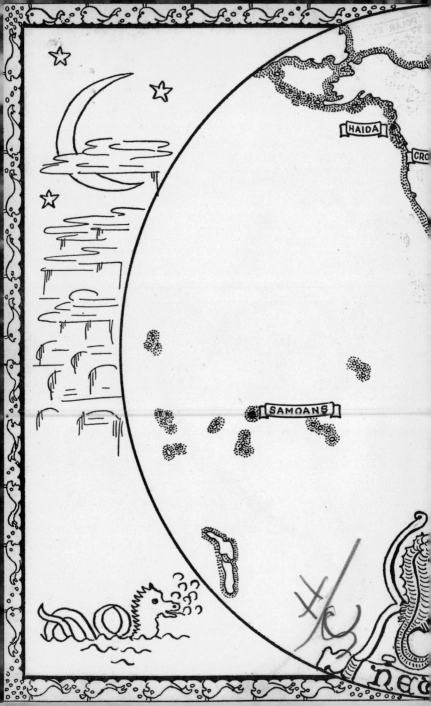